W9-ATZ-744

ITALY GUIDE

YOUR PASSPORT TO GREAT TRAVEL!

ABOUT THE AUTHOR

Having spent eight years living in and traveling through Italy, Douglas E. Morris has finally put his experiences down on paper. Published in a wide variety of media, Mr. Morris gives you the most accurate, up-to-date, and comprehensive information about restaurants, hotels, and sights.

ACKNOWLEDGMENTS

Many people assisted considerably in the development of this book, but I wish to extend my special thanks to Heddi Goodrich for her unique insight into the heart of Naples. My parents, Don and Denise, and my brother Dan were invaluable for their support, information, suggestions, and numerous leads. Special thanks for Salguod Sirrom's editorial and creative assistance.

HIT THE OPEN ROAD - WITH OPEN ROAD PUBLISHING!

Open Road Publishing now has guide books to exciting, fun destinations on four continents. As veteran travelers, our goal is to bring you the best travel guides available anywhere!

No small task, but here's what we offer:

• All Open Road publications are written by authors, authors with a distinct, opinionated point of view – not some sterile committee or team of writers. Our authors are experts in the areas covered and are polished writers.

• Our guides are geared to people who want great vacations, great value, and great tips for both standard tourist sights *and* fun, unique alternatives.

• We're strong on the basics, but we also provide terrific choices for those looking to get off the beaten path and *experience* the country or city – not just *see* it or pass through it.

• We give you the best, but we also tell you about the worst and what to avoid. Nobody should waste their time and money on their hard-earned vacation because of bad or inadequate travel advice.

• Our guides assume nothing. We tell you everything you need to know to have the trip of a lifetime – presented in a fun, literate, no-nonsense style.

• And, above all, we welcome your input, ideas, and suggestions to help us put out the best travel guides possible.

ITALY GUIDE

YOUR PASSPORT TO GREAT TRAVEL!

DOUG MORRIS

OPEN ROAD PUBLISHING

OPEN ROAD PUBLISHING

We offer travel guides to American and foreign locales. Our books tell it like it is, often with an opinionated edge, and our experienced authors always give you all the information you need to have the trip of a lifetime. Write for your free catalog of all our titles, including our golf and restaurant guides.

Catalog Department, Open Road Publishing
P.O. Box 20226, Columbus Circle Station, New York, NY 10023

And if snail mail is too slow for you, contact us by e-mail at:
Jopenraod@aol.com

1st Edition

Text Copyright ©1996 by Doug Morris
Maps on pages 13, 25, 106-07, 126-27, 140-1, 226-27, 244-45, 256-57, 324-25, 340-41, 354-55 by Rob Perry; Copyright ©1996 by Open Road Publishing
All Other Maps Copyright ©1996 by Doug Morris
- All Rights Reserved -

Library of Congress Catalog Card No. 96-67033
ISBN 1-883323-31-2

All photos courtesy of Italian Government Tourist Board, New York.
The author has made every effort to be as accurate as possible, but neither the author nor the publisher assume responsibility for the services provided by any business listed in this guide; for any errors or omissions; or any loss, damage, or disruptions in your travels for any reason.

TABLE OF CONTENTS

23. GLOSSARY

INDEX

MAPS

SIDEBARS

1. INTRODUCTION

If you're looking for great fun, serious relaxation, beautiful beaches, unparalleled artwork and dazzling museums, ancient civilizations, world-class accommodations, great sports and recreation, then Italy is the place for you! Besides all of this, Italian food is arguably the best in the world. And don't forget the great wine. Italy has it all.

There is so much to see, so much to do, so many great dishes to try and different wines to sample, that a trip to Italy can be overwhelming. But with this Open Road guide, your days and nights in Italy will be filled with exciting possibilities. I've given you lots of options to tailor the perfect vacation for your particular needs.

In the past five years Italy has overtaken France as the most visited destination from the United States: more than three million people now visit every year, and it is easy to see why so many Americans choose to visit the boot-shaped peninsula that juts into the Mediterranean. From the big tourist cities of Rome, Florence, and Venice to the tiny hill towns, small mountain villages, and breath-taking coastal resorts, Italy has everything a traveler could want and more. Read on!

PANORAMIC VIEWS IN LOVELY FLORENCE

2. EXCITING ITALY!
- OVERVIEW

Italy is generally divided into four main parts: northern Italy, central Italy, southern Italy, and the islands.

NORTHERN ITALY

Northern Italy is dominated by the lowland formed by the **Po River** and its tributaries. The **Alps** form the northern and western boundaries, and the **Apennines** are the southern boundary. In the east, northern Italy is open to the **Adriatic Sea**, mainly from the port of Venezia, and in the west there is access to the **Ligurian Sea**, mainly from the port of Genoa. Good climate and soil composition in the north are favorable for farming. The north of Italy has the largest portion of the nation's population and is the leading agricultural and industrial area.

There are a variety of interesting travel locations in the north. Besides **Venice**, with its fairy tale architecture surrounded by the canals that are the city's roads, you might want to explore the hiking trails of the Alps in the summer, or ski down mountain slopes in the winter. In the north are the majority of Italy's **golf courses**, and I've listed all those close to your destinations for you golf addicts.

If life by the sea is your thing, try the **Cinque Terre**, five little villages cut into the cliffs along the Ligurian coast of the Mediterranean that seem to be withstanding the annual tide of tourists crashing onto Italy's shores. The middle three will give you a glimpse into the past and a respite from the modern world that will refresh and rejuvenate you for years.

CENTRAL ITALY

Central Italy is that part of the peninsula that extends north of Rome. Although only a small part of the area is composed of lowlands, central

Italy plays an important role in farming and in some branches of industry, specifically wine growing. **Florence** and **Rome** are the main tourist cities in Central Italy and they have the best museums, the best churches, and the best sights to see. Even if you're a seasoned Italy traveler you should make a point of visiting either of these two cities to refresh your memory of the historical beauty of Italy.

One small overlooked town that shouldn't be missed while in Florence is **Lucca**. One of only two completely walled medieval cities left in Europe (the other is in, you guessed it, France), the ramparts and battlements that surround the city have been converted into the most romantic tree-lined walkway you will find anywhere. For you romantics, Lucca is a must see.

Another quaint little town, this one a hill town just outside of Rome, is **Frascati**. Every year they have a bacchanalian wine festival celebrating the pressing of the local wine. If you're in Rome during September you have to visit, since Frascati is only a 30 minute train ride away. And if you come any other time of year and want to stay in a small, peaceful, medieval hill town, with wonderful views over the surrounding countryside (vineyards), wonderful little wine bars, plenty of great restaurants, and a quaint ambiance that will be remembered forever, Frascati is the place for you.

SOUTHERN ITALY

Southern Italy is generally considered to be everything south of Rome. There are few lowlands in the area, and only two have importance in farming. One is the lowland surrounding **Naples**, and the other is the lowland of **Apulia**, the segment of the east coast that includes the heel of the Italian boot.

Naples is a vast port city that boasts one of the best museums in Italy. It is a vibrant city, as are all ports, and can be a little dicey at times, if you're out late at night in the wrong place; but if you look beyond its reputation as being less than meets the eye, and look into its heart, Naples is a fun city to visit. In its old section it has the ambiance of a large medieval city with its tiny streets and shops of artisans practicing crafts you would never believe still exist outside of factories. You can find violin makers, doll makers, cabinet makers and similar craftsmen hidden down the side streets and on the second stories of Naple's **centro storico**.

Naples is the perfect stopping-over point on your way to the quaint little island of **Capri**, in the bay of the city; and is the perfect transit stop for visits to **Pompeii** and **Herculaneum**, those ancient cities smothered but preserved by the lava and ash of the local volcano. These two ancient Roman cities have to be visited if you are a student of history.

Farther south in Italy you can find the resting place of **Santa Claus**. Saint Nicholas is buried in the Church of San Nicola deep in the old town of **Bari**. Down in the heel of Italy's boot is the virtually untouristed **Lecce**, which boasts an array of 17th century Baroque architecture. Besides viewing Lecce's architecture, the city is the perfect jumping-off point to explore the **Salentine peninsula**, which is dotted with medieval fortresses and castles. Exploring the base of Italy's heel is like going back in time, but it is an adventure not to be undertaken except by the most experienced travelers. Southern Italy can sometimes be dangerous if you venture off the beaten coastline and into the hills.

THE ISLANDS: SICILY & SARDINIA

The fourth region of Italy includes its two major islands: **Sicily** and **Sardinia**, as well as smaller island groups in the Mediterranean Sea. The only other island of any size, **Elba**, is in the Tyrrhenian Sea with Sardinia. This small isle off the coast of Tuscany once served as Napoleon's place of exile. Much smaller islands groups are the **Pontine Islands** near Naples; the **Lipari Islands** off northeastern Sicily; and the **Egadi Islands** opposite Sicily's northwestern end.

Sicily is a historian's dream. Here you'll find the most complete Greek ruins outside of Greece, located just below the town of **Agrigento**. You can also find ancient medieval hill towns like **Erice**, located 80 km west of Palermo, complete with walls, fortress and even a temple dedicated to Venus. Sicily is also a summer sportsman's paradise, since it has many resorts and is naturally surrounded by water.

To enjoy summer sports or to get away from it all, try the Lipari Islands (also know as the **Isole Eolie**). Some islands cater to tourists, whereas others have only a few hotels and all the peace and tranquillity you can soak up.

EXPERIENCE HISTORY

Home to the ancient world's most powerful empire, Italy is awash in history. Daily life revolves around ruins thousands of years old. Modern buildings incorporate ancient structures into their walls. Medieval streets snake through almost all cities including Rome, Florence, and especially Venice. In Italy you can see the tapestry of history woven directly in front of you. Museums abound with ancient artifacts, beautiful paintings, and stunning sculpture.

You can easily spend an entire trip roaming through museums – or for that matter inside the beautiful churches where you'll see some of the most exquisite paintings and sculptures anywhere on earth!

MOVIES TO SET THE SCENE FOR YOUR TRIP!

As you're planning your trip, you might want to rent a few movies to get you in the mood for your travels (save the novels for the airplane trips and beach visits!). Some modern classics include:
- ***Amarcord**, Fellini's great film about youth and coming of age*
- ***Christ Stopped at Eboli**, about a sophisticated left-wing doctor sent to a small hill town during the Fascist era*
- ***Cinema Paradiso**, about growing up in southern Italy*
- ***The Garden of the Finzi-Cantinis**, tale of what happens to a wealthy Jewish family before and during World War II*
- ***Caligula**, a bit rough and not for kids, but an interesting take on the debauchery of aristocrats in the Roman Empire.*

A FEAST FOR THE EYES!

Even though you could spend an entire trip inside museums or churches, if you decided to do so you would miss out on what makes Italy such a wonderful vacation: its natural beauty, charm, and ambiance. Being in Italy is like walking through a fairy tale. The old winding streets, twisting around the quaint refurbished buildings, leading to a tiny piazza centered with a sparkling fountain seems like something out of a dream. And you'll find a similar scene in virtually every city you visit in Italy.

If cities are not your cup of tea, you can't surpass the natural beauty of Italy's **Alpine** region, the crystal clear **Northern Lakes**, the pristine southern coastline, or the little villages perched on hills scattered across the land. A feast for the eyes awaits you in Italy.

FOOD & WINE

But a feast for the eyes is not all you'll get. Italy has, arguably (pipe down, you Francophiles!), the best food you'll find anywhere in the world. In most cases it's simple food, but with a bountiful taste. Take, for example, a Roman favorite: *abbacchio arrosto*. This is a succulent lamb dish slowly cooked over an open flame until perfectly prepared. It is usually accompanied by *patate arrosto*, roast potatoes cooked with rosemary, olive oil, and salt that makes my mouth water just thinking about them.

And since Italy is surrounded on almost all sides by water you can sample any flavor of seafood imaginable. Usually caught the same day, especially in the small towns along the sea, the seafood in Italy will have you coming back for more.

And don't forget the pasta. You'll find all shapes and sizes covered with sauces of every description and variety. Regions are known for certain pasta dishes and when there you have to sample them all. The area around Bologna is known for the production of the best ham in the world, *Prosciutto di Parma*, which is fed from the scraps of the magnificent cheese they make in the same region, *Parmiggiano Reggiano*. Both of these foods feature prominently in *spaghetti alla bolognese* – smother mine with the locally made parmesan cheese, *Parmiggiano Reggiano*!

To wash down all these savory dishes you need look no further than the local wine list. Italian wines may not be as full-bodied as French or California wines, but they have an intimate, down to earth, simple taste. Order from the wine list or be adventurous and order a carafe of the house wine, which is usually delicious, and more often than not comes from the local vineyards you saw outside the city as you arrived.

SPORTING ACTIVITIES

If you've noticed your waistband stretching a little from all the wonderful food and wine you've been enjoying, have no fear – Italy has plenty of activities for you to shave off some of those unwanted pounds. A land of sea and mountains, you can find some of the best skiing in the world in the **Alps** as well as wonderfully clear water and beaches all along the **Mediterranean Sea** and the **Adriatic Sea**.

You can go waterskiing, snorkeling, skin diving, sailing or just lie on the beach and sunbathe. Many vacation beaches are topless today, an unheard of activity ten years ago, so you'll be treated to an added adventure either trying it or enjoying it.

There are also many top-level golf courses all over Italy, plenty of tennis courts in most major cities, horseback riding in the country, fishing in lakes and sailing in the seas.

ONLY THE BEST FOR YOU!

*Besides offering the many sights to see, museums and churches to visit, and places to go, I've also listed the **best** sights to see while visiting a certain destination. In conjunction I've detailed for you the best hotels from each star category, as well as the restaurants where you'll find the best atmosphere and most satisfying cuisine. And to make sure you can plan your trip perfectly and find everything the instant you arrive, this book offers you the most complete set of city maps you'll find in virtually any travel guide to Italy.*

THE INCREDIBLY BEAUTIFUL TOWN OF NERVI

3. ROMAN ITINERARIES

If you only have a short period of time in **Rome** and you want to fill it up with the best sights, restaurants, hotels, cafes at which to lounge, and pubs from which you can crawl back to your bed, all you have to do is follow the itineraries listed below. The hotels, sights, and restaurants mentioned are all described in more detail in the *Rome* chapter. Simply refer to this chapter to more fully plan your Roman adventure.

The places listed in these itineraries are among my favorites in Rome, but there were plenty of close calls! So follow my advice if you wish, or plow through my chapter on Rome and find the perfect itinerary for you.

THE PERFECT THREE DAYS

Day One

This is going to be a somewhat slow day since you'll have just arrived and will be slightly jetlagged.

- Arrive on direct flight to Rome's Leonardo da Vinci airport at 8:00am.
- Take a cab to the **Hotel Locarno** near **Piazza del Popolo**, shower and unpack.
- Stop at the cafe next to the excellent restaurant **Dal Bolognese** in the Piazza del Popolo and grab a cappuccino, cafe, or espresso to get you going.
- Take the second road on your left, the **Via del Babuino** to the **Spanish Steps**.
- Get your picture taken while you lean over and grab a drink from the fountain in front of the steps.
- Walk to the top of the steps for the magnificent view over the city
- It should be about lunch time now, so walk back down the steps, cross the street, and take a left into the third street at the edge of the piazza, **Via delle Croce**. Follow this to the end, find an outside seat at the superb local restaurant **Pizzeria La Capricciosa**, in Largo dei Lombardi. Try any of their exquisite Roman pasta specialties: *arrabiata*, *amatriciana*, or *vongole verace*.

- After lunch it should be about nap time. But remember to only take a 2-3 hour nap, wake up right away, take a shower and get out again – otherwise you'll sleep until 10:00pm and be wide awake because jet-lag will have set in.
- Now it's time to explore the streets around the **Piazza di Spagna**, **Via della Croce**, **Via del Corso**, **Via dei Condotti** and admire all the different shops.
- After shopping/exploring, take a small walk (or short cab ride) to **Piazza Navona**.
- Stop at **Le Tre Scalini** and sample some of the world famous Italian *gelato* (ice cream). If you sit at the tables outside the cost will double or triple.
- If some liquid refreshment is more your style, exit the Piazza Navona on the other side, cross the **Via Vittorio Emanuele**, visit the **Campo dei Fiori** (where they have a superb market in the mornings which we'll get to in a few days) and stop in at the **Drunken Ship** for some Guiness, Harp, or Kilkenny. Enjoy the lovely English speaking female bartenders. and have a few ales for me.
- From here you are within striking distance of **Trastevere**, the place for Roman nightlife, across the river. Cross the pedestrian bridge **Ponte Sisto** and make your way to **Piazza Santa Maria** in Trastevere.
- If it's too early for dinner (7:30pm or 8:00pm is the beginning time) stop at one of the outdoor cafes and replenish your fluids.
- For dinner stop at **La Canonica** just outside of the piazza, Here you should also try one of the typical Roman pasta specialties, *arrabiata*, *amatriciana*, or *vongole verace*; as well as some *sogliola alla griglia* (grilled sole) for seconds.
- After dinner, if it's not too late, walk down the long road leading to the Piazza, **Via della Lungaretta**, to the large main road **Viale Trastevere**.
- Catch a cab here to either return to your hotel if you're tired, or have the driver drop you off at the **Trevi Fountain**.

Day Two
- Today is museum day. Start off at the best in the city, the **Vatican Museum** and the **Sistine Chapel**. This should take you all morning.
- Instead of a long sit-down meal, stop at one of the cafes around the museum and St. Peters and order a light snack. My suggestion is the *Medallione*, a grilled ham and cheese concoction that is tasty and filling. You don't order at the counter, you first pay for your order with the cashier (order your drink at the same time), then bring the receipt up to the counter and tell the bartender what you'll have. A good tip to leave is about L500.

- After your meal, let's explore **St. Peters**. Guys will need slacks for this adventure and women cannot wear short skirts of tank top-like shirts. Don't forget to walk to the top.
- Once done here, which should be later afternoon, let's stop at **Castel St. Angelo** and explore the ancient armaments museum and fortifications of the fortress that protected the Vatican in the past.
- Now it's time to go home for a 2-3 hour nap, if you need it.
- Dinner tonight is at the nearby **La Buca di Ripetta**, on Via di Ripetta, where you should try either the Lasagna al Forno, Saltimbocca alla Romana, or the Osso buco di Vitello.
- After dinner, if you missed the **Trevi Fountain** last night, go there tonight. It's about a 20 minute walk (if you're staying at the Locarno), or a short cab ride away.
- If not, you must return to the **Piazza Navona** to soak up the ambiance there at night with its fountains lit up. Either bring your own bottle of wine and sit at one of the benches or grab a table at one of the cafes and enjoy a beautiful Roman evening.

Day Three
- Time to explore some serious ruins. On the way, stop at the market in the **Piazza Venezia**.
- From here make your way down **Via dei Foro Imperiali** to the entrance to the Forum on the right hand side. Up ahead you'll see the **Coliseum**, our next destination.
- View the Coliseum.
- Lunch. Time to hail a cab and go back up the Via dei Foro Imperiali, to Piazza Venezia, then on to **Gino ai Funari** on Via dei Funari. This is a small local place in the Jewish Ghetto that makes the Roman pasta specialties perfectly (carbonara, amatriciana, vongole verace, and arrabiata). Or you can try the conniglio alla cacciatore (rabbit hunter style made with brandy tomatoes and spices). It is superb.
- After lunch, before we go back up the Via di Teatro Marcello to go to the second best museum in Rome – the Campidoglio – since it's so close by, let's pay a visit to the **Isola Tiberina**.
- After a quick exploration of this island, let's get to the **Campidoglio**. Remember to find La Buca della Verita. This should take most of the afternoon.
- When completed, make your way to the **Pantheon** (or back to the hotel if you're tired) and sit at one of the outside cafes and savor the sight of one of Rome's oldest buildings in a quaint medieval square. If it is super hot, sit by the pillars at the entrance of the Pantheon since it is always wonderfully cool there.

- Back to the hotel to freshen up for your meal this evening at **La Carbonara** in **Campo dei Fiori**. Remember you were here on Day One at the Drunken Ship? They make the best *spaghetti alla vongole verace* I've ever had.
- You can stay in Campo dei Fiori for the whole evening and take in the sights and sounds of one of Rome's most popular nighttime piazzas. Most evenings they have live bands playing. You've already been to Navona, Santa Maria in Trastevere, and Trevi, the other three great piazzas where you can get a true taste of Roman nightlife.

THE PERFECT FOUR DAYS

Follow the above itinerary for the first three days, and add Day Four immediately below.

Day Four
- Time to go to church (you don't have to pray if you that's not your thing). To get to these churches you're going to need to take the metro and buses or rely on Roman taxis. Our first stop is **Saint Paul's Outside the Wall**. Get your picture taken in the middle courtyard with one of the trees in the background. When you next return to Rome, do the same thing and trace how long it has been by how far the tree has grown. My family has been doing that for over 40 years now.
- From here cab it back into town to **Santa Maria Sopra Minerva**.
- Next is **Santa Maria Maggiore** near the train station.
- On to **San Pietro in Vicolo** close to the Coliseum.
- Located between the Coliseum and San Giovanni in Laterano is our next stop, **Church of San Clemente**
- Our next church is the cathedral of Rome, which isn't St. Peter's, it is **San Giovanni in Laterano**.
- Time to get ourselves to Trastevere for a late lunch, and **Sabatini's** is the perfect choice. Here we can sit in their large outdoor terrace on the Piazza and enjoy a fine meal.
- Most people don't come to Trastevere to look at churches. They come for the more bacchanalian aspects of the area. But we religious types have first come to see **Santa Maria in Trastevere** in the same piazza as Sabatini's, then the **Church of Santa Cecilia in Trastevere**.
- Since you've been traveling all over town, let's return to the hotel for brief siesta, since everything is closed anyway, or stop off at **Babbington's Tea Room** near the Spanish Steps for a "cuppa."
- When the stores reopen, let's do some antique shopping on the nearby streets of **Via del Babuino** and the **Via Margutta**, Rome's best for antiques.

- If you want to buy a book, stop into the Lion Bookshop at Via del Babuino 181.
- For dinner try the ever popular **Otello Alla Concordia** at nearby Via Della Croce 81, where you can get some of the most succulent *abbacchio alla griglia* anywhere in Rome.
- For an after-dinner vino, sample **Antica Bottigleria Placidi,** a great wine bar on the same street.

THE PERFECT SEVEN DAYS

Follow the above itinerary for the first four days, then add Days Five through Seven immediately below.

Day Five

- If you don't feel as if you are able to truly appreciate some of the activities listed above, by all means return and enjoy them today, but before you run off and do that we're all starting together by waking up early and going back to the **Campo dei Fiori** to see how different it is in the mornings. Here you'll find one of Rome's best food and flower markets. Don't miss it.
- For lunch, return back into the city and find this great place located between Piazza Navona and the Spanish Steps, Orso "80" at Via dell'Orso. Here they make great *spaghetti alla carbonara* as well as the *abbacchio alla griglia.*
- Now the fun begins. We're going to a terrific town – **Frascati**. If we are lucky and it's September, we may stumble into their wine festival (and definitely stumble out).
- To get to Frascati, go to the train station, buy a ticket, go to track 27, board the small local train (takes 35 minutes and costs L6,500), and enjoy the scenery along the way.
- Enjoy the views, exploring the winding medieval streets and the relative peace and quiet compared to Rome. Don't forget to search out some of the little wine stores. My favorite is **Cantina Via Campania**.
- For dinner, let's give the wild and raucous **Pergatolo** at Via del Castello 20 a try. If you're into something more sedate, **Zaraza** at Viale Regina Margherita 21 should be your choice.
- Once dinner is done, make your way back to Rome.
- After arriving at the train station, let's go to a nearby Irish pub, **The Fiddler's Elbow** on Via dell'Olmata, that serves up fine ales, an authentic atmosphere, English conversation, and a fun evening to end an adventurous day.

Day Six

- Let's start off the day at the nearby **Mercato de Stampe**, at Piazza Fontanella, which is open from 9:00am–6:00pm Monday through Saturday. Here you can find maps, stamps, books, almost anything on the intellectual side.
- When done here, take a cab or stroll the short distance to the **Piazza Barberini** at the base of the **Via Veneto**.
- First we'll stop in the **Palazzo Barberini**, located on the Via Quattro Fontane that leads up the hill from the Piazza. This palazzo is the home of the **National Portrait Gallery**.
- After soaking up the art, walk back almost to the piazza to a small street named Via degli Avignonesi. At the end of it you'll find a great little local place, **Trattoria Da Olimpico**. Stop here for lunch.
- Once lunch is over go back up the street to the piazza, and start up Via Veneto, the street that embodies the good life – *La Dolce Vita*. Halfway up you'll pass by the **American Embassy** on the right hand side. Stop at one of the cafes for refreshment.
- At the top of the steps, go through the massive gate, cross the street and enter the beautiful park, **Villa Borghese**. Let's take a leisurely stroll through the gardens to the **Galleria Borghese** that has portraits, paintings, and sculptures galore.
- Follow the roads to the other entrance to the park and back to the hotel
- Dinner tonight is at **Dal Bolognese** in the Piazza del Popolo. Try their *fritto misto*, a fried mix of veggies, cheese, and meat.
- End the evening by going to the top of the **Spanish Steps** for a view over the city at night.

Day Seven

- Assuming today is a Sunday, you must visit the **Porta Portese** market that lines the Tevere every Sunday. Starting at the **Ponte Sublico**, you'll find all sorts of interesting antiques and junk here. A must visit if you're in Rome on a Sunday.
- After the market, and since it is Sunday and everything is closed (that's right, no museums, hardly any shops, etc.) except restaurants, it's time to return to the restaurant you liked best that you tried before. I always do this wherever I travel. It ensures that one of my last meals is going be great, and it makes me feel somewhat like I belong. Go to one with an outside terrace like **La Carbonara** in Campo dei Fiori.
- Return to your hotel and pack, and afterwards go for a stroll around your new neighborhood.
- End your stroll at the top of the **Spanish Steps** again. Tonight we're going to the terrace restaurant in the **Villa Hassler** for a scenic and romantic last dinner in Rome. Try their specialty *abbacchio al forno*.

4. LAND & PEOPLE

LAND

From the top of the boot to the toe, Italy is a little more than 675 miles (1,090 kilometers) long. The widest part, in the north, measures about 355 miles (570 kilometers) from east to west. The rest of the peninsula varies in width from 100 to 150 miles (160 to 240 kilometers). The peninsula of Italy has a total area of about 116,000 square miles (300,400 square kilometers).

A mountainous country, Italy is dominated by two large mountain systems – the **Alps** in the north and the **Apennines** throughout the peninsula. The Alps, which are the highest mountains in Europe, extend in a great curve from the northwestern coast of Italy to the point where they merge with Austria and Slovenia in the east. Just west of the port city of Genoa, the **Maritime Alps** are the beginning of the chain. Despite mighty peaks and steep-sided valleys, the Alps are pierced by modern engineering marvels of mountain passes that have always allowed commerce between Italy and its northern neighbors to flow freely. These highway and railroad tunnels provide year-round access through the mountains.

The Apennine mountain system is an eastern continuation of the Maritime Alps. It forms a long curve that makes up the backbone of the Italian peninsula. The Apennines extend across Italy in the north, follow the east coast across the central region, then turn toward the west coast, and, interrupted by the narrow Strait of Messina, continue into Sicily.

There are numerous smaller mountains in Italy, many of volcanic ancestry, and thankfully many extinct. The two active volcanoes, **Mount Vesuvius** near Naples and **Mount Etna** in Sicily, are the only active volcanoes on the European continent. Maybe that has something to do with the heated Italian temperament?

PEOPLE

The Italian people are considered to be one of the most homogeneous, in language and religion, of all the European populations. The only significant minority group live in the region called **Trentino-Alto Adige**. These Alpine valleys of the north once made up part of the Austrian province of Tyrol, and the several hundred thousand German-speaking residents still refer to their homeland as South Tyrol. The region was incorporated into Italy after World War I, and both Italian and German are official languages in this region. Obviously, the people of the region have developed their own sense of identity – part of, but separate from, the rest of Italy.

One much smaller minority also lives in northern Italy. This group, the **Valdotains**, dwells in the region called **Valle d'Aosta** in the northwestern corner of the country, and also has two official languages, Italian and French.

About 95 percent of the Italian people speak Italian, while members of the two aforementioned groups make up the other 5%. For more than seven centuries the standard form of the language has been the one spoken in Tuscany, the region of central Italy centered around Florence. However, there are many dialects, some of which are difficult even for Italians to understand. Two of these principal dialects, those of Sicily and Sardinia, sound like a foreign language to most Italians. If you have lived in Italy for a while, it is easy to pick the different accents and dialects and pinpoint where someone is from.

5. A SHORT HISTORY

A short history of the peninsula of Italy is a contradiction in terms. So much has occurred in this narrow strip of land which has affected the direction of the entire Western world that it is virtually impossible to succinctly describe its history in a brief outline. We've had the Etruscans, Romans, Greeks, 'Barbarian' hordes, Holy Roman Emperors, the Papacy (although not the whole time – the seat of the Catholic Church was moved to Avignon, France from 1305 until 1377), painters, sculptors, the Renaissance, Crusaders, Muslim invaders, French marauders, Spanish conquistadors, Fascists, American soldiers, Red Brigades, and much more.

What follows is a brief outline of the major events on the Italian peninsula, concentrating mainly on the Roman Empire, since we've already covered some of the Renaissance in the Art sections. Anyway I don't claim to be an historian, only a mere *scrittore di guidi di viaggio*, so please accept this brief historical background for your travel enjoyment.

ETRUSCANS

Long before Rome was even a glimmer in Romulus' and Remus' eye (legend had it that these two were raised by a she-wolf and eventually became the founders of Rome), Italy was the home of a people with an already advanced civilization – the **Etruscans**. This powerful and prosperous society almost vanished from recorded history because not only were they conquered by Rome but also devastated by marauding **Gauls**. At such times, it is assumed that most of their written history was destroyed, and little remains today.

Because of this, and the fact that the language of the inscriptions on their monuments has been only partially deciphered, archaeologists have gained most of their knowledge of the Etruscans from studying the remains of their city walls, houses, monuments, and tombs.

From their research, archaeologists believe that the Etruscans were a seafaring people from Asia Minor, and that as early as 1000 BC they had settled in Italy in the region that is today **Tuscany** and **Lazio** (basically from Rome's Tiber River north almost to Florence's Arno River). Their rule eventually embraced a large part of western Italy, including Rome.

As a seafaring people, the Etruscans controlled the commerce of the Tyrrhenian Sea on their western border. After losing control of Rome, they strengthened their naval power through an alliance with Carthage against Greece. In 474 BC, their fleet was destroyed by the Greeks of Syracuse. This left them vulnerable not only to Rome, but the Gauls from the north. The Gauls overran the country from the north, and the Etruscans' strong southern fortress of Veii fell to Rome after a ten-year siege (396 BC). As was the Roman way, the Etruscans were absorbed into their society, and eventually Rome adopted many of their advanced arts, their customs, and their institutions.

THE ETRUSCAN KINGS OF EARLY ROME

When Greece was reaching the height of its prosperity, Rome was growing in strength. Rome didn't have any plan for its ascension to world domination, it just seemed to evolve. There were plenty of set-backs along the way, but everything fell into place at the right time.

The early Romans kept no written records, and their history is so mixed with fables and myths that historians have difficulty distinguishing truth from fiction. The old legends say that **Romulus** founded the city in 753 BC when the settlements on the seven hills were united. This date is probably too late for the actual founding of the city. As is the case with many emerging societies, their founders are mythical figures, as was Romulus, but there is some evidence that the kings who followed him actually existed.

Shortly before 600 BC, Rome was conquered by several Etruscan princes. The Etruscans were benevolent conquerors (except for Tarquinius Superbus) and set about improving the Roman lifestyles to match their own.

The first Etruscan king, **Tarquinius Priscus**, drained the city's marshes, improved the **Forum**, which was the commercial and political center of the town, and also founded a temple to Jupiter. He protected Rome by carrying on wars with neighboring peoples.

Under **Servius Tullius**, the second Etruscan king, a treaty was made with the Latin cities which acknowledged Rome as the head of all **Latium**. This was the beginning of the concept of Rome as the center of the universe. At the same time he enlarged the city and built a wall around all seven hills, parts of which still stand today.

The last of the Etruscan kings of Rome, **Tarquinius Superbus**, was a tyrant who oppressed the people and scorned the Roman religions. His activities started the fires of rebellion that would eventually unseat the Etruscans from Rome.

Even with this oppression, the Etruscans built Rome into the center of all Latium. Impressive public works were constructed, like the huge sewer **Cloaca Maxima**, which is still in use. Trade also expanded and prospered, and by the end of the 6th century BC Rome had become the largest and richest city in Italy.

THE NATIVE ROMAN POPULATION REVOLTS

But in spite of all this progress and development, the old Latin aristocracy wanted their power back. **Junius Brutus** led a successful revolt around 509 BC, which expelled the Etruscans from the city. That was when the people of Rome made themselves a **republic**.

The Etruscans tried and failed many times to regain control of the city. Rome's successful thwarting of the Etruscans allowed the young republic to begin its long history of almost constant warfare and conquest. At the time, it was only a tiny city-state, much like the city-states that were flourishing at the same time in Greece, with a population of roughly 150,000. Who would have thought that this small republic would eventually rule the known world?

ROME'S EARLY REPUBLIC

In the beginnings of early Rome, the **patricians** (Rome's aristocracy) controlled the government and ruled the **plebes** or **plebeians** (Common People). Because they were shut out from the government, the plebeians were politically and economically oppressed by their wealthy fellow citizens. The internal history of the republic for the next three centuries is mainly a story of how the plebeians wrested reform after reform from the patricians and gained more and more control over their existence and the eventual direction of Roman politics.

What forced the plebes to seek their freedom was the shackle of the patrician's oppression. The wealthy patricians continued to expand their land holdings, taking the best property and increasing their herds until they monopolized the public pasture. They also continued the practice of lending money at ruinous interest to the small proprietors, eventually reducing the plebes to abject slavery when they could not pay.

At the same time, the population of Rome was increasing too fast for the land and their primitive farming methods could not support it. Also the burden of constant warfare fell most heavily on the plebeians, who had to leave their little farms to fight the state's battles. This didn't allow them to provide for their families or even begin to pay off their debts they incurred to start farming the land.

To right these wrongs the plebeians went on what today would be called a general strike. In 494 BC, they marched out of Rome in a body and threatened to make a new city. At the fear of losing its large labor force, the patricians agreed to cancel all debts and to release people who were in prison for debt. By 350 BC, the plebes gained the ability to participate fully in the Republic's government.

While these important changes were taking place at home, the little city-state had been gradually extending its power. Compelled at first to fight for its very existence against its powerful neighbors (mainly the Etruscans, Aequians, and Volscians), Rome gradually fought its way to the leadership of the Italian peoples. This dependence on military strength helped pave the way for Rome's conquest of the world.

THE GAULS SACK ROME

Rome's progress in leadership of all of the Latin tribes received a temporary setback in 390 BC, when marauding Gauls advanced through the heart of Italy. They decimated the farmland as they went and captured and burned Rome. After a stand-off, with Romans slowly taking their city back, the Gauls accepted a heavy ransom to depart promptly and returned to the valley of the Po.

Although Rome had been burned, the Etruscans had suffered far worse in the invasion and were so weakened that Rome was able to seize their southern possessions. In another century, Rome conquered their whole territory.

ROMAN CONQUEST OF ITALY

Meanwhile the **Latin League** had grown to dislike the growing power and arrogance of their ally and attempted to break away from its control; but Rome won the two years' war that followed (340-338 BC). As a warning, some towns were reduced to being vassals of the new state, while others were given full Roman citizenship and others partial citizenship.

Another strong foe in central Italy still remained to be reckoned with: the **Samnites**, who were also of Italic stock. The truce that was made when the Latin League was feuding was broken a few years later (326 BC), and a wild-fought struggle ensued, with a variety of interruptions, until the decisive battle of **Sentinum** (295 BC), which made Rome supreme over all central and northern Italy.

Southern Italy, still occupied by a disunited group of Greek city-states, still remained independent. Alarmed at the spread of Roman power, the Greek cities appealed to **Pyrrhus**, king of Epirus in Greece who inflicted two telling defeats on the Roman army. He then crossed to Sicily to aid the Greek cities there in eliminating Carthaginian rule. This was a classic example of spreading your forces too thin over an extended battlefield. Encouraged by the arrival of a Carthaginian fleet to combat the Greeks, Rome renewed its struggle for the Greek city-states in southern Italy, and in 275 BC defeated Pyrrhus in the battle of **Beneventum** and a new phrase was born: a Pyhrric victory, where you win a battle but lose the war. Eventually, one by one the Greek cities were taken, and just like that Rome was ruler of all Italy.

KEEPING THE CONQUERED LANDS HAPPY

Rome gradually welded the lands conquered into a single nation, contented and unified. They could have exploited the conquered cities of Italy for its own interests, but instead made them partners in Rome's future success.

Rome granted many of them the privileges of Roman citizenship, in full or in part. As it had done for the Latin cities, they gave them the status of allies or partners. These new conquests were allowed to govern themselves, had the right to trade freely with and intermarry with Roman citizens, which would also make the non-Roman a citizen. These newly conquered people did not, however, have the right to vote.

Rome also set about establishing colonies of its citizens, who still retained their full civil rights, all over Italy. Almost one sixth of all Italy was annexed and distributed among these colonizing Roman citizens. By encouraging this colonization, a common interest in the welfare of Rome spread throughout the Italian peninsula.

THE PUNIC WARS

These centuries of warfare had developed Rome into a nation of soldiers. Its only remaining rival in the western Mediterranean was the Phoenician colony of **Carthage**, the established sea power of the time. Rome obviously was the chief land power. At the time Carthage had a policy of sinking any trading vessel of any other city that dared to bid for a share of the rich commerce of the Mediterranean region. Rome could not abide these restrictions, so a series of **Punic Wars** for Mediterranean supremacy began in 264 BC.

The courage and endurance of Rome were tested to the utmost in this long and disastrous series of wars. After the battle of **Zama** (202 BC), Carthage was reduced to the position of a vassal state. In 146 BC, during the **Third Punic War**, because Carthage was again beginning to flex its military and economic might, Rome once more savagely attacked its defeated rival and razed the city.

WINNING WORLD MASTERY

Now Rome was well on its way to world domination. Emboldened with this sudden rise to power, the new generation of Roman statesmen ignored the just policies of their successful predecessors. Most of the conquered lands were administered by governors (**proconsuls**), and citizens were given little chance to become full Roman citizens. These governors ruled like czars, and through the enormous taxes levied on the local populations, tried to amass in their one year of office enough wealth to last them a lifetime.

These taxes also enriched the greedy collectors (**publicans**), who purchased the privilege of collecting the taxes. Incredible amounts of gold, jewelry, and money in the form of taxes poured into Rome from all over the world, and the ancient simplicity of Roman life gave way to luxury and pomp. Morals were undermined, and vice and corruption flourished. (For an example of the debauchery that ensued, try and get a copy of the movie *Caligula* – not a movie for family viewing, but it will give you an insight into what happened to Rome during this time of expansion.

The suddenly enriched official bureaucrats acquired estates by buying up the small farms of the peasants. Even if they kept their land the peasants were too poor to compete with the hordes of slaves who worked the great plantations. Because of this the streets of the capital grew clogged with ruined farmers, along with discharged soldiers and the poor from all over Italy. These people lived on state and private charity, as well as on bribes that were given by political candidates to vote for them in the next election.

THE END OF THE ROMAN REPUBLIC

Once again a conflict began to brew between the aristocracy (formerly the Patricians) and the vast oppressed poor citizens (formerly the Plebes). Men tried to step forward and right the wrongs that were occurring, but each man who did ended up assassinated for his efforts.

To try and maintain a semblance of order a law was forcibly passed that transferred supreme power from the people to the **Senate**. The aristocrats, who became Senators, however, were too corrupt and feeble to hold power, and so the Roman Republic came to an end.

Two brilliant statesmen, **Gaius Julius Caesar** and his great-nephew **Augustus (Octavian)**, helped save Rome by scrapping the old republican framework and remolded the tottering structure into an empire. All power was gradually concentrated in the hands of a single ruler, who was backed by the might of the Roman legions.

TWO CENTURIES OF PEACE & PROSPERITY

With the establishment of the Empire, two centuries of profound peace developed, only broken by small frontier warfare. In the provinces men held power responsibly, possibly because they feared the omnipotent wrath of the emperor, and in Rome literature and civilization flourished. Increasingly the Mediterranean came to resemble one great nation, with paved roads leading from the south of Italy into what are now France and Germany. Even today fragments of Roman roads and ruins still exist in Britain, aqueducts and bridges can be seen in France, Roman wells are still used in the Egyptian oases of the Sahara Desert, and Roman amphitheaters can be visited in the heart of Tunisia.

Roman citizenship was extended to all free men throughout the Empire, and Roman law was administered in every court. The **Roman Peace** (*Pax Romana*) extended over the civilized world. But signs of decay were everywhere.

The pursuit of a good time once again obsessed the people of Rome. The rich amused themselves by giving splendid feasts. The poor had their circuses where free bread was distributed (you've heard of bread and circuses?). Slave labor had degraded the once sturdy peasantry to the status of serfs or beggars, and the middle class, which once had been the backbone of the nation, had almost disappeared. A welfare mentality overcame the population. Then once again, the Roman governors began to concentrate on sucking the provinces dry instead of keeping abreast of the economic and political climate.

FALL OF THE ROMAN EMPIRE

The strength and discipline of the Roman Empire were being sapped by political decay, economic troubles, and decadent living. At this time, German 'barbarians,' who were a violent people led by warrior chiefs living on the fringes of the empire, began to attack the edges of the empire in the 4th century AD. They defeated unprepared Roman garrison after garrison. These **Goths**, **Vandals** (so that's where the phrase comes from!), **Lombards**, **Franks**, **Angles**, **Saxons**, and other tribes sacked and pillaged the decadent and crumbling empire. With the fall of the Western Roman Empire in AD 476, this was the beginning of the medieval period called the **Dark Ages**. They were so called because these 'barbarians' let Roman civilization collapse along with its artistic and engineering achievements.

What the 'barbarians' did bring with them, however, that helped shape the future of Western civilization, was their belief that the individual was important, more so than the state. In contrast, the Romans believed in the rule of the state over the people – in despotism. The 'barbarians' gave us a rudimentary form of personal rights, including more respect for women, government by the people for the people, and a system of law represented by the people being governed. Kings and chiefs were elected by tribal councils, which also served as courts of law. In essence, they brought with them the beginnings of democracy. So, in 20-20 hindsight, who was civilized and which was barbaric?

AFTER THE ROMAN EMPIRE

In AD 330, when the Roman emperor **Constantine** moved the capital to **Constinantinople** (today's Istanbul in Turkey), the Western Roman Empire decayed and was overrun by waves of 'barbarians.' Rival governors fought over fragments of Italian territory.

Even **Charlemagne**, who had conquered the Lombard rulers and had himself crowned emperor of the **Holy Roman Empire** in AD 800, could not stop the disintegration of everything the Roman Empire had built. The Holy Roman Empire was a union between the Papacy and Charlemagne in which management of the empire was shared.

But Charlemagne's Holy Roman Empire fell apart after his death, only to be refounded by the Saxon **Otto I** in 962, bringing Italy into a close alliance with Germany. The Holy Roman Empire ruled over the lands north of Rome into Austria and Germany until 1806. During that time, the Holy Roman Empire took on many shapes, sizes, and rulers. It included at different times France, Germany, Luxembourg, the north of Italy (because the Muslims, and then the Normans had taken control of Italy south of Naples), Austria, Switzerland, and more. It had rulers from the Saxon Line, Franconian Line, Hohenstaufen Line, Luxembourg Line, and the Hapsburg Line. It may have been constantly in flux but it did last over 1,000 years.

While the Holy Roman Empire expanded and contracted, it eventually contracted itself outside of Italy, leaving government to warring city states. Florence, Venice, Milan, and the Papacy became the strongest of the contending powers. They came to dominate the countryside while feudalism declined. They drew their riches from the produce of their fertile river valleys and from profits generated in commerce between the Orient and Europe. This trade flowed in by way of Venice (and eventually) Genoa, and passed through other northern cities on its way across the Alps.

THE ITALIAN RENAISSANCE

Under the patronage of the Papacy and of the increasingly prosperous princes of the city-states, such as the **Medici** of Florence, the scholars, writers, and artists created the masterpieces of literature, art, and science that made the **Italian Renaissance** one of the most influential movements in history. In this period many splendid churches, palaces, and public buildings were built that still inspire awe in Italians and visitors alike. At the same, these beautiful cities, such as Florence, Pisa, Venice, and Milan, were filled with social strife and political unrest.

PAWN OF STRONG NATIONS

While Italy was torn by struggles between the local rulers and the Papacy, strong nations developed elsewhere in Europe, and the Italy of separate city-states became an area of conquest for the powers struggling for European supremacy. French and Spanish rivalry over Italy began in 1494. **Charles VIII of France** valiantly fought his way through the peninsula to Naples, but by 1544 **Charles I of Spain** had defeated the French three times and had become ruler of Sicily, Naples, and Milan.

For centuries the states of Italy remained mere pawns in other nations' games of power. The city-states passed from one to another of Europe's rulers through war, marriage, death, or treaty. The **Papacy** was, however, usually strong enough to protect its temporal power over the areas in central Italy known as the **States of the Church**, or **Papal States**. The tiny republic of **San Marino** in the northeastern Apennines has remained through the centuries as a relic from this period. Although its 24 square miles are entirely surrounded by Italian soil, it is legally independent of Italy and claims to be the oldest state in Europe.

SPANISH & AUSTRIAN RULE

For some 150 years (1559-1713), Spain was the dominant power in Italy. Then the **Treaty of Utrecht** (1713) ended the **War of the Spanish Succession** and established the Austrian Hapsburgs in place of the Spanish as Italy's paramount power.

As time went by the Spanish began to feel slighted by the amount of land that had been ceded to Austria, so they sought to take back their former possessions. In 1734 **Don Carlos**, son of Philip V of Spain, conquered Naples and Sicily, and ruled the area as **Charles III of Naples**.

During this time, in the 18th century, enormous wealth was held by the few while the masses lived in squalor and ignorance. This disparity was especially noticeable in Italy, where the feudal system lingered on. The peasants were without rights or defenders. They lived in hovels and caves, and as a result crime rates were shocking despite harsh laws and punishments.

Ideas of reform coming from other nations found some response among the intellectuals and the middle class, and the concepts of liberty and equality stirring in France gained many Italian supporters. Many Italians were so blinded with the concepts that they offered assistant to a foreigner, **Napoleon Bonaparte**, as he began his conquest of Italy in the 1790s. As time went by the Italians realized their mistake, and hungered to be free of the yolk of French imperialism.

But even when Napoleon was defeated, most Italian states went back to their former sovereigns. For example, Venetia (Venice) was re-absorbed into Austrian rule, and Naples and Sicily were re-absorbed into Spanish rule. Italy was still a pawn in European politics.

MOVEMENT FOR POLITICAL UNITY

Eventually hatred of foreign rule mounted. With it grew the **risorgimento**, or movement for political unity. Such secret societies as the Carbonari (charcoal burners, the name given from their use of charcoal burners' huts for meeting places), plotted against the Austrians, but the **Carbonari Revolts** were crushed in 1821 and again in 1831 by Austrian troops.

Then the idealistic republican leader, **Giuseppe Mazzini**, organized his revolutionary society, **Young Italy**, and called upon **Charles Albert**, king of Sardinia-Piedmont and a member of the ancient House of Savoy, to head a movement to liberate Italy. By early 1848, revolts had broken out in many regions, and constitutions had been granted to Naples, Piedmont, and Tuscany. When Mazzini drove out the pope and set up a short-lived republic in Rome the French came to the pope's aid, while Austria quelled the revolt in the north. Eventually Charles Albert abdicated his rule in Sardinia-Piedmont in favor of his son **Victor Emmanuel II**.

Under the able leadership of the shrewd diplomat **Count Camillo di Cavour**, the minister of Victor Emmanuel, Sardinia-Piedmont grew strong in resources and in alliances. Cavour had learned that, genuine as was Italian patriotic fervor, Italy would never be unified without help from abroad.

Therefore he cleverly won an alliance with **Napoleon III** of France, and in the spring of 1859 Austria was goaded into declaring war against Sardinia-Piedmont and France. Austria was defeated, and Italy claimed the lands of Lombardy for a united Italy, but the Austrian's allowed France to retain Venetia.

Cavour and Victor Emmanuel lobbied the peoples of Tuscany, Modena, Parma, and Emilia who eventually voted to cast out their princes and join Sardinia-Piedmont. Napoleon III consented to such an arrangement, but only if Savoy and Nice voted to join France. (Politics is too complicated. I'll stick to travel writing).

GARIBALDI TO THE RESCUE

The second step toward a united Italy came the next year, when the famous soldier of fortune **Giuseppe Garibaldi** and his thousand red-shirted volunteers stormed the island of Sicily and the rest of the Kingdom of Naples on the mainland. The people everywhere hailed him as a liberator, and the hated Bourbon king was driven out.

Victor Emmanuel II was proclaimed king of Italy in February 1861, but now only the Papal States and Venetia remained to be joined to the new Italian nation. Venetia was gained in 1866, after Austria was defeated by Prussia in alliance with Italy. The Papal States were now the only ones outside the Italian kingdom, besides San Marino. San Marino was small and isolated, but since they were then about the size the current region of Lazio and not just the small little walled-in city they are today, the lack of that territory was a very real handicap to Italy.

VATICAN CAPTURED - KINGDOM OF ITALY UNITED

But since French troops still guarded the pope's sovereignty, Victor Emmanuel, being the apt pupil of Cavour (who had died in 1861), did not want to attack the French and perhaps undo all that had been accomplished. Then, miraculously in 1870, the **Franco-Prussian War** forced France to withdraw its soldiers from Rome, at which time Italian forces immediately marched in.

Pope Pius IX, in his infinite wisdom and understanding, excommunicated the invaders and withdrew behind the walls of the Vatican. There he and his successors remained 'voluntary prisoners' until the **Concordat of 1929**, or **Lateran Treaty**, between Italy and the Holy See, which recognized the temporal power of the pope as sovereign ruler over Vatican City (all 108.7 acres of it, or about 1/6 of a square mile!). Then, as many would argue now, the Vatican was afraid of adapting to a modern world, and wanted the status quo to remain.

MODERN ITALY - THE BEGINNING

Staggering under a load of debt and heavy taxation, giant steps needed to still be taken for Italy to survive. Leaders of the various regions, always trying to gain an edge, were in constant disagreement – even in active conflict. At the same time citizens, used to the ultimate control of despotic rule, found it difficult to adopt the ways of parliamentary government. As a result, riots and other forms of civil disorder were the rule in the latter half of the 19th century.

Despite all of these problems, in the typical Italian fashion of functioning despite complete political chaos, an army and navy were developed; railroads, ports, and schools were constructed; and a merchant marine was developed. At the same time, manufacturing started to flourish.

But then, in 1900, **King Umberto I** (son of Victor Emmanuel II) was assassinated, and his son, **Victor Emmanuel III**, rose to the throne. Meanwhile, trying to relive the glory days of the Roman Empire, Italian government officials were attempting to gain territory in Africa for colonial expansion. Eventually on Africa's east coast they obtained two colonies, **Eritrea** and **Italian Somaliland**, and on the north coast of Africa they won **Tripoli** after a war with Turkey (1911-12).

Although having joined with Germany and Austria in the **Triple Alliance** in 1882, in the early 1900s Italy began to befriend France and England. With Austria's invasion of Serbia in 1914, after the assassination of Archduke Ferdinand of Austria, Italy declared its neutrality despite being Austria's ally. In April 1915, Italy signed a secret treaty with the **Allies** (Russia, France, and England), and the next month it stated that it had withdrawn from the Triple Alliance. On May 23, 1915, the king declared war on Austria.

When World War I ended in 1918, the old Austro-Hungarian Empire was broken up. Italy was granted territory formerly under Austrian rule, including "unredeemed Italy" of the Trentino in the north and the peninsula of Istria at the head of the Adriatic.

MUSSOLINI & FASCISM

The massive depression after World War I brought strikes and riots, which were fomented by anarchists, socialists, and Communists. The government of Victor Emmanuel III seemed powerless to stop bands of former servicemen lawlessly roaming the country. In these bands, **Benito Mussolini** saw his opportunity. With his gift of oratory he soon molded this rabble into enthusiastic, organized groups in many communities all over Italy, armed them, and set them to preserving the order that they had destroyed. These bands formed the nucleus of his black-shirted **Fascist** party, whose emblem was the *fasces*, the bundle of rods that had symbolized the authority of the Roman Empire.

The party grew rapidly because Mussolini promised everything to everybody. On Oct. 28, 1922, the **Blackshirts**, meeting in Naples, were strong enough, well enough prepared, and willing to march on Rome and seize the government. The king, fearing civil war and his own life, refused to proclaim martial law, forced the premier to resign, and asked Mussolini to form a government.

Within a few years Mussolini, *Il Duce* (The Leader), had reorganized the government so that the people had no voice at all. Mussolini first abolished all parties except his own Fascist party, and took from the

Chamber of Deputies the power to consider any laws not proposed by him. The king remained as a figurehead because he was revered by the people and had the support of many wealthy and important families. In 1939, he replaced the Chamber of Deputies with the Chamber of Fasces and Corporations, composed of all his henchmen. No semblance of popular rule remained. Mussolini even took control of the provinces and cities by naming the prefects of the provinces and the mayors of the cities.

All opposition was crushed by intimidation or violence. Suspected critics of the regime were sentenced to prison by special courts or were terrorized, tortured, or murdered by Blackshirt thugs. News was censored and public meetings could not be held without the government's permission. The new Fascist state was based on the doctrine that the welfare of the state is all-important and that the individual exists only for the state, owes everything to it, and has no right to protection against it. It was a return to the despotism of the later Roman Empire.

A RETURN TO THE ROMAN EMPIRE?

Mussolini, like other Italian leaders before him, longed to create a new Roman empire and to bring back Italy's lost glory. So, in 1935, with his large army and recently expanded navy, he attacked and conquered the weak, backward, and poorly defended African country of Ethiopia.

In October 1936, at Mussolini's invitation, the **Rome-Berlin Axis** was formed between Italy and Nazi Germany to oppose the power of France and England. Strangely enough, at this time Mussolini was considered the stronger ally of the two. Through its military and economic support of Spain, this alliance between Rome and Berlin helped Franco achieve victory in the Spanish Civil War. (Spain was also the training ground for Germany's shock troops that would eventually march through Poland in a matter of days.) In April 1939, Italy invaded Albania, and at that time Italy and Germany became formal military allies.

But when Germany's program of aggression plunged it into war with England and France on September 3, 1939, Italy at first adopted the position of a non-belligerent. But on June 10, 1940, Italian forces attacked southeastern France in an invasion coordinated with German forces in the north. But they had only gotten involved when it was obvious that France was no longer a threat.

DEFEAT IN WORLD WAR II

Italy, however, lacked the military power, resources, and national spirit for fighting a large-scale war. Within six months, Italian armies met defeat in Greece and North Africa. (A running joke during World War II was that Italian tanks had only one gear: reverse.) Italy then humbly accepted the military assistance of Germany. This soon grew into economic dependence, and Italy was forced to let Germany occupy it and control its home affairs, and Mussolini became a German puppet.

After the Allies invaded and won all Italian territory in North Africa as well as Sicily in July 1943, public unrest forced Mussolini to resign. He was arrested and held under guard. The constitutional monarchy was restored, with Marshal Pietro Badoglio as premier.

The Allies invaded Italy's mainland from Sicily on Sept. 3, 1943, and after what some considered to be a token resistance (the soldiers buried beneath the graves of Anzio might beg to differ), Italy surrendered unconditionally that same day, and on October 13 declared war on Germany. Meanwhile, Mussolini had been freed by German paratroopers and had fled into German-held north Italy, where he established a "Republican Fascist State."

The entire length of the mountainous north became a bitter battleground, but eventually enemy forces surrendered their hold on northern Italy on April 29, 1945. Mussolini and his wife were subsequently captured by partisans, hung, shot, and for good measure, beaten until he was unrecognizable.

The end of the war found Italy with a large part of its industry and agriculture shattered. During its occupation, the Germans had almost stripped Italy's industry bare by commandeering supplies. Italian factories, roads, docks, and entire villages were ruined by the Allied bombing raids and during the invasion. To make things worse, as the Germans retreated they had wrecked whatever industries and transportation remained.

Even with the Allies contributing substantial quantities of food, clothing, and other supplies, the people were cold, hungry, and jobless. After the war, the United Nations Relief and Rehabilitation Administration gave more aid to Italy than to any other country. Reconstruction lagged, however, because of internal political turmoil, such turmoil becoming something of a theme in postwar Italian poltics.

POSTWAR POLITICAL CHANGES

During the battle for Italy its people were politically restless, and so a variety of parties representing many political views, from the extreme left to the far right, had been born. The more liberal parties demanded an end to the monarchy, but backed by the Allies, Victor Emmanuel III retained his sovereignty until the liberation of Rome in 1944.

On May 9, 1946, Victor Emmanuel III formally abdicated in favor of his son, who reigned for less than one month as **Umberto II**, because on June 2, 1946, the Italian people voted to found a republic. They also elected deputies to a Constituent Assembly to draft a new constitution.

Finally on February 10, 1947, the peace treaty between Italy and the Allies was ready to be signed. The treaty stripped Italy of its African 'empire' of Libya, Italian Somaliland, and Eritrea. The pact also ceded the Dodecanese Islands to Greece, internationalized Trieste, made minor boundary changes with France, and gave about 3,000 square miles to Yugoslavia, including most of the Istrian peninsula.

Italy had to pay $360 million in reparations, and was also forced to restore independence to Ethiopia and Albania. One lone gain was that **south Tyrol**, which Austria had been forced to cede after World War I, remained with Italy, and eventually, in 1954, **Trieste** was given to Italy by agreement with Yugoslavia.

On January 1, 1948, Italy's newly formed constitution became effective. It banned the Fascist party (unfortunately, there are today plenty of political parties in Italy that go by another name but informally call themselves *Fascisti*) and the monarchy. Freedom of religion was guaranteed, but Catholicism remained the state religion.

But a constitution alone cannot recreate a country. Italian leaders had the double task of creating a stable parliamentary system of government while at the same time restoring the economy. (They still haven't solved the first problem.) The main economic hindrance was the poverty-stricken south contributing little to the improving economy of the north. As a result there were many riots and moments of intense civil unrest.

LAND REFORM

The south was so poor because much of central and southern Italy, Sicily, and Sardinia were among the last aristocratic European strongholds of large-scale landowners. The estates of these landowners covered many thousands of acres and employed only small numbers of laborers, mostly at harvest time. These landless peasants, who had no work during much of the year, lived in nearby villages and small towns and barely made ends meet all year. These citizens either stayed peaceful, contributed to civil unrest, or emigrated to find better employment and living conditions.

In the early 1950s, the Italian parliament passed special land reform laws that divided large private estates into small farms and distributed them to the peasants. The new owners were given substantial government support for their first years on the land, and the previous owners received cash compensation. Thousands of new small farms were created in this way during the 1950s, and farm production, as a result of the land reform and other measures, rose quickly.

The Italian government not only invested large sums of money in land reform but at the same time also started to develop the southern infrastructure to help the farmers. New roads were built to help carry produce to market, and new irrigation systems, needed during the long, dry summers, were constructed. Warehouses and cold storage facilities for farm products were provided, and the government also helped to introduce new crops.

Flower growers in The Netherlands began to send seeds to southern Italy, where they could start growing early while the fields of Holland might still be covered with snow. In spring, Italian growers would ship the young plants back north for final growth. As a result of these changes, farming in central and especially southern Italy began to bounce back.

CHAOS MIXED WITH STABILITY

Even with the south's new-found prosperity, Italy's economic development was mainly due to spectacular gains in industrial production in the north. Then during the mid-1960s, Italy began to suffer from severe inflation. A government austerity program to combat this trend produced a decline in profits and a lag in investments. To add insult to injury, devastating floods – the worst in 700 years – hit the country in 1966, ravaging one third of the land and causing losses of more than $1.5 billion. To make matters even worse, some of the priceless art treasures of Florence were irreparably damaged when the flood waters poured through that city.

In 1971 Italy had its largest economic recession since the country's post-World War II recovery. Strikes affected nearly every sector of the economy as Italian workers demanded social reforms. The problems of inflation, unemployment, lack of housing, and unfavorable balance of payments continued in the 1970s. Nevertheless, the economy showed resiliency for the five-year period ending in 1976 with an increase in gross domestic production.

When Italy was about to pull out of its economic problems, political terrorism escalated, culminating in March 1978, when **Aldo Moro**, leader of the Christian Democratic party and former premier, was abducted in Rome by the **Red Brigades**, an extreme left-wing terrorist group. During the two months that Moro was held, Rome was like an armed camp, with military roadblocks everywhere. Eventually Moro was found murdered and left in the trunk of his car two months later.

In 1980, in Italy's worst natural disaster in more than 70 years, an earthquake killed more than 3,000 persons in the Naples area. As if things could only get worse, in May 1981 a Turkish political dissident tried to kill Pope John Paul II in St. Peter's Square in Vatican City. Also in 1981, a corruption scandal involving hundreds of public servants who were allegedly members of a secret society erupted and brought down the government.

Then for the first time in the 35-year history of the Italian republic, a non-Christian Democratic premier was elected. However, the Christian Democrats regained their power in November 1982, and socialist **Bettino Craxi** served as premier from 1983 to 1987, the longest term of any Italian leader since World War II.

Economic conditions in the early 1980s were affected by growing recession and rising inflation. The Vatican Bank and the Banco Ambrosiano of Milan, Italy's biggest private banking group, were involved in a major banking scandal that forced the liquidation of Banco Ambrosiano in 1982. Two natural disasters, an earthquake and a landslide, caused widespread damage in the regions of Perugia and Ancona in late 1982.

In 1989, another bank became involved in a scandal when it was revealed that an American branch of the Banca Nazionale del Lavoro had loaned billions of dollars to Iraq. Then severe drought occurred throughout Italy in the winter of 1989 and in Venice some canals were unusable because water levels had dropped so low. And currently, the Italian government is under intense investigation for rampant corruption including officials taking bribes from members of the Mafia.

Still, despite these natural and manmade disasters, the Italian economy continued to improve, to the point where it is one of the more successful in Europe. Throughout all of this chaos, Italy perseveres. It's almost as if without a reasonable amount of disorder, Italy could not survive.

6. PLANNING YOUR TRIP

BEFORE YOU GO

CLIMATE & WEATHER

The climate in Italy is as varied as the country itself, but it never seems to get too harsh. Any time is a good time to travel to Italy. Most of the country has a Mediterranean type of climate, meaning cool, rainy winters and hot, dry summers.

The summers are mild in the north, but winters in the north tend to be colder because these regions are in or near the Alps. The Alps protects the rest of Italy from cold northern winds. Because Italy is a peninsula and thus surrounded by water, the entire country tends to be calm and mild except for the south and Sicily. These regions are very hot in the summer, and in the winter, wetter than normal. Winter temperatures along and near the coasts of southern Italy seldom drop to freezing in winter, and summer temperatures often reach 90°F (32°C) or higher.

Winter is the rainy season, when stream beds that remain empty during much of the year fill to overflowing and flash floods are common.

When to Go

With this in mind, anytime is good time to travel to Italy. The climate doesn't vary greatly making Italy a pleasant trip any time of year. Then again I'm biased – I spent eight wonderful years in Italy and I think it's fantastic all year. The busiest tourist season is from May to October, leaving Spring and Autumn as the choice times to have Italy all to yourself.

The sidebar below offers you a breakdown by season of the best regions to visit during those times:

ITALY'S FOUR SEASONS

Spring – *Italy has an early spring. The best places to visit are Florence, around Naples and Sorrento, Sicily, and Rome.*

Summer – *Summer can be a little hot at times, so to cool you down there are plenty of beach resorts along most of Italy's coast, especially in Liguria on the Italian Riviera. But the best place to go is the mountains of Tuscany or the northern regions of Lombardia, Piemonte, or Trentino Alto-Adige. This is not to say that Rome or Venice would not be pleasant, just crowded with tourists and relatively warm.*

Autumn – *This is a pleasant time to visit Rome and other major cities, since they are less crowded and much cooler.*

Winter – *Time for winter sports. You can find ski centers in the Alps as well as the central Appenines near Florence and Rome. Also at this time, the southern regions and Sicily are at their best.*

WHAT TO PACK

One suitcase and a carry-on should suffice for your average week to ten day trip. Besides, there are countless clothing stores from which you can buy yourself any needed item. Also it's advised to pack light so you can move your belongings with ease. In conjunction, you can always find a local *Tintoria* (dry cleaner) to clean any dirty clothes for you, if your hotel does not supply such a service. If you want to do it yourself, it's best to look for a *Lavanderia* instead, your basic coin operated Laundromat.

Remember to pack all your personal cosmetic items that you've grown used to using, since, more than likely, they're not available in Italian stores. The Italian culture just hasn't seemed to grasp the necessity of having 400 types of toothpaste, or 200 types of tampons.

Also important to remember, especially if you're traveling in the winter time, is an umbrella, a raincoat, and water-proof shoes. You never know when the rain will fall in the winter.

PUBLIC HOLIDAYS

Offices and shops in Italy are closed on the dates below. So prepare for the eventuality of having virtually everything closed and stock up on picnic snacks, soda, whatever, because in most cities and towns there is no such thing as a 24 hour a day 7-11. The Italians take their free time seriously. To them the concept of having something open 24 hours a day is, well, a little crazy.

• **January 1**, New Year's Day
• **January 6**, Epiphany
• **April 25**, Liberation Day (1945)

- **Easter Monday**
- **May 1**, Labor Day
- **August 15**, *Ferragosto* and Assumption of the Blessed Virgin (climax of Italian family holiday season. Hardly anything stays open in the big cities through the month of August)
- **November 1**, All Saints Day
- **December 8**, Immaculate Conception
- **December 25/26**, Christmas

Listed below are some dates that may be considered public holidays in different areas of Italy, so prepare for them too:
- **Ascension**
- **Corpus Christi**
- **June 2**, Proclamation of Republic (celebrated on the following Saturday)
- **November 4**, National Unity Day (celebrated on following Saturday)

LOCAL FESTIVAL DAYS & THEIR PATRON SAINTS

Town	Date	Patron Saint
Venice	April 25	St. Mark
Florence	June 24	St. John the Baptist
Genoa	June 24	St. John the Baptist
Turin	June 24	St. John the Baptist
Rome	June 29	Sts. Peter and Paul
Palermo	July 15	Santa Rosalia
Naples	Sept. 19	St. Gennaro
Bologna	Oct. 4	St. Petronio
Cagliari	Oct. 30	St. Saturnino
Trieste	Nov. 3	San Giusto
Bari	Dec. 6	St. Nicola
Milan	Dec. 7	St. Ambrose

MAKING AIRLINE RESERVATIONS

Since airfares can vary so widely it is advised to contact a reputable travel agent and stay abreast of all promotional fares advertised in the newspapers. Once you're ticketed getting there is a breeze. Just hop on the plane and 6-8 hours later you're there. Italy's two main international ariports are Rome's **Fiumicino** (also knowns as **Leonardo da Vinci**) and Milan's **Malpensa**, which handle all incoming flights from North America, Australia, and the United Kingdom.

There are other, smaller regional airports in Bologna, Pisa and Venice that accept flights from all over Europe as well as the Untied Kingdom, but not from North America or Australia. So, if you are only visiting the fairy tale city of Venice and want to fly almost directly there, contact your travel agent and make sure they get you on an airline, most likely British Air, that will allow for a transfer in London and a connection to Venice.

Fares are highest during the peak summer months (June through mid-September) and lowest from November through March (except during peak Christmas travel time). You can get the best fares by booking far in advance. This will also assure you a seat. Getting a non-stop flight to Italy at the last minute is simply an impossibility during the high season. If you are concerned about having to change your schedule at the last minute, and do not want to book far in advance, look into some special **travel insurance** that will cover the cost of your ticket under such circumstances. Check with your travel agent about details and pricing since these, like ticket prices, change almost on a daily basis.

ARRIVALS & DEPARTURES

FLYING TO ITALY

Alitalia is Italy's national airline. As you probably know, most international carriers have amazing service, pristine environments, serve exquisite food and overall are a joy to travel – but to be honest Alitalia is not one of them. If you're up for the adventure of the chaos of Italy's system (take their frequent lack of a government, for example) at 30,000 feet, try flying Alitalia. As another example of Alitalia's disorganization, they are the only major airline in the U.S. without their own toll-free number. Despite their problems Alitalia does have the most frequent direct flights from North America to Italy.

Below is a list of some other major carriers and their flights to Italy:
• **Air Canada**, *1-800-776-3000*. Flights from Canada to London or Paris, then connections on another carrier to Rome or Milan.
• **American Airlines**, *1-800-433-7300*. Direct flights from Chicago to Milan.
• **Delta**, *1-800-221-1212*. Direct flights from New York to Rome or Milan.
• **British Airways**, *1-800-247-9297*. Connections through London's Heathrow to Rome, Milan, Bologna or Venice.
• **United**, *1-800-241-6522*. Direct flights from Washington Dulles to Milan.
• **Northwest**, *1-800-2245-2525*. Flights to Amsterdam connecting to KLM and onto Rome or Milan.

GETTING TO & FROM THE AIRPORTS IN ROME

The Italian transportation system is the complete opposite of their airline: on-time, goes everywhere, and is clean and comfortable.

Rome has a dedicated **train** to wisk you directly to the central train station, where you can get a taxi to your hotel (doing it this way will be much less expensive than taking a taxi straight from the airport and just about as convenient). From the train station, you can also hop on the **Metro** or a **city bus** to take you near your hotel.

When you are departing the country remember to have at least L15,000 on hand to pay the airport tax.

Rome Fiumicino (Leonardo da Vinci) Airport

• **Direct Link** – A new train service is now available from the airport directly to **Stazione Termini** (Rome's Central Railway Station). The trip costs L12,000 and takes 30 minutes). There are 15 trips each day in both directions, basically one train every hour. The trains are air-conditioned.

• **Metropolitan Link** – Train service from the Airport to **Stazione Tiburtina** stopping at the following stations: Ponte Galleria, Muratella, Magliana, Trastevere, Ostiense, and Tuscolana. Departures are every 20 minutes from 6:00 am to 10:00 pm. Trip takes about 45 minutes. Trains are air-conditioned.

Rome Ciampino Airport

Dedicated airport buses can be caught outside of the **Agnina Underground Station**. Time to airport: 15-25 minutes, depending on traffic.

GETTING TO & FROM THE AIRPORTS IN MILAN

Milano Malpensa Airport

There is a bus from the square beside **Milano Centrale Railway Station** every 30 minutes, but only in the morning. Contact the tourist office inside the train station or the airport if you have any questions.

Milano Linate Airport

There is a bus from the square beside **Milano Centrale Railway Station** to and from **Linate** airport every 20 minutes. There is also ATM Municipial Bus Service 73 from Piazza San Babila (corner of Corso Europa) every 15 minutes. Duration for both is 30 minutes.

Contact the tourist office inside the train station or the airport if you have any questions.

PASSPORT REGULATIONS

A visa is not required for US or Canadian citizens, or members of the European Economic Community, who are holding a valid passport, unless s/he expects to stay in Italy longer than 90 days and/or study or seek employment. While in Italy, you can apply for a longer stay at any police station for an extension of an additional 90 days. You will be asked to prove that you're not seeking such an extension for study or employment, and that you have adequate means of support. Usually permission is granted almost immediately.

VACCINATIONS

No vaccinations are required to enter Italy, or for that matter, to re-enter the U.S., Canada, or any other European country.

CUSTOMS REGULATIONS

Duty free entry is allowed for personal effects that will not be sold, given away, or traded while in Italy: clothing, books, camping and household equipment, fishing tackle, one pair of skis, two tennis racquets, portable typewriter (I suppose they mean a portable computer now), record player with 10 records, tape recorder or Dictaphone, baby carriage, two still cameras with 10 rolls of film for each, one movie camera with 10 rolls of film (I suppose they mean 10 cassette tapes now), binoculars, personal jewelry, portable radio set (may be subject to small license fee), 400 cigarettes, and a quantity of cigars or pipe tobacco not to exceed 500 grams (1.1 lbs), two bottles of wine and one bottle of liquor, 4.4 lbs of coffee, 6.6 lbs of sugar, and 2.2 lbs of cocoa.

This is Italy's official list, but they are very flexible with personal items. As well they should be, since technology is changing so rapidly that items not listed last year could be a personal item for most people this year (i.e. Sony Watchmans, portable video games, etc.)

REGISTRATION BY TOURISTS

This is usually taken care of within three days by the management of your hotel. If you are staying with friends or in a private home, you must register in person at the nearest police station within that three day period. Rome has a special police information office to assist tourists, and they have interpreters available. *Tel: 461-950 or 486-609.*

DIPLOMATIC & CONSULAR OFFICES IN ITALY

These are the places you'll need to contact if you lose your passport or have some unfortunate brush with the law. If such situations occur, remember that the employees of these offices are merely your government's representatives in a foreign country. They are not God. They cannot do everything in the blink of an eye, but they will do their best to remedy any unfortunate situation in which you may find yourself.

Embassies
- **US**, *Via Veneto 119A, 00187 Roma, Tel. (06) 46741*
- **Canada**, *Via GB de Rossi, 00161 Roma, Tel. (06) 445-981*
- **Ireland**, *Largho del Nazereno, 00187 Roma,Tel. 06/678-25-41*
- **South Africa**, *Via Tanaro 14, 00187 Roma, Tel. 06/841-97-94*
- **United Kingdom**, *Via XX Settembre 80A, 00187 Roma, Tel. (06) 475 5441 and 475 5551*
- **Australia**,*Via Alessandro 215, 00187 Roma, Tel. 06/852-721*
- **New Zealand**, Via Zara 28, 00187 Roma, Tel. *06/440-2928 or 440-40-35*

US Consulates
- *Lungarno Amerigo Vespucci 38. 1 50123 Firenze, Tel. (055) 239-8276*
- *Piazza Portello 6, 16124 Genova, Tel. (010) 290-027*
- *Via Principe Amedeo 2/10, 20121 Milano, Tel. (02) 290-045-59*
- *Piazza della Republica, 80122 Napoli, Tel. (081) 583-8111*
- *Via Vaccarini 1, 90143 Palermo, Tel. (091) 343-546*

Canadian Consulates
- *Delegation du Quebec, Via XX Settembre 4, 00187 Roma, Tel. (06) 488-4183*
- *Via Vittor Pisani 19, 20124 Milano, Tel. (02) 669-7451 and 669-4970 (night line)*

UK Consulates
- *Via San Lucifero 87. 09100 Cagliari, Tel. (070) 66 27 55*
- *Palazzo Castelbarco, Lungarno Corsini 2, 50123 Firenze, Tel. (055) 21 26 94, 28 41 33 and 28 74 49*
- *Via XII Ottobre 2, 16121 Genova, Tel. (010) 48 33-36*
- *Via San Paolo 7, 1-20121 Milano, Tel. (02) 80 34 42*
- *Via Francesco Crispi 122. 08122 Napoli, Tel. (081) 20 92 27, 63 33 20 and 68 24 82*
- *Via Marchese di Villabianca 9, 90143 Palermo, Tel. (091) 33 64-66*
- *Via Rossini 2, 14132 Trieste, Tel (040) 6 91 35*
- *Corso M. d'Azaglio 60. 10126 Torino, Tel. (011) 68 78 32 and 68 39 21*
- *Accademia 1051, R301 00 Venezia, Tel. (041) 272 07*

ACCOMMODATIONS IN ITALY

HOTELS - WHAT TO EXPECT

Don't be surprised by the excessive hotel taxes, additional charges, and requests for payment for extras, such as air conditioning. Sometimes these taxes/service charges are included in room rates; check upon arrival. Remember to save receipts from hotels and car rentals, as 15% to

20% of the value-added taxes (VAT) on these services may be refunded since you're a tourist. *For more information, call I.T.S. Fabry at 803-720-8646.*

The Italian Government Tourist agency rates all of the hotels in Italy with a star basis, so we will continue their system. A five star deluxe hotel (*****) is the best, a one-star hotel (*) is the least desirable and usually the least expensive too. The term *Pensione* is in the process of being phased out, and is being replaced by hotels with a designation of one-star (*), two-stars (**), or three stars (***).

Hotel Prices

The prices that are listed sometimes include a range, for example L100,000-150,000. The first number in the range indicates what the price is during the off-season, the second price is the going rate during high season. If there is no range that indicates that the hotel either doesn't raise their rate for the off-season, or they are not open during that time.

HOTEL RATING SYSTEM

The star rating system that the Italian Tourist Board officially uses has little to do with the prices of the hotels, but more to do with the amenities you will find in them. The prices for each category will vary according to the locale, so if it's a big city, a four star will be super expensive; if it's a small town, it will be priced like a three star in a big city.

This is what the ratings basically mean by star category:

*****Five star, deluxe hotel**: Professional service, great restaurant, perfectly immaculate large rooms and bathrooms with air conditioning, satellite TV, mini-bar, room service, laundry service, and every convenience you could imagine to make you feel like a king or queen. Bathrooms in every room.

****Four star hotel**: professional service, maybe they have a restaurant, clean rooms not so large, air conditioning, TV-maybe satellite, mini-bar, room service, laundry service and maybe a few more amenities. Bathrooms in every room.

***Three star hotel**: a little less professional service, most probably do not have room service, should have air conditioning, TV and mini bar, but the rooms are mostly small as are their bathrooms. Bathrooms might not be in every room.

Two star hotel: Usually a family run place, some not so clean as higher rated hotels. Mostly you'll only find a telephone in the room, and you'll be lucky to get air conditioning. About 50% of the rooms have either a shower/bath or water closet and sometimes not both together. No amenities whatsoever, just a place to lay your head.

*One star hotel: Here you usually get a small room with a bed, sometimes you have to share the rooms with other travelers. More often than not the bathroom is in the hall. No air conditioning, no nothing. Definitely for budget travelers.

RENTING VILLAS & APARTMENTS

One of the best ways to spend a vacation in Italy is in a rented villa in the country or in an apartment in the center of town. It makes you feel as if you actually are living in Italy and not just passing through. Staying in "your own place" in Italy gives your trip that little extra sense of belonging.

The best way to find a place of your own in Italy is to contact one of the agencies listed below that specialize in the rental of villas and apartments in Italy:

• **At Home Abroad, Inc.**, *405 East 58th Street, New York, NY 10022. Tel: (212) 421-9165, Fax: (212) 752-1591.*

• **Astra Maccioni Kohane** (CUENDET), *10 Columbus Circle, Suite 1220, New York, NY 10019. Tel: (212) 765-3924, Fax: (212) 262-0011.*

• **B&D De Vogue International, Inc.**, *250 S. Beverly Drive, Suite 203, Beverly Hills CA. Tel: (310) 247 8612, (800) 438-4748, Fax: (310) 247-9460.*

• **Better Homes and Travel**, *30 East 33rd Street, New York, NY 10016. Tel: (212) 689 6608, Fax: (212) 679-5072.*

• **CIT Tours Corp.**, *342 Madison Ave #207, New York, NY 10173. Tel. (212) 697-2100, (800) 248-8687, Fax: (212)697-1394*

• **Columbus Travel**, *507 Columbus Avenue, San Francisco, CA 941S3. Tel- (415) 39S2322, Fax: (415) 3984674.*

• **Destination Italia, Inc.** (Excluive U.S. Representative for Cuendet & Cie spa). *165 Chestnut Street, Allendale, NJ 07401. Tel: (201) 327-2333, Fax: (201) 825-2664.*

• **Europa-let, Inc.** *92 N. Main Street or P.O. Box 3537, Ashland, OR 97520. Tel: (503) 482-5806, (800) 4624486, Fax: (503) 482-0660.*

• **European Connection**, *4 Mineola Avenue, Roslyn Heights, NY 11577. Tel: (516) 625-1800, (800) 345 4679, Fax: (516) 625-1138.*

• **Four Star Living, Inc.**, *640 Fifth Avenue, New York, NY 10019. Tel: (212) 518 3690, Fax: (914) 677-5528.*

• **Heaven on Hearth**, *44 Kittyhawk, Pittsford, NY 14534. Tel: (716) 381-7625, Telefax (716) 381-9784.*

• **Hidden Treasure of Italy**, *934 Elmwood, Wilmettw IL 60091. Tel. (708) 853-1313. Fax (708) 853-1340*

• **Hideaways International**, *P.O. Box 1270, Littleton, MA 01460. Tel: (508) 486-8955, (800) 8434433, Fax: (508) 486-8525.*

• **Home Tours International**, *1170 Broadway, New York, NY 10001, Tel; (212) 6894851, Outside New York 1-800-367-4668.*

- **Interhome Inc.**, *124 Little Falls Road, Fairfield, NJ 07004. Tel: (201) 882-6864, Fax: (201) 8051 742.*
- **International Home Rentals**, *P.O. Box 329, Middleburg, VA 22117. Tel: (703) 687-3161, (800) 221-9001, Fax: (703) 687-3352.*
- **InternationalServices**, *P.O. Box 118, Mendham, NJ 07945. Tel: (201)545-9114, Fax; (201) 543-9159.*
- **Invitation to Tuscany**, *94 Winthrop Street, Augusta, ME 04330. Tel: (207) 622-0743.*
- **Italian Rentals**, *3801 Ingomar Street, N.W., Washington, D.C. 20015. Tel: (202) 244-5345, Fax: (202) 362-0520.*
- **Itallan Villa Rentals**, *P.O. Box 1145, Bellevue, Washington 98009. Tel (206) 827-3964, Telex: 3794026, Fax: (206) 827-2323.*
- **Italy Farm Holidays**, *547 Martling Avenue, Tarrytown, NY 10591. Tel: (914) 631-7880, Fax: (914) 631-8831.*
- **LNT Associates**, *Inc., P.O. Box 219, Warren, Ml 48090. Tel: (313) 739-2266, (800) 582 4832, Fax: (313) 739-3312.*
- **Overseas Connection**, *31 North Harbor Drive. Sag Harbor, NY 11963. Tel: (516) 725-9308, Fax: (516) 725-5825.*
- **Palazzo Antellesi**, *175 West 92nd Street #1GE, New York NY 10025. Tel. (212) 932-3480, Fax: (212) 932-9039*
- **The Parker Company**, *319 Lynnway, Lynn MA 01901. Tel. (617) 596-8282, Fax: (617) 596-3125.*
- **Prestige Villas**, *P.O.BOx 1046, Southport, CT 06490. Tel: (203) 254-1302. Outside Connecticut (800) 336-0080, Fax: (203) 254-7261.*
- **Rent a Home International, Inc.**, *7200 34th Avenue. N.W.. Seattle, WA 98117. Tel: (206) 789-9377, (800) 488-RENT, Fax: (206) 789-9379, Telex 40597.*
- **Rentals In Italy**, *Suzanne T. Pidduck (CUENDET), 1742 Calle Corva, Camarillo, CA 93010. Tel: (805) 987-5278, (800) 726-6702, Fax: (805) 987-5278.*
- **Rent-A-Vacation Everywhere, Inc**. *(RAVE), 585 Park Avenue, Rochester, NY 14607. Tel: (716) 256-0760, Fax: (716) 256-2676.*
- **Vacanze In Italla**, *P.O. Box 297, Falls Village, CT 06031. Tel: (413) 528-6610, (800) 533-5405, Fax: (413) 528-6222.*
- **Villas and Apartments Abroad, Ltd.**, *420 Madison Avenue. New York, NY 10017. Tel. (212) 759-1025. (800) 433-3021 (Nationwide), (800) 433-3020 (NY).*
- **Villas Intematlonal**, *605 Market Street, Suite 610, San Francisco, CA 94105. Tel: (415) 281-0910, (800) 221-2260, Fax: (415) 281-0919.*

HOME EXCHANGE

*A less expensive way to have "a home of your own" in Italy is to join a **home swapping club**. These clubs have reputable members all over the world. All you'd need to do is coordinate travel plans with a family in a location you'd like to stay in Italy, and exchange houses. Think of how much money you'd save.*

*The best one that we know is **Vacation Exchange Club**, PO Box, Key West FL 33041, Tel. 305/294-3720, 800/638-3841, Fax: 305/294-1448.*

YOUTH HOSTELS

Youth Hostels (*ostelli per la gioventu*) provide reasonably priced accommodations, specifically for younger travelers. A membership card is needed that is associated with the youth hostel's organization, i.e. a student ID card. Advanced booking is a must during the high season since these low priced accommodations fill up fast. Hundreds of youth hostels are located all over Italy. Contact the Tourist Information office when you arrive in the city to locate them.

GETTING AROUND ITALY

Italy is connected by extensive highway systems, a superb train system, a series of regional airports, and naturally, since Italy is virtually surrounded by water and has a number of islands, a complete shipping service involving ferries, hydrofoils, and liners. Your mode of transportation will depend on how long you're staying in Italy and where you are going.

If you have plenty of time on your hands, there will be no need to fly throughout Italy, and travel by train and car will suffice. If you are going to rural, off-the-beaten path locations, you'll need a car, because even if the train did go to where you're going, the *Locale* would take forever since it stops at every town on its tracks.

GETTING AROUND ITALY BY AIR

You can fly between many Italian destinations quite easily. If you are on business, using air travel makes sense to fly from Milan to Rome, but not if you are a tourist. You could enjoy a relaxing three hour train ride in the morning to Florence, spend a day shopping and sightseeing, then get on another three hour train ride to Rome and get there in time for dinner. And the entire cost would only be around $40, a lot less than if you had flown.

But if you insist on flying, here are a list of towns that have airports that receive service from the larger venues in Rome and Milan: Alghero, Ancona, Bari, Bologna, Brindisi, Cagliari, Catania, Firenze, Genoa, Lamezia Terme, Lampedusa, Napoli, Olbia, Pantelleria, Pescara, Pisa, Reggio Calabria, Torino, Trapani, Trieste, Venice, Verona.

GETTING AROUND ITALY BY BUS

Most long distance travel is done by train, but the regional bus systems can be beneficial for intercity trips to smaller towns, and the pullman buses can be perfect for a very long trip. If you're not a rental car person, and you simply have to get to that beautiful little medieval hill town you saw from the train window, the only way you're gouing to get there is by regional bus. Also, if you're going from Florence to Bari to catch the ferry to Greece, it is more convenient to catch a direct bus since you won't have to stop in the Rome or Naples train station to pick up other passengers.

Conveniently, most bus stations are next door to or near the train station in towns and cities. The Italian transporation system is something to be admired and hopefully replicated since they make it so convenient. And comfortable too. Most long range buses are equipped with bathrooms and some have televisions on them (not that you'd understand what was on). The regional inter-town buses are a little less comfortable but still palatial compared to the same type of bus in Central America.

I suggest sticking to the trains, unless the trains don't go where you want to go, which is about everywhere, then take the bus.

GETTING AROUND ITALY BY CAR

The world's first automobile expressways were built in northern Italy during the 1920s. Today, Italy and Germany have the most extensive networks of fast, limited-access highways in Europe. Motorists can drive without encountering traffic lights or crossroads – stopping only for border crossings, rest, or fuel – from Belgium, Holland, France, or Germany across the Alps all the way to Sicily. Two highway tunnels through the Alps, under the Great St. Bernard Pass and through Mont Blanc, enable motor vehicles to travel between Italy and the rest of Europe regardless of weather. The expressways, called **autostradas**, are super-highways and toll roads. They connect all major Italian cities and have contributed to the tremendous increase in tourist travel.

Driving is the perfect way to see the entire variety of Italy's towns, villages, seascapes, landscapes, and monuments. The Italian drivers may be a little *pazzo* (crazy), but if you drive confidently you should be fine. Still, be alert on Italy's roadways.

Driver's Licenses

US, British, and Canadian driving licenses are valid in Italy, but only when accompanied by a translation. This translation is obtainable from the **AAA**, the offices of the **Automobile club d'Italia** in Italy, at the offices for the **Italian State Tourist Office**, and at the Italian frontier.

- **Automobile club d'Italia**, *Via Marsala 8, I-00185, Roma. Tel. (06) 49 98 99*
- **Italian State Tourist Office**, *in the US: 500 N Michigan Ave, Chicago, IL 60611. Tel. (312) 644-0990; 630 Fifth Ave, Suite 1565, New York, NY 10111. Tel. (212) 245-4822; 360 Post Street, Suite 801, San Francisco CA 94109. Tel. (415) 392-6206; in Canada: Store 56, Plaza 3, 3 Place Ville Marie, Montreal, Quebec., Tel. 866 7667.*

Car Rental

In all major cities there are a variety of car rental locations, and even such American stalwarts as Avis and Hertz (see each city's individual section for specifics). All you need to do to rent a car is contact the agency in question, or have the management of your hotel do it for you. Remember to have had your driver's license translated prior to your arrival (see above). From your car rental place, you will be able to pick up detailed maps of the area in which you want to drive.

Driving through the back roads of Italy can offer you some of the best sights of secluded little hill towns, clear mountain lakes, snow capped mountains and more; but it can also be one of the most expensive items on you trip, not only because of the exorbitant cost of the rental itself, but the cost of $6 or more per gallon of gas. There are ways to keep the cost down, the best of which is making the best use of you car. Don't rent it for your entire trip, allowing it to sit in a garage when you are in a big city and you're getting around on bus, metro, or taxi.

Use a rental car to travel through the isolated hills and valleys in between the big cities and drop off the car once you arrive. Compared to the cost of the rental, drop-off charges are minimal. And of course, make sure you have unlimited mileage (kilometerage?), otherwise the cost will creep up by the kilometer.

Beside the beauty you'll encounter, and the expense you'll incur, be aware of the possible danger you'll also be putting yourself into. Unless you are from Boston and are used to aggressive driving tactics, driving a car to get around Italy should be avoided. The country's train system is so superb that if you're only going to the major cities and towns you won't need a car. So think twice about renting a car. Italian drivers are like nothing you've ever seen.

GETTING AROUND ITALY BY TRAIN

The Italian railroad system, which is owned by the government, provides convenient transportation throughout the country. Ferries link the principal islands with the mainland, and those that travel between southernmost Italy and Sicily carry trains as well as cars, trucks, and people.

The railroad system is most extensive in the north, but main lines run along both coasts, and other routes cross the peninsula in several places. The **Simplon Tunnel**, one of the world's longest railroad tunnels, connects Italy and Switzerland. Other rail lines follow routes across the Alps between Italy and France, Austria, and Slovenia.

Taking the train is one of the best ways to travel throughout Italy. They go almost every place you'd like to see. The efficiency of the railway system in Italy is directly attributed to Mussolini. You may have heard the saying, "He may not have done much else, but he got the trains to arrive on time."

Types of Train Tickets

There are two different levels of seating on most every train in Italy: **first class** and **second class**. The difference in price is usually only a few dollars, but the difference in convenience is astounding. First class ticket holders can make reservations in advance, while second class ticket seating is on a first come first serve basis.

In conjunction, the seating quality is light-years apart. An example of the price difference between first class and second when traveling between Rome and Florence is $35 for first class, $22 for second class.

Ticket Discounts

The Italian Railway System offers a variety of discounts on its tickets. Listed below are some that may fit into your travel plans:

- **Silver Card for Senior Citizens**: Available to all people 60 years and older. It allows for a 30% reduction on all first class and second class tickets. Must be purchased in Italy. A one year pass costs L10,000; A two year pass costs L18,000; a permanent pass costs L24,000.
- **Green Card for Youth Travel**: Available to all persons from 12 to 26 years of age. It allows for a 30% reduction on all first and second class tickets. Must be purchased in Italy. A one year pass costs L10,000; a two year pass costs L18,000.
- **Italy Flexi Railcards**: There are many rules and regulations associated with these cards, but they do not hinder the bearer in any way. Example of some rules: cannot be sold to permanent residents of Italy, card is not transferable, card must be validated at any Italian State Railway station's ticket office before travel can commence,

validation slip must be kept separate from card (kind of like the validation slip for travelers checks), lost or stolen cards can not be refunded or replaced unless bearer has validation slip ... whew. Rules, rules, rules. Here are the prices for the Flexi Railcards:

	1st Class	2nd Class
4 days of travel within 9 days of validity	$170	$116
8 days of travel within 21 days of validity	$250	$164
12 days of travel within 30 days of validity	$314	$210

• **Italian Unlimited Rail Pass** or the "BTLC Italian Tourist Ticket:" all travel and any type of train is unlimited and free, except for the special **TR450** trains where a supplemental fee will be required. The time period begins on the first day of its use. Here are the prices for the Unlimited Rail Pass:

Validity	1st Class	2nd Class
8 days	$226	$152
15 days	$284	$190
21 days	$330	$220
30 days	$396	$264

Types of Trains
• **IC-Intercity**: Both first and second class seating is available with most first class compartments air-conditioned. Dining cars are also available.
• **EC-Eurocity**: These are the trains that are used in international rail service.
• **EXPR-Expresso**: Ordinary express trains usually carry first and second class passengers. No supplemental fare and reservations are necessary, but I recommend you make them.. Food and drink service is available. These are the trains to take. Hardly any stops at all. Kind of like the MetroLiner Service on Amtrak between Washington DC and New York.
• **DIR-Diretto**: Semi-express trains that make plenty of stops. They often have second class seating only. During off-peak hours they are not crowded, but at peak hours they're sardine-city.
• **Locale**: These trains stop everywhere on their route and take forever, but to get to rural locations these are the only options.

BOARDING THE RIGHT TRAIN

When taking the trains to any location in Italy, such as Pisa or Lucca, the ultimate destination of the train you're taking may not be the one to which you are going. For example to get to Pisa, sometimes you have to take a train whose ultimate destination is Livorno. Ask the information desk in the train station when your train is leaving, then try one of two things (or both) to make sure you're boarding the proper train:

*1. Consult one of the large glass-enclosed schedules located in the information offices and usually by the tracks that normally have a crowd of Italians hovering around, gesturing wildly and speaking in tongues (at least it sometimes seems that way). Match your intended departure time with the time printed on the sheet. Then check directly to the right of the time to see the list of all the destinations for the train. If the name of your destination is listed, you're golden. Next write down the ultimate destination of the train so you can check the main board at the station that lists **partenze** (trains leaving) to see which **binnario** (track) you should board.*

*2. If that still doesn't assuage your concerns, get to the track and ask someone waiting or inside the train if it is going to your destination. Ask at least two people, since I've had he experience of asking workers going home at night saying "No," since for forty years they haven't bothered to pay attention to where their train actually stops. Anyway, to politely ask in Italian whether the train is going to your destination say **"Mi Scusi, ma questo treno va al <u>Lucca</u>?"** (Excuse me but does this train go to <u>Lucca</u>?) Obviously substitute the underlined city name for the destination to which you wish to go. This question is asked countless times by many people, including Italians, who shockingly enough are actually riding the train for the first time. Even though I do not dress and look Italian, I get asked for directions and information quite a bit (most Italians think I'm German even when I speak Italian with them; how could they think I have a German accent?).*

*Finally, if you're standing on the platform waiting for the train to come and you suddenly see all the Italians moving away en masse, that usually means that the public address announcer just declared a track change. Ask one of the departing Italians "Has the track for the train to <u>Lucca</u> changed?" (**E cambiato il binnario for il treno per <u>Lucca</u>?**) If s/he says yes (si), either get the number and go there or simply follow them, and as you pass the board that lists the trains leaving, you'll see the change already officially noted.*

7. BASIC INFORMATION

BUSINESS HOURS

Store hours are usually Monday through Friday, 9:00am to 1:00pm, 3:30/4:00pm to 7:30/8:00pm, and Saturday 9:00am to 1:00pm. Most stores are closed on Sunday and on national holidays. Don't expect to find any 24-hour convenience stores just around the corner. If you want to have some soda in your room after a long day of touring you need to plan ahead.

Also, you must plan on most stores not being open from 1:00pm to 4:00pm. This is the Italian siesta time. Don't expect to get a lot done except find a nice restaurant and enjoy a pleasant afternoon.

Banking Hours

Banks in Italy are open Monday through Friday, 8:35am to 1:35pm and from 3:00pm to 4:00pm, and are closed all day Saturday and Sunday and on national holidays. In some cities the afternoon open hour may not even exist. Even if the bank is closed, most travelers checks can be exchanged for Italian currency at most hotels and shops and at the many foreign exchange offices in railway stations and at airports.

CURRENCY

The current rate of exchange is **US $1= 1,660 lire** and Can$1 =1,180 lire. In this book, I have shown lire prices as follows: L1,660.

You cannot bring in any currency that totals more than 20 million lire (approximately $12,000) without declaring it at the customs office. This is also the same amount of money that can be legally exported from Italy without declaring it.

If you arrive in Sicily without Italian currency, the airports have banks and monetary exchange offices *(Ufficio di Cambio)*. Remember to keep your receipts from your monetary exhanges, because at some banks, when you want to change lire back to your native currency, you will need to show proof that you first exchanged your currency for Italian currency.

The monetary unit in Italy is the **lira** (leer-ah), the plural is **lire** (leer-ay). Notes are issued for 1,000, 2,000, 5,000, 10,000, 50,000, and 100,000 lire. Coins come in 50, 100, 200 and 500 lira denominations.

US DOLLAR/ITALIAN LIRE EXCHANGE RATES

US$1 = 1,660 lire

Lire	100	500	1,000	5,000	10,000
US Dollars	6¢	30¢	60¢	$3.01	$6.02

CANADIAN DOLLAR/ITALIAN LIRE EXCHANGE RATES

CDN$1 = 1,180 lire

Lire	100	500	1,000	5,000	10,000
Canadian Dollars	4.26¢	21.3¢	42.6¢	$2.14	$4.27

NOTE: The currency situation vis-avis the US and Canadian dollar is constantly floating. Please check the paper or a bank for the current rates of exchange.

PETS

If you're bringing your precious pooch (unfortunately your dog will have to be on a leash and wear a muzzle in public in Italy) or kitty into Italy with you, you must have a veterinarian's certificate stating that your pet has been vaccinated against rabies between 20 days and 11 months before entry into Italy, and that your pet is in overall good health. The certificate must contain the breed, age, sex, and color of your pet and your name and address. This certificate will be valid only for 30 days. The specific forms that the vet needs to fill out are available at all Italian diplomatic and consular offices.

Parrots, parakeets, rabbits, and hares are also subject to health certification by a vet, and will also be examined further upon entry into Italy. Also Customs officials may require a health examination of your pet if you have just come from a tropical region or that they suspect the pet to be ill. All this means that they can do whatever they want whenever they want, so it might be wise to leave your pet at home.

POSTAL SERVICE

Stamps can be purchased at any post office and tobacco shop. If you send a letter airmail with insufficient postage it will not be returned to sender, but will be sent surface mail, which could take months. So try and mail your letters from a post office and have them check the postage for you. Post offices are open from 8:30am to 2:00pm Monday through Friday. On Saturdays and the last day of every month they close at 12 noon; on Sundays they are closed.

AIR MAIL PRICES	
Postcards to US and Canada	1100 lire
Letter (up to 20 grams)	1250 lire
Each additional 20 grams	400 lire
Aerograms for all countries	850 lire

SAFETY

Italian cities are definitely much safer than any equivalent American city. You can walk most anywhere without fear of harm, but that doesn't mean you shouldn't play it safe. Listed below are some simple rules to follow to ensure that nothing bad occurs:

• At night, make sure the streets you are strolling along have plenty of other people. Like I said, most cities are safe, but it doesn't hurt to be cautious.

• Always have your knapsack or purse flung over the shoulder that is not directly next to the road. Why? There have been cases of Italians on motor bikes snatching purses off old ladies and in some cases dragging them a few blocks.

• Better yet, have your companion walk on the street side, while you walk on the inside of the sidewalk with the knapsack or purse.

• Better still is to buy one of those tummy wallets that goes under your shirt so no one can even be tempted to purse-snatch you.

That's really all you should need, but always follow basic common sense. If you feel threatened, scared, or alone, retrace your steps back to a place where there are other people.

STAYING OUT OF TROUBLE

Staying out of trouble is paramount, because in Italy you are guilty until proven innocent, unlike in the states where it's the other way around. And most importantly, if arrested you are not simply placed in a holding cell. The Italian officials take you directly to a maximum security prison and lock you up.

And that's where you'll stay for as long as it takes your traveling partners to figure out where you are, bribe your case to top of the local judge's pile, and have your case heard. That whole process can sometimes take months.

So if you like your drinks strong and your nights long, remember to keep your temper in check. And don't even think about smuggling any banned substance into the country, or God forbid, buying something illicit when you're in Italy. If you are approached to buy some hashish or something else, simply say politely, *No Grazie* (no thank you) and walk away.

TAXIS

Taxi service is widely available in all major cities in Italy, and a little less so in smaller cities such as Pisa or Lucca, and almost non-existent in remote towns and villages. Rates are comparable to those charged in your basic American city. Generally taxis locate themselves in special taxi stands located at railway stations and main parts of the city, but many are out cruising the streets for fares. At these taxi stands are usually telephones that you can call directly from your hotel, but remember, in Italy, if called, the meter starts at the point of origin, so you'll be paying the cabby to come pick you up.

Fares will vary from city to city, but basically when you get in the cab there will be a fixed starting charge, approximately 2,800 to 6,400 lire, and a cost per kilometer, approximately 1,000 to 1,250 lire. Some extra charges may come into play, like the **nighttime supplement** (between 10:00pm and 6:00am), a **Sunday** and **public holiday supplement**, as well as a **per item luggage charge**. All of these vary from city to city.

There is fierce taxi-cab competition in Italy. Some private citizens dress up their cars to look like cabs, so only take the yellow, metered cabs.

TIME

Italy is six hours ahead of Eastern Standard Time in North America, so if it's noon is New York it's 6:00pm in Rome). Daylight savings time goes into effect each year in Italy usually from the end of March to the end of September.

TIPPING
Hotels

A service charge of 15-18% is usually added to your hotel bill, but it is customary to leave a little something else. The following figures are simply guidelines:
- **Chambermaid**: 1,000 lire per day
- **Concierge**: 3,000 lire per day; additional tip necessary for additional services
- **Bellhop or Porter**: 1,500 lire per bag
- **Doorman** (for hailing or calling you a cab): 1,000 lire

• **Room Service Waiter**: 1,000 lire minimum and a little more depending on the amount ordered

Restaurants

A service charge of around 15% is usually automatically added to all restaurant bills. But if you felt the service was good, it is customary to leave between 5–10% more for the waiter. Also, it is not a requirement that you receive an official receipt, so if you need one please ask.

In cafes and bars, if the bill does not already include a gratuity (and most will so be sure to check) a 15% tip is expected even if you don't eat a meal. Two hundred lire is normal if you're standing at the counter drinking a soda, cappuccino, etc. If you have an alcoholic beverage, something to eat, etc. at the counter, the tip should be 500 lire or more.

Theater Ushers

Yep – they get 1,000 lire or more if the theater is very high class.

Taxis

Give the cabbie 10% of the fare, otherwise they just might drive away leaving you without your luggage. (Just kidding).

Sightseeing Guide & Driver

Give 2,000 lire minimum per person for half day tours, and 2,500 minimum per person for full day tours.

Service Station Attendant

Give 1,000 lire or more for extra service like cleaning your windshield, or giving you directions while also filling up your tank.

WEIGHTS & MEASURES

You guessed it, Italy works under the metric system, where everything is a factor ten. This system of measurement is the simplest and easiest; even England converted their entire country some years ago. The only country in the world to still use an antiquated system of measurement, is, you guessed it, our United States. Canada's now about half metric, half antiquated American, but that's because they're America's largest trading partner, they have to know what we do.

The table on the following page gives you a list of weights and measures with approximate values.

WEIGHTS & MEASURES

Weights

Italy	14 grams	Etto	Kilo
US	1/2 oz	1/4 lb	2lb 2oz

Liquid Measure

Italy	Litro
US	1.065 quart

Distance Measure

Italy	Centimeter	Meter	Kilometer
US	2/5 inch	39 inches	3/5 mile

8. SPORTS & RECREATION

Italians are active sports enthusiasts. Besides soccer they participate in skiing, golf, tennis, scuba diving, mountain climbing, hiking, fishing, hunting, and more. Any sport you can play at home you can enjoy as well if not better in Italy!

SKIING

From December through April, **ski** resorts all over Italy are swarming with people willing to sacrifice life and limb to get the adrenaline flow that only plummeting down a sheer cliff covered with snow can offer them. Most winter sports areas are found in the north of Italy in the Alps; one of the most famous is **Courmayeur**, but there are also some near Rome in the Central Apennines, **Cortino d'Ampezzo** being the most notable.

These same mountain ranges are used as hiking locations during the summer. If you like breathtaking views without the risk of tearing a medial collateral ligament, try hiking the trails of the Italian Alps in the summer.

GOLF

In the summer you can also enjoy some excellent **golf** courses. Located all over Italy, except for the poor south, there are plenty of accessible courses around the main tourist areas of Rome, Milan and Florence (see regional chapters for more information). You can also find courses around the many seaside resort areas that dot Italy's coastline.

Since Constatino Rocca choked in the Ryder Cup in 1994 for the whole world to see, and when in the British Open in 1995 made that miraculous putt after chili dipping his chip (he eventually lost to John Daly), Italian golf has started to get recognition. Maybe not the kind of recognition it wants but nonetheless, the *cognoscenti* have begun to discover some gems of courses all over Italy. It's only natural that a country filled with such natural beauty would provide superb golf.

WATER SPORTS

You'll find scuba diving, sailing, snorkeling, para-sailing, and clay tennis courts galore along Italy's various coasts. Since the country is surrounded on three sides by water, Italians are fanatical about their water sports and activities, which has started to include topless bathing, an unheard of activity 10 years ago. At some beaches frequented by northern Europeans, there are days when not a suit is in sight.

HUNTING & FISHING

If you are looking for the more rustic pursuits like **sport fishing** and **hunting**, Italy has lakes, streams and rivers filled with trout. In the Alpine and Appenine regions you can actually bag a wild boar *(cinghiale)*, which is on the menu at many northern Italian restaurants. Hunting is popular all over Italy but the seasons vary according to region. Contact the Italian Travel Office to find information about the hunting and fishing seasons and how to get licenses for each activity.

SPECTATOR SPORTS

If watching from the sidelines is more up your alley, Italy goes **soccer** crazy every Sunday from September to May. Virtually every city and every town has a team that plays professionally. The exception is Bologna. As a distinguished university town, soccer is below their lofty standards. They do have a pro basketball team.

The Italian league is separated into four divisions, or Serie. The first division is *Serie A*, which plays the best soccer in the world, and the bottom division is *Serie D*. Some cities have several teams, like Rome which has two *Serie A* teams (Lazio and Roma), three *Serie C*, and one *Serie D*. The Serie A and B games are the most fun to go to since the fans are so passionate. Tickets can be hard to come by since the games are so popular, but contact your hotels concierge and s/he may be able to scrape (scalp?) some up for you from a relative.

If you don't want to go into the stadium you might want to go to the game to get some great gifts from the vendors that sell team paraphernalia outside. Certain types of product piracy is legal in Italy, and putting the names and logos of sports teams on unofficial products is one of them. The quality of the shirts, hats, and scarves is just as good and about one fourth the price of the official products.

Another popular spectator sport is **auto** and **motorcycle racing**. At Monza, just outside of Milan, the **Italian Grand Prix** is held every September; and at Imola, near Bologna, you can find the **San Marino Grand Prix** every May. Equally as popular is **cycling**, which culminates in the **Tour d'Italia** in May.

And surprisingly enough, **basketball** and **baseball** both have professional leagues. Most major cities now have teams. Professional baseball has been around for only about fifteen years, and is still at the level of minor league play in the US, but is starting to catch on in popularity. Ask your concierge about upcoming games.

9. SHOPPING

As mentioned earlier, store hours are usually Monday through Friday 9:00am to 1:00pm, 3:30/4:00pm to 7:30/8:00pm, and Saturday 9:00am to 1:00pm. This may vary in Milan and/or Turin, where sometimes the lunch break is shorter so shops can close earlier.

The big Italian chain stores are **La Rinascente**, **Coin**, **UPIM**, and **STANDA**. In Coin, UPIM, and STANDA, you will also find supermarkets filled with all manner of Italian delectables. At the end of this chapter I'll make some suggestions about what you could buy at a local Italian *Supermercato* or *Alimentari* (smaller food store) to bring home with you so you can make a fine Italian meal with authentic ingredients!

Besides food and clothing, Italy has a wide variety of handicrafts. Any one of Italy's crafts would be a perfect memento of your stay. Works in alabaster and marble can be readily found in and around Florence, Milan, and Venice. Wood carvings are the specialty of many of the cities in the south, such as Palermo and Messina. Beautiful glasswork is at its best in and around Venice and Pisa. Embroidery and lace work can be found all over Italy, and rugs from Sardinia rival those of most other European countries. Sardinia is also known for its straw bags, hats, and mats, as is Florence.

Exquisite gold and silver jewelry is a specialty of Florence, where, on the Ponte Vecchio, you'll find shop after shop of jewelry stores. In other parts of Tuscany you can find hand-wrought iron work as well as beautiful tiles.

And finally the main fashion centers in Italy are, of course, Milan, Florence and Rome, with Florence specializing in shoes and gloves, and Milan and Rome everything else. Each regional chapter will describe for you specific places to visit to find the most exquisite and authentic regional handicrafts.

GET YOUR TAX REBATE ON PURCHASES

*If you acquire products at the same merchant in excess of L300,000 (about $180), you can claim an **IVA** (purchase tax) **rebate**. You must ask the vendor for the proper receipt (**il ricetto per il IVA per favore**), have the receipt stamped at Italian customs, then mail no later than 90 days after the date of the receipt back to the vendor. The vendor will then send you the IVA rebate. I know it's complicated, but if you spend a fair chunk of money in Italy on clothing or other items, this is a good way to get some money back.*

SIZES

The chart below is a comparison guide between US and Italian sizes. Many sizes are not standardized, so you will need to try everything on in any event.The following conversions should help you out in your shopping quest:

· Women's Clothing Sizes

US	2	4	6	8	10	12	14	16
Italy	36	38	40	42	44	46	48	50

Continued

	18	20	24
	52	54	56

· Women's Shoe Sizes

US	$5_{1/2}$	$6_{1/2}$	7	$7_{1/2}$	8	$8_{1/2}$	9	10
Italy	35	36	37	38	38 1/2	39	40	41

· Women's Hosiery Sizes

US	Petite	Small	Medium	Large
Italy	I	II	III	IV

· Men's Suites, Overcoats, Sweaters, and Pajamas

US	34	36	38	40	42	44	46	48
Italy	44	46	48	50	52	54	56	58

· Men's Shirts

US	14	$14_{1/2}$	15	$15_{1/2}$	16	$16_{1/2}$	17	$17_{1/2}$
Italy	36	37	38	39	40	41	42	43

· Men's Shoes

US	6	$6_{1/2}$	7	$7_{1/2}$	8	$8_{1/2}$	9	$9_{1/2}$
Italy	30	40	$40_{1/2}$	41	$41_{1/2}$	42	$42_{1/2}$	43

Continued

10	10$_{1/2}$		11-11$_{1/2}$	
43$_{1/2}$	44-44$_{1/2}$		45	

• Men's Hats

US	6$_{7/8}$	7	7$_{1/8}$	7$_{1/4}$	7$_{3/8}$	7$_{1/2}$	7$_{5/8}$	7$_{3/4}$
Italy	55	56	57	58	59	60	61	62

• Children's Sizes

US	1	2	3	4	5	6	7	8
Italy	35	40	45	50	55	60	65	70

Continued

9	10	11	12	13	14
75	80	85	90	95	100

• Children's Shoes

US	4	5	6	7	8	9	10	10 1/2
Italy	21	21	22	23	24	25	26	27

Continued

11	12	13
28	29	30

KEY SHOPPING & BARGAINING PHRASES

Italian	**English**
• *Quanto costa?*	How Much is This?
• *E Troppo*	That's too much
• *No Grazie*	No thank you
• *Voglio paggo meno*	I want to pay less
• *Che lai questo pui grande?*	Do have this in a bigger size?
..... *pui piccolo*	..... in a smaller size
..... *in nero*	..... in black
..... *in bianco*	..... in white
..... *in roso*	..... in red
..... *in verde*	..... in green

WHEN TO BARGAIN

In all stores, even the smallest shops, bargaining is not accepted, just like here in North America. But you can bargain at any street vending location, even if they have placed a sign indicating the price. Don't be afraid to bargain, otherwise you'll end up spending more than you (ahem) 'bargained' for.

Most Italian vendors see foreigners as easy marks to make a few more *lire* because they know it is not in our culture to bargain, while in theirs it is a way of life.

The best way to bargain, if the street vendor doesn't speak English, is by writing your request on a piece of paper. This keeps it personal too in case you're embarrassed about haggling over money. Basically while in Italy try to let go of that cultural bias. "When in Rome..." Anyway, you and the vendor will probably pass the paper back and forth a few times changing the numbers before a price is finally agreed upon. And of course, the Italian vendor will be waving his arms about, jabbering away, most probably describing how you're trying to rip him off, all in an effort to get you to pay a higher price. Remember, this is all done in fun – so enjoy it.

ITALIAN SOCCER ATTIRE

If you or someone you know is a soccer nut, you may want to get them a jersey, hat, or scarf from one of the local teams. Most cities and towns in Italy have a soccer team, whether in the Serie A (First Division) or in the three lower divisions. The games are played from September to June and are the best places to get low cost, high quality merchandise.

Outside of most games vendors are selling everything from key rings to official soccer jerseys, all at a low price. The Italian soccer teams are starting to open their own stores featuring their specially-licensed products, like Milan Point, for one of the teams in Milan, but those prices will be about four times as much as at the stadium.

WHAT YOU'RE ALLOWED TO BRING BACK THROUGH CUSTOMS

See *Planning Your Trip* for more detials, but in short you can bring back to the US $400 worth of goods duty free. On the next $1,000 worth of purchases you will be assessed a flat 10% fee. These product must be with you when you go through customs.

You can mail products duty free, providing the total value of each package sent is not more than $50 *and* no one person is receiving more than one package a day. Also, each package sent must be stamped "Unsolicited Gift" and the amount paid and the contents of the package must be displayed. They'll be able to tell you all this again at the post office.

What you can't bring back to North America are any fruits, vegetables, and in most cases meats and cheeses, even if they're for your consumption alone, and even if they are vacuum sealed. Customs has to do this to prevent any potential parasites from entering our country and destroying our crops. Unfortunately, this means all those great salamis and cheeses you bought at those quaint outdoor food markets and had on one of your picnics will not be let back into the North America.

But there are some things you can buy. In most supermarkets you can find salamis and cheeses that have been shrink-wrapped, which customs should let through. Good luck!

10. CULTURE & ARTS

FROM ETRUSCANS TO THE RENAISSANCE

Italy is perhaps best known for its great contributions to painting and sculpture; and many art lovers have described the country as one vast museum. Italy gave birth to such world renowned artists as Giotto, Donatello, Raphael, Michelangelo, Leonardo da Vinci, and Botticelli, known all over the world.

The oldest works of art in Italy are those of the **Etruscans**, and they date back to the 9th century BC. This mysterious society's main cities and art centers were in the middle of the peninsula, between Rome and Florence, mainly in the province now know as Tuscany (the region was named after them ... Etruscans ... Tuscany). In Tarquinia, Volterra, Cerveteri, and Veio, the Etruscans have left behind magnificent temples, sculptures, and bronzes as well as other fascinating testimonies to their presence. The best museum collections of Etruscan art can be found in Rome's **Etruscan Museum**, Florence's **Archaeological Museum**, the **Bologna Municipal Museum**, and the **Municipal Museum of Volterra**.

Italy is also know as being a repository of ancient Greek art. During the time of the Etruscans, the Greeks established colonies in the south of modern-day Italy. Magnificent ruins of temples exist today in some of these Greek colonies: **Syracuse**, **Agrigento**, and **Taormina** in Sicily; and **Paestu** and **Coma** in Campania. There are good collections of Hellenic art in the **National Museum of Naples**, and in the museums in Palermo, Syracuse, Reggio Calabria, Paestum, and Taranto.

After the Greeks and Etruscans, the Roman Empire left its lasting impression all over Italy. There are still roads, bridges, aqueducts, aches, and theaters built by the Romans. The most extensive excavations have been made at the **Forum** in Rome, at **Ostia** near Rome by the beach, and at **Pompeii** and **Herculaneum**, the cities that the volcanic **Mount Vezuvious** buried. For a first-hand, up-front feel of what life was like in the Roman Empire, don't miss these sites.

After the fall of the Roman Empire, the Byzantine Empire ruled many parts of the southern and eastern regions of Italy. This period left behind many churches, with their glorious mosaics, like those of the 6th century in Ravenna near the east coast; as well as the morbid-but-can't-miss site of the **catacombs** outside of Rome.

Then the Renaissance came. This artistic period, meaning "rebirth," began in Italy in the 14th century and lasted for two hundred years. The Renaissance left us an extensive array of churches, palaces, paintings, statues, and city squares in almost every city of Italy. The main cities of Florence, Rome, Venice, Milan, and Naples have most of the treasures and beauty of this period, but smaller towns like Ferrara and Rimini also have their share. The best museums for viewing Renaissance art are the **Uffizzi Gallery** and **Pitti Palace** in Florence, as well as the **Vatican** and **Borghese Galleries** (in the Borghese Gardens just outside the walls) in Rome.

After the Renaissance, **baroque art** became fashionable. And Rome, more than any other Italian city, contains a dazzling array of churches, paintings, and statues recalling the splendor of such famous artists as Bernini, Borromini, and Caravaggio of the late 16th and 17th centuries.

RENAISSANCE PAINTING

In Italy (with France and Germany soon following suit) during 14th and 15th centuries, the Renaissance was a period of exploration, invention, and discovery. Mariners from all over Europe set sail in search of new lands. Scientists like **Leonardo da Vinci** studied the mysteries of the world and the heavens. Artists found the human body to be a marvel of mechanics and beauty (but had to secretly study it, as Michelangelo did, lest the Church condemn them for heresy). This was undoubtedly one of Italy's most exciting periods in the history of artistic and scientific advancement.

Many consider the birthplace of Renaissance art to be Florence. It seemed to start with a young painter named **Masaccio**, who began introducing many bold new ideas into his painting. He made his paintings vibrantly interesting by drawing each person completely different from another, as well as making each person as realistic as possible. In conjunction with his ability to express the human form, Masaccio used combinations of colors to give the impression of space and dimension in his landscapes. Now every art student studies how brown makes objects appear closer, and blue makes them appear in the distance.

Paolo Uccello, another Florentine, worked at the same time as Masaccio. A mathematician as well as an artist, he expanded on the mechanical and scientific issues of painting rather than on the human and psychological ones.

One of his paintings, *The Battle of San Romano*, circa 1457, celebrated the victory of Florence over Siena some 25 years earlier, and is a brilliant study in **perspective**. His depiction of objects, men, and horses all help to accentuate the sense of real perspective he was trying to achieve. One technique he used, which is now part of any good art school's curriculum, is **foreshortening**. In the left foreground is a fallen soldier with his feet facing the front of the picture. To give this figure a proper perspective, Uccello had to shorten the perceived length of the body, an extremely difficult task, and one not usually seen in other artists' previous works. In conjunction, Uccello drew roads, fields, etc., going back into the painting, to give the impression of distance.

But most definitely three of the most famous Renaissance artists were **Raphael**, **Leonardo da Vinci**, and **Michelangelo**. Raphael was mainly known for his paintings of the Madonna and Child, from which our concept of the Mother of Jesus is largely based. But all of his paintings reflect a harmony that leaves the viewer with a warm feeling.

Leonardo da Vinci is most well known for his *Mona Lisa*, painted in Tuscany in 1505-06 and now hanging in the Louvre, but he was also a versatile architect and scientist as well. Leonardo studied botany, geology, zoology, hydraulics, military engineering, anatomy, perspective, optics, and physiology. You name it, he did it – the original Renaissance Man!

Another versatile artist of the Italian Renaissance, and definitely its most popular (he was always being commissioned to paint or sculpt all the wealthy people's portraits) was Michelangelo Buonarroti. Although he considered himself chiefly a sculptor – he trained as a young boy to become a stone carver – he left us equally great works as a painter and architect. As a painter he created the huge **Sistine Chapel** fresco, encompassing more than 10,000 square feet in area. As an architect he helped complete the designs for **St. Peter's**, where his world renowned statue, *La Pieta*, currently resides.

RENAISSANCE SCULPTURE

Besides painting and architecture, **Michelangelo Buonarroti** was also the pre-eminent sculptor of the Renaissance. By the age of 26 he had carved *La Pieta*, his amazing version of Virgin Mary supporting the dead Christ on her knees; and was in the process of carving the huge and heroic marble *David*. He also created the memorable **Medici tombs** in the Chapel of San Lorenzo, Florence. His greatest but lesser known work is his majestic *Moses* designed for the tomb of Pope Julius II. Today this great statue can be viewed at the basilica of San Pietro in Vincoli in Rome.

Even though Michelangelo was commissioned to create many works by Popes themselves, he had learned his amazing knowledge of the human anatomy by dissecting cadavers in his home town of Florence as a young man, a crime punishable by death and/or excommunication at the time.

During the Renaissance there were many other sculptors of note, but Michelangelo was truly the best. One of the others was **Lorenzo Ghiberti**, who died a few years before Michelangelo was born. For 29 years he labored to produce ten bronze panels, depicting Biblical episodes, for the doors of the Baptistery of Florence. Michelangelo was said to have been inspired to become a great artist because of these beautiful bronze doors.

MUSIC

Italy also has a great tradition in music. Even today, Italian folk music has made a resurgence, mainly because of the theme song for the *Godfather* movie series. Can't you just hear it playing in your head right now?

Besides the folk music and Gregorian chants, Italy is known for its opera. If you are an opera fan you cannot miss taking a tour of the world famous **La Scala** in Milan. Getting a ticket to a performance is another matter. But have no fear, if your appetite cannot be satiated without the shrill explosion of an *aria* there are other famous opera houses in Italy: **The Opera** in Rome, **The San Carlos** in Naples, **La Fenice** in Venice, **The Reggio** in Turin, **The Communale** in Bologna, **The Petruzzelli** in Bari, **The Communale** in Genoa, and **Massimo Bellini** in Catania (see addresses and phone numbers below).

These are also many opera festivals all over Italy virtually year-round.

Italian Opera

Italian opera began in the 16th century. Over time such composers as Gioacchino Rossini, Gaetano Donizetti, and Vincenzo Bellini created **bel canto** opera – opera that prizes beautiful singing above all else. Singers were indulged with *arias* that gave them ample opportunity for a prominent display of their vocal resources of range and agility.

Rossini, who reigned as Italy's foremost composer of the early 19th century, was a master of both melody and stage effects. Success came easily, and while still in his teens he composed the first of a string of 32 operas that he completed by the age of 30. Many of these are comic operas, a genre in which Rossini excelled, and his masterpieces in this form are still performed and admired today. Among them is one you probably recognize (even I know this one): *The Barber of Seville* (1816).

Rossini's immediate successor as Italy's leading operatic composer was **Donizetti**, who composed more than 70 works in the genre. A less refined composer than Rossini, Donizetti left his finest work in comic operas, including *Don Pasquale* (1843) and *Lucia di Lammermoor* (1835).

Although he lived for a shorter time than either Rossini or Donizetti and enjoyed a far briefer career, **Bellini** wrote music that many believe surpassed theirs in refinement. Among the finest of his ten operas are *La sonnambula* (The Sleepwalker, 1831), *Norma* (1831), and *I Puritani* (The Puritans, 1835), all of which blend acute dramatic perceptions with florid virtuosity.

From these roots came Italy's greatest opera composers of all times, **Puccini** and **Verdi**. Giacomo Puccini lived from 1858-1924 and composed twelve operas in all. Considered by many to be a close second to Verdi in skill of composition, Puccini's work will remain alive because of his enduringly popular works such as *Madama Butterfly* and *La Boheme*. Even though Puccini was the fifth generation of musicians in his family, he was mainly influenced to pursue his career after hearing Verdi's still popular *Aida*.

Giuseppe Verdi lived from 1813-1901, and is best know for his operas *Rigoletto* (1851), *Il Trovatore* and *La Traviata* (both 1853), and what could be the grandest opera of them all, *Aida* (1871). Verdi composed his thirtieth and last opera *Falstaff* at the age of 79. Since he mainly composed out of Milan and many of his operas opened at La Scala opera house in that city, today a **Verdi museum** has been established there to honor his work.

Opera, Music, Drama, & Ballet Festivals

As the birthplace of opera, Italy offers visitors a variety of choices during the operatic seasons, which are almost year-round. In the summer months there are wonderful open-air operas presented at the **Terme di Caracalla** (Baths of Caracalla) in the center of Rome near the main train station from July to August, at the **Arena** in Verona from July to August, and at the **Arena Sferisterio** in Macerata in July.

Two of the most spectacular festivals for Italian performing arts are the **Maggio Musicale Fiorentino** with opera, concerts, ballet, and drama performances in Florence from May to June, and the **Festival of Two Worlds** with opera, concerts, ballet, drama performances and art exhibits in Spoleto from mid-June to mid-July.

Other events, by their location in Italy, include:
- **Aosta**, mid-July to mid-August: Organ Music Festival
- **Barga (Lucca)**, mid-July to mid-August: Opera Barga
- **Bolzano**, August: International Piano Competition
- **Brescia**, May and June: Piano Festival
- **Catania**, June to September: music and drama performances at the Greek/Roman theatre
- **Cervo (Imperia)**, July and August: Chamber Music Festival

- **Gardone Riviera (Brescia)**, July and August: drama and concerts in the open air theatre of the Vittoriale degli Italiani
- **Lucca**, April and June: Sacred Music Festival in a variety of churches
- **Macerata**, July and August: opera and ballet season at the outdoor Arena Sferisterio
- **Marlia (Lucca)**, mid-July to mid-August: Marlia Festival of rare and exotic live performances
- **Martina Franca**, July to August: Festival of the Itria Valley. Southern Italy's top performing arts festival
- **Monreale and Palermo**, October and November: Sacred Music Festival
- **Orta San Giulio (Novara)**, June: Cusius Festival of Early Music which features Gregorian chants, madrigals, cantata, Baroque and Rennaissance music, as well as many other more popular works; all performers are in period garb
- **Pavia**, July-August: Concerts on the Certosa. Drama performances outside
- **Perugia**, mid-July to late July: Umbria Jazz Festival. Italy's top Jazz festival
- **Pesaro**, mid-August to mid-September: Rossini Opera Festival
- **Ravello**, July: Ravello Classical Music Festival. These take place in the Duomo of Ravello and in the gardens of Villa Rufolo
- **Ravenna**, July and August: Organ Music Festival in the Basilica of San Vitale
- **Ravenna**, mid-July to early August: opera and ballet are performe in the remains of the majestic Rocca di Brancaleone
- **Rome**, June through August: concerts in the Basilica Maxentius
- **Siena**, August: musical weeks
- **Stresa (Novara)**, August to September: musical weeks
- **Taormina (Messina)**, July and August: music and drama festival
- **Torre del Lago Puccini (Lucca)**, August: Puccini opera in the open air theatre in Lucca
- **Trieste**, July and August: Operetta Festival
- **Urbino**, August: drama and art exhibitions and oncerts in the Rennaissance Theatre
- **Verona**, June to September: drama festival in the Roman Theatre as well as a Shakesperean Festival featuring drama, ballet and jazz
- **Viterbo**, August: Baroque Music Festival

ADDRESSES & PHONE NUMBERS
OF MAJOR OPERA HOUSES

Teatro alla Scala, Via Dei Filodrammatici 2, 20121 Milano. Tel 02/887-9211, Fax 02/887-9297

Teatro dell'Opera, Piazza D. Gigli 1, 00184 Roma. Tel. 06/481-601, Fax 06/488-1253

Teatro La Fenice, Campo S. Fantin 1977, 30124 Venezia. Tel. 041/521-0161, Fax 041/522-1768

Teatro Comunale, Corso Italia 16, 50123 Firenze. Tel. 055/27791 or 2729236, Fax 055/2396954

Teatro San Carlo, Via San Carlo, 80133 Napoli. Tel. 081/797-2111

Teatro Regio do Torino, Piazza Castello 215, 10124 Torino. Tel 011/88151, Fax 011/881-5214

Teatro Massimo, Piazza Verdi, 90138 Palermo. Tel 091/583-600

Arena di Verona, Piazza Bra 28, 37121 Verona. Tel. 045/590-109, Fax 045/590-201

If you wish to obtain tickets to opera performances, concerts, ballet, and other performances you can either write directly to the theater in question or ask your travel agent to obtain the ticket for you. Currently there is no agency in the US authorized to sell concert and/or opera tickets, so this is the only way. When you are in Italy, your hotel should be able to assist you in obtaining tickets for performances in their city.

REGIONAL & NATIONAL FOLK FESTIVALS

Despite the encroachment of the modern world, the traditional festivals and their accompanying costumes and folk music have survived surprisingly well all over Italy. In many cases they have been successfully woven into the pattern of modern life so as to seem quite normal. Despite all possible modern influences these festivals (both secular and religious) have preserved their distinctive character.

Two of the most famous, the secular festivals of the **Palio** in Siena and of **Calcio in Costume** in Florence give foreigners a glimpse into the past customs and way of life of ancient Italians. Both of these festivals pit different sections of their respective cities (Florence and Siena) against each other to see who can earn bragging rights for the year. In Siena, a heated horse race takes place in a crowded city square. In Florence, the Piazza della Signorina is turned into a veritable battleground when a game that is a cross between boxing, soccer, rugby, and martial arts is played.

At these secular celebration the old costumes are still worn.

With Italy the home of the Catholic church, religious festivals also play a large part in Italian life. Particularly interesting are the processions on the occasion of **Corpus Christi**, **Assumption**, and **Holy Week**. In Italy, holiday times such as Easter and Christmas have not lost their religious intent as they have in most other places. In Italy, commercialism takes a back seat to the Almighty.

The items below marked by an asterisk are the ones you simply cannot miss. Plan your trip around them.

JANUARY

- **New Years Day**, *Rome*: Candle-lit processional in the Catacombs of Priscilla to mark the martyrdom of the early Christians
- **January 5**, **Rome*: Last day of the Epiphany Fair in the Piazza Navona. All throughout the piazza a fair filled with food stands, candy stands, toy shops opens to the public. Lasts a week. A must see.
- **January 6**, *Piana Degli Albanesi*: Celebration of the Epiphany according to Byzantine rite.

FEBRUARY/MARCH

During February or March in *San Remo*, the Italian Festival of Popular Songs is celebrated.

- **1st half of February**, *Agrigento*: Almond Blossom Festival. Song, dance, costumes, fireworks.
- **Both Months**: **Viareggio, San Remo, Pisa, Turin and some other towns on the Riviera*: Highlight of the carnival celebrations is the procession of spectacular and colorful floats. **Venice*: Carnival in Venice with costume sand masks, with street mimes, music, and fireworks. A fun time.
- **February 24-26**, *Oristano*: "Sa Sartiglia" medieval procession and jousting of masked knights dressed in Sardinian and Spanish costumes.
- **Friday before Shrovetide**, *Verona*: Gnocco (Festival of Bacchus)
- **19 March**, *Many places*: San Giuseppe (St. Joseph's day)

MARCH/APRIL

During March or April, *Rome* celebrates the Festa della Primavera (Spring Festival).

- **1 April**, *San Marino*: Installation of Regents
- **Palm Sunday**, *Many places, particularly Rome and Florence*: Blessings of palms, with procession
- **Wednesday before Easter**, *Many places, particulary Rome*: Mercoledi Santo (lamentations, Miserere)

- **Thursday Before Good Friday**, *Many places, particularly Rome and Florence*: Washing of the Feet, burial of the sacraments
- **Good Friday**, *Many places, particularly Rome and Florence*: Adoration of the Cross. *Taranto:* Procession of the Mysteries (Solemn procession with many beautiful period costumes).
- **Easter Saturday**, *Many places, particularly Rome and Florence*: Lighting of the Sacred Fire
- **Easter Week**, *Assisi:* Celebration of Spring with rites dating back to ancient times.
- **Easter Day**, *Rome*: Papal blessing; *Florence:* Scopplo dei Carro ("Explosion of the Cart" – A pyramid of fireworks is set off in the Cathedral square to commemorate the victorious return of the first Crusade.
- **End of April**, *Taormina*: Costume festival and parade of floats

MAY
- **1 May**, * *Florence*: Calcio in Costume (historical ball game – A Must See; Can't Miss This One)
- **May 2**, *Asti*: Palio San Secondo – 700 year old ceremony with procession in 13th century costumes and flag throwing.
- **During May**, *Florence*: Maggio Musicale (Music festival of May)
- **Beginning of May**, *Cagliari*: Sagra di Sant'Efisio One of the biggest and most colorful processions in the world. Several thousand pilgrims (wearing costumes from the 17th century accompany the saint on foot, in carts, or on horses.
- **First Saturday in May**, *Naples*: San Gennaro (fest de St. Januarius)
- **May 7**, *Bari*: Festival of St. Nicholas (procession of fishing boats with people in costumes)
- **Second Sunday in May**, *Camogli (Liguria)*: Sagra del Pesce (fishermen's festival frying of fish in giant pan)
- **May 15**, *Gubbio (Umbria)*: "Corsa dei Ceri "(procession with candles). Procession in local costumes with tall shrines. They are carried to the church at the top of Mount Ingino.
- **Next to last Sunday in May**, *Sassari*: Sardinian Cavalcade with a traditional procession with over 3,00 people in Sardinian costumes and some on horseback naked.
- **May 26**, *Rome*: San Filippo Neri
- **Last Sunday in May**, * *Gubbio (Umbria):* Palio dei Balestrieri (shooting with crossbows), medieval crossbow contest between Gubbio and Sansepolcro with medieval costumes and arms.
- **Ascension**, *Florence*: Festival of the Crickets. A lot of fun. You get to take home a cricket in a small cage. Something the Chinese do too, but hey, when in Italy ...; *Sassari (Sardinia)*: Cavalcata Sarda (mounted procession)

• **Corpus Christi**, *Many places, particulary Orvieto (Umbris)*: Processions

JUNE

If you're in *Venice*, don't miss the Biennale art exhibition.

• **First Sunday in June**, *Pisa*: Gioco del Ponte – medieval parade and contest for the possession of the bridge; *Either Pisa, Genoa, Venive, or the Amalfi Coast:* Regatta of the maritime republics. Each year the four former maritime republics of Italy meet to battle for supremacy at sea. The firendly contest takes the form of a historic regatta in which longboats representing each of the republics race for first prize: respect. Site changes between the four cities/regions each year.

• **Mid-June**, *Many places*: Corpus Domini (Ascension processions)

• **Mid-June to mid-July**, *Spoleto (Umbria)*: International Festival of Music, Dancing and Drama

• **Sunday after June 22**, *Nola*: The Lily Festival where flower towers are carried in colorful procession by people in costume

• **June 23-24**, *Rome*: Vigilia di San Giovanni Battista (St. John's Eve, fireworks, eating of snails, song competition)

• **June 29**, *Rome*: Santi Pietro e Paulo (feast of Saints Peter and Paul); *Genoa*: "Palio Marinaro dei Rioni." Rowing race in ancient costumes.

JULY

In *Genoa-Nervi*, see the International Ballet Festival in the park of Villa Gropallo.

• **July 2**, * *Siena (Tuscany)*: Palio delle Contrade (horserace, historical parade). Also held on August 16th.

• **July 10-15**, *Palermo*: Feat of Saint Rosalia with processions, bands, fireworks etc., all decorated in honor of the patron saint of the city.

• **July 16**, *Naples*: Feast of Santa Maria del Carmine

• **July 19-26**, *Rome*: Festa de' Noantri folklore festival of old Rome in Trastevere, Rome's oldest habitable section, which includes a colorful procession, folk dances, songs, carnival floats, and fireworks. Everybody gets real worked up for this. A must see.

• **Third Saturday in July (from that night to Sunday)**, * *Venice:* Festival of Redentore on the Grand Canal. Procession of Gondolas and othe craft commemorating the end of the black plague epidemic of 1575

• **During July/August**, *Verona*: Operatic Festival in Roman amphitheatre

AUGUST

• **Beginning of August**, *Assisi*: Perdono (Forgiveness Festival)

• **First Sunday in August**, **Acoli/Piceno*: Joust of the Qunitana. Historical pageant with over 1,000 people in 15th century costumes.

• **DuringAugust**, *Venice*: Nocturnal Festival on Grand Canal

- **DuringAugust/September,** *Venice*: Film Festival
- **First Sunday in August,** *Ascoli Piceno (Marche):* Quintana
- **14 August,** *Sassari (Sardinia):* Festival of Candles
- **15 August,** *Many places*: Assumption (processions and fireworks)
- **16 August,** *Siena (Tuscany)*: Palio delle Contrade (horse-races and processions in medieval costume)
- **Second Sunday in August,** *La Spezia*: Palio del Golfo. Rowing contest over a distance of 2,000 meters
- **August 26 to September 20,** *Strosa (Piedmont)*: Settimane Musicali (musical festival)
- **August 27th to 30th,** *Nuoro*: Feat of the Redeemer. Colorful procession in Sardinian costume.

SEPTEMBER/OCTOBER

- **First Sunday in September,** *Arezzo*: Giostra del Saracino (joust of the Saracin) - Tilting contest from the 13th century with nights; *Venice*: Traditional competition on the canal between two-oar racing gondolas preceded by a procession of Venetian Ceremonial boats from the time of the Venetian Republic.
- **September 5-7,** *Naples*: Madonna della Piedigrotta Folk Song Festival
- **September 7,** *Florence*: Riticolone (nocturnal festival with lantems)
- **September 8,** *Loreto (Marche)*: Nativity of the Virgin; *Recco (Liguria)*: Nativity of the Virgin (large tirework display, eating of *focaccia*)
- **Second Sunday in September,** *Foligno (Umbria)*: Giostra della Quintane Revival of a 17th century joust with over 600 knights in costume. A historical procession takes place the night before the joust; *Sansepolcro*: Palio Balestrieri. Crossbow contest between Sanselpolcro and Gubbio using medieval arms and costumes.
- **Second Saturday/Sunday in September on even years,** *Marostica*: Partita a Scacchi con Personaagi Viventi (Living Chess Game). Chess game played in town square by living pawns in period costumes.
- **September 13,** *Lucca (Tuscany)*: Luminara di Santa Croce
- **Mid-September,** *Ravenna*: Dante celebrations; *Asti (Piedmont)*: Palio race
- **September 19,** *Naples*: Festival of San Gennaro. Religious cceremony honoring the patron saint of the city.
- **Third Sunday in September,** *Asti*: Palio – ancient festival with over 800 costumed participants and 100 horses. Procession followed by bareback horserace along with flag throwing extravaganza.
- **October 1,** *San Marino*: Installation of Regents

NOVEMBER/DECEMBER
- **November 22**, *Many places*: Santa Cecilia (St. Cecilia's day)
- **December 10**, *Loreto (Marche)*: Santa Casa (procession)
- **December 25**, *Rome*: Papal blessing
- **Mid-December to mid-January**, Many places: Christmas crib (Nativity Scenes)

CRAFTS

Hundreds of thousands of skillful Italian artisans are the heirs of a 2,000-year tradition of craftsmanship. Their products – fashioned of leather, gold, silver, glass, and silk – are widely sought by tourists who flock to Florence, Rome, Milan, and Venice. Cameos made from sea-shells, an ancient Italian art form, are as popular today as they were in the days of the Roman Empire. The work of Italian artists and artisans is also exported for sale in the great department stores of France, Germany, the United Kingdom, and the United States.

Italian clothing designers are world famous, especially for precise tailoring, unusual knits, and the imaginative use of fur and leather.

The best place to see Italian artisans at work is in the glass blowing factories of Venice. There you'll be amazed at how easily they can manipulate molten balls into some of the most delicate, colorful, and beautiful pieces you've ever seen. Each chapter in this book highlights specific traditional crafts by region.

LITERATURE

Perhaps Italy's most famous author/poet is **Dante Aligheri**, who wrote the *Divine Comedy*, in which he describes his own dream-journey through Hell *(l'Inferno)* Purgatory *(Purgatorio)*, and Paradise *(Paradiso)*. At the time it was extremely controversial, since it is a poem about free will and how man can damn or save his soul as he chooses, which was contrary to church teachings. Even today it sparks controversy since it seems apparent that Dante's description of Purgatory is actually describing the life we all lead on earth, and shows his belief in reincarnation.

Two other notable Italian writers (you should remember these for quality cocktail party conversation) are **Petrarch**, famous for his sonnets to Laura, a beautiful girl from Avignon who died quite young, and is known as the "First of the Romantics;" and **Boccaccio**, the Robin Williams of his time (except he wrote, not performed) his famous *Decameron*, a charming and sometimes ribald series of short stories told by ten young people in a span of ten days – sort of the Chaucer of Italy.

Among contemporary Italian writers, **Umberto Eco** stands out on his own. You may know two of his books that have been translated into

English: *The Name of the Rose* and the more recent *Foucault's Pendulum*. If you are looking for complex, insightful, intriguing, and intellectual reading, Eco's your man. Last but not least, one Italian writer whom children all over the world should know is **Calo Collodi**, who wrote *Pinnochio*.

SHAKESPEARE'S ITALY

*The Immortal Bard chose Italy as the setting for a number of his best-known masterpieces: **Othello** takes place in part in Venice, and features both honorable and conniving Venetians; **Two Gentlemen from Verona** and **Romeo & Juliet** take place in Verona (the latter was pretty much lifted from Luigi da Porto's identical story, and today you can visit Juliet's House in Verona);**The Merchant of Venice** of course takes place in Venice; **The Taming of the Shrew** concerns the doings of rich Paduans, Pisans, and Veronans; about half of **A Winter's Tale** takes part in Sicily; all of **Much Ado About Nothing** takes place in Sicily; and finally, **All's Well That Ends Well** has one part set in Florence.*

*Ancient Rome and the ageless themes of power, love, and intrigue also held great allure for Shakespeare: pick up **Julius Caesar**, **Titus Andronicus**, **Troilius & Cressida**, or **Coriolanus** for some light reading about the tragic nature of the men and women who made the Roman Empire the world's first superpower!*

11. FOOD & WINE

FOOD

Most Italian food is cooked with fresh ingredients making their dishes healthy and satisfying. There are many restaurants in Italy of international renown, but you shouldn't limit yourself only to the upper echelon. In most cases you can find as good a meal at a fraction the cost at any *trattoria*. Also, many of the upper echelon restaurants you read about are only in business because they cater to the tourist trade. Their food is good, but the atmosphere is a little hokey.

The traditional Italian meal consists of an **antipasto** (appetizer), pasta or soup course, **il secondo** (main course usually meat or fish), salad, and dessert (which can be cheese or fruit). As you will notice in each regional chapter, I target those restaurants that are superb, and most are not well known to the tourist trade.

Most North Americans think that there is one type of Italian food, and that's usually spaghetti and meatballs. They don't know what they are missing. Region by region Italy's food has adapted itself to the culture of the people and land. In Florence you have some of the best steaks in the world, in the south the tomato-based pastas and pizzas are exquisite; in Genoa you can't miss the pesto sauce (usually garlic and basil); and don't forget forget the roast lamb in Rome.

Listed below is a selection of the main regional specialties that you should try. In each regional section, I have itemized for you some of the best places to find these and other dishes.

- **Piemonte** – *fonduta (cheese with eggs and truffles)*, agnolotti (cheese stuffed pasta), and chocolates and toffees
- **Lombardia** – *risotto all milanese* (rice with saffron), *minestrone* (stock and vegetable soup), *osso buco alla milanese* (knuckle of pork dish), *robiola, gorgonzola, stracchino, Bel Paese* (a variety of cheeses)
- **Venetia** – *risi e bisi* (soup with rice and peas), *polenta* (corn meal dish) *zuppa di pesce* (fish soup), *scampi* (shrimp or prawns)

GLOSSARY OF ITALIAN EATERIES

Bar – *Not the bar we have back home. This place serves espresso, cappuccino, rolls, small sandwiches, as well as sodas and alcoholic beverages. It is normal to stand at the counter or sit at a table when one is available. You have to try the* **Medallione**, *a grilled ham and cheese sandwich available at most bars. A little 'pick-me-up' in the morning is* **Café Corretto**, *coffee corrected by the addition of* **grappa** *(Italian brandy) or Cognac.*

Gelateria – *These establishments offer* **gelato** - *ice cream - usually produced on the premises. Italian gelato is softer than American but very sweet and rich.*

Osteria – *Small tavern-like eatery that serves local wine usually in liter bottles as well as simple food and sandwiches*

Panineria – *A small sandwich bar with a wider variety than at a regular Italian bar, where a quick meal can be gotten. One thing to remember is that Italians rarely use condiments on their sandwiches. If you want mustard or such you need to ask for it.*

Pasticceria – *Small pasty shops that sell cookies, cakes, pastries, etc. Carry-out only.*

Pizzeria – *A casual restaurant specializing in pizza, but they also serve other dishes. Most have their famous brick ovens almost directly in the seating area so you can watch the pizza being prepared. There are many featured excellent pizzerias in this book.*

Pizza Rustica – *Common in central Italy. These are huge cooked rectangular pizzas displayed behind glass. This pizza has a thicker crust and more ingredients than in a regular Pizzeria. You can request as much as you want, since they usually charge by the weight, not the slice. Carry-out only.*

Rosticceria – *A small eatery where they make excellent inexpensive roast chickens and other meats, as well as grilled and roasted vegetables, mainly potatoes. Sometimes they have baked pasta. Carry-out only.*

Trattoria – *A less formal restaurant where many local specialties are served.*

Ristorante – *A more formal eating establishment, but even most of these are quite informal at times.*

Tavola Calda – *Cafeteria-style food served buffet style. They feature a variety of hot and cold dishes. Seating is available.*

• **Liguria** – *minestrone* (stock and vegetable soup), *pasta al pesto* (pasta with with an aromatic garlic basil sauce), *torta Pasqualina* (easter pie filled with spinach, artichokes, and cheese)

- **Emilia Romagna** – *lasagna verde* (lasagna made with spinach), *cappelletti alla bolognese* (small hats pasta covered with a tomatoe meat sauce), *scallope* (scallops) *parmigiano reggiano* (cheese) and a variety of salamis
- **Toscana** – *bistecca all Fiorentina* (large T-bone steaks grilled), *arista* (roast pork), *cacciucco* (fish soup)
- **Lazio** – *abbachio arrosto* (roast lamb), *porcetta* (roast pork), and all type of pastas including *penne al'arrabiata* (literally translated it means angry pasta; a spicy hot, garlic-laden, tomato dish; should not be missed), *Tortellini all Panna* (cheese stuffed pasta in a heavy cream sauce)
- **Campania** – *spaghetti alla vongole verace* (with a spicy garlic oil sauce.), Fantastic pizzas beacuse of their wonderful cheeses (*mozzarella, provola, caciocavallo*)
- **Sicilia** – fresh fruits, pastries like *cannoli alla siciliana*; *caponata di melanzane* (eggplant dish), and seafood

RESTAURANT LISTINGS IN THIS BOOK

Here's a sample listing you'll find in this book in each of our *Where to Eat* sections. The number preceding the name of the restaurant tells you where to find it on the accompanying city or town map:

"**3. LA LEPANTO**, *Via Carlo Alberto 135, Tel. 079/979-116. Closed Mondays in the winter. All credit cards accepted. Dinner for two L140,000.*

A fine place with a quaint terrace located in the heart of the old city, but the preparation of dishes is haphazard. Sometimes it's great, other times so-so. Maybe it's because they try to do too much. The menu is extensive and seems to have everything that surf and turf could offer. I've always been pleased with the *i polpi tiepido con le patate* (roasted octopus in an oil and garlic sauce with roasted potatoes) and the *spaghetti con gamberi e melanzane* (with shrimp and eggplant). For antipasto, try the exquisite *antipasto misto di pesce spada affumicato* (smoked swordfish) or the *insalata mista* (mixed salad) with fresh vegetables from the region."

The restaurant listings indicate which credit cards are accepted by using the following phrases:

- **Credit cards accepted** = American Express, Visa, and Diners Card
- **All Credit cards accepted** = Everything imaginable is accepted, even cards you've never heard of
- **No credit card accepted** = Only cash or travelers checks (if a listing is left without an indication, that means that no credit cards are accepted.)

Each list will also give a ballpark price for a dinner for two in Italian lire. For example: "Dinner for two L80,000." With the exchange rate at roughly $1=L1,600, this example the dollar price would be $50 for the meal. This price includes three courses per person and a bottle of house wine with the meal. In most cases you will get by with one course. Thus the actual price you will pay will be less than indicated.

WINE

Italy is also famous for its wines. The experts say the reds are not robust enough, and the whites are too light, but since I'm not an expert, I love them, one and all. Most importantly, to get a good bottle of wine, you don't have to spend a fortune either. You can find some excellent wines straight out of wine vats in small wine stores in every city in Italy.

ITALIAN WINES BY REGION

PIEMONTE - *Barolo* (red, dry), *Barbera* (red, dry), and *Asti Spumanti* (sweet sparkling wine)

LOMBARDIA - *Reisling* (white, dry), *Frecciarossa* (rose wines)

TRENTINO-ALTO ADIGE - *Reisling* (white, dry), *Santa Maddalena* (red, semi-dry), *Cabernet* (red, dry)

VENETIA - *Soave* (white, dry), *Valpolicella* (red, dry or semi-sweet)

LIGURIA - *Cinqueterre* (named after a section of Liguria you must visit. Cinqueterre is five small oceanside towns inaccessible by car or train, you have to walk. They're simply gorgeous.)

EMILIA ROMAGNA - *Lambrusco* (red, semi-sparkling, several kinds going from dry to sweet), *Sangiovese* (red, dry), *Albano* (white, dry or semi-sweet)

TUSCANY - *Chianti* (red, dry; look for the Chianti Classicos. They're the ones with a black rooster on the neck of the bottle)

MARCHE - *Verdicchio* (white, dry)

UMBRIA/LAZIO - *Orvietto* (white, dry), *Frascati* (white, dry or semi-sweet), *Est Est Est* (white, slightly sweet)

ABRUZZI - *Montepulciano* (red, dry)

SARDINIA - *Cannonau* (red, dry to semi-sweet)

SICILY - *Etna* (red and white, wide variety), *Marsala* (white, dry or sweet)

CAMPANIA, APULIA, CALABRIA, BASILICATA - *Ischia* (red and white, several varieties), *San Severo* (red, dry)

As you read each regional chapter, you notice I mention quite a few. This is because I had to have something to go with our picnic lunches during siesta time. Also, at any restaurant, all you'll need to order is the house wine to have a satisfying and excellent wine. (*Vino di casa*: House Wine. *Roso*: Red. *Biancho*: White).

But if you're a connoisseur, or simply want to try a wine for which a certain Italian region is known, in the sidebar above you'll find a selected list of wines and their regions (if you like red wine, try the **Chianti**, and if it's white you prefer, try **Verdicchio**):

ORDER LIKE A NATIVE: READING AN ITALIAN MENU

Here are a few choice words to assist you when you're ordering from a menu while in Italy. Usually, the waiter should be able to assist you, but if not, this will make your dining more pleasurable. You wouldn't want to order octopus by surprise, would you?

ENGLISH	ITALIAN	ENGLISH	ITALIAN
Menu	*Lista or Carta*	Teaspoon	*Cucchiaino*
Breakfast	*Primo Colazione*	Knife	*Cotello*
Lunch	*Pranzo*	Fork	*Forchetta*
Dinner	*Cena*	Plate	*Piatto*
		Glass	*Bicchiere*
Table setting	*Coperto*	Cup	*Tazza*
Spoon	*Cucchiao*	Napkin	*Tovagliolo*

Antipasto

ENGLISH	ITALIAN	ENGLISH	ITALIAN
Soup	*Zuppa*	Broth	*Brodo*
Fish Soup	*Zuppa di Pesce*	Vegetable soup	*Minestrone*
Broth with beaten egg	*Stracciatella*		

Pasta

ENGLISH	ITALIAN	ENGLISH	ITALIAN
Ravioli with meat stuffing	*Agnolotti*	Egg noodles	*Fettucine*
Large rolls of pasta	*Cannelloni*	Potato-filled, ravioli-like pasta	*Gnocchi*
Thin angel hair pasta	*Capellini*	Thin pasta	*Vermicelli*
Little hat pasta	*Capelletti*	Macaroni-like pasta	*Penne*

Eggs	*Uova*		
soft-boiled	*al guscio*	hard boiled	*sode*
fried	*al piatto*	omelette	*frittata*

Fish	*Pesce*		
Seafood	*Frutti di mare*	Eel	*Anguilla*
Lobster	*Aragosta*	herring	*Aringa*
Squid	*Calamari*	Carp	*Carpa*
Mullet	*Cefalo*	Grouper	*Cernia*

Mussels	*Cozze/Muscoli*	Perch	*Pesce Persico*
Salmon	*Salmone*	Clams	*Vongole*
Octopus	*Polpo*	Bass	*Spigola*
Oysters	*Ostriche*	Mixed fried fish	*Fritto Misto Mare*

Meat	*Carne*		
Spring Lamb	*Abbachio*	Lamb	*Agnello*
Rabbit	*Coniglio*	Chicken	*Pollo*
Small Pig	*Porcello*	Veal	*Vitello*
Steak	*Bistecca*	Breast	*Petto*
Pork	*Maiale*	Liver	*Fegato*
Cutlet	*Costellata*	Deer	*Cervo*
Wild Pig	*Cinghiale*	Pheasant	*Fagione*
Duck	*Anitra*	Turkey	*Tacchino*

Methods of Cooking

Roast	*Arrosto*	Boiled	*Bollito*
On the Fire/ Grilled	*Ai Ferri* *Alla Griglia*	Spit-roasted	*Al Girarrosto*
Rare	*Al Sangue*	Grilled	*Alla Griglia*
Well Done	*Ben Cotto*	Medium Rare	*Mezzo Cotto*

Miscellaneous

French fries	*Patate Fritte*	Cheese	*Formaggio*
Butter Sauce	*Salsa al burro*	Tomato and Meat Sauce	*Salsa Bolognese*
Tomato Sauce	*Salsa Napoletana*	Garlic	*Aglio*
Oil	*Olio*	Pepper	*Pepe*
Salt	*Sale*	Fruit	*Frutta*
Orange	*Arancia*	Cherries	*Ciliege*
Strawberry	*Fragola*	Lemon	*Limone*
Apple	*Mela*	Melon	*Melone*
Beer	*Birra*	Mineral Water	*Aqua Minerale*
Orange Soda	*Aranciata*	7-Up Like	*Gassatta*
Lemon Soda	*Limonata*	Juice (of)	*Succo (di)*

Wine	*Vino*		
Red	*Roso*	White	*Bianco*
House wine	*Vino di Casa*	Dry	*Secco*
Slightly Sweet	*Amabile*	Sweet	*Dolce*
Local Wine	*Vino del Paese*	Liter	*Litro*
Half Liter	*Mezzo Litro*	Quarter Liter	*Un Quarto*
A Glass	*Un Bicchiere*		

12. ROME

ORIENTATION

Lazio, the province that **Roma (Rome)** is in, covers an area of 6,633 square miles, including the provinces of Frosinone, Latina, Roma, and Viterbo, and has a population of over 6 million. Its charms include quaint little seaside resorts nestled in pine groves, pretty lakeside villages, many dominated by castles, and exotic skiing resorts, such as Terminillo, only a few hours drive from Rome's center. Also near the city are many beaches, **Lido di Ostia** being one of the best and most easily accessible.

Other than its encompassing the national capital, Lazio does not get much respect from the average Italian. Northerners lump it together contemptuously with the southern provinces of Campania and Calabria, and the southern Italians consider it a wasteland of swamps and poor mountain regions inhibiting the entrance to most everyone's destination in the area – Roma.

That is precisely Lazio's identity problem. It is completely overshadowed by Rome, but this was not always the situation. Rome was not always the largest and most powerful city in the region. Prior to the Roman Empire, another culture, the **Etruscans**, dominated the area around Rome. **Cervetri** and **Tarquinia**, north of Rome in Lazio, were two of the richest Etruscan cities. Now they are home to magnificent *Necropoli*, or simply, cities of the dead. The Etruscans took great care in laying their dead to rest in cemeteries set up like actual towns; and those found in Tarquinia and Cervetri are two of the finest. Cervetri is the closest, so this may be the best alternative for a quick day trip.

Besides Rome, the other locations, towns, and cities featured in this chapter include **Vatican City**, **Tivoli Gardens**, **Castel Gandolfo**, **Frascati**, **Ostia Antica**, **Lago di Bracciano** and **Cervetri**. Two specific excursions are featured near Rome, and two are further afield not far from Naples: the ancient ruins of **Pompeii** and **Herculaneum**, devoured in volcanic lava and ash nearly 2,000 years ago. Finally, you'll find an excursion to the beautiful **Isle of Capri**.

The Eternal City

Rome is the capital of the Republic of Italy, the region of Lazio, and the province of Rome. As such, it has turned into Italy's largest city, with over 5 million people. The **Tiber River** (**Tevere**), Italy's third longest (after the Po and the Adige), dissects the middle of Rome.

For a millennium and a half, Rome was the cultural center of Europe. At the time of the Empire, it controlled territory extending from Scotland to North Africa, and from the Atlantic Ocean to the Persian Gulf. During and after the Renaissance (14th century AD), Rome was also a center of artistic expression. **Michelangelo** spent much time here, working on the Sistine chapel, helping to design St. Peter's, carving the Pieta, and much more. Hundreds of churches were built by the Vatican, and many artists were sponsored to fill them with beautiful works.

Because of this extensive history, dating all the way back to before the time of Christ, Rome has a wide variety of sights to see, which is why many people describe Rome as a living museum. You'll see ancient Roman ruins resting side by side with buildings built 3 to 4 centuries ago, and sometimes these ruins having been incorporated into the design of the 'new' building.

IF YOU HAVEN'T DONE THIS, YOU HAVEN'T BEEN TO ROME

Rome has so many options that it's easy to neglect seeing a certain sight, or taking the time to go to a specific restaurant, or making an effort to visit a particular spot late in the evening to enjoy the ambiance and charm. Even though I've itemized the best places to stay, eat, and see while you're here, if you only have a little time, you have to go to the places listed below while in Rome.

Even if you are the furthest thing from being religious, make the effort to see **St. Peter's** and the **Vatican Museum**. This will take the better part of a day if you do a proper tour. No church is more magnificent and no museum is more complete. All others in Rome and the rest of Italy will pale in comparison.

That night, make sure you get to the **Trastevere** district and sample the atmosphere of **La Canonica**, a converted chapel and now a restaurant that also has many tables spilling out along the street. Reserve a spot inside since this may be your last chance to have a meal in a quaint converted chapel. Try their *Spaghetti alla Carbonara* (with a light cream sauce, covered with ham, peas, and grated parmesan cheese) for primo and for your main course sample the light fish dish, *Sogliala alla Griglia* (grilled Sole). Then sojourn to one of the cafés in the **Piazza Santa Maria** in Trastevere, grab a drink, and savor the evening.

During another day it is imperative that you visit **Piazza Navona** and grab an ice cream at one of the cafés, and either lounge on their terraces or take it with you and sit on the edge of one of the fountains. The best vantage point is on Bernini's magnificent **Fontana Dei Quattro Fiumi** (Fountain of Four Rivers). The four figures supporting the large obelisk (a Bernini trademark) represent the Danube, the Ganges, the Nile, and the Plata Rivers. Notice the figure representing the Nile. It is shielding its eyes from the facade of the church it is facing, **Santa Agnese in Agone**, which was designed by Bernini's rival at the time, Borromini. An ancient artistic quarrel comes to life everyday in Piazza Navona.

From there, only a few blocks away is the quaint little **Campo di Fiori** where you'll find one of Rome's best fruit and vegetable markets every day until 1:00pm, except Sunday Make sure you get here to shop or just to enjoy the atmosphere of a boisterous Roman market.

Here is where you should enjoy at least one meal, at **La Carbonara** in the square. Even though the name would lead you to believe that the best dish to get is the *Spaghetti alla Carbonara*, I believe you haven't been to Rome if you neglect to sample their exquisite *Spaghetti alla Vongole Verace* (with a spicy oil, garlic, and clam sauce). If you want to sit outside, you'll have to wait until about 2:00pm, until after the debris from the outdoor market has been swept up from the piazza.

Other dishes you need to sample while in Rome are the *penne all'arrabiatta* (literally means angry pasta; it's tubular pasta made with a spicy garlic, oil, and tomato-based sauce), the *tortellini alla panna* (meat filled pasta in a thick cream sauce), and any *abbacchio* (lamb) or *maiale alla griglia* (grilled pork).

In the evening, don't miss the **Trevi Fountain**, all lit up and surrounded by locals and tourists strumming on guitars and drinking wine. It's definitely a party atmosphere. Come here with friends or arrive and meet new ones. For one of your evening meals, there's a place somewhat close by a little past the **Spanish Steps**. If you're here in Spring, stop for a minute and admire the floral display covering the steps.

Then move onto **La Capriciossa** where you can sit in a peaceful little piazza just off the Via del Corso, Rome's main shopping street, while you enjoy your meal. They are known for making excellent pizza (only in the evening) as well as preparing perfect Roman pasta dishes and exquisite meat plates. If you haven't already sampled the *penne all'arabiatta*,do so here, and try the succulent *abbacchio arrosto* (roast lamb), another staple of the Roman diet. And to finish the meal, order a *Sambucca con tre mosce* (literally translated, it means a sweet liquor with three flies, but it actually uses three coffee beans). Remember to bite into the beans as you have the sweet liquor in your mouth. The combination of tastes is exquisite.

There is obviously much more to do in Rome than this, but if you only a little time, make sure you get to the places mentioned above. Then you can say you really have seen Rome.

ARRIVALS & DEPARTURES

By Air

Most travelers will arrive at **Rome's Fiumicino (Leonardo da Vinci)** airport that handles most incoming flights from North America, Australia, and the United Kingdom. If you are arriving from other points in Europe you may arrive at Rome's **Ciampino** airport.

Rome's Fiumicino has a dedicated **train** to whisk you directly to the central train station (**Termini**). To get to the train at the airport simply follow the signs (**Treno**) right after you get through customs. After you leave the arrivals building you'll see the train station about fifty feet in front of you across the street and up a ramp. The trip costs L12,000 and takes 30 minutes. There are 15 trips each day in both directions, basically one train every hour. The trains are air conditioned. From the Termini train station you can get a taxi from the taxi stand outside in front of the station, hop on the Metro, or a take city bus to get close to your hotel.

There is also a **Metropolitana** service from the airport to **Stazione Tiburtina** stopping at the following stations: Ponte Galleria, Muratella, Magliana, Trastevere, Ostiense, and Tuscolana. Departures are every 20 minutes from 6:00 am to 10:00 pm. The trip takes about 45 minutes, and trains are air conditioned.

You can also spend the equivalent of a night in a hotel on a **taxi** ride directly to your hotel. This choice can sometimes take longer depending on the traffic situation at and around the airport. Your best bet is to take the train to Termini station and catch a cab there.

If you are renting a car, you will get explicit directions from your rental company. See the *Renting a Car* section below for more complete information. If they neglect to give you directions, get on the large road – SS 201 – leading away from the airport to the **GRA** *(Grande Raccordo Anulare)*, which is Rome's beltway and is commonly known as the **Anulare**, going north. Get off at **SS 1 (Via Aurelia)** and follow this road all the way into town.

If you arrive at Rome's **Ciampino**, there are dedicated airport buses that leave for the **Agnina Underground Station** every half an hour. They take 15 minutes to get into town. Taking a **taxi** from here also costs an arm and a leg but not nearly as much as from Termini, since this airport is closer to Rome. If you rent a car, simply take **Via Appia** all the way into town. For the scenic view get on the **Via Appia Antica** a kilometer or so after passing the **GRA**.

By Car

To get into Rome you will have to either get on or pass by the **GRA** (*Grande Raccordo Anulare*) which is Rome's beltway and is commonly known as the **Anulare**. If arriving from the north you will be using **Via Cassia** (which can get congested), **Via Flaminia**, **Via Salaria** or the fastest route, the **A1** (*Autostrada del Sole*), which will dump you onto the GRA.

If arriving from the south, the fastest route is the **A2**, also referred to as the *Autostrada del Sole*. A more scenic route is along the **Via Appia**.

Sample trip lengths on the main roads:
- **Florence**: 3 1/2 hours
- **Venice**: 6 1/2 hours
- **Naples**: 3 hours
- **Bari**: 13 hours

By Train

When arriving by train, you will be let off at Rome's **Termini** station. From here you can catch a **taxi** at the row of cabs outside the front entrance, walk down to the **Metro** and catch a train close to your destination, or hop on one of the **buses** in the main square just in front of the station.

Termini is a zoo. Packed with people from all over the world, queuing up to buy tickets, trying to cut in line to get information, and in some cases looking for unprotected belongings. Don't leave your bags unattended in any train station in Italy. The Tourist information office is located near the train tracks (*Tel. 06/487-1270*). You can get a good map here and make a hotel reservation. The railway information office faces the front entrance along with the taxis and buses. If you're planning a trip, you should come here to find out when your train will be leaving. All attendants speak enough English to get by.

Sample trip lengths and costs for direct (*diretto*) trains:
- **Florence**: 2 1/2 hours, L35,000
- **Venice**: 5 hours, L56,000
- **Naples**: 2 hours, L25,000
- **Bari**: 12 hours, L70,000

GETTING AROUND TOWN
BY CAR

Are you nuts? Unless you are from Boston and used to aggressive driving tactics, driving a car to get around Rome is a crazy idea, considering that the public transportation system is so good and that virtually everything is within walking distance. Now if you want to rent a car for a day trip at the beach at Lido di Ostia or another excursion, that's another story. But even in those circumstances, you can still get to those destinations and most others by train from Stazione Termini.

So think twice about renting a car, because Italian drivers are like nothing you've ever seen.

Renting a Car

Cars can be rented at **Fiumicino** or **Ciampino airports**, booked in advance by a travel agent, or rented at many offices in the city, especially at **Termini Station**. Try the following places:

• **Avis**, *Main Office, P Esquino 1c, Tel. 06/478-001 or 478-011. Open Monday through Friday 9am-1:30pm and 2:30pm-6:00pm. Their office at Termini Station is open Monday-Saturday 7:00am-8:00pm, and Sundays from 8:00am-11:00pm (Tel. 06/470-1219). Their office at Fiumicino is open every day from 7:30am-11:00pm (Tel. 06/601-551).*

• **Budget Rent A Car**, *Main Office, Via Ludovisi. Tel. 06/482-0966 or 482-0927. Open Monday through Friday 9am-1:30pm and 2:30pm-6:00pm. The office at Fiumicino airport is open Monday-Saturday 7:00am-8:00pm, and Sundays from 8:00am-11:00pm (Tel. 06/6501-0347 or 06/652-9133). The office at Ciampino holds the same hours (Tel. 06/7934-0137).*

• **Hertz**, *Main Office is on the Via Veneto #156. The phone number is 06/321-6831 or 06/321-6834. It's conveniently located in the underground garage that can be accessed from either the Piazza di Spagna Metro stop or the Via Veneto. In and of itself it's something that should be seen and walked through while you're in Rome. The office is open Monday - Saturday 7:00am-8:00pm and Sun day 8:00am-1:00pm. The office number at Termini station is 06/474-6405; at Fiumicino it's 06/602-448; at Ciampino it's 06/7934-0095.*

The fees usually include the costs for towing, minor repairs, and basic insurance, but you should ask. Also most firms require a deposit equal to the daily cost of the rental, which is usually between L200,000 and L300,000. The minimum age usually is 21 and you must have had a drivers license for at least a year. Rules and regulations will vary according to company. Standard industry business practices haven't hit Italy yet.

BY MOPED

If you are looking for a new experience, a different way to see Rome (or any city in Italy), try renting a moped. Walking, riding a bicycle, driving a car, taking the bus, or riding in a taxi cannot come close to the exhilaration of riding a moped.

A moped gives you freedom. A moped gives you the ability to go from one corner of Rome to another, quickly. Riding a moped makes you feel in tune with the flow of the city. With no plan, no sequence, no itinerary, no boundaries, you can go from the tourist areas to a part of Rome tourists rarely see. You can find monuments and markets in Rome you would never have seen if not on a moped. It makes you feel a part of the city, and this familiarity gives you the confidence to widen your explorations.

Now that I've built it up, think hard about renting a moped. As with cars, a moped is even more dangerous since you have nothing to protect you. Only if you feel extremely confident about your motorcycle driving abilities should you even contemplate renting a moped. This isn't the Bahamas where everyone's polite. The Romans will just as soon run you over as make way for you.

Personally, I find a moped to be the most fun way to get around Rome. They're inexpensive, quick, easy to maneuver, and practical since parking is virtually impossible for a car. But, granted, I have had my accidents. Once, as I was speeding between cars who were stopped at a light, a pedestrian walked in front of me and POW, next thing you know I'm wrapped around a pole. And then there was the time a public bus decided that he had the right of way in a circle and casually knocked me down. Anyway, only if you're *un po pazzo* or very brave should you attempt to rent a moped.

MOPED CAUTION & RATES

If you cannot ride a bicycle, please do not rent a moped. The concept is the same, one vehicle just goes a little faster. Also, start off renting a 50 cc (cinquanta), not a 125 cc (cento venti sei). With more than twice the engine capacity, the 125 cc is a big difference, and in the traffic of Rome it's best to start slow. But if you insist on riding two to a moped, then a 125 cc is necessary. It's the law. (Not that any Italians abide by it). Also you need to be at least sixteen years old to rent a moped, but you don't need a motorcycle license. Just hop on, and ride away ... but don't let Mom and Dad know about it.

A sizable deposit (around L200,000+) is required for each moped. The deposit will increase based on the size of moped you want to rent. Your deposit can be cash in any currency, travelers cheques, or on a credit card. This is standard procedure for all rental companies. Do not worry, you'll get your money back. Daily rates are between L50,000 and L80,000. Renting for a more extended period can be a better bargain. Rates should be prominently posted.

Renting a Moped
• **Scooters for Rent**, *Via Della Purificazione 66, Tel. 488-5685. Open 9:00am-7:30pm, seven days a week.* A centrally located moped rental, just off the Piazza Barberini. After the steep climb up this street, you will definitely want a moped. This is a small, quaint little rental outfit that,

to the best of my knowledge, were the first to start renting mopeds to tourists many years ago. The people here are fun, helpful, and friendly.

- **I Bike Rome di Cortessi Ferruccio**, *Viale Galappatoio, near Via Veneto. Tel. 06/322-5240. Open Monday-Saturday 9:00am-1:00pm and 4:00pm-8:00pm, and Sundays 9:00am-8:00pm.* They rent from the same underground parking garage (connecting the Piazza di Spagna Metro Stop and the Via Veneto) as does Hertz. Maybe that's why you get a 50% discount with a Hertz card.
- **St. Peter's Moto**, *Via di Porto Castello 43, Tel. 06/687-5719. Open Monday-Saturday 9am - 1:30pm and 3:30pm-9:30pm.*
- **Scoot-A-Long**, *Via Cavour 302, Tel. 06/678-0206. Open Monday-Saturday 9:00am-7:00pm, Sunday 10:00am-2:00pm and 4:00pm-7:00pm.*

BY BICYCLE

Bicycles make getting from one spot in Rome to another quicker and easier, but if you haven't been on one in awhile, trying to re-learn on the streets of Rome is not a good idea. And don't even think about having children younger than 14 try and ride around Rome unattended. Not only could they get lost very easily, but the traffic laws are so different they may not be able to adapt very well.

I've seen older teenagers fare very well, especially around the Trevi Fountain, Spanish Steps area. Letting your kids do this gives them a sense of freedom, but reinforce to them how careful they have to be.

Renting a Bike

All four places listed above that rent mopeds also rent bicycles on a daily or hourly basis. The cost for en entire day varies from place to place, and year to year, but the latest price is L25,000 per day and L8,000 per hour, except at the one below, which is only L20,000 a day and L5,000 per hour.

- **Bici e Baci**, *Via Principe Amadeo 2B, Tel. 06/474-5389.* Run by a beautiful and animated Italian *signorina* with bubbling brown eyes who insisted I refer to her as *Laura delle Biciclette* (Laura of the bicycles). Her effervescence is in the name of her business *(Bici e Baci)* which means "Bikes and Kisses." I only got a bike this time. Maybe next time I'll get a kiss. Her rates (for the bicycles) are L5,000 for an hour and L20,000 for a day.

BY TAXI

Taxis are the best, and also the most expensive, way to get around Rome. They are everywhere so flagging one down is not a problem. But since they are so expensive I wouldn't rely on them as your main form of transportation. Use them as a last resort, when you start to get tired from walking. Also have a map handy when a cabby is taking you somewhere. Since they are on a meter, they sometimes decide to take you on a little longer journey than necessary. And also watch out for the fly-by-night operators that don't have a licensed meter. They will really rip you off.

The going rate as of publication was L3,500 for the first 2/3 of a kilometer or the first minute (which usually comes first during the rush hours), then it's L300 every 1/3 of a kilometer or minute. At night you'll also pay a surcharge of L3,000, and Sundays you'll pay L1,000 extra. If you bring bags aboard, say for example after you've been shopping, you'll be charged L500 extra for each bag.

Besides having to rely on flagging down a cab, there are strategically placed **cab stands** all over the city. The ones that will benefit you as a tourist the most are probably the ones in Piazza del Popolo, Piazza della Republicca, Piazza Venezia, and at Piazza Sonino just across the bridge in Trastevere.

BY BUS

At all bus stops, called **fermatas**, there are signs that list all the buses that stop there. These signs also give the streets that the buses will follow along its route so you can check your map to see if this is the bus for you. Also, on the side of the bus are listed highlights of the route for your convenience. Nighttime routes (since many of them stop a midnight) are indicated by black spaces on newer signs, and are placed at the bottom of the older signs. (Italians just aren't as compulsive as we are about changing everything at once. They seem to ween the population into everything more slowly.) In conjunction the times listed on the signs indicate when the bus will pass the *fermata* you're at during the night so you can plan accordingly.

Riding the bus during rush is like becoming a sardine, complete with the odor, so try to avoid the rush hours of 8:00am to 9:00am, 12:30pm to 1:30pm, 3:30 to 4:30pm, and 7:30pm to 8:30pm. Yes, they have an added rush hour in the middle of the day because of their siesta time in the afternoon.

The bus fare costs L1,000 and lasts for one hour. Despite the convenience and extent of the Roman bus system, which helped me get anywhere I wanted to go in Rome for a long time, since the advent of the Metro I recommend taking the underground transport since it is easier, quicker, less crowded, and more understandable.

ATAC Bus Tours & Bus 119

If you are a hardy soul, take the no-frills *Giro di Roma* tour offered by **ATAC**, the intra-city bus company *(Tel. 06/469-51)*. This three hour circuit of the city leaves from the information booth in the middle of the **Piazza Cinquecento** in front of the train station daily at 3pm and at 2:30pm on Saturday, Sundays and holidays. For your L15,000 fee they give you a free map and a semi-guided tour in a kind of half-Italian half-English monologue that lets you see many parts of the city for cheap.

If you really want to be a native, the **regular bus #119** takes you to some of Rome's classic sights. It starts in the Piazza Augusto Imperatore and takes you by the Pantheon, Piazza Colonna, Via del Tritone, Piazza di Spagna, and the Piazza del Popolo. This is a regular bus route, and I know it doesn't sound too exciting, but it takes you through the heart of old Rome and is an inexpensive alternative to a guided bus tour (only L1,000).

You can buy these 1 hour bus tickets and other longer versions at all *tabacchi* in the city. They are indicated by the large "T" sign in the front of their stores.

Bus Passes

If you are staying in Rome for an extended period of time and need to use the buses frequently since your hotel or destinations are not on a Metro line, you can buy one of the following bus tickets:
- **Weekly Ticket** *(Biglietto Settimanale): L24,000*
- **Monthly Pass** *(Bonamente Mensile): L50,000*

By Metro

The Roman *Metropolitana* (**Metro**) has two lines (Linea A and Linea B) that intersect in the basement of Termini station. You'll find these and all other stations marked with a prominent white "M" inside a red square up on a sign outside. **Linea A** is probably the most used by the tourists since it starts at Ottaviano, near St. Peters, and has Piazza del Popolo, Piazza di Spagna, Piazza Barberini, and Piazza della Repubblica as stops. **Linea B** comes in a close second since it takes you to the Coliseum, the Circus Maximus, and the Piramide (which really isn't the greatest sight in the world, but I always return since my family members have been getting their picture taken in front of the Piramide since the 1950's).

Buses used to be the way to get around Rome, quickly, efficiently, and inexpensively, but now it's the Metro. A fare only costs L1,500 and lasts for 75 minutes or a return trip within the time allotted. Which means you can make two trips on the Metro, in less than an hour and 15 minutes, for only about a dollar.

The Metro can get quite crowded around the Stazione Termini and during rush hours. Sardine-like is the best way to describe it, otherwise rides are very pleasant. Always be on the look out for pickpockets – at least that's what the signs in the Metro cars tell you to do.

HOW TO BUY A METRO TICKET

Walk down the steps into the subterranean caverns of the Roman Metro, then buy the ticket at the ever-present ticket booths in any station. To get to the trains you stamp the ticket in an ugly bright orange machine. The stamp received from these hideous looking devices marks the start of your 75 minutes. When you get back on the system just stamp your ticket again. Simple.

*If it's late at night, the ticket booths are usually closed so you'll have to use one of the ever-present ticket machines in all stations. Simply have L1,500 ready, or close to it in bills or coins. Then a touch tone screen awaits your commands. Press the upper left image on the screen to indicate to the machine you want a 75 minute ticket. Then insert your bills or coins as indicated (the machines do not like **Gettone**, the coins that used to be used exclusively for the telephones, and which are about the same size as a L200 coin), and presto your ticket and change (if any) will appear.*

Take the Metro to the Beach!

If you're interested in going to the beach or visiting the ruins at Ostia Antica, take the Linea B Metro to the Magliana stop and transfer to the train that will take you there. You'll have to pay a new fare, since the Metro and the train systems are different animals.

WHERE TO STAY

Hotels in Italy are strictly controlled by a government rating system that categorizes them from "no star" hotels to "four star deluxe" hotels. Each and every hotel must prominently display their official ranking for all visitors to see.

These ratings have little or nothing to do with price. They only indicate what types of facilities are available at each hotel. Also, the stars do not indicate what level of service you will receive, how clean the hotels are, whether management is surly or sweet. Even in hotels with the same rating, the quality of facilities is unequal. The stars only indicate which facilities are available. Listed below is the star ranking (see Chapter 6, *Planning Your Trip*, for more details on accommodations and ratings).

You'll find the stars listed at the end of the italicized basic information section (name of hotel, address, phone, price, cards accepted, etc.) before the review itself begins for each hotel.

*Minimum facilities. Probably no rooms with private bath. No air conditioning. No TV. No phones in the room. Boarding-room style accommodations, unless the hotel is on the cusp of being recognized as a two star.

**Comfortable room with a telephone, many with a private bath. No
air conditioning. No TV. Maybe a breakfast served in the mornings. You
may, however, have TV and air conditioning if the hotel is bucking for
three star status.

***All rooms will have private baths, a color TV, CNN (i.e. satellite
TV), air conditioning, a lobby bar, maybe a restaurant, and will be as
comfortable as a four star, except with smaller rooms and public areas, but
also with much lower prices.

****This is a first class hotel and will have every comfort you expect
to find in a regular North American hotel. There are some very small four
star hotels that can make your stay in Italy much more intimate and
romantic.

*****Four star deluxe hotel. These places have everything you could
possibly imagine and more. The place where the jet-set stays.

NO HOTEL RESERVATIONS?

*If you get to Rome without a reservation and arrive at the train station,
there is a free service located at the end of **track #10** that will get you a room.
There is no fee, but you usually do have to pay them for the first night's stay
up front. They call ahead and book your room, give you a map, and show
you how to get to your badly needed bed. It's a great service for those who like
to wing it or arrived in Rome on a whim. Sometimes the lines are long, so
be patient.*

Near Termini Station

1. ALBERGHO IGEA, *Via Principe Amedeo 97, 00184 Roma. Tel. 06/
446-6913. Fax 06/446-6911. Mastercard and Visa accepted. 42 rooms, 221
doubles, 21 singles, all with shower and WC, air conditioning, and TV. Single
L90,000; Double L120,000; Triple L160,000. Breakfast L8,000 per person.* **

Currently in the process of remodeling some of the rooms but will be
completed by 1996. The rooms are large, clean, and with full bath
facilities, air conditioning and TV in each room, it can't be beaten for the
price. The lobby is large and spacious, completely covered in white marble
making it a pleasant place to relax; and the staff is friendly, knowledgeable, and professional. So why only the two stars and low price? They're
still remodeling and to get three stars you need a mini-bar in the room.
Also, they're around the train station which has a reputation for being not
so hospitable.

Granted there's not much to do around the station, and the restaurants are better almost anywhere else in the city, but if you want a lot of
amenities for a low price, stay here.

2. HOTEL ADLER, *Via Modena 5, 00184 Roma. Tel. 06/488-0940. Fax is same number. Mastercard and Visa accepted. 16 rooms, 10 with bath. Single L85,000; Double L96,000-124,000; Triple L132,000-165,000. Breakfast Included.* **

Located near the Via Nazionale, but off on a side street, this hotel offers a good location for shopping as well as sightseeing. The rooms are spartan but clean, and the staff is wonderfully helpful. Most of them speak more English than the normal tourist does Italian, so you can make yourself understood. They have a person at the desk all night long to let you take care of those late night phone calls from your loved ones. One good feature is a small terrace overlooking an interior courtyard that is not that pretty but is cool and calming and makes you feel a part of Italian life. Check out some of the other two stars before you stay here, but if need be you will be happy here.

3. HOTEL ASTORIA GARDEN & MONTAGNA, *Via Bachelet 8/10, 00187 Roma. Tel. 06/446-9908. Fax 06/445-3329. 30 rooms, 23 with bath. Single L56,000-67,000, Double L97,000-121,000; Triple L134,000-174,000.* **

You cannot beat the prices at this place. A single with a bath for L67,000. Oh, that feels good. This has got to be the best kept secret in Rome in terms of price. But the decor and ambiance are great also. Better than their neighbor Hotel Select that charges through the roof. This place is a little darker, but has more character and their outside enclosed garden doesn't glare out onto an ugly building. This place has loads of old-world charm to spare ... downstairs. But upstairs they have modernized all the rooms, which makes for great comfort.

4. HOTEL BRITANNIA, *Via Napoli 64, 00184 Roma. Tel. 06/488-3153. Fax. 06/488-2343. 32 Rooms all with private baths. Air conditioning. Parking Available. American Express, Diners Club, Mastercard, and Visa accepted. Single L220,000; Double L240,000; Triple L275,000. Breakfast included. Children up to ten share parents rooms for free.* ****

Located just north of the Via Nazionale, this is a small efficiently run hotel with a slightly modern decor downstairs. The rooms tend towards a neo-classic ambiance. The rooms aren't the largest in the world but you have all you could want at your fingertips: TV, phone, air conditioning, minibar, sun lamps. Downstairs you can relax at the comfortable American style bar and mingle with the other guests in the evening. Situated near a Metro stop for easy access to all parts of the city.

5. DIANA, *Via Principe Amedeo 4, 00185. Tel. 475-1541 187 rooms all with private baths. All credit cards accepted. Single L155,000; Double L265,000; Triple L348,000. Suites L275,000. Breakfast, Lunch or Dinner costs an extra L40,000.* ***

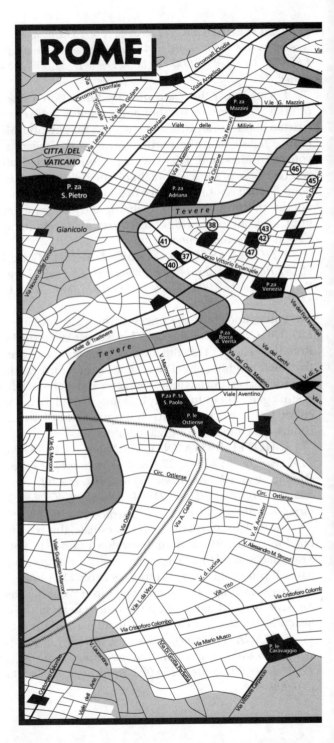

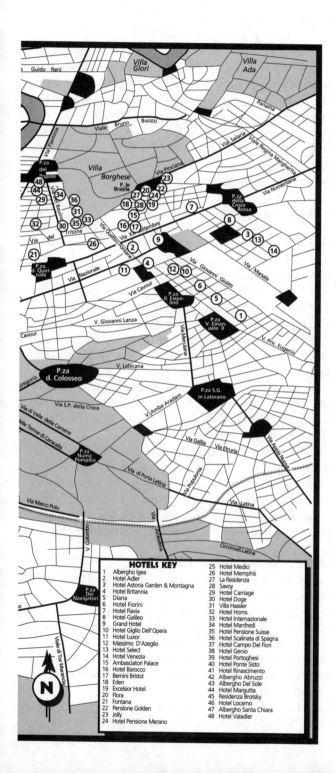

HOTELS KEY

1 Albergho Igea
2 Hotel Adler
3 Hotel Astoria Garden & Montagna
4 Hotel Britannia
5 Diana
6 Hotel Fiorini
7 Hotel Flavia
8 Hotel Galileo
9 Grand Hotel
10 Hotel Giglio Dell'Opera
11 Hotel Luxor
12 Massimo D'Azeglio
13 Hotel Select
14 Hotel Venezia
15 Ambasciatori Palace
16 Hotel Barocco
17 Bernini Bristol
18 Eden
19 Excelsior Hotel
20 Flora
21 Fontana
22 Pensione Golden
23 Jolly
24 Hotel Pensione Merano
25 Hotel Medici
26 Hotel Memphis
27 La Residenza
28 Savoy
29 Hotel Carriage
30 Hotel Doge
31 Villa Hassler
32 Hotel Homs
33 Hotel Internazionale
34 Hotel Manfredi
35 Hotel Pensione Suisse
36 Hotel Scalinata di Spagna
37 Hotel Campo Del Fiori
38 Hotel Genio
39 Hotel Portoghesi
40 Hotel Ponte Sisto
41 Hotel Rinascimento
42 Albergho Abruzzi
43 Albergho Del Sole
44 Hotel Margutta
45 Residenza Brotsky
46 Hotel Locarno
47 Albergho Santa Chiara
48 Hotel Valadier

Located near Stazione Termini and the opera, this is a comfortable well run three star hotel with plain but attractive decor. The rooms are rather large by Roman standards with all the amenities associated with a hotel in its class. The lobby and common areas are an eclectic mixture of marble floors and columns with subtle lighting and paintings.

There is an American style bar with intimate little glass tables that seem straight out of *La Dolce Vita*. It's comfortable and cozy, a good value for your money. Also, they have special rates for groups of 20 or more that will make your stay very cheap if you're arranging for a group. Call for details.

6. HOTEL FIORINI, *Via Principe Amadeo 62, 00184 Roma. Tel. 06/ 488-5065. Fax 06/488-2170. American Express, Diners Club, Mastercard and Visa accepted. 16 rooms, 15 with bath. Single L110,000-135,000; Double 150,000-170,000. Add 35% for each extra person. A sumptuous buffet breakfast included with fruits, cheeses, meats, bread, sweet rolls, coffee, and tea.* **

Even though this hotel is located near the train station and is on the fifth floor, the appeal of this place is not dimmed. The streets it's on is a parade of food, clothing, and shoes stores, as well as outside cafés, bars, and restaurants. After you've taken all you can out of Rome, you can quietly relax in their clean airy rooms, watch a little TV or amble down to their Bar/Breakfast room for a nightcap and a conversation with some other guests. The beautiful proprietor Roberta is charming and friendly.

7. HOTEL FLAVIA, *Via Flavia 42, 00184 Roma. Tel 06/488-3037. Fax 06/481-9129. No credit cards accepted. 30 rooms all with bath. Single L100,000; Double L130,000; Triple L190,000.* **

Located near the Via Veneto and parallel to the Via XX Settembre, this place would be priced higher if (a) they weren't located on the second floor and (b) the building they're in didn't seem to be always under reconstruction. The entrance area is small, as is the breakfast and guest rooms, but for your money you can't ask for much more. You also get the amenities of a three star like mini-bar, TV, direct dial phones, etc., for the price of a two star.

8. HOTEL GALILEO, *Via Palestro 33, 00185 Roma. Tel. 06/444-1205/ 6/7/8. Fax 06/444-1208. Single L139,000; Double L198,000. All credit cards accepted. 80 rooms all with bath. Breakfast included.* ***

They have a lovely garden terrace on the first floor where you can have your breakfast or relax in the end of the day. There are four beautiful floors in this hidden treasure. The only drawback is that the entrance is down a driveway that leads to a garage. But once you're inside everything is transformed to cater to all your needs. The prices are so low for a three star, I think, because of the driveway situation.

9. GRAND HOTEL, *Via Vittorio Emanuele Orlando, 00185 Roma. Tel. 06/4709. Fax 06/474-7307. Single L370,000; Double L550,000; Suites*

L1,500,000. Extra bed costs L85,000. Continental or American Breakfast is extra (can you believe it?). ****

Located between the Piazza della Repubblica and Piazza San Bernardo, near the American speaking church in Rome, Santa Susanna, this top-class luxury hotel has everything you'd ever need. There is a hairdresser service, beauty salons, and saunas. The hotel used to be located in one of the most fashionable quarters but it has long since lost its chic. Nonetheless that doesn't detract from the ambiance of opulence.

The rooms and suites are palatial, some with 16 to 17 foot ceilings. You'll feel like a prince or princess too when they serve you afternoon tea downstairs at 5pm. If tea is not your style, there's a very relaxing but expensive American-style bar.

10. HOTEL GIGLIO DELL'OPERA, *Via Principe Amadeo 14, 00184 Roma. 62 rooms all with bath. Tel. 06/484-401 or 488-0219. Fax 06/487-1425. Single L200,000; Double L250,000.* ***

Close to the opera, this hotel appears as if it houses some of the performers. If you like the longhaired chic crowd that always looks just right, this is the place to stay. The rooms are all attractive in a neo-classic style. The lounge area is large and is perfect for the look they're going for. Also they have a small and intimate area that serves as a bar in the evenings. You'd better know music to get involved in the conversations. Breakfast is served in a spartan, white, brightly lit room off the lobby.

11. HOTEL LUXOR, *Via A. De Pretis 104, 00184 Roma. Tel. 06/485-420, 06/481-5572. Fax 06/481-5571. 27 rooms all with bath. Single L170,000; Double L230,000.* ***

They offer individual discounts if you tell them you want one – up to 25% or so, they told me. Don't tell the Italian Government. Anyway ... this is a small hotel off the Via Nazionale that is small, as you'll see when you enter, but comfortable. The proprietor and her husband will do almost anything to make you happy. It has all the amenities of a three star hotel and you'll just love the classic beds and armoires. Centrally located, near a Metro for all your sightseeing pleasure.

12. MASSIMO D' AZEGLIO, *Via Cavour 18, 00184 Roma. Tel. 460-646. 200 rooms, all with private baths. Single L260,000; Double L350,000.* ****

Located near Stazione Termini, this hotel first opened in 1875 and still continues in its old fashioned ways, which give the place its charm. They have all the modern amenities to be rated a four-star in Italy, but the look and feel of the place is definitely 1950s. The best part is the *Cantina* restaurant downstairs that looks like a wine cellar. There are lots of nooks and crannies in which to get lost. But if you're going to spend the money, stay on the Veneto or another better located place, but do come and visit, especially the restaurant.

THE TEN BEST HOTELS IN ROME

You'll find plenty of great hotels when in Rome, but for a truly relaxing stay here is a list of my ten best, so your stay in the Eternal City will be even better.

**Two star hotels

3. HOTEL ASTORIA GARDEN & MONTAGNA, *Via Bachelet 8/10, 16 rooms, 10 with bath. Single L85,000; Double L96,000-124,000.*

37. HOTEL CAMPO DEI FIORI, *Via del Biscione 6, Four singles with shower each L115,000; Nine Doubles with shower each L170,000, 14 doubles without shower each L100,000.*

44. HOTEL MARGUTTA, *Via Laurina 34, 24 rooms all with bath. Single or Double L140,000*

24. HOTEL PENSIONE MERANO, *Via Vittorio Veneto 155, 30 rooms all with bath. Single L95,000; Double L138,00.*

***Three star hotels

46. HOTEL LOCARNO, *Via della Penna 22, 38 rooms all with bath. Single L170,000; Double L250,000; Suite L420,000.*

36. HOTEL SCALINATA DI SPAGNA, *Piazza Trinita Dei Monte 17, Only 15 rooms all have baths. Single L300,000; Double L380,000.*

14. HOTEL VENEZIA, *Via Varese 18, 61 rooms all with bath. Single L135,000; Double L180,000.*

****Four star hotels

16. HOTEL BAROCCO, *Piazza Barberini 9 (entrance on Via della Purificazione 4), 28 rooms all with bath. Single L280,000; Double L380,000.*

31. VILLA HASSLER, *Piazza Trinita Dei Monti 6, 80 rooms all with bath. Single L420,000-450,000; Double L620,000-900,000.*

*****Five star hotels

18. EDEN, *Via Ludovisi, 49, Single L390,000; Double L550,000, Suites L1,100,000. Continental breakfast is L28,000 extra, buffet breakfast is L43,000.*

13. HOTEL SELECT, *Via V. Bachelet 6, 00187 Roma. Tel. (06)6994-1349. Fax 06/6994-1360. American Express, Mastercard and Visa accepted. 19 rooms all with bath. Single L195,000; Double L225,000; Triple L300,000.* ***

Located just off the Piazza Indipendenza this hotel has a pleasant outside garden except for the building it faces. Still, a good place to relax after touring. The lobby lounge and bar are also a good place to lift up your feet for a while. The rooms are made to seem larger with the mirrors strategically placed on the armoires; each room has the necessary amenities for a three star. Quiet and calm, but for your money I'd stay next door at the Hotel Astoria (see above) with the same accommodations (save for the rooms without a bath) for a much lower price. But if this is where you can get in, the staff will make sure you enjoy every minute.

14. HOTEL VENEZIA, *Via Varese 18, 00184 Roma. Tel. 06/445-7101. Fax 06/495-7687. American Express, Diners Club, Mastercard and Visa accepted. 61 rooms all with bath. Single L135,000; Double L180,000; Triple, L245,000.* ***

If you have to or simply desire to stay near the Stazione Termini, this is the place to stay. For a three star the prices are so low and the service so high at this wonderful hotel you can't go wrong. Located on a side street away from all the noise, ask for a room on the fifth floor with a balcony (all singles). Here you can relax and enjoy the wonderful Roman evenings. The rest of the rooms are just as nice. Some have showers to cater to Americans, others have a bath for the Japanese.

The hotel caters also to business customers as well as visiting professors (the University is just around the corner) and there's an office with computer, printer, copier, and fax machine for your use. They're contemplating the introduction of e-mail service also. You'll love the 16th century altar that serves as buffet table for breakfast and bar at night, as well as the 16th century table that centers their conference room. Say hello to the charming, beautiful, and ever hospitable owner and operator, Patrizia Diletti, for me when you get there.

Trevi Fountain/ Via Veneto area

15. AMBASCIATORI PALACE, *Via Vittorio Veneto 62, 00187 Roma. Tel. 06/47-493. fax 06/474-3601. 103 rooms and 8 suites, all with private bath. All credit cards accepted. Single L350,000; Double L460,000; Suite L700,000. Buffet breakfast L21,000 extra.* *****

Virtually in the center of the Via Veneto, this hotel deserves its luxury rating since it has impeccable service, palatial rooms, and a top class restaurant *La Terrazza* to complement its fine ambiance. Your every need can be taken care of her: massage, evening companion, theater reservations, travel arrangements, etc. If you're looking for deluxe treatment at a deluxe price, look no further.

16. HOTEL BAROCCO, *Piazza Barberini 9 (entrance on Via della Purificazione 4), 00187 Roma. Tel. 06/487-2001/2/3, 487-2005. Fax 06/485-994. 28 rooms all with bath. Single L280,000; Double L380,000.* ****

If you're looking for an intimate four-star experience and don't want to get lost in the crowd at the Excelsior or the Eden, this is the place for you. All rooms are elegantly furnished with enough space for you to relax. If that's not good enough go on up to their roof terrace where you can bring your drink from the downstairs bar and soak in the Roman night.

Centrally located with the Trevi Fountain, Spanish Steps, Via Veneto all around the corner. A great place to spend an entire vacation, or simply the last night of a long one.

17. BERNINI BRISTOL, *Piazza Barberini 23, 00187 Roma. Tel. 06/ 488-3051. Fax 06/482-4266. 124 rooms all with private baths. Single L315,000; Double L440,000; Suite L1,100,000. Continental Breakfast Buffet L25,000. VAT excluded.* *********

The hotel is located in the Piazza Barberini at the foot of the Via Veneto facing Bernini's Triton Fountain. This is another hotel that deserves its luxury rating. Perfectly located for shopping and sightseeing, you can get to the Spanish Steps and Trevi Fountain in minutes. The upper rooms have grand views as does the attractive roof garden, which is a great place to unwind after a long day. The rooms are not furnished with the faux antique look as are other deluxe hotels, they are more modern and seemingly more comfortable.

18. EDEN, *Via Ludovisi, 49, 00187 Roma. Tel. 06/474-3551. Fax 06/ 482-1584. 100 rooms all with private baths. Single L390,000; Double L550,000, Suites L1,100,000. Continental breakfast is L28,000 extra, buffet breakfast is L43,000.* *********

Located west of Via Veneto in the exclusive Ludovisi section, the Eden is a long-established top ranked hotel. It has a high class of service and amenities virtually unmatched the world over. Located off the crowded Via Veneto is an advantage since it makes your stay at the Eden much quieter. The terrace restaurant where you can have your breakfast, lunch, or dinner has a beautiful view of the city and the Villa Borghese. Also available is a complete gym for working out with everything from cardiovascular equipment to free weights. The Eden is truly luscious.

19. EXCELSIOR HOTEL, *Via Vittorio Veneto 125, 00187 Roma. Tel. 06/4708. Fax. 06/482-6205. All 244 doubles, 38 singles, and 45 suites have private baths. Single L 320,000; Double L480,000, Suite L1,200,000. An extra bed costs L90,000. Continental breakfast is L27,000 extra and American breakfast is L42,000.* *********

This superb hotel is located on the east side of the Via Veneto not far from the walls that lead to Villa Borghese. All rooms and common areas are done up with ornate moldings and elegant decorations. A truly palatial experience. They have a world renowned restaurant, *La Cuppola*, as well as a piano bar at night. You can do anything and get anything here, even rent the CIGA corporate jet!

20. FLORA, *Via Vittorio Veneto 191, 00187 Roma. Tel. 489-929. Fax 06/ 482-0359. All 8 suites and 167 rooms have private baths. All credit cards accepted. Single L270,000; Double L360,000, Suites L600,000.* ********

Located immediately at the top of the Via Veneto by the old Roman walls, this old-fashioned hotel has first class traditional service. The public rooms are elaborately decorated with antiques, oriental rugs, and soothingly light color schemes. The rooms are immense and some have wonderful views over the walls into the lush greenery of Villa Borghese. Try and request one of those rooms, since Borghese is beautiful at night.

This hotel offers everything you could want: location, service, great rooms.

21. FONTANA, *Piazza di Trevi 96, 00187 Roma. Tel. 06/678-6113, 06/679-1056. Single L180,000; Double L250,000. All credit cards accepted.* ***

The location of this hotel is great, but is not secluded or tranquil because it is in the same square as one of Rome's most famous monuments, the Trevi Fountain. You can hear the cascading waters and ever-present crowds far into the night. If you're a heavy sleeper this hotel's location is perfect, but if not try elsewhere. The rooms are sparse but comfortable and since this is a converted monastery, some rooms have been made by joining two monk's cells together. There is also a pleasant roof garden from which you can sip a drink and gaze over the rooftops of Rome.

22. PENSIONE GOLDEN, *Via Marche 84, 00187 Roma. Tel. 482-1659. 12 of the 13 rooms have private baths. All credit cards accepted. Single L140,000; Double L180,000.* **

Kind of an upscale pensione since it has air-conditioning, TV, phone, and mini bar in every room. It's located on the first floor of an old house, on a quiet street off of the Via Veneto. The stark white breakfast room that serves you your mini-buffet in the mornings doubles as the bar/lounge in the evenings. All the amenities of a three star, with the location of a one star at the prices of an upscale two star.

23. JOLLY, *Corso d'Italia 1, 00198 Roma. Tel. 06/8495. Fax 06/884-1104. All 200 rooms have private baths. Al credit cards accepted. Single L315,000; Double L415,000. Breakfast an extra L45,000.* ****

You haven't seen anything like the Jolly. Its ultra-modern, Buck Rogers glass and steel architecture contrasts sharply with the ancient Aurelian wall just across the street. Located just outside of the old wall overlooking the Villa Borghese. Jolly sits in a perfectly serene position. If you like the standards of comfort and efficiency associated with North American hotel chains, and don't mind a rather impersonal modern atmosphere, then this is the hotel for you. The rooms are relatively small but all their amenities make up for it. Try to get a room with a view of the Borghese Gardens, otherwise you'll end up looking at the Aurelian wall and be woken up by the traffic on the Corso D'Italia.

24. HOTEL PENSIONE MERANO, *Via Vittorio Veneto 155, 00198 Roma. Tel. 06/482-1796. Fax 06/482-1810. American Express, Diners Club, Mastercard and Visa accepted. 30 rooms all with bath. Single L95,000; Double L138,00; Triple L178,000.* **

Another great find. Perfect location on the Via Veneto at rock bottom prices. The only reason the prices are so low is that you have to ride an elevator up to the third floor of a building to get to the hotel. The entranceway is dark and dingy but the rooms are warm and cozy. Everything is spic and span in the bathrooms, and you don't have to worry about remembering to buy your drinks for the evening. They sell beer, soda, and water. If you want to enjoy Rome inexpensively, this is one of the better places from which to do it.

25. HOTEL MEDICI, *Via Flavia 96, 00187 Roma. Tel. 06/482-7319/ 487-1802. Fax 06/474-0767. All credit cards accepted. Single L140,000; Double L200,000; Triple L240,000. Includes breakfast.* ***

The lobby is a little worse for wear but the sedate garden in the back makes up for it. The rooms are spartan and seem to have just made the three star rating, but that doesn't mean they're not comfortable. And the hotel is ideally situated near the Via Veneto and within walking distance of all the major sights. Also, they have a working relationship with three local restaurants to be able to offer you meals at a discount.

26. HOTEL MEMPHIS, *Via degli Avignonesi 36-36A, 00187 Roma. Tel 06/485-849. fax 06/482-8629. 24 rooms all with bath. Single L235,000; Double L300,000. Extra bed costs L90,000. Breakfast is L23,000 extra.* ****

This is a small four star hotel that has begun to develop a reputation worldwide. There are plenty of mirrors everywhere to make the place look bigger. All they did to me was offer me a fright whenever I passed by. It has all the amenities of a four-star and a great location. If you stay here, try the Tube Pub just up the street. Great darts, drinks, and conversation.

27. LA RESIDENZA, *Via Emilia 22-24, 00187 Roma. Tel. 06/488-0789. Fax 06/485-721. Mastercard and Visa accepted. 27 rooms all with bath. Single L248,000; Double L280,000. Full American Buffet breakfast offered.* ***

Wonderfully located just off of the Via Veneto, La Residenza offers well appointed and large rooms, a cozy American-style bar where you can sink into the leather chairs after a few drinks, an intimate roof terrace for those late night escapades, and one of the best buffet breakfasts around. You'll find a few Roman cats strolling around the grounds regally ignoring your presence unless you throw them a scrap of food. The only reason it's not a four star is because its entrance way is a little jumbled looking. Everything inside is perfect.

28. SAVOY, *Via Ludovisi 15, 00187 Roma. Tel. 474-141. All 135 rooms have private baths. All credit cards accepted. Single L320,000; Double L380,000; Triple L650,000; Suite L650,000.* ****

Located in the upscale Ludovisi section west of Via Veneto, this is a comfortable and well run hotel and features an excellent restaurant, offering both a la carte ordering and a superb buffet for quick dining, and a lively but still relaxing bar downstairs. The service is impeccable as it should be and the decor is elaborately expensive. The rooms that face off of the Via Veneto are quiet and comfortable. The location is perfect, especially if you're a spy – the hotel is almost directly across the street from the American Embassy.

Piazza di Spagna area

29. HOTEL CARRIAGE, *Via delle Carrozze 36, 00187 Roma. Tel. 06/679-3312. Fax 06/678-8279. American Express, Diners Club, Mastercard, and Visa accepted. 24 rooms all with bath. Single L215,000; Double L270,000; Triple L330,000; Suite L660,000. 30 rooms all with bath. Breakfast included.* ***

Located near the Piazza di Spagna, this elegant little hotel is luxuriously furnished with a variety of antiques but is still quite comfortable. They have a lovely roof garden terrace from which you can have your breakfast or an evening drink. There's not much of a view, but just being above the street level with the open sky above you has a calming effect. The bathrooms are immaculately clean.

30. HOTEL DOGE, *Via Due Macelli 106, 00187 Roma. Tel 06/678-0038. Fax 06/679-1633. American Express, Mastercard and Visa accepted. 11 rooms all with bath. Single L100,000; Double L147,000; Triple L185,000. Breakfast included.* **

The accommodations here are clean and spartan as well as comfortable, and you'll notice the prices are pretty good considering this is one block from the Spanish Steps. It's located on the fourth floor of an apartment building that you enter by walking through the entrance/retail show space of a local sports store. The prices are so low because it doesn't have it's own entrance. A good value for your money in a prime location. Only 11 rooms, so reserve far in advance.

31. VILLA HASSLER, *Piazza Trinita Dei Monti 6, 00187 Rome. 06/678 2651. Fax 06/678-9991. No credit cards accepted. 80 rooms all with bath. Single L420,000-450,000; Double L620,000-900,000. Continental breakfast L30,000 extra. Buffet breakfast L45,000 extra.* ****

In many traveler's opinions, this is the best hotel in Rome. And even if it's not, people come here to see each other and be seen. Located at the top of the Spanish Steps, with its own garage, a relaxing courtyard restaurant in the summer, and an excellent (but expensive) roof garden restaurant with the best view of the city. Remember to request one the nicer apartments facing the church belfry and the Spanish Steps. That's the whole point of staying here: the beautiful view. Even if you don't stay here, come to the restaurant, sample the food, and enjoy the superb view.

32. HOTEL HOMS, *Via Delle Vite 71-71, Tel. 0/679-2976. Fax 06/678-0482. All credit cards accepted. 50 rooms all with bath. Single L155,000; Double L240,000; L320,000.* ***

Located on the same street as the great Tuscan restaurant *Da Mario* and just across from the Anglo-American bookstore, as well as being virtually in between the Trevi Fountain and the Spanish Steps, this hotel has a quaint, pleasant ambiance and decor. Since Via Delle Vite is not well traveled you also escape the traffic noise. The lobby area is dark, but the rooms are light and airy.

33. HOTEL INTERNAZIONALE, *Via Sistina 79, 00187 Roma. Tel. 06/6994-1823. Fax 06/678-4764. American Express, Mastercard and Visa accepted. 42 rooms all with bath. Single L200,000; Double L285,000; Extra bed L90,000. Buffet Breakfast included.* ***

Located just a stone's throw away from the top of the Spanish Steps, you can hardly find a better location at a better price. The building itself is a part of history, having been redone and built upon since the first century BC. The lobby is small and without heart, but don't fret: once you move into your rooms and the other public areas, the antiques and tasteful decorations abound.

34. HOTEL MANFREDI, *Via Margutta 61, 00187 Roma. Tel. 06/320-7676. Fax 06/320-7736. American Express, Mastercard and Visa accepted. 17 rooms all with bath. Single L200,000; Double L280,000; Triple L370,000. American style breakfast buffet with ham, eggs, cheese, fruit etc. included.* ***

If you only stay for the breakfast it's worth it. The prices quoted above are those they offer as a perpetual discount because they do not agree with the rates the Italian Government Travel Service has forced upon them. So when you make your reservations tell them you read it here in this book and you'll receive the prices above.

This cozy, accommodating hotel is located near the Spanish Steps and has all the charm, service, and amenities of a four-star hotel, but it is on the third floor of a local building. They even have VCRs in some rooms as well as movies to rent at the front desk for your convenience. The street they're located on is cute, quiet, and home to some of Rome's best antique stores and at galleries.

35. HOTEL PENSIONE SUISSE, *Via Gregoriana 54, 00187 Roma. Tel. 06/678-3649, 06/678-6172. Fax 06/678-1258. No credit cards accepted. 14 Rooms, only 9 with private baths. Single L85,000-100,000; Double L120,000-150,000; Triple L165,000-200,000. Breakfast included.* **

Located near the Spanish Steps, this long-running and efficiently run small hotel is on two floors of an old building. It used to be part of two buildings but their lease ran out on one (for those of you that remember her before 1990).

The rooms are large, spotlessly clean, and comfortably furnished. There is also a public room in which to relax as well as a breakfast room. The staff is superb, especially the matriarch who is a little hard of hearing but will assist you in any way she can, in four languages.

36. HOTEL SCALINATA DI SPAGNA, *Piazza Trinita Dei Monte 17, Rome. 06/679 3006 and 06/679 0896.Fax 06/684-0598 American Express, Mastercard and Visa accepted. Only 15 rooms all have baths. Single L300,000; Double L380,000; Triple 450,000. Suite for 5 people L600,000. Breakfast included.* ***

Just across the Piazza from the Hassler, this used to be a moderately priced, quaint little pensione. But since it received a three star rating its prices have sky-rocketed. Nothing much else has seemed to have changed so the proprietor must be making up for lost time by bringing in all the money he can. The best feature of this hotel is it's location at the top of the Spanish Steps and the superb view of the city from the roof terrace. The roof is open in the summer months for breakfast, as well as for your own personal nightcaps for the evening. Having a roof terrace makes this place wonderful and will make your stay in Rome so much more pleasant and intimate.

Piazza Navona and Campo dei Fiori area
37. HOTEL CAMPO DEI FIORI, *Via del Biscione 6, 00186 Roma. Tel. 06/687-4886. Fax 06/687-6003. All credit cards accepted. Four singles with shower each L115,000; Nine Doubles with shower each L170,000, 14 doubles without shower each L100,000.* **

All the amenities of a three star with the best, I repeat, the best roof terrace in Rome, all at two-star prices. Why? The hotel is on six floors in a sliver building without an elevator. Also there's no air conditioning, which could be a problem in August. But at any other time this is the place to stay in Rome, bar none, if you're on a budget or not.

You have a great location only a few blocks away from the Trastevere area and its nightlife. Here you are in the perfect location to visit the best outdoor market in the city, the Campo dei Fiori, eat at some of the best restaurants (*La Carbonara* in Campo dei Fiori), a great bar/pub nearby (*The Drunken Ship* in Campo dei Fiori), and the best sights just around the corner. You also have the wildest, craziest, friendliest staff, as well as inexpensive prices, and the terrace to beat all terraces. Breakfast is served in a basement dining area, but you are free to bring it to the roof with you. The only real drawback is that it's not near a Metro line, but plenty of buses do pass this way.

38. HOTEL GENIO, *Via Zanardelli 28, Roma 00186. Tel 06/683-2191,06/683-3781. Fax 06/6830-7246. American Express, Mastercard, and Visa accepted. 61 rooms all with bath. Single L150,000-185,000; Double L200,000-270,000 An extra bed costs L70,000. A large breakfast buffet is included.* ***

Located almost in the Piazza Navona you get a great location in the Old City of Rome. Most of the guests are from Scandinavia and Germany so you may not rub elbows with any Americans here. The rooms are well appointed with tasteful paintings, Persian rugs, and cream colored wall coverings. The lobby/common areas seem a little worse for the wear but the roof garden terrace has a spectacular view. This is where you'll be served your breakfast in the morning. A great way to wake up, gazing at the Dome of St. Peter's.

39. HOTEL PORTOGHESI, *Via dei Portoghesi 1, 00186 Roma. Tel. 686-4231. Fax 06/687-6976. Mastercard and Visa accepted. 27 rooms all with bath. Single L130,000; Double L210,000. Suite L230,000-260,000. An extra bed costs L50,000.* ***

Between Piazza Navona and the Mausoleum of Augustus, nestled beside the church of Sant'Antonio, and on a narrow medieval style street, this small hotel's central location is ideal. It may be not be near a Metro line but the restaurants, shops, food stores, small streets, and sights all around it make its location perfect. There are a smattering of antiques all over the hotel to give the place a feeling of old world charm that matches its unique location. The rooms are large and airy but the common areas are a little cramped. Not to worry: there are great restaurants all over the place where you can relax. A great place to stay.

40. HOTEL PONTE SISTO, *64 Via dei Pettinari, 00186 Roma. Tel. 686-8843. Fax 06/6830-8822. All credit cards accepted. Single L152,000; Double L199,000; Triple L241,000. Over 100 rooms all with bath. Breakfast included.* ***

Located close to the walking bridge Ponte Sisto that gives you access to Trastevere, the Renaissance quarter, this is a well situated and finely appointed hotel. The hotel is spartan but very comfortable, and the rooms and common areas are spacious. I especially love the central outside terrace garden with its fountain and palm trees. The perfect place to relax at the end of hard day. Try to get a room on a higher floor so you can have great views from your window. The staff is superbly professional and are fluent in many languages.

41. HOTEL RINASCIMENTO, *122 Via Del Pellegrino, 00186, Rome. Tel. 687-4813. Fax 06/683-3518.. All credit cards accepted. 20 rooms all with bath. Single L128,000. Double L200,000. L72,5000 for an extra be. Breakfast included.* **

Perfectly situated for the sightseer. It's five minutes from the Piazza Navona (where you can get gelato at *Tre Scalini*), Campo dei Fiori (where you can shop for local produce in the mornings), and 10 minutes from the Pantheon and the Vatican (in different directions). There is mostly a German clientele here, but that is changing as we speak. The rooms and bathrooms are clean but a little small. There is a large buffet breakfast served in the mornings.

Piazza del Popolo to the Pantheon

42. ALBERGO ABRUZZI, *Piazza della Rotunda 69, 00186 Roma. Tel. 06/679-2021. No credit cards accepted. 25 rooms on four floors all without bath. 2 bathrooms in every corridor. Single L75,000; Double L100,000.* **

Even though you don't have a private bathroom, you do have a great location at a great price. Besides, there is a sink in every room. This place decided not to upgrade its facilities like the Albergho del Sole (see below) and is content being a small, clean, and comfortable *pensione* for travelers who like to stay cheap. There is no common area, but the rooms are large enough to relax in. If not, the piazza in front of the Pantheon is a great place to kick back with a bottle of wine, or if you're more upscale you can sit at a nearby sidewalk café.

43. ALBERGHO DEL SOLE, *Piazza dell Rotunda 63, 00186 Roma. Tel. 06/78-0441. Fax 06/6994-0689. All credit cards accepted. 62 rooms all with bath. Single LL320,000; Double L450,000; Suite L530,000-600,000.* ****

This is a place that used to be a small well appointed *pensione* that upgraded its rooms prior to the new "star" ratings and voila: we have a four-star hotel. But it did upgrade quite a bit. The clean white walls and delicate furniture attest to the changes made under new ownership. Most of the furniture is of the neo-classic mold but leaning towards almost modern. Some of the rooms have a view over the Pantheon, which can be beautiful but also noisy in the mornings. The service is exquisite and everything conforms to the highest standards, making this a well-located fine little four-star hotel.

44. HOTEL MARGUTTA, *Via Laurina 34, 00186 Roma. Tel. 06/322-3674. American Express Diners Club, Mastercard and Visa accepted. 24 rooms all with bath. Single or Double L140,000; Triple L180,000. #s 50/52 have a terrace L170,000. #59 is great L180,000. Breakfast included.* **

The prices are great since it's a two star, and it has that rating because there is no TV or mini-bar in the room, and no air conditioning which is a must in August. The hotel has been totally renovated and is as modern as can be. There's a relaxing lounge area and the rooms are all spacious and airy (except in August).

And it's location, ooh la la, right between the Piazza del Popolo and the Spanish Steps. Who could ask for more? That, coupled with the excellence of the accommodations and the low prices, make this place a definite rare gem.

45. RESIDENZA BROTSKY, *Via del Corso 509, 00186 Roma. Tel. 06/ 361-2339. No credit cards accepted. 24 rooms, 10 with bath. Single with bath 90,000-100,000. Single with out bath L60,000. Double with bath L105,000-115,000. Double without bath L90,000. Triple with bath L140,000-150,000. Triple without bath L125,000. Quad with bath 175,000-185,000. Quad without bath 160,000. L35,000 for each extra person.* **

This is a dark, dingy little place, but the proprietor is friendly and helpful and he makes sure the place stays clean as a whistle. It's located on the third floor of an apartment building off one of Rome's most famous streets. This is a favorite of students and those who travel on the cheap, where they all gather in the evenings on the roof gardens and share a bottle of wine and the stories of their day. Ah, to be young again.

46. HOTEL LOCARNO, *Via della Penna 22, 00186 Rome. Tel. 06/361-0841. Fax 06/321-5249. American Express, Mastercard and Visa accepted. 38 rooms all with bath. Single L170,000; Double L250,000; Suite L420,000. Breakfast included.* ***

Situated between the Piazza del Popolo and the Tiber River, in a nice neighborhood of stores and galleries, this hotel is perfectly situated for those of you that love to shop. It has a very relaxing American-style bar, spacious common areas, a small garden patio, and a roof terrace where breakfast is served in good weather. On top of all that, the rooms are tastefully decorated to make you feel right at home: not too many faux antiques here. There are excellent restaurants all around, *Da Bolognese* for example, which means you won't have to wander far for your gastronomic pleasures. A little off the beaten path too, so it offers a respite from the hectic pace of Rome.

47. ALBERGHO SANTA CHIARA, *Via Santa Chiara 21, 00186 Roma. Tel. 06/687-2979. Fax 06/687-3144. All credit cards accepted. Single L200,000-225,000; Double L250,000-290,000.* ***

A three star that should be a four star. Once you enter the lobby you feel as if you've been whisked away to a palace. Everything is marble. The ceilings reach to the sky. The rooms are all tastefully decorated and the ones on the top floors get great breezes, if you don't want to use your air conditioning. You also have some good views over the roof tops. The service is impeccable. The place is great. If you want four star accommodations for a three star price, stay here.

48. HOTEL VALADIER, *Via della Fontanella 15, 00187 Roma. Tel. 06/361-0592, 361-0559, 361-2344. Fax 06/320-1558. 50 rooms and suites all with bath. Single L270,000-330,000; Double L370,000-450,000, Suite L400,000-600,000. All credit cards accepted.* ****

The first word that comes to mind is opulent. There is black marble everywhere, and it is doubled by the placement of the many mirrors and shining brass fixtures. But you ain't seen nothing yet. The wood paneling here sparkles, it's so well shined. The rooms are no less ostentatious with lights, mirrors (some on the ceiling ... but only slightly over the bed so don't get too excited), and the ever-present marble. If you want to feel like an oil sheik who has money to burn, spend your stay in Rome here.

The hotel is between the Piazza del and the Spanish Steps, so you're in walking distance to many of the sights and shops.

WHERE TO EAT

Before I guide you to the wonderful restaurants Rome has in store for you, below I've prepared an augmented, Rome-specific version of Chapter 11, *Food & Wine*.

Roman Cuisine

"Italian Food" is definitely a misnomer, because each region of Italy has its special dishes, and in most cases so do each province and locality. As a rule, Roman cooking is not refined and is considered a poor man's cuisine. The food is basic, simple, and enjoyable. Gone are the days of the Roman Empire's lavish banquets.

Authentic Roman dishes today are often based on rudimentary ingredients, such as tomatoes, garlic, hot pepper, and parmesan cheese, and the results are magnificent. Some favorite dishes, like brains, tripe, oxtail, and pig's snout, never seem to find their way onto the plate of squeamish foreigners like myself. Instead we get treated to the omnipresent pasta and grilled meats.

Besides these staples, Romans enjoy the harvest of seafood from the shores just 15 miles from their city, and prepare excellent grilled seafood dishes and the famous *spaghetti alla vongole verace* (spicy clam sauce), as well as other pastas brimming with other fruits from the sea. The Roman countryside provides exquisite fresh greens and vegetables, which arrive daily at their open air markets. Also in never-ending supply are the local cheeses, *pecorino*, made from sheep's milk, and plump *mozzarella* balls, generally made from the milk of water buffaloes.

The Jewish ghetto has made a lasting impression on Roman cuisine. The most memorable dish to come from there is the *carciofo alla giudia*, a small artichoke flattened and fried. What I'm trying to say is that it is very difficult not to eat well in any one of Rome's 5,000-plus restaurants.

In case you didn't know, lunch hour is usually from 1:00pm to 2:00pm, and dinner any where from 7:30pm to 10:00pm. So enjoy your meal and remember to take your time. Meals are supposed to be savored, not rushed through.

Traditional Roman Fare

You don't have to eat all the traditional courses listed below. Our constitution just isn't prepared for such mass consumption, so don't feel embarrassed if all you order is a pasta dish or an entrée with a salad or appetizer.

ANTIPASTO - APPETIZER

• **Bruschetta** – garlic bread brushed with olive oil

- **Antipasto Misto** – Mixed appetizer plate. Differs from restaurant to restaurant
- **Tomate, Mozzarella ed olio** – Tomato and mozzarella slices covered in olive oil with a hint of basil

PRIMO PIATTO – FIRST COURSE
Pasta
- **Spaghetti alla carbonara** – Spaghetti tossed with bacon, garlic, peppers, grated cheese, and a raw beaten egg
- **Bucatini alla matriciana** –Thin tubes of pasta with red pepper, bacon, and pecorino cheese
- **Penne all'arrabbiata** – Literally means angry pasta. It is short ribbed pasta tubes with a hot and spicy tomato base, garlic and parsley sauce (this is my favorite, but if your stomach can't handle spicy food, steer clear of this delicacy)
- **Fettucine all'burro** – fettucine with butter and parmasan
- **Spaghetti alla puttanesca** – Litrerally translated it means whore's spaghetti! So named because the ingredients, peppers, tomato, black olives and garlic, are so basic that prostitutes could quickly create a meal between tricks

Zuppa – Soup
- **Stracciatella** – a light egg-drop soup
- **Pasta e ceci** – a filling pasta and chick pea soup
- **Zuppa di telline** – soup made from tiny clams

SECOND PIATTO – ENTRÉE
Carne – Meat
- **Abbacchio** – Milk-fed baby lamb. Can be grilled (alla Griglia), sautéed in a sauce of rosemary, garlic, onions, tomatoes, and white wine (alla Cacciatore), or roasted (al Forno)
- **Saltimbocca alla romana** – veal fillets that are covered in sage and prosciutto and cooked in butter and white wine
- **Pollo alla cacciatore** – same dish as the lamb above but replaced with chicken
- **Pollo all romana** – Chicken stewed with yellow and red dell peppers
- **Pollo al diavolo** – so called because the chicken is split open and grilled over an open fire and flattened by a weight placed on top of it. I guess it's what Romans think hell would be like.
- **Fritto misto** – a selection of mixed deep-fried meats and seasonal vegetables
- **Lambata di Vitello** – Grilled veal chop

- **Porchetta** – Tender suckling pork roasted with herbs
- **Maile arrosto can patate** – Roasted pork with exquisite roast potatoes

Pesce – Fish
- **Soliola alla griglia** – Thin sole lightly grilled
- **Ciriole** – Small tender eels dredged from the Tiber

Contorno – Vegetable
- **Carciofi alla guidia** – Jewish–style artichokes, pressed flat and fried. Usually served with a an anchovy garlic sauce
- **Peperonata** – Stewed red and yellow bell peppers
- **Patate arrosto** – Roasted potatoes that usually come with a grilled meats but can be ordered separately
- **Insalata Mista** – mixed salad. You have to prepare your own olive oil and vinegar dressing. American's lust for countless types of salad dressings hasn't hit Italy yet

Wines

Romans prefer 'local' wines from the **Castelli Romani** area: **Frascati**, **Marino**, **Velletri**, etc. These are soft, well-rounded simple white wines that most anyone can appreciate. They do well in countering the aggressive flavors of the Roman food. In most restaurants you can also get better known wines such as Chianti, Orvieto, Verdiccio, Pinto Grigio, and Barolo, but the best bet if you're not a wine expert is to simply try the *vino da casa* (house wine) of the restaurants you visit. You will find this to be not only less expensive but usually as enjoyable as a more expensive bottle.

The house wine can be ordered in liters *(un litro)*, halves *(mezzo litro)*, or quarters *(quarto do un litro)*.

Sambuca liqueur

You have to try the Sambuca, an anise-flavored after dinner drink, served with three coffee beans. It's called *Sambuca con tre mosce*, Sambuca with three flies. If you blur your vision a little they do look like flies floating in the drink. When sipping this small drink get one of the beans in your mouth and chew on it. It's bitter taste compliments the sweetness of the liqueur perfectly. The best brand of Sambuca is **Molinari**, and the next is **Romana**, which is better known in the States because of the company's aggressive marketing campaign.

Explaining the Reviews

The reviews below are arranged by specific sections in Rome. Each entry mentions a price for dinner for two. This indicates what the cost of a meal would be if two people order two dishes apiece (i.e., a pasta and a meat for one person and an antipasto and a fish dish for the other, etc.) and a liter of house wine. Obviously, if you only choose to eat one dish per sitting, which we Americans are apt to do, the actual price for your meal will be significantly less than what is indicated in this guide.

ROME'S TEN BEST RESTAURANTS

You'll find plenty of good restaurants in Rome, but for a truly great meal every time, here is a list of my ten best.

1. LA CANONICA, *Vicolo dei Piedi 13, Dinner for two L80,000.*

5. SABATINI I, *Piazza Santa Maria in Trastevere 13, At least L100,000 for two.*

7. TAVERNA DEL MORO, *Via del Moro 43, Dinner for two L55,000.*

10. PIZZERIA LA CAPRICCIOSA, *Largo dei Lombardi 8, Dinner for two L75,000.*

22. OTELLO ALLA CONCORDIA, *Via Della Croce 81, Dinner for two L80,000*

24. LA CARBONARA, *Campo dei Fiori 23, Dinner for two L90,000.*

27. ORSO "80", *Via dell'Orso 33, Dinner for two L85,000.*

32. LA BUCA DI RIPETTA, *Via di Ripetta 36, Dinner for two L70,000.*

33. LA NUOVA COMPANNINA DA ENRICO E VITTORIO, *Piazza delle Coppelle 8, Dinner for two L60,000.*

38. LA CIOTTOLA, *off of the Via Cassia Nuova outside of town on an unnamed dirt road. Tel. 06/267-324. Dinner for two L85,000.*

Trastevere

This is the perfect place for exploring the way Romans actually live. **Trastevere** literally means "across the river," and this separation has allowed the area to remain virtually untouched by the advances of time. Until recently it was one of the poorest sections of Rome, but now it is starting to become gentrified. These changes have not altared Trastevere's charm. You'll find interesting shops and boutiques, and plenty of excellent restaurants among the small narrow streets and *piazzetta* (small squares). The maze of streets is a fun place to wander and wonder where you're going to end up.

This area offers some of the best dining and casual nightlife in town. Here you can sit in a piazza bar, sipping Sambuca or wine and watch the life of Rome pass before your eyes. To accommodate this type of activity, many stores have begun to stay open later.

1. LA CANONICA, *Vicolo dei Piedi 13, just off of the Piazza Santa Maria in Trastevere. Closed Mondays. Major credit cards accepted. Tel. 580-3845. Dinner for two L80,000.*

In the capital of the Catholic world, what better way to dine than in a deconsecrated chapel transformed into one of Rome's most entrancing restaurants. Located across from Rome's only exclusive English language movie theater, *La Pasquino*, at Vicolo del Piede 13, La Canonica's Baroque facade is delicately covered with vines and flowers. In the summer months tables are set outside (and around the corner into the adjacent street) to enjoy this beautiful display and the warm Rome evenings. The best place to sit is inside; it's always cool and you can soak in the atmosphere of a renovated chapel that now has meats, kegs, and bottles hanging from the ceiling.

The menu is dominated by seafood and pasta. My recommendations: *Spaghetti alla Vongole Verace* (spaghetti with spicy clam sauce of garlic, basil, oil, and hot peppers) or the *Spaghetti alla Carbonara* (spaghetti with a light cream sauce, covered with ham, peas, and grated parmesan cheese). For the main course, try the light fish dish of *Sogliala alla Griglia* (grilled Sole). The *Grigliato Misto di Pesce* (mixed grilled fish) is also good and is sold by the *etto*, which is about a quarter of a pound.

2. CAMPARONE, *Piazza in Piscinula 47. Tel 06/581-6249. Closed Mondays. Credit cards accepted. Dinner for two L75,000.*

This restaurant owns the entire block, starting with the bar/café on the left, this restaurant in the middle, and the pizzeria/birreria on the right. The outside seating at the restaurant is the best pace to enjoy a Trasteverian evening. Their food includes an excellent rendition of *osso bucco alla romana*. They do it with *fungi* (mushrooms). Mmm, good. They are mainly known for their grilled meats and some of their pastas.

3. DA CENCIA, *Via della Lungaretta 67, 00153 Roma. Tel. 06/581-2670. Credit cards accepted. Closed Sundays and Mondays for lunch. Dinner for two with wine L75,000.*

They have crowded outside seating in a side area under an awning, but it's perfect for people watching. Inside is small but the tables are spaced a little farther apart. Inside is where you'll find all the locals sitting and savoring the restaurant's fine food.

Try any of their pastas for a primo (*arrabiatta, amatriciana, vongole,* etc.). They are all Roman specialties and are made perfectly. Then move onto the *fritto misto mare* (mixed fried fish) and you won't be disappointed.

4. GINO IN TRASTEVERE, *Via Della Lungaretta 85, 00153 Roma. Tel. 06/ 580-3403. 06/580-6226. Closed Wednesdays. Dinner for Two L80,000.*

The spacious and bright interior makes you want to sit outside under their awning on the side or in the front by the main road. Wherever you

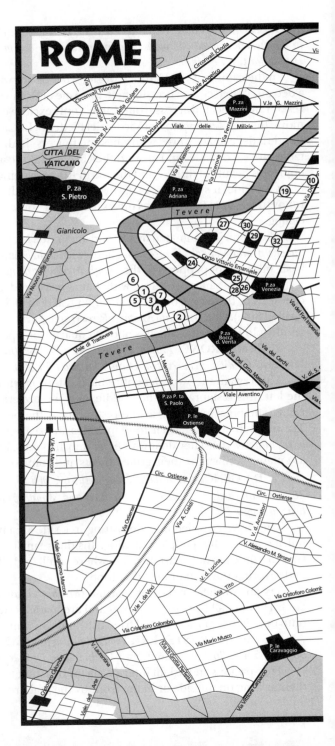

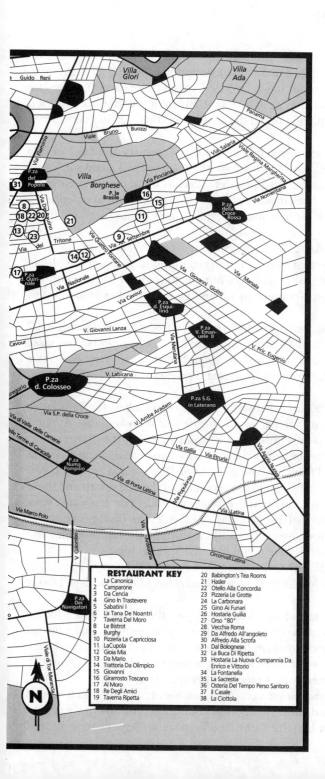

Guido Reni

Villa
Glori

Villa
Ada

Panama

Viale Bruno Buozzi

Via Salaria

Viale Regina Margherita

Via Flaminia

P.za
del
Popolo
(31)

Villa
Borghese

Via Pinciana

Via Nomentana

P. le
Brasile

(16)

(15)

P.za
della
Croce
Rossa

(8)

(18) (22) (20)

Via D'Azeglio

(21)

(11)

(13)

(23)

Via del

Tritone

Via Quattro Fontane

(9) XX Settembre

(14) (12)

(17) P.za
d. Quiri-
nale

Via Nazionale

Via Cavour

Via Giovanni Giolitti

Via Manala

Cavour

V. Giovanni Lanza

P.za
d. Esqui-
lino

Via Meridiana

P.za
V. Eman-
uele II

V. Pric. Eugenio

P.za
d. Colosseo

V. Labicana

Gregorio

Via S.P. della Croce

V. Amba Aradam

P.za S.G.
in Laterano

Via di Valle delle Camene

Via Gallia

Via Etruria

Via Appia Nuova

elle Terme di Caracalla

P.za
Numa
Pompilio

Via di Porta Latina

Via Popolonia

Via Marco Polo

Via Latina

Via Colombo

Circonvall.Latina

P.za
Dei
Navigatori

Viale di Tor Marancia

N

RESTAURANT KEY

1 La Canonica
2 Camparone
3 Da Cencia
4 Gino In Trastevere
5 Sabatini I
6 La Tana De Noantri
7 Taverna Del Moro
8 Le Bistrot
9 Burghy
10 Pizzeria La Capricciosa
11 LaCupola
12 Gioia Mia
13 Da Mario
14 Trattoria Da Olimpico
15 Giovanni
16 Girarrosto Toscano
17 Al Moro
18 Re Degli Amici
19 Taverna Ripetta
20 Babington's Tea Rooms
21 Hasler
22 Otello Alla Concordia
23 Pizzeria Le Grotte
24 La Carbonara
25 Gino Ai Funari
26 Hostaria Guilia
27 Orso "80"
28 Vecchia Roma
29 Da Alfredo All'angoleto
30 Alfredo Alla Scrofa
31 Dal Bolognese
32 La Buca Di Ripetta
33 Hostaria La Nuova Compannia Da
   Enrico e Vittorio
34 La Fontanella
35 La Sacrestia
36 Osteria Del Tempo Perso Santoro
37 Il Casale
38 La Ciottola

end up the food will be exceptional. One of the proprietors, Paulo, will greet you at the door and make sure everything is perfect all night long. Since it's popular it tends to get crowded, so get there early (7ish) or late (10ish) otherwise you may be in for a wait. But later is better because then you can watch the parade of people pass by on their way to Piazza Santa Maria.

They have an extensive fish and meat menu: try the *Sogliola alla Griglia* (grilled sole), or the *saltimboca alla romana* (veal shanks in sauce and spices) for seconds. Your primo piatto has to be one of their great Roman pasta dishes like *arrabiata* (tomato-based with garlic and peppers), or *vongole verace* (clams in a spicy oil, garlic, and basil sauce). Or if the desire for pizza hits you, it's great here.

DA MEO PETACA, *Piazza dei Percanti 30. Do Not Go Here.*

This is a real tourist trap. I'm not even going to give you the phone number. If someone asks you to go, or your tour guide has been bribed to take you there, just politely say no and go to any other restaurant in Trastevere.

5. SABATINI I, *Piazza Santa Maria in Trastevere 13, Tel. 06/581-8307 (outside seating) or 06/581-2026 (inside seating with an entrance on side). Closed Wednesdays, and two weeks in August. But at that time their other restaurant is open. No credit cards accepted. Very expensive. At least L100,000 for two.*

Besides the excellent fish dishes here, you can soak up the Trastevere life-style, especially in summer when outside seating is available. At night the floodlights keep the church at the opposite end of the piazza aglow. Try the *spaghetti cozze* (mussels), *zuppa di pesce*, the *spiedino misto di pesce al forno* (mixed grilled fish), and the grilled sole (*sogliola alla griglia*). If you want to see the fish grilled go to the very back of the restaurant and there they'll be roasting over an open fire, scales and all. (You can watch your meal being de-boned, de-headed and de-tailed). The inside is cozy and comfortable and they have singers walking through the tables serenading the customers, which is nice if you like that sort of thing.

6. LA TANA DE NOANTRI, *Via della Paglia 1-2-3, 00158 Roma. Tel. 06/580-6404 or 06/589-6575. Credit cards accepted. Closed Tuesdays. Dinner for two L75,000.*

Located past Piazza Santa Maria and past the tables laid out for La Canonica, this superb restaurant has rather boring seating inside, but oh so wonderful places outside in the Piazza di san Egidio which they take over at night. You can sit under awnings in the quiet piazza and savor dish after dish of succulently seasoned Roman specialties.

I've had the *pizza con salsiccia* (with sausage) as a primo, then moved onto the *Bracioline di abacchio* (literally translated it means "little arm of lamb"). My partner had the *Tortellini alla crema di funghi* (cheese stuffed tortellini with cream sauce and mushrooms). Even though we were too full to go on, we lingered over a bottle of white wine then ordered some *spaghetti alla carbonara* to close out the night. It was a real feast in a great atmosphere.

7. TAVERNA DEL MORO, *Via del Moro 43, Tel. 06/580-9165. Closed Mondays. Dinner for two L55,000. No credit cards accepted.*

A great inexpensive place to eat and enjoy an evening in Trastevere after you go pick up a novel at Clair Hammond's Corner Bookstore just up the road. Here you'll find the pizza superb, as well as their pasta's and meats. On Fridays they have Egyptian night in the back complete with belly dancers and more. A fun local place. When in the area, give this small, charming place a try. Their *spaghetti alla carbonara* is as great as is their *alla vongole*.

Trevi Fountain & Via Veneto area

The **Trevi Fountain** is the place where you toss a coin at Neptune's feet for a guarantee that you will one day return to Rome. It is a powerful 18th century baroque statue that dominates the square it is in. In fact, it seems overbearing for so small a space, especially at night when it is lit up by floodlights.

All around Trevi are shoe stores and small *pizzerie*. Then you have the **Via Veneto**, backdrop for the 1959 film *La Dolce Vita*. It used to be the chic gathering place for international movie stars but now it's simply an expensive place to stay, shop, and eat.

Besides these two places in this section, the area is modern, hectic, and devoid of many real sights. There are exceptions like the **Baths of Diocleslan** and the **Economy Bookstore**, the latter selling English-language new and used books, but overall, Trevi and Via Veneto are the places to see in this section.

8. LE BISTROT, *Via dei Greci 5, Tel. 967-97704. Open evenings only from 8pm -2am. Closed Sundays and three weeks in August. Dinner for two L80,000.*

If you're interested in trying some good French food during your stay in Italy, give Le Bistrot a try. Even though the name is French, they also have some Italian pasta dishes since the place is owned by an Italian. Furnished in authentic Art Nouveau style. I'm not a big fan of French food but I found the *Soupe a l'oignon* (onion soup) a worthwhile light meal in the early evening.

9. BURGHY, *Via Barberini 2-16, Tel. 465-107. Closed Sundays. No credit cards accepted.*

What used to be The Piccadilly, Rome's version of an American diner, is now a fast food place specializing in – you guessed it – burgers. I normally wouldn't write about this, but if you're dying for a burger and don't want to go to McDonalds out of guilt since you're in Italy, try an

Italian version of a fast food burger. You'll be surprised. I tried them and thought they were better than Micky D's, which is not hard to do. Give it a shot if you have that Big Mac Craving.

10. PIZZERIA LA CAPRICCIOSA, *Largo dei Lombardi 8 just off of the Via Del Corso. Telephone numbers: 6794027/6794706. Open lunch and dinner (until 1 am). Closed Tuesdays. Dinner for two L75,000.No credit cards accepted.*

Do not be fooled by the name. This is no ordinary pizzeria. This is a large, wonderfully authentic Italian restaurant with over 25 tables inside. At night and on weekends, the restaurant expands into the Largo dei Lombardi. Through a white marble retail arcade are some ruins your kids can play in while you dine in peace. Beside the ruins, La Capricciosa is in a convenient location directly in the middle of Rome's premier shopping area, Via del Corso. So after an evening of shopping, stop in. But remember to bring cash, because La Capricciosa doesn't accept American Express, Visa, or Mastercard.

The beginning feature is a large selection of antipasto with all sorts of prepared vegetables, ham, salami, and mozzarella. Mainly a pasta and pizza restaurant (pizza served only in the evenings), specializing in the gargantuan *Pizza Cappricciosa*. This is a pizza with everything, Italian style. Give it a try. They also make all of the Roman pasta staples perfectly: *arrabiatta, amatriciana,* and *vongole.* One pasta dish that was a little different but really good was the *spaghetti al burro con funghi* (with butter and mushrooms). Try the *mezzo pollo all'diavolo* (half chicken cooked over the flames) if you're in the mood for poultry.

11. LA CUPOLA, *in the Hotel Excelsior, at Via Veneto 125, Tel. 4708. Credit cards accepted. Open 7 days a week. Dinner for two L100,000.*

This is the restaurant in the Hotel Excelsior where I first had *spaghetti al burro* when I was a kid. It's expensive and the French Empire style decorations are ostentatious, but you can have your basic Roman-style dishes, like *penne all'arrabiata, amatriciana, or carbonara,* some nouvelle cuisine the chef creates, or anything your little heart desires. If you want to feel like you're part of *La Dolce Vita,* eat here. Otherwise try something else.

12. GIOIA MIA, *Via degli Avignonesi 34. Tel. 06/462-784. Closed Wednesdays. Credit cards accepted. Dinner for two L70,000.*

A small family-run pizzeria which serves excellent *calzone, bruschetta* (garlic bread made with olive oil), and pizza. They can also make you a *crostino* sandwich that they roast in their oven. Another favorite in this restaurant is their roasted or grilled meats. The *abbacchio* (lamb) is great.

13. DA MARIO, *Via della Vite 55, Tel. 678-7381. Closed Sundays and August 5-30. Dinner for two L80,000.*

You can tell the specialty of this restaurant by the stuffed game birds in the window. Da Mario serves unpretentious Tuscan food. I suggest trying the *ribollita* (thick cabbage soup) and the staple of all Tuscan restaurants, the *Bistecca alla Fiorentina*, which is big enough for two. Try all of this with a bottle of the house wine (excellent Chianti) and you should be able to get a meal for a good price. If you order two dishes apiece you'll match the price listed above.

14. TRATTORIA DA OLIMPICO, *Via degli Avignonesi 37. Credit cards accepted Closed Tuesdays. Dinner for two 60,000.*

Located just up the road from the Hotel Memphis, this is a great inexpensive place to eat. The street it's on is not well traveled, so they lure people in to sample their succulent dishes by offering great prices. Their *pizza margherita* (tomatoes and cheese) and other pizzas are made the perfect Roman Way. If you only eat the pizza and have a bottle of wine you could get out of here with only a L30,000 meal.

15. GIOVANNI, *Via Marche 64, Tel. 482-1834. Closed Saturdays and the entire month of August. Credit cards accepted. Dinner for two L150,000.*

Close to the hustle and bustle of the Via Veneto is this good restaurant with an Adriatic flair. The owners are from Ancona and they serve fresh fish brought in from there. The soups in their restaurant are also very good, so if you've had your fill of pasta, come here and try the seafood and soups. I really like the *Calamaretti ai ferri* (small shrimp cooked over and open flame). The house White, from the Verdicchio region is quite good.

16. GIRARROSTO TOSCANO, *Via Campania 29, Tel. 493-759. Closed Wednesdays. No credit cards accepted. Dinner for two L120,000.*

Located in the cellar of a huge building facing onto the Aurelian Wall, this is a first class restaurant that accepts orders until 1am. An ideal place to come back to after a night of revelry if you have a lingering hunger. The food is mainly veal and beef grilled on a spit over an open wood fired oven. Prior to the meats you can indulge in melon, Parma ham and *ovoline* (small mozzarella cheeses). The servings are large and so are the prices, and befitting its location near the Via Veneto the service is excellent.

Beside the food you'll enjoy the rustic atmosphere, with hams hanging in the entrance way along with a table filled with fresh produce. In the dining area bottles of wine line the walls above the tables, and the wood paneling adds to the peasant appeal at princely prices.

17. AL MORO, *Vicolo dell Bollette 13 (off Via del Lavatore), Tel. 678-3495. Closed Sundays and the entire month of August. No credit cards accepted. Dinner for two L110,000.*

The food is excellent in the Roman style, the ingredients are all fresh and of the highest quality, but the prices are a little high, and since this a popular eating establishment you'll need to make reservations. I swear the *Spaghetti al Moro* (a light carbonara sauce with cheese, egg, bacon, and red pepper flakes) is the best I've tasted. They make an excellent *all'arrabiata* (hot and spicy sauce) too. I also enjoyed the *Scampi alla Moro* (broiled

Shrimp). Other excellent dishes are the *abbacchio romanesco al forno con patate* (roasted lamb with superb roasted potatoes with a sprinkle of rosemary).

The inside front room is dominated by a large picture of Moro himself, long since passed away. The other two rooms have wine bottles surrounding the walls above the tables and are relatively roomy. If you want to sit outside you'll be crowded against a wall on a lightly traveled little *via*. I recommend the inside seating.

18. RE DEGLI AMICI, *Via della Croce 33b, Tel. 679-5380 or 678-2555. Credit cards accepted. Closed Mondays and the last three weeks in June.*

This *trattoria* close to the Spanish Steps has been serving traditional Roman food for years. If you don't want a full meal their antipasto bar will more than suffice. After 7:30pm, you can get one of their excellent pizzas. My favorite is the one named after the restaurant, made with sausage, mozzarella, oregano and tomatoes. The pasta dishes here are also something that shouldn't be missed. Try any of the Roman specialties: *carbonara, amatriciana,* or *arrabiata.*

19. TAVERNA RIPETTA, *Via di Ripetta 158, Tel. 06/6880-2979. Credit cards accepted. Dinner for two L75,000.*

This is small restaurant with a Middle Eastern flair. They have couscous, falafel, shish kebab, and tabule as well as a Roman staple such as *sogliola alla griglia* (grilled sole). This is a good place for a light but filling meal with a twist. Vegetarians should love this place since many of the dishes are meatless.

Piazza di Spagna area

The **Piazza di Spagna** is where it all happens in Rome. You have the best shops, great restaurants, beautiful sights. Stately *palazzos* lining the streets look like an ideal place to live, but today much of the housing has been replaced by offices, shops, boutiques, or restaurants. Only the lucky few can afford an apartment in this location.

This area is home to the **Spanish Steps**, which gets its name from the Piazza, which gets its name from the Spanish Embassy in the square that has been its residence since 1622. The area was adopted by British travelers in the 18th and 19th century, because it was not yet a popular location. Their presence is still here in the form of **Babbington Tea Rooms**, an expensive but satisfying establishment in the piazza; as well as a plaque commemorating the house where Keats died in 1821. The area used to called *il ghetto degli inglesi* – the English ghetto.

At the beginning of Spring, the steps are laden with banks of flowers that make the whole area look like a garden. This is the only time it's difficult to do what most do at the Spanish Steps ... simply sit down and watch the world go by, with a nice chilled bottle of wine of course.

20. BABINGTON'S TEA ROOMS, *23 Piazza di Spagna, Tel. 678-6027. Credit cards accepted. Closed Thursdays.*

Really a place to grab a spot of tea, except in the mornings when they serve massive breakfasts of scones, shepherd's pie, and other British delights (if there is such a thing). This ancient café, with its heavy furniture, musty decor, and creaky floors has been serving customers for several centuries. The service is out of the eighteenth century, but the prices are from the 21st. Expect a cup of tea to cost over $5.

21. HASLER, *Piazza Trinita dei Monti 6, Tel. 678-2651. Credit cards accepted. Open 7 days a week. Dinner for two L120,000.*

If you have the money to spend, the view down the Spanish Steps from the glassed-in and air-conditioned terrace is worth every penny. You can pick out the Castel Sant'Angelo, the Jewish Ghetto's synagogue, the Pantheon, and the Quirinale Palace from the terrace. The food used to be passable, but now its Italian and Continental menu has begun to sparkle. The multilingual waiters will tell you that the *abbacchio al forno* is excellent, and I'd agree. There are many fine dishes on the menu, so you can order anything, but remember it's expensive.

22. OTELLO ALLA CONCORDIA, *Via Della Croce 81. Tel. 679-1178. No credit cards accepted. Closed Sundays. Dinner for two L80,000*

This is a family-run, formerly small trattoria off of the Via della Croce. It's set off the road, which used to render it unnoticed, but now it seems to be crowded all the time. And with good reason – the food is excellent. You go through a tiny entrance off the main road then through a small shady garden to get to the restaurant. They have now made the garden eating area enclosed in removable glass, so people can eat out here all year round. In the summer it's especially nice.

On the inside the walls are filled with countless oil paintings, many received as trade for a good meal by a struggling artist. The prices are perfect and the food is simple, basic, and good. I loved the *abbacchio arrosto can patate* (roast lamb with grilled potatoes). The pasta dishes are not that good, which is strange for Rome, but if you stick with the meat fishes and vegetables you'll have a great meal. They open at 7:30pm. Make sure you get there early or else you'll have a wait. The help is surly, but in a typical Roman way.

23. PIZZERIA LE GROTTE, *Via delle Vite 37. Credit cards accepted. Dinner for two L70,000.*

This place has a dark rustic appearance complete with partially wood walls. They are known for their excellent antipasto bar that could fill you up for the rest of the meal. I've had the *spaghetti alla vongole verace* (spicy clam sauce) and the *pollo arrosto* (spit roasted chicken) and loved them both. The food is down-to-earth peasant in the Roman fashion, and mixes well with the decor.

Piazza Navona & Campo dei Fiori area

Piazza Navona is the perfect place to explore Rome's historical tapestry. Just outside Navona in the **Piazza Tor di Sarguinana**, you'll find ancient Roman ruins completely surrounded by the "modern" baroque buildings of Piazza Navona. The square itself has a charm that makes you want to come back over and over again. It is like a living architectural gallery, with its baroque churches and buildings lining the square and the immense statues standing majestic in the square itself.

On a hot day, the fountains here are a visitor's oasis, allowing for needed foot soaking refreshment. But before you take your shoes off and relax your sore feet by soaking them in one of the fountains, stroll to the center of the piazza and take note of the magnificence of Bernini's **Fontana Dei Quattro Fiumi** (Fountain of Four Rivers). Navona is filled with wonders. You'll find some of the ice cream Navona has become famous for, as well as the carnival of life swirling around you. You might see fire-eaters, painters, jugglers, caricaturists, tourists, rampaging Italian children, and much more here.

And from mid-December to mid-January, the square becomes a giant Christmas market with booths and stalls selling stuffed animals, toys, handicrafts, and candy that looks like coal.

This Navona area is basically an extension of the Campo dei Fiori area in character. They are both genuinely picturesque and intriguing neighborhoods,with a maze of interconnecting narrow streets and *piazzetta* (small squares), and each has a reputation of becoming a haven for hashish sellers late at night. This commercial aspect goes hand in hand with the Campo die Fiori (literally translated means "field of flowers") flower and produce market every morning. Both areas evoke a feeling of what Rome used to be like many centuries ago, with the centuries-old buildings and the peddlers, carts, and small stores lining the narrow streets.

24. LA CARBONARA, *Campo dei Fiori 23, Tel. 654-783. Credit cards accepted. Closed Tuesdays. Dinner for two L90,000.*

Located in the best piazza for dining, and the food's not bad either. As could be expected, *pasta alla carbonara* is the house specialty so give that a try here. Here it is prepared to perfection with *rigatoni* in a rich peppery sauce of egg, cheese, and bacon. They also make the best *spaghetti alla vongole verace* (spicy clam sauce) I've ever had. The *fritto misto* (lightly fried mixed vegetables and cheese) is excellent since most of the produce comes in directly from the *mercato* in the square. The market can be a problem at early lunch since there are still discarded veggies on the ground where the tables should be. There's no smell, but the sight isn't too appetizing. As always, I loved the *abbacchio alla griglia* (roast baby lamb) and the roasted potatoes.

25. GINO AI FUNARI, *Via dei Funari. Closed Wednesdays. American Express accepted. Dinner for two L65,000.*

Another inexpensive place, this one located in the Jewish ghetto. The decor is simple and basic but the food is good and cheap. They have the basic Roman pastas (*carbonara, amatriciana, vongole verace, and arrabiata*) but I jumped over them to try the *conniglio alla cacciatore* (rabbit hunter style made with brandy tomatoes and spices). It is superb.

26. HOSTARIA GUILIA, *Via della Barchetta 19, Tel. 06/6880-6466. Dinner for two L65,000.*

They have a beautiful arched interior with brown tiled floors that emits all the character of Rome. The dishes are basic but great Roman fare too, like the *Penne all'arrabiata* or the *Spaghetti alla Vongole*. Besides the pasta they have fresh fish and grilled meats. These guys are off the beaten track and their prices are great. Give them a try if you're in the neighborhood.

27. ORSO "80", *Via dell'Orso 33, Tel. 06/656-4904. Credit cards accepted. Closed Mondays. Dinner for two L85,000.*

This is a fine Roman restaurant, a place to come for some classic pasta dishes, good fresh fish, and juicy meats. They bake their breads on-site in their red-brick pizza oven. Basically this is a restaurant with a little bit of everything for everybody. Pasta, pizza, fish, grilled meats, home-made breads, extensive antipasto, etc. I really like the Roman favorite *spaghetti alla carbonara* as well as the *abbacchio alla griglia* (grilled baby lamb). The place always seems to be crowded even though it's large, so try to get there early. Located near Piazza Navona, Pantheon, and Campo dei Fiori.

28. VECCHIA ROMA, *Piazza di Campitelli 18, Tel. 656-4604. No credit cards accepted. Closed Wednesdays. Dinner for two L85,000.*

The setting of the piazza with its Baroque church and three beautiful palazzos makes your meal worthwhile, even if the buildings are covered in grime. This menu changes constantly, but the basics are the wide variety of antipasto (which could be a meal in itself), as well as *agnello* (lamb) and *capretto* (goat) or their grilled artichokes. You have to try the artichok, since this is the Jewish ghetto and the dish is a local favorite.

Piazza del Popolo to the Pantheon

This historic area shares many of the flavors of the bordering Piazza Navona area. It is filled with a delightful mixture of artisan's shops and modern commercial stores. When you stray off the Via del Corso, this section's eastern boundary, you'll enjoy meandering through narrow streets lined with small shops and boutiques.

The focal point of the area is the **Pantheon**, built almost two thousand years ago by Consul Marcus Agrippa as a pantheistic temple, hence its name. The city's population was centered in this area during the Middle

Ages, and except for the disappearance of a large fish market, the area has remained virtually unchanged.

29. DA ALFREDO ALL'ANGOLETO, *Piazza Rondanini 51 Tel. 686-8019, 06/686-1203. Credit cards accepted. Closed Mondays and August 11-15. Dinner for two L100,000.*

A vibrant and noisy trattoria specializing in fish. Try to resist the lure of the innumerable, mouth-watering *antipasti* or you won't have room for the superbly fresh fish, the enormous Mediterranean prawns, or the still live lobsters in the display case awaiting your cooking instructions. This tentatively can be called the best seafood restaurant in Rome. Mushrooms are another Alfredo specialty from late summer to late autumn. I recommend you try any of their seafood dishes, roast meats, or pastas.

There is outside seating on a small piazza as well as air-conditioned inside seating. The decor is simple, with wine bottles lining the shelves set above the tables. Come here for great food and go away satisfied.

30. ALFREDO ALLA SCROFA, *Via della Scrofa 104, Tel. 654-0163. Closed Tuesdays. Credit cards accepted.*

There are photographs of the very rich and famous literally papering the walls. The restaurant has been in business for over half a century and was even frequented by Douglas Fairbanks and Mary Pickford. All the pasta dishes are superb, especially *Fettucine al triplo burro* (with triple butter sauce). The wine list is excellent and so are their house variations. If you like music with your meal, there is a strolling guitarist inside.

31. DAL BOLOGNESE *Piazza del Popolo 1-2, Tel. 361-1426., 06/322-2799. Closed Mondays and Sunday evenings, and August 9-25. Credit cards accepted. Dinner for two L85,000.*

The cooking is Bolognese in style, which some claim is the best in Italy. Why? Because of the *Parmigianno Reggiano* cheese and the *Prosciutto di Parma,* as well as their affinity for pastas that use one or both of these ingredients. They have a menu in English to help you search through their great dishes. The *fritto misto alla Bolognese,* which includes fried cheeses, meats and vegetables, is great. The *Misto di Paste* (mixed pasta and sauces) was filling enough for two. By ordering this dish you get to sample a variety of dishes while only ordering one. They have outside seating, perfect for people watching, but the intimacy of their inside rooms decorated with a fine collection of modern paintings appeals to me more. Also inside, you don't have to breathe exhaust fumes while you eat.

32. LA BUCA DI RIPETTA, *Via di Ripetta 36, Tel. 678-9528. Closed Mondays and the whole month of August. No credit cards accepted. Dinner for two L70,000.*

This is a very small, friendly trattoria, where you must arrive early if you have not made a reservation. It is popular for its food and the reasonable prices. Also, the jovial *padrone* is in constant attendance. The food is basic, straightforward Roman fare. Try the *Lasagna al Forno, Saltimbocca alla Romana,* and the *Osso buco di Vitello.* The restaurant consists of one room only, its high walls covered with cooking and farming paraphernalia like enormous bellows, great copper pans, etc.

33. HOSTARIA LA NUOVA COMPANNINA DA ENRICO E VITTORIO, *Piazza delle Coppelle 8, Tel. 06/6880-3921. Dinner for two L60,000.*

This is a country restaurant transplanted into the city, with country prices and country accents. I couldn't understand the waiters half the time and I speak Italian. They have outside seating in a little *piazza* that helps you escape the hordes of tourists. If for nothing other than the quaint small *piazza*, come here for a meal. A perfect respite from a day's touring. Try the *vitello arrosto con funghi* (roasted veal with mushrooms) or the *Ossobucco alla Romana.* Did I forget the primo? Yes.

This place makes great meats, but they don't know diddly about pasta. So stick to an antipasto and a secondo.

34. LA FONTANELLA, *Largo Fontanella Tevere 86, Tel. 678-3849. Closed Mondays. Credit cards accepted. Dinner for two 85,000.*

A simple enjoyable restaurant with a distinctive Tuscan flair. Their specialties are game when it's in season. The charm of the restaurant is distinctively old world, with a gleaming wood floor and flowers on every table. Their pastas are also good and they have all the basic Roman staples: *Tortellini alla panna, penne all'arrabiata,* etc.

35. LA SACRESTIA, *Via del Seminario 89, Tel. 679-7581. Closed Wednesdays. No credit cards accepted. Dinner for two L85,000.*

Close to the Pantheon, this restaurant has over 200 places for seating, and offers good food at reasonable prices. The decorations leave much to be desired, especially the garish ceiling and fruit clustered grotto. Come for their pizzas, served both during the day and at night, an unusual offering for an Italian restaurant. They also serve good cuts of grilled meat, and the pasta is typically Roman also, which naturally makes it good.

36. OSTERIA DEL TEMPO PERSO SANTORO, *Via dell'Oca 43, Tel. 06/322-4841, 6/322-0947. No credit cards accepted. Dinner for two L65,000.*

Great rustic, peasant fare, a stone's throw away from the Piazza del Popolo – and at great prices too. The restaurant is in a small area enclosed by planters in which you can eat your meals on papered wooden tables. This place is not haute cuisine, but it has great pizzas and pastas. Come here for the Roman specialties *carbonara, arrabiata, and amatriciana.* You can get your pizza with virtually anything on it, just ask. You want salami, they'll put salami.

Outside of Town

Motivating yourself at the end of a tiring day to sample these restaurants may be difficult, but I believe they will be worth your while. The food at each is stupendous, and the settings uniquely Roman, making for a fabulous dining experience!

37. IL CASALE, *Located 10 kilometers outside of Rome on the Via Flaminia. Tel. 06/457-986. Best way to get there is simply hail a cab. Cost for the cab should be around L10,000 each way. Dinner for two L90,000.*

Excellent outdoor dining, especially during the summer months since the restaurant's location offers a respite from the hectic Roman crowds. Housed in a renovated farm house with roaring fires, looking out over expansive grounds, creates a terrific ambiance for a wonderful evening. The grounds are perfect for children to explore while their parents wile away the hours with a good Italian wine after dinner.

An enormous table of antipasto is the perfect first course, since you can help yourself as often as you want. For the main course, grilled meats are the specialty, especially veal, lamb, and beef. All are prepared with exquisite care, and could be the finest servings of succulent meat south of Florence.

My recommendations for a pasta dish are either the *Penne All'Arrabiatta* or *Tortellini alla Panna* (Cheese tortellini in a thick cream sauce.)

Recommendations for meat dishes: *Lambata di Vitello* (Veal Chop), *Lambatta alla Griglia* (Grilled Veal), *Maiale all Griglia* (Grilled Pork), *Miallino all Griglia* (grilled baby pork, more juicy and flavorful than *Miale*).

38. LA CIOTTOLA, *off of the Via Cassia Nuova outside of town on an unamed dirt road. Tel. 06/267-324. Dinner for two L85,000.*

This place is situated down a small, deserted country road and is located in an old farmhouse. It has a great country ambiance and is a perfect escape from the rigors of inner city Rome. The outside seating in the summertime is a great place to spend an afternoon. It can be cold inside in the winter (this is an old farmhouse, remember) so dress for warmth.

Their specialty is *Pasta Strudel* served in a rustic soup-like bowl. You'll need plenty of bread to soak up the sauce. If you have room left, try their roasted wild chicken.

SEEING THE SIGHTS

There are several approaches to sightseeing in Rome. The chief difficulty, most visitors find, is that there is so much to see in this mammoth and historic city, so that even a month's concentrated touring would only scratch the surface.

If your time is limited, a sightseeing tour, or series of tours by bus, is perhaps the one way you can be sure to see at least the greatest sights in Rome and its environs. There are a variety of tours available through **CIT** (the official Italian company), *located at Piazza della Repubblica 64*; **American Express**, *at Piazza di Spagna 38*; **Thomas Cook**, *Via Vittorio Veneto 9/11*; or **Wagon-Lits**, the French travel company, *at Via Boncompagni 25.*

---

10 MUST-SEE SIGHTS IN ROME

The Vatican Museums alone can take you an entire day to work through, so don't believe that you can do all of these places justice in a few short days. Also, when you visit Piazza Navona, Piazza di Spagna, and Trevi Fountain, you will get a different experience depending on the time of day you go. At night each of these places livens up with Italians of all ages strolling, chatting, sipping wine, strumming guitars, while during the day they may only be swarmed by tourists.

Take your time – don't do too much. These ten could easily last you a week.

Sistine Chapel *– Site of Michelangelo's magnificent frescoed ceiling and walls.*

Vatican Museums *– Everything you could imagine including Egyptian, Greek & Roman artifacts, as well as the best collection of paintings and sculpures anywhere in the world.*

St. Peter's *– The world's largest cathedral, exquisitely decorated.*

Castel Sant'Angelo *– The fortress that used to protect the Vatican, now houses a wonderful armaments museum.*

Imperial and Roman Forums *– The center of ancient Roman life. A great place for people of all ages to explore.*

Capitalone Museum on the Campidoglio *– The second best museum in Rome, with many fine sculptures and paintings as well as the Boca della Verita (Mouth of Truth).*

Piazza Navona *– In what used to be the place for naval gladiatorial battles is now a lively piazza filled with wonderful fountains, churches, and palazzi as well as good cafés and restaurants.*

Piazza di Spagna *– Walk to the top and get a great view of the city. Sit by the fountain during siesta and enjoy Rome as it passes you by.*

Trevi Fountain *– One of the most beautiful fountains in Italy. At night, when lit up it is a magnificent sight..*

Saint Pauls Outside the Walls *– Location of many buried Saints, some fine sculptures and mosaics.*

If you have more time, or prefer to set your own pace, the best approach —indeed the only workable approach in Rome — is to choose

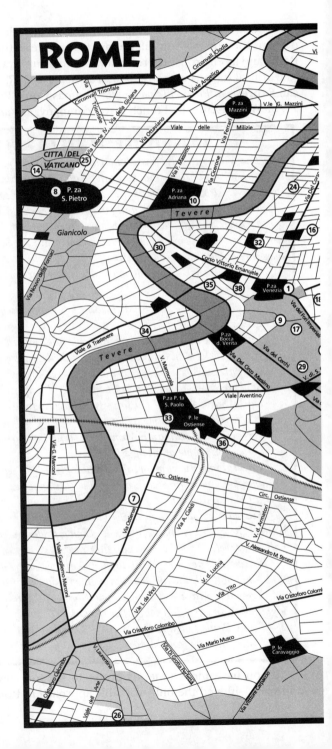

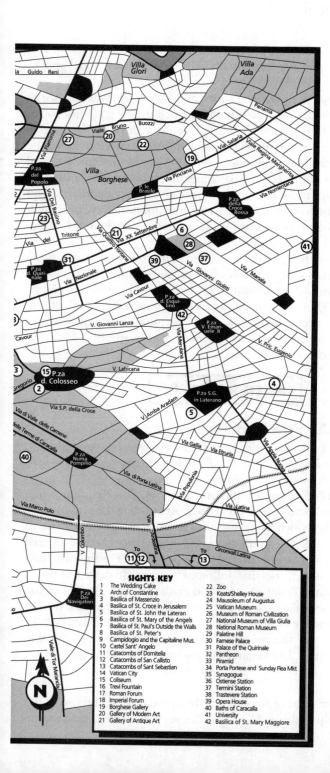

SIGHTS KEY

1   The Wedding Cake
2   Arch of Constantine
3   Basilica of Massenzio
4   Basilica of St. Croce in Jerusalem
5   Basilica of St. John the Lateran
6   Basilica of St. Mary of the Angels
7   Basilica of St. Paul's Outside the Walls
8   Basilica of St. Peter's
9   Campidoglio and the Capitaline Mus.
10 Castel Sant' Angelo
11 Catacombs of Domitella
12 Catacombs of San Callisto
13 Catacombs of Sant Sebastian
14 Vatican City
15 Coliseum
16 Trevi Fountain
17 Roman Forum
18 Imperial Forum
19 Borghese Gallery
20 Gallery of Modern Art
21 Gallery of Antique Art

22 Zoo
23 Keats/Shelley House
24 Mausoleum of Augustus
25 Vatican Museum
26 Museum of Roman Civilization
27 National Museum of Villa Giulia
28 National Roman Museum
29 Palatine Hill
30 Farnese Palace
31 Palace of the Quirinale
32 Pantheon
33 Piramid
34 Porta Portese and Sunday Flea Mkt
35 Synagogue
36 Ostiense Station
37 Termini Station
38 Trastevere Station
39 Opera House
40 Baths of Caracalla
41 University
42 Basilica of St. Mary Maggiore

only what you're really most interested in and not force yourself to visit something that doesn't appeal to you merely because "everybody" goes to see it.

A map of Rome, some walking shoes, and a spirit of adventure are all you need to explore the innumerable *piazzas*, churches, galleries, parks, and fountains of this unique city. If you saunter through the narrow streets of old Rome, behind the **Piazza Navona**, for example, or along the **Via Giulia** or near the **Pantheon**, you'll get many unexpected and revealing glimpses of flowerhung balconies, inner courtyards, and fountains. Here, perhaps more than in the impressive ruins of antiquity, you will get a little of the feeling of this city where civilizations have been built on the ruins of the previous ones for centuries, an ancient city whose vitality seems to be renewed perpetually.

And remember, most, if not all, of these sights follow the Italian siesta system, which means that they will open at 9:00am until 1:00pm, then close from 1:00pm to 3 or 4:00pm. This goes for the museums, sights, monuments, etc. Thereafter they will stay open until 6:00pm or 7:00pm. So plan your tours accordingly. Also, all of the museums, buildings, and monuments will charge a small fee to enter, mostly around L5,000 (or $3.00), so be prepared for that also.

ANCIENT ROME

THE IMPERIAL FORUMS

Via dei Fori Imperiali. Admission L4,000. Open Tuesday–Saturday, 9:00am–1:30pm and Sunday 9:00am–1:00pm. In the summer they are also open Tuesdays–Saturdays from 4:00pm 7:00pm.

The **Imperial Forums** were built in the last days of the Republic, when the Roman Forum became inadequate to accommodate the ever-increasing population. These forums were used as meeting places for Romans to exchange views, as lively street markets, or as places where official announcements could be proclaimed to the populace. The first was built by Julius Caesar, and those that followed were created by Augustus, Vespasian, Domitian, Trajan, Nerva, and Hadrian. After the fall of the Roman Empire, these places of great import fell into disrepair and during the Middle Ages and the Rennaissance all that was left are the ruins we see today. Gradually, over the centuries, these monumental ruins became covered with soil until they began to be excavated in 1924.

Trajan's Forum

Located below current street level, this is the most grandiose of the Forums of the imperial age. Here you can see one of the finest monuments in these Imperial Forums, **Trajan's Column**, built to honor the Victories of Trajan in 113. It is over 30 meters high and is covered with a series of spiral reliefs depicting the military expoilts of the Emperor against the Dacins in the 1st century AD.

At the summit of this large column is a statue of St. Peter that was placed there by Pope Sixtus V in the 17th century.

Trajan's Market

This is a large and imposing set of buildings attached to Trajan's Forum, where people gathered and goods were sold. In the vast semi-circle is where the merchants displayed their wares.

Forum of Caesar

Located to the right of the Via dei Fori Imperiali (the road itself was built in 1932 on the site of a far more ancient road to more adequately display the monuments of Ancient Rome), this was the earliest of the Imperial Forums. It was begun in 54 BC to commemorate the Battle of Pharsalus, and finished in 44 BC. Trajan redesigned many parts of this Forum to meet his needs in 113 AD.

For example, Trajan added the **Basilica Argentaria** (Silver Basilica) that was a meeting place for bankers and money changers. Originally a bronze statue of Julius Caesar stood in the center of this Forum; currently it is located in the Campidoglio.

Forum of Augustus

Built around the time of Christ's birth, this Forum commemorates the deaths of Brutus and Cassius (the traitors who allied agianst Caesar) at the Battle of Philippi in 42 BC. Here you'll find some remains of the **Temple of Mars Ultor**, the god of war, including a high podium and some trabeated (horizontal) columns. To the side of the temple you'll find the remains of two arches of triumph and two porticos.

Forum of Nerva

Constructed in 96 AD, this Forum was generally known as the **Forum Transitorium** since it served as a passageway between the **Forums of Augustus** and **Vespasian**. Here you'll find two large columns projecting up from the walls of the **Temple of Minerva**. Little is left of the Forum of Vespasian, at least anything that is identifiable.

Basilica of Maxentius & Constantine

This large building was begun by Maxentius between 306-312 AD and eventually completed by Constantione. It was used as a court of law and a money exhange, as were all Roman basilicas. It faces the Coliseum and is one of the best preserved of the buildings in the Imperial Forums. In its prime, the building was 100 meters long and 76 meters wide and divided into three naves, most of which remains to this day.

THE COLISEUM

Piazza Colosseo. Admission L8,000. Hours in the summer 9:00am–4:00pm. In the winter 9:00am–7:00pm. Catch buses 11, 27, 81, 85, 87 or get off at the Colosseo Metro stop.

The **Coliseum** (*Ampitheater Flavium*) remains the most memorable monument remaining from ancient Rome. Its construction bgean in 72 AD by Vespasian on the site of the Stagnum Neronis, a lake near Nero's house, and was eventually dedicated by Titus in 80 AD. It is recorded that at this dedication, which lasted three months, over 500 exotic beasts and many hundreds of gladiators were slain in the arena. These types of spectacles lasted until 405 AD, when they were abolished by the Emperor. The building was severly damaged by an earthquake in the fifth century AD and since then it has been used a a fortress and as a supply source for construction material for papal buildings.

What we see today is nothing compared to what the building used to look like. In its prime it was covered with marble, and each portico was filled with a marble statue of some important Roman. The Coliseum used to be fully elliptical and could hold over 50,000 people. The first tier of seats was reserved for the knights and tribunes, the second teir for citizens, and the third tier for the lower clsses. The Emperor, Senators, Government Officials and Vestal Virgins sat on marble thrones on a raised platform that went around the entire arena.

Today in the arena we can see vestiges of the subterranean passages that were used to transport the wild beasts. They employed human powered elevators to get the animals up to the Coliseum floor. At times the arena was flooded to allow for the performance of mock naval battles.

Arch of Constantine

Piazza Colosseo. Catch buses 11, 27, 81, 85, 87 or get off at the Colosseo Metro stop.

Located near the Coliseum, this monument was built in 315 to commemorate the Emperor's victory over Maxentius at the Ponte Milvio, is comprised of three archways, and is the largest and best preserved in Rome. Even though this is the Arch of Constantine, the bas-reliefs refer to deeds performed by Trajan, Hadrian, and Marcus Aurelius. The upper reliefs facing the Coliseum represent Marcus Aurelius in his battle with the Dacians, and on the opposite side there are episodes of deeds by Marcus Aurelius and Constantine.

THE ROMAN FORUM & NEARBY SIGHTS

Via dei Fori Imperiali. Tel. 699–0110. Admission L12,000. Open Tuesday–Saturday 9:00am–1:30pm, and Sunday 9:00am–1:00pm. In the summer also open Tuesdays–Saturdays from 4:00pm–7:00pm. Catch buses 11, 27, 85, 97, 181, 186, 718, and 719.

The best way to get an overall view of the **Roman Forum** is to descend from the Piazza del Campidolglio by way of the Via del Campidoglio, which is to the right of the Senatorial Palace. Here you get a clear view of the Forums in the front, with the Coliseum in the background, and the Palatine hill on the right.

In the Roman Forum you'll find the following sights and more:

Arch of Septimus Severus

Built in 203 AD to celebrate the ten years of the Emperor Septimus Severus' reign, it is constructed with three archways and is one of the most imposing sturctures from ancient Rome. Over the side arches are bas-reliefs depicting scenes from victorious battles fought by the Emperor over the Parthians and the Mesopotamians.

Rostra

Located directly to the left of the Arch of Septimus Severus, this building was decorated with the beaks of ships captured by the Romans at Antium in 338 BC. It was the meeting place for Roman orators. In front of it is the **Column of Phocas**, erected in honor of the Eastern Emperor of the Roman Empire in 608 AD. The column was the last monument to be erected in the Forum.

Temple of Saturn

Built in 497 BC, it was restored with eight ionic columns in the 3rd century AD. In the temple's basement was the Treasury of State.

Basilica Giulia

Started in 54 BC by Julius Caesar and completed by Augustus, it was destroyed by fire and restored by Diocletian in 284 AD. The building served as a large law court.

Basilica Emilia

Located to the right of the entrance to the Forum, it was erected in 179 BC, and because of the ravages of fire, destruction by "barbarian hordes" and neglect, little remains today. Together with the Basilica Giulia, it was one of the largest buildings in Rome and was used by money-changers and other other business people.

The Curia

Founded by Tullus Hostilius, this was the house of the Senate during the Late Empire. It used to be covered with exquisite marble. Today all that remains are two balustrades called the **Marble Walls of Trajan** that are sculpted with bas-reliefs of animals and episodes from the life of Trajan.

Temple of Anthony & Foustina

Built by Antonius Pius in honor of his wife Faustina, the temple was later converted to a church in the 11th century, **San Lorenzxo in Miranda**. All that remains of the original Roman temple are the ten monolithic columns that are 17 meters high, and an elegant frieze. The baroque facade is from the 1600s.

Temple of Caesar

Near the Arch of Augustis and past the Temple of Casot and Pollux you'll find the Temple of Caesar, built in 42 BC by Octavius. It was on this site that Caesar's body was cremated.

Temple of Castor & Pollux

Built in 484 BC and restored by Hadrian and Tiberius. The three Corinthian columns in the podium are from that period of restoration. It was originally built to pay homage to the Gods Castor and Pollux who, according to legend, aided the Romans against their enemies.

House of the Vestal Virgins

This is where the vestal virgins lived who dedicated themselves to maintaining the sacred fires in the nearby **Temple of Vesta**. A portico of two stories adorned with statues of the Vestals surrounded an open court that was decorated with flowerbeds and three cisterns. In the court you can still see the remains of some of the statues and the pedestals on which they sat.

Arch of Titus

Erected to commemorate the vistories of Vespasian and Titus, who conquered Jerusalem. The arch contains bas-releifs of the Emperor and of soldiers carrying away the spoils of Jerusalem. One of the most imposing structures remaining from ancient Rome.

Temple of Romulus

Built by the Emperor Maxentius who dedicated it to his deified son Romulus. A circular building that was converted to a church in the sixth century.

The Palatine Hill

This is one of the seven hills of Rome and was the residence of the Roman Emperors from the Golden Age and Imperial Period. It was here, in 754 BC, that Romulus is said to have founded the city of Rome. Noble families also resided here, leaving behind wonderful architectural relics that have mostly all been excavated today, making the Palatine Hill one of the must-see places when you tour the Forum.

Here you'll find the baths of Septimus Severus, the Stadium of Domitian, the Farnese Gardens, the House of Livia, the Flavia Palace, the House of Augustana, and more. Most of the ruins are covered with grass, and bushes grow wild making a walk through the ruins quite a relaxing natural adventure.

BATHS OF CARACALLA

Via di Terme Caracalla, Tel. 575-8626. Admission L8,000. Hours Monday–Saturday 9:00am–3:00pm. Sundays 9:00am–1:30pm. Catch buses 90, 90b, 118 or get off at the Circo Massimo Metro Stop.

Constructed in 217 AD by the Emperor Caracalla, these baths were second in size only to the Baths of Diocletian. They were used until the sixth century when they were destroyed by Gothic invaders. They used to be rich with marble, statues, stuccoes, and more. Today, on cool summer evenings, opera perfromances are held among the ruins of the **Calidarium**, the circular vapor bath area.

BATHS OF DIOCLETIAN

Catch buses 57, 64, 65, 75, 170, 492, and 910 or get off at the Repubblica Metro stop.

These were the most extensive baths of their times. More than 3,000 bathers could be accommodated at one time. They were built by Maximian and Diocletian fromn 196–306 AD. Today the **National Museum** is located within their walls, as is the **Church of Santa Maria Degli Angeli**.

CAMPIDOGLIO

Catch buses 94, 95, 713, 716.

One of the seven hills of Rome. Today it houses the **Capitalone Museum**, **Senatorial Palace**, the **Palace of the Conservatori**, and the **Church of Santa Maria D'Arcoeli** (formerly the Temple of Juno Moneta). To ascend the hill, take the steep stairway that leads to the church, the winding ramp of the Via delle Tre Pile, or from between the two of these by way of the monumental stairs, Cordonate, which were designed by Michelangelo. At the entrance to these stairs you'll find two imposing Egyptian lions and at the top the statues of Castor and Pollux.

Try to visit the museums on this hill, since they are second in magnificence only to Vatican Museums, and are even better in certain exhibits.

CIRCUS MAXIMUS

Catch buses 15, 90, 90b, 94 or get off at the Circo Massimo Metro.

One of the most perfectly conserved monuments of anceint Rome. It was erected in 309 AD by the Emperor Maxentius in honor of his deified son Romulus, whose temple is nearby.

CATACOMBS OF SAINT CALLIXTUS, SAN SEBASTIAN, & SANTA DOMITILLA

Catch buses 118 and 218.

Located next door to one another on the Via Appia Antica south of the city, these tombs were originally an ancient Roman necropolis, then they were used by the early Christians as a meeting place as well as a place of worship, and a haven from prosecution. Here you can visit the **crypts of the Popes**, the crypt of Saint Cecilia, the crypt of Pope Eusebius, as well as frescoes dating back to the 3rd century AD. All three are an eerie reminder of the time before Christianity dominated the Western world.

CHRISTIAN ROME

CASTEL SANT'ANGELO

Lungotevere Castello. Admission L8,000. Open 9:00am–6:00pm. Last entrance time is 1 hour before closing. Catch buses 23, 34, 64, 280, 982.

Also known as the **Mausoleum of Hadrian** since it was built for Hadrian and his successors. For eighty years it was used as a funeral monument where the ashes of the Roman emperors were stored. Subsequently the structure was used as a fortress, a residence for popes and princes, a prison, and as a military barracks.

In the Middle Ages it was transformed into what it is now, the **Papal fortress**. A covered walkway leads from Saint Peter's to the Castel Sant'Angelo and, because of the volatile political siuation in Italy for many centuries, this walkway was used more than once to protect the Pope.

On the summit of the building is the statue of an angel (hence the name of the castle), and rumor has it that in 590 AD, Gregory the Great saw a vision with an avenging angel sheathing its sword at the summit of the castle. He took this to mean the plague that had ravaged Rome was over. To commemorate this event he placed an angel on top of the building. Today the castle houses a museum with one of the best collections of articles of war from the Stone Age to the present ever assembled. There are also some non-descript art exhibits and luxuriously preserved Papal apartments.

PROPER ATTIRE, PLEASE!

When you're visiting most museums and monuments in Italy, follow these necessary rules:

Women: *don't forget to wear either long pants or a long skirt or dress, and a top with sleeves.*

Men: *wear long pants and no tank tops.*

You will be denied entry to St. Peter's for sure, and to many other sights as well if you're wearing shorts!

SAINT PETER'S

Piazza San Pietro. Hours 9:00am–6:00pm. Catch the Metro to Ottaviano or buses 19, 62, 64, or 492.

Located in the monumental square **Piazza San Pietro**, a masterpiece created by **Bernini** between 1656 and 1667, sits Saint Peter's, the largest church in the world. The square itself is oval and 240 meters at its largest diameter. It is composed of 284 massive marble columns, and 88 pilasters forming three galleries 15 meters wide. Surrounding the square, above the oval structure are 140 statues of saints.

In the center is an oblesik 25.5 meters high with four bronze lions at its base, all of which were brought from Heliopolis during the reign of Caligula (circa 40 AD) and which originally stood in the circus of Nero. It was placed here in 1586. Below the monument you can see the points of the compass and the names of the winds. To reach Saint Peter's you must pass the obelisk and walk up a gradual incline.

The church rises on the site where Saint Peter is buried. The early Christians erected a small oratory on the site of the tomb, but that was destroyed in 326 when Constantine the Great erected the first Basilica on this site. Over the centuries the church began to expand and became incongrously and lavishly decorated, so that by 1452 Nicholas V decided to make it more uniform. He commissioned Bernardo Rossellino to deisgn a new structure. When the Pope died three years late this work was interrupted, but in 1506 Pope Julius II, with the assistance of Bramante, continued the work on a grander scale.

Bramante died before his work could be finished. His successors were Raphael, Baldassare Peruzzi, and utlimately Antonio de Sangalloo the Younger. Eventually, the project was taken over and modfied by **Michelangelo** in 1546. After he died, his plans too were changed by Vignola, Pizzo Ligorio, Giacomo dell Porta, Domenico Fontana, and finally Carlo Maderno, who designed the facade. On November 1, 1626, **Urbano VIII** dedicated the Basilica as we know it today.

The Facade

Rounding off, the **facade** is 115 meters long and 45 meters high, and is approached by a gradually sloping grand staircase. At the sides of this staircase are the statues of **Saint Peter** (by De Fabis) and **Saint Paul** (by Adamo Tadolini). On the balustrade, held up by eight Corinthian columns and four pilasters, are the colossal statues of the Savior and St. John the Baptist surrounded by the Apostles, excluding Saint Peter.

There are nine balconies, and from the central one the Pope gives his Christmas and Easter benedictions. There are five doors from which to enter the chruch, but today only the large central one is used.

The Interior

The church is more than 15,000 square meters in area, 211 meters long and 46 meters high. There are 229 marble columns: 533 of travertine, 16 of bronze, 90 of stucco, and 44 altars. On the floor of the central nave you'll find lines drawn identifying where other churches in the world would fit if placed in Saint Peter's. Kids love to explore this aspect of the basilica.

Also on the floor, near the front entrance, is a disk of red porphyry indicating the spot where **Charlemagne** was crowned Holy Roman Emperor by Leo III on Christmas Day in 800 AD. To the right of this, in the first chapel, is the world famous *Pieta* created by Michelangelo when he was on 24, in 1500 AD. In the niches of the pilasters that support the arches are statues of the founders of many religious orders. In the last one on the right you'll find the seated bronze statue of Saint Peter. The statue's foot has been rubbed by so many people for good luck that it has almost disappeared.

Just past the statue is the grand **cupola** created by Michelangelo. One of the most amazing architectural wonders of all times, it is held up by four colossal spires which lead to a number of open chapels. Under the cupola, above the high altar rises the famous **Baldacchino** (or Grand Canopy) made by Bernini. It's made from bronze taken mainly from the Pantheon. In front of the altar is the **Chapel of Confessions** made by Maderno, around which are 95 perpetually lit lamps illuminating the **Tomb of Saint Peter's**. In front of the shrine is the kneeling statue of Pius VI made by Canova in 1822.

Throughout the rest of the Basilica you'll find a variety of superb statues and monuments, many tombs of Popes, and a wealth of chapels, not the least of which is the **Gregorian Chapel** designed by Michelangelo and executed by Giacomo della Porta. It is rich in marbles, stuccos, and mosaics, all put together in the creative Venetian style by Madonna del Soccorso in the 12th century.

If you grow tired of the many beautiful works of art and wish to get a bird's eye view of everything, you can ascend into Michelangelo's Cupola either by stairs (537 of them) or by elevator. If you come to Saint Peter's, you should do this.

VATICAN CITY

Piazza San Pietro. Catch the Metro to Ottaviano or buses 19, 62, 64, or 492. City is generally inaccessible except for official business. Can look into gardens from cupola of Saint Peters.

Vatican City sits on the right bank of the Tiber river, in the foothills of the Monte Mario and Gianicolo section of Rome. In ancient Rome this was the site of the Gardens of Nero and the main circus where thousands of Christians were martyred. Saint Peter met his fate here around 67 AD. Today it is the world center for the Catholic Church, rich in priceless art, antiques, and spiritual guidance.

The Vatican (officially referred to as The Holy See) is a completely autonomous state within the Italian Republic and has its own radio station, railway, newspaper, stamps, money, and diplomatic representatives in major capitals. Though it doesn't have an army, the **Swiss Guards**, who are volunteers from the Swiss armed forces, guard the Vatican day and night.

PIAZZAS, FOUNTAINS, MONUMENTS, PALAZZI & GARDENS

PIAZZA NAVONA

Catch buses 70, 81, 87, 90.

The piazza is on the site of a stadium built by Domitian that he used for naval battles and other gladiatorial contests, as well as horse races. The style of the piazza is richly Baoroque, featuring works by two great masters, **Bernini** and **Borromini**. Located in the middle of the square is Bernini's fantastic **Fontana Dei Quattro Fiumi** (Fountain of Four Rivers), sculpted from 1647-51. The four figures supporting the large obelisk (a Bernini trademark) represent four rivers: the Danube, the Ganges, the Nile, and the Plata Rivers.

Besides the statue's obvious beauty, Bernini has hidden a subtle treasure in this sculpture. Notice the figure representing the Nile. Some historians interpret the shielding of its eyes from the facade of the church it is facing, **Santa Agnese in Agone**, as a statement of revulsion. This church was designed by Bernini's rival at the time, Borromini, and

Bernini, as the story is told, playfully showed his disgust with his rival's design through the sculpted disgust in his statue. Others claim the revulsion comes from the fact that the church, originally a family chapel for Pope Innocent X's Palazzo Pamphili, was built on the location of an old neighborhood brothel.

To savor the artistic and architectural beauty, as well as the vibrant nightlife of the Piazza, choose a table at one of the local bars or cafés and try some ice cream, grab a coffee, or have a meal. Navona is one of Rome's many gathering spots for people of all ages. You'll find local art vendors, caricaturists, hippies selling string bracelets, and much more. This is a place you cannot miss if you come to Rome.

PIAZZA DI SPAGNA

Catch buses 52, 53, 56, 58, 60, 61, 62, 71, 81 or get off at Piazza di Spagna Metro stop.

This is one of the most beautiful and visited spots in Rome. It is named after the old Spanish Embassy to the Holy See that used to stand on the site. The 137 steps are officially called the *Scalinata della Trinita dei Monti*, and are named for the church which they lead to at the top. But most people just call them the **Spanish Steps**. The fountain in the middle of the piazza is known as the **Barcaccia** and was designed by Pietro Bernini in commoration of the big flood of 1598. To the right is the column of the **Immaculate Conception** erected in 1865 by Pius IX.

The Spanish Steps, besides being the location of fine works of art and architecture, are also a favorite meeting spot for Italians of all ages, and the place can get quite crowded at night. You'll find musicians, artists, caricaturists, palmists, tourists, and many others assembled together making this place perfect for people watching. Grab a bottle of wine (yes, you can drink in public in Italy) and sitby the fountain for an afternoon or an evening and watch the world pass by.

CAMPO DEI FIORI

Catch buses 46, 62, 64.

This is a typically Roman piazza that hosts a lively flower and food market every morning until 1:00pm. Here you'll find the cries of the vendors blending with the bargaining of the customers. A perfect place to see and smell the beauty of Rome. This used to be a square where heretics were burned at the stake and criminals were hanged. The monument in the middle is in memory of Giordano Bruno, a famous philosopher who was burned here in 1600.

This is another place to come at night, since there are plenty of impromptu concerts and a great restaurant, **La Carbonara**, that serves the best *Spaghetti alla Vongole Verace* I've ever had, and a great Irish Pub, **The Drunken Ship**.

TREVI FOUNTAIN

Catch buses 52, 53, 56, 58, 60, 61, 62, 71, 81.

Another meeting place for Italians in the evenings. You'll always find an impromptu guitar solo being performed as well as wine being drunk by many. A great place to hang out in the evenings and make new friends. This is the largest and most impressive of the famous fountains in Rome. It is truly specatacular when it is lit up at night. Commissioned by Clement XII, it was built by Nicola Salvi in 1762 from a design he borrowed from Bernini. In the central niche you see Neptune on his chariot drawn by marine horses preceded by two tritons. In the left niche you see the statue representing Abundance, to the right Health.

There is an ancient custom, or legend, or rumor, that says that all those who throw a coin into the foutain are destined to return to Rome. So turn your back to the fountain and throw a coin over your left shoulder with your right hand into the fountain and fate will carry you back. By the way it is completely illegal, and severely enforced, to walk in the fountain, especially to try and get wine money from the many coins in the pool of the fountain.

PANTHEON

Catch buses 70, 81, 87, 90.

The **Pantheon** is one of the most famous and definitely the best preserved monuments of ancient Rome, located in another piazza frequented by the locals and tourists all day. There some expensive restaurants and cafés/bars to grab a quick meal or drink from around the piazza in which the Pantheon sits. Besides the architectural beauty, the entrance area to the Pantheon is by far the coolest place in Rome during the heat wave of August. So if you want to relax in seemingly air conditioned comfort in the middle of a hot day, park yourself here.

First construdcted by Agrippa in 27 BC, it was restored after a fire in 80 AD and returned to its original rotunda shape by the Emperor Hadrian. In 609 AD, it was dedicated as a Christian Church called Santa Maria and the Martyrs, and in the Middle Ages it served as a fortress. A variety of Popes stole its bronze ceiling and melted it into the cannons for Castel Sant'Angelo, as well as for the Baldacchino in Saint Peter's. The building is made up of red and grey Egyptian granite. Each of the sixteen columns is 12.5 meters high and is composed of a single block.

You enter the building by way of the cool and comfortable portal area and the original bronze door, and you can feel the perfect symmetry of space and harmony of its architectural lines. This feeling is somewhat lessened by the fact that the Roman authorities in their infinite wisdom have started charging for entrance to the building, and have placed a ticket booth inside along with a small souvenir stand. Sad. Nonetheless you will still be awed by the marvelous dome (diameter 43 meters) with the hole in the middle.

There are three niches in the building, two of which contain **tombs**: the tomb of **Victor Emmanuel II** (died 1878), one of Italy's few war heros, and the tombs of **Umberto I** (died 1900) and **Queen Margherita** (died 1926), and in another niche the tomb of reknowned artist **Raphael Sanzio** (died 1520).

VILLA BORGHESE

Catch buses 95, 490, 495, 910.

The most picturesque park in Rome, complete with bike and jogging paths (you can rent bikes in the park), a lake where you can rent boats, a wonderful museum – **Galleria Borghese** – lush vegetation, large grass fields, the Roman **zoological park**, a large riding ring, and more.

This is the perfect place to come and relax in the middle of a hard day of touring. Kids of all ages will love to wander all over the park or simply cuddle up together and take a quick siesta.

The Borghese Gardens

This is a great sanctuary just outside the ancient walls of Rome. If you only want an afternoon's respite from the sights of the city, or you're tired of spending your time in your hotel room during the siesta hours, escape to the luscious and spacious **Borghese Gardens**.

To get to the gardens is simple enough: either exit the old walls of Rome through the gates at the Piazza del Popolo or at the top of the Via Veneto. From the Piazza del Popolo exit, the gardens will be on your right through the iron gates just across the busy Piazzale Flaminio. Once you enter you will be on the Viale Washington. Anywhere to the left of you, after a few hundred meters, will be prime park land. From the Via Veneto exit, cross the major thoroughfare in front of you and you're in Borghese. From here stroll to your right and you will instantly find a pleasant area to picnic or take a small nap for the afternoon.

Borghese houses Rome's **zoo**, several museums (including Galleria Borghese and the Galleria Arte Moderna), playing fields for calcio, a small lake, an amphitheater, and many wooded enclaves to have a wonderfully secluded picnic (look out for those heated Italian couples).

Galleria Borghese

One of Rome's finest museums is in the Borghese Gardens, the **Galleria Borghese**. For those of you that entered the Gardens from Piazza del Popolo, it will be a long hike up the Viale Washington to the lake, and around it to the Viale Dell'Uccelleria (the zoo will be on your left) which leads directly to the Galleria Borghese.

From the Via Veneto it is not quite as long. From where you first entered the gardens, there is a road, Viale Del Museo Borghese, on your right. Take this all the way to the Galleria.

The Galleria Borghese was built by Dutch architect Hans van Santes during the 1820's. It houses a large number of rare masterpieces from many disciplines and countries. There are classical works of Greeks and Romans, along with 16th and 17th century paintings by such notables as Raphael, Titian, Caravaggio, and Antonella da Messina. Sculptures are also featured with works by Lorenzo Bernini, Pietro Bernini, and Houndon.

For more details, see the Galleria Borghese description below under *Museums*.

ROMAN NEIGHBORHOODS

PIAZZA DEL POPOLO
Catch buses 90, 119 or get off at Flaminio Metro stop.

This impressive piazza, and the ascent to the **Pincio**, was designed by G. Valadier at the beginning of the 19th century. The piazza is decorated on its sides with two semi-cycles of flowers and statues, and in the center is the **Egyptian Obelisk** that is 24 meters high and came from Egypt during the time of Ramses II in the 8th century BC. The obelisk was removed from Heliopolis by order of Augustus and initially erected in the Circus Maximus. Then in 1585, Sixtus V had it placed here in its present location.

There are two symmetrical baroque churches at the south end of the piazza flanking the intersection of the Via del Corso. These two churches, **Santa Maria dei Miracoli** (1678) and **Santa Maria in Monesanto** (1675) both have picturesque cupolas that were begun by C. Rainaldi and finished by Bernini and Carlo Fontana.

Eerie Roman Trivia: There is a movie theater directly next to Santa Maria dei Miracoli that played the first run release of the *Exorcist* when it came out in the 1970's. During the first showing of the film, the cross on the top of the church dislodged itself from its perch and shattered itself directly in front of the movie theater. No one was hurt. This is a true story.

VIA VENETO
Catch buses 52, 53, 56, 58 or get off at the Barberini Metro stop.

Definitely the most famous and most fashionable street in Rome. It used to be the center of all artistic activities as well as the meeting place for the jet set, but it doesn't quite have the same allure it used to. Nonetheless, it's still a great place to wander up the road, which is flanked by hotels, stores, and cafés.

At the bottom of the street in the **Piazza Barberini**, where you'll find the graceful **Fontana delle Api** (Fountain of the Bees) made by Bernini. Up a little ways on the right you will find the famous Church of Bones, **Santa Maria della Concezione**, which has a macabre arrangement of over 4,000 friars that have died over the centuries in the adjoining convent. The bones are located below the church in the **Cappucin crypt**. Up a little way is the grandiose **Palazzo Margherita**, built by G Koch in 1890 and now the home of the American Embassy. You'll recognize it by the armed guards hanging around out front.

VIA APPIA ANTICA

Catch buses 118 and 218.

This celebrated of all Roman roads was begun by Appius Claudius Caecus in 312 BC. The road has been preserved in its original chracter as have the original monuments. Originally it was the chief line of communication between Rome and Southern Italy, Greece, and the eastern possessions of the Roman Empire.

Now it is a well travelled picturesque road to the country and the famous Roman/Christian **catacombs**.

TRASTEVERE

Catch buses 44, 75, 170, 710, 718, 719.

This is the perfect place for exploring the way Romans actually live. **Trastevere** literally means "across the river" and this separation has allowed the area to remain virtually untouched by the advances of time. Until recently it was one of the poorest sections of Rome, but now it is starting to become gentrified. Yet these changes have not altered Trastevere's charm. You'll find interesting shops and boutiques, and plenty of excellent restaurants among the small narrow streets and *piazzette* (small squares). The maze of streets is a fun place to wander and wonder where you're going to end up.

During the month of July the *Trasteverini* express their feeling of seperation from the rest of Rome with their summertime festival called **Noiantri**, meaning "we the others," in which they mix drunken revelry with religious celebration in a party of true bacchanalian proportions. *Trasteverini* cling to their roots of selling clothing and furnishings to make ends meet by continuing to hold the **Porta Portese** flea market on Sundays. Today, the goods sold are of much higher quality, especially the antiques, but the event is true Trastevere.

This area offers some of the best dining and casual night life in town. Here you can sit in a piazza bar sipping Sambuca or wine and watch the life of Rome pass before your eyes. To accommodate this type of activity many stores have begun to stay open later. Trastevere is a great place to enjoy for a day or even more, because it is the way Rome used to be.

ISOLA TIBURTINA

Catch buses 44, 75, 170, 710, 718, 719.

Halfway across the river going towards Trastevere, this island used to be a dumping ground for dead and sick slaves. Then the Romans had a cult of healing *(aesculapius)* here in the 3rd century BC, and currently half its size is taken up by a hopsital. One of the bridges to the mainland, **Ponte Fabricio**, is the oldest in Rome. This is a good place to cross the Tiber going towards Trastevere if you've been exploring the Jewish Ghetto.

JEWISH GHETTO

Catch buses 780, 774, 717.

Located west of city center, next to the Tiber just across from Trastevere, you'll find the old **Jewish Ghetto** where Rome's Jewish population was forced to live for centuries. To find out more about this period check out the **Jewish Museum** in the **Sinagoga Ashkenazita** *(Tel. 06/687-5051)* that has a plan for the original ghetto, as well as artifacts from the 17th century Jewish community and more.

Besides learning about the history of the ghetto, you can find some of Rome's truly great restaurants here as well as see many ancient Roman buildings, arches, and columns completely incorporated into modern day buildings. It seems as if many structures were better preserved here, since the locals did not have the resources to tear them down and replace them.

PALAZZO BARBERINI

Via Quattro Fontane, 13. Tel. 854-8577. Admission L4,000. Hours 9:00am–7:00pm, Holidays 9:00am–1:00pm. Closed Mondays. Catch buses 95, 490, 495, 910.

Located just off the Piazza Barerbini on the Via Quattro Fontane, this baroque palace was started by Carlo Maderno in 1625 with the help of Borromini and was finished in 1633 by Bernini. The palace is the site of the **National Portrait Gallery**. Besides the wonderful architecture which shouldn't be missed, the gallery has many wonderful paintings such as *Marriage of St. Catherine* by Sodoma, *Portait of a Lady* by Piero di Cossimo, and *Rape of the Sabines* by Sodoma.

PALAZZO FARNESE

Piazza Farnese. Hours 9:00am–Noon. Monday–Thursday. Catch buses 23 and 280.

This palace represents one of the high points of Rennaissance architecture. It was started in 1514 by Antonio da Sangallo the Younger for Cardinal Alessandro Farnese (later Pope Pius III), and was continued by Michelangelo who added the large window, the molding on the facade, the thrid floor of the court, and the sides. It was finally finsihed by Giacomo della Porta. As well as being an architectural wonder, there is a first floor galery of frescoes depicting mythological subjects by the painters Carracci, Domenichino, and Reni.

GIANICOLO

Catch bus 41.

Offering one of the best panoramas of Rome, **Gianicolo hill** is located between Trastevere and the Vatican, across the river from the old city of Rome. At the terrace of the Piazzale del Gianicolo, you'll find the equestrian statue of Giuseppe Garibaldi and a perfect photo opportunity. The walk may be a little tiring but the view is calming and serene, as is the lush vegetation.

CHURCHES

SAINT PAUL'S OUTSIDE THE WALLS

(San Paolo Fuori le Mura). Via Ostiense. Church open 7:00am–7:00pm. Cloisters Open 9:00am–1:00pm and 3:00pm–6:00pm. From the Piramide stop on the Metro take buses 23, 170, or 673.

Located a mile or so beyond the Porta Paolo, **St. Paul's Outside the Walls** (San Paolo Fuori le Mura) is the fourth of the patriarcal basilicas in Rome. It is second only in size to St. Peter's and sits above the tomb of St Paul's. It was built by Constantine in 314 and then enlarged by Valentinian in 386 and later by Theodsius. It was finally completed by Honorius, his son.

In 1826 the church was almost completely destroyed by a terrible fire and many of its great works of art were lost. Immediatley afterward, its renovation began and today it seems as magnificent as ever. So much so that every time my family returns to Rome we line up just inside the entrance to the *quadroportici* with its 150 granite columns and get our picture taken with one of the palm trees in the background. We've been doing this since the 1950's and in that time the palm in the background has grown from a stubby bush into a gigantic tree. Along with the exterior with its beautiful garden surrounded by the great rows of columns, the palms growing in the center, the gigantic statue of St. Paul, and the facade with mosaics of four prophets (Isaiah, Jeremaih, Ezekial, and Daniel) the interior of the basilica is quite lovely.

The interior is 120 meters long and has four rows of columns and five naves. The columns in the central nave are Corinthian that can be identified by their splendidly ornate capitals. The walls contain Medallion Portraits of the Popes from Saint Peter to Pius XI. On the High Altar still sits the ancient Gothic tabernacle of Arnolfo di Cambio (13th century) that was saved from the fire in 1826. Saint Paul rests beneath the altar in the confessional. The mosaic in the apse, with its dominating figure of Christ, was created by artists from the Republic of San Marino in 1220.

To the left of the apse is the **Chapel of St. Stephen**, with the large statue of the saint created by R. Rainaldi, and the **Chapel of the Crucifix** created by Carlo Maderno. This chapel contains the crucifix which is said to have spoken to Saint Bridget in 1370. Also here is St. Ignatius de Loyola, who took the formal vows that established the Jesuits as a religious order. To the right of the apse is the **Chapel of San Lorenzo**, the **Chapel of Saint Benedict** with its 12 columns. One other place of note in the church are the cloisters that contain fragments of ancient inscriptions and sarcophagi from the early Christian era.

SANTA MARIA SOPRA MINERVA

Piazza della Minerva (behind the Pantheon). Hours 7:00am–Noon and 3:30pm–7:00pm. Catch buses 70, 81, 87,90.

Built on the pagan ruins of a temple to Minerva (hence the name Saint Mary above Minerva) this church was begun in 1280 by the Dominican brothers Sisto and Ristoro, who also began the beautiful Santa Maria Novella in Florence. The facade was created during the Rennaissance by Meo del Caprino in 1453.

The interior is divided into three naves, seperated by pilasters with ogival vaulting. You can find many tombs of famous personages of the 15th through the 16th centuries as well as valuable works of art. Saint Catherine of Siena, who died in Rome in 1380, lies beneath high altar. To the left of the altar is the statue of *Christ Carrying the Cross* created by the great Michelangelo in 1521.

Behind the altar are the tombs of Pope Clement VII and Leo X which were created by the Florentine sculptor Baccio Bandanelli. In the Sacristy is a chapel covered with frescoes by Antoiazzo Romano, brought here in 1637 from the house where Catherine of Siena died.

SAN PIETRO IN VICOLO

Piazza di San Pietro in Vicolo. Hours 7:00am–12:30pm and 3:30pm–6:00pm.

Located only a few blocks from the Coliseum, this church was founded in 442 as a shrine dedicated to preserving the chains with which Herod bound St. Peter in Jerusalem. Its single, completely unforgettable work is the seated figure of *Moses* created by the master Michelangelo himself. This statue captures the powerful personification of justice and law of the Old Testament.

In fact, Moses appears as if he is ready to leap to his feet and pass judgement on you. You can almost see the cloth covering his legs, or the long beard covering his face move in the breeze. Because of this one work, this church cannot be missed.

SANTA MARIA MAGGIORE

Piazza di Santa Maria Maggiore. Hours 8:00am–7:00pm. Catch buses 4, 9, 16, 27, 714, 715.

Like St. Paul's Outside the Walls, St. Peter's, and St. John Lateran, this is one of the four patriarchal basilicas of Rome. It is called *Maggiore* since it is the largest church in Rome dedicated to the Madonna. The facade, originally built in the 12th century, but badly tampered with in the 18th century is nothing to look at and so many people pass this church by.

But the interior, in all its 86 meters of simplistic splendor, is interesting and inspiring mainly because of the 5th-century mosaics, definitely the best in Rome, and its frescoes. On the right wall of the Papal Altar is the funeral monument to Sixtus V and on the left wall the monument to Pius V, both created by Fontana with excellent bas-reliefs. Opposite this chapel is the **Chapella Paolina**, sometimes referred to as the **Borghesana** since the sepulchral vaults of the wealthy Borghese family lie beneath it. Here you'll view the beautiful bas-relief monumental tombs to Paul V and Clement VIII on its left and right walls.

SAN GIOVANNI IN LATERANO

Via dei Querceti. Hours 6:00am–12:30pm and 3:30pm–7:00pm. Catch buses 16, 85, 87, and 650.

Another of the great basilicas of Rome, this is the actual cathedral church of Rome and of the whole Catholic world, and not St. Peter's. Bet you didn't know that? The simple and monumental facade of the church, created by Allessandro Galiliei in 1735, is topped by fourteen colossal statues of Christ, the Apostles, and saints. It rises on the site of the ancient palalce of Plautinus Lateranus (hence the name), one of the noble families of Rome many eons ago.

To get inside, you must pass through the bronze door that used be attached to the old Roman Senate house. The interior of the church, laid out in the form of a Latin cross, has five naves filled with historical and artistic objects. In total it is 150 meters long, while the **central nave** is 87 meters long. This central nave is flanked by 12 spires from which appear 12 statues of the Apostles from the 18th century. The wooden ceiling and the marble flooring are from the 15th century.

The most beautiful artistic aspect of the church is the vast transept, which is richly decorated with marbles and frescoes portraying the *Leggenda Aurea* of Constantine. This is here because the Emperor Constantine, after he became converted to Christianity, donated the building to the Catholic church. One piece of historical interest is the table of wood, on which it is said that Saint Peter served mass, which you'll find in the **Papal Altar**.

CHURCH OF SAN CLEMENTE

Via di San Giovanni Laterano. Admission L3,000. Hours to visit the basement 9:00am–1:00pm. Not on Sundays. Catch bus 65.

Located between the Coliseum and St. John Lateran is the beautiful **San Clemente**. One of the better preserved medieval churches in Rome, it was originally built in the fifth century. The Normans destroyed it in 1084 but it was reconstructed in 1108 by Pachal II. Today when you enter you are in what is called the **Upper Church**, a simple and basic basilica divided by two rows of columns. The altar is intricately inlaid with a variety of 12th century mosaics.

The thrill of this church is that all you have to do is descend a set of stairs to the **Lower Church**, which was discovered in 1857, and immediately you have left the Middle Ages and are now surrounded by early Christian frescoes and a small ancient altar. Then you can descend a shorter set of stairs and go to the third level where a small temple and a meeting room still exist from the days when Christians had to practice their religion below ground for fear of prosecution. The temple is of Mithraic, a lost religion known for their evil blood rites. Below this level are still more ruins that are in the process of being excavated. This church is perfect for a descent into four different levels of Roman/Christian history.

CHURCH OF SANTA CECILIA IN TRASTEVERE

Via dei Genovesi. Hours 10:00am–Noon and 4:00pm–6:00pm. Catch buses 181, 280, 44, 75, 717, 170, 23, 65.

Normally visitors don't go to Trastevere to visit churches. Instead they are attracted by the more secular delights of this part of Rome. But if you're interested in beautiful churches, **Santa Cecilia** is one to visit in Trastevere; the other is Santa Maria.

Santa Cecilia was founded in the fith century and had a make-over in ninth century as well as the 16th. A baroque door leads to a picturesque court, beyond which is a baroque facade, with a mosaic frieze above the portico, and a beautiful bell tower erected in the 12th century. There are several important works of art to be found in the church, not the least of which is the expressive statue of Santa Cecilia by Stefano Maderno. It represents the body of the saint in the exact position it was found when the tomb was opened in 1559.

Another place of interest to visit on the church grounds is the Roman house where Santa Cecilia suffered her martyrdom by being exposed to hot vapors. There are two rooms preserved, one of them the bath where she died. It still has the pipes and large bronze cauldron for heating water. A great church to visit, not just for the art, but also for the history.

SANTA MARIA IN TRASTEVERE

Piazza Santa Maria in Trastevere 1. Hours 7:00am–7:00pm. Mass at 9:00am, 10:30am, noon, and 6:00pm. Catch buses 181, 280, 44, 75, 717, 170, 23, 65.

A small church in Trastevere, in a piazza of the same name that is the most frequented by locals and tourists alike, making the church one of the most visited. Around this church are some of the best restaurants and cafés in all of Rome, the only dedicated English language theater, a handsome 17th century fountain where hippies hang out at all night long, and the Palace of San Calisto.

This was one of Rome's earliest churches and the first to be dedicated to the Virgin. It was built in the 3rd century and remodeled between 1130-1143. It is best known for its prized mosaics, especially the 12th and 13th century representation of the Madonna which adorns the facade of the church. The romanesque bell-tower was built in the 12th century. The interior is of three naves separated by columns purloined from ancient Roman temples.

On the vault you'll find exquisite mosaics depicting the Cross, emblems of the Evangelists, and Christ and the Madonna enthroned among the Saints (created by Domenichino in 1140). Lower dwon, the mosaics of Pietro Cavallini done in 1291 portray, in six panels, the life of the Virgin.

MUSEUMS

CAPITOLINE MUSEUM

Piazza del Campidoglio. Tel. 6710-2071,Admission L10,000. Hours 9:00am-1:30pm. Sundays 9:00am-1:00pm. Tuesdays and Saturdays also open from 5:00pm to 8:00pm. Closed Mondays. Catch buses 44, 46, 56, 57, 90, 90/ , 94, 186, 710, 713, 718, 719.

Actually the **Capitoline Museum** is actually two museums, the **Capitolone** and the **Palazzo dei Conservatori**.

The **Capitalone** is the perfect place to come to see what ancient Romans looked like. Unlike Greek sculpture, which glorified the subject, Roman sculpture captured every realistic characteristic and flaw. There are rooms full of portrait busts dating back to the republic and imperial Rome, where you have many individuals of significance immortalized here, whether they were short, fat, thin, ugly. Here they remain, warts and all. Because of these very real depicitions of actual Romans, and many other more famous sculptures, this museum has to rank second only in importance to the Vatican collections.

Besides the busts, you'll find a variety of celebrated pieces from antiquity including *Dying Gaul, Cupid and Psyche*, the *Faun*, and the nude and voluptuous *Capitalone Venice*. Then in the **Room of the Doves** you'll find two wonderful mosaics that were taken from Hadrian's Villa many centuries ago. One mosaic is of the doves drinking from a basin, and the other is of the masks of comedy and tragedy. Besides these items in the interior, the exterior itself was designed by none other than the master himself, Michelangelo.

The **Palace of the Conservatori** is actually three museums in one, the **Museum of the Conservatori**, the **New Museum**, and the **Pinocoteca Capitolina**. It too was also constructed by a design from Michelangelo. Their draw to me, and most people young at heart, are the largest stone head and stone foot you're ever likely to see. A great place to take a few pictures. These pieces are supposed to be fragments from the statue of Constantine. Wouldn't that have been a sight to see?

You could wander here among the many ancient Roman and Greek scultptures and paintings but remember to see the famous *Boy with a Thorn*, a graceful Greek sculpture of a boy pulling a thorn out of his foot, the *She-Wolf of the Capitol*, an Etruscan work of Romulus and Remus being suckled by the mythical wold of Rome, the death mask bust of Michelangelo, the marble *Medusa* head by Bernini, the celebrated painting *St. Sebastian* by Guido Reni that shows the saint with arrows shot into his body, and the famous Caravaggio work, *St. John the Baptist*.

And don't forget to find *La Buca della Verita*, the mouth of truth. This is one museum you simply cannot miss while in Rome.

NATIONAL MUSEUM - MUSEUO DELLE TERME

Baths of Diocletian, Viale di Terme. Admission L2,000. Hours 9:00am–2:00pm. Sundays until 1:00pm. Closed Mondays. Catch buses 57, 64, 65, 75, 170, 492, 910.

If you like sculpture you'll love this collection of classical Greek and Roman works, as well as some early Christian sarcophagi and other bas-relief work. Located in the **Baths of Diolcletian**, which are something to see in and of themselves, this museum is easily accesible since it is located near the train station and right across from the Republicca Metro stop. Since there are so many fine works here, you should spend a good half day perusing the items, but remember to start with the best, which are located in the *Hall of Masterpieces*. Here you'll find the *Pugilist*, a bronze work of a seated boxer, and the *Discobolus*, a partial sculpture of a discus thrower with amazing muscle development.

At the turn of the century this collection was graced with the Ludovisi collection, collected by Cardinal Ludovico Ludovisi, and by a number of Roman princes. There are many fine works of art, the most inspiring of which is the the celebrated *Dying Gaul and His Wife*, a colossal sculpture from Pergamon created in the thrid century BC. The collection also contains the famous Ludovisi throne, created in the 5th century BC and is adorned with fine Greek bas-reliefs.

Another must-see in the museum is the *Great Cloister*, a perfectly square space surrounded by an arcade of one hundred Doric columns. It is one of the most beautiful achitectural spaces in Rome, which is something to say. Rumor has it that it was deisgned and built by Michelangelo in 1565, which may be the case, but since he was so busy many experts believe that it is actually the work of one of his more famous, and possibly intimate pupils, Jacopo del Duca.

Another great museum to see in Rome.

GALLERIA BORGHESE

Villa Borghese, Piazza dell'Uccelliera 5. Tel. 845–8577. Admission L4,000. Hours 9:00am–7:00pm. Holidays 9:00am–1:00pm. Closed Mondays. Catch buses 95, 490, 495, 910.

Located in the most picturesque public park in Rome, this is a gallery to visit before or after a nice picnic lunch in the shade of the many trees or by the large man-made lake in the center of the park. On the ground floor of the museum is their sculpture collection, which would be superb if not for the fact that it is located in Rome, but the main draw of this museum is the beauty of the gallery of paintings on the first floor.

Before you abandon the sculptures, take note of the reclining *Pauline Borghese*, created by Antonio Canova in 1805. She was the sister of Napoleon, married off to one of the wealthiest families in the world at the time to ensure poeace and prosperity. She looks quite enticing posing half naked on a lounge chair. Another work not to miss is *David and the Slingshot* by Bernini in 1619. It is actually a self-portrait.

On the first floor there are many great works especially the *Madonna and Child* by Bellini, *Young Lady with a Unicorn* by Raphael, *Madonna with Saints* by Lotto, and countless works by Caravaggio.

MUSEUM OF VILLA GIULIA

Piazza di Villa Giulia. Admission L8,000. Hours 9:00am–7:00pm. Holidays 9:00am–1:00pm. Closed Mondays. Catch buses 19b or 30b.

Located in the Palazzo di Villa Giulia, which was built in 1533 by Julius III. This archaeological museum contains ancient sculptures, sarcophogi, bas-reliefs, and more, and is separated into five sections consisting of 34 rooms. Items of interest include the archaic statues created in the 5th century BC of a *Centaur*, and *Man on a Marine Monster*; Estruscan clay sculptures of *Apollo*, *Hercules with a Deer*, and *Goddess with Child*; objects from the necropoli at Cervetri including a terracotta work of *Amazons with Horses* created in the 6th century BC and a sarchophagus of a "married couple," a masterpiece of Etruscan sculptur created in the 6th century BC.

VATICAN MUSEUMS

Viale Vaticano. Tel. 6988-3333. Admission L13,000. Summer hours 8:45am–1:00pm. Winter hours 9:00am–4:00pm. Saturday 9:00am–1:00pm. Closed Sundays. The last Sunday of every month they are open and entrance is free. Catch buses 19, 23, 32, 45, 51, 81, 492, 907, and 991.

Pinacoteca Vaticana

A wonderful collection of masterpieces from many periods, covering many styles all the way from primitives to modern paintings. Here you can find paintings by Giotto (who was the great innvoator of Italian painting since prior to his work Italian paintings had been Byzantine in style), many works by Raphael, the famous *Brussels Tapestries* with episodes from the Acts of the Apostles created by Pieter van Aelsten in 1516 from sketches by Raphael, and countless paintings of the Madonna, Virgin, Mother and Child, etc.

Pius Clementine Museum

Known mainly as a sculpture museum, it was founded by Pius VI and Clement XIV. You can also find mosaic work and sarcophogi from the

2nd, 3rd and 4th centuries. One mosaic in particular is worth noting, the *Battle between the Greeks and the Centaurs*, created in the first century AD. The bronze statue of Hercules and the **Hall of the Muses** that contain statues of the Muses and the partons of the arts are also worth noting. Here you can also find many busts of isslustrous Romans including Caracalla, Trajan, Octavian and more.

In the **Octagonal Court** are some of the most important and the beautiful statuies in the history of Western art, especially the *Cabinet of the Laocoon*. This statue portrays the revenge of the gods on a Trojan priest, Laocoon, who had invoked the wrath of the goids by warning his countrymen not to admit the Trojan horse. In revenge the gods sent two enormous serpents out of the sea to destroy Laocoon and his two sons.

Chiaramonti Museum

Founded by Pope Pius VII, whose family name was Chiaramonti, this museum includes a collection of over 5,000 Pagan and Christian works. Here you can find Roman Sarcophogi, *Silenus Nursing the Infant Bacchus*, busts of Caesar, the Statue of Demosthenes, the famous *Statue of the Nile* with the 16 boys representing the 16 cubits of the annual rise of the Nile, as well as a magnificent Roman chariot recreated in marble by the sculpture Franzone in 1788.

Etruscan Museum

If you can't make it to any of the necropoli around Rome, at least come here and see the relics of a civilization that preceded Ancient Rome. Founded in 1837 by Gregory XVI, it contains objects excavated in the Southern part of Etruria from 1828-1836, as well as pieces from later excavations around Rome. Here you'll find an Etruscan tomb from Cervetri, as well as bronzes, gold objects, glass work, candelbra, necklaces, rings, funeral urns, amphora and much more.

Egyptian Museum

If you can't make it to Cairo to see their splendid exhibit of material excavated from a variety of Egyptian tombs, stop in here. Created by Gregory XVI in 1839, this musem contains a valuable documentary of the art and civilization of ancient Egypt.

Here you will find sarcophogi, reproductions of portraits of famous Egyptian personalities, works by Roman artists who were inspired by Egyptian art, a collection of wooden mummy cases and funeral steles, mummies of animals, a collection of papyri with hieroglyphics, and much more.

Library of the Vatican

Founded through the efforts and collections of many Popes, this museum contains many documents and incunabula. Today the library contains over 500,000 volumes, 60,000 ancient manuscripts, and 7,000 incunabuli. My favorite are the precious manuscripts, especially the *Codex Vaticanus B* or the 4th century Bible in Greek.

Appartamento Borgia

Named after Pope Alexander VI, whose family name was Borgia, since he designed and lived in these lavish surroundings. (What about that vow of poverty?) From the furnishings to the paintings to the frescoes of Isis and Osiris on the ceiling, this little "museum" is worth a look.

Sistine Chapel

This is the private chapel of the Popes but it is famous for some of the most wonderful masterpieces ever created, many by **Michelangelo** himself. Michelangelo started the ceiling in 1508 and it took him four years to finish it. On the ceiling you'll find scenes from the Bible, among them the *Creation*, where God comes near Adam, who is lying down, and with a simple touch of his hand imparts the magic spark of life. You can aslo see the *Separation of Light and Darkness*, the *Creation of the Sun and Moon*, *Creation of Trees and Plants*, *Creation of Adam*, *Creation of Eve*, *The Fall and the Expulsion from Paradise*, the *Sacrifice of Noah and his Family* and the *Deluge*.

But on the wall behind the altar is the great fresco of the *Last Judgment* by Michelangelo. It occupies the entire wall (20 meters by 10 meters) and was commissioned by Clement VII. Michelangelo was past 60 when he started the project in 1535. He completed it seven years later in 1542. Michelangelo painted people he didn't like into situations with evil connotation in this frescoe. The figure of Mides, with asses' ears, is the likeness of the Master of Ceremonies of Paul III, who first suggested that other painters cover Michelangelo's nude figures. This eventually was done by order of Pius IV, who had Daniele da Volterra cover the most prominent figures with cloth. These changes were left in when the entire chapel underwent its marvelous transformation a few years back, bringing out the vibrant colors of the original frescoes that had been covered by centuries of dirt and soot.

Rooms of Raphael

Initially these rooms were decorated with the works of many artists of the 15th century, but because Pope Julius II loved the work of Raphael so much, he had the other paintings destroyed and commissioned Raphael to paint the entire room himself. He did so, but spent the rest of his life in the task. Not nearly as stupendous as the Sistine Chapel work by Michelangelo, but it still is one of the world's masterpieces.

Chapel of Nicholas V

Decorated with frescoes from 1448-1451 by Giovanni da Fiesole. The works represent scenes from the life of Saint Stephan in the upper portion and Saint Lawrence in the lower.

The Loggia of Raphael

Divided into 13 arcades with 48 scenes from the Old and New Testaments, these were executed from the designs of Raphael by his students, Giulo Romano, Perin del Vaga, and F. Penni. The most outstanding to see are the *Creation of the World, Creation of Eve, The Deluge, Jacob's Dream, Moses Receiving the Tablets of Law, King David*, and the *Birth of Jesus*.

Grotte Vaticano

The Vatican caves seem to be a well-kept secret even though they've been around for some time. I think that's because you need special permission to enter them, and if you haven't made plans prior to your arrival it is quite difficult to gain access at short notice. To gain permission you need to contact the **North American College** in Rome *(Via dell'Umita 30, Tel. 672-256 or 678-9184)*. The entrance to the Grotte is to the left of the basilica of St Peter's where the Swiss Guards are posted. The Grotte were dug out of the stratum between the floor of the actual cathedral and the previous Basilica of Constantine. This layer was first excavated during the Rennaissance. After passing fragments of inscriptions and mosaic compositions, tombstones, and sarcophogi, you descend a steep staircase to get to the Lower Grottos, also called the **Grotte Vecchie** (the Old Grottos).

Here you'll find pagan and Christian necropoli dating from the 2nd and 3rd century. The Grotte are divided into three naves seperated by massive pilasters that support the floor of St. Peter's above. Along the walls are numerous tombs of popes and altars adorned with mosaics and sculputes. At the altar is the entrance to the **Grotte Nuove** (New Grottos), with its frescoed walls, marble statues, and bas-reliefs.

MUSEO DELLA CIVILITA ROMANA

Get off at the EUR stop on the Metro.

Always wanted to see a scale model of ancient Rome? If so, a perfect replica of Rome during the height of empire in the 4th century BC is in the **Museum of Roman Civilization** in EUR. This piece, called *Plastico*, is an exquisitely detailed plaster model that brings ancient Rome to life.

Even if you are not a museum person, this exhibit is well worth seeing. Ideal for kids of all ages.

WALKING TOUR OF MICHELANGELO'S ROME

Even though he was Tuscan born and bred, and is still considered Florence's native son. Rome helped develop **Michelangelo Buonarotti** into the world's greatest artist, and in Rome he spent most of his adult life. Michelangelo specialized in four distinct art forms – sculpture, painting, architecture, and poetry. Rome at that time was a run-down faded city, but it was where Michelangelo became the wonder of his time, and the master of all ages.

The Fabric of Rome in the Mid-Fifteenth Century

At the age of 21, in June 1436, Michelangelo Buonarotti arrived in the city of Rome. The contrasts between Rome, a dirty, noisy, chaotic place, practically in a state of complete disrepair, and Florence, where order, reason, and beauty were cherished and cultivated, were immense. Many tourists today still consider this to be true.

This once vast city had turned to pasture lands outside the Roman walls. Sheep grazed among the ruins of ancient Rome, and the population, which had shrunk to a mere 50,000 from its height of over 1 million inhabitants, was beset with disease and a lack of potable water. But even in this setting Michelangelo blossomed, and Rome is where he created many of his most memorable masterpieces. Uncovering these works from the many corners of Rome can be the highlight of any trip to Italy, and I've laid it out for you in a special walking tour of Michelangelo's Rome.

The Search

For most people, the **Vatican** and **St. Peter's** offer the extent of Michelangelo's influence on Rome. But Vatican City holds just the beginning of the fabric Michelangelo wove into the tapestry of Roman life. It is true that nothing yet conceived can rival the magnificence of the **Sistine Chapel**, which is dominated by Michelangelo's powerful ceiling, made even more so by the recent cleaning that again allow the colors to jump out at you. And you also shouldn't miss the apocalyptic *Last Judgment*, located on the immense wall above the main altar. Every time I return to Rome I visit these two masterpieces to reassure myself that their beauty is not just a figment of my imagination.

These two works seem to epitomize the contrasts of Michelangelo's long career, which seems to coincide with the rise and fall of the Renaissance itself. The *Last Judgment*, begun when Michelangelo was in his 60's, marks the end of his life's work, and the Renaissance's magnificence, while the glorious Sistine ceiling commemorates the peak of excellence.

These two works, coupled with *La Pieta*, located just to the right of the entrance inside St. Peter's, completes for most visitors to Rome the extent of Michelangelo's influence on the Eternal City. Remember to wear long pants, men, otherwise the Vatican guards will not allow you entrance into St. Peter's. By the way, this holds true for most, if not all, monuments and museums in Rome.

Other Works

Michelangelo's Roman tapestry spreads over the entire city. To attempt to see every piece of Michelangelo's work would be virtually impossible, therefore we cover only the most important pieces in this little tour. Get your walking shoes on.

To begin, return to the Vatican, to the art works overlooked by most. The **Vatican Museum** houses two definite musts for any Italian expert and lover. The beautiful sculpture *Apollo Belvedere* should be viewed even if you will be visiting, or have seen, the godlike *David* in Florence. The Apollo's importance stems from the fact that it was Michelangelo's inspiration for his ageless *David*.

Palazzo Farnese

To get to our next destination, cross the **Ponte Vittorio Emmanuelle** and walk down the Corso Vittorio Emmanuelle on the right hand side. Follow this street, then turn into **Campo dei Fiori** after you pass the Palazzo Della Cancelleria. The Campo dei Fiori was once the site of brutal executions, but now is the home to a beautiful open air market every morning.

Walk through the Campo dei Fiori and you'll find the **Palazzo Farnese** at the other end. Situated in one of Rome's most picturesque quarters, the Palazzo Farnese is one of the most unexplored examples of Michelangelo's work, since it now houses the French Embassy.

The Palazzo was begun in 1514 by Antonio Sangano, The Younger, and was then passed onto Michelangelo's creative genius and imagination to develop the finishing touches. Just prior to overall completion, Michelangelo handed over the reins of design to Giacamo Della Porta, but many of the master's inclusions were left untouched. The most apparent Michelangelo marks are the pieces above the main doorway, but if you have any diplomatic pull (possibly a brother or cousin who happens to be a US Senator) or more realistically try to get a note from your Congressman, you should be able to get yourself inside to see the elegant third floor. A bribe to the French won't help, incidentally, since the French government rents this exquisite building for the incredible fee of only 1 lira a year.

Since it is hard to get inside, go around the left of the building to the **Arch of the Palazzo Farnese** over Via Guilia. This bridge was designed by Michelangelo and connects the Piazza Farnese with its satellite houses that were originally on the river's edge, but now are restricted by the high walls and roadway of the Lungotevere. Michelangelo's plan had been to connect the Palazzo Farnese with its cousin in Trastevere, the Villa Farnesina, by a private bridge. Unfortunately for the French, and the rest of us, the bridge was never built.

On to the Piazza Navona

From here stroll through the aforementioned Campo dei Fiori, across the Via Vittorio Emmanuelle II, onto the small Via Cuccogno and into the elegant **Piazza Navona**. On a hot day, the fountains here are a visitor's oasis, allowing for needed foot-soaking refreshment. But before you take your shoes off and relax your sore feet by soaking them in one of the fountains, stroll to the center of the piazza and take note of the magnificence of **Bernini's Fontana Dei Quattro Fiumi** (Fountain of four Rivers). The fours figures supporting the large obelisk (a Bernini trademark) represent four rivers, the Danube, the Ganges, the Nile and the Plata Rivers; see the story behind this statue in the *Piazza Navona* section above.

Even though this has close to nothing to do with Michelangelo, it is one of the many pieces of Roman history intertwined almost inconspicuously with its present. And it's a good place for a refreshing break. Try the *gelato* (ice cream) at the small *gelateria* a few paces down the small unnamed road to the left of **Le Tre Scalini**, one of Rome's best attractions. True, the *gelato* at Le Tre Scalini is also good, if you are willing to pay an exorbitant price for a small scoop. That's why it's wise to simply walk down the road to a smaller, better, less expensive gelato place. With ice cream in hand you can sit in the piazza, soak your feet if you wish, and partake in the Roman tradition of people watching.

Santa Maria Sopra Minerva

The last stop on today's *passegiatta* involves a short walk to the **Piazza Della Minerva** and the church of **Santa Maria Sopra Minerva**. To get there, leave the Piazza Navona via the exit directly across from Le Tre Scalini. As you exit, bear to your left and go down the Via di Crescene to the piazza directly in front of the imposing **Pantheon**. If you haven't seen the Pantheon yet, stay awhile and go inside. It's a beautiful sight and pleasantly cool in the interior. The Piazza Della Minerva is around the left of the Pantheon.

Santa Maria Sopra Minerva is a combination of an early Renaissance exterior and an austere Gothic interior. Besides displaying splendid frescoes by Fillipino Lippi and elaborate marble tombstones made by Michelangelo of two Medici popes (Leo X and Clement VII, who played large roles in the sculptor's life), the masterpiece of the church to the left of the main altar is Michelangelo's *Christ Bearing the Cross*. This obviously spiritual sculpture epitomizes how much the church meant to Michelangelo, even though some historians claim he was a closet homosexual.

More Buried Treasure

The next day's itinerary is much shorter and begins at the church of **San Pietro in Vincolo** near the Cavour Metro stop. Here you can admire Michelangelo's glowering, biblical figure *Moses*, which emphatically demonstrates the qualities of excellence, perfection, and intensity that make Michelangelo's works so memorable.

From here, grab the Metro at Cavour and take it to Termini. From Termini transfer to Linea A and go one stop to Repubblica. In the **Piazza della Repubblica** is the church of **Santa Maria Degli Angeli**, whose interior was created by Michelangelo out of the ruins of the enormous **Diocletian Baths**. Even though the interior was modified in the 18th century, Michelangelo's creative transformation is still very apparent.

The monumental task of reconstructing a church's interior contrasts well with our next stop, a virtually unknown and infinitely smaller creation. Go up the Via VE Orlando to the **Piazza San Bernardo**, where you'll find the national Catholic church of Americans in Italy, **Santa Susanna**. Its baroque exterior and interior, rich paintings, stucco work, and ornaments has played host to many a visiting American dignitary, with OJ Simpson and George Wallace balancing out the spectrum. (I got both their autographs when they were visiting. I think OJ's might be worth something now.) Also, in case you were paying attention, as we go through the Piazza San Bernardo, there is a copy of the figure *Moses* we just saw.

The paintings inside Santa Susanna's, though created many years after the life of Michelangelo, and have nothing to do with this tour except to show you some more of Rome's glory, are exquisitely beautiful and can be fully enjoyed with the realization that many casual visitors to Rome never witness their grandeur. What we came to see is not these paintings, but the small **well** in the adjacent courtyard. Surrounded by what was once the convent of the sisters of San Bernardo, this well is one of the smaller threads of Michelangelo's tapestry in Rome. The architrave (main form and structure) and pilaster (rectangular column work on the well) were created by the master himself. And to think that after Mass every other Sunday, we the parishioners of Santa Susanna would congregate here for coffee and donuts. Isn't Rome magnificent?

Well, that's the last stop. As you can see, Michelangelo's works spread like a tapestry over all of Rome. I hope you enjoyed finding them. If you find others along the way, please send me your information.

NIGHTLIFE & ENTERTAINMENT

Rome is filled with many discos, pubs, and *birrerias* (bars) where you can spend your evening hours having wild and raucous times. If that's what you want to do, I've compiled a list of the best places to go. But if you want to do like (most of) the Romans do, seat yourself at a bar/café or restaurant, and savor the beauty that is Rome. Linger in the evening air while recalling the day's events or planning tomorrow's. Slow down your pace. Adapt to the culture. Be one with the Force, and so on. You get the picture.

Anyway, there are a few places in Rome in which you can do just that, become part of the culture. The best is in **Trastevere** at one of the little open air cafés where you can either stay all night sipping a few glasses of wine, or visit after you've had your dinner in one of the restaurants around the piazza (see Trastevere, *Where to Eat*). This is definitely THE best place to go for a night out in Rome.

Another is **Campo dei Fiori**, which also has many cafés and restaurants where you can sit while you watch the life of Rome amble past. The other nightspot is around **Piazza Navona**, of course, where you can admire the fine sculpture, the beautiful people, and the many different life forms comprising the streetlife of Rome.

But if this sedate, appreciative, slow-paced lifestyle is not for your, by all means try one of the following. I found them all perfect for letting off some steam.

Bars & Clubs

JACKIE O, *11 Via Bon Compagni, Tel. 06/488-5457.*

This place has been famous for years and the fact that it is located just off the Via Veneto makes their prices sky high. The place is a combination, in three different areas, of a piano bar, a disco, and restaurant, so conceivably you can go to dinner, grab an after dinner drink, then dance the night away at the same place. It claims to be Rome's most prestigious and best loved nightclub, with members of the jet set visiting whenever they're in Rome, and from the atmosphere I can see why. Besides the high class but bawdy decor, you can expect discreet and professional service while at Jackie O's.

BIRRERIA LOWENBRAU MUNCHEN, *Via delle Croce 21, Tel. 06/ 679-5569.*

You can eat here if the need for Viennese cuisine creeps up on your stomach (you'll find plenty of German tourists here enjoying the staples from their homeland), but I find it's a perfect place to have the best German beer on tap. It's a festive place to throw down a few pints with your travel partners. They serve their large beers in glass boots which adds to the charm of this *birreria*. In conjunction you're in one of the best nighttime areas in Rome, around the Piazza di Spagna, where you can go for a casual stroll before or after your drinking adventure.

FLAN O'BRIEN'S PUB, *Via Napoli 29/34. Tel. 06/488-0418. Pints L8,000, Half Pints L5,000, Panini L4,000. Open all day from 9:00am to 1:00am.*

There's a café/bar store front on Via Nazionale, but this place is in the back on Via Napoli. Run by Italians, but has the look and feel of a real Irish pub. Definitely not of the same ilk as the one I know by the same name in Boston, since that one is a hole in the wall.

There are two bars, both serving Harp Lager and Stout, Kilkeny, and Guiness on tap. The menu is relatively meager but you can get a *Panino* (sandwich) of ham and cheese, which is good. All wood decor, a little brightly lit, with polished brass fitting, framed pictures of vaguely Irish origin, and stained glass and floral pattern wallpaper. There are tables and plenty of places to pull up a stool, and they play great music by which to enjoy a pint or two. The Hotel Britania just across the street contributes to the flow of people that can truly appreciate its ambiance. It gets fairly crowded on Friday and Saturday nights.

NED KELLY'S, *Via delle Copelle 13. Pints L8,000, Half pints L5,000. Open 12:30am - 3:30pm and 6:00pm - 1:00am.*

As you guessed, this is an Aussie pub. At lunch they serve amazing salads with a beer and mineral water for only L10,000-15,000. If you're a foreign student you get discounts in the evening by buying a membership card for the night, for only L2,000. You'll save that on your first pint. For all of you who know and love the camaraderie and festivities associated with Australian people, you'll want to check this place out. It's located near the Pantheon, so it's in the center of everything and very hard to miss.

THE TUBE PUB, *Via Avignonesi 10A. Pints L8,000. Half Pints L5,000.*

A real hole in the wall – actually a real bottom of the basement. Located just off the Piazza Barberini in the basement of a building down this dark and dingy street, this place has a lot of character and a dart board to boot. Two separate areas, one near the bar with booths which is frequented by the younger set, and the other with tables frequented by many ex-pats from abroad living in Rome.

NIGHT AND DAY, *Via dell'Oca 50. Pints L8,000. Half Pints L5,000. Open until 5am.*

Yes, it's open until 5am, so put your drinking hat on. They also serve a lovely lunch from 12:30pm until 3:30pm with great salads and shepherd pies. You'll find your Guiness on tap for strength, as well as a nice assortment of local Frascati wines graciously served to you by the owners Stefano and Simone.

FIDDLER'S ELBOW, *Via dell'Olmata 43. Tel. 06/487-2110. Open 7 days a week 4:30pm - 1:15am. Pints L8,000 Half Pints L5,000.*

Located just off the Piazza Santa Maria Maggiore near the train station, this place claims to be Rome's oldest pub, and it sure looks like it. That slightly ratty ambiance helps to give it a truly Irish flavor. The Guiness helps too, as do the crowds of Anglophones. So if you're looking for a taste of home, or just want to hear another English speaking person, "come on down." No food is actually served so if you're hungry you'll have to make do with chips, peanuts, or salami sticks. They also have places in Florence and Venice, so you can have a pint at the "Elbow" throughout Italy.

OLD MARCONI, *Via Santa Prassese 9c, 00184 Roma. Tel. 06/486-636. Open until 1:30am.*

Located near it's brother pub, The Fiddler's Elbow, this one serves fine English fare like fish and chips. You'll find Guiness, Harp, and Kilkeny on tap (pint L7,000, half-pint L4,000), and pleasant company all around. This and Fiddler's are the main hangout for Anglo's in the city, but they'll accommodate a Yank if you've got a sense of humor.

BIRRERIA TRILUSSA, *Via Aruleno Cello Sabino 29P, Tel. 06/7154-2180. Pints L8,000. Half Pints L5,000.*

Located a stone's throw away from the Campo dei Fiori, you can see a few shady characters in here, but all are having fun. So if you want a little adventure, and desire to be a part of the in-crowd in Rome, give this place a try. (But do not buy anything illegal from anyone in there, no matter how nicely they offer. The laws are very strict in Italy, i.e. incarceration for many months before you even go to trial. Here you're guilty until proven innocent). That being said, have a pint for me.

THE DRUNKEN SHIP, *Campo de' Fiori 20/21, Tel. 06/6830-0535. Open 10am - 2:00am. Pints of Guiness, Harp, Kilkenny L6,000.*

Located in one of Rome's best piazzas for night life, the Campo dei Fiori. This is in the opinion of many the only real Irish bar in town. The place has European style and plays American music. The "frat boy types" in the crowd will love their Jello shots and cute American female bartenders. The decor is dark wood and the whole place has slight tilt to it befitting, I suppose, a drunken ship. No outside seating but the inside is fun enough. In the evening, every evening, this little piazza fills up with quite a few counterculture Italians and ex-pats. A fun place to be.

PIPER 90, *Via Taglimanento 9, Tel 06/841-4459 or 06/855-5398.*

This place only really gets going on the weekends with its video screens, live bands, and rockin' DJs. A place to really let your hair own, your body drench with sweat, and your money flow like water.

RADIO LONDRA, *Via di Monte Testaccio. No telephone ... how chique can you get.*

Recommended to me by a wine importer friend, who said it was wild. Well, he was way off base. It's totally insane, and crowded, and loud, and completely out of this world. You have segments of all parts of society here, making for a complete viewing pleasure. If the goings-on inside the inferno gets too hot, you can always sojourn to one of the tables on the terrace. A great place to meet other single people, not necessarily tourists.

Movies in English

Look for listings for both of these in local papers or contact each cinema for a list of movies.

PASQUINO, *Vicolo del Piedo 19A, Tel. 06/580-3622.*

Located just off the Piazza Santa Maria in Trastevere, this is the only true English language cinema in Rome since this is all they show. So if you are in need of a little touch of back home, come here and enjoy. Beware of the changing of the reels in inclement weather. Since there is only one projector, they have to change reels when one ends, and when they do they usually open the skylight roof and sometimes forget it's pouring outside.

Despite the possibility of a drenching by coming to the Pasquino, you will probably witness the last remaining true intermission, complete with intermission girls walking around selling popcorn, candy, and ice cream anywhere I've found in the Western World.

ALCATRAZ, *Piazza Merry del Val, Tel 06/588-0099.*

They show English language films that have not been dubbed, but since they also show French, German, Indian, and other films in their original language, they are really a multilingual cinema.

SPORTS & RECREATION

There are many different sporting activities to participate in and around Rome, since the city is only 15 miles from the beach and 65 miles from great skiing country. Below is a list of possible activities:

Amusement Park

For people with a lot of money in their pockets, there is a permanent amusement park, **Luna Park**, in EUR. To get there take the Metropolitana on Linea B to the EUR stop. EUR stands for *Esposizione Universale Romana*, a grandiose project sponsored by Mussolini as a permanent exhibition to the glory of Rome. The park is to your left as you enter EUR along the Via Cristoforo Colombo.

Bicycling

Reckless Roman drivers can make biking on the city streets dangerous if you're not careful, and especially if you're a young North American used to the defensive drivers in the States and Canada.

But you can rent bicycles at many different locations (see *Getting Around Town*) and take them for a trip through the **Borghese Gardens** (see *Seeing the Sights*, above).

Boating

Rowboats can be rented at the **Giardino del Lago** in the Villa Borghese. You can also rent dinghies at **Lago di Bracciano** and **Lido di Ostia** (see *Day Trips & Excursions* below).

Bowling

There are two particularly good bowling alleys *(bocciodromi)* in Rome. Unless you have your own car, both of these places are far outside of the old walls of the city and thus rather difficult to get to except by taxi.
• **Bowling Brunswick**, *Lungotevere Aqua Acetosa, Tel. 396-6696,* and
• **Bowling Roma**, *Viale Regina Margherita 181, Tel. 861-184.*

Golf

There are a variety of 18 hole and 9 hole courses all around Rome:
• **L'Eucalyptus Circolo del Golf**, *Via della Cogna 3/5, 04011 Aprilla. Tel. 06/926-252. Fax 06/926-8502.* Located 30 km from Rome, this is an 18 hole par 72 course that is 6,372 meters long. It is open all year except on Tuesdays. They also have a small executive course, driving range, pro shop, tennis courts, swimming pool, guest quarters, and a restaurant/bar.
• **Golf Club Torvalaianica**, *Via Enna 30, 00040 Marina di Ardea. Tel. 06/ 913-3250. Fax 06/913-3592.* Located 25 km from Rome this is a 9 hole par 31 course that is 2,208 meters long. It is open all year except Mondays. They have a driving range as well as a restaurant/bar.
• **Golf Club Castel gandolpho**, *Via Santo Spirito 13, 00040 Castelgandolpho. Tel. 06/931-2301. Fax 06/931-2244.* This is an 18 hole par 72 course near the Pope's summer residence that is 5,855 meters long. It's open all year except on Mondays. They have a driving range, carts, pro shop, swimming pool, and a restaurant/bar.
• **Circolo del Golf di Fioranello**, *Via della Falcognana 61, 00134 Roma. Tel. 06/713-8080 or 731-2213. Fax 06/713-8212.* Located 17 km from the center of Rome, this is an 18 hole par 70 course that is 5,417 meters long. It is open a year except for Wednesdays. They also have a driving range, pro shop, swimming pool, and a bar/restaurant.

- **Macro Simone Golf Club**, *Via di Marco Simone, 00012 Guidonia. Tel. 0774/370-469. Fax 0774/370-476.* Located 17 km from Rome, this is an 18 hole par 72 course that is 6,360 meters long. It is open all year except for Tuesdays. They also have an 18 hole executive course, driving range, pro shop, swimming pool, tennis courts, massage room, sauna, gymnasium, and an excellent restaurant and bar.
- **Golf Club Parco de' Medici**, *Viale Parco de' Medici 20, 00148 Roma. Tel. 06/655-33477. Fax 06/655-3344.* Located 10 km outside of the city center, this is an 18 hole par 72 course that is 5,827 meters long. It is open all year except on Tuesdays. They also have a driving range, swimming pool, tennis courts, and a restaurant/bar. This is the course most accessible and nearest the city center.
- **Circolo del Golf di Roma – Acqua Santa**, *Via Appia Nuova 716 or Via Dell'Aquasanta 3, Roma 00178, Tel. 06/780-3407. Fax 06/7834-6219.* Located 11 km from Rome, this is an 18 hole par 71 course that is 5,825 meters long. It is open all year except on Mondays. They have a driving range, putting green, swimming pool, and a restaurant/bar.
- **Olgiata**, *Largo Olgiata 15, Roma 00123, Tel. 06/378-9141. Fax 06/378-9968.* Located 19 km from the center of Rome, in a housing development similar to many golf courses in the U.S. At Olgiata there is an 18 hole par 72 course that is 6,396 meters long and a 9 hole par 34 course that is 2,968 meters long. The course is open all year except on Mondays. They have a driving range, pro shop, swimming pool and a bar/restaurant.

River Trips

In July and August you can take a river trip through central Rome. The trips are organized by the **Amici del Tevere**. Check the journal *This Week in Rome* for details, available in most hotels.

Swimming

The major outdoor pool in Rome is at the **Foro Italico** (*Tel. 396-3958*), open June to September. An indoor pool at the Foro Italico is open November to May.

The best beach is at **Lido di Ostia**, less than an hour west-northwest of Rome. The beaches are clean and large. They have plenty of *cabanas* to rent where you can change you clothes, and there are some excellent seafood restaurants where you can leisurely eat, sip wine, and enjoy the beautiful Italian summers.

Tennis

The following public courts require reservations:

• **Circolo Montecitorio**, *Via Campi Sportivi 5, Tel. 875-275*
• **EUR**, *Viale dell'Artigianato 2, Tel. 592-4693*
• **Foro Italico**, *Tel. 361-9021*
• **Tennis Belle Arti**, *Via Flaminia 158, Tel. 360-0602*

SHOPPING

Because the very best of Italian design and craftsmanship are conveniently located in one small area, Rome is one of the finest shopping cities in the world. You can find beautifully made items made from the very best material, and as such this is not the place to look around for cut-price bargains. Leather and silk goods predominate, but Rome is also an important location for jewelry, antiques and general top of the line *pret-a-porte* (ready to wear) fashion.

ITALIAN DEPARMENT STORES

It's always fun to go to supermarkets and department stores in other countries to see what the natives like. Even if you don't buy anything, it's still fun to browse and not be followed around the store, as you would in one of the smaller boutiques by one of the vulture-like owners or staff. Both STANDA and UPIM are designed for the Italian on a budget, while Rinascente is a little more chic.

STANDA, Viale di Trastevere 60 and Via Cola di Rienzo 173.

Italy's largest food market, the perfect place to find that food product to bring back to the States with you. Since most of their stuff is vacuum sealed and pre-packaged you should not have any problems with customs. Standa also has a large selection of housewares and clothing. This is the combined K Mart and Safeway of Italy, with slightly better quality products.

UPIM, Via Nazionale 111, Piazza Santa Maria Maggiore and Via del Tritone 172.

This department store is just like STANDA, except without the food.

LA RINASCENTE, Piazza Colonna on the Via del Corso and Piazza Fiume.

This is much more upscale than the other two and has about the same prices as boutiques, and even has some of the vultures hanging around too.

The main shopping area is a network of small and large streets containing the famous **Via Condotti**. The shopping area boundaries extend over to **Via della Croce** in the north to **Via Frattina** in the nouth, and **Via del Corso** in the west to **Piazza di Spagna** in the east.

Romans, like other Italians, prefer to shop in boutiques, and the Via Condotti area has these quaint little shops selling everything from shirts to gloves. This specialization originates in the craft shops from which the smart shopping village has grown, and generally ensures top quality and personal service. In Italy, **department stores** are the exception rather than the rule, but in this shopping area there are some that warrant a look, like **La Rinascente**, **Standa**, **Upim**, and **Coin**.

To get the instant smile and respect you expect when you shop in most stores in America, you may have to dress the part here in Italy. It's not like in the malls back home where it doesn't matter how you dress; here in Rome the wealthier you look the better assistance you'll get. Unfortunately as tourists we usually leave our best attire back home, but try the best you can. Shorts and tank tops usually will get you no respect at all, particularly if you're shopping on the Via Condotti and Via Borgognona. This holds true, and I can vouch for this personally, if you're shopping on some of the parallel streets like Via Frattina, some of the little cross-streets, and even in Piazza di Spagna or Via del Babuino.

SHOPPING STREETS

Top of the Line Shopping – Via Condotti, Via Borgognona, Via Bocca di Leone

Middle Range Fashion – Via Nazionale, Via del Corso, Via Cola di Rienzo, Via del Tritone, and Via Giubbonari

Antiques – Via del Babuino, Via Guilia, Via dei Coronari.

Food Stores – Via del Croce

Inexpensive Shoes – Fontana di Trevi area

Leather goods and apparel – Via due Macelli, Via Franscesco Crispi

Straw and Wicker Products – Via dei Deiari, Via del Teatro Valle

---

Other shopping districts are less formal, and many of these are worth investigating if you have time, for here is where you'll find the real bargains. **Via del Tritone** and the streets around the **Trevi Fountain**, **Via Cola di Rienzo** across the Tiber and north of the Vatican, **Piazza San Lorenzo** in Lucina and the streets around **Piazza Campo dei Fiori** are all areas where you will find cheaper leather bags and shoes. **Via Veneto** also has more of an international flavor, but boy, is it expensive.

Besides these areas, Rome also has many colorful street markets offering a vast selection of top quality fruit, flowers, vegetables, prosciutto, salami, cheeses, meat and fish, as well as cheap (that's inexpensive and sometimes just plain cheap) clothes. Because of this proliferation of shops and markets, and the Italian penchant for shopping in them, there are few department stores or supermarkets in the city center.

Straight bargaining is an accepted practice in clothes markets, but elsewhere transactions are conducted in a more roundabout way. At food stalls, cheeses and other weighed items have *prezzi fissi* (fixed prices), and in nearly all clothes shops, you can try asking for a *sconto* (discount). Reasons for meriting a *sconto* may be numerous – buying two articles at once is a good example – but if you are bold you will ask for a *sconto* for no good reason at all, and will usually get one. This practice applies to all but the very grandest of shops.

Surprisingly few shopkeepers speak English, but in the larger shops there is usually one person on hand who understands enough to be able to help you. Try to get your shopping done in the morning hours, when the stores are not so busy. At night, traditionally when Italians shop, it is so crowded it is difficult to get assistance.

Antiques

Today, the typical Roman antique can be either a precious Roman artifact or pieces in the baroque and neoclassical style. There are also many French and English antiques masquerading as Italian. One thing that they all have in common is that they are extremely expensive.

The best antique shops in Rome can be found in the **Via del Babuino** and the **Via Margutta**. Other shops can be found on the **Via dei Coronari**, and the **Via Guila**. And don't forget to check out the **Porta Portese** Sunday market *(open 6:30am–2:30pm)*. You'll find some interesting and inexpensive antiques there.

Outdoor Markets

Many natives buy their vegetables, fruits, flowers, meats and cheeses from one of the many street markets held daily all over the city. Stalls of inexpensive clothing are also available, but there are whole markets devoted specifically to clothing. The food and flower markets are the best, and I advise you not to miss the opportunity to wander through one in the mornings, since they are usually closed in the afternoons.

Here are some of the better markets:

Campo dei Fiori, *Piazza Campo dei Fiori. Open 6am–2pm. Closed Sunday.*

Rome's oldest market held in the cobblestoned square in the center of Rome's old medieval city. You can buy flowers (the name Campo dei Fiori means fields of flowers), fruits and vegetables, all delicately presented under makeshift awnings or giant umbrellas. Surrounding the square are some *Alimentaris* where you can pick up cold cuts, cheeses, and bread for picnics.

Piazza Vittorio Emmanuele, *Open 7am–2pm. Closed Sundays.*

Stretching all the way around this large piazza is the city's largest market. Clothes and leather goods are displayed along the south side, with some fine bargains to be found. The food stalls on the north side are known by their specialization: one stall will sell only fresh tuna, another calves livers, another tangerines. The crowing of the cocks and scuttling of crabs really adds to the atmosphere of this market. You can find some very unusual food in these stalls as well as some exquisite cheeses and salamis.

Porta Portese, *Ponte Sublico. Open 6:30am–2:30pm, Sundays only.*

This flea market stretches along the Tiber from Ponte Sublico (where the Porta Portese is) in the north to the Ponte Testaccio in the south. That's basically south of Trastevere along the river and not even on most maps, but tell a cab driver where you're going and he'll know. The clothes and accessories are inexpensive but of cheap quality, as befits most flea markets. This is a true Roman market and not many tourists venture here, but it's safe, and if you like flea markets, a whole lot of fun.

Via Andrea Doria, *Open 8am–1pm. Closed Sundays and Mondays.*

Filling almost the entire length of the Via Andrea Doria, as well as spilling into many side streets, this is a large and lively food market. The stalls are laid out in artistic arrangements to attract buyers. You can find strings of onions, cheeses, bottled oils, salamis, sausages, cheeses, etc. all laid out perfectly for the customer.

Via Sannio, *Open Monday through Friday 8am–1pm, Sat 8am–7pm. Closed Sundays.*

Most of these clothes sellers move their wares to the Porta Portese on Sundays, so if you can't make it there try to make it here. To get here by Metro, go two stops past the Piazza Vittorio Emmanuele.

Mercato de Stampe, *Piazza Fontanella Borghese, Monday–Saturday 9:00am–6:00pm.*

A small outdoor market based at the end of the square that specializes in old prints, stamps, postcards, assorted books, and knickknacks that could be considered antiques. The prices tend to be high, especially if you're pegged as a tourist, so bargaining is essential.

Bookstores with English Language Titles

American Book Shop, *Via della Vite 27 & 57, Tel. 583-6942. American Express, Diners Club, Mastercard and Visa accepted. Open Monday 4:00pm–8:00pm, Tuesday–Saturday 10:00am–1:00pm and 3:30pm–7:30pm.*

A small English-language only new bookstore that has almost everything you could want. It's a little pricy but that's to be expected.

Ancora Book Shop, *Via della Conciliazione 63, Tel. 656-8820. American Express, Diners Club, Mastercard and Visa accepted. Monday-Friday 9:00am–1:00pm, and 3:30pm–7:30pm. Saturdays 9:00am–1:00pm.*

Mainly a Catholic religious bookstore, but they have English language titles upstairs as well as a good selection of travel guides.

Anglo-American Bookstore, *Via delle Vite 102. Tel. 06/679-5222. Credit cards accepted. Monday–Friday 9:00am–1:00pm, and 3:30pm–7:30pm. Saturdays 9:00am–1:00pm.*

Located between the Spanish Steps and the Trevi Fountain, this bookstore caters to all manner of bibliophiles and computer nerds too. As well as a full selection of travel books, paperbacks, history books, etc. They have a multimedia computer center too.

The Corner Bookshop, *Via del Moro 48, Tel. 583-6942. Mastercard and Visa accepted. Open Monday 3:30pm–7:30pm, Tuesday–Saturday 10:00am–1:00pm and 3:30pm–7:30pm.*

Located in Trastevere, this is a relatively new bookstore featuring English-language titles exclusively. Owned by the very knowledgeable, helpful, and friendly Claire Hammond, you can almost always find what you want. They're stocked with hardbacks, paperbacks in non-fiction, fiction, general interest and more. A great place to meet other ex-pats or fellow travelers. Say hello to Claire for me when you see her.

Economy Bookstore and Video Center, *Via Torino 136, Tel. 474-6877. Credit cards accepted. Monday 3:00pm–7:30pm, Tuesday–Saturday 10:00am–1:00pm and 3:30pm–7:30pm.*

The best place to find a novel in English, and now they rent movies too. This mainstay of the English-speaking community for the past three decades has recently moved from Piazza di Spagna to this new location (I almost didn't find it again). They buy and sell second-hand English language paperbacks and have an excellent selection of both new and used books, including everything from fiction to non-fiction, children's, science fiction, best sellers and mysteries. They also carry a complete range of guide books on Rome and Italy.

Lion Bookshop, *Via del Babuino 181, Tel. 360-5837. Credit cards accepted.*

This is the largest English-speaking bookstore for new books. Has a definite Anglo bent to it, while the Economy Bookstore is more for people from across the pond. Since the Economy Bookstore has recently left its abode at the Spanish Steps for a much larger location near the Train station, this is the best English language bookstore in Rome's prime tourist area.

Libreria Internazionale Rizzolo, *Largo Chigi 15, Tel. 679-6641. Credit cards accepted.*

The largest store of Italy's largest bookstore chain. It has a great selection of artistic and cultural books. On the ground floor and in the basement there is also an adequate selection of guidebooks and paperbacks in English.

Newspapers

The *International Herald Tribune* is published jointly by the Washington Post and The New York Times and printed in Bologna for distribution throughout Italy. You can also find a condensed version of *USA Today*.

Besides these two, you can find newspapers from all over the world at almost any newsstand.

Food Stores & Markets

As mentioned above in the section on outdoor markets, the best places to get your fresh fruit, cheese, salami, ham, turkey, and bread for a picnic would be at any of the markets mentioned above in this section under *Outdoor Markets*. If you can't make it to one of these, here's a list of some small *Alimentaris* and wine stores from which you can get all you need.

Campo dei Fiori, *Open Air Market, Piazza Campo dei Fiori. Open 6am–2pm.*

You can get salamis, cheeses, breads, and fruit here. A few stores on and around the Via Sistine.

Piazza Vittorio Emmanuele, *Open 7am–2pm. Closed Sundays.*

You can find many specialty food items here, especially cheeses, breads, and salamis.

One small store is on Via Laurina. Another small store, near both entrances to the Borghese Gardens, is in the middle of the Via Della Croce.

Wine

Antica Bottigleria Placidi, *Via del Croce 76, Tel. 679-0896. Expensive. All credit cards accepted. Closed Sundays.*

Opened in 1860, until a few years ago this was an old fashioned, ancient really, wine store selling local vintages directly from large vats. You would walk past the huge wooden doors and into the cool, dark, and damp store lined with shelf upon shelf of wine and oil, and it would seem as if centuries had been erased. Now it's a yuppified fern-filled wine bar. They actually have plants in the vats where once I was served some of the choicest vintages. Not that it's all that bad, for a faux wine bar, they do serve palatable side dishes. I just wish they had kept the vats in use.

Interesting Little Shops

Check out **Cartolerie**, the perfect places to buy unique school supplies for the kids, or yourself, such as pens, notebooks, stationary, pencils, etc. I've been using foreign made notebooks bought in these shops for my journal entries for over six years. They're all over town.

Try also: **Ai Monestari**, *Piazza delle Cinque Lune 76*. A tiny shop of monk-made products including my favorite, **L'Amaro Francescano di Assisi** liqueur. Another fun place is **Terecotte Persiane**, *Via Napoli 92. Tel. 06/488-3886. Open 10:00am–1:30pm and 3:30pm–8:00pm*. Eclectic mix of terra cotta figures, tiles, masks, planters and post boxes. Located in a small courtyard, the place is packed with everything terra cotta you can imagine. Even if you don't want to buy, come and browse.

ALIMENTARI

These are small shops that serve up Italy's famous salamis, meats, cheeses, and breads for you to snack on or take on a picnic. I've listed some of my favorites that are dispersed all over the city, but you only need to find one closest to your hotel for a culinary treat.

Via Principe Amadeo 61 (Termini). *Next to Fiorino Hotel.*

Valeria Basconi, Via Firenze 53 (Via Nazionale). *Near Hotel Alda.*

Salumeria, Via Sardegna 20 (Via Veneto/Trevi Fountain).

Via degli Avignonesi 25 (Via Veneto/Trevi Fountain)

Via Laurina 36 (Piazza di Spagna) *– Meats, cheeses, breads*

Via Laurina 39 (Piazza di Spagna) *– fruits and vegetables and wine*

Via di Ripetta 233A (Pantheon/Navona) *– large meat, cheese, bread, and wine store.*

Via della Scrofa 100 (Piazza Navona/Pantheon) *– meats and cheeses. If you want some prosciutto this small shop will have it cut by hand for you in the window for all to see.*

Via della Scrofa 32 (Piazza Navona/Pantheon)– *hot and cold take out of pastas and souffles as well as salami, cheese and wine.*

PRACTICAL INFORMATION

Bank Hours & Changing Money

Banks are open Monday through Friday from 8:30am to 1:30pm and some do reopen from 2:30pm or so to 3:30pm or so. Some exceptions to that rule are:

- **American Express**, *Piazza di Spagna 38, Tel. 67-64-1. Open weekdays 9:00am to 5:30pm, and Saturdays from 9:00am to 12:30pm.*
- **Banco Nazionale del Lavoro**, *Via Veneto 11, Tel. 475-0421. Open 8:30am to 6:00pm Monday through Saturday.*
- **American Service Bank**, *Piazza Mignanelli 15. Open 8:30am to 6:30pm Monday through Saturday.*

Besides banks, there are plenty of exchange bureaus around (*casa di cambio*). One that is open until 9:00pm on weekdays, and until 2:00pm on Saturdays, is in the **Stazione Termini**. But use this as a last resort since the lines are always horrendously long.

Another option, if all else is closed, is to simply change your money at your hotel or any of the four star hotels that line the Via Veneto. You won't get the best rate but at least you'll have money.

Business Hours

From October to June, most shops are open from 9:00am to 1:00pm and from 3:30pm to 7:30pm, and are closed all day Sundays and on Monday morning. Then from June to September, when it really starts to get hot in Rome, the morning hours remain the same, but the mid-day siesta time is slightly extended to 4:00pm and sometimes 4:30pm, which then pushes closing time back to 7:30pm or 8:00pm. In conjunction with the Sunday/Monday mornings closed, shops also close for half days on Saturday. Is that clear?

Food stores, like an *alimentari*, generally are open from 8:30am to 1:30pm (so stock up on your picnic supplies before you need them) and from 5:00pm to 7:30pm, and during the winter months they are closed on Thursdays.

Church Ceremonies in English
- **All Saints'** (Church of England), *Via del Babuino 153b, Tel.06/679-4357. Sunday Mass 8:30am an 10:30am*
- **St. Andrews** (Scottish Presbyterian), *Via XX Settembre 7, Tel. 06/482-7627. Sunday mass at 11:00am*
- **St. Patrick's** (English Speaking Catholic), *Via Boncompagni 31, Tel. 06/465-716. Sunday ass at 10:00am*
- **St. Paul's** (American Episcopal), *Via Napoli 58, Tel. 06/488-3339. Sunday Mass 8:30am and 10:30pm (sung)*
- **San Silvestro** (English speaking Catholic), *Piazza San Silvestro, Tel. 06/679-7775. Sunday Mass at 10:00am and 5:00pm. Weekdays Mass at noon*
- **Santa Susanna** (American Catholic), *Piazza San Bernardo, Tel. 06/482-7510. Sunday Mass at 9:00am, 10:30am, and noon. Weekdays at 6:00pm*

Doctors & Dentists (English-speaking)

In case of need, the **American Embassy** *(Via Vittorio Veneto 119, Tel. 06/467-41)* will gladly supply you with a recommended list of English-speaking doctors and dentists (That's why I can't supply it here, they wouldn't give it to me because I hadn't had an accident!).

A hospital where English is spoken, **Salvator Mundi**, is at *Viale della Mura Gianicolensi, Tel. 500-141.* I had my tonsils out here so it can be trusted.

Embassies & Consulates
- **United States,** *Via Veneto 199, Tel. 06/467-41*
- **Canadian Embassy,** *Via Conciliazione 4D, Tel. 06/68-30-73-16*
- **United Kingdom,** *Via XX Settembre 90, Tel. 06/482-5441*
- **Australia,** *Via Alessandro 215, Tel. 06/852-721*
- **New Zealand,** *Via Zara 28, Tel. 06/440-2928 or 440-40-35*

• **Ireland**, *Largho del Nazereno, Tel. 06/678-25-41*
• **South Africa**, *Via Tanaro 14, Tel. 06/841-97-94*

Festivals in Rome

• **January 1**, Candle-lit processional in the Catacombs of Priscilla to mark the martyrdom of the early Christians.
• **January 5**, Last day of the Epiphany Fair in the Piazza Navona. A carnival celebrates the ending.
• **January 21**, *Festa diSant'Angese*. Two lambs are blessed then shorn. Held at Sant'Agnese Fuori le Mura.
• **March 9**, *Festa di Santa Francesca Romana*. Cars are blessed at the Piazzale del Coloseo near the church of Santa Francesca Romana.
• **March 19**, *Festa di San Giuseppe*. The statue of the saint is decorated with lamps and placed in the Trionfale Quarter, north of the Vatican. There are food stalls, sporting events and concerts.
• **April**, *Festa della Primavera* (festival of Spring). The Spanish Steps are festooned with rows upon rows of azaleas.
• **Good Friday**, The Pope leads a candlelit procession at 9pm in the Coliseum.
• **Easter Sunday**, Pope gives his annual blessing from his balcony at noon.
• **April 21**, Anniversary of the founding of Rome held in Piazza del Campidoglio with flag waving ceremonies and other pageantry.
• **May 1**, *Festa del Lavoro*. Public Holiday
• **First 10 days of May**, international horse show held in the Villa Borghese at Piazza di Siena.
• **May 6**, Swearing in of the new guards at the Vatican in St Peter's square. Anniversary of the sacking of Rome in 1527.
• **Mid-May**, Antiques fair along Via dei Coronari
• **First Sunday in June**, *Festa della Repubblica* involving a military parade centered on the Via dei Fori Imperiali. It's like something you'd see in Moscow during the Cold War.
• **June 23-24**, *Festa di San Giovanni*. Held in the Pizza di Porta San Giovanni. Traditional food sold: roast baby pig and snails.
• **June 29**, *Festa di San Pietro*. Festival to Saint Peter. Very important religious ceremony for Romans.
• **July**, *Tevere Expo* involving booths and stalls displaying arts and crafts, with food and wine lined up along the Tiber. At night there are fireworks displays and folk music festivals.
• **July 4**, A picnic organized by the American community outside Rome. Need to contact the American Embassy *(4674)* to make reservations to get on the buses leaving from the Embassy.
• **Last 2 weeks in July**, *Festa de Noiantri* involving procession, other festivities, feasting and abundance of wine all in Trastevere.

- **July & August**, Open air opera performances in the Baths of Caracalla.
- **August 15**, *Ferragosto*. Midsummer holiday. Everything closes down.
- **Early September**, *Sagra dell'Uva*. A harvest festival with reduced price grapes and music provided by performers in period costumes held in the Roman Forum.
- **Last week of September**, Crafts show held in Via del'Orso near Piazza Navona.
- **Early November**, Santa Susanna Church Bazaar. Organized by the church for the Catholic American community to raise money for the church. Great home-made pies and cookies as well as used books and clothes. Auction of more expensive items held also.
- **December 8**, Festa della Madonna Immacolata in Piazza di Spagna. Floral wreaths inlaid around the column of the Madonna and one is laid at the top by firefighters.
- **Mid-December**, Start of the Epiphany Fair in the Piazza Navona. All throughout the piazza a fair filled with food stands, candy stands, toy shops opens to the public. Lasts a week. A must see.
- **December 20-January 10**, Many churches display elaborate nativity scenes.
- **December 24**, Midnight Mass at many churches. I recommend the one at Santa Maria Maggiore.
- **December 25**, Pope gives his blessing at noon from his Balcony at St. Peters. The entire square is packed with people.
- **December 31**, New Years Eve. Much revelry. At the strike of midnight people start throwing old furniture out their windows into the streets, so be off the streets by that time, or else your headache from the evening's festivities will be much worse.

Laundry Service

- **Uondo Blu**, *Principe Amadeo 70, near Termini Station.* Coin operated laundry open until 1am. If you need clean clothes, this is the only place to come that is inexpensive. Otherwise it's the wash-in-the-sink-action-and-let-them-dry-for-days scenario.

Papal Audiences

General audiences with the Pope are usually held once a week (Wednesday at 11am) in Vatican City. To participate in a general audience, get information through the **North American College** (*Via dell'Umita 30, tel. 672-256 or 678-9184)*, the American seminary in Rome. Catholics are requested to have a letter of introduction from their parish priest. During the audience women should dress modestly, with arms and head covered, and dark or subdued colors are requested. Men are asked to wear a tie and a jacket.

During the latter part of the summer, because of the heat in Rome, and now moreso for tradition, the Pope moves to his summer residence at **Castel'Gandolpho** in the Alban Hills about sixteen miles southeast of Rome. Audiences are also regularly held there.

Postal Services

You can buy stamps at local tobacconists (they are marked with a "T" outside) as well as post offices. Mail boxes are colored red. Post offices are open from 8am to 2pm on weekdays. The two exceptions to this rule are: the **main post office** (Palazzo delle Poste) at Piazza San Silvestro, which is open Monday through Friday from 8am to 9pm, and Saturday from 8am to noon; and the branch at **Stazione Termini** that keeps the same hours.

Tourist Information & Maps

You can buy maps and guide books at most newsstands and bookstores. This may be necessary even though the tourist offices give away free maps for the subway, buses, as well as an extensive map of the streets of Rome. Most of the time, especially in high season, they are out of all of the above. And in Grand Italian Fashion, nothing gets done about it. So newsstands are your only recourse.

Below are some sources for tourist information:
• **American Express**, *Piazza di Spagna 38, Tel. 06/676-41*
• **Rome Provincial Tourist Board** (**EPT**), *Via Parigi 5, Tel. 06/488-3748*
• **EPT Termini**, *between tracks #2 and 3, Tel. 06/487-1270*
• **EPT Fiumicino**, *just outside customs, Tel. 06/601-1255*
• **Italian Government Travel Office** (ENIT), *Via Marghera 2, Tel. 06/49711*
• **Enjoy Rome**, *Via Marghera 2, Tel. 06/446-3379 or 444-1663*
• **Centro Turistico Studentesco e Giovanile**, *66 Via Nazionale, Tel. 06/467-91*

Tour Companies

• **American Express**, *Piazza di Spagna 38, Tel. 06/676-41*
• **Wagon-Lit**, *Via Gradisca 29, Tel. 06/8-54-38-86*
• **Thomas Cooke Travel**, *Piazza Barberini 21A 06/482-81-82*

Supermarkets

• **Maxi Sidis**, *Via Isonzo 21D*
• **Supermex**, *Viale Liegi 29*
• **Standa**, *Viale Regina Margherita 117*

DAY TRIPS & EXCURSIONS

I've planned some fun excursions for you: **Tivoli Gardens, Castel Gandolfo, Frascati, Ostia Antica, Lago di Bracciano** and **Cervetri**. And if you've got the time, visit the incredible ancient ruins of **Pompeii** and **Herculaneum**. And if that's not enough, you'll find an excursion to the beautiful **Isle of Capri**.

TIVOLI GARDENS

Modern day **Tivoli** has about 45,000 inhabitants. It stands on the **Aniene**, a tributary of the Tiber, and overlooks Rome from its place on the **Sabine hills**. This town is where the wealthy Romans built their magnificent summer villas. The three main attractions are **Villa Adriana** (Hadrian's Villa), **Villa d'Este**, and **Villa Gregoriana**.

The **Villa Adriana's** main attraction is its huge grounds, where you and lizards can bask in the sun. There are plenty of secluded spots to relax or enjoy a picnic on the grass. The building itself was begun in 125 AD and completed 10 years later, and was at the time the largest and most impressive villa in the Roman Empire. From his travels **Hadrian**, an accomplished architect, found ideas that he recreated in his palace. The idea for the **Poikile**, the massive colonnade through which you enter the villa, came from Athens. And the **Serapeum** and **Canal of Canopus** were based on the Temple of Serapis near Alexandria, Egypt.

The **Villa D'Este's** main draw are its many wonderful fountains. The villa itself was built on the site of a Benedictine convent in the mid-16th century. The **Owl Fountain** and **Organ Fountain** are especially beautiful, as is the secluded pathway of the **Terrace of the Hundred Fountains**. If you make it out to Tivoli, these gardens and their fountains cannot be missed, especially at night during the months of May through September when they are floodlit.

The **Villa Gregoriana** is known for the **Grande Cascata** (the Great Fall), which is a result of Gregory XVI diverting the river in the last century to avoid flooding. The park around the cascade has smaller ones as well as grottoes. This is the least interesting of the three villas.

The addresses and hours of the three villas are:
- **Villa Adriana**, *Bivio Villa Adriana, 3.5 miles southwest of Tivoli. Open Tuesday–Sunday, 9:30am–1 hour before sunset. Closed Mondays. Small fee required.*
- **Villa D'Este**, *Viale delle Centro Fontane. Open Tuesday–Sunday, 9:30am to 1.5 hours before sunset. May–September also open 9–11:30pm with the garden floodlit. Closed Mondays. Small fee required. Sundays free.*
- **Villa Gregoriana**, *Largo Sant'Angelo. Open Tuesday–Sunday 9:30am to 1 hour before sunset. Closed Mondays. Small fee required. Sunday free.*

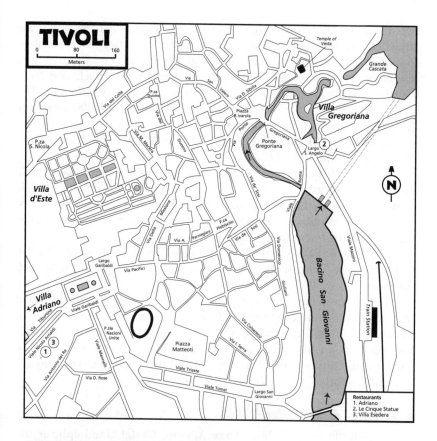

ARRIVALS & DEPARTURES

Tivoli is about 23 miles east of Rome.

By Car

Take the Via Tiburtina (SS5). The Villa Adriana lies to the right about 3.5 miles before the town.

By Train

From Stazione Termini the trip takes about 40 minutes.

WHERE TO EAT

Tivoli simply abounds with restaurants, many offering a magnificent panoramic view of Rome. Here are some of my suggestions.

1. ADRIANO, *(near Hadrian's Villa), Via di Villa Adriana 194, Tel. 0774/529-174. Closed Sunday nights. All credit cards accepted. Dinner for two L130,000.*

Basically at the front of the entrance to Hadrian's Villa, this restaurant attached to a hotel has a beautiful garden terrace. They make excellent *crostini di verdure* (fried dough with vegetabales in side), *raviolini primavera con ricotta e spinaci* (ravioli with spring vegetables, spinach and fresh ricotta), *tagliata di coniglio alle erbette* (rabbit with herbs) and more. The prices are a little rich for my blood, especially with the L6,000 for *coperto* (just sitting down and ordering).

2. LE CINQUE STATUE, *Largo S Angelo 1, Tel. 0774/20366. Closed Fridays. Dinner for two L110,000. All credit cards accepted.*

In front of the entrance to Villa Gregoriana this place has outside seating where you can enjoy the local cuisine. They make many of their pastas in house so they're sure to be fresh. They also specialize in meats, especially the *maialino* (baby pork) and *abbacchio* (lamb) *arrosto* as well as their *verdure fritte* (fried vegetables).

3. VILLA ESEDRA, *(near Hadrian's Villa), Via di Villa Adriana 51, Tel. 0774/534-716. Closed Wednesdays. Dinner for two L70,000. All credit cards accepted.*

You can get some interesting anitpasti like the *insalatine di pesce* (small fish salad), then you can move on to their pastas, which are all made in house, and are all superb, especially the *spaghetti all'amatriciana* (with tomatoes, cream and spices) and the *penne all'arrabiatta* (with tomatoes, galric oil and hot pepper). The meats are a little suspect, so you may get away with a less expensive bill if you only try the pastas.

CASTEL GANDOLPHO

Beautifully located above **Lake Albano, Castel Gandolpho** is the summer residence of the Pope. From up at the Castel Gandolpho, you can enjoy a wonderful view of the wooded slopes that fall swiftly down into the murky waters of a volcanic crater.

The one real sight to see is the **Palazzo Papal** (Papal Palace), built in 1624. During the summer months when the Pope is in residence, every Sunday at noon His Eminence gives an address in the courtyard of the palace. No permit is required to enter. First come, first servedis the rule.

ARRIVALS & DEPARTURES

Castel Gandolpho is about 15 miles east of Rome.

By Car

Take the Via Appia Nuova (SS7) for about 30 minutes.

By Train

From Stazione Termini, it's about 35 minutes. From the station you will have to take a local taxi up to the Castel, unless you feel adventurous and want to walk the three kilometers uphill. Just follow the signs on the side of the road.

WHERE TO EAT

ANTICO RISTORANTE PAGANNELLI, *Piazza A Gramsci 4, Tel. 06/ 936-0004. Closed Tuesdays. Dinner for two L90,000. All credit cards accepted.*

This restaurant with a nice view of the lake has been in existence since 1882, and they still serve all the traditional dishes made with produce from the local countryside. They make a wonderful *strozzapreti all'amatriciana* (pasta with tomatoes, cream and spices), *risotto al'erbe* (rice dish with herbs), *maialino arrosto* (roast baby pork), *bracciole di cinghiale* (roast boar "arms"), and other savory dishes. Rumor has it that the Pope even has stopped in once of twice.

FRASCATI

If wine is what you're looking for, **Frascati** is where you want to be. This town's wine is world famous, and something you simply cannot miss. The ambiance of this hill town is magnificent.

Frascati is a great place to stay while visiting Rome if you can't stand the urban hustle and bustle. Since it's only 30 minutes and $5 away, Frascati's relaxing pace, scenic views, quaint little wine shops, excellent local restaurants, and winding old cobbletstone streets should be seriously considered as an alternative to downtown Rome.

Since this is still primarily an excursion, I've listed the restaurants first and hotels second for this beautiful town – even though I hope some of you will opt to stay here and enjoy Frscati's many charms.

ARRIVALS & DEPARTURES

Frascati is roughly 14 miles southeast of Rome.

By Car

Take the Via Tuscolana (SS215) up to the hill town (25 minute drive).

By Train

From Stazione Termini, board a local train that leaves every forty minutes or so from Track 27. The ride lasts a little over 35 minutes. Cost L4,500.

CONSIDER FRASCATI!

Even though I spent 8 years living in Rome, and have grown to love it, the city can be a bit overwhelming both for a first time visitor and the Roman veteran. It's large, congested, noisy, polluted and challenging while also being one of the most beautiful, charming cities filled with some of the world's most well-known sights and prized artistic treasures. Prices at most hotels and restaurants seem to have gone through the roof.

*So if you are someone who would rather not experience the hectic pace of a big city, but you still want to see all that Rome has to offer, stay in **Frascati**. This quaint, charming, quiet, little hill town is the perfect place to get away from it all while still having access to everything. The town is only 35 minutes away by train (the fare is L4,500) and the trains run every 45 minutes or so until 10:00pm. Granted there might be a concern if you want to take a nap in the middle of the afternoon, but that is what the **Borghese gardens** are for. Bring a picnic lunch and take a little siesta in the shade in one of the prettiest and peaceful gardens in any city in the world.*

In Frascati, you'll be able enjoy many good restaurants, sample the fine local wines from quaint little wine stores that are located all over the city. They serve you glasses or carafes from huge vats. You'll also be able to savor the ambiance of an ancient medieval town, with its cobblestone streets and twisting alleys. Here you'll be able to gaze out your windows and see lush valleys below, instead of looking out onto another building as you would probably do in Rome. And if you come in October, you'll be able to experience a wine festival of bacchanalian proportions.

So if you are used to the calm serenity of country life, but still want to experience the beauty that Rome has to offer, Frascati may be your answer.

WHERE TO STAY

1. ALBERGHO PANORAMA, *Piazza Carlo Casini 3, Frascati 00044. Tel. 06/942-1800 or 941-7955. 9 rooms, two with bath. Double with bath L85,000; Single with bathj L75,000. Double without bath L75,000; Single without bath L65,000. L15,000 for an extra bed. L30,000 for all meals. No credit cards accepted. **

Situated in the centro storico with a beautiful panoramic view of Rome. This is a small but comfortable hotel for those on a budget. Say hi to the proprietress, Laura, for me. The view from the hotel is stunning.

2. BELLAVISTA, *Piazza Roma 2, 00044 Frascati. Tel. 06/942-1068 or 942-6320. Fax 06/942-1068. 13 rooms all with bath. Double L130,000-160,000. Breakfast L10,000. All credit cards accepted. ***

You have room service, TV in your room, and a hotel bar, as well as a nice view of the valley. The rooms are clean and comfortbale as befits a good country three star. The building is quite quaint, and old but restored perfectly for your comfort. I love the high ceilings in the rooms, making them feel much larger.

3. HOTEL FLORA, *Via Vittorio Veneto 8 00044 Frascati. Tel. 06/941-6110. Fax 06/942-0198. 33 rooms only 30 with bath. Double L150,000; Single L120,000. Breakfast L12,000. All credit cards accepted.* ***

An old hotel decorated with style, located in a central position in Frascati. Much better amenities than the Bellavista, but not as good a view. Located a little ways outside of town, this hotel is set in a wonderfully tranquil environment. A good place to stay.

4. PINNOCCHIO'S, *Piazza del Mercata 20, Tel. 06/941-7883. Fax 06/941-7884. Single L80,000 (Double used as a single); Double L130,000. Seven rooms all with bath, mini-bar, and TV. No credit cards accepted.* **

Large comfortable rooms with gigantic bathrooms. Upstairs from the restaurant, so you can grab yourself a snack until late in the evening. The office is in the restaurant so you'll need to enter there to get your key.

Perfectly located on the central market square. A sight you have to see while in Frascati and a great place to get some fruits, vegetables (you can even get fresh bags of mixed salad), meats, and cheeses. The place is alive with bargaining and local greetings.

WHERE TO EAT/WINE BARS

Some of the wine bars are so small and so nonchalant about the tourist trade that they don't even have names. Also many of the places do not have telephones. One of the owners explained to me, *"Why should we have telephones when we can walk over and talk in person?"* That makes sense, since Frascati is such a small intimate little town.

Don't be put off by this casual hill town attitude, since the ones without names or phones are some of the best places to visit. Enjoy.

5. CANTINA FARINA, *Vini Propri, Via Cavour 20. No Telephone.*

A real wine bar, not a fern infested one. With a tile floor, collapsible wooden tables and chairs and great wine served from vats, here you can get a real taste for how the Italians enjoy life. Located near a school, so it can get periodically noisy during the day.

6. CANTINA VIA SEPULCRO DI LUCURO, *Via Sepulcro di Lucuro 6. No Telephone.*

Located just off the main road (Via Catone), this place has a small area for seating outside separated from the rest of the world by large planters. The inside is quite cool, like a wine cellar. Just inside the door is an antique wine press that they still use during the pressing season. Inside or out you'll get some of the best wines Frascati has to offer here.

7. CANTINA VIA CAMPANIA, *Via Campania 17. No Telephone.*

Just down the road from the wine bar listed above, this place has one and a half of its four inside walls covered with wine vats, and the rest of the space taken up with strange looking tools used in the wine trade, as well as large empty bottles that you only wish you could take home with you ... full. The owner is quite friendly and if it's not too crowded will sit down and chat. Great wine. Wonderful atmosphere.

8. CANTINA VIA VILLA BORGHESE, *Via Villa Borghese 20. No Telephone.*

Small wine store filled with large 1,000,000 liter barrels called *botte*, and 500,000 liter barrels called *mezza botte*. Each cask is numbered and initialed with the vineyard it came from. Not very scenic atmosphere and no tables to sit at, but they will sell you a bottle of their finest for only L2,000. That's $1.50 for an excellent bottle of Frascati wine.

9. PIZZERIA/BIRRERIA PINNOCCHIO, *Piazza del Mercato 20, Tel. 06/941-6694 or 942-0330. Dinner for two L55,000.*

A large statue of Pinnocchio advertises this superb restaurant in Frascati's quaintest and most vibrant square (it's actually a triangle). There is outside seating with large planters separating you from the pace of this market-dominated piazza. Inside you'll find tiled floors and wood panelling giving the place a nice rustic flair. They serve great *canneloni ai quattro formaggi* (with four cheeses), as well as great Roman staples such as *amatriciana, carbonara, and vongole.*

For seconds try their *scampi alla griglia* (grilled shrimp) which is reasonably priced at only L16,000. If you find you've lingered too long over your Sambuca, Pinnocchio's has some wonderful rooms upstairs.

10. PERGATOLO, *Via del Castello 20, Tel. 06/942-04-64. L13,000-Cold plate with wine and bread; L20,000-First course of pasta, pizza, or meat, second course of the cold plate with wine and bread.*

Wild and fun atmosphere, a little on the touristy side with singers serenading the diners. You can either enjoy or ignore it in this large and spacious restaurant that has a deli counter displaying all the available meats, cheeses, breads, salamis, etc., that you'll be served. There are roaring fires behind the counter where your meats are all prepared.

If you've come to Frascati for the day or the week, this is one place you have to try, just for the fun of it. Say hi to the beautiful manager Tiziana for me.

11. TRATTORIA/PIZZERIA DA GABRIELE, *Via Solferino 5. No telephone. No credit cards. Dinner for two L35,000.*

You ladies will love the charming part owner Rapaaele. He looks like something out of a movie with his piercing dark eyes and sultry glances. You can get pizza until 1:30am at wonderfully inexpensive prices. Just off the main piazza, this is a fun place to come in the late evening. Try their *pizza can salsiccia* (with sausage) or *con porcini* (mushrooms). I asked them to put both together, with extra cheese, and the pizza came out wonderfully.

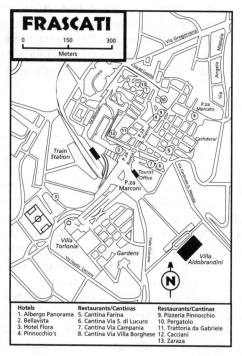

FRASCATI

0   150   300
Meters

Hotels
1. Albergo Panorama
2. Bellavista
3. Hotel Flora
4. Pinnocchio's

Restaurants/Cantinas
5. Cantina Farina
6. Cantina Via S. di Lucuro
7. Cantina Via Campania
8. Cantina Via Villa Borghese

Restaurants/Cantinas
9. Pizzeria Pinnocchio
10. Pergatolo
11. Trattoria da Gabriele
12. Cacciani
13. Zaraza

12. CACCIANI, *Via Alberto Diaz 13, Tel. 06/942-0378. Closed Mondays. Holidays January 7-15 and 10 days after ferragosto. Dinner for two L110,000. All credit cards accepted.*

One of the most famous restaurants in this region. It has a beautiful terrace that offers a tranquil and serene atmosphere. For starters, try the *crostini con verdure* (baked pastry appetizer filled with vegetables). Then try the home-made *fetuccine alla romana* (made with tomatoes, chicken and spices) or *spaghetti con le vongole verace* (with clams in a hot oil and garlic sauce). For the entré try the *fritto misto di carne* (mixed fried meats) the *saltimbocca*, or any of their grilled fish.

13. ZARAZA, *Viale Regina Margherita 21, Tel. 06/942-2053. Closed Mondays and the month of August. Dinner for two L70,000. Visa accepted.*

Traditional *cucina romana* where you can get *bucatini al'amatriciana* (pasta with tomatoes, cream and spices), *gnocchi al ragu* (potatoe dumplings with tomato-based meat sauce), *capaletti in brodo* (pasta shaped like little hats in soup), *trippa alla romana* (tripe with a tomato-based sauce) *abbacchio al forno* (grilled lamb), as well as some other Roman specialties such as *spaghetti all'amatriciana* and *penne all'arrabiata* (with a hot spicy tomatoe based sauce), as well as *lombata di vitello* (grilled veal chop) and *misto arosto* (mixed roast meats).

A simple rustic atmosphere with a few tables outside offering a limited view of the valley below. Inside tables are located in the basement of (but seperate from) the Albergho Panorama hotel. It's warm and inviting in the winter, with the heat from the kitchen, the brick pillars, the whitewashed arched walls, and the friendly family service.

SEEING THE SIGHTS

If you've driven, you've seen the lovely scenic route to Frascati along the old **Appia Antica**, past the Catacombs and ruined tombs. The town is perched halfway up a hill, and on a clear day you will have splendid views of all of Rome and its scenic countryside.

Besides the great views, the wine, and the chance for some relaxation, Frascati has a wealth of villas and spacious parks that were formerly residences of princes and popes. One of these residences, **Villa Aldobrandini**, sits just above the town, and has a magnificent garden in which you can find solitude. To enter the villa's grounds you need to first get a free pass from the **Aziendo di Soggiorno e Tourismo**, in Frascati's Piazza Marconi. *The hours are Monday–Friday 9:00am–1:00pm.*

Besides the beauty of its old villas, many of which were damaged in Allied bombings because the Germans had taken over the town for their headquarters, Frascati's draw is the fine **white wine** that bares its name. All wines seem to lose a special *qualcosa* when they travel, so if you are a wine lover, do not miss out on this chance to drink Frascati's wine directly at the source.

To enjoy this succulent nectar, there are old, dark wine stores, with heavy wooden tables and chairs located all over town. At one of these you can sip and enjoy this unspoiled and inexpensive wine, the way the natives have been doing it for centuries. The **Cantina Vanelli**, just off Piazza Fabro Filzi, is a prime example of one such wine store, and a fine traditional location to sample Frascati's produce. Just ask for a *bicchiere di vino* (glass of wine). An alternative to the cramped quarters of these wine stores but with quite a bit less atmosphere would be to sit at one of the sidewalk cafés offering superb views along with great wine.

Frascati is the perfect place to wander through, getting lost in the alleys, side streets, steps leading nowhere, and winding roads (all cobblestoned). If you follow the sporadically placed yellow signs that say *Ferario Pedonale,* you'll be guided through all the major sights and sounds of this hill town. One distinguishing feature is that there seem to be more *alimentaris* (little food stores) per person than in any other city I've ever seen.

If you are fortunate enough to be in Frascati in the fall, specifically during the month of October, the town celebrates a **wine festival** of pagan proportions that lasts several days and nights. Come out to witness and partake in the debauchery, but please do not drive back to Rome afterwards – take the train.

LAGO DI BRACCIANO

Bracciano is a place to visit if you're desperately need to go swimming, or entertain the kids for a little while. There are sights to see in the main town, with its imposing castle, but the distance and time to get here, and lack of adequate restaurants makes it a destination only if you feel the need to swim in fresh water. Even so, **Ostia Lido** is closer and much more easily accessible if you want to go swimming.

One of the best sights on the way to Bracciano, whether by car or train (since the train follows the roadway) is a still functional ancient **Roman aquaduct** that slices through lush green fields. When you get to the town Bracciano, you need to drive or walk down the hill to get to the **lake**. It's about a 15 minute walk and a three minute drive.

The lake is about 22 miles in circumference, and its shoreline boasts the town of **Bracciano**, standing high above the lake; the picturesque village of **Trevignano**; and the popular resort of **Anguillara**. The shores of the lake, planted with pine and olive groves, make pleasant picnic spots and swimming areas. Bracciano seems dominated by the **Castello Orsini**, the castle of the former landlords of the town. The structure, completed around 1485, is a magnificent example of a private Rennaissance castle. It has a polygonal shape accompanied by five slender circular towers rising from it. Many rooms open to public still display the original frescoes and contain some quite good Etruscan relics and a fascinating collection of arms and armor. *Tel. 902-4003. Open Tuesday to Sunday 10:00am–Noon and 3:00pm–6:00pm in the summer, and Tuesday – Sunday 9:00am–Noon and 3:00pm–5:00pm in the winter. Admission L7,000.*

While at Bracciano you can also rent dinghies and paddle out on the water. There's not much to do or see, and the beach space is relatively limited, so try to come during the week and not on the weekends.

ARRIVALS & DEPARTURES

Bracciano is 26 miles north northwest of Rome.

By Car

Drive about 45 minutes up the Via Cassia (SS2) to Madonna di Bracciano, then take route 493 to the lake.

By Train
From Stazione Ostiense it takes about 1 and a quarter hours and costs L8,400. In Rome, take the metro to the Piramide stop, and walk through the underpass at the "Ple Partigiani" exit to the Ostiense station. Buy your ticket at this station.

WHERE TO EAT

In all honesty I cannot recommend any of the restaurants in Bracciano, but if you haven't prepared a picnic lunch or didn't buy supplies in the town to bring down to the beach area, there are plenty of little bars and cafés lining the main road around the beach, and a few floating restaurants you might brave.

CERVETRI

Cervetri used to be the Etruscan capital of **Caere**, which the Romans at one point overran on their rise to power long before the Roman Empire. But Cervetri is not known today for the town of the living, but the towns of the dead the Etruscans built. These **necropoli** are large circular mounds of tombs laid out in a pattern of street like houses in a city.

Today their round roofs are densely covered with grasses and wild flowers. Inside they have been furnished with replicas of household furnishings carved from stone. Most of the original artifacts are in the **Villa Giulia Museum** or the **Vatican Museums** in Rome. *The site is open Tuesday to Sunday 9:00am–4:00pm. Admission L6,000.*

After viewing the necropolis you can settle down among the mounds and have a picnic lunch, and imagine what life would be like during that time. After sightseeing you can return to the town by taxi, or by car if you have one, and take in the limited sights the little town has to offer. From the crowded main piazza you can climb steps to a **museum** with a lovely medieval courtyard.

ARRIVALS & DEPARTURES

Cervetri is about 28 miles west northwest of Rome.

By Car
A 45 minute drive up the Via Aurelia (SS1), which will give you a more scenic view, or the Autostrada A12, which connects to the 'beltway' around Rome by route 201.

By Train
From Stazione Termini it takes 1 hour and 10 minutes; from Roma Tiburtina it takes 50 minute to get to Cervetri-Ladispoli. Once in the town,

to reach the **Necropolis** you can grab a local taxi, or take the two kilometer walk along a quiet little road. There are signs on the road to guide you where you're going. If in doubt stay to the right at the fork in the road.

WHERE TO EAT

DA FIORE, *near Procoio di Ceri, Tel. 06/9920-4250. Closed Wednesdays. Dinner for two L60,000. No credit cards accepted.*

A simple little local *trattoria* in the open country not far from the ruins and only four kilometers from the Via Aurelia. They make great pastas like *penne al funghi* (with mushrooms) *al ragu* (with tomatoe and meat sauce) or *con salsiccia* (with sausage), as well as grilled meats and their famous *brushetta* (garlic bread as an appetizer) and pizza – all cooked in a wood burning oven.

OSTIA ANTICA & LIDO DI OSTIA

Ostia Antica

Founded in the fourth century BC, **Ostia Antica** feels about as far away from Rome as you can get. As with excursions to Pompeii or Herculaneum, you get the sensation that the clock has been turned back nearly 2,000 years. But actually it is only 15 miles southwest of the city, a mere 45 minutes by subway (don't take your car or you'll defeat the purpose of relaxation).

This city was once the bustling port of Ancient Rome, but today it is calm and serene, and it is only busy with quiet. It is well preserved despite having been subject to repeated attacks by pirates and hostile navies. The only invasions it undergoes now are from packs of marauding Italian school children, on their cultural outings, rampaging through its archaeological excavations – the main reason to come here (see below).

ARRIVALS & DEPARTURES

Ostia Antica is about 15 miles southwest of Rome.

By Car

Take the Via del Mare (SS8) for about 25 minutes.

By Metro & Train

Buy a metro ticket and take Linea B to the Magliana station, and catch the train to Ostia Antica or continue to Lido di Ostia (the beach). It takes about 45 minutes from Stazione Termini. You'll have to pay a new fare (L3,000) to take the beach train since the Metro and the train systems are different animals.

WHERE TO EAT

There's really only one to reccommend if you haven't packed yourself a picnic lunch. All the other restaurants are by the beach, so if you're heading that way see the listings under Lido di Ostia.

IL MONUMENTO, 18 *Piazza Umberto I, Tel. 06/565-0021. Closed Mondays. Holidays Aug 15 - Sept 15. Dinner for two L90,000. Credit cards accepted.*

A simple seafood restaurant with quaint outside seating on the main piazza. Try the *spaghetti "Monumento"* with seafood and shrimp, as well as the *spaghetti con cozze* (with muscles) either in their light white sauce or their spicy red sauce. For seconds try any of the fish, which they either bake in the oven or grill on an open fire.

SEEING THE SIGHTS

You enter the excavations in Ostia at the **Porta Romana** from which you follow the **Decumanus Maximus**, the old city's main street. You will encounter the well-preserved old **Theater**. From here you overlook the **Piazzale dei Corporazione** (Corporation Square), a tree-lined boulevard once filled with over seventy commercial offices of wine importers, ship owners, oil merchants, or rope makers. The well-preserved laundry and wine shop should be visited. These offices are tastefully decorated with mosaic tiled floors representing the trades of each location (If you will not have a chance to visit Pompeii, this will give you the taste and feel, on a smaller scale, of that famous city). The chief commodity was corn, but there were also such imported luxuries as ivory (depicted by an elephant).

Farther down the Decumanus Maximus you arrive at the **Capitolium**, a temple dedicated to Jupiter and Minerva, located at the end of the **Forum**. The **insulae** (apartment blocks) are of particular interest since they are often four or five stories high. This is where the regular people and smaller merchants lived. Only the most wealthy of the merchants were able to build themselves villas. The *insulae* were well lighted, had running water, and had a means for sanitation (i.e., garbage removal) on each floor.

Two private home of interest that should be visited are the **House of the Cupid and Psyche**, which is west of the Capitolium, and the **House of the Dioscuri**, which is at the southwest end of town.

The site is open daily 9:00am–6:00pm in summer, 9:00am–4:00pm in winter. Admission L10,000.

Lido di Ostia

Lido di Ostia is the beach about four kilometers from the ruins of Ostia Antica. Take the same route that you took to the ruins but continue on a little farther either by car or by train (see *Arrrivals & Departures* above for more details). This is a perfect place to visit after a tough day of walking through the buildings and necropoli of the Old City.

Treat yourself to a seaside celebration. There are rafts to rent, umbrellas to use, *cabanas* to change in, restaurants to go to, and hotels to stay at if you get to tired and don't want to get back to Rome. Lido di Ostia is a typical Italian beach and it's close to Rome. But don't go on the weekend unless you like mobs of people.

WHERE TO STAY

If you find you've lingered over the wine and the seafood a little too long, here are some hotel suggestions:

ROME AIRPORT PALACE HOTEL, *Viale Romagnoli 165, Lido Di Ostia. Tel. 06/569-2341. Fax 06/569-8908. 260 rooms, 230 with bath. All credit cards accepted. Double L320,000; Single L200,000.* *****

Don't let the name fool you, this place is quiet and it is also close to the beach. Also it's the only five star deluxe hotel in the area. They have everything you could need or want like a bar, restaurant, reading room, air conditioning, and more.

SATELLITE PALACE HOTEL, *Via delle Antille 49, Lido Di Ostia. Tel. 06/569-3841. Fax 06/569-8908. 283 rooms all with bath. All credit cards accepted. Single L200,000; Double L320,000. Air conditioning.* ****

Even though the star rating is one below it's cousin just around the corner, the Rome Airport Palace Hotel, the service and prices are exactly the same. They even have more, like a disco, swimming pool, audio video equipment, a sauna, a solarium, and so on, so I don't know why they don't have that last and final deluxe star.

HOTEL KURSAAL 2000, *Via F D'Aragona 10, Lido Di Ostia. Tel. 06/567-0616. Fax 06/567-0547. 38 rooms, 8 suites, all with bath. All credit cards accepted. Double L125,000; Suite L250,000.* ***

A good deal in a very tranquil location right near the beach. They have their own piano bar and restaurant so you don't have to stray too far at night. The rooms are all air conditioned, clean and tidy, and each has the necessary amenities to make this a three star hotel.

HOTEL RIVA, *Piazzale Mageliano 22, Lido Di Ostia. Tel. 06/562-2231. Fax 06/562-1667. 15 rooms all with bath. Single L105,000-115,000; Double L118,000-148,000. All credit cards accepted.* ***

Located near the beach, this is a good but not great three star hotel that overlooks the sea in the front and has a tranquil garden in the back. You also have prompt room service, air conditioning, a good restaurant and a small but comfortable bar.

WHERE TO EAT

LA CAPANNINA DA PASQUALE, *Lungomare Vespucci 156, Tel. 06/ 567-0143. Closed Mondays. Holidays in November. All credit cards accepted. Dinner for two L110,000.*

A little expensive but the location is supreme, especially the outside seating right on the sea. They have a superb antipasto table which could serve as your whole meal if you're not too hungry. Their pastas and rice dishes are also good since many of them have been home-made at the restaurant. Try the *risotto ai frutti di mare* (rise with seafood ladled over the top). They are known for their seafood dishes so try anything *al forno* (cooked over the grill), with their wonderfully grilled potatoes. The service is stupendous, as it should be based on the price.

CHIARALUCE, *Via Ponte di Tor Boacciana 13, Tel. 06/569-1302. Closed Wednesdays. No credit cards accepted. Dinner for two L60,000.*

A little off the beaten track with tranquil outside seating. This is a small local place that prides itself on making superb food. They make a great *saute di vongole* (sauteed clams) as well as *spaghetti con vongole* (with clams), and a huge mixed fried seafood platter (*frittura mista*). They also make perfectly grilled fish that goes well with their excellent house wine. The food is very good here.

PECCATI DI GOLA, *Corso Regina Maria Pia 19, Tel. 06/560-1233. Closed Mondays. No credit cards accepted. Dinner for two L70,000.*

On a street parallel to the beach, this is (surprise) another great fish restaurant that also serves well prepared meat dishes. You can watch through the glass partition as the cooks make each dish. If you're looking for light fare try their *insalata di mare* (mixed seafood salad).

TRE PULCINI, *Viale della Pineta di Ostia 30, Tel. 06/562-1293. Closed Mondays. Dinner for Two L110,000. All credit cards accepted.*

A simple family run place with mama Antonietta in the kitchen and Renato in the restaurant. Here you'll experience some true down home Italian cooking. Try their *saute di cozze e vongole* (sauteed muscles and clams), *zuppa di pesce* (fish soup), or their *fritto misto* (mixed fried seafood). You can also get some home-made *gelato* (ice cream) as dessert which is made daily by the daughter Cristina. You can enjoy all of this either outside on the balcony or in the air conditioned comfort of the interior.

VILLA IRMA, *Corso Regina Maria Pia 67, Tel. 06/560-3877. Closed Tuesdays. Holidays December 20-30. Dinner for two L 150,000. All credit cards accepted.*

Super expensive but superb restaurant, some say the best in Ostia. You can enjoy the ambiance of the patio or the comfort of air conditioning inside while you dine on the wonderfully prepared seafood dishes. Anything here on the grill (*alla griglia*) or fried (*fritta*) is great. The service is four-star perfect. The place to come if you want to be treated like royalty.

POMPEII & HERCULANEUM

If you have any free time while in Rome, try to visit these two ancient cities. They are truly a major wonder of the world: two cities trapped in time by a devastating volcanic eruption. What more could you ask for?

Two thousand people died and thousands more lost their homes when **Vesuvius** erupted in 79 AD, and submerged **Pompeii**, **Herculaneum**, and **Stabiae** with lava. The lava created an almost perfect time capsule, sealing in an important cross-section of an ancient civilization for many centuries.

ARRIVALS & DEPARTURES

Since these ancient towns are a good 150 miles away from Rome, and could easily take three hours each way, I'd suggest you take a tour to see the ruins.

By Tour

Contact one of the following tour operators:
- **American Express**, *Piazza di Spagna 38, Tel. 6764*
- **Appian Line**, *Via Vittorio Veneto 84, Tel. 474-1641*
- **CIT**, *Piazza della Repubblica 68, Tel. 479821* (they'll help you find your own tour guide.)

By Car

Take the Autostrade A2 to Naples, then the S18 to the S70.

By Train

From Stazione Termini to Napoli Centrale, then go one floor below the Central Station to the Circumvesuviana station for a local high speed train to Ercolano (Herculaneum) or Pompeii Scavi (3 1/2 to 4 hours total journey). Purchase one of the inexpensive maps available so you can find your way through the two ruined cities.

Pompeii

Before the catastrophe, **Pompeii** was an old established city with a diverse population of about 25,000 that reflected successive waves of colonization. By 80 BC, it was a favorite resort of wealthy Romans.

Although the ruins were discovered in the 16th century and rudimentary excavations began in 1763, systematic excavations did not get under way until 1911. Since then only about three fifths of the site has been freed from the death grip of the lava.

Strolling through this dead city is quite ominous. You can easily imagine yourself living here. Many pieces of regular life remain: the walls are covered in graffiti, ranging from erotic drawings to political slogans, since a local election was taking place when the eruption occurred. There are also abundant frescoes depicting mythological scenes in the wealthier homes, as well as frescoes indicating what form of work the owners of the house partook in.

Some of the best homes to see are the **House of the Faun** and the **House of the Vettii**, both in the residential area north of the Forum. Other homes of interest are the **House of the Melander** (located to the east of the Forum), the **Villa of the Mysteries** (located to the west of the main town), and the **House of Pansa** (located to the north of the Forum) that also included rented apartments.

Also in evidence in the remains are symbols of the cult of Dionysos. But this cult was only one of many that flourished in the city. The **Temple of Isis** (to the East of the Forum) testifies to the strong following that the Egyptian goddess had here. The public **Ampitheater**, in the east of the city, should not be missed. There are locations on the stage area that if a whisper is spoken, even a person standing at the top-most part of the seating area can hear it clearly. Other attractions are the footprints left in time, the mummified bodies trying to shield themselves from the lava, and more. Everything about Pompeii is a wonder to behold.

Gates to the site open year round 9:00am to 1 hour before sunset. Admission L10,000.

Herculaneum

Seventeen miles northeast of Pompeii is the smaller town of **Herculaneum**. At the time of the eruption it had only 5,000 inhabitants, compared to the 25,000 in Pompeii, had virtually no commerce, and its industry was solely based on fishing. The volcanic mud that flowed through every building and street in Herculaneum was different from that which buried Pompeii. This steaming hot lava-like substance settled eventually to a depth of 40 feet and set rock-hard, sealing and preserving everything it came in contact with. Also the absence of the hail of hot ash that rained down on Pompeii, which smashed its buildings, meant that many of the inhabitants of Herculaneum were able to get away in time, and that complete houses, with their woodwork, household goods, and furniture were preserved.

Although Herculaneum was a relatively unimportant town compared with Pompeii, many of the houses that have been excavated were from the wealthy class. It is speculated that perhaps the town was like a retirement village, populated by prosperous Romans seeking to pass their retirement years in the calm of a small seaside town. This idea is bolstered by the fact that the few craft shops that have been discovered were solely for the manufacture of luxury goods.

Archaeologists speculate that the most desirable residential area was in the southwest part of town which overlooked the ocean in many different housing terraces. Here you will find the **House of the Stags**, famous for its beautiful frescoes, sculpted stags, and a drunken figure of Hercules.

Farther north you can find the marvelously preserved **House of the Wooden Partition**. It is one of the most complete examples of a private residence in either Pompeii or Herculaneum. (Remember that this town was recently discovered which allowed for better preservation efforts, unlike Pompeii which was discovered in the 16th century) Near this house to the north are the **Baths**, an elaborate complex incorporating a gymnasium and assorted men's and women's baths.

Gates to the site open year round 9:00am to 1 hour before sunset. Admission L10,000.

CAPRI

Capri is an island geared completely for the reaping of tourist dollars. That doesn't mean that it is not beautiful, like the **Blue Grotto**, but remember that in the summer the population of Capri fluctuates perhaps more than any other island in the world. This increase is a result of many tourists from the mainland and all over the world, and temporary residents who summer on the island. In winter, life reverts to the dreamy pace that has been so characteristic of Capri over the centuries. So if you want to see a relatively pristine part of paradise unsoiled by rampant tourism, try to visit in the winter months. Many tourist stores and restaurants will be closed, but you'll have the island almost to yourself.

ARRIVALS & DEPARTURES

By Tour

Since this beautiful island is over 125 miles away from Rome, and could easily take three hours each way, I recommend taking a tour to see the beauty of the place. Contact one of the following tour operators:

• **American Express**, *Piazza di Spagna 38, Tel. 6764*
• **Appian Line**, *Via Vittorio Veneto 84, Tel. 474-1641*
• **CIT**, *Piazza della Repubblica 68, Tel. 479821* (they'll help you find your own tour guide.)

By Car

Take the Autostrade A2 to Naples down to the ferry or hydrofoil docks (they only run in the summer). Go to the Mole Beverello to catch the ferry or hydrofoil (tourist cars are not allowed on the island, so you'll have to leave it in Naples. Not a good idea.)

By Train
From Stazione Termini to Napoli Centrale takes about 2 hours and 30 minutes. Then take a taxi to Molo Beverello in the harbor to catch the ferry or hydrofoil to the island.

WHERE TO STAY

1. QUISISANA E GRAND HOTEL, *Via Camerelle 2, 80073Capri, Tel. 081/ 837-0788. Fax 081/837-6080. 143 rooms, 15 suites all with bath. All credit cards accepted. Double L330,000-550,000; Single L225,000-325,000.* *****

An ultra-luxurious hotel with swimming pool, health club, tennis courts, sauna, a great restaurant, as well as excellent views of the whole island. Here you'd be staying in the lap of luxury. The rooms are large and comfortable and have all the amenities you could expect: mini-bar, TV, air conditioning, room service, hairdryers and more. If you have the money, this is a great place to stay.

2. EUROPA PALACE HOTEL, *(Anacapri) Via Capodimonte, 80071 Capri. 081/837-0955. Fax 081/837-3191. 93 rooms all with bath. Double L270,000-460,000; Single L180,000-250,000. All credit cards accepted.* ****

They have an outdoor pool as well as a covered swimming pool, a health club, a weight room, a sauna, a private beach, a sun room, a piano bar, a great restaurant with a scenic view and almost everything you could want while on Capri. The location in Anacapri is splendid, away from the crowds. The rooms are large and comfortable with spotless bathrooms.

3. LA LUNA, *Via Matteoti 3, 80073 Capri. Tel. 081/837-0433. Fax 081/ 837-7459. 50 rooms all with bath. Double L220,000-430,000; Single L165,000-200,000. Suites 430,000-550,000. Breakfast included.* ****

If you get tired of the pool and the topless bathing that is allowed here, or the panoramic view from the restaurant/bar, you can always go upstairs and numb your mind with satellite TV. But why would you want to do that in Capri, when there are beautiful sights to be found? If you don't want to walk they have a bus that can take you all over the island.

4. LA PINETA, *Via Tragara 6, 80073 Capri. Tel. 081/837-0644. Fax 081/837-6445. 36 rooms all with bath. Double L170,000-290,000; Single L80,000-160,000. All credit cards accepted.* ****

If you want to gain weight, then get back in shape all in the same day, stay here. Their restaurant serves superb food complimented by a stunning view over the sea. After you've gorged yourself you can either work out in the health club or weight room, take a few laps in the pool, or go for a swim in the sea. Then you can rest on their private beach, soak up the sun, and then do it all over again. The rooms are large, clean and comfortable and contain all the amenities of a four star: air conditioning, TV, mini-bar, radio, room service, etc.

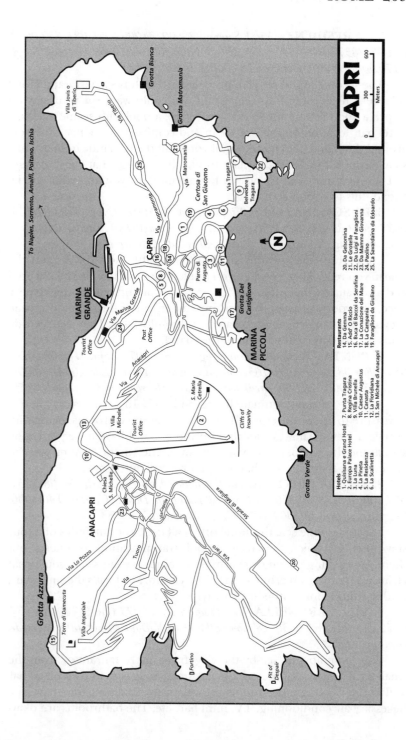

CAPRI

5. LA RESIDENZA, *Via F Serena 22, 80073 Capri. Tel. 081/837-0833. Fax 081/837-7564. 114 rooms all with bath. All credit cards accepted. Single L170,000-200,000; Double L260,000-320,000.* ****

The second largest hotel on the island (the Quisisana e Grand Hotel is larger), here you'll find everything you could want for your stay on Capri: a good restaurant with a great view, a pool with scenic guests, a hotel bar, location on the sea, clean and comfortable rooms, transport around the island, and more. But if you want the romantic intimacy of a smaller hotel, this is not the place to stay. It's so large that guests can get lost in the crowd. But if you want anonymity for you and your special friend, this is a good choice.

6. LA SCALINATELLA, *Via Tragara 10, 80073 Capri. Tel. 081/837-0633. Fax 081/837-8291. 30 rooms, 2 suites, all with bath. Double L350,000-580,000; Single L230,000-350,000. All credit cards accepted.* ****

Located on the sea, this small intimate little hotel offers you the charm you're looking for when you think of Capri. They also have a pool and a restaurant that offers perfect views for an intimate dining experience. The rooms are slightly small, but this enhances the intimate appeal; they are clean, eclectically decorated, and comfortable. They also provide transportation for guests around the island.

7. PUNTA TRAGARA, *Via Tragara 57, 80073 Capri. Tel. 081/837-0844. Fax 081/837-7790. 16 rooms all with bath. Double L280,000-400,000; Suite L380,000-520,000. Breakfast included. All credit cards accepted.* ****

A prime, elegant, intimate hotel. With only 16 rooms every guest is a treasure to the proprietors. They offer small serene rooms, many with excellent views. They are located on the sea and have a weight room, sauna, and thermal baths for your pleasure. Then in the evening you can either enjoy their disco or bar, or go for a walk into Capri.

8. REGINA CRISTINA, *Via F Serena 20, 80073 Capri. Tel. 081/837-0744. Fax 081/837-0550. 55 rooms all with bath. Double L160,000-400,000; Single L130,000-180,000. All credit cards accepted.* ****

Located on the sea, this hotel offers all the basic amenities of a four star hotel. It's quiet, they have a pool, transportation for guests, but there's something missing – charm. The rooms are fair sized, somewhat clean, and comfortable, but – again – no charm. Maybe it's the surly staff, or that things look a little in disarray.

9. VILLA BRUNELLA, *Via Tragara 24, 80073 Capri. Tel 081/837-0122. Fax 081/837-0430. 18 rooms all with bath. Double L300,000. All credit cards accepted.* ****

You can enjoy the sea by the view from the restaurant or from the small local beach a few meters away. A small hotel with its own piano bar and cocktail lounge, the rooms are relatively small but they have the necessary air conditioning, TV, mini bar, etc. The bathrooms are okay-sized but immaculately clean. Located a little way outside of Capri, it's only a short walk to get into the center of town.

10. CAESAR AUGUSTUS *(Anacapri), Via G. Orlandi 4, 80071 Capri. Tel. 081/837-1421. Fax 081/837-1444. 58 rooms, 4 suites all with bath. Double L100,000-350,000; Single L60,000-150,000; Suite L350,000. Breakfast L15,000. All credit cards accepted.* ***

This is *La creme de la creme* of the three stars on Capri. The rooms are large with well appointed bathrooms. They have a pool that seems to attract some of the best bathing beauties around, and the hotel also has a stupendous view of the sea and parts of Capri. The only thing really missing is a restaurant, but you're within walking distance of Anacapri so you can sample the many restaurants there.

11. CANASTA, *Via Campo di Teste 6, 80073 Capri. Tel. 081/837-8298. Fax 081/837-8933. 17 rooms all with bath. Double L120,000-200,000; Single L90,000-110,000. All credit cards accepted.* ***

A quaint little three star that has all the amenities and charm of many of the four stars without the exorbitant prices. Located on the sea, this is a small romantic hotel that only lacks a restaurnat so guests don't have to go out for dinner. With the restaurant, this place would be a four star.

12. LA FLORIDIANA, *Via Campo di Teste 16, 80073 Capri. Tel. 081/ 837-0166. Fax 081/837-0434. 36 rooms all with bath. Double 125,000-240,000; Single L60,000-120,000; Suite 380,000. Breakfast L30,000. All credit cards accepted.* ***

An intimate three star with a good restaurant that has a fantastic view. Some of the quiet rooms share this same view of the sea. In the evenings you can sit sipping a room service cocktail from your plain but attractive room and reflect on the beauty that is Capri. Since you're right on the sea your bathing opportunities abound.

13. SAN MICHELE DI ANACAPRI, *Via G Orlandi 3, 80071 Capri. Tel. 081/837-1427. Fax 081/837-1420. Double L140,000-200,000; Single L100,000-120,000. Breakfast included. All credit cards accepted.****

Oh my, what a view. Located on the edge of a cliff, almost all the rooms have the most spectacular view you could find anywhere. The excellent restaurant and swimming pool share the same scenery. It doesn't have the intimacy of a smaller hotel, but it has worlds of charm. The rooms are large and comfortable and bathrooms are immaculate.

WHERE TO EAT

14. DA GEMMA, *Via Madre Serafina 6, Capri, Tel. 081/837-0461. Closed Mondays and November. Dinner for two L50,000. All credit cards accepted.*

In the hot summer months, come here to enjoy the cool air-conditioned comfort and great food. Even though Gemma is no longer around to run the place, her family continues the tradition of classic

Italian food with just enough flair to make them unique and interesting. They are famous for their *spaghetti alla vongole* (with clam sauce) and the *"fritto alla Gemma"* (fried food alla Gemma with mozzarella and zucchini and other vegatables).

15. ADD' 'O RICCIO, *Locanda Gradola, Via Grotta Azzurra 4, Tel. 081/ 837-1380. Open all week. Closed for holidays November 10 - March 15. Dinner for two L110,000. All credit cards accepted.*

Come here for the food as well as the beautiful terrace overlooking the water, the rocks, and the Grotta Azzurra (Blue Grotto). They make a superb *risotto al mare* (seafood rice dish) and grilled or baked fish.

16. BUCA DI BACCO DA SERAFINA, *Via Longano 35, Tel. 081/837- 0723. Closed Wednesdays and November. Dinner for Two L80,000. All credit cards accepted.*

This is a small pizzeria *trattoria* with the wood burning oven the center of attention in the place. As you guessed, they make great pizzas. Try one of their specials, loaded with mozzarella and ricotta cheeses. They also make great pasta dishes, including a *pennette alla peperoni* (small tubular pasta in a tomatoe and sausage sauce). Since they're on Capri, they also serve a variety of seafood dishes for good prices.

17. LA CONAZONE DEL MARE, *Via Marina Piccola 93, Tel. 081/837- 0104. Only open for dinner. Holidays November to March. Meal for two L110,000. All credit cards accepted.*

Located at the small marina with a beautiful terrace overlooking everything. The perfect place to enjoy a meal and watch the people go by. You can get a variety of food here, including toast (bruschetta) loaded with mozzarella, tomatoes and olive oil, as well as a scrumptious club sandwich. Any of their *antipasti di mare* (seafood appetizers) are superb. Try their *spaghetti con pomodor e basilico* (with tomatoes and basil) or their *spaghetti ai frutti di mare* (with seafood). For seconds they have a great selection of fresh fish, either grilled, cooked in the oven, or *all'aqua pazza* (in crazy water, i.e. boiled).

18. LA CAMPANINA, *Via delle Botteghe 12, Tel. 081/837-0732. Closed Wednesdays and November to Easter. Dinner for two L140,000. All credit cards accepted.*

A fine family run, upscale, but rustic establishment. You'll enjoy the air conditioning in the heat of the summer. Try their linguine *ai frutti di mare* (with seafood) and their *coniglio "alla tiberiana"* (rabbit stewed with tomatoes and spices). Here you'll get peasant fare for a princely sum.

19. FARAGLIONI DA GIULIANO, *Via Camarelle 75, Tel. 081/837- 0320. Closed Mondays and Nover 15 to March 15. Dinner for two L110,000. All credit cards accepted.*

You can enjoy the traditional cooking either in air conditioned comfort inside or out on their terrace overlooking the street. They make a good *risotto alla pescatore* (rice with seafood), *spaghetti ai frutti di mare* (with seafood) and any of their grilled fish dishes, especially the sole.

20. DA GELSOMINA *(Anacapri) Via Belvedere Migliari, Tel. 081/837-1499. Closed Tuesdays and January 20-31. Dinner for two L70,000. All credit cards accepted.*

Off the beaten path, and quite a hike from Anacapri or Capri, but it's worth the journey. Great peasant food served on a beautiful veranda overlooking the ocean and the lights from Capri below. Try their *spaghetti alla cozze* (with muscles) or their great antipasto table for primo. Then sample their great *coniglio alla cacciatore* (rabbit with a tomato, brandy, and mixed spices – you have to try it).

21. LE GROTELLE, *Via Arco Naturale 5, Tel. 081/837-5719. Closed Thursdays and December 1 - January 3. Dinner for L 100,000. All credit cards accepted.*

Out in the middle of a virtual nature preserve, from the terrace you have a spectacular view of the sea, the stars, and nature. Here you get typical local fare like *pasta e fagioli, ravioli alla caprese*, and fish either fried or grilled. If you sit inside, these delicious smells permeate the rooms making your meal all the more enjoyable.

22. DA LUIGI AI FARAGLIONI, *Strade dei Faraglioni, Tel. 081/837-0591. Open only for dinner. Dinner for two L120,000. All credit cards accepted.*

The best terrace in Capri. Out on a small peninsula off the island, you can try some wonderfully prepared seafood dishes like *sauté di vongole* (sautéd clams), or *pomodoro "alla Luigi"* (with mozzarella e basil) or *pizza "Monacone"* (filled with vegetables). Come for the romantic view (remember to reserve a spot) and stay for the food.

23. DA MAMMA GIOVANNA *(Anacapri) Via Boffe 3/5, Tel. 081/837-2057. Closed Mondays and the ten days after Christmas. Dinner for two L80,000. All credit cards accepted.*

Located in the heart of Anacapri, this is a small, quaint, local trattoria that makes great pizzas as well as grilled or oven cooked meats and fish. They have a terrace from which you can watch the night pass as you sip your dry house wine and enjoy the food.

24. PAOLINO, *Via Palazzo a Mare 11, Tel. 081/837-6102. CLosed Mondays and January 15 to Easter. Dinner for two L120,000. All credit cards accepted.*

They've got old stoves and other cooking devices for the bases of the tables, which lends the place a nice down to earth touch that seems to go well with their sky high prices. Try their *ravioli alla caprese, spaghetti con pomodoro*, or *rucola e gamberi* for primo. For seconds try any of their seafood on the grill.

25. LA SAVARDINA DA EDOARDO, *Via Lo Capo Tiberio 8, Tel. 081/837-6300. Closed November to March. Dinner for two L75,000. All credit cards.*

You can only get here on foot, but it's worth the hike. Some of the best food on the island as well as some of the best prices. The terraces looks out over lemon and other fruit trees making the meal quite tranquil. They make great *fiori di zucchine fritte* (fried zucchini flowers) and *conniglio alla cacciatore* (rabbit cooked in tomatoes, brandy, and spices). A nice place to come for a change of pace.

SEEING THE SIGHTS

To get to the town of Capri after you've made it to the **Marina Grande**, the main harbor on the island, take the funicular (kind of like a trolley rising up the mountain). From here you can enjoy a memorable view from **Piazza Umberto I** over the **Bay of Naples**. You can walk – granted it's a long way – northeast to the ruined **Palace of Tiberius**, and along the way enjoy the breathtaking views.

The Palace is perched on an imposing hilltop from which the Emperor is said to have thrown his enemies (and if you've read any Roman history this is probably true). *Open daily 9:00am until 1 hour before sunset. Admission L5,000.* On the south edge of town is the **Certosa di San Giacomo**, a 14th century Carthusian monastery now largely in ruins, as well as the **Parco Augusto** that offers you fine views to the south of the island. *Both are open 24 hours.*

From here you can follow a road that leads to the **Marina Piccola** (small harbor). From the harbor southeast along the shoreline you can venture a dip in the water from the rocks (in the summer of course).

My favorite part of the island is the town of **Anacapri**. It is perched high up on a rocky plateau, its flat-roofed buildings obviously Moorish in style. Here you can find the 18th century **Church of San Michele** (*open daily 7:00am–7:00pm*) and the **Villa San Michele**, which is known for its beautiful gardens and vast collection of classical sculpture. *Open summer 9:00am–6:00pm, winter 10:00am–3:00pm. Admission L12,000.* From Anacapri you can walk or take a chair lift up to **Monte Solaro**, which has amazing views over the entire island and toward another Island, **Ischia**

Finally, the famous **Grotta Azzura** or **Blue Grotto**. To get there you have to take a motorboat from Marina Grande, then transfer to rowboats to enter the grotto. The silver-blue color of the water is caused by refraction of light entering the grotto from an opening beneath the surface. I know it seems cheesy and touristy, but if you've made it this far, the Blue Grotto really is worth seeing. *Open 24 hours. Boat trips from Marina Grande go from 9:00am–6:00pm.*

Walking is by far the best way of getting about the island, but horse-drawn carriages and buses operate, the latter linking Capri and Anacapri, and Marina Grande and Marina Piccola. And if you're walking during the summer months, remember to rest frequently; the hills can be steep. Bring along some water to prevent dehydration.

13. FLORENCE

A visit to Italy is not complete without a trip to **Firenze** (**Florence**), one of the most awe-inspiring cities in all of Europe. The Renaissance reached its full heights of artistic expression here, and it was here in Florence that countless master artists, writers, inventors, political theorists and artisans lived and learned their craft - Michelangelo being only the best known outside of Italy. But I'll wager you've also heard of Leonardo da Vinci, Dante, Petrarch, Machiavelli, Giotto, Raphael and many other learned and talented Florentines.

Strolling through the cobblestone streets of Florence, it's like your walking in an art history book come to life. The sights, smells, and sounds of this wonderful medieval place have got to be experienced first-hand. So read on, and I'll guide you through the amazing, lovely city of Florence!

Alive with History – Beautiful Firenze!

At first Florence was only the market square for the ancient Etruscan town of **Fiesole**, located on a hill about three miles (five kilometers) to the northeast. Farmers displayed their fruits and vegetables on the clearing along the **Arno**, and the Fiesole people came down to buy. About 187 BC, the Romans built a road through the marketplace, and later a military garrison was established here.

As the Roman roads extended through central and northern Italy, Florence grew and prospered. It became a trade center for goods brought down from the north as a resort. Invaders sought to conquer Florence. In 401, a horde of Ostrogoths besieged the city, and in 542 the Goths made an unsuccessful attack. Soon after, the Lombard conquest swept over Florence, and the city became the capital of a dukedom. In time, Charlemagne drove the Lombards out and in 799 ordered new fortifications. Charlemagne's death in 814 ended the Holy Roman Empire's hold on Florence, and it became a virtual city-state.

With its new-found freedom, Florence expanded rapidly. The Florentines became energetic merchants and bankers, expert workmen, brave soldiers, and shrewd statesmen. By the 1100s their guilds were among the most powerful in Europe, and Florentine textiles were sold throughout the continent. Florentine bankers financed enterprises in many countries. In 1252, the city coined its first gold pieces, called **florins**. These became the accepted currecny for all of Europe.

AN INCREDIBLE STATUE, AN INCREDIBLE INN!

If this is your first visit to fair Italy, you must visit Florence. The small Renaissance streets, the countless art galleries, the friendly people, and the fine food all make this city a joy to visit. But not in high season. Florence in the summer is a zoo of tourists (not quite as bad as Venice, but close) all crammed together or queued for blocks to see the main sights. Florence definitely should be visited in the off-season, not only to save on your hotel bills (hotels drop their rates dramatically in the off-season) but also to make your entire stay more enjoyable and relaxing.

*It is one thing to savor the excellence of Michelangelo's **David** virtually alone, and almost believe that you could see it move, and it is another thing entirely to have to fight your way through a crowd jut to get loose enough to try and see. But no matter when you visit, if you're looking for some peace and tranquillity, try the unmatched **Torre Di Bellosguardo**, one of my favorite hotels anywhere.*

Located above the city, you'll find the best views of Florence from anywhere. It is a supremely romantic spot filled with gardens, olive trees where horses graze, an open lawn in front, and a pool with a bar all overlooking this magnificent city. But there are only 16 rooms in this medieval castle, so if you want to stay here you have to plan far, far in advance.

Although Florence was largely self-governing, for a long time the city was the property of German princes. The last to hold it was Countess Matilda of Tuscany. At her death in 1115, the countess bequeathed Florence to the papacy. In the early 1200s, the papal power was supported by a political group called the **Guelfa**, and the claims of the German emperor were backed by another group, the **Ghibellines**. In 1215 the rival factions tried to seize control. The struggle lasted for more than 100 years.

Aided by several popes, the Guelfa held power in the city until 1260, when their army was almost wiped out at the nearby town of Siena. The Ghibellines then held the reins for six years. In 1266, Charles of Anjou, the champion of Pope Clement IV, marched down from France and smashed the forces of the German emperor at the battle of Benevento. The Guelfa exiles were able to return to Florence.

In 1293, the **Ordinances of Justice** were passed. These laws excluded from public office anyone who was a member of a Florentine guild. Many powerful people were barred from holding public positions, and the strength of the merchant-nobles was thus reduced for a time. Florence remained a republic for about 150 years. The control of the city, however, soon passed back into the hands of the wealthy.

The **Medici** family gradually took possession of Florence, installing their puppets in city offices. Giovanni de' Medici was the first of this family to gain wealth and influence. His son Cosimo was the real ruler of Florence for many years; it was he who brought exiled Greek scholars to the city. Under Cosimo's grandson **Lorenzo the Magnificent**, Florence ascended to its greatest heights as a cultural center.

REBIRTH OF ART & SCIENCE IN FLORENCE

*Florence, rather than Rome, was the cradle of the Italian **Renaissance**. This rebirth of classical knowledge soon gave way to new creativity in art and literature, and Florentines led the procession. **Dante's** magnificent poetry made the Tuscan dialect the official language of Italy. **Francesco Petrarch** composed his lovely sonnets that still live today, and **Giovanni Boccaccio** wrote his Decameron Tales here. **Niccolo Machiavelli**, another Florentine, set down his brilliant, cynical observations on politics.*

***Giotto** was the first of many immortal Florentine painters and sculptors. **Michelangelo** worked by day on the city's fortifications and by night on his paintings and statues. **Ghiberti** labored almost a lifetime on the doors for the Florentine Baptistery. Many other great artists studied or worked in Florence, among them **Leonardo da Vinci, Donatello, Raphael,** and **Luca della Robbia**.*

After Lorenzo died in 1492, the city's excesses brought on a reform movement. Heading the movement was Girolamo Savonarola, a Dominican friar. The Medici were expelled in 1494. Savonarola then ruled Florence himself until 1498, when a reaction set in, and he was put to death.

In 1512 the Medicis were restored, and Florence became a duchy. In 1537 it became part of the Grand Duchy of Tuscany. Upon the death of the last Medici in 1737, Tuscany passed to the Austrian Hapsburgs. In 1861 it was formally annexed to the newly formed Kingdom of Italy, of which Florence was the capital from 1865 to 1870.

In World War II, Florence was again a battleground. Italy entered the war on the German side in 1940, and soon after German troops occupied the city. When the Allies advanced in 1944, the Germans declared Florence an open city. Yet in retreating they destroyed all the bridges except the Ponte Vecchio, and they demolished many medieval dwellings. Later the Allied Military Government restored the less seriously damaged structures. In 1966, Florence's artworks suffered their most devastating loss when the Arno River overflowed its banks, rising as high as 20 feet (6 meters) in some places. Many of the more important damaged works have since been restored, but thousands of irreplaceable treasures were lost.

IF YOU MISS THESE PLACES, YOU HAVEN'T BEEN TO FLORENCE

After spending all your time and money to come to this Renaissance paradise, there are a few sights you that if you don't see you can't really say you've been to Florence. The first of which is hard to miss: the **Duomo** with its campanile and baptistery. The next is a gem of Medieval and Renaissance architecture, the **Ponte Vecchio** with all its gold shops. And if you miss Michelangelo's **David** in the Accademia you shouldn't show your face back in your home town. That work of art is as close to sculpted perfection as any artist will ever achieve.

Last but not least is the art collection in the **Uffizzi Gallery**. To actually do this museum justice you may need to spend close to one day wandering through its many rooms. And don't forget to sample the *panini* at **Nerbone**, a small local eatery inside the **Mercato Centrale** that serves the most succulent boiled meat sandwiches, prepared right in front of you.

There are countless other wonderful sights to see and places to go in Florence. Walking the streets is like walking through a fairy tale. But if you haven't seen the items above, you haven't been to Florence.

ARRIVALS & DEPARTURES

By Bus

There are many different bus companies in Italy, each serving a different set of cities and sometimes the same ones. Buses should be used only if the train does not go to your destination since traffic is becoming more and more of a problem in Italy.

The most convenient bus company in Florence is located directly next to the train station in **Piazza Adua**, called **LAZZI** *(055/215-154)*. They have over 50 arrivals and departures a day to and from a variety of different locations like Pisa, Lucca, Prato, and Pistoia.

By Car

If arriving in Florence from the South, for speed you will probably be on the **A1** (**E35**). If you were looking for a more scenic adventure, you would be on the **Via Cassia** which you take all the way from Rome. If arriving from the North in a hurry, you would also take the **A1** (**E35**), but if in no rush you would probably take the **SS 65**.

Sample trip lengths on the main roads:
- **Rome**: 3 1/2 hours
- **Venice**: 4 hours
- **Bologna**: 1 1/2 hours.

If you need to rent a car while in Florence, please refer to the *Getting Around Town* section of this chapter, below.

By Train

The station, **Santa Maria Novella**, is located near the center of town and is easily accessible on foot to most hotels. The **tourist information office** in the station *(Tel. 055/278-785)* is open daily from 7:00am to 10:00pm and is your first stop if you don't have a reservation at a hotel. The **railway office**, at the opposite end of the station from the tourist information office is your destination to plan your trip from Florence. You need to take a number to get information.

The wait can be quite long, but it is entertaining watching Italians become completely confused about having to take a number, wait in a queue, and actually do something in an organized fashion. First your average Italian will attempt to assert his Latin ego to an information officer, whether they are serving someone else or not, get rebuffed, attempt to do it again with another information officer, get rebuffed again, finally look at the machine spitting out numbers and the directions associated with it, stare as would a deer trapped in an oncoming car's headlights, turn and glare at the long line formed since they attempted their folly, then ultimately strut out of the office without getting the information they need. I've seen it happen too many times!

There are **taxis** located just outside the entrance near the tourist information office as well as **buses** that can take you all over the city.

Sample trip lengths and costs for direct *(diretto)* trains:
- **Rome**: 2 1/2 hours, L35,000
- **Venice**: 3 1/2 hours, L27,000
- **Bologna**: 1 hour, L15,000.

GETTING AROUND TOWN

By Bicycle & Scooter

There is one reputable company in Florence to get either motorbikes or bicycles:
- **Noleggio dell Fortezza** *(two locations),Corner of Via Strozzi and Via del Pratello, Open 9:00am to 8:00pm, the 15th of March to 31st of October; and Via Faenza 107-109r. Tel. 055/283-448.* **Scooter prices**: *1 hour L9,000/ half day L20,000/ 1 day L38,000.* **Bicycle prices**: *1 hour L3,000/ half day L8,000/ 1 day L15,000.*

By Bus

There is no need to go by bus in Florence unless you're going up to Fiesole. But if you need to, first get information from the booth at the Piazza della Stazione across the piazza from the station itself. Here they can give you all the information you need to go anywhere you want to go. A ticket costs L1,400 and is reusable within an hour.

At all bus stops, called **fermatas**, there are signs that list all the buses that stop there. These signs also give the streets that the buses will follow along its route so you can check your map to see if this is the bus for you. Also, on the side of the bus are listed highlights of the route for your convenience. Nighttime routes (since many of them stop a midnight) are indicated by black spaces on newer signs, and are placed at the bottom of the older signs. In conjunction, the times listed on the signs indicate when the bus will pass the *fermata* during the night so you can plan accordingly.

Riding the bus during rush is very crowded, so try to avoid the rush hours of 8:00am to 9:00am, 12:30pm to 1:30pm, 3:30 to 4:30pm, and 7:30pm to 8:30pm. They have an added rush hour in the middle of the day because of their siesta time in the afternoon.

By Car

Renting a car is relatively simple, as things go in Italy, but it is somewhat expensive. You can rent a car from a variety of agencies all over Florence. All prices will vary by agency so please call them for an up-to-date quote.

- **Budget**, *Borgo Ognissanti 134r, Tel. 055/29.30.21 or 28.71.61.*
- **Euro Dollar**, *Via il Prato 80r, Tel 055/238-24-80. Fax 055/238-24-79.*
- **Avis**, *Borgo Ognissanti 128r, Tel 055/21-36-29 or 239-8826*
- **Avis**, *Lungarno Torrigiani 32/3, Tel 055/234-66-68 or 234-66-69*
- **Hertz**, *Via Maso Finiguerra 33, Tel. 055/239-8205. Fax 055/230-2011*
- **Maggiore**, *Via Maso Finiguerra 11r, Tel. 055/21-02-38*

Most companies require a deposit that amounts to the cost of the rental, as well as a 19% VAT added to the final cost, which can be reimbursed once you're home (see Chapter 7, *Basic Information*). A basic rental of a Fiat Panda costs L120,000 per day, but the biggest expense is gasoline. In Italy it costs more than twice as much per gallon as it does in the States.

Also if you're adventurous enough to think of renting a car, remember that the rates become more advantageous if you rent for more than a week.

By Moped

Since Florence is so small, the areas in Tuscany I'm recommending quite close together, and the drivers are not quite as crazy as Romans, a moped (50cc) or *vespa* (125cc) is one of the best ways to get around and see the countryside. But this isn't a simple ride in the park. Only if you feel extremely confident about your motorcycle driving abilities should you even contemplate renting a moped.

Rentals for a moped (50cc) are about L40,000 per day, and for a 125cc (which you'll need to transport two people) about L70,000 per day. Some companies you can rent even bigger bikes, but I would strongly advise against it. You can also rent the cycles for an hour or any multiples thereof.

• **Firenze Motor**, *Via Guelfa 85r. Tel 055/280-500. Fax 05/211-748. Located in the Centro section to the right of the station and north of the Duomo.*

By Taxi

Taxis are the best, and also the most expensive, way to get around Florence if you're tired of walking. They are everywhere, except on the streets designated for foot traffic only, so flagging one down is not a problem. But since they are so expensive I wouldn't rely on them as your main form of transportation. Also have a map handy when a cabby is taking you somewhere. Since they are on a meter, they sometimes decide to take you on a little longer journey than necessary. And also watch out for the fly by night operators that don't have a licensed meter. They will really rip you off.

The going rate as of publication was L3,500 for the first 2/3 of a kilometer or the first minute (which usually comes first during the rush hours), then its L300 every 1/3 of a kilometer or minute. At night you'll also pay a surcharge of L3,000, and Sundays you'll pay L1,000 extra. If you bring bags aboard, say for example after you've been shopping, you'll be charged L500 extra for each bag.

There are strategically placed cab stands all over the city.

WHERE TO STAY

Centro Storico

The **Centro Storico** is the very heart of Florence. Anywhere you stay, shop, eat, or drink will be relatively expensive, since this is the prime tourist area of Florence. In this area you have the **Duomo** dominated by Brunelleschi's huge dome; the **Baptistery** next door with its beautiful bronze doors; the **Piazza della Signoria** with its copy of Michelangelo's *David* and, under the cobble stones, Bronze age relics proving that Florence is centuries older than anyone ever thought; the **Uffizzi Gallery** with it many art treasures; the **Ponte Vecchio** which was built in 1345 and used to house butchers, blacksmiths, green-grocers, tanners and leather workers but is now home to with its many gold shops; the **Piazza della Repubblica** that once was the site of a Roman Forum; the **Jewish ghetto**, and until the end of the 19th century, an open air market; the **Mercato Nuovo** or Straw Market with its many fine examples of Tuscan craftsmanship; and the Fifth Avenue of Florence, the **Via Tornabuoni**, where it even seems expensive to windowshop.

1. HOTEL ALDINI, *Via Calzaiuoli 13, Firenze. Tel 055/214-752. Fax 055/216-410. Mastercard and Visa accepted. 15 rooms all with private bath, telephone, and air conditioning. Single L105,000; Double L160,000; Triple L220,000. Breakfast Included.* **

Centrally located, some of the rooms have views of the Duomo. You can't beat the price for a double with air conditioning anywhere. A bargain if I ever saw one.

2. HOTEL AUGUSTUS, *Piazzetta dell'Oro 5, 50123 Firenze. Tel. 055/283-054. Fax 055/268-557. American Express, Diners Club, Mastercard and Visa accepted. 62 rooms all with private bath. Single L200,000-275,000; Double L270,000-390,000; Suites L360,000-510,000.* ****

Sister hotel to the Continental and Lungarno, I would recommend them over this one mostly because of the superior views. The locations, service, amenities, etc. are all the same, except that this beauty is not on the Arno. Use this as a fall-back position for your top-class hotel, but try the other two first.

3. PENSIONE BRETAGNA, *Lungarno Corsini 6, 5123 Firenze. tel. 055/289-618. Fax 055/289-619. 28 rooms, 14 with private bath. Single L60,000-70,000; Double L95,000-115,000 Triple L145,000-160,000.* **

If you can get room #30 with its separate entrance hall, bathroom, large bedroom, and two windows facing onto a quiet courtyard, by all means stay here. For L115,000 it's a steal, since you're a stones throw from the Ponte Vecchio and everything else in Florence. The rooms are on two floors of an old building which you'll fall in love with once you step foot into their large lobby and common area. The wood floors, tall ceilings, paintings and furniture all hark back to days gone by. The other rooms are nice too, but only one overlooks the Arno.

4. HOTEL BERCHIELLI, *Lungarno Acciaioli 14, 50123 Firenze. Tel. 055/264-061. Fax 055/218-636. American Express, Diners Club, Mastercard and Visa accepted. 74 rooms all with private bath. Single L220,000-270,000; Double L320,000-380,000. Extra bed L100,000.* ****

A glossy, neo-classic, ultra-modern, blue-tinted hotel. As you can tell, I found the decor rather garish, but the courtyard terraces are fine. Located right beside the Ponte Vecchio, the look and feel of the place is more business than tourism. I would suggest trying one of the other hotels nearby: Augustus or Continental.

THE FIVE BEST HOTELS IN FLORENCE

*One star hotels

8. ALBERGO FIRENZE, *Piazza Donati 4 (Via del Corso), Firenze. Tel. 055/268-301. Fax 055/212-370. No credit cards accepted. 60 rooms, 35 with private bath. Single L50,000-60,000; Double L74,000-86,000. Breakfast included.*

**Two star hotels

11. HOTEL LA SCALETTA, *Via Guicciardini 13, Firenze. Tel. 055/283-028. Fax 055/289-562. Mastercard and Visa accepted. 12 rooms, 11 with private bath. Single L80,000: Double L125,000; Triple L165,000; Quad L185,000. Breakfast included.*

***Three star hotels

9. HOTEL HERMITAGE, *Vicolo Marzio 1 (Piazza del Pesce), 50122 Firenze. Tel. 055/287-216. Fax 055/212-208. Mastercard and Visa accepted. 29 rooms all with private bath. Single L120,000-160,000; Double L190,000-240,000. Breakfast included.*

****Four star hotels

38. HOTEL TORRE DI BELLOSGUARDO, *Via Roti Michelozzi 2, Firenze. Tel. 055/229-8145. Fax 055/229-008. 16 room all with bath. Single L250,000; Double L330,000; Suites L430,000-530,000. All credit cards accepted. The best hotel in Florence ... bar none.*

*****Five star hotels

21. EXCELSIOR HOTEL, *Piazza Ognissanti 3, 50123 Firenze. Tel. 055/264-201. Fax 055/210-278. Toll free number in American 1-800-221-2340. All credit cards accepted. 200 rooms all with private bath. Single L290,000-340,000; Double L420,000-490,000' Suite L800,000-L1,300,000. Continental breakfast L26,000. American breakfast L41,000.*

5. HOTEL SOGGIORNO BRUNORI, *Via del Proconsolo 5, Firenze. Tel 055/289-648. No credit cards accepted. 9 rooms, 1 with private bath. Double L62,000-78,000; Triple L87,000-110,000; Quad L110,000-138,000. *

Leonardo (the thick heavy set guy) and Giovanni (the thin witty one) will do anything to make your stay at their hotel more pleasurable. Call a taxi, book train reservations, etc. You name it they'll do it. The rooms aren't spectacular but there are some with balconies that overlook the busy street and give you some decent views.

But look at the prices. They are continuing to upgrade the facilities but as they do all is still very accommodating here. If you call for a reservation and they don't have a room for you, they'll put you in touch with other places with similar prices just to keep you happy. These guys really go the extra mile.

6. HOTEL CALZAIUOLI, *Via Calzaiuoli 6, Firenze. Tel 055/212-456. Fax 055/268-310. American Express, Mastercard and Visa accepted. 45 rooms all with private bath, TV, Telephone, mini-bar, and air conditioning. Breakfast included. Single L85,000-120,000; Double L120,000-L180,000. Extra bed L50,000.* ***

Some rooms have great views of the Duomo and with that view, its location, and all the amenities it offers the prices do seem rather good. The rooms have a nice floral and ribbon print motif if that's your cup of tea. You can't beat the location or the service.

7. HOTEL CONTINENTAL, *Lungarno Acciaioli 2, 50123 Firenze. Tel. 055/282-392. Fax 055/283-139. American Express, Diners Club, Mastercard and Visa accepted. 48 rooms all with private bath. Single L 270,000; Double L350,000; Penthouse suite L630,000. Breakfast L25,000.* ****

If only I could afford the penthouse suite I would be in heaven. One rung below that fantasy is the hotel's superb terrace with breathtaking views of the Arno and the Ponte Vecchio. I mean breathtaking since they're basically right on top of the old bridge. You can't go wrong with the location, the ultra-modern rooms, the exquisite service. At the Continental you can truly live the experience of being in Renaissance Florence with all the modern amenities to keep you happy.

8. ALBERGO FIRENZE, *Piazza Donati 4 (Via del Corso), Firenze. Tel. 055/268-301. Fax 055/212-370. No credit cards accepted. 60 rooms, 35 with private bath. Single L50,000-60,000; Double L74,000-86,000; Triple L100,000-115,000. Breakfast included.* *

This is two different hotels. One is new, the other's left in a time warp from the 1950s. My recommendation is based on the new section, so call in advance to get your reservations.

Even though this place doesn't have air conditioning, it shouldn't be a one star. The lobby is all three star, as are the rooms in the new wing. Room 503 caught my fancy since it has a great view of the Duomo from the bed. So when you wake up in the morning, open your eyes, and there's the Duomo right in front of you. Besides the beauty and comfort of the new wing, the lobby and breakfast area is of a much higher standard than any other one star I've been in. It's beautiful and its inexpensive. They speak English, so make sure you tell them that you want to stay in the new wing.

9. HOTEL HERMITAGE, *Vicolo Marzio 1 (Piazza del Pesce), 50122 Firenze. Tel. 055/287-216. Fax 055/212-208. Mastercard and Visa accepted. 29 rooms all with private bath. Single L120,000-160,000; Double L190,000-240,000. Breakfast included.* ***

Only steps from the Ponte Vecchio but located above the tourist noise, this 20 room *pensione* is on the top three floors of an office building and is reached by a private elevator. It has the most wonderful roof

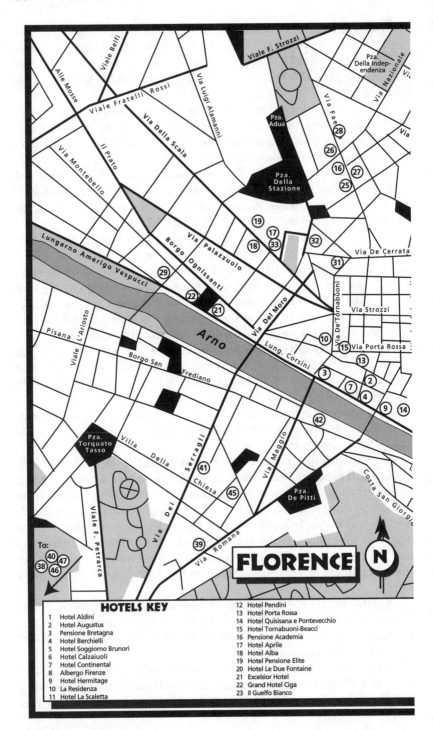

HOTELS KEY

1   Hotel Aldini
2   Hotel Augustus
3   Pensione Bretagna
4   Hotel Berchielli
5   Hotel Soggiorno Brunori
6   Hotel Calzaiuoli
7   Hotel Continental
8   Albergo Firenze
9   Hotel Hermitage
10 La Residenza
11 Hotel La Scaletta
12 Hotel Pendini
13 Hotel Porta Rossa
14 Hotel Quisisana e Pontevecchio
15 Hotel Tornabuoni-Beacci
16 Pensione Academia
17 Hotel Aprile
18 Hotel Alba
19 Hotel Pensione Elite
20 Hotel Le Due Fontaine
21 Excelsior Hotel
22 Grand Hotel Ciga
23 Il Guelfo Bianco

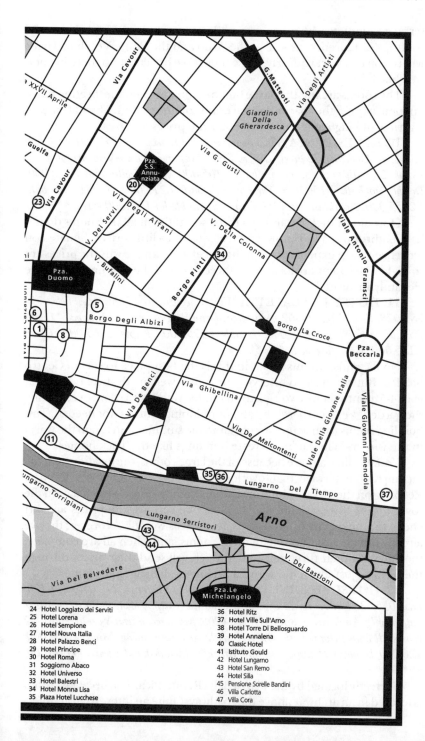

24 Hotel Loggiato dei Serviti
25 Hotel Lorena
26 Hotel Sempione
27 Hotel Nouva Italia
28 Hotel Palazzo Benci
29 Hotel Principe
30 Hotel Roma
31 Soggiorno Abaco
32 Hotel Universo
33 Hotel Balestri
34 Hotel Monna Lisa
35 Plaza Hotel Lucchese
36 Hotel Ritz
37 Hotel Ville Sull'Arno
38 Hotel Torre Di Bellosguardo
39 Hotel Annalena
40 Classic Hotel
41 Istituto Gould
42 Hotel Lungarno
43 Hotel San Remo
44 Hotel Silla
45 Pensione Sorelle Bandini
46 Villa Carlotta
47 Villa Cora

terrace, complete with greenery and flowers and a wonderful view of the rooftops of Florence, as well as the Arno and the Ponte Vecchio. That's where you can start your day, since they serve breakfast up there in good weather.

The rooms are not that large but the ambiance and the location make up for it, as does the spacious terrace and common areas. The staff speaks a variety of languages. For a three star the prices are great.

10. LA RESIDENZA, *Via Tornabuoni 8, Firenze. Tel. 055/218-684. Fax 284-197. American Express, Diners Club, Mastercard and Visa accepted. 25 rooms, 20 with bath. Single no bath L105,000; Single with bath L130,000; Double no bath L150,000; Double with bath L215,000. Triple with bath L2855,000. Breakfast included. dinner available for L35,000 extra.* ***

How did a hotel in Italy get a three star rating if all the rooms do not have bathrooms? Who knows? A nice hotel but a little pricey. Situated on Florence's most expensive shopping street, you can see why the prices are so high. The rooms are located on three floors of the building and all are elegantly furnished.

11. HOTEL LA SCALETTA, *Via Guicciardini 13, Firenze. Tel. 055/ 283-028. Fax 055/289-562. Mastercard and Visa accepted. 12 rooms, 11 with private bath. Single L80,000: Double L125,000; Triple L165,000; Quad L185,000. Breakfast included.* **

No ifs, ands, or buts about it; this is the best place to stay in Centro Storico. But you have to reserve your rooms well in advance. Let's say at least 4-5 months before you go, to guarantee you'll get a room overlooking the garden! Yes, yes there's no air conditioning, but it's not needed. This building seems to suck up the cold air in the summer and retain the warm in the winter. Why can't we create buildings like this back home?

You should stay here because of the large rooms, the location, and the incomparable terrace that overlooks all the best sights of Florence. Relaxing on the terrace alone or with your fellow guests after a day on the town makes this stay sublime. And let's be serious, the prices are dirt cheap for the quality offered. But these prices won't last forever; they've already put air conditioning in three rooms, and when all are complete, they may get their three star rating which will send their prices through the terrace, just like it did with La Scalinetta di Spagna in Rome.

12. HOTEL PENDINI, *Via Strozzi 2, 50123 Firenze. Tel. 055/211-170. Fax 055/-281-807. E-Mail pendini@dad.it (http://www.dada.it/pendini/ hotel.html). American Express, Diners Club, Mastercard and Visa accepted. 42 rooms all with private bath. Only 25 with air conditioning. Single L100,000-120,000; Double L150,000-180,000. Breakfast included. Extra bed costs L60,000.* ***

Perfectly located by the Piazza della Repubblica. The breakfast room is located in an archway above the roadway. Quite an interesting architectural quirk. Thinking about it can make you a little nervous at breakfast. They have twelve rooms that overlook the piazza and all are beautiful. The staff is more than accommodating, and they speak perfect English. An ideally central location for your stay in Florence.

13. HOTEL PORTA ROSSA, *Via Porta Rossa 19, 50123 Firenze. Tel. 055/287-551. Fax 055/282-179. American Express, Diners Club, Mastercard and Visa accepted. 80 rooms all with private bath. Double L175,00.* ***

Don't even think of staying here. Yes it's quaint, yes the rooms are large, yes the prices are inexpensive, but the place is so run down and the staff is so surly and unnaccomodating that it makes even a one night stay unbearable.

14. HOTEL QUISISANA E PONTEVECCHIO, *Lungarno Archibusieri 4, 50122 Firenze. Tel. 055/216-692. American Express, Diners Club, Mastercard and Visa accepted. 37 rooms, 34 with private bath. Double with bath L135,000.* ***

The rooms that overlook the bridge are the best, and if you've ever seen the movie *A Room With A View*, you will be instantly reminded of certain scenes when looking out the windows.

15. HOTEL TORNABUONI-BEACCI, *Via Tornabuoni 3, Firenze. Tel. 055/212-645. Fax 055/283-594. American Express, Diners Club, Mastercard and Visa accepted. 28 rooms all with private bath. Single L150,000; Double 240,000. Extra bed L50,000. Buffet breakfast included.* ***

Located on the top three floors of a 14th century palazzo on the famous shopping street, Via Tournabuoni. There is a wonderful rooftop garden terrace that will make you fall in love with Florence every evening you spend up there. Try to get the rooms facing the garden to avoid the noise of the busy shopping street below. A much better deal with infinitely better atmosphere than La Residenza. This place is coordinated like an old castle, with nooks and crannies everywhere, and plenty of common space besides the terrace to sit and write your postcards home.

Centro

This section of town is north of the Duomo and west of the Via Tornabuoni, and is home to many reasonably priced hotels, restaurants, and stores. Here you'll find the **Mercato of San Lorenzo**, a huge daily outdoor clothing market, and the **Mercato Generale**, Florence's main food market where you can find everything from swordfish to buffalo-milk *mozzarella*.

Also located in the Centro is the train station from which you'll be embarking on the terrific excursions I've planned for you to Fiesole, Pisa, Siena, and Lucca.

16. PENSIONE ACADEMIA, *Via Faenza 7, Firenze. Tel. 055/293-451. American Express, Mastercard and Visa accepted. 16 rooms, 13 with private* *bath. Single L70,000-75,000; Double L155,000; Triple L156,000. For an extra person add 35% of the double price. Breakfast included.* *

They have beautiful stained glass entrance doors and clean quiet rooms. The singles and triples are the best values here. The doubles seem to be a little overpriced. So if you're traveling alone or with two friends, stay here.

17. HOTEL APRILE, *Via della Scala 6, 50123 Firenze. Tel. 055/216-237. Fax 055/289-147. American Express, Mastercard and Visa accepted. 29 rooms, 25 with private bath. Single L75,000-90,000; Single with bath or shower L125,000-140,000; Double L120,000-150,000; Double with bath or shower L165,000-195,000. The first price listed above is without breakfast the second is with breakfast.* ***

On a quaint side street of Piazza Santa Maria Novella that has plenty of shops, bars, cafés, and other hotels, this is a delicately decorated three star with all necessary amenities. Try to get a room that overlooks the quiet courtyard garden, so when you open the windows you can escape the onslaught of the moped noise.

18. HOTEL ALBA, *Via della Scala 22-38r, 50123 Firenze. Tel. 055/282-610. fax 055/288-358. Single L140,000; Double L200,000. Extra bed L65,000. Breakfast included.* ***

Another nice three star hotel on the Via Scala. You have all the amenities here and a great location for sightseeing, shopping, eating, dancing at Space Electronic, or drinking at the Fiddler's Elbow. The common area rooms are done up in bright colors with plants and flowers as an accessory. There is a lobby bar and a quaint little breakfast room. The rooms are a little crowded but still comfortable, and the prices are good.

19. HOTEL PENSIONE ELITE, *Via della Scala 12. Tel 055/215-395. 10 rooms all with bath or shower. Single with shower L80,000; Single with W/ C L90,000. Double L110,000; Double that shares a bathroom with another double, a perfect family arrangement L90,000 per room.* **

Beautiful small hotel located on a great street in a perfect area for sightseeing, shopping, or dining. You'll love the wooden staircase that takes you from the lobby and breakfast salon up to your quiet and spacious rooms. The prices really can't be beat, nor can the quality of accommodations and service.

20. HOTEL LE DUE FONTANE, *Piazza SS. Annunziata 14, 50123 Firenze. Tel. 210-185. American Express, Mastercard and Visa accepted. 48 rooms all with private bath. Single L 135,000; Double L245,000, Suite for 2 or 3 people L335,000. Extra bed L60,000. Buffet breakfast included.* ***

This is a modern hotel situated in an old palazzo, so it has limited charm except for the piazza. Really a businessman's hotel that caters to tourists as well. If you were to stay on this piazza, I'd recommend the Hotel

Loggiato dei Sevititi instead. No offense to this inn, but the ambiance just doesn't cut it.

21. EXCELSIOR HOTEL, *Piazza Ognissanti 3, 50123 Firenze. Tel. 055/264-201. Fax 055/210-278. Toll free number in American 1-800-221-2340. American Express, Diners Club, Mastercard and Visa accepted. 200 rooms all with private bath. Single L290,000-340,000; Double L420,000-490,000' Suite L800,000-L1,300,000. Continental breakfast L26,000. American breakfast L41,000.* *******

Directly across from its sister, The Grand Hotel CIGA, both of these hotels are run by the Ciga organization. Some rooms in this hotel are decorated similarly to those in the Grand Hotel, but the size and decor of the rooms here varies widely – but they are all of the highest standard. I mean, this is the Excelsior. The best feature of this hotel is its roof garden/restaurant where you can have your meal or sip an after dinner drink, listen to the piano player, and gaze out at the splendor that is Florence. You don't have to stay here to enjoy the view; just come for dinner.x

22. GRAND HOTEL CIGA, *Piazza Ognizzanti 1, 50123 Firenze. Tel. 055/288-781. Fax 055/217-400. Toll free number in American 1-800-221-2340. American Express, Diners Club, Mastercard and Visa accepted. 106 rooms all with private bath. Singe L360,000-400,000; Double L510,000-580,000; Suite L900,000-1,600,000. Continental breakfast L26,000. American breakfast L41,000.* ******

Aptly named, this hotel is wonderfully quiet, even though it is on a main thoroughfare, and extremely elegant. Housed in a pale yellow and gray palazzo, the reception rooms have all been restored to their former brilliance. Each bedroom has beautiful neo-classic furniture and elegant decorations and frescoes. More pleasant and comfortable than the Excelsior since its modernization, but remember to go to the Excelsior for their roof-bar restaurant.

23. IL GUELFO BIANCO, *Via Cavour 29, Firenze. Tel. 055/288-3301. Fax 055/295-203. American Express, Mastercard and Visa accepted. 29 rooms all with private bath. Single L155,000-200,000; Double L200,000-215,000; Triple L260,000; Quad L300,000. Continental breakfast included.* *****

Not my favorite area of Florence, but there's something about this hotel that catches my heart. Maybe it's room 24, with the only terrace located on the inside courtyard. A perfect place to unwind after a day of sightseeing. Or maybe number 27 and 28, two large doubles that are basically suites with living and sleeping space. If you stay here, call well in advance to book either of these rooms. They also have two different courtyards downstairs where you can relax or start your day with breakfast.

24. HOTEL LOGGIATO DEI SERVITI, *Piazza SS. Annunziata 3, 50122 Firenze. Tel. 055/289-593/4. Fax 055/289-595. American Express,*

Diners Club, Mastercard and Visa accepted. 29 rooms all with private bath. Single L110,000-170,000; Double L190,000-240,000; Suite for 2 L300,000-500,000. Breakfast included. L80,000 for an extra bed. ***
Located in a 16h century loggia that faces the beautiful Piazza della SS Annunziata. The interior common areas consist of polished terra cotta floors, gray stone columns and high white ceilings. The rooms are pleasant and comfortable and are generally filled with antique furnishings. All designed to make you feel like you just walked into the 17th century, and it works. But they do have the modern amenities necessary to keep us weary travelers happy, especially the air conditioning in August. If you want to feel as if you're a part of history, stay here and you'll love it.

25. HOTEL LORENA, *Via Faenza 1, 50123 Firenze. Tel. 055/282-785. Fax 055/288-300. 16 rooms, 10 with bath. Single L50,000-95,000; Double L90,000-120,000; Triple L160,000; Quad L180,000. All credit cards accepted. Continental Breakfast an additional L7,500. Hotel closes its doors from 2am to 6pm so don't get left out in the cold.* **
A pleasantly run hotel located just off of the large Lorenzo market. Perfectly located for shopping and sightseeing. The rooms are nondescript but comfortable and the prices are good, if you can reserve yourself a room with a bath.

26. HOTEL SEMPIONE, *Via Nazionale 15, Tel. 055/212-462. fax 055/212-463. 24 rooms all with bath and breakfast. Single L80,000; Double L130,000; Triple L175,000; Quad L200,000. Extra person L45,000.* **
There's a nice breakfast room on the ground floor to start your day as well as a laundry service to help you feel fresh for it. The rooms on top have vistas of the Duomo and Florentine rooftops and one, room 53, has a pleasant balcony. Their is no bar area, but they do serve beverages in your rooms or in the breakfast area.

27. HOTEL NUOVA ITALIA, *Via Faenza 26, Firenze. Tel. 055/287-508. Fax 055/210-941. American Express, Mastercard and Visa accepted. 21 rooms all with private bath. Single L90,000; Double L135,000; Triple L185,000. Breakfast included.* **
Despite the absence of air conditioning, the fans in every room do a great job except in August. Each room is plainly but comfortable furnished. This family run hotel is located ideally near most of the sights and night spots, and the prices are very good. You'll just love the old Mama as she caters to you during your meals in the breakfast area, which looks just like a *trattoria* in the country.

28. HOTEL PALAZZO BENCI, *Via Faenza 6, Firenze. Tel. 055/217-049. Fax 055/288-308. American Express, Diners Club, Mastercard and Visa accepted. 26 rooms all with private bath. Single L150,000; Double L220,000; Triple L260,000. Breakfast included.* ***

There's a hole in the ground as you walk in – but it's actually excavated ruins that they put a glass viewer over so you can see what once was ancient Florence. They have a pleasantly quiet courtyard terrace where you can enjoy breakfast or an evening drink. The decorations are a rough combination of neo-classic and ultra-modern, but the rooms are spacious and comfortable.

29. HOTEL PRINCIPE, *Lungarno Amerigo Vespucci 34, 50123 Firenze. Tel. 055/284-848. Fax 055/283-458. American Express, Diners Club, Mastercard and Visa accepted. 20 rooms all with private bath. Single L140,000-280,000; Double L190,000-380,000. Breakfast included. ****

Just down the from the tourist center, this is a quaint little hotel that caters to the discerning guest. More intimate than one of the larger high class hotels, you'll find the rooms a little plain but very comfortable with air conditioning, mini-bar, and all the other trappings of a four star hotel. They have a pleasant garden in the rear where you can enjoy a quiet afternoon.

30. HOTEL ROMA, *Piazza Maria Novella 8, 50123 Firenze. Tel. 055/ 210-366. Fax 055/215-306. American Express, Diners Club, Mastercard and Visa accepted. 60 rooms all with private bath. Single L138,000 - L275,000; Double L187,000 - L373,000. ****

The reason for the disparity in prices between low and high season is that the main draw of this hotel is the roof terrace which overlooks the beautiful Santa Maria Novella piazza. All the rooms are completely modern and spartan in appearance. The common areas are ostentatiously decorated with marble, columns, frescoes with an omnipresent blue shade. You walk into this hotel and you're instantly mellow because of the color. Even the desk staff seems to be put to sleep by it. Try it in the off-season, because their prices are great then.

31. SOGGIORNO ABACO, *Via dei Bianchi 1, 500123 Firenze. Tel. 055/238-1919. 6 rooms 1 with bath. Single L40,000-50,000; Double 60,000-70,000; Big Double 70,000-120,000. The big double is the only one with bath. Extra person L20,000. Breakfast an extra L5,000. *

For the low-budget crowd that wants the most for your money. A small intimate affair with a proprietor, Bruno will do almost anything to make your stay more pleasant. For groups or eight or more people, he will gladly cook a superb Tuscan meal of your choosing for between L5,000 and L10,000 per person. The price cannot be beaten and his culinary skills are unmatched.

There are two full baths for the five rooms that don't have the facilities, and in one, they have installed a coin operated laundry machine so you don't have to venture out in the wilds to find one. The rooms are large and accommodating and you're right in the middle of everything here. The place is like a country inn.

32. HOTEL UNIVERSO, *Piazza Santa Maria Novella 20, 50123 Firenze. Tel. 05/281-951. Fax 055/292-335. 45 rooms, 31 with bath. Single L60,000-100,000; Double L90,000-110,000; Triple L110,000-130,000; Quad L149,000-179,000; Quint L187,000-227,000.* **

A double on this picturesque square for only L110,000 with bath cannot be beat, except in August since they do not have air-conditioning. Simple and basic in style, you also get a 10% discount in the off-season. The rooms are not spectacular but they are convenient and comfortable. Remember to request a room with bath and, if you don't like noise, one that faces away from the piazza. Great location and great prices.

Santa Croce

This is the area of Florence in which Michelangelo played as a child before he was sent to the country to live with a stone carver, from whom he learned the fundamentals for his amazing ability to carve figures from slabs of marble. Located to the east of the Centro Storico and the Centro sections of Florence, Santa Croce is more of an authentic, residential, working class neighborhoodand seems far from the maddening crowds, even though it's just around the corner from them. The church that gives this area its name, Santa Croce, is home to the graves of Michelangelo, Galileo, and other Italian greats.

This is also the area in which Florentines come to dine at regular Tuscan restaurants or some of the newer restaurants offering nouvelle cuisine. The area is also home to another food market, the **Mercato Sant'Ambrogio**, located in the Piazza Ghiberti. There is also a prime picnic location, not nearly as nice as the Boboli Gardens but still a respite from the crowds, in the Piazza Massimo D'Azeglio.

33. HOTEL BALESTRI, *Piazza Mentana 7, 50122 Firenze. Tel. 055/ 214-743. Fax 055/239-8042. American Express, Diners Club, Mastercard and Visa accepted. 50 rooms all with private bath. Single L160,000; Double L220,000; Triple L290,000. Breakfast included.* ***

The best part of this hotel is that the view is great. And don't forget the extensive buffet breakfast every morning. Situated on the Arno, there are three rooms that overlook the river and the Ponte Vecchio that have terraces. Remember to request them when you book far in advance. If the noise gets to you, try four of the rooms in the rear with terraces. A good three star that is delicately appointed.

34. HOTEL MONA LISA, *Borgo Pinti 27, 50121 Firenze. Tel. 055/247-9751. Fax 055/247-9755. American Express, Diners Club, Mastercard and Visa accepted. 30 rooms all with private bath. Single L108,000-216,000; Double L145,000-290,000. Breakfast L25,000.* ****

A short walk from the Duomo, this hotel is on the ground floor of a Renaissance palazzo, and some of the rooms seem as if they have not been redecorated since that period. The common area opens onto a garden which unfortunately is also a parking area. But since this is outside of the Centro, all the rooms are quiet and tranquil, not to mention romantic. You won't find all all the amenities of a four star here; I think they are a four star because of the large size of the rooms and the old building the hotel is in.

35. PLAZA HOTEL LUCCHESI, *Lungarno della Zecca Vecchia 38, 50122 Firenze. Tel. 055/26236. fax 055/248-0921. 87 rooms all with bath. Single 153,000-280,000; Double L228,000-400,000; Suite L520,000. Breakfast included. Extra bed costs L75,000. All credit cards accepted.* ****

Located on the Arno across the river from the Piazzale Michelangelo just outside of the hustle and bustle of the center. Here you are within walking distance of all the sights, but are far enough away that you don't feel swamped by it all. All the amenities of a four star, including a piano bar and an excellent but expensive restaurant. The rooms are all air conditioned and have cable TV for your late night viewing pleasure.

36. HOTEL RITZ, *Lungarno della Zecca Vecchia 24, 50122 Firenze. Tel. 055/234-0650. fax 055/240-863. 32 rooms all with bath. Single L142,000-170,000; Double L195,000-260,000; Suite L270,000-310,000. Breakfast L18,000. All credit cards accepted.* ****

Same location as the Plaza Hotel Lucchesi above. A small, intimately romantic hotel. Perfect for young lovers. Not as many amenities as a larger four star, as reflected in the price, but the rooms are sizable and comfortable. Rooms have air conditioning, TV, mini-bar, and room service.

37. HOTEL VILLE SULL'ARNO, *Lungarno Colombo 3, 50122 Firenze. Tel. 055/67-09-71. Fax 055/678-244. 47 rooms all with bath. Single L95,000-190,000; Double L145,000-290,000. Breakfast included. All credit cards accepted.* ****

Located away from the center of things, which makes the hotel very quiet and tranquil. They have a pool and a lovely garden and a bus which can transport you to and from your destinations. You're also only a very short cab ride from everywhere. The rooms are large and comfortable with all the amenities of a four star, including air conditioning and cable TV.

Oltrarno

Oltrarno, literally "the other side of the," is home to many of Florence's artisans, leather workers, etc. It is looked upon as a city unto itself since it wasn't encompassed into the walls of Florence until the 14th century (people remember their history in Europe). Most of the beautiful architecture was destroyed during World War II, not only by the Germans but also by the Allied bombings. Thankfully both sides spared the Ponte

Vecchio, The Duomo, and the other great pieces of architecture on the other side of the river.

Also spared was the **Palazzo Vecchio** (also known as the **Medici Palace**) and the **Boboli gardens**, where Michelangelo first began his serious artistic training with the support of the Medici family. Beyond these sights and the artisans shops, the only other place to visit is the **Piazza Santo Spirito** that boasts its 15th century church with the unfinished facade by Brunelleschi. The piazza is also home to a small fresh **produce and flower market** every morning.

38. HOTEL TORRE DI BELLOSGUARDO, *Via Roti Michelozzi 2, Firenze. Tel. 055/229-8145. Fax 055/229-008. 16 room all with bath. Single L250,000; Double L330,000; Suites L430,000-530,000. All credit cards accepted.* ****

If you have the money, this is the place to stay in Florence – you'll feel like you stepped back in time to the Renaissance. Simply the best view of the city from anywhere around the city. Their grounds are filled with gardens, olive trees where horses graze, an open lawn in front, and a pool with a bar – all overlooking the magnificent city of Florence below.

The rooms are in an old castle that was once the small English language school, St. Michael's, that catered to 100 students. So you can imagine that with only sixteen rooms the size of your accommodations are quite large; and the interior common areas are like something out of a movie script, with vaulted ceilings and arches, as well as staircases leading off into hidden passages. You're a short distance outside of the old city walls but you'll get romance, peace, and tranquillity. The hotel is so magnificent that you have to reserve well in advance, since they are booked solid most of the glorious spring, summer, and fall months. I can't say enough about the view. If you aren't already in love, you'll find it or rekindle it in this wonderful hideaway.

39. HOTEL ANNALENA, *Via Romana 34, 50125 Firenze. Tel. 055/ 222-402. Fax 055/222-403. American Express, Diners Club, Mastercard and Visa accepted. 20 rooms, 16 doubles, four singles all with bath. Single L100,000-145,000. Double L170,000-195,000. Breakfast included.* ***

This place has at times been a convent, a school for young ladies, a gambling casino, during WW II a safe haven for many Italian Jews, and now it has become the Hotel Annalena. It takes over the entire floor of a beautiful Florentine palazzo and has all the necessary amenities of a good three star hotel. The lobby area doubles as breakfast room and evening bar space. The rooms are large with high ceilings an seem to be "fresco" all year round. Located just beyond the Palazzo Pitti, the only real sight nearby, except for a hidden sight, the Museo Zoologico la Specola at Via Romana 17, which houses some life-like colored wax figures and body parts that were used for anatomical study back in the 12th century.

40. CLASSIC HOTEL, *Viale Machiavelli 25, 50125 Firenze. Tel. 055/ 229-3512. Fax 055/229-353. American Express, Mastercard and Visa accepted. 20 rooms all with private bath. Single L120,000; Double L170,000; Triple L200,000. Breakfast included. Without breakfast take off L10,000 per room.* ***

Located in a quaint little old palazzo outside the old city walls, here you can get a taste of Florentine life without the constant clamoring of mopeds riding past your bedroom window. Piazzale Machiavelli is an exclusive address and this hotel shows it. The lush garden in the rear (there's a glassed-in section for winter guests) is your breakfast location as well as your mid-afternoon slumber spot, and there's a small bar just off the garden for evening drinks.

Your rooms are palatial, with immense ceilings and clean bathrooms. Each room is furnished quite differently. Some have antique furniture, others have newer but sill attractive pieces. The diversity lends a spot of charm. I would recommend this gem to anyone that likes to tour and then escape the hectic pace of the city. One minor note, they do not have air conditioning, but when I was there on a 90 degree day each room was very cool. These old palazzi were built to keep cool in the summer and remain warm in the winter. Don't ask me how, it just works.

41. ISTITUTO GOULD, *Via dei Serragli 49, 50125 Firenze. Tel. 055/ 212-576. Fax 055/280-274. No credit cards accepted. 25 rooms, 20 with private bath. Single L40,000; Double L30,000 per person.* *

If you don't have your own bath here you're still okay, since you only have to share two toilets and two showers with four other rooms. The office is on the ground floor and there are limited office hours (9:00am–1:00pm and 3:00pm–7:00pm) but they give you your own key so you can go in and out as your please. A rarity in Florence for one-stars. The rooms, on the second and third floors scattered all over the place, are quite large. My single easily should have been a double. In your search here you'll find an immense common room with comfortable chairs and a quaint little terrace overlooking some rooftops in the rear, which is a great place to relax with a glass of Chianti and some salami.

The best part of your stay is that the Istituto Gould is a home for wayward children (their quarters are far removed from your own and the kids I met seemed just to want to practice their English and play soccer), and your payment goes to assist in their care and well-being. They separate the more mature budget travelers from the younger crowd, so the late night adventures of the younger set don't keep us old folks awake.

42. HOTEL LUNGARNO, *Borgo S Jacopo 14, 50125 Firenze. Tel. 264-211. Fax 055/268-437. American Express, Diners Club, Mastercard and Visa accepted. 66 rooms all with private bath. Single L210,000-L275,000; Double L280,000-L390,000; Junior Suite L360,000-L540,000.* ****

An excellent location right on the river, only a few meters from the Ponte Vecchio, and situated down a quaint, Florentine side street with some great restaurants and food shops a few stores away. Even though most of the hotel is modern, it is a quaint establishment. The lounge just off the lobby offers a relaxing view of the river and the Ponte Vecchio.

An ancient stone tower is part of the hotel, with a great penthouse suite, in the old tower. If you want the atmosphere of the tower, specify this upon making your reservation. Some of the rooms have terraces overlooking the river, which makes for a perfect place to relax after a tough day of sightseeing. Get a confirmation to ensure you will be staying exactly where you want.

43. HOTEL SANREMO, *Lungarno Serristori 13, 50125 Firenze. Tel. 055/234-2823. Fax 055/234-2824. American Express, Diners Club, Mastercard and Visa accepted. 40 rooms all with bath. Single L100,000-130,000; Double L150,000-170,000; Triple L180,000-200,000, Quad L190,000-240,000. Breakfast included.* ***

You can either request the rooms with a view of the Arno and the Ponte Vecchia and get woken up by traffic in the morning if you're a light sleeper, or take the tranquil *camere* (rooms) in the back. The rooms are all delicately appointed and have all the necessities for a three star including air conditioning. They have a "grotto" restaurant downstairs where you can eat your breakfast in old world charm. With the bricked archways and ceiling it seems as if you're in the basement of a castle. They also have a small bar area to get a drink after you finish your nights wanderings.

44. HOTEL SILLA, *Via dei Renai 5, 50125 Firenze. Tel. 055/234-2888. Fax 055/234-1437. American Express, Diners Club, Mastercard and Visa accepted. 54 rooms all with private bath. Single L140,000; Double L190,000; Triple L230,000.****

Located on the first floor of an old palazzo. To get to it enter from the little traveled side street just off the Lungarno and walk up the red carpet covering the middle of the white marble stairs. It makes you feel very presidential. The rooms are quite big with high ceilings and all the amenities of a good three star.

45. PENSIONE SORELLE BANDINI, *Piazza Santo Spirito 9, 50125 Firenze. Tel 055/215-308. Fax 055/282-761. No credit cards accepted. 13 rooms, 5 with private bath. Double (for one or two people) L110,000-140,000 Triple L150,000-186,000; Quad L184,000-232,000. Breakfast included.* *

Usually occupied by art students from a variety of different American universities, you can usually find a room before May and after June. And what a place this is! The maze of staircases, floors, passageways intertwining with balconies, and the look of the rooms makes you feel as is you've suddenly found yourself in a medieval castle. It's definitely for the stay on the cheap set, but if you can get one of the rooms with a bath, stay here for the balcony and the prices. The balcony extends around two sides of the palazzo, offering you some great vistas of Florence. The rooms are all large, and as mentioned the clientele are mostly of university age, which makes it fun for geezers like me. Breakfast is served to all. Only dinners go to the students, but like the cats do, you too can sneak in if you want to try.

46. VILLA CARLOTTA, *Via Michele di Lando 3, 50125 Firenze. Tel. 055/233-6134. Fax 055/233-6147. American Express, Diners Club, Mastercard and Visa accepted. 27 rooms all with private bath. Five more under construction in a gatehouse building. Singles L170,000-250,000; Double L240,000-350,000. Breakfast included. Can also get another meal at their fine restaurant or L48,000.* ****

Viviana asked me to put her directors name in here (Fabrizio Gheri) instead of hers, but since she was so kind and made my stay so welcome I decided to do both. The hotel is like something out of a dream, with its sunlit tea room used for breakfast, its small garden on the side with fish swimming in the fountain, and elegant dining in the magnificent restaurant below. To top it all off you have a real bar with stools from which you can get any type of concoction your heart desires.

The location is perfect for those that like to get away from the places they just walked through. And the rooms are all pleasantly furnished with all necessary amenities.

47. VILLA CORA, *Viale Machiavelli 18-20, 50125 Firenze. Tel. 055/ 229-8451. Fax 055/229-086. American Express, Diners Club, Mastercard and Visa accepted. 47 rooms all with private bath. Single L280,000-380,000; Double L400,00-600,000; Deluxe Double Room L500,000-700,000; Suites L700,000-1,800,000. A full buffet breakfast included.* *****

You'll find this extravagant and ornately decorated hotel that was once a nineteenth century palazzo on a residential street that curves up to the Florentine hills. It is truly magnificent with its chandeliers, statues, bas-relief covered walls, gilded mirrors and staff that will wait on you hand and foot. If you want to stay in the lap of luxury and are willing to pay for it, this is the place for you. There is a poolside restaurant, Taverna Machiavelli, where you can eat and relax after a hard day's touring. Another important feature is the rooftop terrace garden, offering excellent views of Florence. And the rooms are superb, stupendous, *fantavolosso* – think of an adjective and the rooms will surpass it!

WHERE TO EAT

Before I guide you to the culinary delights you'll encounter in Florence, I've prepared an augmented version of Chapter 11, *Food & Wine,* for you to better enjoy the wonders of Tuscan cuisine. *Buono appetito!*

Tuscan Cuisine

During the Renaissance, Florence and Tuscany experienced a burst of elaborate cuisine, much the result of Catherine de Medici importing a brigade of French chefs, but today that type of cuisine has given way to more basic fare. Tuscan cooking has its roots in the frugal peasant fare that was the result of the region being agriculturally poor for so many centuries. The food is simple but healthy, with the emphasis on fresh ingredients which accentuates the individual tastes of each dish.

Grilled meats are a staple of the Florentine diet, with *Bistecca alla Fiorentina* rivaling anything Texas could dream of producing. The Florentines tend to over-salt their vegetables and soups, but you can ask for them to be prepared *senza sale*, without salt, and no one will be insulted at all. You'll also find beans and olive oil prominently used in many dishes, as well as many types of game that populate the hills of Tuscany. And if you like cheese, my favorite is the full flavored *pecorino* made from sheep's milk.

Tuscany is not really known for their pasta dishes, but they do make an excellent *Pasta alla carrettiera*, a pasta dish with a sauce of tomato, garlic, pepper, and parsley. If you want a simple, filling, healthy meal, you'll find one in Tuscany. Just don't expect some extravagant saucy dish. For that go to France.

Suggested Tuscan Cuisine

You don't have to eat all the traditional courses listed below. Our constitution just isn't prepared for such mass consumption, so don't feel embarrassed if all you order is a pasta dish or an entrée with a salad or appetizer.

ANTIPASTO - APPETIZER

- **Crostini** – Chicken liver pate spread on hard, crusty bread
- **Pinzimonio** – Raw vegetables to be dipped in rich olive oil
- **Bruschetta** – Sliced crusty bread roasted over a fire covered with olive oil and rubbed with garlic; sometimes comes with crushed tomatoes, or another version has an egg on top (*Aqua Cotta*)

PRIMO PIATTO - FIRST COURSE

Zuppa – *Soup*
- **Ribollita** – means reboiled. A hearty mushy vegetable soup with beans, cabbage, carrots, and chunks of boiled bread.
- **Panzanella** – A Tuscan gazpacho (cold soup) made with tomatoes, cucumbers, onions, basil, olive oil, and bread.

Pasta
- **Pappardelle alla lepre** – Wide homemade pasta with a wild hare sauce
- **Pasta alla carrettierra** –Pasta with a sauce of tomato, garlic, pepper and parsley
- **Tortelli** – Spinach and ricotta ravioli with either cream sauce or a meat sauce
- **Turtui cu la cua** – Tortellini filled with marsapone, ricotta, and spinach with a butter and basil sauce.

SECOND PIATTO - ENTRÉE
Carne – *Meat*
- **Bistecca alla fiorentina** – T-bone steak at least 2 inches thick cooked over coals charred on the outside and pink in the middle. Welcome to Texas!
- **Fritto misto** –Usually lamb, rabbit or chicken, with peppers, zucchini, artichokes dipped in batter and deep fried
- **Arista di Maile** – Pork loin chop cooked with rosemary and garlic
- **Spiedini di maile** – Pork loin cubes and pork liver spiced with fennel and cooked on a skewer over open flames
- **Francesina** – Meat, onions, and tomatoes stewed in red wine
- **Trippa alla fiorentina** – Tripe mixed with tomato sauce and served with a variety of cheeses

Pesce – *Fish*
- **Bacca all fiorentina** – Salted cod cooked with tomatoes and spices (usually garlic and fennel)
- **Seppie in Zimino** – Cuttlefish simmered with beans

Contorno – *Vegetable*
- **Fagioli all'ucceletto** – White beans with garlic and tomatoes and sometimes sage
- **Insalata Mista** – mixed salad. You have to prepare your own olive oil and vinegar dressing. American's lust for countless types of salad dressings hasn't hit Italy yet.

Formaggio – *Cheese*
  - **Pecorino** – Cheese made from sheep's milk

Tuscan Wines
   Tuscany is known for its full bodied red wines, especially its **Chianti**. There are plenty of wine cellars and *enoteche* (wine bars) in every Tuscan city for you to sample the regional offerings. Some Tuscans say that their

food is so bland so that they can enjoy the wine with their meals more. Whatever the reason, you'll love sampling the different varieties.

Most Italian wines are classified by the type of grape used and the district from which the wines are produced. Some of the best wines come with a **DOC** (*Denominazione di Origine Controllata*) label that indicates the wine comes from a specially defined area and was produced according to specific traditional methods. If the label reads **DOCG** (G stands for *Garantita*) the wine will be of the highest quality, guaranteed.

The best wines are called *Classico*, which means they come from the oldest part of the production zone. If the wine is a Chianti Classico red you'll find a black rooster label on the neck of the bottle that designates such a wine. There are also *Riserva* and *Superiore*, which indicates that the wine has been aged for quality.

THE BEST DINING IN FLORENCE

3. LA BUSSOLA, *Via Porta Rossa 58, 50123 Firenze. Tel. 055/ 293-376. Visa and Mastercard accepted. Closed Mondays. Dinner for two L90,000.*

8. NERBONE, *Mercato Centrale. No telephone. No credit cards accepted. Meal for two L10,000.*

10. BUCA LAPI, *Via del Trebbio 1, 50123 Firenze. Tel. 055/213-768. American Express, Diners Club, Visa and Mastercard accepted. Closed Sunday for dinner and Mondays. Dinner for two L70,000*

19. TREDICI GOBBI (*13 Hunchbacks*), *Via Porcellana 9R. Dinner for two L100,000. Credit cards accepted.*

20. ZI ROSA, *Via dei Fossi 12, 50123 Firenze. Tel. 055/287-062. American Express, Diners Club, Visa and Mastercard accepted. Closed Thursdays and Friday for lunch. Dinner for two L55,000.*

25. TRATTORIA MOSSACCE, *Via del Pronconsolo 55, 50122 Firenze. Tel. 055/294-361. No credit cards accepted. Closed Sundays. Dinner for two L65,000.*

From the Chianti region you should try the following red wines: **Castello di Ama, Castello di Volpaia**, and **Vecchie Terre di Montefili**. Outside the region try some **Rosso delle Colline Luchesi** from the hills around Lucca, **Morellino di Scansano** from the hills south of Grosseto, and **Elba Rosso**, made on the island of Elba.

Some whites you might enjoy are a dry **Montecarlo** from the hills east of Lucca or a dry **Bolgheri** from the coast. The red wines mentioned above also have some excellent white wines to complement them.

Some of these wines may a bit pricey in restaurants so you may want to buy them at a store and sample them back in your hotel room or on a picnic. At restaurants, in most cases the house wines will be locally produced and of excellent quality, so give them a try.

Centro Storico

1. ANTICO FATTORE, *Via Lambertesca 1-3, 50123 Firenze. Tel. 055/ 261-225.*

I'm sorry to say that this wonderful Tuscan restaurant was virtually destroyed when terrorists bombed the Uffizzi Gallery. In time I'm confident they will return serving their fantastic food again. Virtually on the spot of this restaurant, or should I say where this restaurant used to be on Via Lambrusco is a gate with flowers and memorials for the people that lost their lives because of this foolish terrorist gesture. Come see so you can remember the senseless damage that terrorism creates.

2. BUCA DELL'ORAFO, *Volta de' Girolami 28, 50123 Firenze. Tel. 055/213-619. No credit cards accepted. Closed Sundays and Mondays. Dinner or two L85,000.*

Look just down the street and you'll see construction underway to repair the damage done from the bombing of the Uffizi. Bring a flower and place it on the fence as tribute. Afterwards push aside the brown beads and enter the basement room that houses this restaurant and try their *tortellini alla panna* (with rich cream sauce) or *straciatella* for starters. Then move onto the *petti di pollo al pepe verde* (chicken breasts with green peppers) or an *insalata mista*.

3. LA BUSSOLA, *Via Porta Rossa 58, 50123 Firenze. Tel. 055/293-376. Visa and Mastercard accepted. Closed Mondays. Dinner for two L90,000.*

You can get superb pizza in this pizzeria/ristorante/tavola calda, as well as pasta. The waiters and ambiance of this place is like something out of a movie set, especially in the back. They have a marble counter where you sit and watch the pizza master prepare the evening's fare in the wood heated brick oven. Or, if you're into the formal dining scene, try the back with tablecloths, etc. Wherever you sit the food will be excellent.

For pasta, try the *capricciossa*, *quattro formaggi*, or the *tortellini all panna*. You can get any type of pizza you want here. Even ask to mix and match ingredients. The pizza master is more than willing to accommodate. You won't need to leave too large of a tip since they tack on a *coperto* of L9,000.

4. RISTORANTE/PIZZERIA/BIRRERIA IL BOCCALE, *Borgo SS Apostoli 33r, Tel 055/283-384. Two pizzas and two beers L30,000.*

Great prices, surly service, good pizza, and tasty brews, Catering mainly to the German tourist contingent, this is the perfect place to come with kids for lunch or dinner since it's really inexpensive, down to earth (nobody cares how rowdy your kids get) and the food and beer are scrumptious. If you're into a flower coated, candle-lit dinner atmosphere,

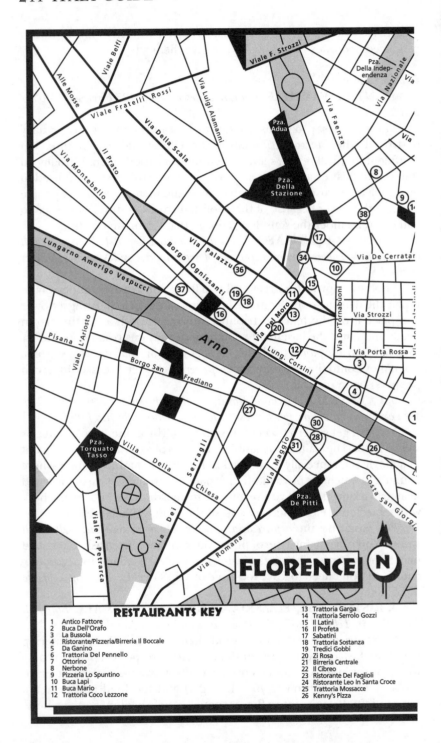

RESTAURANTS KEY

1   Antico Fattore
2   Buca Dell'Orafo
3   La Bussola
4   Ristorante/Pizzeria/Birreria Il Boccale
5   Da Ganino
6   Trattoria Del Pennello
7   Ottorino
8   Nerbone
9   Pizzeria Lo Spuntino
10 Buca Lapi
11 Buca Mario
12 Trattoria Coco Lezzone

13 Trattoria Garga
14 Trattoria Serrolo Gozzi
15 Il Latini
16 Il Profeta
17 Sabatini
18 Trattoria Sostanza
19 Tredici Gobbi
20 Zi Rosa
21 Birreria Centrale
22 Il Cibreo
23 Ristorante Del Faglioli
24 Ristorante Leo In Santa Croce
25 Trattoria Mossacce
26 Kenny's Pizza

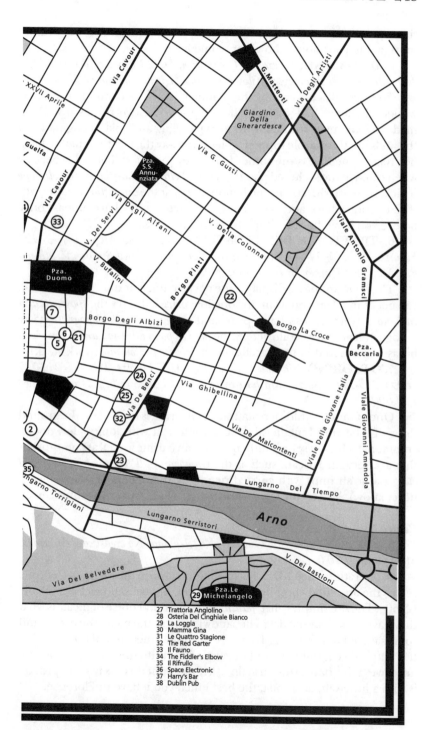

27 Trattoria Angiolino
28 Osteria Del Cinghiale Bianco
29 La Loggia
30 Mamma Gina
31 Le Quattro Stagione
32 The Red Garter
33 Il Fauno
34 The Fiddler's Elbow
35 Il Rifrullo
36 Space Electronic
37 Harry's Bar
38 Dublin Pub

this one room *birreria* won't cut it. If you want good food without mortgaging your house, however, come here.

5. DA GANINO, *Piazza dei Cimatori 4, 50123 Firenze. Tel. 055/214-125. All credit cards accepted. Closed Sundays. Dinner for two L75,000*

The best place to sit in the summer is at the communal outside wooden benches hedged in by flower pots. The two rooms inside are made to look rustic with their wooden paneling and yokes hanging from the walls but the marble topped tables give away the fact that they're faux, not real. Nonetheless the somewhat pricey food is still great, especially when eaten in the secluded piazza. Try the *Petto di pollo alla crema di limone* (chicken breast with cream and lemon sauce) or the *conniglio e verdure fritte* (fried country hare and vegetables). You have to try hare at least once before you leave Italy, so it might as well be here.

6. TRATTORIA DEL PENNELLO, *Via Dante Aligheri 4, 50123 Firenze. Tel. 055/94-848. No credit cards accepted. Closed Sunday for dinner and Mondays. Dinner for two L L60,000.*

The huge antipasto display is the perfect lunch or dinner repast. You can get as much as you want for one low price. Also try the *spaghetti alla carbonara* (with cheese ham, peas, and an egg) or *alla bolognese* (tasty bologna meat sauce), followed by the *petti di pollo alla mozzarella* (chicken breasts smothered in mozzarella) or the *bistecca di maiale* (pork steak)

7. OTTORINO, *Via delle Oche 12-16, 50123 Firenze. Tel. 055/218-747 or 055/215-151. Visa and Mastercard accepted. Closed Sundays. Dinner for two L95,000.*

One of the city's oldest restaurants, Ottorino is located on the ground floor of a beautiful medieval tower, brightly lit with long pale wooden communal tables. It serves authentic Tuscan cuisine as well as some dishes that are very un-Tuscan, such as the *Gamberoni all'Americana con riso al curry* (large shrimps with curried rice. Why they call it *all'Americano* I'll never know). Also try the *tagliatelli al coniglio* (light pasta in a rabbit sauce).

Centro

8. NERBONE, *Mercato Centrale. No telephone. No credit cards accepted. Meal for two L10,000.*

In operation since 1872, this small food stand in the Mercato Centrale serves the absolutely best boiled pork, beef, or veal sandwiches for only L3,500. They're simply called *panini* and your only choice of meats is what they have boiled for the day. The sandwich is just the meat, the bread, and some salt, but it is amazing. They take the boiled meat out of the steaming hot water, slice it right in front of you, ladle it onto the meat, pour a little juice over it for flavor (they usually ask if you want this ... say yes), sprinkle it with a little salt, and voila, the best lunch you'll have in Florence.

You can stand at the counter and sip a glass of wine or beer, or take your meal to the small seating area just across the aisle from Nerbone. They also serve pasta, soups, salads, etc., but everyone comes here for their terrific *panini*.

9. PIZZERIA LO SPUNTINO, *Via Canto de' Nelli 14-16, Tel. 055/210-920. No credit cards accepted. Meal for Two L18,000.*

Located in the square with the San Lorenzo market, the specialty is inexpensive but excellent thick crust pizza. They serve many varieties by baking huge trays of them in ovens in the back, displaying them in the front so you can choose. Once you've selected one they pop your piece into a toaster oven to re-heat it, even though it doesn't need it, then it's yours. They make great sausage pizza, ham pizza, vegetable pizza, and more. A great place to come for a quick snack, lunch, or dinner. They have seating at a counter as well as at benches, and serve a variety of wines and beers.

10. BUCA LAPI, *Via del Trebbio 1, 50123 Firenze. Tel. 055/213-768. American Express, Diners Club, Visa and Mastercard accepted. Closed Sunday for dinner and Mondays. Dinner for two L70,000*

One of the very best restaurants Florence has to offer. On a small street, down in the basement of an old building, Buca Lapi treats you to the food of a lifetime (and the spectacle of a lifetime too). There is a small open kitchen surrounded on two sides by tables from which you can see all the food being prepared. The decor is bizarre in a fun way, with travel posters covering the walls and ceiling.

Try the *spaghetti al sugo di carne e pomodoro* (with meat and tomato sauce) for starters, then try either the *pollo al cacciatore con spinache* (chicken cooked in tomato-based spicy sauce with spinach) or the *cingulae con patate fritte* (wild boar with fried potatoes). A superbly intimate restaurant with wonderful culinary and visual experiences.

11. BUCA MARIO, *Piazza Ottoviani 16, 50123 Firenze. Tel. 055/214-179. No credit cards accepted. Closed Wednesdays. Dinner for two L70,000.*

Situated in a small square off the Piazza SM Novella, this is a small basement *trattoria* that serves up some succulent meat dishes. The atmosphere and food is all Tuscan and the portions are big enough to keep you happy for hours. Try the *lombata di vitello* or the *bistecca alla fiorentina* and you can't go wrong. A wonderful place to try.

12. TRATTORIA COCO LEZZONE, *Via dei Parioncino 26, 50123 Firenze. Tel. 055/287-178. No credit cards accepted. Closed Saturdays and Sundays in the Summer and Tuesdays for dinner. IN the winter closed Sundays and Tuesdays for dinner. Dinner for two L75,000.*

Located in what was once a dairy, Coco Lezzone's long communal tables contrast sharply with the white tiled floors. Despite the strange decor, Florentines pack themselves in to enjoy the authentic Tuscan cuisine. The portions are pleasantly large, the meats are amazingly good, especially the *arista al forno* (pork loins on the fire). Also try the *Piccione* (pigeon) cooked over the grill; don't worry, they're farm raised – they don't go out to the piazza and catch the dinner. Where else will you be able to eat pigeon?

13. TRATTORIA GARGA, *Via del Moro 9, 50123 Firenze. Tel. 055/ 298-898. American Express, Diners Club, Visa and Mastercard accepted. Closed Sundays and Mondays. Dinner for two L90,000.*

If you want to get in on some of the best pasta in Florence, look no further. Try the *Pennette al Gorganzola e zucchine*. For seconds, try the *petto di pollo al pomodoro e basilico* (chicken breast with tomato and basil) or the *scalippina di vitella al limone* (veal with light lemon sauce). The food and the ambiance touch the edge of nouvelle cuisine, so if you're interested in trying something different in a unique atmosphere this place is great.

14. TRATTORIA SERROLO GOZZI, *Piazza San Lorenzo 8, 50123 Firenze. No telephone. No credit cards accepted. Closed Sundays. Dinner for two L45,000.*

This inexpensive, small, rustic *trattoria* is situated smack dab in the middle of the bustling San Lorenzo market. The seating is at long communal tables that line the walls with benches on one side and chairs on the other. Being just across the street from the food market, Mercato Generale, guarantees you'll have the freshest ingredients. The fare is purely Tuscan. I liked the *Arrista di Maiale al forno* (pork grilled over the fire) and the *vitello arrosto* (roasted veal). Super inexpensive, completely authentic, and very satisfying.

15. IL LATINI, *Via Palchetti 6, 50123 Firenze. Tel. 055/210-916. No credit cards accepted. Closed Mondays and Tuesdays for lunch. Dinner for two L65,000.*

The hams hanging from the ceiling and a huge oxen yoke should give you a good idea of what type of food to expect. They specialize in meat dishes but you can complement that with one of their *insalata mista* (mixed salad). The service is brusque in the Tuscan manner and the location down a little street makes the ambiance so authentic. Try the *Spiedini Misti* (mixed meat grill) or the *pollo arosto* (roasted chicken) and you won't be sorry.

16. IL PROFETA, *Via Borgognissanti 93, 50123 Firenze. Tel. 055/212-265. American Express, Diners Club, Visa and Mastercard accepted. Closed Sundays and Mondays. Dinner for two L75,000.*

A cheerful unpretentious place with simple, basic food served to you by friendly waiters. The kitchen is visible at the end of the dining room so the sound of pots and pans clattering adds a rustic touch to your meal. They make good pastas, especially the *penne carettiera* (garlic, tomatoes and pepper) which is a little like *penne all'arrabiata* in Rome, and the house special *penne profeta* (with cream, ham, and mushrooms). Next, sample the finely cooked *lombatina di vitella* (veal cutlet) or the ever present *bistecca alla fiorentina*.

17. SABATINI, *Via Panzani 9, 50123 Firenze. Tel. 055/211-559. American Express, Diners Club, Visa and Mastercard accepted. Closed Mondays. Dinner for two L100,000.*

Very high class establishment even though it is no longer *the* place to go in Florence. Most critics don't think the food here is a good value for the money spent, and I concur, but if you have a craving for a large succulent omelet made to order, this is the only place I found that would make one. Not for breakfast, mind you, but for lunch. Also try the *Spaghetti all vongole verace* (with a clam sauce of oil and garlic) or the *petti di pollo al curry* (curried chicken breast).

18. TRATTORIA SOSTANZA, *Via della Porcellana 25, 50123 Firenze. Tel. 055/212-691. No credit cards accepted. Closed Saturdays for dinner and Sundays. Dinner for two L65,000*

Aptly named "Sustenance," this down to earth, tiny little restaurant is frequented by all the *conoscenti* (those in the know). You enter this place by pushing aside the tacky beads that line the entrance. The dining area is narrow and crowded and the noises from kitchen in the back add to the charm. The waiters are brusque, but that's part of their schtick; the plates land in front of you with a thud, but everyone has a great time. Try any of their meat dishes made in the perfect Tuscan manner. Other than salads that's what they do well. Come here for a taste of a non-tourist *trattoria* and a sampling of true Florentine cuisine.

19. TREDICI GOBBI *(13 Hunchbacks), Via Porcellana 9R. Dinner for two L100,000. Credit cards accepted.*

Mainly Florentine cuisine, with a little Hungarian dishes added for spice. A moderately priced restaurant with some pricey dishes, which are mostly the excellent *Bistecca Fiorentina* and other beef dishes. The pasta is average. One endearing quality is the thicker spaghetti used which gives the pasta an exotic texture. The atmosphere is sophisticated and superb.

Tredici Gobbi's walls are crammed with paintings received in payment from impoverished Florentine artists in exchange for the restaurants fine food. If you are captivated by one, it is usually for sale. After enjoying your *Bistecca*, soaking up the delightful atmosphere, and admiring the many paintings, it's time for the dessert cart. These well-presented delicacies and a steaming cup of café will round out an excellent meal.

20. ZI ROSA, *Via dei Fossi 12, 50123 Firenze. Tel. 055/287-062. American Express, Diners Club, Visa and Mastercard accepted. Closed Thursdays and Friday for lunch. Dinner for two L55,000.*

Intimate little pizzeria with great food at superb prices. If you like pizza, *crostini* (sandwiches), or *calzone* you'll will fall in love with this place.

All the food is prepared quickly and with the best of care. Try the pizza con *salame piccante* (with spicy salami), *calzone con salsiccia* (with sausage) or the *crostini con mozzarrella e rucola* (with two types of cheese). All are baked to excellence. After a few sips of wine you'll be in the mood to try another delicacy from their oven.

Santa Croce

21. BIRRERIA CENTRALE, *Piazza Cimatori 1, 50122 Firenze. Tel. 055/211-915. American Express, Diners Club, Visa and Mastercard accepted. Closed Saturday for lunch and Sundays. Open noon until midnight.*

As the name suggests (*birreria* means beer garden) this really is not a restaurant, but a place to grab a beer or a glass of wine and a snack. Their menu is not extensive at all, so I suggest coming here for a light lunch. They make a good Roman specialty, *Pizza margherita* (with cheese and tomato sauce) and a scrumptious *Gran Toast* (sandwich toasted with ham and cheese and a salad on the side). They have outside and inside seating. In good weather try the outside since this place is located on a secluded little piazza.

22. IL CIBREO, *Via dei Macci 118, 50122 Firenze. Tel. 055/677-394. American Express, Diners Club, Mastercard and Visa accepted. Closed Sundays and Mondays. Dinner for two L75,000.*

This is a combination traditional and nouveau cuisine and it is excellent. If you like pasta, though, don't come here – there's none on the menu. Their mushroom soup is excellent as is the typically Roman buffalo-milk mozzarella. All the ingredients are basic and simple, but it seems to be prepared in a whole new way. If you want to try the *cibreo*, the restaurant's namesake, a Tuscan chicken stew made from parts of the bird that are usually discarded, you need to order it at least a day advance while making reservations. If you want the same food for half the price, simply go to the *vineria* on the other side of the kitchen, sit down and place your order.

23. RISTORANTE DEL FAGIOLI, *Corso dei Tintori 47, 50122 Firenze. Tel. 055/244-285. American Express, Diners Club, and Visa accepted. Closed Sundays. Dinner for two L60,000.*

A straightforward Tuscan *trattoria* with great food for a good value. The rustic appearance with the wood paneling and antlers hanging on the walls reflects the peasant cuisine served. The menu is not that extensive but you can get a quite good *salsicce alla griglia* (grilled sausage) for a dinner and some *fagiole and zucchini* as an appetizer. Their specialty is grilled meats.

24. RISTORANTE LEO IN SANTA CROCE, *Via Torta 7r, 50122 Firenze. Tel. 055/210-829. Fax 055/239-6705. All credit cards accepted. Closed Mondays. Dinner for two L85,000.*

A brightly lit, trying-to-be-upscale restaurant near the church of Santa Croce that actually serves good food. They prepare dishes from all over Italy so you're not confined to the normal Tuscan peasant fare. You can get the *antipasto di casa* and be filled for a while, or you can try a good rendition of the Roman favorite *spaghetti all carbonara* (ham, cheese, mixed with an egg). Consider also the *cordon bleu* or the *filetto di pepe verde* (beef with green peppers).

25. TRATTORIA MOSSACCE, *Via del Pronconsolo 55, 50122 Firenze. Tel. 055/294-361. No credit cards accepted. Closed Sundays. Dinner for two L65,000.*

Great prices for great food. The meats are especially exquisite, especially the *osso bucco*. Try the *ribollita* as a beginner. I suggest you sit all the way in the back around the "L" of a dining area so you can sit in front of the small open kitchen and watch the cooks prepare your meal. That alone makes this restaurant a lof of fun. It's basically a place for locals but they accept the occasional tourist in their midst.

PIZZA DELIVERY

If you're too tired to go out or just want a mid-day snack brought to your door, you can get some great pizza delivered:

26. KENNY'S PIZZA, *Tel. 055/287-903.*

*Their territory is basically all of Florence's Centro Storico, Centro, Oltrarno, and Santa Croce, and they deliver within 30 minutes. You get a choice of **Normale** or **Gigante** pizzas. The normale is about 12 inches, the gigante is about 16. My suggestion is to order the basic **pizza margherita** that comes with tomato sauce and cheese, and add toppings at will. Each topping for the Normale costs L1,500 extra and for the gigante they cost L2,500 extra. The toppings they have are mozzarella (extra cheese), peperoni, prosciutto (ham), salame piccante (spicy salami), salsiccia (sausage) and funghi (mushrooms).*

My advice would be to get extra cheese and salsicia, which is great. You also can have sodas and beers delivered, as well as ice cream and hamburgers or chicken sandwiches. If you want utensils, you'll have to ask for them and pay an extra L1,000 per person.

Oltrarno

RISTORANTE ALFREDO SULL'ARNO, *Via dei Barbi 46r, 05/283-808. Dinner for two L90,000.*

I haven't numbered this one, because I'm not recommending it. Here's why: Located a few paces from the Ponte Vecchio on the south side of the Arno, this restaurant's only saving grace is its view. The atmosphere is plain, the service is slow and surly, the prices are extraordinarily high, and the portions are minuscule. The food is good, but there is not enough of it. They are definitely playing for the tourist crowd.

With the restaurant located on the Arno overlooking the Ponte Vecchio, at least you're able to enjoy some scenery if you choose to dine here. One other shortcoming is that only those ordering complete meals, i.e. antipasto, pasta, and entrée, can sit on the terrace with the view. I witnessed many groups of startled tourists who were asked to move inside even after settling down, having a few drinks, and eating an antipasto. The motto of this story is: Do not dine at a restaurant that tells you how much you can eat and where you can eat it.

One saving grace is that the restaurant is located directly across from a garage that sells a wide variety of creative Italian signs and bumper stickers. These make the perfect gifts because they are easy to transport, are very Italian, and do not cost very much. So, if you choose not to eat here, at least visit the garage across the street.

27. TRATTORIA ANGIOLINO, *Via Santo Spirito 36, 50125 Firenze. Tel. 055/239-8976. Mastercard and Visa accepted. Closed Mondays. L60,000.*

A large and vibrant local *trattoria* that serves basic Tuscan fare. You'll love the wood stove in the middle of the room, as well as the wrought-iron light fixtures an he full hams hanging in the entranceway. This place is definitely rustic. If you come in the winter try to get a seat in the back where you can watch the action in the open kitchen. In the heat of the summer that wouldn't be such a good idea. The food is your basic peasant fare at peasant prices. Try the *tortellini alla panna* (cheese stuffed pasta in a cream sauce) or the *taglietelli con funghi* (pasta with mushrooms), then the *Lombata di vitello* (veal chop roasted) or the ever present *bistecca all fiorentina*.

28. OSTERIA DEL CINGHIALE BIANCO, *Borgo San Jacopo 43, 50125 Firenze. Tel. 055/215-706. Mastercard and Visa accepted. Closed Tuesdays and Wednesdays.*

Wild game is the specialty here as befitting a place named The White Boar, so get ready to enjoy some fine peasant dishes. I tried the wild boar cold cuts but liked the assorted salamis of Tuscany better. The chicken breast cooked with ham and cheese was not Italian, but it was great. I like the wrought-iron motif that dominates the place, especially the the old cooking pot hanging from the ceiling.

29. LA LOGGIA, *Piazzale Michelangelo 1, 50125 Firenze. Tel. 055/234-2832. Fax 055/234-5288. American Express, Diners Club, Mastercard and Visa accepted. Closed Wednesdays. L110,000.*

Come for the view of Florence, stay for the food, try to escape from the prices. This ideally located restaurant and café has a great panoramic view of Florence, which seems to make your meal that much better, until the bill arrives, then cardiac arrest sets in. Make sure you come dressed for success otherwise the other customers will give you the once-over. The staff treated me with the utmost respect though. Try the *Pollo al diavolo* (chicken cooked over and open fire) after the *spaghetti al frutti di mare* (with seafood).

30. MAMMA GINA, *Borgo S Jacopo 37, 50125 Firenze. Tel. 055/239-6009, Fax 055/213-908. American Express, Diners Club, Mastercard and Visa accepted. Closed Sundays. Dinner for two L 85,000.*

A very small place with great food. I tried their *tortellini all crema* with apprehension since I do not believe that Florentines know how to make good pasta, and was pleasantly surprised. Then I had the *petti di pollo alla griglia* (chicken breasts o the grill). You might also try the *Penne strascicate alla Fiorentina* (a meat and tomato based pasta) and the *petti di pollo al cogna can funghi* (chicken breast cooked in cognac with mushrooms ... it gives it kind of a cacciatore taste).

31. LE QUATTRO STAGIONE, *Via Maggio 61, 50125 Firenze. Tel. 055/218-906. Mastercard and Visa accepted. Closed Sundays. Dinner for two L65,000.*

A very small restaurant that tourists avoid since there's no view of the Arno. The decor is basic, with a few paintings of Florentine scenes on the walls, but what makes this place great is their food. Try the *Scaloppini Moda Chef* (veal with mushrooms, tomatoes, and cream), the *fritto di mare* (mixed fired seafood) or the *Pollo arrosto* (roasted chicken). For starters they make a good *insalata mista*.

SEEING THE SIGHTS

The sights of Florence are fascinating, incredible – add your own superlatives after you've seen them! The sights below are numbered and correspond to the *Florence Sights* map.

1. STATUE OF DAVID AT THE ACADEMIA

Via Ricasoli 60. Open 9:00am–2:00pm Tuesday–Saturday. Sunday 9:00am–1:00pm. Admission L10,000.

Granted the **Accademia** is filled with a wide variety of paintings by artists from the Tuscan school of the 13th and 14th centuries, but the museum's main draw is a must-see for you in Florence, Michelangelo's perfect *David*. Michelangelo finished sculpting this wonderful statue at the age of 25 in the year 1504, after four years of labor. It was originally in front of the Palazzo della Signoria, but was replaced with a substitute in 1873 to protect the original from the elements.

Leading up to the David are a variety of other works by Michelangelo, most unfinished. These are called *The Prisoners,* since the figures appear alive and to be trapped in stone. These were destined for the Tomb of Pope Giulio II, but Michelangelo died before he could bring the figures to life. Also included in this wonderful exhibit of Michelangelo's sculptures is the unfinished *Pieta*. Many art critics have spent their entire lives comparing this Pieta with the more famous one in St. Peter's in Rome. Comparing these two works, you can see how Michelangelo's worked progressed through the years.

2. PIAZZA & CHURCH OF SS ANNUNZIATA
Open 7:00am–7:00pm.

Just around the corner from the Accademia, this piazza is relatively isolated from the hustle and bustle of Florence's tourist center, and when you enter it you feel as if you walked back into Renaissance Florence. This is how all the piazzas must have looked and felt back then, no cars, only people milling around sharing the Florentine day.

In the center of the square you'll find the equestrian *Statue of the Grand Duke Ferdinando I* by **Giambologna** and **Pietyro Tacca** (1608). The two bronze fountains with figures of sea monsters are also the work of Tacca (1629).

The church was erected in 1250, was reconstructed in the middle of the 15th century by **Michelozzo**, and was again re-done in the 17th and 18th centuries and remains today as it was then. The interior is a single nave with chapels on both sides and is richly decorated in the Baroque style. The ceiling is carved from wood and is wonderfully intricate. Throughout this small church you'll find simple but exquisite bas-reliefs, frescoes, sculptures and more.

3. PONTE VECCHIO

Literally meaning *Old Bridge*, the name came about because it's been around since Etruscan times. The present bridge was rebuilt on the old one in the 14th century by **Neri di Fiorvanti**. Thankfully this beautiful bridge with its shops lining each side of it was spared the Allied and Axis bombardments during World War II. Today the shops on the bridge belong to silversmiths and goldsmiths. In the middle of the bridge are two openings that offer wonderful views of the Arno. On the downstream side of the bridge is a bust of **Benvenuto Cellini**, a Renaissance Goldsmith and sculptor, done by Raffaelle Romanelli in 1900. At night on the bridge you'll find all sorts of characters hanging out, sipping wine, and strumming guitars.

From the Ponte Vecchio to the Pitti Palace there used to be a beautiful street lined with wonderful old palazzi. Unfortunately the bombers in World War II didn't avoid these buildings as they did the Ponte Vecchio itself. Even so, today the street is filled with lovely reconstructed buildings erected just after the war.

4. PITTI PALACE

Piazza dei Pitti. Open 9:00am-2:00pm Tuesday-Saturday. Sunday 9:00am-1:00pm. Admission L10,000.

Built for the rich merchant **Luca Pitti** in 1440, based on a design by Filippo Brunalleschi. Due to the financial ruin of the Pitti family, the construction was interrupted until the palace was bought by **Eleonora da Toledo**, the wife of Cosimo I. It was then enlarged to its present size. Currently it is divided into five different museums: **The Palatine Picture Gallery**, famous for its Raphaels and its Titian and Rubens; **The Silver Museum** that houses Lorenzo di Medici's vases; **The Costumer and Porcelain Museums**; **The Gallery of Modern Art**, which exhibits paintings by Tuscan artists that are similar to French impressionists; and **The Museum of Precious Stones**.

This is another wonderful place to come if you're tired of looking at all that religious art in the Uffizzi and elsewhere. Even though some of the Medici clan were elected Pope, their taste in art was more secular in nature, so you'll find a good complement of both religious and secular works.

5. DUOMO & BAPTISTERY, CAMPANILE, & CATHEDRAL MUSEUM

All located at the Piazza del Duomo. Hours: Duomo – Church open 7:00am-7:00pm. Entrance to the dome open Monday-Saturday 10:00am – 5:00pm. Admission L6,000. The Baptistery – Open Monday – Saturday 1:00pm-6:00pm andx Sunday 9:00am-1:00pm. The Campanile– Open 9:00am-5:00pm, Summer 8:30am-7:00pm. Admission L6,000. Cathedral Museum (Museo dell'Opera del Duomo) – Open 9:00am-6:00pm Tuesday-Saturday. Until 7:30pm in the summer. Holidays open 9:00am-1:00pm.

Duomo

When you're in Florence the one sight you have to see is the **Duomo**, Florence's cathedral. It was consecrated in 1436 by Pope Eugenio IV as **Santa Maria del Fiore** (Saint Mary of the Flowers), and that is still its official name, but everybody calls it "The Duomo." It was started in 1296 by Arnolfo di Cambio on the spot where the church of Santa Reparata existed. After di Cambio's death in 1301, the famous Giotto took over the direction of the work, but he dedicated most of his attention to the development of the Bell Tower (*Campanile*).

When Giotto died in 1337, Andrea Pisano took over until 1349 (he didn't die, he just moved on to other projects). By 1421 everything else was finished except for the dome, which **Brunelleschi** had won a competition to design and build. It took 14 years just to build the gigantic dome.

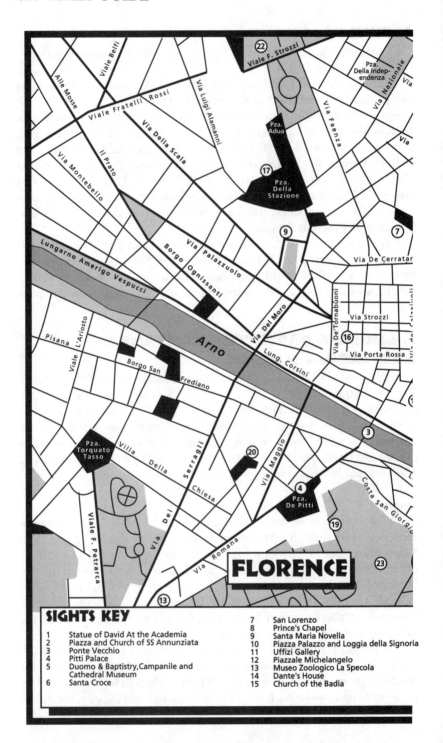

SIGHTS KEY

1 Statue of David At the Academia
2 Piazza and Church of SS Annunziata
3 Ponte Vecchio
4 Pitti Palace
5 Duomo & Baptistry, Campanile and Cathedral Museum
6 Santa Croce
7 San Lorenzo
8 Prince's Chapel
9 Santa Maria Novella
10 Piazza Palazzo and Loggia della Signoria
11 Uffizi Gallery
12 Piazzale Michelangelo
13 Museo Zoologico La Specola
14 Dante's House
15 Church of the Badia

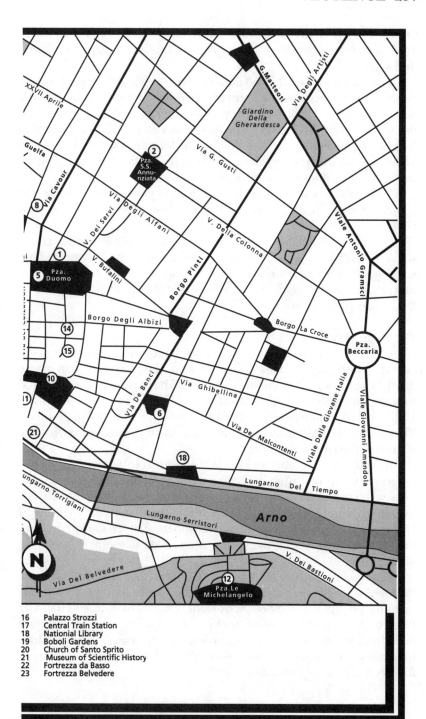

16 Palazzo Strozzi
17 Central Train Station
18 Nationial Library
19 Boboli Gardens
20 Church of Santo Sprito
21 Museum of Scientific History
22 Fortrezza da Basso
23 Fortrezza Belvedere

Over the years, slight modifications and changes have been made, and in 1887, the current facade of the Duomo was finished by architect **Emilio de Fabris**.

The interior of the Duomo is 150 meters long and 38 meters wide at the nave and 94 meters at the transept. There are enormous gothic arches, supported by gothic pillars, which gives the interior a majestic quality. The dome is 90 meters high and 45.5 meters in diameter and is decorated with frescoes representing the Last Judgment done by Giorgio Vasari and Federico Zuccari at the end of the 16th century. In the niches of the pillars supporting the dome are statues of the Apostles.

The central chapel is home to the **Sarcophagus of San Zanobius** that contains the saints relics. The bronze reliefs are the work of Lorenzo Ghiberti (1442).

When you've finished wandering through and admiring the art and stained glass windows, you can go up to the top of the Duomo and get some great views of Florence. The way up is a little tiring, but the magnificent photo opportunities – both inside and out – are fabulous. Don't miss these views!

The Baptistery

Definitely considered one of the most important works of art in the city, the **Baptistery** was built on the remains of a paleo-Christian monument, as well as an early Roman monument. The Baptistery was dedicated to Saint John the Baptist, the patron saint of Florence and was built in the 10th and 11th centuries. Up until 1128, it was the cathedral of Florence. That's why they built the Duomo; this small structure just didn't reflect the stature of the city of Florence.

Its shape is octagonal and is covered with colored marble. On the pavement by the Baptistery you'll find the signs of the Zodiac taken off of oriental textiles in the 13th century. Inside is the tomb of Giovanni XXIII by Donatello and Michelozzo in 1427. Next to the altar, you'll see the *Angel holding the Candlestick* by Agostino di Jacopo in 1320. To the left between the Roman sarcophagi is the wooden statue *Magdalen* by Donatello in 1560.

But the bronze paneled doors by **Ghoberti** and **Andrea Pisano da Pontedera** are the true masterpieces of the Baptistery. The door that is open to the public is the **Southern Door**, created by Andrea Pisano da Pontedera and is of least interest. The east and north doors are far more beautiful and intricate. Michelangelo described the east door as "the door to paradise." On it you'll find stories of the Old Testament, beginning as follows from the top left hand side:

• Creation of Adam; original sin; expulsion of Adam and Eve from Paradise
• Stories of Noah and the universal deluge (strangely enough some of these panels were almost lost in the flooding of 1966)
• Jacob and Esau; Rachel and Jacob; Isaac blesses Jacob
• Moses receives theTen Commandments on Mount Sinai
• The battle against the Philistines; David and Goliath.

From the top right hand side:
• Adam works the soil; Cain and Abel at work; Cain kills Abel
• Three angels appear to Abraham; Abraham sacrifices Isaac
• Joseph meets his brothers in Egypt; Stories of Joseph
• Joshua crosses the Jordan river; The conquering of Jericho
• Solomon receives the Queen of Sheba in the Temple.

The Campanile

Giotto died while he was attempting to complete the **Campanile**, but after his death **Andrea Pisano** and **Francesco Talenti** both scrupulously followed his designs until its completion. The only part they left out was the spire that was to go on top, which would have made the Campanile 30 meters higher than its current 84. The tower is covered is colored marble and adorned with bas-reliefs by Andrea Pisano and Luca della Robbia and Andrea Orcagna. Sculptures by Donatello, Nanni di Bartolo, and others used to be in the sixteen niches but are now in the Cathedral Museum.

Cathedral Museum (Museo dell'Opera del Duomo)

This is the place where many pieces of artwork that used to be in the Cathedral or the Campanile are now located. This was mainly done to help preserve them from the environment and the onslaught of hordes of tourists. Most of the items are statues and bas-relief work. The most famous ones to keep an eye out for are *St. John* by **Donatello**, *Habakkuk* by Donatello, *Virgin with Infant Jesus* by Arnolfo, and *Choir Gallery* with many scenes by Donatello.

6. SANTA CROCE

Piazza Santa Croce. Open 8:00am–12:30pm and 3:00pm–6:30pm.

The church of **Santa Croce** sits in the Piazza Santa Croce, surrounded by ancient palazzi renowned for the architecture. The one opposite the church is the **Palazzo Serristori** by Baccio D'Agnolo in the 16th century. Facing the church on the right hand side at #23 is the **Palazzo dell'Antella** built by Giulio Parigi in the 17th century.

The frescoes on the facade were created in only 20 days by 12 painters working non-stop. In the center of the square is a statue of **Dante Aligheri**, he of *Divine Comedy* fame, sculpted by Enrico Pazzi in 1865. This is a wonderfully ornate yet simple church belonging to the Franciscan Order. Consturction was begun in 1295 but its modern facade was created in 1863 by Nicolo Matas. It has a slim bell tower whose Gothic style doesn't seem to fit with this modern exterior. The interior, on the other hand, fits perfectly with the simple stonework of the bell tower.

Initially the walls inside had been covered with exquisite frescoes created by Giotto but these were covered up by order of Cosimo I in the 16th century. What remains is a basic monastic church that conveys piety and beauty in its simplicity. Of the many Italian artistic, religious, and political geniuses that lie buried beneath Santa Croce, the most famous has to be that of **Michelangelo** himself.

Besides the beautiful bas-reliefs, exquisite sculptures, and other works of art in Santa Croce you can find an excellent and inexpensive **leather school** *(Scuola del Cuoio)*. To get there go through the sacristy and you'll end up in the school that was started by the monks more than three decades ago. Here you'll find all kinds of leather goods for sale in what was once cells for the monks. The prices and selection are good even if the atmosphere is completely touristy *(Tel. 244-533, Tuesday–Saturday, 9:00am–12:30pm and 3:00pm–6:00pm. American Express, Mastercard, and Visa accepted)*.

7. SAN LORENZO

Piazza San Lorenzo. Open Monday–Saturday 9:00am–Noon and 3:30pm–5:00pm.

One of the most ancient basilicas in Florence. The architecture is the work of **Filippo Brunelleschi**, done from 1421-1446, but the church was finished by his pupil **Antonio Manetti** in 1460. The facade was never completed even though Michelangelo himself submitted a variety of designs for its completion.

The interior is made up of three naves with chapels lining the side walls. In the central nave at the far end are two pulpits that are the last two works of **Donatello** who died in 1466 after completing them. You'll find plenty of works by Donatello in this church, including:
• The stucco medallions in the Old Sacristy that represent the *Four Evangelists*
• The stucco medallions in the Old Sacristy that are *Stories of Saint John the Baptist*
• The terracotta *Bust of Sant Laurence* in the Old Sacristy
• The bronze doors with panels representing the *Apostles and Fathers of the Church* in the Old Sacristy.

8. PRINCES' CHAPEL

Piazza San Lorenzo. Open 10:00am–1:00pm and 3:00pm–7:00pm Monday, Tuesday, Thursday through Saturday. Sunday 10:00am– Noon. Wednesdays closed.

Just around the corner from the church of San Lorenzo, this octagonal building's construction was begun in 1604 on a design by Prince Giovanni dei Medici. It houses the tombs of a variety of Medici princes from which it gets its name. It is of interest to many tourists because of the tombs in the New Sacristy which were created by Michelangelo himself. *The Tomb of Lorenzo, Duke of Urbino* (created by Michelangelo) has a statue of the duke seated and absorbed in meditation as well as two reclining figures that represent Dawn and Dusk. On the opposite wall is the *Tomb of Giulano, Duke of Nemours* (also created by Michelangelo) which shows a seated duke replete in armor, ready for action, as well as two reclining figures that represent night and day. Another Michelangelo work in the New Sacristy is the unfinished *Madonna and Child*.

If you like Michelangelo's sculpture but want to avoid the crowds that congregate at the museum that houses the David, this is the place to come.

9. SANTA MARIA NOVELLA

Piazza Santa Maria Novella. Open 7:00am–Noon and 3:30pm–5pm Monday–Saturday and Sunday 3:30pm–5:00pm.

Built in 1278 by two Dominican friars, **Fra Ristoreo** and **Fra Sisto**, the church was created in the Gothic style with green and white marble decorations that are typically Florentine in character. The church was completed in 1470. To the left and right of the facade are tombs of illustrious Florentines all created in the same Gothic style as the church.

The interior of the church is in a T shape with the nave and aisles divided by clustered columns that support wide arches. Down the aisles are a variety of altars created by **Vasari** from 1565 to 1571.

As a young artist, Michelangelo worked on many of the frescoes as commissioned by his teachers. This is where he got his initial training that helped him create the now famous frescoes in the Sistine Chapel in Rome.

You can spend hours in here admiring the magnificent frescoes done by many Florentine artists including **Domenico Ghirlandaio** (Chapel of High Altar), **Giuliano da San Gallo** (Gondi Chapel), **Giovanni Dosio** (Gaddi Chapel), **Nardo di Cione** (Strozzi Chapel) and more. And if you're tired of sightseeing and need a little break, Florence's best pub, The Fiddler's Elbow, is in the piazza outside the church.

10. PIAZZA, PALAZZO, & LOGGIA DELLA SIGNORIA
Piazza della Signoria

This piazza, with the Palazzo, the Loggia, the fountain, the replica of the statue of David, and more is incomparable in its beauty. Over the centuries great historical and political events, as well as the lives of average Florentines, have been worked out here.

Today the square is the site of the annual event, **Calcio in Costume** (soccer played in period garb), where the different sections of the city vie for dominance in a game that is a cross between soccer, rugby, and an all-out war. This annual contest used to be played in the square of Santa Croce but was moved here during modern times. If you are in Florence during June, when the event covers three of the weekends in that month, you definitely have to try and get tickets. The entire piazza is covered with sand, and stadium seats are put up all around the makeshift field. A truly memorable experience.

In the small square on the left is **Ammannati's Fountain** with the giant figure of *Neptune*. He's commonly called *Biancone* (Whitey) by the locals because of his bland appearance. Giambologna created the equestrian statue representing *Cosimo I dei Medici* on the left of the square.

Palazzo della Signoria – Palazzo Vecchio

Piazza della Signoria. Open Monday–Friday 9:00am–7:00pm, and Sunday 8:00am–1:00pm. Admission L10,000 for upstairs galleries.

The most imposing structure in the square is the **Palazzo Signoria**. It is 94 meters past the fortified battlements to the top of **Arnolfo's Tower**. The entire structure is rather severe, but at the same time elegant. Its construction began in the late 13th century but took hundreds of years to finish. It was once the home of **Cosimo de Medici** and other members of the Medici family before the Pitti Palace was completed.

In front of the building on the platform at the top of the steps, ancient orators used to harangue the crowds, and for this reason this section of the building is called *Arringhiera* (The haranguing area). Located here are several important sculptures including the *Marzocco* (a stone copy of the original which sits in the National Museum, a lion which symbolizes the Florentine Republic); *Judith and Holofernes* created by Donatello in 1460, which is a record of the victory over the Duke of Athens; the copy of Michelangelo's *David* (the original is in the Accademia), and *Hercules and Cacus* created by Baccio Bandinelli.

Above the main door is a frieze with two lions and a monogram of Christ with the inscription *Rex Regum et Dominus Dominantium* (King of Kings and Lord of Lords), which records the time that the Florentine republic elected Christ as their King in 1528. The inscription used to read as follows *Jesus Christus Rex Florentinei Populi S P Decreto Electus* (Jesus Christ elected by the people King of Florence) but was changed in 1851.

The interior is mainly filled with artwork glorifying the Medici family that ruled Florence and much of Italy for centuries. So if you're need a break from religious art and all those paintings of the Madonna and Child, this is the respite you've been asking for. Everything is elaborate and ornate, as befitting the richest family in the world at that time.

You enter through the courtyard which was designed by Michelozzo in 1453. The elaborate stucco decorations on the columns and frescoes on the arches were added in 1565 on the occasion of the wedding between Franscesco dei Medici and Joan of Austria. The fountain is the center of a *Graceful Winged Cupid* was done by Verrochio in 1476. From here most of the art to see is upstairs, so either take the staircase up or use the elevator. What follows is a description of the important works to see in each room:

Hall of the Five Hundred – Salone dei Cinquecento

The most splendid and artistic hall in Florence. It was designed for public meetings after the Medicis had been thrown from power. When Cosimo I regained the family's control over Florence, he had the hall enlarged and used it for his private audiences. On the wall opposite the entrance you'll find three large magnificent paintings by Baccio D'Agnolo, Baccio Bandinelli and Giorgio Vassari: *The Conquest of Siena; The Conquest of Porto Ercole; The Battle of Marciano*. On the wall across from this you'll find: *Maximilian Tries to Conquer Livorno; The Battle of Torre San Vincenzo; The Florentines Assault Pisa*. Underneath these painting you'll find sculptures by Vincenzo de Rossi representing *Hercules Labors*.

The ceiling is divided into 39 compartments with paintings by Giorgio Vasari that represent *Stories of Florence and the Medici*. The coup de grace is in the niche of the right wall at the entrance. Here you'll find Michelangelo's unfinished work, *The Genius of Victory*, which was designed for the tomb of Pope Julius II. If you only have a little time, spend it here. This rooms is magnificent.

Study of Francesco I de Medici

Here you'll find the work of many of Florence's finest artists crammed into as small a space as imaginable. The walls and even the barrel shaped ceiling are covered with paintings, and niches are filled with a variety of bronze statues. Elaborate and ostentatious.

Hall of the Two Hundred – Salone dei Duecento

It is called thus since this is where the Council of two hundred citizens met during the time of the Republic for their important decisions. The walls are adorned with tapestry, the ceiling is ornately decorated, chandeliers hang low, and statues and busts adorn any free spot. The center of the room is occupied by the seating used by the Council of 200.

Monumental Quarters – Quartieri Monumentali

These are a series of rooms that get their names from a member of the Medici family. Each are elaborate in their own right, filled with paintings, sculptures, frescoes, and more. From here you'll find many more interesting rooms and paintings as you explore, both on this floor and the one above, but this is the bulk of the beauty in the Palazzo Signoria.

The Loggia della Signoria

In the Piazza, on the right of the Palazzo, is the expansive and airy **Loggia della Signoria**, a combination of Gothic and Renaissance architecture. It was built by Benci di Cione, Simone Talenti and others during the years 1376–1382. At either end of the steps are two marble lions, one of which is very old, the other made in 1600.

Underneath the arch are some wonderful sculptures: *Persius* by Cellini in 1553 under the left hand arch; *The Rape of the Sabines* by Giambologna in 1583 under the right arch; *Hercules and the Centaur* by Giambologna in 1599 under the right arch also. There is also *Menelaus supporting Patroclus* and a few other less important works. All of them, since they are open to the elements and pollution, have been stained and discolored, but all are excellent studies in human anatomy.

11. UFFIZZI GALLERY

Piazza del Uffizzi. Open Tuesday to Saturday 9:00am–7:00pm and Sunday 9:00am–1:00pm. Admission L10,000.

The building housing the **Uffizi Gallery** was begun in 1560 by Giorgio Vasari on the orders of the Grand-Duke Cosimo I. It was originally designed to be government offices, but today holds the most important and impressive display of art in Italy, and some would say the world. The gallery mainly contains paintings of Florentine and Tuscan artists of the 13th and 14th centuries, but you'll also find paintings from Venice, Emilia, and other Italian art centers as well as Flemish, French, and German works. In conjunction there is a collection of numerous ancient sculptures.

These fabulous works of art were collected first by the Medici family, then later by the Loraine family. After the Gastone, the last of the Medici, the last inheritor, Anna Maria Luisa donated the entire Gallery to the Tuscan state in 1737 so that the rich collection gathered by her ancestors would never leave Florence. Not everything would go as planned, since in the 18th century some pieces were stolen by Napoleon's marauding forces, but most of these were later ransomed for their return. Some items were damaged in the great flood of 1966 (see the section below *Walking the Path of the Flood of 1966*), and still others were damaged in 1993 when a terrorist car bomb ripped through parts of the Gallery. Even with all these occurrences, the Uffizzi is still one of the finest galleries in the world.

It's collection is so rich and so vast that it has caused some tourists to grow queasy, feel faint, and generally feel ill. A medical study has determined that some people become completely overwhelmed with the large amount of artistic beauty and cannot handle the input; while others postulate that it is the abundance of religious paintings, mainly of the Madonna and child, that make people disoriented by the constant repetition of the same theme. Whatever the reasons for the symptoms, if you start to feel queasy, don't be shy to ask for a place to rest.

It is interesting to see, as you enter the Uffizzi, the statues of Cosimo the Elder and Lorenzo the Magnificent, as well as several busts of the rest of the Medici rulers, since when they ruled most Florentines despised their despotic ways. But now they are immortalized in time because of the philanthropic gesture of their last heir. Anyway, it would be virtually impossible to list all the paintings and sculptures exhibited, so let me make a list of those that you absolutely must see if you visit the gallery:
• *Madonna of the Pomegranate* - Botticelli - Room X
• *Self Portraits of Titian, Michelangelo, Raphael, Rubens, Rembrandt and more* - Third Corridor
• *Madonna of the Goldfinch* - Raphael - Room XXV
• *Holy Family* - Michelangelo - Room XXV
• *Venus of Urbino* - Titian - Room XXVIII
• *Young Bacchus* - Caravaggio - Room XXXVI
• *Portrait of an Old Man* - Rembrandt - Room XXXVII
• *Portrait of Isabelle Brandt* - Peter Paul Rubens - Room XLI

12. PIAZZALE MICHELANGELO

From this piazza you have a wonderful view of the city of Florence dissected by the river Arno. Remember to bring your camera for the best public view of the city. The best private view is from the Hotel Torre di Bellosguardo, but if you want to see it you have to stay there and it's in the high price range. At the center of the Piazzalle Michelangelo is a monument to **Michelangelo** dominated by a replica of the statue of *David*. Round the pedestal are four statues that adorn the tombs of famous Medicis which Michelangelo created.

If you don't want to walk up the steep hill to the Piazza, take bus number 13 from the station.

13. MUSEO ZOOLOGICO LA SPECOLA

Via Romana 17. Closed Wednesdays. Open Sundays 9:00am–1:00pm, and all other days 9:00am–12 noon.

This is an outing for the entire family, especially little boys. They have vast collection of stuffed animals from all over the world, some extinct, as well as bugs, fish, crustaceans, and more. Unfortunately some ignorant tourists have started using a hollowed out elephant foot as a trash can.

You won't believe the extent of this collection, and that's just the animals. The best part of the exhibit are the over 500 anatomical figures and body parts that were made in very life-like colored wax between 1175 and 1814. Every part of the body has been preserved separately and in whole body displays. They even left the hair on the female bodies to make them look more realistic. One exhibit you may not want your kids to see is the part on reproduction, which gets pretty graphic. That room is at the end so you can march ahead and steer your loved ones into another room.

The other stuff is very tame. The last room has miniature wax scenes that are completely realistic depcitions of the toll taken by the Black Death (the Plague). One particular tiny image of a rat pulling on a dead man's intestine is quite intense. Look at these pieces as art, not the anatomy tools they were used for, and you'll appreciate them as much as the many art students I encountered sketching the wax figures.

THE BOBOLI GARDENS

Located behind the Pitti Palace. Open 9am until one hour before sunset.

Hidden behind the Pitti Palace is your respite from the Florentine heat and its hectic pace. Began in 1549 by Cossimo I and Eleanor of Tudor, the gardens went through many changes, additions, and alterations before they reached their present design. Among its many pathways and well-placed fields, the **Boboli Gardens** are the only true escape from the sun, humidity, and crowds that swarm through Florence in July and August. If you are inclined to walk in a calm, peaceful garden, far from the bustling crowds, or if you wish to enjoy a relaxing picnic, the Boboli is your place.

In the groves and walks of the Boboli you can find many spots to sit and enjoy a picnic lunch, or you can simply enjoy the platoons of statuary lining the walks. Some of the most famous works here include: *Pietro Barbino Riding a Tortoise*, commonly called Fat Baby Bacchus riding a turtle (you'll find reproductions of this statue in almost every vendor's stall in Florence); a Roman amphitheater ascending in tiers from the Palazzo Pitti, designed as a miniature Roman circus to hold Medici court spectacles; and *Neptune's Fountain* at the top of the terrace, created in 1565 by Stoldo Lorenzi.

From this fountain a path leads to the adorable **Kaffeehaus**, a boat-like pavilion that offers a fine view of Florence and drinks to quench your thirst. Keep going up until you reach the **Ex Forte di Belvedere**, which offer magnificent views of all of Florence, and Cypress Alley, lined with statues of many different origins.

La Limonaia

Even if you are not looking for it, you can't miss the **Limonaia**, a room 340 feet long and 30 feet wide that became the 'hospital' for all the devastated works of art during the Flood of '66 (see story below). Originally used to house the Boboli Gardens' lemon trees during the winter months, this room, many experts felt, was the savior of the Florentine masterpieces, because of its insulation from the Florentine humidity. Most of the art treasures from the disastrous flood of '66 were brought here to be rehabilitated. I guess you could say that all art lovers can be thankful that the Medicis, who built the Boboli Gardens and the Limonaia, had a passion for lemons.

Porta Romana

This garden stretches seemingly forever, and it hides some of the best green spaces at its farthest corners, near Florence's **South Gate** (**Porta Romana**).

WALKING THE PATH OF THE FLOOD OF 1966

Standing at the center of the Ponte Vecchio, surveying the incomparable beauty and serenity of the sights of Florence, makes it difficult to imagine the city virtually blanketed with oily, muddy surging walls of water. This image was reality not long ago, when Florence's last massive flood occurred and devastated the world with its historic and artistic calamity.

On November 3, 1966, the normally complacent **Arno** turned into a life threatening, destructive river, coursing through the labyrinth of Florence's many streets. On that night, and the subsequent days, despite the valiant efforts of an army of students from all over the world and the courageous Florentines, the world lost many priceless art treasures, and many irreplaceable documents and manuscripts.

Not the First

But this was not Florence's first experience with a flood's devastation. For many centuries Florentines had been ravaged by the power of nature, a power which had been enhanced by the meddlesome hand of man.

What remains of these past floods are the commemorative plaques, all over the city, indicating the high water marks from each of the individual disasters.

How could such calamity occur to one of the world's most historic cities? How could it have been prevented?

Leonardo da Vinci clearly saw the cause of these periodic floods, and even made excellent recommendation for their remedy. He designed projects to develop water impoundments in the hills around Florence, to develop tributaries off the Arno, to develop chambers beneath Florence to hold excess flood waters. In conjunction, a proposal was made to initiate a government-sponsored reforestation plan, first by Gianbattista Vico del Cicerto, and later by many other visionaries.

Centuries of De-Forestation

But each and every suggestion went unheeded by those in power. Why? Mainly because the trees around Florence were needed to support the growing population's demand for fuel and construction material. Couple this with the root destruction caused by grazing goats and sheep, which helped support the successful wool trade, and this left the surrounding hills, once thick with impenetrable forests, barren and desolate and open to rain water run-off that helped stimulate the devastating Florentine floods.

Since the massive flood of 1333, moderate floods have occurred in Florence every 24 years, major floods every 26 years, and massive floods (like the one in 1966) every 100 years. As we take our flood tour of Florence, keep a watchful eye up at the 15-20 foot level on most buildings, because that is where the commemorative flood markers of November 4, 1966; November 3, 1844; and November 4, 1333 and others are located.

This tour is not meant to glorify these natural disasters, of course, but to act as a reminder that history ignored has a tendency to repeat itself.

Where to Start

Starting on the **Ponte Vecchio**, try and imagine trees and automobiles being hurled by the Arno into this living masterpiece, destroying the gold shops in its wake. For centuries these periodic floods may have been considered a necessary cleansing process, for the Ponte Vecchio was lined with butcher shops and leather tanners before gold took over.

Our first stop is the **Uffizi Gallery**, the reigning king of the Renaissance museums. The cellars of the gallery, which were designed as government offices for the Medicis, were completely submerged. Many works of art, in conjunction with the State Archives containing valuable papers of the Medici family and the Florentine governments, were covered in water and fuel oil. This fuel oil was a modern addition to the

Florentine floods. It was used as heating for Florentine homes, and was dredged up all over the city by the swirling waters of the Arno.

La Biblioteca Nazionale

Walking along the river we reach the **Horne museum**, which lost an extensive collection of paintings, sculptures, and furniture, all drowned in over 13 feet of water. A little farther up from there is the Italian equivalent of the Library of Congress, the **Biblioteca Nazionale Centrale**. Here, arguably, the most devastation occurred, when close to one and a half million of nearly three million volumes disappeared from the miles of shelving into the waters.

Past the left of the library we enter the **Piazza Santa Croce** where the church of Santa Croce almost lost the bones of Michelangelo, Machiavelli, Galileo, and the composer Rossini to the muddy Arno water. The museum next door had its *Crucifix* by Giovanni Cimabue battered and eventually destroyed by the black tide.

Michelangelo & Mud?

Out the Piazza and to the right, down the Via Dei Benci, the **Bargello**, sculptures equivalent to the Uffizi, was awash with 14 feet of oil, mud and water. Many of Michelangelo's works found here were completely covered, and had to be blanketed with clouds of talcum powder to extract all the potentially damaging oil.

Il Duomo

Now follow the Via del Proncosolo to the **Piazza del Duomo** and the **Baptistery**, which is covered on three sides by its beautiful bronze doors. The door on the east side, containing magnificent scenes from the Old Testament, had five of its panels pried loose, luckily to be saved by a protective gate that surrounded the monument.

Obviously I could go on virtually forever, following the path of the disastrous flood of 1966 as it twisted through the web of Florence; but I could never fully describe the toll the Arno inflicted on the citizens of Florence, and on the treasures of the Renaissance. Almost every museum, library, and residence was affected in some way by the flood of 1966.

I have not even discussed the loss of human life, and have only touched on the courage and determination of the students and of the Florentines. But now, with better river water management, through the proper use of dams and improved communication between the two major dams above Florence, the effects of centuries of deforestation can be better controlled. And hopefully, history, in this case, will not repeat itself.

LEARN TO COOK IN FLORENCE

Since 1973, Giuliano Bugiali has been teaching Italian cooking to visitors in Florence, and its all in English. To get information about how to spend an enjoyable culinary experience while in Florence, contact **Guiliano Bugialli's Cooking in Florence**, *PO Box 1650, Canal Street Station, New York, NY 10013-0870. Tel. 212/966-5325. Fax 212/226-0601.*

NIGHTLIFE & ENTERTAINMENT

Florence is definitely not known for its nightlife like Rome or Milan are. Local Florentine activities usually include some form of late night eating and drinking at a restaurant that stays open late. Heated dancing and wild debauchery don't seem to part of the Florentine make-up.

Here are some places to go if you get that itch to be wild; the numbering follows the restaurants on the *Florence Restaurants* map.

32. THE RED GARTER, *Via de Benci 33r, Tel. 055/234-4904. Serve Heineken, McFarland, Guiness, margaritas and an any other drink you could want. Open 8:30pm - 1:00am. Happy hour 8:30pm - 9:30pm.*

A raunchy, wild and fun-filled place with live music in the back and a bar up front. Their pitchers cost L24,000-30,000, Liters L14,000-18,000, and half-pints L7,000-10,000. A place to come and be wild. Why else would they serve pitchers?

33. IL FAUNO, *Via Cavour 89. Tel 055/471-682. Open 5:00pm - 2:00am. Happy hour 5:00pm - 10:00pm.*

Yes, they have a loooong happy hour (five hours). Enjoy the half-priced drinks in a not so authentic Irish pub. Fiddler's is where the ex-pats hang out, so if you're into a pseudo Irish time, and want to save some bucks give this place a try. If it's no good, after happy hour, hop over to Fiddler's.

34. THE FIDDLER'S ELBOW, *Piazza Santa Maria Novella 7R, Tel. 055/215-056. Open 3:00pm- 1:15pm every day.*

If you want to wallow in a true Irish pub outside of Ireland, you've found it. They serve Harp, Kilkenny, Guiness and some Inch's Stonehouse Cider. A pint costs L7,000, a half-pint L4,000 and the lovely Irish and English bartenders will gladly serve you a shot or two of your pleasure. There is no food served, and there is seating outside but no service for the tables.

But to actually feel as if you're in Ireland, step into the air conditioned comfort, sit among the hanging musical instruments, belly up to the dark wooden bar, eye yourself in the mirror, and have a pint. For snacks (you have to pay for them), they have peanuts, salami sticks for the Italians, and four types of Highlander Scottish potato chips (they call them crisps):

Roast Beef Taste, Cheddar & Onion, Caledonian Tomato, and Sea Salt. If you want to be a part of the ex-pat community here in Florence this is one of the places to go. They also have bars in Rome and Venice. Mr. Fiddler has really become a businessman.

35. IL RIFRULLO, *Via San Niccolo 55, Tel. 055/213-631. Large beer L5,000, small beer L3,000, Crepe L5,000. Open from 8:00am to midnight.*

Located in the centro, this is a charming and relaxing place where you can enjoy a drink in the garden in the summer, in front of the fireplace in the winter, or up at the bar whenever you please. The atmosphere in the front room is all pub, in the back room all *taverna*, and in the garden, all party. They have a bar set into ancient struts that hold up the building; the tables are under an overhead canopy. They serve Whitbread Pale Ale, Campbells Scotch Ale, Stella Antois (Belgian) and Leffe (and Belgian Double Malt on tap), as well as some of the largest and most scrumptious crepes around. Come early; remember that Florence closes down early even on weekends.

36. SPACE ELECTRONIC, *Via Palazzuolo 37, 50123 Firenze. tel. 055/292-082. Fax 055/293-457.*

The largest and loudest discotheque in the city. They've had videos playing here before anybody knew what videos were (I remember), and they continue to be the trendsetters when it comes to club antics. What they are into now I'll keep quiet, so maybe you'll come check them out. They play all sorts of music, so no one is left out. A fun place.

37. HARRY'S BAR, *Lungarno a Vespucci 22, 50123 Firenze. Tel. 055/239-6700. American Express, Mastercard and Visa accepted. Closed Sundays.*

Based on the famous Harry's Bar in Venice (see the Venice Section in this book), but with no business connections (Italians obviously have different trademark laws than we do), this is now the place to find the best burgers in Florence. They also mix some strong drinks in the evening, so if you have nothing to do and just want to get out of the hotel room, pop in here.

38. DUBLIN PUB, *Via Faenza 27r. Tel. 055/293-049. Closed Mondays. Open from 5pm to 2:00am*

A true Irish pub, dark and dingy and open only at night. They serve Kilkenny, Harp, Guiness for L7,000 a pint and L4,000 a half pint; as well as some Bulmers Cider. A hopping nightlife spot with true Irish ambiance. I prefer Fiddler's Elbow, but they're close enough together that you can try them both. This one is near the outdoor San Lorenzo Market and the Mercato Centrale.

Movies in English

Try **Cinema Astro**, P*iazza San Simone (near Santa Croce; closed July 10–August 31 and Mondays. Ticketc cost L8,000.* There's a student discount on

Wednesdays for L6,000. There are films in English here every night. Either call for the schedule or stop by and pick one up.

There's also a movie poster listing the films playing at Cinema Astro just inside the **Fiddler's Elbow** pub (see above in this section).

SPORTS & RECREATION

Balloon Rides in Tuscany

Contact **The Bombard Society**, 6727 Curran Street, McLean VA 22101-3804, US, Tel. 800/862-8537, Fax. 703/883-0985. In Virginia or outside, Tel. 703/448-9407; you can call collect. Call for current price and information about the most spectacular way to view the most spectacular scenery in the world.

Bicycling

Florence is the perfect city to explore on a bicycle and there are a few rental places available.
- **Free Motor**, *Via Santa Monaca 6-8, Tel. 055/295-102, in the Oltrarno area.*
- **Motorent**, *Via San Zanobi 9, Tel. 055/490-113, in the Centro area.*
- **Sabra**, *Via Artisti 8, Tel. 055/576-256, in the Oltrarno area.*

Golf

- **Circolo Golf dell'Ugolino**, *Via Chiantigiano 3, 51005 Grassina, Tel. 055/320-1009. Fax 055/230-1141.* Located 9km from Florence this is a par 72, 18 hole course that is 5,728 meters long. Open all year round except on Mondays. They have tennis courts, a swimming pool, a pro shop, a nice bar and a good restaurant.
- **Poggio de Medici Golf & Country Club**, *Via San Gavino 27, 50038 Scarperia. Tel. 055/83-0436/7/8. Fax 055/843-0439.* Located 30km from Florence this is a 9 hole, par 36, that is 3,430 meter long course, open all year round except for Tuesdays.. They have a driving range, putting green and a club house with snacks and drinks.

Swimming

There are three public pools in Florence:
- **Piscine Bellariva**, *Lungarno Colombo 6, Tel. 677-521, located outside the city.*
- **Piscine Costoli**, *Viale Poali, Tel. 055/669-7444, located outside the city.*
- **Piscine Pavoniere**, *Viale degli Olmi, Tel. 055/367-506*

Tennis

- **Associazione Sportiva**, *Viale Michelangelo, Tel. 055/681-2686*

SHOPPING

Antiques

Many of the better known antique stores have been located in the **Via dei Fossi** and **Via Maggio** for years, but there are some interesting little shops in the **Borgo San Jacopo** and the **Via San Spirito**, all located in the **Oltrarno** section of Florence across the river.

When shopping for antiques in Florence, there is one important thing to remember: the Florentines are excellent crafts people and as such have taken to the art of antique fabrication and reproduction. How can they do this legally? Under Italian law, furniture made from old wood is considered an antique. These products can be exported. But if you find a 'real' antique by American standards, it is usually stamped so that it cannot be taken out of the country.

Artisans

If you want to see some of this fabrication and reproduction work, as well as genuine restoration in progress, you need venture no further than across the river to the **Oltrarno** section. In these narrow streets you'll find small workshops alive with the sounds of hammers and saws, intermingled with the odors of wood, tanning leather, and glue. When I lived in Florence this was my favorite area to come to. Watching someone creating something out of nothing has always been a relaxing adventure, and besides, not many tourists even venture into these tiny alcoves of Florentine culture.

Some of the most well known shops are located in the **Via Santo Spirito**, **Viale Europa**, **Via Vellutini**, **Via Maggio** and the **Via dello Studio**. Strangely enough, on these same streets are your reputable antique shops. How convenient to have the fabricators and reproducers next door to the 'legitimate' antique dealers.

Books & Newspapers in English

BM Bookshop, *Borgo Agnissanti 4r, Tel 055/294-575. American Express, Mastercard and Visa accepted. Open Winter: Monday 3:30pm-7:30pm, Tuesday-Saturday 9:00am-1:00pm and 3:30pm-7:30pm. Open Summer: 9:30am-1:00pm and 3:30pm-7:30pm daily.*

An extensive collection of English language books in both hardcover and paperback. This is also one of the meeting places for the English-speaking community in Florence. Located in the *Centro* area.

English Bookstore Paperback Exchange, *Via Fiesolana 31r, Tel 247-8154. American Express, Diners Club, Mastercard and Visa accepted. Open Monday-Saturday 9:00am-1:00pm and 3:30pm-7:30pm. Closed in August. Closed Mondays November–February.*

The unofficial English speaking expatriates meeting place, this store has the largest and best priced selection of English-language paperbacks in Florence. It's the Florentine equivalent of the *Economy Bookstore* in Rome. You will get paid for any used paperbacks you want to get rid of, or they'll credit the amount to any purchases you want to make. Located in the *Santa Croce* section of Florence.

Libreria Internazionale Seeber, *Via Tornabuoni 68r, 055/215-697. Mastercard and Visa accepted.*

This is a quaint old fashioned bookstore that's been around since the 1860s to serve the expatriate community. An entire room is devoted to foreign books, not all of which are in English. Even if you can't find what you want, this is a fun place to browse.

THE PAPIERMACHE STORE

*One store you simply cannot miss is the small studio/gallery of the artist Bijan, **Firenze of Papier Mache, Piazza Pitti 10, 50125 Firenze, Tel. 055/230-2978, Fax 055/365-768.** He makes some beautiful masks covered with intricate sketchings of famous paintings, as well as beautiful anatomical forms all from papiermache. Even if you don't buy anything, simply browse and savor the beauty of his work. Since the shop is near the Palazzo Pitti, one of your 'must see' destinations while in Florence, there's no reason why you shouldn't stop here.*

Cartoleria - Stationary Stores

L'Indice Scrive, *Via della Vigna Nuova 82r. Tel. 055/215-165. Mastercard and Visa accepted.*

A wide variety of stationary products and unique pens are featured in this store. Most of the items are hand-made, including the diaries, ledgers, guest books, desk sets. etc. A great place to get a gift for someone back home.

Il Papiro, *Piazza Duomo 24r, Tel. 055/215-262. Credit cards accepted.*

If you like marbleized paper products, this is the store for you. You can get boxes, notebooks, picture frames, pencil holders, basically anything you could imagine. The prices are a little high but that's because of the great location and high quality products.

Markets

The markets in Florence are all hustle and bustle, especially in the high tourist season. But despite the crowds you can have a great time browsing and shopping. And of course, the prices are sometimes close to half what they are in stores. Remember to bargain if you want something.

Mercato Centrale, *immediately north of Piazza San Lorenzo, near the Duomo, open Monday–Saturday, 7am–1pm, 4–7:30pm.*

This is Florence's main food market for wholesale and retail fish, fresh meat, vegetables, cheeses, oils, breads, and many other delicacies. The meat and fish section is on the ground floor, with a few vegetable stands thrown in, but if you're into healthy food, make your way upstairs to their fruit and vegetable market. The aroma is enough to make you want to come back every day you're in Florence. Try to find some *caciotta* (sheep's milk cheese) and *finocchiona* (salami flavored with fennel) because they are an exquisite local delicacy. This is the best place to shop for your picnic supplies. A must see while in Florence. The market itself is surrounded by the large clothing market of San Lorenzo.

When you visit the Mercato Centrale, don't think of leaving without getting a sandwich at **Nerbone's** (see review above in *Where to Eat*). In operation since 1872, this small food stand serves the absolutely best boiled pork, beef, or veal sandwiches, for only L3,500. They're simply called panini and your only choice of meat is what they have boiled for the day. The sandwich is just the meat, the bread, and some salt, but it is amazing. You can stand at the counter and sip a glass of wine or beer, or take your meal to the small seating area just across the aisle.

Mercato di San Lorenzo, *located near the Duomo, open Monday–Friday, 7am–2pm, Saturdays and holidays 4–8 pm.*

This is the largest and most frequented street market in Florence, and it completely dominates the church of San Lorenzo and its piazza, as well as spilling into most adjacent streets. You can find everything from shoes to pants, T-shirts, belts, and much more, most at prices close to half of what you would pay in a store. Both Florentines and tourists come here looking for bargains. Again, remember to bargain, because once a merchant marks you as a tourist the price quoted is usually higher than that quoted to Italians.

Mercato Nuovo, *located in the Logge del Mercato Nuovo off the Via Por San Maria near the Piazza del Signoria, open daily 9am–5pm.*

This is the famous Straw Market. They sell traditional products made from straw but also exquisite leather products, ceramics, linens (like table clothes and napkins), statues, and other hand-made Florentine crafts.

Mercato Delle Piante, *located in the Piazza della Repubblica in front of the Central Post Office, open Thursday 7am–1pm.*

This beautiful flower market can calm any soul. Even if you do not want to buy any plants, simply walk through the many different flowers and enjoy the sights and smells.

Mercato dell Pulci, *located in the Piazza dei Compi about four blocks north of the church of Santa Croce, open Tuesday–Saturday, 8am–1pm, 3:30pm–7pm, and the first Sunday of each month from 9am–7pm.*

This is Florence's famous flea market. If you want antiques and junk at obviously trumped up prices, come here. They think tourists will pay anything for a true Italian antique – so remember to bargain. The next market, Mercato di Sant'Ambrogio, is located just to the east of this market.

Mercato di Sant'Ambrogio, *located in the Piazza Lorenzo Ghiberti between the Via Dell' Agnolo and the Borgo La Croce, open weekday mornings.*

This is another of Florence's food markets. It has a less hectic and more intimate atmosphere than the larger Mercato Centrale. Also a good place to sit at their lunch counter, try some food, and settle down with a nice cappuccino.

Mercato delle Cascine, *located in the Cascine park along the Arno river on the outskirts of Florence to the west, just off of the Piazza Vittorio Veneto, open Tuesdays, 7 am–1pm.*

This is like a huge outdoor department store. For sale are mainly clothing and household products, but even if you're not going to buy anything, this is an interesting insight into Italian culture and society.

Picnic & Food Supplies

If you can't make it to the **Mercato Generale** or the **Mercato di Sant'Ambrogio** for your Boboli Gardens or day trip picnic supplies, here's a small list of food stores from which you can get almost everything you want. The perfect amount of meat for a sandwich would be *mezzo etto*, and same goes for your cheese. Also, at most bars you can order a sandwich to go if you're too lazy to make your own sandwich, as well some *vino* or *birra* to take with you.

Alimentari, *Via Luigi Alimani #6.*

Located right next to the train station. Actually it's housed in the same building but the entrance to this place is outside. A perfect place to pick up a snack before you go on a day trip.

Vera, *Piazza Frescobaldi 3r, Tel 055/215-465. No credit cards accepted.*

Located in the Oltrarno section of Florence, this store is a food connoisseur's delight. It is indisputably Florence's best stocked food store, conveniently located close to the Boboli Gardens. It has the best fresh cheeses, salamis, hams, roasted meats, freshly baked breads, olive oil, soups and salads. If you want fresh fruit you're also in luck – but not here, in the store across the street.

Alimentari, *Via Arione 19r, 055/214-067. No credit cards accepted. Closed Wednesday afternoons.*

Located in the Centro area of Florence near the Piazza San Trinita, this is your basic Italian grocery store. There's a sandwich counter from which you can have the sandwich of your choice made with a wide variety of meats (try the *prosciutto*), cheeses (get some of the fresh buffalo-milk *mozzarella*), salamis, and fresh bread. You can also get *vino* to go here. If you want to eat or enjoy a glass of Chianti at the bar, upside-down barrels serve as seats.

Cibreo Alimentari, *Via del Verrocchio 4, 50122 Firenze. Tel. 055/677-298.*

A deli-type store in the Santa Croce area that is associated with the Cibreo restaurant in the same area. They sell authentic and fresh local delicacies for take-out.

Vino e Olio, *Via dei Serragli 29r, Tel. 055298-708. No credit cards accepted.*

You can find any type of wine or olive oil you could dream of in this store. Since it is slightly expensive you may not want to get your wine for the picnic here, but it is a great place to buy gifts for friends at home. If you don't want to carry them with you on the rest of your trip, the owner will arrange to have them shipped to wherever you choose.

Alessi Paride, *Via delle Oche 27-29r, Tel. 055/214-966. Credit cards accepted.*

This store is a wine lovers paradise. They have wines from every region of Italy and there's one room entirely of Chianti. This store may also be a little expensive for picnic supplies, but you can get any manner of wine imaginable here, as well as selected liquors, chocolates, marmalades, and honeys.

POLICE CHIC SHOPPING!

Il Tricolore, Via della Scala 32, is a moderately priced Italian army navy store, with a few American items thrown in. You can get Caribinieri (Italian military police) hats, T-shirts, knives, pins, badges, jackets, bags, etc., all from the Italian police or military services. Some items they can't sell to you since they are official army and/or police issue, but the stuff you can buy will make some great gifts for yourself or others.

PRACTICAL INFORMATION

Bank Hours & Changing Money

Banks are open Monday to Friday, 8:30am–1:20pm and 3pm–4pm, and are closed Saturdays, Sundays and national holidays. You'll need your passport when changing money or travelers checks at a bank as well as at a hotel or foreign exchange office (*ufficio di cambio*).

You'll find the best rates at banks and *cambio*. To get the most for your money try to avoid changing it at the American Express office or at a hotel.

Business Hours

Shops are generally open 9am–1pm and 3:30pm or 4pm to 7pm or 7:30pm, although some in the *Centro Storico* area stay open all day to cater to the tourists. And an even more accommodating gesture towards the almighty dollar is that some stores even open on Sundays. I can remember when nothing was open in Florence on a Sunday except the restaurants.

In the winter, most shops are closed on Monday morning, except the food stores which close on Wednesday afternoon. (Why? Who knows?) In the summer, some stores close all day Saturday, but remain open on Monday morning. The rules change constantly.

Church & Synagogue Ceremonies in English
• **St. James**, American Episcopal Church, *Via Rucellai 9, Tel. 055/294-417.* Located in the *Centro* section of Florence.
• **St. Marks**, Church of England, *Via Maggio 16, Tel. 055/294-764.* Located in the *Oltrarno* section of Florence.
• **Synagogue**, *Via L.C. Farini 4, Tel. 055/245-251/2.* Located in the *Santa Croce* section of Florence.

Consulates
• **British Consulate**, *Lungarno Corsini 2, Florence, Tel. (055) 284-133*
• **United States Consulate**, *Lungarno Amerigo Vespucci 38, Florence, Tel. (055) 239-8276*

If you're Canadian, Irish, or another nationality, you'll need to contact your embassy in Rome (see our *Rome* chapter, *Practical Information* section).

Local Festivals & Holidays
• **January 1**, New Years Day
• **April 25**, Liberation Day
• **Ascension Day**
• **Easter Monday**, Cricket Festival with floats and many little crickets sold in cages. Kids love this festival. You won't be able to bring the crickets back to the states though.
• **May 1**, Labor Day
• **Month of May**, Iris Festivals
• **May and June**, *Maggio Musicale Fiorentino*
• **Mid-June to August**, *Estate Fiesolana*. Music, cinema, ballet and theater
• **Three Weekends in June**, *Calcio in Costume*
• **June 24**, St. John the Baptist's Day celebrated with fireworks
• **August 15**, *Ferragosto*
• **First Sunday in September**, Lantern Festival
• **November 1**, All Saints Day *(Ognissanti)*
• **December 8**, Conception of the Virgin Mary *(Immacolata)*
• **December 25 & 26**, Christmas

Laundry

After you're on the road for a few days, and especially if you're going to be on the road for quire a while, you're definitely going to need to do some laundry, quickly, easily, and cheaply. If you're staying at a four star hotel don't bother reading this because you've already sent your clothes down to be starched and pressed by the in-house staff.

For the rest of us, we need to find a good coin operated laundry, and in Florence they have just the thing. Actually, there are four of them, all branches of the same outfit, plus one lone entrepeneur.

• **Wash & Dry**, *Open seven days a week from 8:00am to 10:00pm. Last wash allowed in at 9:00pm. General number 055/436-1650. L6,000 for wash, L6,000 for dry, L2,500 for detergent. At the following locations: **Via dei Serragli 87/R** (in the Oltrarno); **Via della Scala 52/54R** (by the train station) – has air conditioning; **Via dei Servi 105/R** (by the Duomo) – has air conditioning; **Viale Morgagni 21/R** (Quite a ways away from the tourist center. You'll probably never get out this far).*

• **Laundrette**, *Via del Guelfa 33. Open seven days a week from 8:00am to 10:00pm. Wash L5,000, Dry L3,000, Detergent L5,000.*

Postal Services

The **central post office** in Florence *is at Via Pietrapiana 53-55, in the Santa Croce section of town*; but stamps can be bought at any tobacconist (store indicated by a T sign outside), and mailed at any mailbox, which are red and marked with the words *Poste* or *Lettere*. You can send duty free gift packages (need to be marked "gift enclosed") home to friends or relatives as long as the cost of the gift(s) in the package does not exceed US$50.

If you need to mail a package of material which you brought with you on you trip, you need to mark the package "American goods returned."

Tourist Information & Maps

• **Information Office**, *Via Manzoni 16, Tel. 055/247-8141.* Located in the Santa Croce area of Florence. Provides city maps, up-to-date information about Florence and the Province of Florence, which includes museum hours, event, and bus and train schedules.

• **Information Office**, *at the Train Station, Via Stazione 59r. Open 7am to 10pm. Tel. 055/278-785.* They can book hotel rooms for you here. You have to pay the first night's stay in advance plus a fee of L10,000 for a deluxe hotel, L6,000 for a four-star, L5,000 for a three-star, L4,000 for a two star, and L3,000 for a one star. There's an attached form that you need to fill out so that they can find just the room for you.

• **American Express**, *Lungarno Guicciardini 49, Tel. 055/288-751.* Located in the *Oltrarno* section of Florence. You don't need to be a card holder or be in any way related to American Express to ask for assistance.

Tour Operators
- **American Express**, *Via Dante Aligheiri 22r, Tel. 055/50981.* Located in the *Centro Storico* section of Florence.
- **Wagon-Lit**, *Via del Giglio 27r, Tel 055/21-88-51.* Located in the Centro section of Florence.
- **World Vision Travel**, *Via Cavour 154/158r. Tel 055/57-71-85. Fax 055/582-664; and Lungarno Acciadi 4. Tel. 055/29.52.71. Fax 055/215-666.*
- **CIT**, *Via Cavour 56-59, Tel. 055/294-306.* Located in the Centro section of Florence.

DAY TRIPS & EXCURSIONS

If you have the time, there are a number of great day trips and longer excursions in the region. For many, a trip to Italy is not complete without visiting one of the most famous sights in the world – the **Leaning Tower of Pisa**, located, you guessed it, in **Pisa**!

There's also the charming walled city of **Lucca**; the winding medieval streets of **Siena**, with one of the most impressive clock towers in Italy; and the ancient town of **Fiesole**, once the Roman Empire's dominant town in Tuscany.

PISA

Located 56 miles west of Florence, with a population of a little over 100,000 people, **Pisa** is mainly known for its leaning tower. But it is rich in history with many beautiful architectural landmarks, decorated with intricate ornamentation.

The famous **Campo dei Miracoli** is in the northwestern part of the city. In this square are the **baptistery**, a circular church building used for baptisms; the **cathedral**, built from 1063 to 1160; and **marble bell tower**, known to the world as the **Leaning Tower of Pisa**. It is thought that in the cathedral the astronomer **Galileo** first made the observation that later became known as the principle of the motion of a pendulum. The bell tower, which is 179 feet (55 meters) high and 50 feet (15 meters) wide, was built on unstable ground. It began to tip during its construction and is now 15 feet (4.6 meters) out of perpendicular. Other monuments include a cemetery, the Church of Santa Caterina, several museums, and many libraries. The city suffered considerable damage during World War II, but its art treasures still attract a large number of tourists from all over the world.

A naval base under Roman control, Pisa became a Roman colony after 180 BC. The town had a Christian bishop by 313 AD. Pisa's greatest time was back in the 12th century, when its population was greater than 300,000. Pisa was considered a city of marvels because Pisa's merchants,

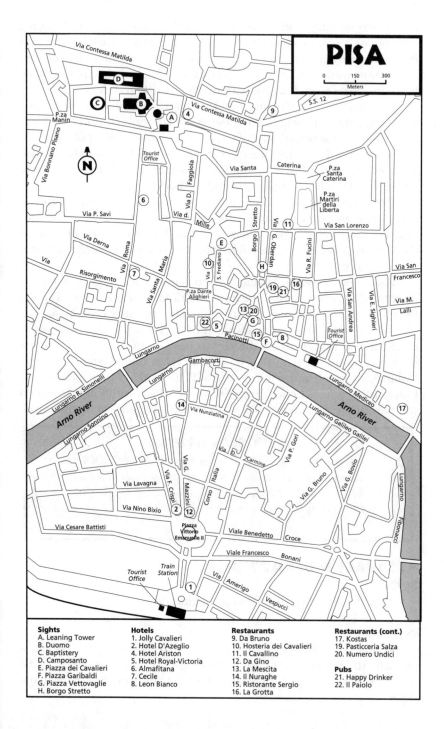

PISA

0   150   300
Meters

Via Contessa Matilda

S.S. 12

D

C   B

P.za
Manin   A   4

Via Contessa Matilda   9

Tourist
Office

Via Bonnano Pisano

N

Via Santa   Caterina   P.za
Santa
Caterina

Via D. Faggiola

P.za
Martiri
della
Liberta

6

Via P. Savi   Via d. Mille

Via San Lorenzo

11

Via Derna   E   Borgo Stretto   Via G. Oberdan   Via R. Fucini

Via San
Francesco

Via   10   Via S. Frediano   H   19   16   Via San Andrea   Via E. Sighieri   Via M.
Lalli

Risorgimento   Via Roma   Via Santa Maria   7   P.za Dante Alighieri   13   20   21

22   5   G   Tourist
Office

Pacinotti   15   F   8

Lungarno   Gambacorti

Lungarno   Lungarno Mediceo

Lungarno R. Simonelli   14   Via Nunziatina   Lungarno Galileo Galilei   Arno River   17

Arno River   Lungarno Sonnino   Via G. Mazzini   Via Carmine   Via P. Gori   Lungarno Fibonacci

Via Lavagna   Via G. Crispi   Via B.   Via G. Bruno   Via G. Bovio

Via Nino Bixio   2   12   Corso Italia

Via Cesare Battisti   Piazza
Vittorio
Emanuele II   Viale Benedetto   Croce

Viale Francesco   Bonani

Tourist
Office   Train
Station   1   Via   Amerigo

Vespucci

Sights	**Hotels**	**Restaurants**	**Restaurants (cont.)**
A. Leaning Tower	1. Jolly Cavalieri	9. Da Bruno	17. Kostas
B. Duomo	2. Hotel D'Azeglio	10. Hosteria dei Cavalieri	19. Pasticceria Salza
C. Baptistery	4. Hotel Ariston	11. Il Cavallino	20. Numero Undici
D. Camposanto	5. Hotel Royal-Victoria	12. Da Gino	
E. Piazza dei Cavalieri	6. Almafitana	13. La Mescita	**Pubs**
F. Piazza Garibaldi	7. Cecile	14. Il Nuraghe	21. Happy Drinker
G. Piazza Vettovaglie	8. Leon Bianco	15. Ristorante Sergio	22. Il Paiolo
H. Borgo Stretto		16. La Grotta	

and its strong navy, had traveled all over the Mediterranean, bringing back not only new products but new ideas and styles in art. The famous **Pisan Romanesque** architecture, with its stripes and blind arcades, had its orignins in the Moorish architecture of Andalucia in Spain, whose ideas and styles were brought back by Pisa's world travelers.

During this successful time, the **Duomo** was built and the Baptistery and Campanile were begun. But these weren't the only glory of Pisa. It has been described as being a city of ten thousand towers, most of which do not exist today. How unfortunate that the one which has survived leans. Most of the other Pisan monuments no longer with us today were destroyed in the bombings at the end of World War II.

Pisa historically aligned itself with the rulers of Tuscany, mainly in Florence, if only for expediency. Their navy was vast and fierce and they were constantly at war somewhere in the Mediterranean, usually against the Muslim world, even if they did adapt their science and architecture to their own uses.

Pisa's decline began in 1284, when the mercantile port of Genoa devastated the Pisan navy at the **Battle of Meloria** near Livorno. But the final blow to Pisa's Mediterranean dominance was delivered by nature. The silt from the Arno gradually filled in the Pisan port and the cost of dredging was too great for the city to bear. From that point on Pisa became a pawn that the other Italian city states traded back and forth. Eventually coming under the control of Florence, the Medici dukes gave Pisa a lasting gift, Florence's own university. This institution helped Pisa stay alive and vital, and in touch with the changes going on in the world.

BEST EATS IN PISA

If you only eat at one restaurant while in Pisa, make it Il Cavallino (#11 on the map). They serve wonderful pasta, meat, and fish dishes at great local prices. Located on the edge of a peaceful piazza away from the tourist area of Pisa, this is the perfect place to experience the real city, not just its sights.

ARRIVALS & DEPARTURES

By Car

Take the A11 directly to Pisa from Florence.

By Train

Trains from Florence arrive at the Stazione Centrale, which is pleasant 10-15 minute walk to the leaning tower and the other tourist sights. Or if you are a little tired, take the No. 1 bus from the station to the sights.

WHERE TO STAY

I am not recommending that you actually stay in Pisa. I'm suggesting that you take a day trip up this way from Florence, spend the day, see the sights, explore the old city by the Arno, have lunch and maybe dinner, then catch one of the frequent trains home. But if you happen to tarry a little longer than expected, here's a concise list of hotels in a variety of price ranges that are worthy.

1. JOLLY CAVALIERI, *Piazza della Stazione 2, 56125 Pisa. Tel. 050/ 43290. Fax 050/502242. 100 rooms all with bath. Single L220,000-260,000; Double L260,000-350,000. Breakfast included. All credit cards accepted.* ****

Located near the train station and a ways away from the main sights, this could be an option if you've lingered too long over a long dinner and don't want to take the train back to Florence or have missed the last one. All the amenities of a four star including air conditioning, cable TV, piano bar and more. It's location is not so hot in terms of tourist sights, but if you've missed the last train this wonderful first class hotel will put you at ease.

2. HOTEL D'AZEGLIO, *Piazza V Emmanuele II 18b, 56125 Pisa. Tel. 050/500-310. Fax 050/28017. 29 rooms all with bath. Single L148,000; Double L190,000. Breakfast L13,000. All credit cards accepted.* ****

Yes, there is air conditioning, cable TV, and mini-bars, and room service, and laundry service, and more, but the place is a little run down and quite a distance away from anything of importance in Pisa. Truly a dirt cheap four-star hotel that is clean and comfortable, but seems to lack charm and ambiance. But if you want to save a little money and still get certain amenities, here's the place to stay.

4. HOTEL ARISTON, *Via Cardinale Maffi 42, Tel. 050/561-834. Fax 050/561-891. 33 rooms all with bath and TV. Single L78,000; Double L110,000. Breakfast L10,000. All credit cards accepted.* ***

5. HOTEL ROYAL-VICTORIA, *Lungarno Pacinotti 12, Tel. 050/940-111. Fax 050/940-180. 67 rooms, 48 with bath. Single L30,000-100,000; Double 35,000-120,000. Breakfast included. All credit cards accepted.* ***

Not a bad choice. Your typical three star in a smaller town.

6. ALMAFITANA, *Via Roma 44, Tel. 050/29-000. Fax 050/25-218. 21 rooms all with bath, TV, and air conditioning. Single L50,000-60,000; Double 80,000-85,000.* **

This is the best place at the best price to stay if you've had to make an unplanned stop-over in Pisa. They have all the amenities of a three star but with the price of a two star, including air conditioning, TV, bar, and more. The rooms are comfortable if not too quiet on the weekday mornings, but for the price you can't go wrong. It's also in the center of everything so if you want to grab one last look at Pisa, this is a good place to stay.

7. CECILE, *Via Roma 54, Tel. 050/29-328. Fax is the same. 19 rooms, 15 with bath and TV. Single L30,000-60,000; Double L40,000-80,000. All credit cards accepted.* **

8. LEON BIANCO, *Piazza del Pozzetto 6, Tel. 050/543-673. 28 rooms, 17 with bath. Single L33,000-48,000; Double L48,000-73,000. No credit cards accepted.* **

WHERE TO EAT & DRINK

9. DA BRUNO, *Via Luigi Bianchi 12, Pisa. Tel. 050/560-818. American Express, Diners Club, Visa and Mastercard accepted. Closed Mondays for dinner and Tuesdays. Dinner for two L90,000.*

Located outside the walls a few blocks northeast of the Campo dei Miracoli. Definitely catering to the tourist crowd since it's so close to the sights, but ignore that and enjoy the ambiance of brick archways, wooden ceilings and all kinds of knick-knacks on the walls. The farm tools indicate they serve good Tuscan meats, the sailing regalia indicate they also cater to the seafood lovers, but I preferred the meat dishes. Try either the *Agnello arrosto* (roasted lamb) or the *Conniglio al forno* (rabbit cooked over flames on a grill).

10. HOSTERIA DEI CAVALIERI, *Via San Frediano 16, Pisa. Tel. 050/ 49-008. Closed Saturdays for lunch and Sundays. Credit cards accepted. Dinner for two L65,000.*

A small place near a public high school (right around lunch the place empties out to the sounds of excited kids and their motorbikes). They have good pasta dishes here such as *con funghi porcini* (with mushrooms), *conniglio e asparagi* (rabbit and asparagus) or *vongole verace* (clams in a garlicky red sauce). For secondo, try either the *conniglio al origano* (rabbit made with oregano) or the *fileto di pesce fresco can patate e pomodoro* (fresh fillet of the catch of the day with roasted potatoes and tomatoes).

11. IL CAVALLINO, *Via San Lorenzo 66, Pisa. Tel. 050/432-290. Closed Mondays. No credit cards accepted. Dinner for two L45,000.*

You have to try this place. If you only eat at one restaurant in Pisa make it this one. Frequented by locals, it's an amazingly inexpensive place just off the beaten path, with spartan inside seating but a nice outside terrace overlooking a grass-filled quiet piazza. The owner has some Roman heritage; that's why the pastas here are so good.

Try the pe*nne all'arrabiata* (tomato based with garlic, olive oil, parsley and hot peppers) or the *penne ai quattro formaggi* (a thick sauce of four cheeses). For secondo, try the *sogliola alla griglia* (grilled sole) or the *petti pollo alla griglia* (grilled chicken breast. If you order any dish that has *gamberoni* (large shrimps) in it, your bill will escalate dramatically. Stick to the staples and have an authentic Italian meal with great ambiance outside.

12. DA GINO, *Piazza Vittorio Emanuele 19, Pisa, Tel. 050/23-437. Dinner for two L50,000. Credit cards accepted.*

Located near the train station with a basic bar/café type of atmosphere. You can select either inside or outside seating but with the traffic noise and definite lack of ambiance I'd suggest inside. I wouldn't recommend going out of your way for this place, even though the food is good, but if you're waiting for a train, pop in here and grab some quick pasta dishes or pizza. They have all kinds of pizza including *prosciutto e funghi porcini* (ham and mushrooms) as well as an excellent *capricciosa* (mushrooms, ham, and artichoke). Their pasta is good with a seafood bent. Try the *Spaghetti allo scoglio* (with clams) or the *alla marinara* (with a mixed bag of seafood).

13. LA MESCITA, *Via Cavalca 2, Pisa. Tel. 050/544-292. Closed Saturdays for lunch and Sundays. Credit cards accepted. Dinner for two L75,000.*

The price listed above is if you sample either their land or sea meal combinations. You'll get a salad, soup, and either a meat or seafood dish, along with a dessert for between L30,000 and L35,000. The meat and seafood choices for this place change daily depending on the catch and the availability at the butcher in the square. If you come for lunch you may walk right by this place since it is just outside of the Piazza Vettovaglie, where the market is located on the Via d. Cavalca. If this is full, try one of the other three or four local *trattorias* on the street.

14. IL NURAGHE, *Via Mazzini 58, Pisa. Tel 050/443-68. Closed Mondays. Credit cards accepted. Dinner for two L 45,000-50,000.*

Located on a main street leading from the station to the Arno, you can get some good *tortellini alla panna* (cheeses stuffed pasta with thick cream sauce) for primo and the *gran misto di pesce all'eriste aromatiche* (mixed fish spiced to excellence). The atmosphere is down to earth and rustic.

15. RISTORANTE SERGIO, *Lungarno Pacinotti 1 Tel. 050/48-245. American Express, Diners Club, Visa and Mastercard accepted. Closed Sundays and Monday for lunch. An expensive place. Dinner for two L150,000.*

Great fresh food prepared in exquisite Pisan style in an environment that looks like something out of an old castle. They have large keys and porcelain dishes hanging on the walls interspersed among the haphazardly placed paintings. If you try any of the *antipasti* it should be enough for a meal. Two such dishes are the *salumi tipici toscani con crostini* (Tuscan salami with crostini) or the *pesce spada con insalata di stagione* (swordfish with salad). If you try any of their meats or seafood dishes your price will easily meet the anticipated L100,000.

16. LA GROTTA, *Via San Francesco 103, Tel. 050/578-105. No credit cards accepted. Dinner for two L70,000. Closed Sundays and in August.*

An old Pisan restaurant built in 1947 and made to look like a cave. As such the atmosphere is unique and compliments the rustic Pisan cuisine.

Try the *risotto ai fiori di zucchini* (rice with zucchini flowers), the *spaghetti alla vongole* (with clam sauce), then for later try either the *conniglio* (rabbit) or the *vitello* (veal). If you're up late, this place stays open until 1 or 2am and becomes a wine bar serving drinks and cold plates after 11pm.

17. KOSTAS, *Via del Borghetto 39, Tel. 050/571-457. All credit cards accepted. Dinner for two L85,000. Closed Sundays and lunch on Mondays.*

A simple basic restaurant owned by a Greek but that has an Italian chef so the food is true Pisan. Here you can sit in air conditioned comfort while you dine on *tagliatelli al ragu* (pasta with meat and tomato sauce) or the *tagliolini al nero* (pasta with squid's ink sauce). After that all their roast meats are exquisite. A little distance away from the station, the center, and the sights, so only stop in here if you happen to be in the neighborhood, since most of the other restaurants mentioned are better.

19. PASTICCERIA SALZA, *Borgo Stretto 44/46, Tel. 050/28296. No credit cards accepted. Closed Sundays. Dinner for two L75,000.*

Open only for dinner. Don't let the name and entrance fool you. This still is a pastry shop, the most famous in Pisa, but it is also a restaurant that serves good pastas and a memorable *salmone alla griglia con le erbe* (grilled salmon smothered in herbs and spices) or *vitello farcito con patate* (grilled veal with roast potatoes). And of course, you have to try at least one of their pastries for dessert.

20. NUMERO UNDICI, *Via Cavalca 11. No telephone. No credit cards accepted. Closed Saturdays at dinner and Sundays. Dinner for two L45,000.*

A small local place with an outside patio. Located near the old market in Pisa this is the perfect place to sample Pisan home cooking. They make great *lasagnas*, *crepes*, and *foccace* (a crepe like concoction with meats, cheeses, and vegetables baked inside the crisp doughy exterior), but my favorite was a dish of assorted salamis.

Pubs

21. HAPPY DRINKER, *Vicolo del Poshi 5-7. Open from 4am to 12 midnight.*

An authentic Irish atmosphere serving up great pints of Guiness, Harp, or Caffreys for L6,000. Inside seating only.

22. IL PAIOLO, *Via Cortatone e Montanara 9. Open for lunch and dinner.*

The look and feel of a German beer garden with the communal wooden tables. Outside it's just another café. They serve the German beer Weininger for L6,000 a pint. They also have a limited *trattoria* type menu for those desiring to have some food with their ale.

SEEING THE SIGHTS

Much of the main tourist area centers around the **Campo dei Miracoli** (Square of Miracles) and its famous Leaning Tower, but Pisa has other attractions that you should excplore as well. The sights below are lettered and correspond to the letters on the map of Pisa.

PIAZZA DEL MIRACOLI

It is called the **Square of Miracles** because of the stupendous architectural masterpieces filling the square. These are living testimony to the greatness that the city of Pisa reached at the height of its glory. The square is surrounded by imposing walls begun in 1154. Today these walls are surrounded by countless vendors selling a wide variety of trinkets for the tourists.

The following items are on display in the piazza:

A. THE CAMPANILE, OR THE LEANING TOWER

Closed indefinitely until they figure out how to stop it from leaning.

The most unique tower in the world because of the angle in which it leans. There are other leaning towers in Italy, but none has the beauty and charm of this one, nor are any others on the verge of falling over as is this one. Today the base is like a construction site as the Italians, with their famed organizational skills and speed, are attempting to make sure one of their country's main tourist attractions doesn't fall and shatter itself on the ground. Once you were able to walk up the 293 steps to the top of the tower, but today you have to be content with snapping photos of the structure from the outside. The best place to get a shot is at a distance, beside the Baptistery.

The list in the tower was not planned, but it was noticed when the tower reached a height of 11 meters. Even so the builders continued to build even though they realized that the foundation was unstable. It was begun in 1174 by Bonanno Pisano and finished in 1350 by Tomaso Pisano, so the family spent many years trying to discover ways to eliminate the list. The tower is 55 meters, 22 centimeters high, and its steepest angle is almost 5 meters. This angle appears to be increasing at almost a millimeter a year.

During its useful days the tower was employed by **Galileo Galilei** when he conducted experiments with the laws of gravity. Today the tower, with its six galleries each surrounded by arches and columns, as well as the bell cell located at the top, is only used for drawing the tourist trade to Pisa.

B. THE DUOMO

Open 8:00am–12:30pm and 3:00pm–6:30pm. In January only open until 4:30pm.

Started in 1063 by Buschetto, it was finally consecrated in 1118 after Rainaldo finished the work. The bronze doors are reproductions, by 16th century Florentine artists, of the originals that were lost in the fire of 1569. The facade is covered with many columns and arches as was the Pisan style at the time.

The interior contains numerous sculptures and mosaics, among which is the famous mosaic *Christ and the Madonna* started by Francesco of Pisa and continued by Cimabue. The celebrated pulpit is the work of Giovanni Pisano, of the same family that built the Campanile. There is also the famous lamp that hangs in the center of the nave that was created by Stolto Lorenzi. It is called the **Lamp of Galileo**, who, as rumor has it, discovered through observation and experiment the oscillation of pendulum movements. Last but not least is the statuette in ivory by Giovanni Pisano of the *Madonna and Child*.

C. BAPTISTERY

Open 9:00am–1:00pm and 3:00pm–6:30pm. In January only open until 4:30pm.

Begun in 1153 by the architect Diotisalvi, it is circular in form with a conical covering. Later the facade was adapted by Nicola Pisan and his son Giovanni to fit the other works in the square. The interior has five baptismal fonts created by Guido Bigarelli of Como in 1246 and the masterpiece of a pulpit created by Nicola Pisano in 1260.

D. CAMPOSANTO

Open 8:00am–6:30pm. In January open from 9:00am–4:30pm. Admission L5,000.

A rather serene and unpretentious cemetery, very unlike the foreboding "city of the dead" found in Genoa. This one was started in 1278 by Giovanni di Simone. It was enlarged in the 14th century and stands today like an open air basilica with three aisles. The center soil is rumored to have been brought from the Holy Land, about fifty three gallons. The corridor around the earth is formed by 62 arches in a Gothic style of white and blue marble.

You'll also find some beautiful frescoes along the walls and floors that were partially destroyed during World War II but have since been restored.

E. PIAZZA DEI CAVALIERI

This is the most harmonious piazza in the city after the famous Piazza dei Miracoli with its leaning tower. Literally translated the name means square of the knights, and it is named for the **Knights of St. Stephen**, an order established by Cosimo I de Medici to defend Florence and her holdings from pirates. The statue above the fountain by Francavilla in 1596 that is opposite the Palazzo dei Cavalieri (Knights Palace) is dedicated to this order. On its facade you'll find floral displays, symbols, coats of arms as well as sacred and profane images which are described as graffito style decorations. In niches above the second row of windows you'll find six busts of Tuscan Grand-dukes, from Cosimo I to Cosimo III de Medici.

The other buildings in this irregularly shaped 'square' were built in the 16th and 17th centuries and include the **Church of St. Stephen's**, next to the Palazzo Cavalieri on the eastern side. On the western sides is the **Palazzo del Collegio Puteano** built in 1605. The southern side is occupied by the **Palazzo del Consiglio** (Council Chambers) of the order of the Knights of St. Stephen. On the northern side is the **Palazzo dell'Orologio** (Clock Palace). In the same piazza, next to the Palazzo del'Orologio, the infamous **Muda Tower** (Tower of Hunger) used to sit. This was where Count Ugolino della Gherardesca was imprisoned with his sons and nephews in 1288 and left to starve to death. This situation was recorded for all to remember in Dante's *Inferno*.

If you're walking from the train station to the Leaning Tower you will most probably walk through this piazza. It's a nice place to sit and watch Pisan life pass you by.

F. PIAZZA GARIBALDI

This piazza is at the end of the Borgo Stretto with its covered walkways, and is brimming with real Pisan life – not the tourist trap situation like at the Piazza dei Miracoli. From here you are mere meters away from the Piazza Vettovaglie with its outdoor market. From here and the **Ponte de Mezzo**, you can see the beautiful palazzi lining the Arno as it meanders towards the sea. If you are walking from the train station you will most probably pass over this bridge and through this piazza to get to the Piazza dei Miracoli. The area around the Piazza Garibaldi will give you a genuine feel for the real life in Pisa.

G. PIAZZA VETTOVAGLIE

There's a market in the square every morning from 7am to 1:30pm. Just off the Via Stretto, here you'll find the hustle and bustle of a small Italian market, with vendors hawking their wares to attract customers.

You'll find everything from produce to used clothes. Also around the piazza are little shops that compliment the food being sold outdoors. You'll have butchers, and *alimentaris*, and bakers so that the Pisan housewife can get all she needs here to make her family's daily dinner.

The market spills out onto the Via Domenio Cavalca and around the corner. Great sights, sounds, and smells to remember Pisa by. Also, the street just mentioned has a variey of different little restaurants to sample if the market's wares have tempted your appetite.

FABBRICHE DI CAREGGINE - A 13TH CENTURY TOWN THAT REAPPEARS EVERY TEN YEARS!

Located in the mountainous region northwest of Pisa is a 13th century village buried between the waters of **Lake Vagli**. *This watery grave was created by the 350 foot dam on the* **Edron River** *built in 1947 when Italy was in dire need of plentiful electricity. But every 10 years or so, the waters that cover the village must be drained so that repairs can be made on the dam.*

This event occurred last in the fall of 1993, and lasted for seven months, and the well-preserved Romanesque church and bell tower, as well as the other buildings and streets, were visible for all to see and visit.

The nearest town, **Vagli Sotto**, *which also borders Lake Vagli, drummed up publicity for the event, bringing back former residents to view their old town one more time (many of them are now in their nineties) as well as encouraging visitors. In all over 100,000 people came to witness the city buried beneath the lake. So, if you're interested in seeing a sight in Italy, that very few people have ever laid their eyes on, and you're going to be in Italy in the fall of 2003, this is the place to visit!*

Contact the mayor of Vagli Sotto, Ilio Giorgi, for more information.

H. BORGO STRETTO

If you can't get to Bologna to see their famous covered streets, this little *via* has something similar. The sidewalks are covered so this street is always hopping whatever the weather. Just look out for the motor scooters and bicycles. Some of them pop up on the sidewalk to get away from the rain. You'll also find street performers and mimes entertaining the bustling crowds. Here you can either people watch or shop at the many delightful stores. The market mentioned above is just off of this street.

TOURIST INFORMATION

• **Piazza Duomo**, to the right of the Camposanto, Tel. 050/560-464.
• **Piazza Stazione**, Tel. 050/42-291. Just as you exit the doors of the station

the office is located directly on the left. They can give you a map to guide your way through the streets to the sights.

LUCCA

Try not to miss this city. Instead of making this a one day adventure, I highly recommend staying at least one or two days to savor its beauty and charm. Located 46 miles west of Florence and 14 miles northeast of Pisa, **Lucca** is closer to Pisa than to Florence and it is still one of the least visited cities in Tuscany, but we guidebook writers are starting to change that.

Most motorists coming from the north drive past in their haste to get to Pisa, and most people arriving from Florence fail to take the hour ride further north because Lucca doesn't have an architectural anomaly like the Leaning Tower of Pisa. But what Lucca has, even with a slowly growing tourist trade, is charm, and lots of it.

Lucca's Walls

Lucca is surrounded by walled fortifications, which were designed to keep marauding Florentines at bay, but which are now a flowering greenbelt around the city. This tree-lined garden boulevard extends clear around the city and is perfect for a *passegiatta* (slow stroll) that is safe, peaceful, and enchanting any time of the day. The garden walkway has a thin sliver of asphalt which makes it a bicyclists and a roller bladers paradise. But on either side of the walkway is grass, countless trees and shrubs that make this city a lovers paradise.

At the battlements, of which there are 10, each conveniently shaped like a heart, there are plenty of places to cuddle with your loved one, or sit at a wooden table and have a calming afternoon picnic. If you're with a family, the kids can roam free, exploring the nooks and crannies of the walls, while you and your spouse enjoy a small second honeymoon.

Besides the walls, which with Ferrarra's are the best preserved in Italy, Lucca offers a tight grid road system, a remnant of its Roman occupation, which now gives it the feel of a compact Renaissance town. I love exploring the many intimate little streets and revel in the enjoyment of making new discoveries in the maze. In this labyrinth of a city is **San Michel in Foro**, which is located on what used to be Lucca's Forum. Every column is different, some are intertwined like corkscrews, some doubled, and some carved with medieval looking monsters.

Often confused with San Michel is Lucca's **Cathedral**. The Duomo rests at the end of the Via Duomo in Piazza San Martino. This structure is perhaps the most outstanding example of the Pisan style of architecture outside of Pisa. Its porch with three arches, and three levels of colonnades, give it an unusual facade, but typically Pisan.

Explore Lucca!

Besides these sights, Lucca is a city to explore. You can walk its labyrinth of tiny streets and feel a part of the Renaissance. Through your exploration you will find the busy shopping area around **Via Fillungo**, the 12th century church of San Frediano, the Roman **amphitheater** (a must-see so you can compare the different centuries and cultures combined into modern day life), the **Torre Giungi**, which is the tower that overlooks the city. It has one special feature, a garden complete with full-grown trees on the top. Here you can take fine panoramic pictures of the area. There are plenty of other discoveries waiting for you in Lucca.

BEST EATS IN LUCCA

When in Lucca there is really only one place to eat. **Da Leo Fratelli Burelli** *has great atmosphere; it's boisterously local with friends calling to each other across the crowded dining space inside. Don't sit outside at the narrow strip of terrace; only tourists bother to sit there. Inside is where the action and ambiance are. As you enter you'll pass by their kitchen where you can see two or three female chefs slaving over hot stoves preparing their scrumptious meals. Seeing how hard they work makes you appreciate even more the fantastic food they prepare. When in Lucca, don't miss this place.*

ARRIVALS & DEPARTURES

By Car

Car is quickest, about one hour away from Florence on the A11 past Prato and Pistoia, two excellent journeys on their own. When driving in Italy always remember *Fare il Pieno* (fill 'er up) whenever you stop for gas, because sometimes gas stations are few and far between.

By Train

Trains from Florence take between an hour and an hour and a half depending on how many stops the train has to make. As of press time the trains that depart Florence for Lucca are at 9:42am, 1:42pm, 3:42pm, 4:42pm, 5:13pm, 5:42pm, 6:45pm, and 8:35pm. Returning to Florence you'll find many trains in the evening, also usually leaving every two hours: 3:00pm, 5:00pm, 7:00pm, and 9:00pm. Make sure you check all this information prior to your departure if you're going for a one day adventure.

To get to inside the city walls when you arrive by train you can either take the adventurous/native route or the more mundane. The native route from the station is to walk straight out of the station and keep going straight on the left hand side of the Piazza Ricasoli. Cross the road carefully and follow the path into a passageway into the walls. At night it's very well lit and safe. When you enter the stairs inside the ancient walls, despite the graffiti covering them, you'll feel as if you've walked back into the Middle Ages. Follow the stairs to the wooded walkways on top of the walls. From here descend to the walled city below and you're on your way to exploring. The more mundane way to enter the city would be to go through the elaborate and imposing **Porta San Pietro**, which was built around 1566, just a short distance down the main road in front of the station to the left. The gate still has Lucca's proud motto of independence, *Libertas*, etched over the top.

Sights
A. Duomo of St. Martin
B. San Michele in Foro
C. Piazza dell'Antifeatro
D. Torre Guinigi
E. San Frediano

Hotels
1. Cinzia
2. Hotel Diana
3. La Luna
4. Piccolo Hotel Puccini
5. Hotel Ilaria
6. Universo

Restaurants
7. L'Antico Sigillo
8. Pizzeria Italia
9. Il Giglio
10. Pizzeria K2
11. Da Leo Fratelli Buralli
12. Ristorante Puccini

Restaurants (cont.)
14. Da Carolina

Alimentari
15. Il Mercantino

WHERE TO STAY

The only hotels listed here are the ones that are inside the walls of the old city. If you come to Lucca there is no point in staying anywhere else since all the flavor, ambiance, and romance is inside the city walls.

1. CINZIA, *Via della Dogana 9, Lucca. Tel 0583/491-323. No credit cards accepted. 12 rooms, 3 with bath. Single 20,000-31,000; Double 35,000-45,000.* *

On a quaint little street that has ivy covering the sign on the door, you'll find very inexpensive lodging here, but everything is spic and span. Usually booked well in advance, so call to make reservations.

2. HOTEL DIANA, *Via del Moinetto 11, Lucca. Tel. 0583/492-202. Fax 0583/47-795. Credit cards accepted. 9 rooms, 8 with bath. Single 26,000-42,000; Double 60,000-95,000.* **

Great prices in a great location down a cute side street. If you want to stay inside the walls of Lucca for a great price, you'd better book in advance, because with these prices and the ambiance of the location this hotel is in great demand.

3. LA LUNA, *Via Fillungo, Corte Compagni 12, Lucca. Tel. 0583/493-634. Fax 0583/490-021. American Express, Diners Club, Mastercard, an Visa accepted. 30 rooms all with bath. Single L80,000-115,000; Double L150,000-160,000.* ***

Located in the same small square as the Pizzeria Italia, this is a professionally run small hotel with beautiful rooms done up in antiques and a comfortable lobby bar area in which to relax. The prices aren't as good as the Hotel Puccini but the service may be a bit better. But is that worth L45,000 extra?

4. PICCOLO HOTEL PUCCINI, *Via di Poggio 9, 55100 Lucca. Tel. 0583/55-421 or 53-487. Fax 0583/534-87. 14 rooms all with bath. Single L68,000-78,000; Double L100,000-113,000. Credit cards accepted.* ***

Located right up from the Piazza San Michelle, this is a beautifully appointed little three star hotel that even has a TV in the rooms (but did you really come all this way to watch TV?) The lobby is small with a stairway in the area that leads to all the rooms. You'll find the accommodations intimate, comfortable and cozy; and the classical music in the lobby area soothing. This is the place to stay in Lucca.

5. HOTEL ILARIA, VIA DEL FOSSO 20, LUCCA. *Tel 0583/47-558. 17 rooms, 13 with bath. Credit cards accepted. Single 42,000-54,000; Double 87,000.* **

Located on Lucca's baby canal, this hotel seems a little worse for wear. Even with the canal area this is not Lucca's most alluring location. The prices are good, and it's inside the walls, so I shouldn't complain. But try some of the others first.

6. UNIVERSO, *Piazza del Giglio 1 (next to the Piazza Napoleone), Tel. 0583/493-678. Fax 0583/954-854. Credit cards Accepted. 60 rooms 52 with bath. L50,000-195,000; Double L75,000-260,000.* ***

This place has been in business well over a century and it sure shows. On the Piazza del Giglio, not one of Lucca's prettiest squares, it can get rather noisy. It's ideally located near the station but its prices are a little much in the high season. Its saving grace is a wonderful little bar with seating on the square. Best to look elsewhere if you can. If not, enjoy the ambiance of a slightly run-down, formerly first class hotel.

WHERE TO EAT

7. L'ANTICO SIGILLO, *Via degli Angeli 13, 55100 Lucca. Tel 0583/ 91-042. Credit cards accepted. Dinner for two L50,000.*

Try the pizza here, and if you don't have an antipasto, cut the price above in half. They have good *margherita* (plain cheese) and *quattro formaggi* (four cheeses) but limited atmosphere. For that and just as good pizza, go to Pizzeria Italia very close by. They have a larger selection too.

8. PIZZERIA ITALIA, *Corto Compagni 2, 55100 Lucca. Tel 0583/ 493012. Credit cards accepted. Dinner for two L45,000.*

You'll only reach the price limit if you have two pizzas, or *calzone* each. Otherwise cut the above price in half. The second best place in Lucca, not really for the local flavor that you find at Da Leo, but come for the good food and cheap prices.

Their menu is gargantuan with countless pizzas and *calzones* (brick oven baked strudel-like concoction with ingredients in the middle). Try the *pizza arrabiata* (with tomatoes, garlic, pepperoncini, and chili) if you like it hot, or maybe the *wurstel* (with tomatoes, cheese, and wurstel sausage). They have a *calzone speciale* with ham, mushrooms, salami and sausage that makes my mouth water remembering it. Complete with outside seating on a quiet little piazza, as well as rustic seating inside around and behind the brick pizza oven.

9. IL GIGLIO, *Piazza del Giglio 2, 55100 Lucca. Tel 0583/494-058. fax 0583/55-881. Dinner for two L90,000.*

Lucca's best seafood place, with seating on a relatively busy piazza and a plain indoor seating area. Try the *sogliola alla griglia* (grilled sole) or the *trote al carbone* (grilled trout). If fish doesn't grab you sample the *agnello al forno* (grilled lamb) or the *arista di maiale al forno* (grilled pork). An expensive meal, but if you want fish or meat this is the best place to eat in Lucca. Located next door to the Universo hotel.

10. PIZZERIA K2, *Via del Anfiteatro 107. Tel 0583/47-170. Closed Wednesdays. Dinner for tow L45,000. No credit cards accepted.*

If you order only one pizza, split the price above in half. Not quite the same quaint atmosphere as Pizzeria Italia and their prices are higher too. A good fall back position if the Italia is full. Their outside seating may be better for people watching but their menu is so limited compared to the Italia. They are both near each other, so why don't you check out which place suits your needs best?

11. DA LEO FRATELLI BURALLI, *Via Tegrimi 1. Tel 0583/492-236. Closed Sundays. No credit cards accepted. Dinner for two L50,000.*

This place is perfect. If you're going to have one meal (or two, or three) have it here, but not outside in the thin sliver of seating area on a small side street. You have to come inside and truly the enjoy the vibrancy of this Luccan delicacy. Friends will call to each other across the room, the food will come clattering down in front of you as it is served.

From the open kitchen you pass by on your way, where you can see the frenzied female cooks preparing the food for hundreds of people each evening, this place is the best. And the prices are so inexpensive. All *primi piatti* are L6,000. Try the fettucine all rucola e gamberi (with cheese an shrimp) or the *pasta al pomodoro e ragu* (with tomato and meat sauce). For seconds sample the *pollo arrosto con patate* (roasted chicken with potatoes), a cold dish of *prosciutto e mozzarella* (ham and mozzarella), or some *pollo fritto e zucchini* (fried chicken and zucchini).

12. RISTORANTE PUCCINI, *Corte San Lorenzo 1, Tel 0583/316-116. Fax 316-031. Dinner for two L110,000.*

An expensive but pleasant restaurant that has a somewhat modern ambiance. Try the *Antipasto di mare* (seafood antipasto) or the *penne agli scampi* (pasta with shrimp). For seconds, I recommend the *grigliatta mista* (mixed grilled meats from Tuscany). A definitely high class eatery but go with Da Leo (see above) if you're only going to have one meal (or two) in Lucca.

14. TRATTORIA "DA CAROLINA," *Via Pescheria #3. Tel 0583/49-681. Dinner for two L60,000. Credit cards accepted.*

Down a quiet side street with seating outside, this is a fine *trattoria* (despite its slightly incongruous name). The inside is acceptable also since it's usually home to many locals sampling the great food served here. They make great pastas as well as meats. Try the *tortellini alla panna* (cheese filled pasta with thick cream sauce) or the *penne all'arrabiata* (macaroni-like pasta made with a spicy tomato and garlic sauce) for primi. For secondi move onto the *petti di pollo alla griglia* (chicken breast on the grill) or the *bistecca di maiale* (pork steak). If you want some fish (and this will increase the price a little), try the *fritto misto di mare* (mixed fried seafood). All in all, a great atmosphere with good food.

15. IL MERCANTINO, *Via SS Paulino 23.*

This is an alimentari, not a restaurant, but I'm listing it here because it's a real find! You can buy anything and everything your little culinary heart desires. With the hams hanging from the ceiling for inspiration, inch your way around this tiny store and find the source of your gastronomic pleasure. A great place for picnic supplies (salami, prosciutto, bread, cheese) or to get gifts to bring back to friends.

SEEING THE SIGHTS

Lucca is a small walled city that has a few memorable sights to see, but the most important is the entire package itself. Lucca is like a medieval town come to life, with its tiny twisting streets and its converted walls and battlements. It is a great place to explore. You'll get lost without a map for sure, but since the walled city is so small you'll eventually find something you recognize, especially the walls.

If you come to Lucca, stroll and picnic along these glorious tree-lined promenades. It will be a romantical and memorable experience.

EXPLORE LUCCA BY BIKE!

Cicli Barbetti, Via Anfiteatro 23. Tel. 0583/854-444 is located near the ampitheater, and is the only place to find bicycles to rent in the city. There really isn't a need to rent one, since the city is so small, but if you like to ride, this is your place.

A. THE DUOMO OF ST. MARTIN

Open 7:00am–7:00pm.

This is perhaps the most outstanding example of Pisan style outside of Pisa. It was begun in the 11th century and completed in the 15th. The facade has three levels of colonnades with three different sized arches. Behind and on the arches are beautiful 12th and 13th century bas-reliefs and sculptures. If you look hard enough you can find a column carved with the tree of life with Adam and Eve crouched at the bottom and Christ at the top, a variety of hunting scenes with real and fantastic animals, dancing dragons, and more, all created by anonymous artists.

The dark interior is a showcase for Lucca's most famous artist, **Matteo Civitali** whose work has not escaped beyond the walls of Lucca. Rumor has it that until his mid-thirties, a ripe old age for some at that time, he was a barber, when he then decided he'd rather be a sculptor. His most famous work is the octagonal *Tempietto* done in 1489. It is a marble tabernacle in the middle of the left aisle. It contains a cedar crucifix, The *Volto Santo* (Holy Image) is said to have the true portrait of Jesus sculpted on it by Nicodemus, an eyewitness to the crucifixion. Every September 13th the image is removed to join a candlelight procession around town.

Further up the left aisle you can find Fra Bartolomeo's *Virgin and Child Enthroned* as well as the *Tomb of Ilaria del Caretto*, a magnificent work by the Siennese artist Jacopo della Quercia. You will also find the Madonna *Enthroned with Saints* by Domenico Ghirlandaio and a strange *Last Supper* with a nursing mother in the foreground and what look like cherubs floating above Christ's head.

B. SAN MICHELE IN FORO

Open 7:00am – 7:00pm.

This church is so grand that most people mistake it for Lucca's cathedral. It is located in the old Roman Forum and is a masterpiece of Pisan Gothic architecture. The huge facade rises above the level of the roof, making the church look even larger and grander. You'll notice that every column in the five levels of Pisan style arcading is different. Some will be twisting, some doubling, some carved with relief monsters and more.

While the entire facade is quite ornate and elaborate, the interior is more austere. It is best known for the place where Puccini started his musical career as a choirboy. As a reminder of this, just down the small road directly in front of the church is a wonderfully intimate place to hang your hat, the Piccolo Hotel Puccini. Besides the memory of Puccini, the interior of San Michelle in Foro contains a glazed terra cotta *Madonna and Child*, a 13th-century *Crucifixion* hanging over the high altar, and a memorable painting of saints that lived during the plague years.

C. PIAZZA DELL'ANTIFITEATRO

A remarkable relic dating from Lucca's ancient Roman past is the **Roman Amphitheater**. Today it is lined with modern shops and medieval houses, and only the barest of outlines of the ancient arches can still be seen. Any marble that was once here was used to build the Cathedral and San Michele.

This place seems like an oasis from the past filled with modern comforts where you can lounge at a café and watch the Italian children playing their never ending game of *calcio* (soccer).

D. TORRE GUINIGI

Open 9:00am–7:00pm in the summer and 10:00am–4:00pm in the winter. Admission L5,000.

A tower rising above a neighborhood that has scarcely changed in 500 years. Here the medieval ancestors of the **Guinigi** family had their stronghold with the tower as their look out. One of Lucca's landmarks, it is one of the most elaborate medieval family fortresses. From the top you have the greatest views over all of Lucca. It's just a short walk up the 230-plus steps to reach the lush garden on the top, complete with trees sprouting from the ramparts. Remember to bring your camera and take some great pictures.

E. SAN FREDIANO

Open 7:00am–7:00pm.

A rather tall church with an even taller *campanile (bell tower)*, both built in the 12th century and completed with colorful mosaics in the 13th century. The interior contains a magnificent baptismal font which is covered with bas-reliefs. The chapels around the central nave are elaborately decorated.

Also inside is the **mummy of St. Zita**, patroness of domestic servants. She was canonized in 1696, long after her birth in 1218. She put in many years of service as a servant for a rich family in Lucca with whom she stayed with until her death. She is revered for her selfless acts of charity towards the poor, and now she is pickled in a coffin in Lucca.

TOURIST INFORMATION

• **APT**, *Vecchia Porta San Donato/Piazzale Verdi. Tel 0583/419-689. Hours 9:00am–7:00pm.* They have everything you need here. You can get a map, a list of hotels, or better yet, they can actually help you find the hotel you want and point you in the right direction. Very helpful, very professional (by Italian standards), and ideally located for people arriving by bus or car. For those of you arriving by train, it's a little walk from the station.

SIENA

Siena is generally described as the feminine counterpart to the masculine Florence, and even its nickname, **City of the Virgin**, belies this feminine quality. Located 42 miles south of Florence, this picturesque walled city is known for its many quality buildings, narrow streets, immense churches, and quaint little restaurants; but the two reasons why I love Siena are that cars are banned from the center of the city, making for a pleasant automobile-less environment (similar to Venice but without the water), and also for the bi-annual event called the **Palio**.

The well-preserved walls with towers and bulwarks of Siena are seven kilometers long and were built from the 13th to the 15th centuries. The ramparts on the outskirts are now used as public gardens. They are beautiful but not nearly as romantic or inviting as those from Lucca.

Siena was once a prosperous, stable, and artistic city in its own right even before she was absorbed into the grand duchy of Tuscany in 1559, which was ruled by Florence, after years of siege by Cosimo de Medici. Once it became a part of Florence, Siena was not allowed to continue to pursue its previously prosperous banking activities, nor were they allowed to continue their flourishing wool trade. Because of these actions, and the general despotic rule of Florence, Siena fell into a long period of decline. But today, as other Italian cities have also, Siena has learned how to succeed by marketing its ancient charm.

ARRIVALS & DEPARTURES

By Car

Either take the Florence-Siena Superstrada or the slower but more scenic Route 22 that runs through the heart of the Chianti wine region.

From Rome take the A1 to the Via di Chiana exit, then head west on route 326 into Siena. You'll have to leave your car at one for the many parking lots on the outskirts of the city center, since no automobiles are allowed into the city.

HIGHLIGHTS OF SIENA

Siena is a beautifully quaint little town with winding medieval streets and charming old buildings. There's really not too much to do here except absorb the atmosphere and ambiance, and find a place to settle down for a good meal, which is enough in and of itself. The best places to eat here are:

16. PIZZERIA/TAVOLA CALDA IL CAVALLINO BIANCO, Via di Citta 20. Tel. 0577/44-258. Closed Wednesdays. Two slices of pizza each and a large beer L24,000. Open late. No credit cards accepted.

10. RISTORANTE/PIZZERIA SPADA FORTE, Piazza del Campo 12. Credit cards accepted. Dinner for two L65,000.

*Obviously if you can get to Siena while the **Palio** is in session, you simply must do it. The pageantry, the horse race, the costumes, the intensity all evoke a time long gone and will sweep you back through the centuries. Held bi-annually on July 2 and August 16, plan well in advance to get a place to stay and a ticket to the horse race that is held in the **Campo**.*

*If you only have a little while in Siena the Campo is where you will head anyway, the gathering place for the locals, young and old alike. You'll also want to see the **piazza**, with its sloped surface of stone that seems to float down to the **Palazzo Pubblicco**, a building regal in bearing and boasting one of the most imposing clock towers in Italy. This tower, the **Torre del Mangia**, must be scaled while you're in Siena. If you're fit enough, the 112 meters and more than 400 small confined steps can be taken easily. Once at the top you will be treated to the most amazing panoramic view over the town and the surrounding countryside.*

By Train

From Florence there are over a dozen trains a day. The trip takes 1 1/2 hours. The train station is located one mile from the center of the city, but do not fear. Just exit the station, stand on the curb and catch either bus 15, 2, or 6 and they will all take you to a dropping off point near the information desk, from which you can get a map (L500) and hotel reservations if needed. Everything else from that point on is walking distance.

If, or should I say when, the blue bus ticket machine in the lobby of the train station is out of order, simply go to the train ticket window and purchase a ticket for L1,200. It's good for an hour once you punch it in the machine on the bus. I recommend buying your return fare in advance if you're not going to stay the night, so you don't have to worry about that detail on your return to the station in the evening. If you don't want to catch the bus, the old town is a short walk up the hill.

Renting a Car

If you're staying in Siena for a while and want to view the magnificent countryside, you can always rent a car, van, or moped.

There's one place just outside the walled city where you can do this:
• **General Cars**, *Vialle Toselli 20/26. Tel. 0577/40-518. Fax 0577/47-984.*

WHERE TO STAY

1. HOTEL ATHENA, *Via P Mascagni 55, 53100 Siena. Tel. 0577/286-313. Fax 0577/48153. 101 rooms all with bath. Single L65,000-130,000; Double L100,000-200,000. Breakfast included. All credit cards accepted.* ****

Even though it is located in the Centro, this hotel is a little walk from the main sights of Siena. Nonetheless it is quite a nice place to stay if you like the look and feel of a large well-run hotel. They have air conditioning in the rooms, a great restaurant and bar. What more could you ask for?

2. CANON D'ORO, *Via Montanini 28, 53100 Siena. Tel. 0577 44-321. Fax 0577/28-08-68. Credit cards accepted. 32 rooms all with bath. Single L35,000-74,000; Double L47,000-95,000. Breakfast L9,000 extra.* **

The oldest hotel in the city, it is located down a small white walled entrance way. The rooms are quiet since the hotel is located in part of the *zona pedonale* (walking area). Situated on two stories of a 12th century palazzo, this hotel has the feel of a three star with superb prices. Definitely the place to stay while your in Siena. But you have to book well in advance for the luxury of these accommodations.

3. HOTEL TOSCANA, *Via C Angiolieri 12, 53100 Siena. Tel 0577/46-097. Fax 0577/270-634. 42 rooms all with bath. Single L38,000-68,000; Double L52,000-100,000. Credit cards accepted.* ***

Located on a quaint side street, you can't find a better location or such good prices for a three star. My choice would be the Cannon D'Oro, but this comes in a very close second.

4. HOTEL MINERVA, *Via Garibaldi 72, 53100 Siena. Tel. 0577/284-474. Fax 0577/284-474. 49 rooms all with bath. Single L57,000-78,000; Double L91,000-110,000. Breakfast L9,000. All credit cards accepted.* ***

Located just on the outskirts of the center of town, this is a decent three star that could use some fixing up. Rooms are comfortable but some are not that clean. Limited amenities also.

5. HOTEL CENTRALE, *Via Cecco Angiolieri 26, 53100 Siena. Tel. 0577/280-379. Fax 0577/42-152. 7 rooms, 6 with bath. Double L55,000-95,000.* **

A small place than is clean, quiet, and kept up nicely. To get a room here you have to book many months in advance since the location is excellent and the rooms are few. The proprietor knows he's sitting on a gold mine, but is still as pleasant as can be. A wonderful place to stay if you have the foresight to plan your trip well in advance.

6. HOTEL DUOMO, *Via Stalloreggi 34-38, 53100 Siena. Tel. 0577/ 289-088. Fax 0577/43-043. Credit cards accepted. 25 rooms all with bath. Single L61,000-115,000; Double L92,000-160,000.* ***

Comes with all the amenities for a three star, including cable TV for those in need of such entertainment. Located in part of an old palazzo just a little distance away from the Campo, this is a good place to stay within reach of all major sights.

7. JOLLY HOTEL EXCELSIOR, *Piazza La Lizza. Tel. 0577/284-448. Fax 0577/41-272. US toll free number 1-800-221-2626. American Express, Diners Club. Mastercard and Visa accepted.* ****

A good four star in the Jolly tradition. Located where the buses drop off the passengers from the station, it is just outside of all the activity but close enough for you to be able to amble over and enjoy it. The rooms are somewhat small but the hotel offers all the necessary amenities.

8. PICCOLO HOTEL ETRURIA, *Via delle Donzelle 3, 53100 Siena. Tel. 0577/288-088. Fax 0577/288-461. Credit cards accepted. 15 rooms, 13 with bath. Single L 48,000-58,000; Double L85,000.* **

Perfectly located on a little side street just near the Campo. This place has great prices and modern but spartan rooms. A perfect place to stay because of the location and the charming environment.

9. TRE DONZELLE, *Via delle Donzelle 5, 53100 Siena. Tel 0577/280-358. 27 rooms, 11 with bath. No credit cards accepted. Single 32,000-53,000; Double L56,000-70,000. No breakfast available.* *

To get one of these quaint little rooms on a beautiful side street near the Campo you have to book well in advance, especially for the Palio. A very clean and well taken care of one star. If you can get one of the rooms with a bath, you'll be in a prime location with a great room.

WHERE TO EAT

Since Siena is a university town, snack and fast food places abound, but there are also some excellent restaurants. Siena specialties include *cioccina* (a special variation on pizza) *pici* (thick Tuscan spaghetti with a sauce from ground pork), and *pancetta* (sausages and chicken breast added to tomatoes and cooked with red wine).

Siena is also known for its different varieties of salamis that you can buy at any *alimentari*. I recommend the alimentari Morbidi *at Via Banchi di Sotto 27.*

Soppressata, either sweet or hot, is an excellent boiled salami made from a mixture of rind and gristle with black peppercorns added. Don't let this description fool you. The sweet *soppressata* is the best.

Buristo is a cooked salami made from the blood and fatty leftovers of sausages. It is heavily spiced.

Finocchiona is a salami made of peppered sausage meat seasoned with fennel seeds.

Salsiccioli secchi are made from lean crusts of pork or boar, spiced with garlic and black or red pepper.

10. RISTORANTE/PIZZERIA SPADA FORTE, *Piazza del Campo 12. Credit cards accepted. Dinner for two L65,000.*

If you're at the top of the Campo looking down at the Palazzo Pubblico, this place is on your right at the end of the wall. They have scenic outside seating from which you can watch the goings on in the Campo, as well as inside seating in a typically spartan Sienese restaurant environment. They have a huge antipasto menu which should satisfy you for lunch. If not, try one of their pizzas.

The *barrocciaia* (tomatoes, sausage and garlic), and the *salsiccia* (tomato, mozzarella and sausages) are both good. If you're into meats, try the *cinghiale alle senese* (wild boar cooked over the open flame) or the ganello arr*osto* (roasted lamb). The best prices in the Campo with a better location, a little out of the way.

11. DA VASCO, *Via del Capitano 6/8. Tel 0577/288-094. No credit card accepted. Dinner for two L45,000.*

Small quaint little place just down from the Duomo. The atmosphere is typically austere with brick ceiling and whitewashed walls. The food is good and inexpensive. Try the *penne all'arrabiatta* (with a tomato, garlic, pepper sauce), the *spaghetti alla carbonara* (with cheese, ham, and egg), or the *ravioli all quattro formaggi* (thick sauce with four cheeses). For secondo, try the *bistecca di maiale* (pork steak) or the *omelette al formaggio* (cheese omelet). This is the only place in Siena where you can get an omelet.

12. OSTERIA DELL'ARTISTA, *Via Stralloreggi 11, Tel 0577/28-03-06. Closed Thursdays. No credit cards accepted. Dinner for two L45,000-50,000.*

Small place only with inside seating that has your typical brick ceiling and whitewashed wall decor. Good food, though, at great prices. Try the *Penne alla crema di formaggio* (with cream sauce and ham) or the *lasagna al forno* (thick lasagna cooked in the oven. For seconds the *bistecca di maiale* (pork steak) is good as is the *costellette di agnello fritte* (fried veal cutlets).

13. L'OSTERIA, *Via dei Rossi 79/81. Tel. 0577/287-592. No credit cards accepted. Dinner for two L45,000-50,000.*

Literally translated it's "The Restaurant" and it seems to be very popular with the locals. Located down a side street past two other more touristy places away from the thundering crowds. Squeeze through the worn hanging beads and cram yourself in here to enjoy a wonderfully local atmosphere will superbly prepared food. Try the *penne con melanzone e peperoni* (eggplant and pepperoni salami) for primo, and either the *pollo ai peperoni* (chicken with pepperoni), the *bistecca di vitella* (veal steak), or the *bistecca di maiale* (pork steak) for secondi. You won't be disappointed.

14. RISTORANTE VITTI, *Via Monatanini 14-16, Tel. 0577/28-92-91. No credit cards accepted. Dinner for two L55,000-60,000.*

Tranquil outside seating off the main road as well as in the *zona pedonale* (walking zone). Your food is passed through a window from the kitchen to the waiter. The inside is uncomfortably small with only a counter and standing room only, but the Sienese seem to enjoy the food so they cram themselves in for lunch, leaving the outside seating to tourists. In the window of the place are some dishes that are not on the menu, so if one of them catches your fancy (this is where they hide the pre-cooked fish, prawns, deep fried veal in batter, and more) ask to order something from the *finestra* (window). From the menu try some of their pasta, particularly the *Tortellini alla panna* (cheese stuffed pasta in a rich cream sauce) or the *lasagna al forno* (oven baked lasagna) for primo. For secondo try the rare *petto di tacchino arrosto* (roasted turkey breast).

15. RISTORANTE IL BIONDO, *Via del Rustichetto 10, Tel. and Fax 0577/280-739. Closed Wednesdays. Dinner for two L80,000.*

Another place you should think of trying, since the ambiance at the outside seating is so peaceful and colorfully local and the food is great. You can get a good seat inside in a plain whitewashed Sienese style restaurant, but try the outside. They make some good pasta here including Spaghetti *alla Vongole* (with clam sauce) and *penne alla puttanesca* (literally translated it means whore's pasta, made with tomatoes, garlic, black olives, olive oil and meat). For seconds, try the *Saltimbocca alla Romana* (veal shank stewed in tomatoes and spices) or the *bistecca alla griglia* (beef steak cooked on the grill that would make a Texan proud).

16. PIZZERIA/TAVOLA CALDA IL CAVALLINO BIANCO, *Via di Citta 20. Tel. 0577/44-258. Closed Wednesdays. Two slices of pizza each and a large beer L24,000. Open late. No credit cards accepted.*

The pizza is great, the prices are cheap, and the atmosphere is fun. They cook up the large square pizzas in the back at their huge ovens, then display them at the front. You choose the one you want and they throw it in a small toaster oven to reheat it. The choice is excellent, from sausage to salami to mushrooms, onions, or a combination of both. The atmosphere upstairs where the locals sit is boisterous and fun.

SEEING THE SIGHTS
The Palio Race
The best time to visit because of the sights to see, and the worst time to visit because of the crowds, is during the bi-annual **Palio**, held on July 2 and August 16. To the uninitiated the Palio is all colorful banners, historic pageantry, and the wild bareback horse race three times around

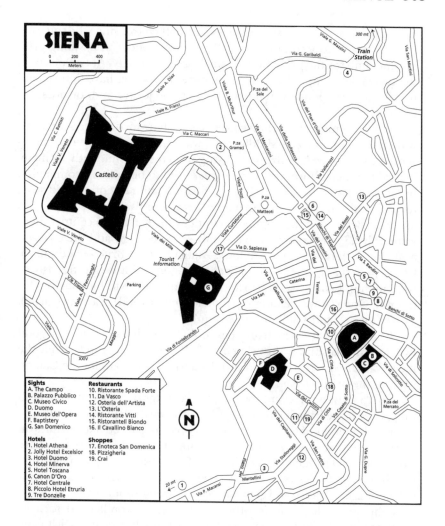

SIENA

0   200   400
Meters

Castello

P.ze del Sale

Train Station

Tourist Information

Parking

XXIV

Sights
A. The Campo
B. Palazzo Pubblico
C. Museo Civico
D. Duomo
E. Museo del'Opera
F. Baptistery
G. San Domenico

Hotels
1. Hotel Athena
2. Jolly Hotel Excelsior
3. Hotel Duomo
4. Hotel Minerva
5. Hotel Toscana
6. Canon D'Oro
7. Hotel Centrale
8. Piccolo Hotel Etruria
9. Tre Donzelle

Restaurants
10. Ristorante Spada Forte
11. Da Vasco
12. Osteria dell'Artista
13. L'Osteria
14. Ristorante Vitti
15. Ristorantell Biondo
16. Il Cavallino Bianco

Shoppes
17. Enoteca San Domenica
18. Pizzigheria
19. Crai

20 mt

the **Piazza del Campo** that lasts all of 90 seconds but will generate
memories to last a lifetime.

A *palio* literally is an embroidered banner, the prize offered for
winning the race. The first official Palio was run in 1283, though many say
the custom dates back farther than that. During the Middle Ages, besides
the horse races, there were violent street battles, bloody games of
primeval rugby (which you can see today in Florence twice a year) and
even bullfights (because of the Spanish control of Italy for many centuries).

The contestants in the horse race itself are jockeys from the seventeen
neighborhood parishes or *contrade* in Siena (during one Palio, ten horses

ride in the first race and seven horses ride in the next, since the square is not big enough to accommodate all the horses at once), who willingly risk life and limb for the pride of their small area of the city. At two places in the Piazza del Campo there are right angles the horses have to turn, and usually at these points you'll have at least one jockey and/or horse go flying.

But this is more than a horse race. It is really a sanctioned community-wide regression into the Middle Ages, with the coats-of-arms that represented each *contrade* at that time being displayed prominently by members of that neighborhood. The *contrade* used to be military companies, but these became outdated when the Spanish and Florentines laid siege to Siena and conquered it. At that time there were 59 *contrade*, but plagues and wars decimated the population until by the early 18th century there were only 23 left. Today there are only seventeen left and the coats-of-arms for each *contrade* is as follows: Aquila (eagle), Bruco (caterpillar), Chiocciola (snail), Civetta (owl), Drago (dragon), Giraffa (giraffe), Istrice (porcupine), Leocorno (unicorn), Lupa (she-wolf), Nicchio (shell), Oca (goose), Onda (wave), Pantera (panther), Selva (wood), Tartuca (turtle), Torre (tower), and Valdimontone (ram).

Prior to the race, which only has room for ten horses, there is a good two hour display of flag throwing by the alf*eri* of each *contrada*, while the medieval *carroccio* (carriage), drawn by a white oxen, circles the Campo bearing the prized *palio*.

But to witness this event you have to plan way in advance, since at both times of year the Palio is jam packed. You can see the Palio in one of three ways: in the center of the Piazza where people are packed like sardines on a first come first serve basis; in the viewing stands which cost anywhere from L200,000 to L350,000; or in one of the offices or apartments that line the piazza. To get a seat in the viewing stand you'll need to plan at least 6-9 months in advance and get your tickets through your travel agent. To view the spectacle from an office or apartment you'll need to have connections. Maybe the company you work for has dealings with the banks and other companies whose offices line the square. But however you witness this blast from Siena's medieval past, you will go away with memories for a lifetime.

A. THE CAMPO

Eleven streets lead into the square where, in the past, the people of Siena used to assemble at the sound of the **Sunto bell** to learn the latest news. Today it still is the gathering place for all the locals and tourists. It is concave and irregular with a ring of rather austere buildings surrounding, but even so it a marvel of architectural harmony. On the curved side of the Campo sits the fountain called **Fonte Gaia** (Gay Fountain) made by Jacopo della Quercia.

On the map the Campo looks flat, but it's actually a gradually sloping surface with bricks that seem to float down to the Palazzo Pubblico. You'll find groups of teenagers and tourists lounging on the bricks at all hours of the day, since the slope is perfect for either lying down or sitting. A great place to grab a bite to eat at one of the many restaurants, sip a drink at one of the cafés, or to simply rest your tired tourist feet by relaxing on the cobblestone slope.

B♦ PALAZZO PUBBLICO

At the Campo. Tower open 10:00am–dusk. In the winter open only until 1:30pm. Admission L5,000.

One of the most attractive and imposing Gothic buildings in all of Tuscany. Most of it was built between 1297 and 1340, with the top story being raised in 1639. This building reflected the wealth and success of the Siennese. Did you know that near the middle of the 14th century Siena was almost the same size as London and Paris? The little chapel underneath the tower was offered by the town to the Virgin Mary when the terrible plague known ever since as the *Morte Nera* (Black Death) came to an end. In Siena alone, 65,000 people died of the plague in the summer of 1348. That was over half of their population. Anyway, the wrought-iron gate that covers the entrance was made in 1445.

The best part of this building is the **Torre del Mangia**. It offers the greatest sights in all of Siena. Unfortunately you have to climb up 400 small confined steps to top of the bell tower. It's 112 meters high, was built in 1334, and is still in amazing shape. The clock was made in 1360 and the huge bell was raised to its present position in 1666. Imagine having to haul a bell that weighs 6,764 kilos up a pulley system to the top of the tower? Remember to bring your camera because the views of the countryside and the city are stupendous. You can see past the old walls, look over the terra cotta tiles of the city roofs, lush fields, and forests for as far as the eye can see. A definite must-see when in Siena.

C♦ MUSEO CIVICO

At the Campo. Open 9:30am–7:30pm Monday–Saturday. Open Sunday 9:30am–1:30pm.

Inside the Palazzo Pubblico is the **Museo Civico**, which is filled with many wonderful paintings, frescoes, mosaics, and tapestries. Upstairs is the famous **Sala del Mappamondo** (Hall of the Map of the World). From its large windows you can look out onto the market square. The other three walls are frescoed with scenes of the religious and civil life of the

Siena Republic. In this museum you'll find many examples of the some of the finest Sienese art anywhere.

D. THE DUOMO

Piazza del Duomo. 7:30am–1:30pm and 3:00pm to dusk from December to March. From March to November open 9:00am–7:30pm. Admission L6,000.

The combination of Gothic and Romanesque architectural elements in the Cathedral of Siena is a result of the large amount of time spent completing it. Nonetheless it doesn't appear as if the two styles contrast too much with each other. Despite being incredibly elaborate the facade seems quite harmonious and attractive. The side walls and steeple are striped black and white like the *Balzana* that is the standard of the town. It was started in 1200 and finished in the 1400s.

Inside the cathedral there are even more elaborate and rich decorations. It has three naves and is 90 meters long and 51 meters high, and the walls are covered with the white and black *Balzana* stripes also. All around the nave you'll see a row of 172 busts of Popes, from Christ to Lucius III, all made in 1400. Beneath them are 36 busts of Roman Emperors. The graffito and inlaid floor is a succession of scenes from the Old Testament, which took from 1372 to 1551 to complete. The earlier ones are done in black and white, and the later scenes have a touch of gray and red in them.

You can't miss the intricate and elaborate pulpit which was made by **Nicola Pisano** from 1265 to 1268. It is of white marble and supported by nine columns resting on nine lions. There are 300 human figures and 70 animal figures decorating this delightful work. Besides the pulpit there are countless remarkable paintings, sculptures, reliefs, and stone coffins all attributed to famous Italian masters. The statues on the Piccolo altar have been attributed to **Michelangelo**. In the **Piccolomini Library** you'll find beautiful frescoes of the life of Pope Pius II made by the master Pinturicchio. As you leave the library you'll see the monument to Archbishop Bandini's nephews made in 1570 by Michelangelo.

There were plans to have made this cathedral but a small part of a much larger place of worship. Those plans were stunted for a variety of reasons, including the plague and the eventual Florentine conquest of the city. But today a few pillars and walls remain from the blue prints of that grandiose church.

E. MUSEO DEL'OPERA DEL DUOMO

Piazza del Duomo. 7:30am–1:30pm and 3:00pm to dusk from December to March. From March to November open 9:00am–7:30pm. Admission L6,000.

In the **museum of the cathedral** is a valuable collection of the treasure of paintings, statues, and fragments the cathedral once displayed. One of the best paintings is Duccio di Buoninsegna's M*aesta* (1308-1311) that was originally on the high altar. You'll find a group of three sculptures, the *Three Graces*, which are Greek works of the 2nd century BC that were once in the Piccolomini Library. And you can't miss the exquisitely beautiful goldsmith's work, *Rosa D'Oro* (Golden Rose) that was given to the city of Siena by Alessandro VIII in 1658. Another work of interest is the plan of the unfinished facade of the Baptistery by Giacomo di Mino del Pelliciaio.

F. BAPTISTERY OF SAN GIOVANNI

Piazza del Duomo. Open 9:00am–1:00pm and 3:00pm–5:00pm year round. In the summer open until 7:00pm.

This is really the **crypt** of the Cathedral. Here you can find the baptismal fonts by Jacopo della Quercia, the bronze bas-relief of Bishop Pecci by Donatello, and many bronze reliefs of the Old and New Testament. The Baptistery was begun in 1315, but its facade has never been finished.

G. CHURCH OF SAN DOMENICO
& THE SANCTUARY OF SANTA CATERINA

Costa San Antonio. Church is open from 9:00am–6:00pm. The Sanctuary is closed 12:30pm–3:30pm Monday–Saturday and all day Sunday.

The Basilica is indelibly linked with the cloistral life of the local saint. It rises monumental and solitary overlooking the surrounding landscape and city. It's simple brick architecture of the 13th century was modified in the 14th and 15th centuries but still remains more like a fortress than a church. You can't miss the **chapel of St. Caterina** inside where the Saint's head is preserved today in the silver reliquary. In the other chapels of the church you'll find paintings by Sienese artists of the 14th through 16th centuries.

The house where St. Caterina used to live is now **Caterina Sanctuary**. The rooms she lived in as a youth have been frescoed by artists of all times with scenes from her life. It is a simple home but it is of cultural significance, since St. Caterina is one of the patron Saints of Italy.

TOURIST INFORMATION

• **Piazza San Domenico**, *Tel 0577/940-809. Place to get maps and hotel reservations if needed. Open 9:00am to 7:00pm.*

SHOPPING

The shops below are numbered and can be found on the *Siena* map.
17. Enoteca San Domenica, *Via del Paradiso 56. Tel.05/77-27-11-81.*
Right near where the bus lets you off from the station you can buy gifts of great Chianti wine for only L6,500. They also have other wonderful

gifts of local products. There are a number of these little shops all over Siena, but this one is the best and the best located.

18. Pizzigheria, 95 *Via della Cita.*

Look for the boar's head outside with a pair of glasses resting on his snout. Enter here and enjoy the greatest food smells you could ever imagine. A good place to buy any picnic supplies you may need, but there's a less expensive place up the road. Just stop here for the sight and smell of the sweet salamis hanging.

19. Crai, *Via di Citta 152-156.*

A small supermarket/*alimentari* where you can get great food supplies of all sorts at a better price that the Pizzigheria just down the street. But no atmosphere, just a good supply of everything you'll need to make a picnic in the Campo.

FIESOLE

Fiesole is five miles east of Florence on a hill overlooking the city. Well before Florence existed, Fiesole dominated this part of the Arno valley. Fiesole was one of the 12 important towns of ancient **Roman Etruria** from the 80 century BC on, and later was named the capital city of Roman Etruria. But in 1125 AD, all this dominance came to an end when Florence sacked and began its control of Fiesole and all of Tuscany. After the takeover, Fiesole was used by many of the Medici family as a refuge from the toil of governing, and the heat of the summer.

Even today Fiesole is a great respite from the heat or the hectic pace of Florence. Remember to bring a jacket because it is quite a bit cooler up in the hills. This is the place to stay if you want to get away from everything after you've finished your touring. It's only a 20 minute bus ride away (they leave from the station every 15 minutes). This is a tranquil location for a family vacation that offers access to Florence quickly and easily. If you're one to be bothered by traffic noise or a hectic pace, I would seriously suggest staying up here and commuting to Florence every day.

Besides being a refuge, Fiesole offers visitors a small glimpse into the ancient past with their archaeological excavations. There are also many fine churches and vistas to enjoy. You'll really feel above it all here, since almost every road offers a perfect panorama of Florence below.

ARRIVALS & DEPARTURES

By Bus or Taxi

The easiest and least expensive way to get to Fiesole from Florence is to take the #7 bus from the Piazza della Stazione. The ride takes only 20 minutes (with a soundless but still intrusive advertising video playing the whole time). If you take a taxi it'll cost you about $25. Both rides will offer you glimpses of fine villas and gardens as you weave through the winding road up to Fiesole.

Remember to pack yourself a picnic lunch which you can create from the ingredients you buy at one of the street markets or the *alimentaris* listed in this section of the book. If you forgot, there are a number of bars, cafés, and restaurants to choose from. Look out for the little birds, I think they were starlings, that imagine themselves cars that sweep two feet above the road pavement on the hills of Fiesole. A beautiful sight to see.

You catch the bus at the side of the station under the awnings. Tickets are sold at the *Giornalaio* inside the station or at the ticket office catty-corner to the bus stop outside. Tickets cost L1,400.

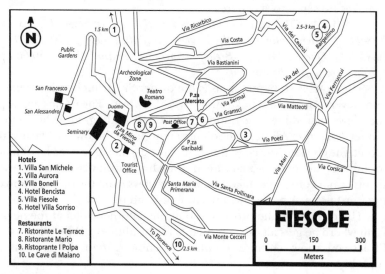

WHERE TO STAY

1. VILLA SAN MICHELLE, *Via Doccia 4, 50014 Fiesole. Tel. 055/59-451. Fax 055/598-734. Single L510,000; Double L910,000. Breakfast included. 36 rooms all with bath. American Express, Diners Club, Mastercard and Visa accepted.* *****

Located in a converted monastery that has a facade attributed to Michelangelo. If nothing else this hotel will allow you to bring stories of beautiful views, ancient habitations, and opulent surroundings back home. The reception area of the hotel is an old chapel, and the dining room bar is made from an ancient Etruscan sarcophagus (imagine if a bar in Washington, DC was made from the coffin of a soldier in the Civil War ... ah, the Italian culture is so laid back).

Each room has a four poster bed but all else is simple and basic. The best rooms overlook the gardens that surround the hotel. This is *the* hotel for those of you with plenty of disposable income. Here you can enjoy an outdoor pool during the day, a wonderfully scenic view from the restaurant in the evening, and a boisterous piano bar at night.

2. VILLA AURORA, *Piazza Mino de Fiesole 39, 50014 Fiesole. Tel. 055/ 59-100 or 59-292. Fax 055/59-587. American Express, Diners Club, Mastercard and Visa accepted. 26 rooms all with bath. Single L120,000-190,000; Double L160,000-290,000. Breakfast cost L18,000.* ****

Here you've got everything a four star could offer, but then again so does the Villa Bonelli, which is a three star, for a much better price. But if you want to stay in the central square this is the place to stay. It's really not a bad hotel but when you have the Bonelli just up the road (see below), it makes no sense to stay here.

3. VILLA BONELLI, *Via Francesca Poeti 1. Tel. 055/59-513. Fax 055/ 598-942. 20 rooms all with bath. Single L110,000; Double L170,000; Triple L215,000; Quad L240,000. Breakfast included. Dinner about L30,000 per person extra ... and its worth it.* ***

The hotel is stupendous, as is the owner Sr. Brunelli, who seems to know everyone there is to know all over the world. The rooms are large, the views incredible, the tranquillity worth bottling, and the food at dinner *fantastico*. All the ingredients come from the owners' farms: the rabbit, the chicken, the eggs, the oil, the wine, you name it, he has it made for him. A truly amazing man, and the best hotel around for the best price. If you're not convinced, take a look at the views from the dining room on the third floor. A perfect way to start and end the day.

The owner's in the process of building another hotel at the nearby farm where he gets all the ingredients for his dinners. When that opens I'll let you know, because the plans he showed me indicate it will be superb.

4. HOTEL BENCISTA, *Via Benedetto da Maiano 4, 50014 Fiesole. Tel. 055/59163. Fax is the same. 42 rooms all with bath. Single L200,000; Double L230,000. Breakfast L15,000. No credit cards accepted.* ***

Not many amenities except for clean and comfortable rooms in the middle of the hills surrounding Fiesole. It's quiet, romantic, the restaurant is good, but here you're married to your car. Fiesole is a long walk away, and besides the only way to get here is to drive out. Try the Bonnelli.

5. VILLA FIESOLE, *Via Beato Angelico 35, 50014 Fiesole. Tel. 055/597- 252. 28 rooms, all with bath. Single L110,000-180,000; Double L160,000- 320,000. Breakfast included. All credit cards accepted.* ***

Here you have peace and tranquillity since this place is truly in the middle of the Tuscan hills. Located in an historic building, the Villa Fiesole is great romantic getaway that has a pool and not much else. A good place to come on a second honeymoon if all you want to do is lounge around.

6. HOTEL VILLA SORRISO, *Via Gramsci 21, 50014 Fiesole. Tel. 055/ 590-27. Fax is the same. Seven rooms, 6 with bath. Double L70,000-98,000. Breakfast included. *

A great one star on the main road just up from the central square. Some of the rooms have great views overlooking a nearby valley, but not of Florence. But that's alright, the view is superb. The rooms are all clean and comfortable and you're right next door to a good restaurant, Pizzeria Le Terrace. Another plus is that the rooms are air conditioned. A perfect low-price getaway spot.

WHERE TO EAT

7. RISTORANTE PIZZERIA LE TERRACE, *Viale Gramsci 19, 50014 Fiesole. 055/59-272. Closed Tuesdays. Dinner for two L50,000. Credit cards accepted.*

This is a huge place with both indoor and somewhat cramped outdoor seating, but with stupendous views of a lush green valley below. Ignore the tacky wooden, life-sized waiter at the entrance and come for the view and the inexpensive food. As you enter you'll pass by the brick wood burning oven where they'll make your pizzas. There are plenty of varieties to please even the most discerning eater.

Besides pizza they make good pastas. Some recommendations: *Tortellini alla panna e prosciutto* (with cream and ham), and *tagliatelli della casa* (house favorite made with onions, sausage, saffron in a thick cream sauce). If you're interested in meat dishes, try their *pollo fritto* (chicken fried in olive oil), or the *coniglio fritto* (rabbit fried in olive oil) and compare whether rabbit really does taste like chicken.

8. RISTORANTE MARIO, *Piazza Mino #9. Credit cards accepted. Dinner for two L75,000.*

They have two different menus rolled into one. A traditional menu and one they call a *cucina creativa* (creative cooking) menu. Both are rather sparse, so check them out in the window before you stop here to see if you want anything. They have outside seating on the main square, as well as a few tables inside. Some of the more creative dishes are the *ravioline salmone e vongole* (little ravioli with a salmon and clam sauce), and the *filetto o coniglio alle mele* (thin slices of rabbit served with melon).

9. RISTORANTE TRATTORIA I POLPA, *Piazza Mino #21/22. Dinner for two L60,000.*

Try their country style *bruschetta*. They brush the coarse toasted garlic bread with succulent olive oil and cover it with fresh tomatoes. Then sample their *pennette all fiesolana* (with cream sauce and ham). If the meat bug hits you try the *scaloppini ai funghi porcini* (veal with porcini mushrooms).

10. LE CAVE DI MAIANO, *Via delle Cave 16, Tel. 055/59133. Closed Thursdays and Sunday nights. Dinner for two L 100,000. All credit cards accepted.*

One of the most popular restaurants for Florentines escaping their hectic, tourist-jammed city during the summer time. You'll need a car, or grab a cab from Fiesole, to get here, since it is about 3-4 kilometers outside of the town of Fiesole proper. You'll be served typical Tuscan food in a truly rustic atmosphere. The restaurant is blessed with a perfect garden environment. They specialize in all types of grilled, roasted, and fried meats. A great place to try if you've made the 20 minute bus ride up to Fiesole.

SEEING THE SIGHTS

Cathedral of San Romulus, *in the Piazza della Cattedrale (also Piazza Mino di Fiesole). Open daily 7:30am–Noon and 4:00pm–7:00pm.*

Built in the 11th century, the best part of this church is the bell tower whose chimes toll the half hour and the hour. You can hear it all over the countryside informing you of your place in the universe.

The Archeological Zone, *Open Winter 9:00am–6:00pm, Summer 9:00am–7:00pm. Closed on Tuesdays.*

The museum itself houses epics from prehistoric, Etruscan, Roman and medieval times; but the best part of this place is the **Roman Theater**, partially restored, that dates back to the 1st century BC. It's like a mini-Pompeii or Roman Forum.

The steep five minute climb (if you're fit) from the west end of **Piazza Mino** up to the **Church of San Francesco** will give you wonderful views of Florence and the Arno valley, especially from the benches near the **Church of San Alessandro** *(Open daily 7:30am–Noon and 4:00pm–7:00pm.)* Remember to bring your camera. The Church of San Francesca itself is relatively non-descript, but the cloisters are worth seeing as is the small museum that has a few Etruscan remains and relics collected by Franciscan missionaries in the Orient many years ago. Below the church you can see the public gardens and the **Basilica of S Alessandro**, which is on the site of the ancient **Roman temple of Bacchus**. *Gardens open 7:00am – 7:00pm. Basilica open same hours.* Cheers.

You can see everything there is to see in Fiesole in less than a day, so you can spend the rest of your time soaking up the great panoramic views, eating wonderful food, and celebrating the tranquillity with some Chianti. But remember, you are only 20 minutes away from the center of Florence by a bus that leaves at least twice an hour. So let me reiterate: if you like the splendor of Florence but can't seem to be able to stomach the noise and congestion, stay here in Fiesole. It will make your tour that much more pleasant and rewarding.

14. VENICE

City of Canals & Bridges

Venice is one of the great cultural centers of Europe, and as such attracts tens of thousands of tourists each year. It serves as the capital of the province of Venice (**Venezia**) and the **Veneto region**, which includes the towns of **Padua**, **Verona**, and **Vicenza**.

The historic center of Venice that everyone comes to see is built on a group of islets and mudbanks in the middle of **Laguna Veneta**, a crescent-shaped lagoon separated from the **Adriatic Sea** by a barrier of narrow islands and peninsulas. The modern city covers the whole 90 mile (145 km) perimeter of the lagoon and includes ten principal islands, in addition to those of the mother city and two industrial boroughs of **Mestre** and **Marghera** on the mainland.

The main core of Venice includes the islands of **La Giudecca** with its floating cafés and restaurants; **San Giorgio Maggiore**, with its famous 16th century church of the same name; and **San Michele** with its famous cemetery. Other islands include the **Lido**, a resort built in the 19th century, with casino, hotels, and beaches; **Murano**, noted for its glass-works; **Burano**, famous for its lace; and **Torcello**, site of the remains of the **Santa Maria Assunta** cathedral. Venice is separated from the sea by natural and artificial breakwaters, but flooding is common from November through March of each year, so if you visit then, remember to bring some galoshes.

Because of this water, Venice is world renowned as a city of canals and bridges. These facilitate internal transportation and have a beauty and charm that draw countless visitors each year. Chief among these arteries is the **Grand Canal**, which starts at the railway station at **Piazza Roma** and ends at **Piazza San Marco** (**St. Mark's Square**). Altogether there are more than 200 canals, which are literally the streets and avenues of Venice. Crossing the waterways are about 400 bridges, the most famous of which is probably the **Rialto** with its many shops, and the daily market near its base in the **San Polo** section. Other well known bridges include the **Scalzi**, the **Accademia**, and the infamous **Bridge of Sighs**, which leads from the upper story of the **Doges' Palace** to the republic's prison. It's called the Bridge of Sighs because centuries ago prisoners went over it sighing in trepidation of their torture and death.

Within the Venetian islands, canals, and lagoons, commodities move by barges and tugs, while passenger movement is primarily by *vaporetti* (water buses). The world-famous black *gondolas*, propelled by professional gondoliers, are narrow with high prows and sterns and are used mainly for short canal passages. Now they are mainly the vehicles of merchants, politicians, and especially tourists.

The Early Years

As competing history books will tell you, **Venice** was either founded on fear and cowardice, or brilliant necessity and creative ingenuity. With the fall of the Roman Empire, the "barbarian" states – Goths and Ostrogoths – swept over Italy in the 5th and 6th centuries AD. Instead of facing this onslaught, the people of the Veneto region found shelter on the scores of offshore islets in the lagoons off the coast, which had previously been inhabited by small numbers of fishermen. There the future Venetians built their houses on pilings on the partially flooded islands and learned to move about by poling in shallow boats, which have evolved into *gondolas*.

The "barbarians" were good horsemen, but bad boatmen, so they continued to wreak havoc on shore, leaving the lagoons to the Venetians. Over the centuries Venice grew into a great maritime power. This success developed because of the astuteness of its merchants and rulers, as well as its centuries-old political, military, and commercial ties with the Byzantium world in Constantinople, now Istanbul.

Early Venice was a society ruled by its **Doges**, who were first elected in 727AD. They were chosen by the **Council of Ten**, elected by nobles and rich merchants who accounted for only six percent of the population. Not really a prime example of democracy, but remember, this was the 8th century!

The city-state's chief maritime competitors were Genoa and the Amalfi Coast towns south of Naples, but Venice had the advantage of easier access through low Alpine passes to the heart of Western and Central Europe. Venice learned to put aside moral issues and profit from any venture sent its way.

For example, not only did the Doges make money off the Crusades by outfitting ships bound for the Holy Land, and then some say warning their Muslim friends of the impending arrivals; but in 1204 they also cut a deal with the Crusaders to attack and destroy Constantinople, their erstwhile Muslim partners in trade. This led to a great increase in Venice's profitability since they had cut out the middle man in their trading.

After years of bitter conflict between the two city states, Genoa was defeated in 1381. The Venetians trapped the Genoan fleet inside the Chioggia lagoons south of the city and forced its surrender. At the height of the republic's power, Venice controlled Corfu, Crete, and the Peloponnesus in what is today Greece. On the mainland it acquired the land westward almost to Milan. Also, because of the defeat of Constantinople, the Black Sea and the eastern Mediterranean were now open for Venetian vessels.

A variety of problems, however, contributed to a sharp decline in the republic's stature from the 16th century on. One of the main problems was their situation on the lagoon. What earlier had assited them would now bring about their decline. Because of its location on sedentary water, the population of Venice was decimated over three centuries by outbreaks of plague. In one, from 1347 to 1349, three-fifths of its inhabitants died. Then the **Turks**, who had captured Constantinople in 1453, noticed Venice's weakness and began to take over Venice's Greek lands and possessions.

Venice later was defeated by the **League of Cambria** in 1508, but then later temporarily regained its maritime power. This ended when the Portuguese opened the Cape Route around Africa, which meant that they had access to the spices the Venetians were trading, but the Portuguese were able to get them from the source.

In 1797, the city was conquered by **Napoleon** and later ceded to Austria. In 1848 there was an unsuccessful revolt against the Austrians. Venice finally became part of a unified Italy in 1866, and, with the opening of the Suez Canal in 1869, the city regained a direct route to the East, but it never fully recovered its commercial supremacy.

ARRIVAL & DEPARTURES
By Bus
When arriving by bus you have to disembark at Piazza Roma, then either walk or catch some form of water transport to your destination. The main local bus service is **ACTV** *(Tel. 041/528-7886)*. They have a tourist office in Piazza Roma where you can get maps, tourist information about Venice, and reserve bus seats to a variety of different cities in the region including Mestre, Padua, Mira and Treviso.

By Car
If you arrive in Venice by car, be prepared for long waits near **Piazza Roma** before you can deposit your automobile for the duration of your stay. One of the beauties of Venice is that it is automobile free. The only

way to get to Venice by car is through the mainland town of **Mestre**, then over the bridge (made by Mussolini) to the parking lots around the Piazza Roma. Once you get rid of your car, you can either walk to your destination or hop on the *vaporetto* at the Piazza Roma stop on the canal. You will also be able to catch water taxis or gondolas from this location.

Sample trip lengths on main roads:
• **Padua**: 50 minutes
• **Bologna**: 2 hours
• **Florence**: 4 hours
• **Rome**: 6 hours.

If you want to rent a car, try **Avis**, *Piazza Roma 496/H, 041/522-5825* or **Hertz**, Piazza Roma, 496/E, *041/528-4091*.

By Train

Arriving by train is the most convenient way to get to Venice. The **Stazione di Santa Lucia** is located on the northwestern edge of the city. From here you'll need to either walk to your hotel through the maze of medieval streets, take a *vaporetto* (a water bus), hire a water taxi, or go in style (and expense) in a gondola. All of these transportation services are located on the canal directly in front of the train station.

The **tourist information office** *(041/719-078)*, on the left, and hotel information *(041/715-016)*, on the right, are located side by side near the front entrance of the station. If you need a hotel reservation get in the right line. If you just want information about upcoming events in Venice, a map, etc., get in the left line.

Sample trip lengths and costs for direct *(diretto)* trains:
• **Padua**: 45 minutes, L4,000
• **Bologna**: 1 1/2 hours, L15,000
• **Florence**: 3 1/2 hours, L27,000
• **Rome**: 5 hours, L56,000.

ORIENTATION

Venice is conveniently broken up into six **sestieri**, or sections, and the houses are numbered consecutively from a point in the center of each section, making finding specific locations an adventure in and of itself. The six *sestieri* are:
• **Cannaregio**, where the Jewish Ghetto is located; not too many tourists here.
• **Santa Croce**, along with San Polo is still considered the 'other side of the canal,' even though the Rialto bridge was built back in 1588 to connect this section of Venice with the more influential San Marco section.

- **San Polo**, site of the famous food marketnear the foot of the Rialto bridge that is open every morning except Sunday and Monday.
- **San Marco**, which is the cultural and commercial center of Venice and the location that most tourists never leave.
- **Dorsoduro**, where you can have a relaxing meal on the **Zattere**, the series of quays facing the island of **La Guidecca**, and watch the sun go down.
- **Castello**, the location of the **Arsenale**, where many of Venice's ships have been built.

AN INSIGHT INTO VENICE

Venice was the late Walt Disney's favorite city. With its scenic canals, ornate bridges, and grandiose palazzi and piazzi, it easy to see why Venice grabbed his heart. Not only is it stunningly beautiful, but the whole tourist section of the city has an amusement park feel to it. It's almost as if what you're seeing is too magnificent, too stunning to be real.

Then suddenly, if you're here in high season, you encounter the hordes of tourists from all over the globe, and as you thrust your way through the crowds some of the luster starts to wear off. Then you start to notice that every doorway, every building front, every available space on every little street is packed with stores you can find in any mall in America. It seems as if parts of Walt Disney's favorite city have turned into one of the ugly strip malls that have grown like mold around his theme parks.

Because of the crowds and the tacky commercialism that comes with them, Venice is definitely a place to visit in the off-season. You'll share the city almost completely with the locals, and you'll be able to stay in a much better hotel since all accommodations virtually cut their rates in half during the off-season. You'll also miss the stench that sometimes seeps its way from the canals during the heat of July and August. And by coming in the off-season you may be lucky enough to be in Venice during one of their rare snow storms that blanket the city with a powdery decoration, turning a gorgeous city into a magical one. One so much so that it is easy to see Walt's affection for it.

GETTING AROUND TOWN

By Vaporetti – Water Buses

The least expensive way to travel around Venice and the most efficient is via a **vaporetti**. If you're staying longer than a week you may want to invest in a **Carta Venezia** pass, which enables you to take the *vaporetti* for one-third the regular fare. You can buy these at most tobacconists, the same place you buy your stamps. Some of the *vaporetti* may be quite crowded so be prepared to act like a sardine sometimes.

The main lines are as follows:

- **Accelerato No. 1** – Stops at every landing spot on the **Grand Canal**. Obviously this one takes a little time.
- **Diretto No. 2** – Fastest way to get from the **train station** and **Piazzale Roma** to **Accademia**, **Rialto**, and **San Marco** stops. Often very crowded and as their name suggests, *diretti* are direct trips.
- **Diretto No. 4** – Summer time *vaporetto* that basically follows the same path as the No. 2.
- **Motoscafo No. 5** – The circle line that travels in both directions around the periphery of Venice and to the smaller islands around Venice, **Isola San Michele** and **Murano** (see Day Trips & Excursions section of this chapter for more details). A great ride in and of itself for you to see the peripheral areas of Venice from the water.
- **Vaporetto No. 12** – Goes to **Murano**, **Burano**, and **Torcello**, all smaller islands around Venice (see Day Trips & Excursions section of this chapter for more details); departs from the **Fondamenta Nuove** stop just across from the Isola San Michele.
- **Vaporetti 6 & 11** – Goes to the resort of **Lido** and leaves from the **Riva Degli Schiavoni** stop to the east of Piazza San Marco.

By Traghetti – Gondola Ferries

At many points along the Grand Canal, basically near many of the regular *Vaporetti* stops, you can cross by using the inexpensive public gondola ferries called **traghetti** that are rowed by pairs of gondoliers. The times for each varies for each departure based on whether the gondoliers have enough passengers. In these boats there is standing room only, which causes you to unlearn everything you've ever been taught about boat etiquette. You'll be packed in with crowds of locals, workmen, business people with their briefcases, art students, and others while you're poled along.

By Gondola

Gondolas are privately operated boats operated by professional **gondoliers**. This is the most delightful way to admire Venice at a leisurely pace. Granted they are expensive (a half hour ride costs over $50) but they're still fun and romantic if you're so inclined. There are only a little over 400 licensed gondoliers in Venice and the licenses, though theoretically open to everyone, are in practice restricted to the sons (not the daughters) of gondoliers.

If you are going to hire a gondola, take one with a specific destination in mind, like going to a specific restaurant or specific site instead of just asking the gondolier to pole you around for a while. Even though gondoliers are trained to take you to the prettiest places for your money, by bringing you to a specific destination you and gondolier become part of the Venice of old, because in the not so distant past gondolas were the main form of transportation for all the elite Venetians when they went out to dinner or the opera.

You can also hire a gondola for *serenate* (group rides in which the gondolas feature an accordionist and a singer) at night. These rides can be very expensive, but if it's your honeymoon or a special occasion who cares?

Remember to bargain with the gondolier for each ride, whether it's a regular trip or a *serenate*. Their prices are not set in stone.

By Water Taxi

There are plenty of **water taxis**, but they too are extremely expensive. If you don't want to be part of the maddening crowds, however, this is the quickest way to get from point A to point B. If you want to get picked up at a certain place at a certain time, *call 523-2326 or 522-2303.*

By Foot

Let's be serious. Venice is comparable in size to New York City's Central Park, so it's possible for you to walk anywhere you want, as long as you're not in a hurry, or worried about getting lost. I've done that plenty of times when I forgot to bring my map with me, but I usually found some out-of-the way shop or café to enjoy on my journeys.

The true beauty of this city is the absence of cars or buses. The streets are the way they should be, designed for walking. This fact alone makes life in Venice seem calmer and more serene than anywhere else. Many Venetians are proud of the fact that throughout their entire lives they have never owned an automobile. Not having owned one for more than six years now, I can understand their pride.

WHERE TO STAY

If you are unable to make suitable reservations prior to arriving in Venice, you should stop by the train station and consult with their friendly, multi-lingual **hotel finders service**, *Santa Lucia Train Station, Tel. 041/715-016.* They'll book you a room based on your specifications: for example,you can request a double with bath in the Desoduro section. During the summer high season you may not have much of a choice, but at least you'll get a room.

Venice is very popular all over the world, so if you want to stay in the perfect place, please reserve at least six months or more in advance. Most of the lower budget hotels in Venice subscribe to the service at the station. In the same office space, but not the same entrance is the **general**

information office for tourists *(Tel. 041/522-6356)*, where you can get maps, directions, and all sorts of necessary information if you're in a bind.

When applicable, each hotel reviewed here also lists the closest water taxi *(vaporetto)* stop for your planning purposes.

THE FIVE BEST HOTELS IN VENICE

*One star

25. ANTICO CAPON, *Campo Santa Margherita 3004B, Venezia. Tel. 041/528-5292. No credit cards accepted. 7 rooms, all with bath. Single L50,000-77,000; Double L62,000-100,000.*

**Two star

14. HOTEL CAMPIELLO, *Campiello del Vin 4647, Venezia. Tel. 041/520-5764. Fax 041/520-5798. 16 rooms 15 with bath. Single L55,000-120,000; Double L120,000-170,000.*

***Three star

7. HOTEL FLORA, *Calle Larga 22 Marzo 2283A, Venezia. Tel. 041/520-5844. Fax 041/522-8217. 44 rooms, 43 with bath. Single L125,000-195,000; Double L165,000-260,000.*

****Fourt star

15. HOTEL DANIELI, *Riva degli Schiavoni 4196, Venezia. Tel. 041/522-6480. Fax 041/520-0208. 235 rooms all with bath. Single L 240,000-480,000; Double L350,00-700,000. Suites L1,158,000-2,698,000.*

*****Five star

26. HOTEL CIPRIANI, *Fondamenta San Giovanni 10, La Guidecca, Venezia. Tel. 041/520-7744. Fax 041/520-3930. 98 rooms all with bath. Single L 340,000-680,000; Double L495,000-990,000.*

San Marco

Directly in the center of Venice, **San Marco** is the commercial and tourist center. Most people that visit Venice hardly ever leave this section of the city. For good reason. If you only have a little time, even the most seasoned traveler will be able to find everything s/he desires right here.

The **Piazza San Marco** is the center of this stage, where people vie with pigeons for space. The most frequently followed path is from this piazza down the busy main tourist shopping street to the **Rialto Bridge**. You can find everything you'll need right here: history, architecture, restaurants, cafés, shops, sights, fun, and many people.

1. HOTEL ALA, *Campo Santa Maria dei Giglio 2494, Venezia. Tel. 041/ 520-5333. Fax 041/520-3690. American Express, Diners Club, Mastercard and Visa accepted. 85 rooms all with bath. Single L115,000-160,000; Double L160,000-220,000; Triple L205,000-280,000. Breakfast included.* ***

Vaporetto Stop – *Santa Maria del Giglio.*

This is close to the famous and expensive Gritti Palace, where rooms go for over $350 a night. The hotel's location makes it seem exclusive, especially since it has its own dock on the adjacent canal, but the inside decor clarifies any lingering doubts about why this is only a three star. Though beautiful, the common areas just don't seem to mix together. I think they added the suit of armor to make the hotel seem more palatial.

The rooms are large with TVs, air conditioning, mini-bars, and direct dial phones, and the bathrooms are as modern as you'll find anywhere. The setting along the canal is what makes this hotel so beautiful and romantic, as well as a great deal for its location. You'll especially enjoy the roof garden for evenings of relaxation.

2. HOTEL BEL SITO, *Campo Santa Maria del Giglio 2517, Venezia. Tel. 041/522-3365. Fax 041/520-4083. American Express, Diners Club, Mastercard and Visa accepted. 38 rooms, 34 with bath.* ***
Vaporetto Stop – *Santa Maria del Giglio.*

Handsomely furnished, centrally located, but still off of the beaten path so you can get away from the crowds. Professionally managed to make your stay as pleasant as possible. They have a quiet little outdoor café to enjoy in the evenings. The rooms are small and all but 15 of them overlook the intimate church of Santa Maria del Giglia in the local piazza, which unfortunately is currently under renovations.

3. HOTEL BONVECCHIATI, *Calle Goldoni 4488, Venezia. Tel. 041/528-5017. Fax 041/528-5230. American Express, Diners Club, Mastercard and Visa accepted. 86 rooms, 80 with bath. L70,000-200,000; Double L100,000-280,000; Suite L150,000-350,000.* ***
Vaporetto Stop – *San Marco.*

The best rooms are on the top floor since they offer a semblance of a view over the canals and the city. Get one that faces out onto the peaceful canal and you'll truly enjoy your stay in Venice. I love the stained wood floors covered with Persian carpets and the antique furnishings. Perfectly located for access to everything. It seems a little long in the tooth at first glance, but the ambiance and comfort will grow on you.

4. HOTEL SANTA MARINA, *Campo Santa Marina 6068, Tel 041/523-9202. Fax 041/520-0907. 19 rooms all with bath. Single L80,000-180,000; Double L130,000-270,000.* ***
Vaporetto Stop – *Rialto.*

In a small square, you get a combination of local flavor and tourist amenities all around you. You're in the middle of everything but still a part of the true life of Venice. The staff here is amazingly helpful and your room, though small, is comfortable and quiet. Each room is decorated in its own color scheme, which makes each stay here different. A good choice for a veteran Venetian traveler or an adventurous first-timer.

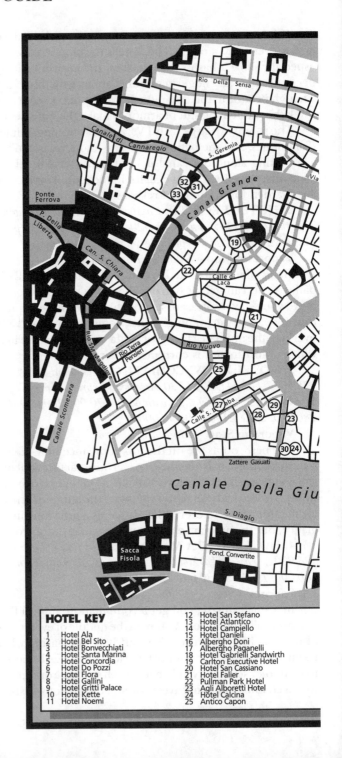

HOTEL KEY

1 Hotel Ala
2 Hotel Bel Sito
3 Hotel Bonvecchiati
4 Hotel Santa Marina
5 Hotel Concordia
6 Hotel Do Pozzi
7 Hotel Flora
8 Hotel Gallini
9 Hotel Gritti Palace
10 Hotel Kette
11 Hotel Noemi

12 Hotel San Stefano
13 Hotel Atlantico
14 Hotel Campiello
15 Hotel Danieli
16 Albergho Doni
17 Albergho Paganelli
18 Hotel Gabrielli Sandwirth
19 Carlton Executive Hotel
20 Hotel San Cassiano
21 Hotel Falier
22 Pullman Park Hotel
23 Agli Alboretti Hotel
24 Hotel Calcina
25 Antico Capon

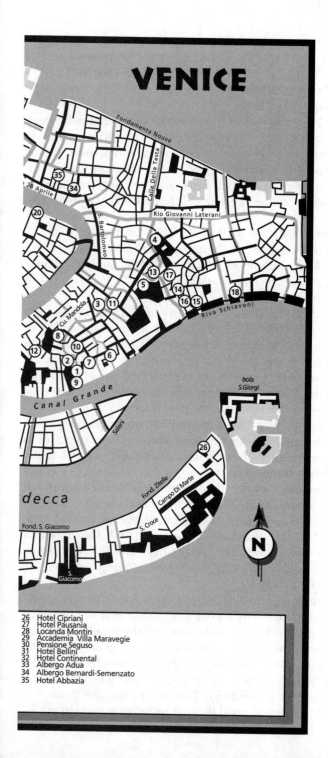

26 Hotel Cipriani
27 Hotel Pausania
28 Locanda Montin
29 Accademia Villa Maravegie
30 Pensione Seguso
31 Hotel Bellini
32 Hotel Continental
33 Albergo Adua
34 Albergo Bernardi-Semenzato
35 Hotel Abbazia

5. HOTEL CONCORDIA, *Calle Larga San Marco 367, Venezia. Tel. 041/520-6866. Fax 041/520-6775. American Express, Mastercard and Visa accepted. 57 rooms all with bath. Single L150,000-280,000; Double L210,000-410,000. Extra bed costs L65,000-85,000. Breakfast is L25,000 extra.* ****
Vaporetto Stop – *San Marco.*

The hotel has 20 rooms that overlook the Piazzetta dei Leoni which is part of the Piazza San Marco. Decor is Starship Enterprise modern in the lobby. The rooms attempt to combine modern and pseudo antique with a yellow color scheme that doesn't really work. There are better four-stars in less hectic surroundings, but if you want a view over the Piazzetta and don't mind noise until the wee hours of the morning, you might like this place.

6. HOTEL DO POZZI, *Via XXII Marzo 2373, Venezia. Tel. 041/520-7855. Fax 041/522-9413. American Express, Diners Club, Mastercard and Visa accepted. 35 rooms all with bath. Single L110,000-160,000; Double L160,000-220,000; Triple L210,000-260,000. Breakfast included.* ***
Vaporetto Stop – *San Marco.*

Don't get put off by the samurai sword in a display case right as you enter. This is a very peaceful and relaxing hotel. Located in the middle of everything but set off on its own small side street. They have a garden in the tiny piazza in which you can enjoy your breakfast or drinks in the afternoon. You also have air conditioning, phones, mini-bars, room service for breakfast, TVs, and a laundry service, everything a first class hotel can give you – but these aren't first class prices.

You can also get lunch or dinner for only L30,000 more per person at the restaurant Da Raphaele, which is a steal. The rooms are spartan and clean with little ambiance, but are quite comfortable. They left the ambiance in the lobby common areas.

Hint: Even if you don't stay here, come and relax in their courtyard during the day. It's a nice respite from the thundering herds.

7. HOTEL FLORA, *Calle Larga 22 Marzo 2283A, Venezia. Tel. 041/520-5844. Fax 041/522-8217. American Express, Diners Club, Mastercard and Visa accepted. 44 rooms, 43 with bath. Single L125,000-195,000; Double L165,000-260,000. Breakfast included. Closed November through January.* ***
Vaporetto Stop – *San Marco.*

The garden setting, where breakfast and afternoon drinks are served in the summer, is dominated by an old well and several old pieces of statuary. This area, the breakfast room service, and the general ambiance lend an old fashioned sense of hospitality to this hotel. A great place in the thick of things where you can still feel you've gotten away from it all. To get to the rooms, some of which are very small, you go up a painted stairway that is something to behold. The best rooms are those that overlook the serene garden. A good deal for its location and charm.

8. HOTEL GALLINI, *Calle della Verona 3673, Venezia. Tel. 041/520-4515. Fax 520-9103. Mastercard and Visa accepted. 50 rooms, 35 with bath. Single L60,000-130,000; Double L75,000-180,000. Breakfast included. Closed November 15 through March 1.* **

Vaporetto Stop – *San Marco or San Angelo.*

The hotel has been in the owner's family for over 50 years, and they make sure everything is as perfect as it can be. There's not much they can do since the hotel has little charm in and of itself. But even so the place is immaculately clean and your stay here will be in a perfect location for a good price, especially in the low season, which is really the best time to come to Venice.

9. HOTEL GRITTI PALACE, *Campo Santa Maria del Giglio, Venezia. Tel. 041/794-611. Fax 041/520-0942 . American Express, Diners Club, Mastercard and Visa accepted. 96 rooms all with bath. Single L290,000-548,000; Double L371,000-742,000.* *****

Vaporetto Stop – *Santa Maria del Giglio.*

Definitely a top-notch, high-class, deluxe hotel, with lots of local charm. You are treated like royalty, since many of their guests actually are. Located in a fifteenth century palace that still looks and feels like a private residence, you'll find Murano chandeliers everywhere as well as Burano lace table linens. There's really no words to describe the splendor of this place. Enjoy a night here if you're not worried about spending the equivalent of a monthly car payment. Or if you only want to feel like royalty for a little while, simply have a drink at their bar on the canal or enjoy a fine dinner at their lovely adjacent terrace restaurant. If you want romance, this is your place in Venice.

10. HOTEL KETTE, *Piscine San Moise 2053, Venezia. Tel. 041/520-7766. Fax 041/522-8964. American Express, Diners Club, Mastercard and Visa accepted. 69 rooms, all with bath. Single L100,000-170,000; Double L160,000-250,000. Breakfast included.* ***

Vaporetto Stop – *Santa Maria del Giglio.*

If you want luxury for less this is the place to stay. You have air conditioning, TVs, mini-bars, phones in the room, a picturesque landing on the canal for gondolas and water taxis, and friendly and efficient service like you'd expect in North America. It's also somewhat off the beaten path so you can enjoy a peaceful night's rest.

The public area is filled with comfortable chairs and international magazines where you can relax outside of the comfort of your room and get a little down time or mingle with the other guests. The rooms are all tastefully decorated, even though each has different furnishings. Unfortunately, some rooms face onto close walls from adjacent buildings, but except for this the place is great. Near enough to everything but still far enough away.

11. HOTEL NOEMI, *Calle de Fabbri 909, Venezia. Tel. 041/523-8144. Fax 041/522-5238. American Express, Diners Club, Mastercard and Visa accepted. 15 rooms none with bath. Single L50,000; Double L70,000; Triple L87,000. No breakfast served.* **

This is your typical two-star hotel with hardly any amenities, including no private bathrooms, which is really a drawback. The furnishing is a mish-mash collection, and the walls are thin, so if you have noisy neighbor you could be in for a sleepless night. Basically, if this is a last resort, go for it, otherwise find someplace else. Even though it is ideally located, in Venice this should not always be your priority because everything is within walking distance anyway.

12. HOTEL SAN STEFANO, *Campo Santo Stefano 2957, Venezia. Tel. 041/520-0166. Fax 041/522-4460. Mastercard and Visa accepted. 11 rooms and with bath. Single L80,000-150,000; Double L130,000-200,000; Triple L200,000-250,000. Breakfast included.* ***

Vaporetto Stop – *San Angelo.*

There are TVs in every room, as well as phones and hairdryers, and air conditioning available for L10,000-15,000 extra. Located on the colorful local Campo Santa Stefano close to the Accademia and Piazza San Marco, this hotel is a good place for its price. Many rooms have a view onto the square, but if you're a light sleeper don't ask for one of these since it can get noisy at night. The *campos* in Venice are the locals' gathering place in the evenings, which makes your stay more colorful, but if you face the Campo it will be nosiy at night. There is also a charming little garden patio for unwinding after a day of being a tourist. A good choice for anyone who wants to come to Venice.

Castello

This part of town offers the perfect chance to escape from the tourist hordes and discover the real Venice. There are plenty of quiet residential neighborhoods here, where old Italian ladies chat with each other from windows overhead while putting out their laundry to dry. If you're looking to shop this isn't the section of Venice for you, but there are some excellent and relatively inexpensive restaurants. Avoid the Riva degli Schiavoni to find the best prices for restaurants.

Castello is home to the **Arsenale** (where many of Venice's boats have been made) and the **Giardini Publici** (Public Gardens), which are a great place to come and relax.

13. HOTEL ATLANTICO, *Calle del Rimedio 4416, Venezia. Tel. 041/520-9244. Fax 041/520-9371. Mastercard and Visa accepted. 36 rooms, 29 with bath. Single L40,000-98,000; Double L45,000-180,000. All the singles are with bath.* **

Vaporetto Stop – *San Zaccharia.*

A well run, clean little hotel tucked in behind the San Marco section. On a street with no shops, so this is your chance to get away from all the consumer pressure of the tourist part of Venice. Some of the rooms overlook the Bridge of Sighs on a quaint little canal. Request these rooms if you choose to stay here. At night you can hear the sighs of the long dead condemned men drifting into your window ... The prices for doubles are a little high.

14. HOTEL CAMPIELLO, *Campiello del Vin 4647, Venezia. Tel. 041/ 520-5764. Fax 041/520-5798. American Express, Diners Club, Mastercard and Visa accepted. 16 rooms, 15 with bath. Single L55,000-120,000; Double L120,000-170,000.* **

Vaporetto Stop – *San Zaccharia.*

A friendly, quiet, and clean hotel located just behind the Riva degli Schiavoni. Consider this hotel if you like luxury on a budget. It is inexpensive, near everything, yet still on a quiet little canal. You can't ask for more. The rooms are all clean and quiet and the assistance you get from the owners is stupendous. They actually seem to like us tourists.

15. HOTEL DANIELI, *Riva degli Schiavoni 4196, Venezia. Tel. 041/ 522-6480. Fax 041/520-0208. American Express, Diners Club, Mastercard and Visa accepted. 235 rooms all with bath. Single L240,000-480,000; Double L350,00-700,000. Suites L1,158,000-2,698,000.* *****

Vaporetto Stop – *San Zaccaria.*

First opened in 1882 with only 16 rooms, the Danieli has expanded to encompass many surrounding buildings. The lobby, which is built around a Gothic courtyard, with its intertwining staircases and columns is spectacular. You feel as if you're in a castle. The largest hotel in Venice as well as the most romantic. The best place for breakfast, lunch, or dinner in all of Venice is their rooftop dining room which has an exquisite view of the Lagoon. If you can't afford to stay here, at least romance yourselves with a dinner or light lunch.

16. ALBERGHO DONI, *Calle del Vin 4656, Venezia. Tel. 041/522-4267. No credit cards accepted. 13 rooms none with bath. Single L45,000-55,000; Double L55,000-85,000. Extra bed L35,000. Breakfast included. Closed December 20 through March 15.* *

Vaporetto Stop – *San Zaccaria.*

Located just off the Riva Schiavoni and near Piazza San Marco and the church of San Zaccaria, this little hotel is a gem in a prime location. The views from the rooms overlook either a beautiful canal usually filled with gondolas or a small garden in the rear. The rooms are larger than would be expected and the prices are good. You can have your breakfast taken off of your bill for an extra L10,000 which will make it even a more pleasant stay. A perfectly romantic and serene place to stay for those on a low-budget. Close to my favorite restaurant in all of Venice, the Rivetta.

A hangout for all the gondoliers whose boats are in the canal in front of the hotel. The perfect place for budget travelers, but book well in advance.

17. ALBERGHO PAGANELLI, *Campo San Zaccaria 4687, Venezia. Tel. 041/522-4324. Fax 041/523-9267. American Express, Mastercard and Visa accepted. 7 rooms only 2 with bath. Single L90,000-120,000; Double L120,000-180,000.* **

Vaporetto Stop – *San Zaccaria.*

The biggest draw for this place (if you can get a room with a bath) is its isolated location in the middle of everything. Located on a Campo that neither the locals or tourists frequent, you'll have your peace after a hard day's touring. The rooms are all clean and the service is good. The prices are a little high even in off season, but the owner's know the value of a serene location.

18. HOTEL GABRIELLI SANDWIRTH, *Riva degli Schiavoni 4110, Venezia. Tel. 041/523-1580. Fax 041/520-9455. American Express, Diners Club, Mastercard and Visa accepted. 100 rooms all with bath. Single L120,000-295,000; Double L180-470,000. Closed mid-November to mid-March. Breakfast included.* ****

Vaporetto Stop – *San Zaccaria.*

Located in a Gothic palace with a beautiful rose garden in its center where you can take a drink from the bar. You can also roast in the sun on the roof terrace that overlooks the lagoon while enjoying your drink. This is the place to come for luxury on the lagoon. The best views are over the water. You don't have to worry about noise, since this is a bit off the main tourist track. All the rooms are tastefully decorated with antiques, chandeliers, and the ever-present roses. A less expensive option for luxury travel.

Santa Croce & San Polo

For purposes of clarity we have combined these two geographically connected sections of Venice into one. Still considered to be "the other side of the canal," even though the **Rialto bridge** was built back in 1588 to connect these two sections with the more influential San Marco. Beyond the area around the Rialto, you can find small little pizzerias that serve great good for an excellent price.

There are also plenty of tiny artisan's shops along with your regular touristy stores. **Campo San Polo** is the second largest in Venice and is a center for social life in these two neighborhoods. This is a great area just to roam through the back streets and discover the secrets of Venice.

19. CARLTON EXECUTIVE HOTEL, *Santa Croce 578. Tel. 041/718-488. Fax 041/719-061. 122 rooms all with bath. All Credit cards accepted. Single L140,000-210,000; Double L205,000-325,000. Breakfast L20,000 extra.* ****

Vaporetto Stop – *San Stae.*

A little off the beaten path, but the calm serenity makes up for that. As you can see, this is quite inexpensive for a four star hotel in Venice. A good opportunity to live in luxury for less. Their little garden is a perfect place to relax after a tough day of vacationing.

20. HOTEL SAN CASSIANO, *Calle della Rosa 2232, Venezia. Tel. 041/ 524-1768 Fax 041/721-033. American Express, Mastercard and Visa accepted. 35 rooms all with bath. Single L65,000-198,000; Double L85,000-283,000.* ***

Vaporetto Stop – *San Stae.*

Located in a Gothic palazzo on the Grand Canal, with its own dock from which you can arrive or depart by water taxi. At this same dock area they have a few tables where you can sit and enjoy the passing boats on the canal and feel completely free of the thundering herds of tourists. The rooms are all elegantly furnished with antiques, and there are chandeliers everywhere. The building seems a little down on its luck but that makes the stay quaint and romantic. They have *USA Today* available every morning so you can keep abreast of news at home.

21. HOTEL FALIER, *Salizzada San Pantalon 130, Venezia. Tel. 041/ 522-8882. Fax 041/520-6554. Mastercard and Visa accepted. 19 rooms all with bath. Single L60,000-150,000; Double L70,000-170,000. Breakfast included.* **

Vaporetto Stop – *San Toma.*

Near the Campo dei Frari and the Frari church, this hotel used to be an excellent value for a two-star in Venice. Now its prices have risen to another level. The best part of the hotel is that the area is not touristy. Instead the area is filled with real Venetian shops, cafés, and restaurants that make you feel like part of the life here. The rooms are on the small side but they are all wonderfully appointed, with plenty of space for you and your clothing. It's tough to find, but that adds to the charm.

22. PULLMAN PARK HOTEL, *Santa Croce 245. Tel. 041/528-5394. Fax 041/523-0043. 100 rooms all with bath. Single L120,000-240,000; Double L150,000-320,000. Breakfast included.* ****

Another inexpensive four star hotel. That's because this one and the previous one are located outside of the main tourist areas of Venice. But remember everything here is within walking distance and safe. Located off the beaten path, you'll still find plenty of excellent local restaurants nearby that serve superb food. The accommodations are perfectly four star. A great place to stay if you want luxury for less.

Dorsoduro

If you want to try and get away from it all while in Venice, this section of the city is great. There are few stores but many real Venetian sights. You'll find artisans, locals buying fruit from a boat that comes daily from the mainland, as well as ritzy hotels and museums. The best place in this section is the **Zattere**, "rafts" that are home to a variety of different and excellent restaurants. Eating on the water, looking out over the island of La Guidecca, you will be amazed at the beautiful sunsets over the island.

23. AGLI ALBORETTI HOTEL, *Rio Terra Antonia Foscarini, Accademia 884, Venezia. Tel. 041/523-0058. Fax 041/521-0128. American Express, Mastercard and Visa accepted. 20 rooms all with bath. Single L95,000-120,000; Double L146,000-180,000. Breakfast L10,000 extra. Lunch or dinner L45,000 extra.* **

Vaporetto Stop – *Accademia.*

I love the little garden off the lobby where you can have breakfast in the mornings or relax in the evenings for dinner or drinks after a hard day of touring. The rooms are not quite so spacious, but they're comfortable. Located in the shadows of the Accademia, you are a bridge away from all the major sights, but still have the comfort of a tranquil setting and air conditioning to boot, a rarity for two-star hotels.

24. HOTEL CALCINA, *Fondamenta Zattere dei Gesuati 780, Venezia. Tel. 041/520-6466. Fax 041/522-7045. American Express, Diners Club, Mastercard and Visa accepted. 30 rooms, 23 with bath. Single 35,000-95,000; Double L90,000-200,000.* ***

Vaporetto Stop – *Zattere.*

The hotel has views over the large canal in front, a side canal, and the boring rear. Try to get a great view in the front overlooking La Guidecca. The sunsets are spectacular. They also have a floating terrace out front from which you can enjoy breakfast or an afternoon cocktail. The rooms are clean and comfortable without any true distinguishing feature, except for the tranquillity and calm. A great location for joggers.

25. ANTICO CAPON, *Campo Santa Margherita 3004B, Venezia. Tel. 041/528-5292. No credit cards accepted. 7 rooms, all with bath. Single L50,000-77,000; Double L62,000-100,000.* *

A super deal in the best local area in Venice. The Campo Santa Margherita and its environs have everything you'll need while staying in this tourist-plagued city. Most mornings there is a small market selling fruit, vegetables, and fresh fish in the piazza. You'll also find places for pizza, pastries, a supermarket, an Irish Pub, a laundry, and more. The hotel is directly in the middle of all this Venetian life, and three of the rooms face this hustle and bustle while the other four face the uninspiring rear. The rooms are large but the bathrooms are quite small. The shower is located above the toilet.

If you've been to Venice before and disliked the crowds, this is the place for you to stay. It is truly a respite from insanity. The perfect antidote for the crowds of Venice.

26. HOTEL CIPRIANI, *Fondamenta San Giovanni 10, La Guidecca, Venezia. Tel. 041/520-7744. Fax 041/520-3930. American Express, Diners Club, Mastercard and Visa accepted. 98 rooms all with bath. Single L 340,000-680,000; Double L495,000-990,000. ******
Vaporetto Stop – *Zitelle.*

This exquisite hotel occupies three beautiful acres at the east end of La Isola del Guidecca. There is a swimming pool, saunas, Jacuzzis, a private harbor for yachts, a private launch to ferry guests back and forth from the center, an American-style bar with every drink imaginable, and two superb restaurants. Sixty rooms overlook the lagoon, while many others look out over the pool.

This hotel is probably as close to heaven on earth as you'll find in Venice. There are even private suites that can be rented by the week which have their own butler assigned to them. If you can't afford to stay here, simply come out and enjoy a drink by the pool.

27. HOTEL PAUSANIA, *Rio di San Barnaba 2824, Venezia. Tel. 041/522-2083. fax 041/420-178. American Express, Mastercard and Visa accepted. 24 rooms all with bath. Single L80,000-170,000; Double L110,000-250,000. Breakfast included. ****
Vaporetto Stop – *Ca' Rezzonico.*

Near Campo San Barnaba and the floating markets on barges, the location on the San Barnaba Canal is perfect for getting a feel for real Venetian life. To get to the lobby you need to pass through a beautiful medieval courtyard, and the breakfast room opens up onto a well tended garden. The rooms are large, air conditioned, with direct dial phones, a mini-bar, hair dryer, TV and radio, basically everything your money has paid for. And you get the pleasure of peace and quiet in the evenings too.

28. LOCANDA MONTIN, *Fondamenta di Borgo 1147, Venezia. Tel. 041/522-7151. Fax 041/520–0255. American Express, Diners Club, Mastercard and Visa accepted. 9 rooms none with bath. Single L35,000-45,000; Double L65,000-85,000; Triple L95,000. (No Stars)*
Vaporetto Stop – *San Toma.*

Conveniently located just off the Piazza Santa Barbara, the hotel is entered through a huge, local restaurant. If you're too tired to go out to eat, just go downstairs and enjoy great Italian food in their huge restaurant. Eclectic furnishings, but everything is clean and comfortable. Perfect for low budget travelers. Two rooms have teeny tiny balconies covered with flowers that overlook the canal. Perfect for budget travelers.

29. ACCADEMIA VILLA MARAVEGIE, *Fondamenta Bollani/Marevegie 1058, Venezia. Tel. 041/521-0188. Fax 041/523-9152. American Express, Diners Club, Mastercard and Visa accepted. 27 rooms, 25 with bath. Single L65,000-130,000; Double L110,000-200,000; Triple L225,000. Breakfast included. ****

This is a perfect spot for post-touring relaxation. This impressive 17th century villa, formerly the Russian consulate, is surrounded by beautiful gardens and is just off the Grand Canal. There is a patio with chairs and tables and many plants on one side of the villa facing the Grand Canal.

The inside is simply beautiful, and its amazing that you can find a room here for so cheap. You also have an upstairs tea-room as well as breakfast room that overlooks a flower garden. All the rooms are large, save number 8 which is a tiny single. Obviously because of the location and ambiance, reservations are sometimes necessary over a year in advance!

30. PENSIONE SEGUSO, *Zattere dei Gesuati 779, Venezia. Tel. 041/528-6858. Fax 041/522-2340. American Express, Mastercard and Visa accepted. 36 rooms, 18 with bath. Single L50,000-130,000; Double L110,000-270,000. Breakfast included. In high season your room comes with either a lunch or a dinner.* **

Vaporetto Stop – *Zattere.*

In the front you can enjoy a tiny terrace set with chairs, tables, and umbrellas. The view of the Canal and Guidecca island is especially beautiful when the sun is setting. Unfortunately the prime rooms that overlook the canal don't have their own baths, which may explain why this is only a two star. All the rooms are simply decorated and the atmosphere is very much like a bed and breakfast.

A great location for peace and quiet, and if you're a jogger you're in a perfect spot to churn out a few miles along the uncrowded canal in the morning. Slightly expensive for a two star, but the view is great.

Cannaregio

This section in the north of the main island is where the **Jewish ghetto** is located. This was the first place in Europe that Jews were isolated from the rest of the population and have it named a ghetto. Three of the synagogues in the main square of the tiny island (which comprised the first ghetto) are worth seeing. Here you'll find some of the tallest buildings in Venice, because once the Jewish population started to increase, the only place they could find more space was to build up.

Compared to the rest of Venice the place looks a little run down, but the place is alive with local shoppers buying their supplies for the day, with beautiful side streets and canals away from it all.

31. HOTEL BELLINI, *Cannaregio 116/a. Tel. 041/715-095. Fax 041/715-193. 69 rooms all with bath. 3 suites. Single L170,000-250,000; Double L230,000-360,000. All credit cards accepted. Breakfast included.* ****

Located near the train station in an antique palazzo that has been completely restored. There are many rooms with a view of the Grand Canal. This place has all the amenities of a four star hotel, but is not in the greatest location. A last resort for you luxury travelers.

32. HOTEL CONTINENTAL, *Lista di Spagna 166. Tel. 041/715-122. Fax 041/524-2432. 93 rooms all with bath. Single L 70,000-175,000; Double L130,000-240,000. Breakfast included. All credit cards accepted.* ***
Not in a great location, but the old building housing the hotel is a tranquil and romantic setting. Their restaurant has a wonderful view of the Grand Canal. All the amenities you'd want to find in a three star at less than three star prices. That's because of the location near the train station.

33. ALBERGO ADUA, *Lista di Spagna 233A, Venezia. Tel. 041/716-184. American Express, Diners Club, Mastercard and Visa accepted. 18 rooms, 4 with bath. Single L40,000; Double L50,000-80,000; Triple L70,000-100,000. Breakfast is L8,000 extra.* *
Vaporetto Stop – *Bar Roma.*
You have to walk up two flights of stairs from a busy street to get to the reception area. This hotel is small but comfortable, and has been in business now for close to 20 years. I could have done without the red carpeting in the rooms, but the view from my room onto the street made up for it. The rooms in the back aren't so lucky, with a view of a blank wall. For its price, in this, the costliest city in Italy, it's a good hotel.

34. ALBERGO BERNARDI-SEMENZATO, *Calle del Oca, SS. Apostoli 4363-4366, Venezia. Tel. 041/522-7257. 041/522-242. Credit cards accepted. 15 rooms, 7 with bath. Single without shower L32,000-L58,000; Double without shower L45,000-70,000; Double with shower 65,000-98,000. Breakfast L7,000 extra.* *
Vaporetto Stop – *Ca' D'Oro.*
This place has changed quite a bit in the last few years. It's now a super renovated, extremely clean, and wonderfully inexpensive little hotel in a great location. They even have a roof terrace that overlooks Venetian rooftops for you sun worshippers, or those of you that wish to grab a quiet drink at the end of the evening. Getting up there is kind of rough, and the clothes lines can get in the way, but for a one star to have a roof deck in Venice, ignore it. If you are a budget traveler and choose not to stay here, you made a big mistake. They're in the process of putting in air conditioning and TVs in the rooms in hopes of getting upgraded to a two star by 1998. If they do everything right, they'll end up a three star instead. So enjoy them while you can, because the prices are going to shoot through the roof soon.

35. HOTEL ABBAZIA, *Calle Priuli 68, Venezia. Tel. 041/717-333. Fax 041/717-949. American Express, Diners Club, Mastercard and Visa accepted. 31 rooms, 23 with bath. Single L85,000-170,000; Double L113,000-225,000. Breakfast included.* ***
Vaporetto Stop – *Ca' D'Oro.*
This place has many amenities that you wouldn't expect to find for the price, like air conditioning (a must in August) mini-bars, TVs, hair dryers,

and direct dial phones. This used to be part of a monastery until about 15 years ago when the monks sold this section of their property. Once inside, you'll be amazed at the beautiful but simple decor. I desperately want one of the wooden abbey benches that line the perimeter of the lobby.

The space in the rooms is amazing compared to most other hotels that don't cost an arm and a leg. So if you're traveling on a budget and want some great inexpensive accommodations, consider this place very seriously.

WHERE TO EAT

When applicable, each restaurant reviewed below also lists the closest water taxi (vaporetto) stop.

THE BEST RESTAURANTS IN VENICE

1. AL BACARETO, *Calle Crosera 3447, Venezia. Tel. 89-336. American Express, Mastercard and Visa accepted. Closed Saturdays for dinner and Sundays. Dinner for two L75,000.*

12. ALLA RIVETTA, *Ponte S Provolo 4625, Venezia. Tel. 528-7302. American Express, Mastercard and Visa accepted. Closed Mondays. Dinner for two L55,000-60,000.*

19. HOSTERIA DA FRANZ, *Fondamenta San Isepo 754, Venezia. Tel. 522-0861 or 522-7505. American Express, Mastercard and Visa accepted. Closed Tuesdays and in January. Dinner for two L180,000.*

22. AL MASCARON, *Calle Lunga Santa Maria Formosa 5225, Venezia. Tel. 522-5995. No credit cards accepted. Closed Sundays and mid-December to mid-January and 15 days in August. Dinner for two L70,000.*

24. TAVERNA "CAPITAN UNCINO" (Captain Hook), *1501 Campo San Gaicomo del'Orio. Credit cards accepted. Closed Wednesdays. Open until midnight. Dinner for two L65,000. Tel. 041/72-19-01. Dinner for two L90,000.*

25. TRATTORIA/PIZZERIA ANTICO CAPON, *Piazza Santa Margherita 3004, Tel. 041/528-525. Credit cards accepted. Dinner for two L 50,000.*

30. POSTE VECHIE, *Pescheria 1608, Venezia. Tel. 721-822. American Express, Mastercard and Visa accepted. Closed Tuesdays. Dinner for two L100,000.*

38. SAN TROVASO, *Fondamenta Priuli 1016, Venezia. Tel. 520-3703. American Express, Mastercard and Visa accepted. Closed Mondays. Air conditioned. Dinner for two L65,000.*

41. TRATTORIA ALTANELLA, *Guidecca Calle delle Erbe 270. Tel. 041/522-7780. No credit cards accepted. Closed Mondays and Tuesdays as well 15 days in August. Dinner for two L 90,000.*

Venetian Cuisine

Venice is not generally known for its cuisine, especially reasonably priced cuisine, but they do know how to prepare some great seafood dishes. The seafood usually comes placed over a bed of *risotto* (rice), and even though pasta is not used as often as in other regions of Italy, the Venetians make really good *spaghetti alla vongole* (clams) or *alla cozze* (mussels). Another favorite is the *zuppa di pesce* (fish soup), that mixes together every kind of fish that could be found at the market. You can't go wrong with fish here, except maybe on Sundays and Mondays when the *pescheria*, the seafood market at the Rialto, isn't open, which means your fish won't be fresh, but, (gasp) horrors, one or two days refrigerated.

Honestly, eating most anywhere in Venice you won't get the bang for your buck that you'd get somewhere else in Italy. Most of the restaurants have been created to cater specifically to the tourists and as such they charge ridiculously high prices. Even the natives go to the mainland to find themselves a good inexpensive meal. But with this word of warning, you can also find some great little pizzeria that cater to the local population. I'll list some later in this section.

Suggested Venetian Cuisine

Traditional Venetian fare is listed below. Our constitution just isn't prepared for such mass consumption, however, so don't feel embarrassed if all you order is a pasta dish or an entrée with a salad or appetizer.

ANTIPASTO - APPETIZER

• **Insalata di mare** – Seafood salad of shrimp, squid, and clams in a zesty oil, vinegar and herbs sauce.
• **Antipasto misto di mare** – Seafood appetizers taken from a buffet

PRIMO PIATTO - FIRST COURSE

• **Zuppa di pesce** – Seafood soup with any fish you can imagine cooked into it.
• **Spaghetti alla vongole verace** –Spaghetti with an olive oil, garlic and clam sauce
• **Risotto con cozze** – A rice and mussels dish pumped with a variety of spices

SECOND PIATTO - ENTRÉE

Pesce (Fish)
• **Grigliatta mista di mare** – An assortment of grilled seafood based on whatever the seasonal catch is.
• **Bisato, anguilla alla veneziana** – Eel cooked with onion, oil, vinegar, garlic and a little bay leaves

• **Coda di Rospa** – Monkfish either broiled or grilled.

• **Fritto Misto** – Assorted deep fried seafood

Carne (Meat)
• **Fegato alla veneziano** – Calf's liver sautéed with onions
• **Torresani** – Tiny pigeons served grilled on a spit

Formaggio (Cheese)
• **Asiago** – A dry, sharp cheese from the Veneto mainland

Regional Wines
You'll probably recognize many of the white wines from this region, especially the **Friuli** wines, such as **Pinot Brigio** and **Pinot Bianco**, and the incomparable **Soave's** which can be found in your stores at home. The reds are not so recognizable except for the **Cabernet**, and they're not nearly as good as the reds from the Chianti region around Florence. But then again, not many reds can compare to a Chianti.

San Marco
1. AL BACARETO, *Calle Crosera 3447, Venezia. Tel. 89-336. American Express, Mastercard and Visa accepted. Closed Saturdays for dinner and Sundays. Dinner for two L75,000.*
Vaporetto Stop – *San Samuele.*
Located on the corner of Salizzada San Samuele, this authentic neighborhood *trattoria* serves excellent Venetian dishes. There are a few tables outside from which you can not only enjoy your meal but revel in the sights and sounds of the local neighborhood. The seating inside is warm, with a dark wooden beamed ceiling where you'll notice many local customers indulging in their favorite meal.

You can get their specialty *Fegato alla veneziano* (calf's liver sautéed with onions) or any of their great seafood dishes for seconds. Then try their *risotto pesce* (rice mixed with seafood) or the *zuppa di pesce* (fish soup) for starters.

2. TRATTORIA DA "ARTURO," *Calle degli Assassini 3656A. Tel. 041/528-6974. Dinner for two L100,000. Credit cards accepted.*
Vaporetto Stop – *Rialto.*
An expensive place catering to tourists, thus the hamburger on the menu. Nonetheless it is a quaint little place on a small side street that emits local charm and ambiance despite the prices. The dark wood paneling only enhances the charm. So settle down and enjoy some good Italian, not necessarily Venetian food, like *spaghetti alla carbonara* (with ham, cheese, and eggs) or a *scaloppini al Porto* (veal cutlet cooked in port wine).

3. ANTICO MARTINI, *Campo San Fantin 1983, Venezia. Tel. 522-4121. American Express, Mastercard and Visa accepted. Closed Tuesdays and Wednesdays for lunch. Dinner for two L150,000.*
Vaporetto Stop – *Santa Maria Del Giglio.*

Snuggled in a back street of Venice, this is an excellent restaurant, but it is quite expensive, so save coming here for a special occasion or if you have money to blow. Not only can you order Italian and Venetian dishes, but the menu is in four languages. They make superb seafood and grilled meats but again, the prices are sky high.

4. LEON BIANCO, *Salizzada San Luca 4153, Venezia. Tel. 522-1180. No credit cards accepted. Closed Sundays. Open Monday - Saturday 9:00am - 1:00pm and 4:00pm to 9:00pm. Meal for two L35,000.*
Vaporetto Stop – *Rialto.*

A surprising inexpensive little wine bar in Venice's most expensive area, San Marco. There's a wide variety of *tramezzini* sandwich fillings to go along with your wine choice. My favorites were *prosciutto e formaggio* (ham and cheese), *prosciutto e funghi* (ham and mushrooms), and *prosciutto e uovo* (ham and egg, a great breakfast). But basically you can request your own combinations, as long as you speak a little Italian. The perfect place to come for a midday snack and a cold glass of wine or an ice cold draft beer, as well as for a light dinner.

5. RISTORANTE AL BUSO, *Ponte di Riallo 5338, Tel. 041/528-9078. Dinner for two L 65,000. Credit cards accepted.*
Vaporetto Stop – *Rialto.*

Located right beside the Rialto bridge down on the water by the Grand Canal. It only has a few tables set outside for the great canal-side views, but its worth the wait. Your red jacketed waiters will serve from the nearby restaurant with a variety of appetizing meals. Their pizza and pasta are both good and inexpensive. To be Venetian for the night, try their *pizza ai frutta di mare* (seafood pizza) or the *spaghetti con pesce* (with seafood). Then for *doppo* (seconds), try the grilled sole, a wonderful finish to any meal.

6. CLUB DEL DOGE DELL' HOTEL GRITTI, *Campo Santa Maria del Giglio 2467, Venezia. Tel. 041/794-611. American Express, Mastercard and Visa accepted. Dinner for two L180,000.*
Vaporetto Stop – *Santa Maria Del Giglio.*

You don't have to stay at the Gritti to enjoy their restaurant, so if you have some money left over from your trip and want to share a romantic meal with your significant other, this is the place to come. The Gritti's open air terrace is directly on the Canale della Guidecca which offers a great view of the sunset. Their classic Italian cuisine is superb. Even though the menu changes almost daily, they'll always have succulent meats, perfectly grilled or fried fresh fish and delicious pastas. After

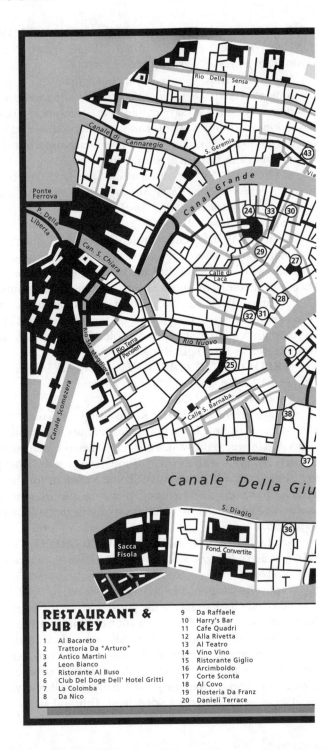

RESTAURANT & PUB KEY

1 Al Bacareto
2 Trattoria Da "Arturo"
3 Antico Martini
4 Leon Bianco
5 Ristorante Al Buso
6 Club Del Doge Dell' Hotel Gritti
7 La Colomba
8 Da Nico

9 Da Raffaele
10 Harry's Bar
11 Cafe Quadri
12 Alla Rivetta
13 Al Teatro
14 Vino Vino
15 Ristorante Giglio
16 Arcimboldo
17 Corte Sconta
18 Al Covo
19 Hosteria Da Franz
20 Danieli Terrace

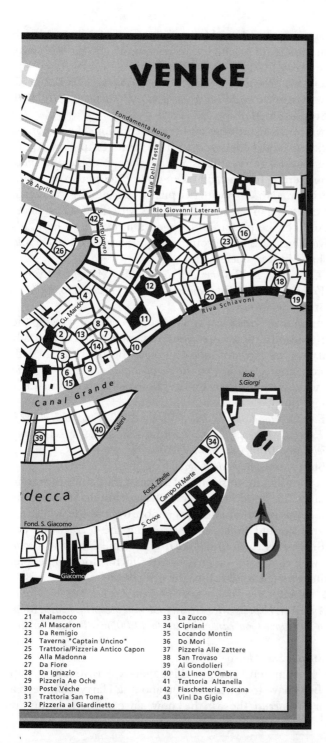

VENICE

21	Malamocco	33	La Zucco
22	Al Mascaron	34	Cipriani
23	Da Remigio	35	Locando Montin
24	Taverna "Captain Uncino"	36	Do Mori
25	Trattoria/Pizzeria Antico Capon	37	Pizzeria Alle Zattere
26	Alla Madonna	38	San Trovaso
27	Da Fiore	39	Ai Gondolieri
28	Da Ignazio	40	La Linea D'Ombra
29	Pizzeria Ae Oche	41	Trattoria Altanella
30	Poste Veche	42	Fiaschetteria Toscana
31	Trattoria San Toma	43	Vini Da Gigio
32	Pizzeria al Giardinetto		

dinner, linger here over a Sambuca Molinari, or a glass of wine and watch the sunset. If you want to go to a high class restaurant, choose this place, not the faux chic Harry's Bar.

7. LA COLOMBA, *Piscina di Frezzeria 1665, Venezia. Tel. 522-1175. American Express, Mastercard and Visa accepted. Closed Tuesdays. L100,000.*
Vaporetto Stop – *San Marco.*

Mainly known for its fish dishes and fine decorations, La Colomba also has a wide variety of grilled, baked, or fried meats. Sitting on a quiet street with some outdoor tables, this is a good place to come and relax until late into the evening (orders still taken up to 11:00pm). You might want to try the large *scampi al curry* with rice pilaf, not originally a Venetian specialty until the city began having vast dealings with the Far East many centuries ago. And yes, be prepared to spend a little money here; it's slightly expensive. They also make some good pastas, like *spaghetti alla carbonara* (with ham, butter, cheese, and egg).

8. DA NICO, *Frezzeria 1702, Venezia. Tel. 522-1543. American Express, Mastercard and Visa accepted. Closed Mondays. Dinner for two L80,000.*
Vaporetto Stop – *San Marco.*

The menu emphasizes fresh fish and pasta. I recommend trying the *antipasto di pesce* (seafood antipasto), so you can sample much of the daily catch. After that give the *tagliatelle alla "boscaiola"* (a superb pasta with mushrooms, bacon, and tomatoes) or the *sogliola alla nostrana mugnaia* (sole with a light wine and butter sauce). They both make my mouth water just thinking about them.

9. DA RAFFAELE, *Fondamenta delle Ostreghe 2347, Venezia. Tel. 523-2317. American Express, Mastercard and Visa accepted. Closed Thursdays and January to mid-February. Dinner for two L75,000.*
Vaporetto Stop – *San Maria del Giglio.*

Even though your first impression is of a tourist trap, since the menu is in four languages, the food here is actually very good. Actually, the Venetians frequent this restaurant but they choose to sit inside, where it's endowed with marble and much cooler, leaving the terrace for the tourists. And the terrace is a beautiful place to enjoy a meal. Try the *Risotto Raphaele* (made with clams and other seafood) which is for two people. Then later try the assorted fried fish or the grilled sole.

10. HARRY'S BAR, *Calle Vallaresso 1323, Venezia. Tel. 528-5777. Fax 041/520-8822. American Express, Mastercard and Visa accepted. Closed Mondays. 10:30am to 11:00pm (you can order up to 11:00pm). Dinner for two L160,000.*
Vaporetto Stop – *San Marco.*

I really don't recommend going to this super-expensive tourist trap bar/ristorante, but I have to at least tell you about it. Harry's has been a place to come for *i conoscenti* (those in the know) since before Hemingway was killing brain cells here. The downstairs bar is for drinking (if you've money for $6 drinks) and people watching. If you're going anyway, try the *Bellini* for which Harry's is famous, made with fresh peach juice and white wine. The restaurant upstairs is very expensive and has a pseudo-sophisticated air. This is a nouveau-riche hangout – but the food is excellent and there is a wide selection to choose from, especially in the meat and fish department. Remember to bring your credit card!

11. CAFÉ QUADRI, *Piazza San Marco 120-124, Venezia. Tel. 22-105. Credit cards accepted. Closed Mondays.*

Vaporetto Stop – *San Marco.*

This is a landmark in Venice, along with its fellow musically inclined cafés in the Piazza San Marco, such as the Florian or the Gran Café Chioggia. You might want to give this one or the others a try. Expensive, but if you want to say you've been here, have a drink and enjoy the music.

12. ALLA RIVETTA, *Ponte S Provolo 4625, Venezia. Tel. 528-7302. American Express, Mastercard and Visa accepted. Closed Mondays. Dinner for two L55,000-60,000.*

Vaporetto Stop – *San Zaccaria.*

Tucked away at the foot of a bridge this place is largely overlooked by tourists since many people don't bother to look down as they cross the canal. A hangout for some of the gondoliers as a drinking hole (they have a bar that faces onto the small canal where the gondoliers park their craft) and for many of the locals because of the food, location, and prices.

Their menu is in four languages so you'll be able to order what you desire, but here are some suggestions: *antipasto di pesce* (seafood antipasto), then the *spaghetti alla bolognese* (with veal, cream and tomatoes), and finally either the *fritto misti di mare* (mixed fried seafood) or the *cotolette alla milanese* (breaded veal cutlet). The atmosphere is all Venetian and the menu is from all over Italy. Enjoy both together.

13. AL TEATRO, *Campo San Fantin 1916, Venezia. Tel. 522-1052. American Express, Mastercard and Visa accepted. Closed Mondays and in November. Last orders can be placed at midnight. Dinner for L85,000.*

Vaporetto Stop – *Santa Maria del Giglio.*

Al Teatro stays open late to cater to the exiting theater customers (hence the name). It's actually a ristorante, pizzeria, and bar all rolled into one that has great local flavor. They have seating outside under canopies in the piazza and plenty of seating inside. The atmosphere is best outside. Try the *spaghetti alla vongole* (with a spicy olive oil-based clam sauce or the *risotto di pesce* (seafood rice dish). Then grab some *scampi e calamari fritti* (fried squid and shrimp for seconds).

14. VINO VINO, *Calle Veste 2007A, Venezia. Tel. 522-4121. American Express, Mastercard and Visa accepted. Closed Tuesdays. Open 10:00am - 2:30pm and 5:00pm to 1:00am.*

Vaporetto Stop – *Santa Maria del Giglio.*

A late night wine bar open by the owners of the Antico Martini (see number 3 above) to cater mainly to the late night theater crowd and others just leaving their restaurant when it closes at 10:00pm. They serve salads, sandwiches, as well as meat dishes like chicken and lamb all prepared by the kitchen at the Antico Martini and for a much better price (about one quarter as expensive). These two places are bookends for another Martini special, a piano bar that serves late night drinks and entertainment.

15. RISTORANTE GIGLIO, *Campo Santa Maria dei Giglio 2477 (next to the Hotel Ala). Tel. 041/523-2368. Dinner for two L80,000.*

Vaporetto Stop – *Santa Maria del Giglio.*

Enclosed piazza seating for any kind of weather. They have a menu in English for easy ordering. Try the Risotto with seafood, which is served for two people. Then make sure you try the curry chicken with rice pilaf and you'll have had a great culinary experience. For later, try Haig's Grill, there attached bar/café, for a drink outside under the stars in the isolated piazza.

Castello

16. ARCIMBOLDO, *Calle dei Furlani 3219, Venezia. Tel. 86-569. No credit cards accepted. Closed Tuesdays. Dinner for two L60,000.*

Vaporetto Stop – *Riva Degli Schiavoni.*

Located on a small canal, off the beaten path near the Scuola di San Giorgio degli Schiavoni. You'll love the local flavor and quiet ambiance of the outside seating. Hardly a tourist around, save for yourself. Try their exquisite *scampi al curry* with rice pilaf and any of their grilled meats. A wonderful place to get away from it all. But bring your map – this is a tough one to find.

17. CORTE SCONTA, *Calle del Pestrin 3886, Venezia. Tel. 522-7024. American Express, Mastercard and Visa accepted. Closed Sundays and Mondays. Dinner for two L70,000.*

Vaporetto Stop – *Arsenale.*

Located near the Piazza San Giovanni in Bragora, this restaurant has a plain decor but interesting patrons. Their menu changes with the tide, i.e., whatever the catch is that day, but they always seem to have a well stocked but diverse *fritture mista di mare* (mixed fried seafood). Since this is a very popular, high end local restaurant, reservations are required.

18. AL COVO, *Campiello della Pescaria 3968, Venezia. Tel. 522-3812. American Express, Mastercard and Visa accepted. Closed Wednesdays and Thursdays and 15 days in August. Dinner for two L130,000.*

Vaporetto Stop – *Riva Degli Schiavoni.*

The perfect place to eat is on their patio. The service is quite attentive and the food prepared perfectly. Located near San Giovanni in Bragora, this is true Venetian cuisine. Try the *spaghetti al nero di seppia* (with octopus ink), the fried vegetables for seconds, and the wonderful atmosphere.

19. HOSTERIA DA FRANZ, *Fondamenta San Isepo 754, Venezia. Tel. 522-0861 or 522-7505. American Express, Mastercard and Visa accepted. Closed Tuesdays and in January. Dinner for two L180,000.*
Vaporetto Stop – *Giardini.*

Located in a tranquil neighborhood area of Venice, way off the beaten path, this is a fantastic culinary adventure. Owned by Gianfranco Gasperini, the menu offers many Venetian dishes, especially seafood like *antipasto ai crostacei* (crustacean antipasto) and *gamberetti con salsa al curry* (baby shrimps in a curry sauce). Their rice dishes are also exquisite. Try either the *risotto di pesce* (rice with fish) or *ai frutti di mare* (with mixed seafood). For seconds your mouth will water anticipating the grilled fish, the delicately fried shrimp or mixed seafood dish. Expensive but world renowned. Take a water taxi here and back since it is quite a hike.

20. DANIELI TERRACE, *Riva degli Schiavoni 4196, Venezia. Tel. 26-480. American Express, Mastercard and Visa accepted. Open 7 days a week. Dinner for two L160,000.*
Vaporetto Stop – *Riva Degli Schiavoni or Daniele (their private pier if coming by taxi).*

Located in the gigantic (by Venetian standards) Danieli hotel. To get to the restaurant you pass through the magnificent hotel courtyard and lobby. From the restaurant you can get a great view of the sunset over the Lagoon.

This is a first class restaurant all the way, from their table settings to the wait service. The menu features international favorites but the Venetian cuisine here is excellent. The house specialty, *fettucine alla buranella* (fettucine with sole and shrimp in a cream sauce) is out of this world. For dessert, many people order flaming crepes. I guess for the show. But, once again in Venice, be prepared to pay dearly for the food.

21. MALAMOCCO, *Campiello del Vin 4650, Venezia. Tel. 27-438. American Express, Mastercard and Visa accepted. Closed Thursdays and in January. Dinner for two L90,000.*
Vaporetto Stop – *Zaccaria.*

Located just off of the Riva Schiavoni, this pleasant little restaurant is set in a quiet, tiny piazza with its own enclosed seating area outside. Enjoy the weather, the local flavor, and the superb seafood and meat dishes. Try the *sogliola al burro* (butter fried sole), the *medaglioni di vitello con crema e funghi* (veal medallion in a cream and mushrooms sauce ... exquisite), or the *scampi all'indiana* (shrimp with a curry sauce).

22. AL MASCARON, *Calle Lunga Santa Maria Formosa 5225, Venezia. Tel. 522-5995. No credit cards accepted. Closed Sundays and mid-December to mid-January and 15 days in August. Dinner for two L70,000.*

Located near Santa Maria Formosa and SS Giovanni e Paolo, this is a rough and plain bar/*trattoria* with a truly rustic atmosphere that serves great food. You can get great boiled or roasted vegetables as an appetizer or a side dish. If you don't mind a wait, order the *pennette al pesce spada* (small noodles with a sauce of swordfish), then for seconds any of their fish on the grill.

23. DA REMIGIO, *Salizzada dei Greci, Venezia. Tel. 523-0089. Credit cards accepted. Closed Monday dinners and Tuesdays. Dinner for two L120,000.*
Vaporetto Stop - *Arsenale.*

A true family style Venetian *trattoria* that is frequented mainly by Venetians. The food is not specatular, but it is tasty and filling and the atmosphere is rustic and down to earth. As in most Venetian restaurants the specialty is fish. Their mixed seafood grill is scrumptuous as are their grilled fish. I would try Al Mascaron first, but if you have another chance at dinner give this place a try.

Santa Croce/San Polo
24. TAVERNA "CAPITAN UNCINO" (Captain Hook), *1501 Campo San Gaicomo del'Orio. Tel. 041/72-19-01. Credit cards accepted. Closed Wednesdays. Open until midnight. Dinner for two L65,000. Dinner for two L90,000.*
Vaporetto Stop - *Riva di Biasio.*

Exquisite food in a local restaurant on a beautiful piazza, completely off the beaten path. You'll want to buy the colored glass fishnet floats hanging from the ceiling, as well as the other implements of the sea hanging around. As long as there is no soccer game of importance being played, they don't turn the TV on that sits in one corner. Even so, watching a soccer game with frenzied Italians can add to the ambiance. The seafood is great. I like the *spaghetti alla vongole* (with clams) and their *frittura di scampi e calamari* (deep fried shrimp and squid).

25. TRATTORIA/PIZZERIA ANTICO CAPON, *Piazza Santa Margherita 3004, Tel. 041/528-525. Credit cards accepted. Dinner for two L50,000.*
Vaporetto Stop - *Ca' Rezzonico.*

Located right next to and below the great one star hotel of the same name, this is a perfect place to enjoy the life of a Venetian Piazza. Sit under the awnings or in the sun, but enjoy some good pizza or *crostine* (sandwiches). The *crostino con funghi, prosciutto, e mozzarella* (with mushrooms, ham, and mozzarella) is great, as is the *crostino al inferno* (literally translated it means hell's sandwich). It has tomatoes, mozzarella, hot salami, mushrooms, and *pepperoncini* and is quite tasty, if a little spicy).

26. ALLA MADONNA, *Calle dell Madonna 594, Venezia. Tel. 522-3824. American Express, Mastercard and Visa accepted. Closed Wednesdays and in January. Dinner for L100,000.*

Vaporetto Stop – *Rialto*.

Located near the Rialto bridge, you get a good mix of locals and tourists here for both lunch and dinner. It is a simple but superb *trattoria* where you can pick out your own fish from the refrigerated display of the catch bought at the morning market nearby. If you don't want any fish they have a variety of grilled and roast meats based on availability. I liked the *maialino arrosto* (baby roast pork). Besides the excellent food, the atmosphere is loud and boisterous which tends to make the meal fun and authentically Venetian. They also have excellent *risotto ai frutti di mare* (rice with seafood) and and a superb *fritto misto di mare* (mixed fried seafood).

27. DA FIORE, *Calle del Scaleter 2202, Venezia. Tel. 041/721-308. American Express, Mastercard and Visa accepted. Closed Sundays and Mondays, and during August and Christmas. Dinner for two L150,000.*

This is an elegant but at the same time simple old Venetian *trattoria* that offers great fresh seafood. You'll find some *cucina nuova* influence here (nouvelle cuisine, that is) since they have a different menu every day and try to make each meal a magical journey. One of their staples is *risotto di scampi e funghi porcini* (rice with shrimp an mushrooms) that serves two people. After you've digested this, try their *frittura mista al'Adriatico* (mixed seafood from the Adriatic). It's not meant for two, but after the rice dish, it should suffice.

28. DA IGNAZIO, *Calle Saoneri, San Polo 2749, Venezia. Tel. 523-4852. American Express, Mastercard and Visa accepted. Closed Saturdays and 2 weeks in March and July. Dinner for two L100,000.*

Vaporetto Stop – *San Toma*.

Located near San Polo and the Frari, this is a basic Venetian fish restaurant with great character. Along with the beautiful central garden and the charming rooms with wood beam ceilings, you'll get quality seafood at a reasonable price. They display some of the fish in the window to entice you to come in. Try the *zuppa di pesce* (fish soup) or *spaghetti alla vongole* (with clams) for starters. Then indulge yourself in the *fritto misto del'Adriatico* (mixed fried seafood from the Adriatic) for seconds.

29. PIZZERIA AE OCHE, *Calle del Tintor 1552A, Venezia. Tel. 041/524-1161. American Express, Mastercard and Visa accepted. Closed Mondays. Dinner for two L45,000*

Vaporetto Stop – *San Stae*.

Located near the Campo San Giacomo dell'Orio in Santa Croce, this is another inexpensive pizzeria frequented by many young Venetians who seem to appreciate the seemingly countless varieties of pizza, and I agree with them. My favorite was the *pizza mangia fuoco* (literally meaning 'eat fire,' a spicy pizza with salami and hot peppers). For other spicy pizzas, go for the *Diavolo* or *Inferno*.

As always the best seating is outside where you can watch the Venetians go by. The booths inside are also comfortable, but not quite so scenic. Besides pizza, you can get an *omelet a piacere* (made any way you want). Too bad they're not open for breakfast.

30. POSTE VECHIE, *Pescheria 1608, Venezia. Tel. 721-822. American Express, Mastercard and Visa accepted. Closed Tuesdays. Dinner for two L100,000.*

Vaporetto Stop – *Rialto.*

Huddled in the corner of the vast *pescheria* fish market (hence the address), and located near the old post office (hence the name). To get here you follow a private wooden bridge that leads to this old converted inn with its low ceilings and dark wooden beams. This restaurant is known for its perfectly prepared fish, especially the grilled variety, and its bountiful antipasto table. In the summer you can dine in the splendid garden that has vines and leaves hanging overhead. Try their *risotto di pesce* (rice with seafood for two people), then try their exquisite *sogliola ai ferri* (grilled sole).

31. TRATTORIA SAN TOMA, *Campo San Toma, San Polo 2864A, Venezia. Tel. 041/523-8819. American Express, Mastercard and Visa accepted. Closed Tuesdays. Dinner for two L60,000*

Vaporetto Stop – *San Toma.*

Pizza is their specialty, so try a great *pizza rustica* (with mozzarella, tomatoes, salami, and egg). Or indulge yourself in a staple of Venetian cuisine, *risotto di pesce* (rice with seafood, and kind of *paella*-like concoction). The outside seating is best on this out of the way little piazza. You can enjoy your meal and *vino* under the stars or inside in their rustic, wood paneled environment. With the absence of automobiles, the terrace is best.

32. PIZZERIA AL GIARDINETTO, *Rio della Frescada 2910. Tel 041/522-4100. Credit cards accepted. Dinner for two L65,000.*

Vaporetto Stop – *San Toma.*

Located just off a quaint little canal under a blanket of vines in their little garden (hence the name). If you have to sit inside, admire the framed painted dinner plates they have on display and enjoy a variety of pizzas that will make you ache for more. Try the *prosciutto and funghi* pizza (ham and mushrooms) and ask for extra mozzarella (*doppia mozzarella*) and you will be very satisfied.

33. LA ZUCCA, *Calle del Megio 1762, Venezia. Tel. 041/524-1570. Credit cards accepted. Closed Sundays. Dinner for two L50,000.*

Vaporetto Stop – *San Stae.*

Zucca means pumpkin, and you guessed it, their specialty pasta in the winter is pumpkin pasta. Surprisingly enough, it is rather delicious, especially with a cream sauce. They also have fresh fish, chicken, and salads but not too much red meats. So if you're a supreme carnivore, this healthy menu will discourage you. The owners and staff all have this radiant glow, which is what eating healthy food will do to you. Enjoy a small table outside or one of their inside tables with views of the canal. You won't regret it.

Dorsoduro
34. CIPRIANI, *Fondamenta San Giovanni 10, La Guidecca, Venezia. Tel. 707-744. American Express, Mastercard and Visa accepted. Dinner for two L150,000.*
Vaporetto Stop – *Zitelle.*
Super expensive and extremely elegant, this restaurant is part of the magnificent Cipriani Hotel. You can have a restful pool-side lunch with bountiful antipastos and your basic but tasty club sandwich. Dinner is served in the elegant dining room and the menu contains everything you could possibly desire. If you are late for dinner, have a drink on the terrace or spend some time in their intimate piano bar. Just going their for a drink is well worth the trip, and the price of the drink.
35. LOCANDO MONTIN, *Fondamenta Eremite 1147, Tel. 041/522-7151. Closed Tuesday evenings an Wednesdays. Dinner for two L65,000.*
Vaporetto Stop – *Ca' Rezzonico.*
A humongous local place, but the old woman who runs the joint leaves much to be desired. Even so, it has a good atmosphere and decent prices if you stick to pasta and less expensive meat dishes. The seating under the canopy is the best, but at times this place does get packed so you can't be choosy. Try the *tortellini in brodo* (tortellini in soup) for primo and *braciola di vitello ai ferri* (veal "arms" grilled) for seconds.
36. DO MORI, *Fondamenta del Ponte Piccolo 558, La Guidecca, Venezia. Tel. 522-5452. No credit cards accepted. Closed Sundays. Dinnfer tow L85,000*
Vaporetto Stop – *Guidecca.*
The plain ambiance inside doesn't reveal the excellence of the cooking. They have a superb *zuppa di pesce* (fish soup) or *zuppa di verdure* (vegetable soup) as well as a great *frittura di pesce* (mixed fried seafood). The best place to eat all this is not in the local hangout inside but on the water outside. If you want a peaceful respite from the tourist hordes, take the *vaporetto* over and enjoy.
37. PIZZERIA ALLE ZATTERE, *Zattere ai Gesuati 795, Venezia. Tel. 041/520-4224. Credit cards accepted. Closed Tuesdays. Dinner for two with only pizza L40,000.*
Vaporetto Stop – *Zattere.*
This a favorite local pizzeria near the Campo San Agnese, not only for its many varieties of pizza but also for its excellent view of Guidecca island from the pizzeria's tables on the Zattere's floating rafts. A perfect place to

eat when the sun sets. You can get almost any type pizza here, including *margherita* (with sauce and cheese), *verdure* (with grilled vegetables), and I would imagine they could put any topping on you ask for. Give it a try. They oblige me here by putting extra cheese, salami (they didn't have pepperoni), and a sprinkle of oregano on mine. There are also seafood salads and seafood pastas from which to choose.

38. SAN TROVASO, *Fondamenta Priuli 1016, Venezia. Tel. 520-3703. American Express, Mastercard and Visa accepted. Closed Mondays. Air conditioned. Dinner for two L65,000.*

Vaporetto Stop – *Accademia or Zattere.*

If they put you in the side room or upstairs with the locals, you feel as if you entered a heated discussion since everyone seems to be talking at once. Couple this with the clatter of pans and the occasional dropped glass or plate from the kitchen and this place has a great local feel to it. And the food is great, otherwise the locals wouldn't come, right? Try either the *Spaghetti Newburg* (with shrimp, tomatoes sauce an cream) or the *spaghetti alla carbonara* (with ham, cream and egg). For secondo they have plenty of reasonably priced meats and fish. Take your pick, they're all good.

39. AI GONDOLIERI, *Dorsoduro 366. Tel. 041/528-6396. Closed Tuesdays. Credit cards accepted. Dinner for two L120,000.*

Vaporetto Stop – *Santa Maria Della Salute.*

Here you can find any type of meat and a really great house wine, as well as a superb wine list. Start with one of their homemade patés if you're into that, or maybe a mushroom soup (*zuppa di porcini*), or possibly some exquisitely prepared vegetables. And for dessert try something from their extensive cake cart. Located near the Peggy Guggenheim Museum.

40. LA LINEA D'OMBRA, *Punta della Dogana-Zattere 19. Tel. 041/ 528-5259. Credit cards accepted. Closed Sunday nights and Wednesdays. Dinner for two L160,000.*

Vaporetto Stop – *Santa Maria Della Salute.*

Extremely romantic. This is a traditional Venetian restaurant, which means they serve lots of fish dishes, but they also try to be a little creative with their cooking. Inside is where all the locals and interesting people sit, but outside on their terrace you get great views of the Canal looking towards La Guidecca. A great place to watch the sun set. You'll find light cream sauces covering their salmon, and you'll find spaghetti mixed with shrimp and zucchini. But you'll also find a mixed fried seafood extravaganza if you can't make up your mind. Come for the food, stay for the view. Extremely romantic.

41. TRATTORIA ALTANELLA, *Guidecca calle delle Erbe 270. Tel. 041/522-7780. No credit cards accepted. Closed Mondays and Tuesdays as well 15 days in August. Dinner for two L 90,000.*

Vaporetto Stop – *Guidecca.*

Located just off the main waterfront walkway, Fondamenta del Ponte Longo, here you'll find a tranquil setting and wonderful food. Getting here is an adventure since you have to take the ferry and then walk to this local neighborhood spot. There's a peaceful outside seating, but the inside is as pretty and more fun with all the locals bantering about. This is a typical Venetian restaurant with seafood and pasta and both inter-mixed. You can't go wrong with any of their grilled fish or pasta mixed with seafood like *spaghetti alla vongole verace* (with clams in a spicy oil sauce).

Cannaregio
42. FIASCHETTERIA TOSCANA, *Calle Giovanni Cristomo 5719, Tel 041/528-5281. Closed Tuesdays and July. Dinner for two L100,000. Credit cards accepted.*
Vaporetto Stop – *Rialto.*

Located near the church of San Giovanni Cristomo this place has pleasant outside seating just across the street in a piazza. But it's only used during the high season. Inside seating is elegant and bright, with the best seats by the window so you can watch the parade pass by. They specialize in seafood here, and if you've been to the Rialto seafood and vegetable market you'll understand why many restaurants in Venice do. They also have international offerings, like sandwiches and such . My favorite though is their *spaghetti alla vongole verace* (with a spicy oil & clam sauce) and then their *fritto misto al mare* (mixed fried seafood). But if you're sick of seafood, try their filets of beef.

43. VINI DA GIGIO, *Cannaregio San Felice 3628/a. Tel. 041/528-5140. Closed Mondays and 15 days in January. All credit cards accepted. Dinner for two L100,000.*
Vaporetto Stop – *Ca'D'Oro.*

Located a little off of the tourist path, this is a simple local wine bar and *trattoria*. They offer more than 300 different wine choices with your meal of typical Venetain cuisine. Try their *antipasto di frutti di mare* (antipasto of sea food), then some *tagliatelle nere con sugo di scampi* (dark pasta with shrimp sauce) then a *fritto misto di mare and verdure* (mixed fried seafood and vegetables). If you're tired of seafood there is an extensive menu of grilled meats.

SEEING THE SIGHTS

Some people say that Venice is dead, that it is really only a museum of itself, but that's what makes it perfect for tourists. Everywhere you look you see something so beautiful, so awe inspiring that Venice at times seems like a living amusement park. I guess that is probably why this was the late Walt Disney's favorite city.

Medieval in layout and design, this city built on pilings in a marshy lagoon has everything you could imagine for a vacation, except, during high season, reasonable prices. You can find exquisite churches, beautiful synagogues, pristine *palazzi*, spacious *piazze*, magnificent museums, deserted islands only a *vaporetto* ride away, skilled crafts people blowing glass or making masks right in front of you, superb restaurants, relaxing hotels, and so much more.

The Quiet Side of Venice

During the summer months Venice is literally crammed with tourists, and at some point you'll need to take a break from them. If you're in need of a little solitude, basically anywhere away from Piazza San Marco, the Piazzale Roma, and the Rialto Bridge you can find a more serene experience.

And as you're walking (or taking the *vaporetto* then walking) to these isolated areas, don't be afraid of getting lost. You'll always find your way back, every place in Venice is perfectly safe virtually all day and all night long, and you'll also find some charming piazza or café that will seem as if it hasn't been touched by a single tourist. So strap on your walking shoes and get going.

Cannaregio – This section in the north of the main island is where the Jewish ghetto is located. Three of the synagogues in the main square of the tiny island are worth seeing. Here you'll find some of the tallest buildings in Venice, because once the Jewish population started to increase, the only place they could find more space was to build up. Compared to the rest of Venice the place looks a little run down, but the neighborhood is alive with local shoppers buying their supplies for the day, and beautiful side streets and canals away from the big crowds.

Castello – There's not much to see or do in this section of Venice, but they do have some of the best restaurants. In and around the **Arsenale** you'll find real Venetian neighborhoods, with grandmas chatting at each other from window sills above the canals, children playing in the narrow streets, and life peacefully devoid of the rumble of tourist crowds.

Dorsoduro – By simply walking from the Accademia to the Piazzale Roma in a meandering fashion you'll wander through some of the best neighborhoods that offer a taste of local color. You'll find artisan's shops, lovely houses, and of course narrow medieval streets and calm canals. And for food, wine, and a calming atmosphere, you can sit for hours on the *Zattere*. Literally meaning rafts, these open air restaurants are anchored off the eastern edge of the Dorsoduro and face the Isola della Guidecca. Try one of these restaurants for a real treat. It is an experience you'll cherish, especially if you stay long enough to see the sun go down. The glow is magnificent.

Isola della Guidecca – This a thriving neighborhood where everybody seems to know everyone else. If you're interested in gondolas, here you'll find the main gondola repair shop on the **Rio del Ponte Lungo**. This is a great place just to walk, watch, and listen.

BUY A MAP

*Venice is one big interconnecting alleyway with little to no address organization or structure. Sometimes street names are repeated in different districts of Venice and many times there are no street signs on the walls. Venice is confusing to get around and the only way I was able to before I figured out the city was to buy a map. I reccomend the **F.M.B. Piante di Citta** with its ugly orange/yellow cover for L8,000.*

---

1. ACCADEMIA

*Located in Campo della Carita, Dorsoduro. Tel 522–2247. Open Monday–Saturday 9am–7pm in the summer and 9am–4pm in winter. Sunday and holidays 9am–1pm. **Vaporetto** – Accademia.*

Five hundred years of unequaled Venetian art are on display at the **Accademia**. The collection began in 1750 when the Republic of St. Mark's decided to endow the city with an academy to feature local painters and sculptors (*Accademica di Pittori e Scultori*). The original academy occupied the current Port Authority building located by the gardens of the royal palace overlooking the harbor of St. Mark's.

During the French occupation of 1807, the collection was moved to the School and Church of the Carita (in Campo della Carita) as well as the former monastery of the Lateran Canons. Since then it has grown and expanded immensely and is a must-see for anyone visiting Venice who is interested in art.

There are far too many excellent paintings and sculptures to list them all, but these are the ones you should definitely discover on your own:
• *St. George* – Montegna (Room 4)
• *The Madonna degli Alberelli* (Madonna among the little trees) – Giovanni Bellini (Room 5)
• *The Tempest* – Giorgione (Room 5)
• *The Miracle of the Slave* – Jacopo Tintoretto (Room 10)
• *Banquet in the House of Levi* – Veronese (Room 10)
• *The Pieta* – Titian (Room 10) The last work of this famous artist before his death
• *Legend of St. Ursula* – Vittore Carpaccio (Room 21)
• *Detail of the Arrival of The Ambassadors* – Vittore Carpaccio (Room 21)
• *Presentation at the Temple* – Titian (Room 24)

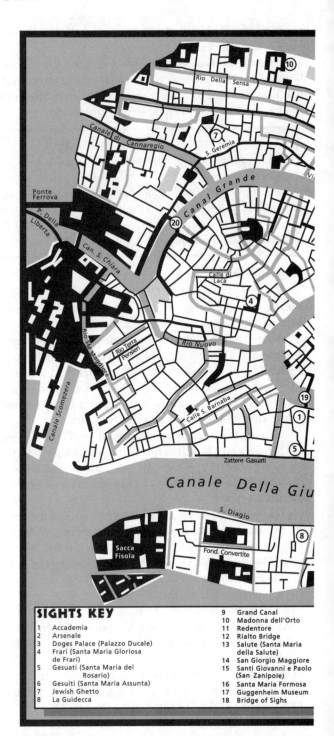

SIGHTS KEY

1   Accademia
2   Arsenale
3   Doges Palace (Palazzo Ducale)
4   Frari (Santa Maria Gloriosa de Frari)
5   Gesuati (Santa Maria del Rosario)
6   Gesuiti (Santa Maria Assunta)
7   Jewish Ghetto
8   La Guidecca

9   Grand Canal
10 Madonna dell'Orto
11 Redentore
12 Rialto Bridge
13 Salute (Santa Maria della Salute)
14 San Giorgio Maggiore
15 Santi Giovanni e Paolo (San Zanipole)
16 Santa Maria Formosa
17 Guggenheim Museum
18 Bridge of Sighs

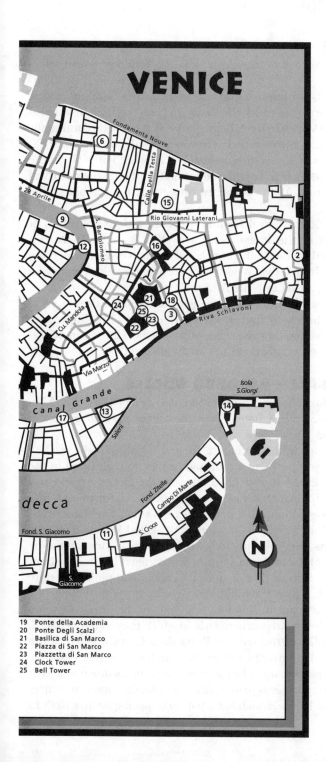

VENICE

19 Ponte della Academia
20 Ponte Degli Scalzi
21 Basilica di San Marco
22 Piazza di San Marco
23 Piazzetta di San Marco
24 Clock Tower
25 Bell Tower

2. ARSENALE

Open 9:00am–Noon and 3pm–7pm Monday–Saturday. **Vaporetto** – *Arsenale.*

The **Arsenale** is an imposing group of buildings, landing stages, workshops, and more from which the Venetian Navy was built. It was also the shipyard for the Venetian fleet. Begun in 1100, it has been continually enlarged over the years. Surrounded by towers and walls, the Arsenale has an imposing Renaissance entrance created by Giambello in 1460. In the front of the entrance is a terrace with statues that symbolize the victory of the Battle of Lepanto. At the sides are four lions, the symbol of the Venetian city state.

Inside you'll find the **Naval History Museum** with its collection of relics and trophies of the Italian Navy as well as Venice. There is a wonderfully detailed model of the last *Bucintoro*, the vessel in which the Doge of Venice celebrated the "Wedding of the Sea" between Venice and the sea by throwing a ring into the Adriatic.

This is a great place, not only since you have to trek through real Venetian neighborhoods to find it, but also because of its impressive collection of armaments, models, relics of modern craft used in World Wars I and II. Kids especially seem to like the displays.

3. DOGES PALACE – PALAZZO DUCALE

Located in St. Mark's Square (Piazzetta San Marc o), San Marco. Tel. 522–4951. Open Monday–Sunday 8:30am–7pm in the summer and 8:30am–2pm in the winter. **Vaporetto** – *San Marco.*

Another must-see while in Venice. To view it all will take the better part of a day if you perform a thorough inspection. Finished in the 1400s after being started in the 9th century by the Doges Angelo and Giustiniano Partecipazio, this was the seat of the government, the residence of the **Doge**, Venice's supreme head of state. The flamboyant Gothic style was mainly created by a family of skilled Venetian marble craftsmen, the **Bons**. It is still a joy to behold despite the devastation by fire in 1577 of one of the building's wings. Since then it has been rebuilt in its original form. It has a double tier of arcading and pink and white patterned walls which gives the building a delicate open air feeling.

Everywhere you roam in this building you will be amazed by the combination of styles and the ornate style in which they were prepared. As you enter you will pass through the **Porta della Carta**, created by the Bon family, with its flamboyant Gothic style. You'll see the statue of *Doge Frascari kneeling before the winged lion* and the statue of a woman seated at the tallest spire that represents Justice. After passing through you'll enter the courtyard of the Palace, which has a pair of imposing bronze wells in the middle. The one closer to the Poscari Portal is by Alfonso Alberberghetti (from 1559) and the other is by Niccolo del Conti in 1556. Stand here a moment and soak in the typically blended Venetian style of architecture, where they combine Gothic with Renaissance. Also enjoy the countless archways, the exquisite sculptures, and inspiring staircases.

One such staircase is *The Staircase of the Giants*, so named because of the two colossal statues of Mars and Neptune on either side of the landing made by Sansovino and his pupils. The new Doges were officially crowned on the landing at the top of the stairs.

You will also find some of the most beautiful plaster relief ceilings, marble relief fireplaces, paintings, sculptures, tapestries, medieval weapons rooms and ancient dungeons anywhere in Europe.

4. FRARI - SANTA MARIA GLORIOSA DE FRARI

Campo dei Frari, San Polo. Tel. 522-2637. Open Monday–Saturday 9:30am–Noon and 2:30pm–6pm. Sun open 2:30pm–6pm. **Vaporetto – San Toma.**

This Romanesque-Gothic style Franciscan church contains tombs of many famous Venetian figures. The church was begun by Franciscan monks in 1250 from a design by Nicola Pisano and was later made a little more ornate by Scipione Bon, a member of the famous Venetian family of sculptors in 1338. It was finally finished in 1443. I guess the monks didn't have much money, so they took their time completing it.

Today the unadorned facade is not much to look at but is beautiful in its simplicity. It is divided into three sections by pilaster strips surmounted by pinnacles. Over the central portal are statues attributed to Alessandro Vittorio in 1581. There is a Romanesque bell tower that is the second largest in Venice after that of St. Mark's.

The interior is as simple and as equally beautiful as the exterior. It is laid out in a Latin cross with single aisles set off by twelve huge columns. The main draw for this simple church is the tomb of the grand master Titian, who died of plague in 1576. There are two works by Titian featured inside, *Assumption of the Virgin* done in 1518 hanging over the main altar, and *Pesaro Altarpiece* done in 1526, depicting the Virgin with members of the Pesaro family over the second altar. Another work to note is the statue of *St. John the Baptist* by Donatello in the altar of the first chapel.

5. GESUATI - SANTA MARIA DEL ROSARIO

Fondamenta delle Zattere, Dorsoduro. **Vaporetto** – *Accademia or Zattere.*

This church was erected between 1726 and 1743 for the Dominican friars, and was built over a 14th century monastery called "Monastery for the poor Gesuati." *Gesuati* are Jesuits, by the way. The exterior is simple and tasteful in the basic Classical style. This elliptical shaped church has no aisle, making it seem larger than it really is, and contains superb frescoes on the ceiling of the dome by GB Tiepolo.

The first altar contains the *Virgin in Glory with Three Saints,* a masterpiece done in 1747 by Tiepolo. The second altar has a work by GB Piazzetta, *St. Dominic,* done in 1739. The third altar has the *Crucifixion* created by Tintoretto in 1741.

6. GESUITI - SANTA MARIA ASSUNTA

Campo dei Gesuiti, Cannaregio. Vaporetto - Fondamenta Nuova.

This grandiose church was given to the Jesuits (Gesuiti) in 1656, but it was built in the 12th century. It was remodeled between 1715 and 1730 with a Baroque facade designed by Fattoretto. It contains the statues of the 12 Apostles by Penso, the Groppellio brothers, and Baratta.

This is a single-aisled church laid out in a Latin Cross Style and is decorated with a variety of colored marble inlays. The main draw to this church are two outstanding paintings: the *Assumption of the Virgin* by Jacopo Tintoretto and the *Martyrdom of St. Lawrence* by Titian.

7. JEWISH GHETTO

Near the train station, Cannaregio. Guided tours of the synagogues available every hour on the hour from 10am–4pm, and Sunday 10am–Noon. Tours not available Saturday and holidays. Vaporetto - San Marcuola.

This was the first Jewish Ghetto in Europe. The word itself, ghetto, originated in Venice. The location was established by Ducal decree in 1516 and remained an enforced enclave for the Jews in Venice until 1797, with Napoleon's victory over the Republic. The Jews were moved here originally from the section of the city known as La Guidecca (see below) so the government could keep an eye on them.

Here you'll find five synagogues, three of which are open to the public: **Sinagoga Grande Tedesca**, **Sinagoga Spagnole**, and **Levantina**. The small museum, **Museo Ebraica** *(Tel. 71-53-59) in the Campo del Nuovo Ghetto,* the main square in the ghetto, contains information about the five centuries of Jewish presence in Venice.

8. LA GUIDECCA

Vaporetto - Guidecca.

This populous suburb was once the neighborhood set aside for the Jews of Venice prior to their move to the Jewish Ghetto in 1516 – hence its name, which roughly means *The Jewish Area.* A brief excursion here is a wonderful respite from the hectic pace of tourist Venice. You'll find real Venetian neighborhoods, top-of-the-line hotels along the **Fondamenta**

Zitelle, abandoned factories, and more. There are not many sights to see, but you can take a relaxing stroll without running into hardly any tourists.

9. GRAND CANAL

The **Grand Canal** is shaped like a large upside down "S" bisecting the city. It is almost 2 1/2 miles long, 15 feet deep, and ranges anywhere from 100 to 150 feet across. Usually calm and serene, the canal has become more and more menacing and rough since the introduction of huge ocean liners docking close by.

Lining this wonderful waterway are tremendous old buildings, palaces, and homes dating from every time period and epitomizing every architectural style. You'll also see small canals thrusting off into the darkness, and beautiful gateways and entrances blackened by and beginning to be covered by the water. The best way to see the canal is to take the *vaporetto* around a few times and simply enjoy the view.

10. MADONNA DELL'ORTO

Campo Madonna dell'Orto, Cannaregio. Open 9am–5pm. **Vaporetto** *– Madonna dell'Orto.*

This is a simple little church that contains the remains of **Jacopo Robusti**, known as **Tintoretto**, who was buried here in 1594. There are also some exquisite works by the grand master himself, **Titian**. These paintings are in the choir: *Last Judgment, Adoration of the Golden Calf, Moses Receiving the Tablets of the Law.* The tomb of Tintoretto is marked by a simple stone plaque and is just to the right of the choir.

11. REDENTORE

Campo Redentore. Open 9am–5pm. **Vaporetto** *– Redentore.*

Built between 1577 and 1592 by Andrea Palladio and Antonio Da Ponte, as part of a thanksgiving for the end of another of the many plague epidemics that struck Venice. Across Europe more than a third of the population died because of the plagues.

A huge staircase leads up to the facade and the entrance to the church. Inside you'll find the same simple harmony as the outside as well as a magnificent Baroque altar adorned with bronzes by Campagna. In the sacristy you'll find *Virgin and Child* by Alvise Vivarini, *Baptism of Christ* by Veronese, *Virgin and Child with Saints* by Palma the Younger, and a variety of works by Bassaro.

12. RIALTO BRIDGE

One of the best places to view the traffic along the **Grand Canal** and all its charm. This is the oldest of the three bridges spanning the canal and was originally made of wood. It collapsed in 1440 and was rebuilt in wood but still remained rather unstable, so in the 16th century the Doges decided to build a more stable bridge. Michelangelo himself submitted a design for the bridge but a local boy, Antonio Da Ponte, was awarded the contract to design and build the bridge. The bridge was finished in 1592. The Rialto spans 90 feet and is 24 feet high. There are 24 shops lining the bridge separated by a double arcade from which you can walk out onto the terraces and get those superb views for which it is richly famous.

Every morning, except Sunday on the San Polo side of the Rialto, the **Fish** and **Vegetable market** is held. A sight that should not be missed while in Venice, especially the **Pescheria** (Fish Market).

13. SALUTE - SANTA MARIA DELLA SALUTE

Campo delle Salute. Open 9am–5pm. **Vaporetto** *– Salute.*

One of the sights you'll see from St. Mark's square across the canal is this truly magnificent church. Adorned with many statues sitting atop simple flying buttresses, this octagonal church is topped with a large dome, and a smaller one directly above it. It was erected as thanksgiving for the cessation of a plague that struck Venice in 1630. During its construction it had a variety of mishaps like the foundation sinking, the walls being unable to support the dome, and other simple engineering problems like that.

Inside are six chapels all ornately adorned. On the main altar you'll find a sculpture by Giusto Le Court that represents *The Plague Fleeing The Virgin*. The church is replete with Titian's work, including *The Pentecost* to the left of the third altar, *Death of Abel* on the sacristy ceiling, *Sacrifice of Abraham* in the sacristy, *David and Goliath* on the sacristy ceiling, and an early work *St. Mark and The Other Saints* over the altar in the sacristy.

14. SAN GIORGIO MAGGIORE

Isola San Giorgio Maggiore. Open 9am–12:30pm and 2:30pm–6:30pm. **Vaporetto** *– San Giorgio.*

On an island just off the tip of La Guidecca, this magnificent church by Palladio can be seen and admired from St. Mark's Square, but you should go out and visit because the view of the lagoon and the city from its bell tower are priceless and unforgettable.

The church's white facade makes it stand out wonderfully from the ochre and brown colored monastery buildings surrounding it. It was finished in 1610 by Scamozzi from the plans of the master Palladio. The facade is distinctly his, with its three sections divided by four Corinthian columns. In two niches between the columns are statues of *Sts. George* and *Stephen,* and on either side are busts of *Doges Tribuno Mommo* and *P Zini* all by Giulio Moro. The bell tower we mentioned earlier was erected by

Benedetto Buratti from Bologna (a city known at the time for its many towers) in 1791 to replace an older one that collapsed in 1773. The interior is simple yet majestic. It has a single aisle and is shaped like an inverted Latin cross. Three works to admire are: *Crucifix* by Michelozzo in the second altar on the right, and *Last Supper* and *Shower of Mana* by Tintoretto at the main altar.

15. SANTI GIOVANNI E PAOLO - SAN ZANIPOLO
Campo Santi Giovanni e Paolo, Castello. Open 9am-5pm. Vaporetto - Rialto or Fondamenta Nuova.

Started by the Dominican monks in 1246, **Santi Giovanni e Paolo** was not finished until 1430, probably due to lack of funds just like their Franciscan counterparts when they were building Santa Maria Gloriosa dei Frari. Like that church, it contains the tombs of many well-known Venetian citizens. The church's style is known as Venetian Gothic with its combination of Gothic and Renaissance styles. Unfortunately, the facade was never finished, but it is still beautiful in its simplicity.

The inside is filled with monuments, sculptures, and paintings depicting a large number of Doges and their families. Don't miss the magnificent 15th century Gothic window by Bartolomeo Vivarini.

16. SANTA MARIA FORMOSA
Campo Santa Maria Formosa, Castello. Open 9am-5pm. Vaporetto - Rialto or San Zaccaria.

This church was starting to be rebuilt in 1492 (when Columbus sailed the ocean blue) and has two 16th century facades and a 17th century belfry. It is in the shape of Latin cross and has no aisles. The walls are covered with wonderful works by such artists as Vivarini and Palma the Elder. A simple, small church that sits in a part of Venice that most tourists never find. The piazza is filled with the sights and sounds of true modern day Venetian life.

17. GUGGENHEIM MUSEUM
Palazzo Venier dei Leoni, Dorsoduro 701, Calle Cristoforo. Tel. 520-6288. Open March-October, Wednesday-Monday 11am-6pm and Saturday 11am-9pm. Closed Tuesday Admission L10,000. Vaporetto - Accademia.

This is a magnificent 20th century art collection developed by the intriguing American heiress and art aficionado Peggy Guggenheim. It is exhibited in Ms. Guggenheims old home, where she lived until her death in 1979. Here you'll find all the 20th century movements including cubism, surrealism, futurism, expressionism, and abstract art. There are works by Dali, Chagall, Klee, Moore, Picasso, Pollock and many others.

18. THE BRIDGE OF SIGHS

From the canal side of Ponte della Paglia you can look directly at this covered bridge connecting the Doges Palace and Prigione Nuovo (New Prison). It was built in the 17th century to transport convicts from the palace to the prison to face their punishment. The name presumably derives from the sighs of prisoners as they crossed the bridge.

19. PONTE DELLA ACCADEMIA

The least attractive and most modern bridge in Venice, it is one of three that traverses the Grand Canal. It is a metal and wood construction that seems to fit, but not quite, with the fairy tale images all around it. It's as if a pioneer style bridge was placed in Snow White's scenes at Disneyland.

Nothing magnificent to see but convenient to use to go from San Marco to the Accademia.

20. PONTE DEGLI SCALZI

Also known as the **station bridge** since it is right near the station, this is the first bridge you'll cross if you're walking from the station to St. Mark's. But don't walk - take the *vaporetto*. A simple, single span bridge made of white Istrian stone, it was erected in 1934 to replace a metal bridge built in 1858. The bridge is approximately 130 feet long and 23 feet above water level.

21. BASILICA DI SAN MARCO

Piazza San Marco. Open 9:30am–5:30pm. Vaporetto - San Marco.

The church is so large and magnificent that a day's adventure is normal for an art and architecture lover.

The building was built to house the remains of the republic's patron saint, St. Mark, as well as to glorify the strength of Venice's sea power. The structure was begun in 829, a year after St. Mark's remains were brought back from Egypt. By 832 the church had all its main structures and by 883 it was fully decorated. Its beauty was slightly marred in 976 from a fire that was set in the Doges Palace. Then in 1000 the church was demolished because it was not grand enough. The church we know and love today was started in 1063 and was originally a Byzantine plan. It was finished in 1073 and then for centuries it was adorned with superb mosaics, precious marbles, and war spoils brought back by merchants, travelers, and soldiers, so that today the church is a mix of Byzantine, Gothic, Islamic and Renaissance materials.

It is magnificent inside and out. A description of all the art and architecture in this incredible place would fill another book, so you might want to hire a local tour guide or purchase one of the local guide books inside the church specifically for the Basilica.

22. PIAZZA SAN MARCO

Vaporetto – San Marco.

When the Basilica of St. Mark and the Doge's Place were being erected, the grassy field in front of them was filled in and paved (around 1172-1178). On either side of the pavement, elegant houses were built with arcades running the length of them. Many were taken over by government magistrates, called *Procurati*, which gives these buildings their name today, *Procuratie*. In 1264 the square was repaved with bricks in a herringbone pattern. Then in 1723 it was paved again with gray trachyte and white marble.

The square is 569 feet long, 266 feet at the side of St. Mark's, and 185 feet long at the side facing St. Mark's. The piazza is alive with orchestra music being played by competing cafés and is wonderful place to stroll and people watch. You won't find many Venetians here, unless it's the off-season.

23. PIAZZETTA DI SAN MARCO

Vaporetto – San Marco.

Directly in front of the Doges Palace, this little piazza blends into the larger Piazza San Marco and is sometimes lumped together with it. Originally it was a market place for food stuffs, but in 1536 the Doge mandated that it remain clear for public executions. The two columns at the dock (one with the *Lion of St. Mark* atop and the other with a statue of *St. Theodore*) were brought back from the Orient in 1125 and erected in 1172. Here you'll find some peaceful but expensive outside cafés.

24. CLOCK TOWER

*Piazza San Marco. Tel. 523-1879. Admission L5,000. **Vaporetto** – San Marco.*

Facing St. Mark's, the **Clock Tower** is directly on your left. No, it's not the tall brick structure in the middle of the piazza; that's the Bell Tower). It was built between 1496 and 1499, and the wings were added from 1550-1506. Above the tower is an open terrace upon which stands a bell with two male figures on either side that hammer the bell to indicate the time. These figures have been performing their faithful service for over 500 years and as a result have taken on a dark weather-beaten appearance. Because of this, they are called the Moors.

Beneath the terrace that houses these figures is the symbol of Venice, a golden winged lion. Below the lion is a niche that contains a statue of the Virgin and Child that has been attributed to Alessandro Leopardi sometime in the early 1500s. The clock, just below this, in addition to just telling the time, also indicates the changing of the seasons, the movements of the sun, as well as the phases of the moon.

25. THE BELL TOWER

Piazza San Marco. Tel. 522-4064. Open 9:30am–10pm. Admission L6,000. **Vaporetto** *– San Marco.*

Built over old Roman fortifications, the **Bell Tower** has been added to off and on since 888. It withstood floods and earthquakes, but it finally gave in to less than perfect craftsmanship. On July 14, 1902, it collapsed but was reconstructed and re-opened to the public in 1912. It is the most convenient place to get a birds-eye view of the city and the lagoon. (The next best place is the bell tower of the church of San Giorgio Maggiore). An elevator can take you to the top where there are five bells that toll on special occasions.

In the past a cage used to jut from the wall on the piazza side that would occasionally contain criminals to be exposed to the elements as punishment. This practise was abolished in the 16th century. Another tradition was to stretch a rope between the tower and the Doges Palace and have an acrobat walk the span.

NIGHTLIFE & ENTERTAINMENT

THE FIDDLER'S ELBOW, *3847 Cannaregio (near Ca' d'Oro Vaporetto stop). Tel. 041/523-9930. Open from 5:00pm - 1:30am. Closed Wednesday but not in the summer.*

Come here for a taste of old Ireland. You'll find Harp, Guiness, and Kilkenny on tap (Pint L7,000 half pint L4,000), as well as almost any other drink you can imagine. The Irish lads and lassies behind the bar will serve you up proper, so enjoy a pint or two for the homeland (well, their homeland anyway). The meeting place for Anglophiles in Venice.

THE GREEN PUB, *Campo San Margherita 3053A, Tel. 041/520-1993. Pints inside: Harp L6,500; Guiness and Kilkenny L7,000. Pints outside: Harp L7,500; Guiness, Kilkenny L8,000.*

Great outside seating on the perfect piazza in Venice, but it's usually packed so get here early and try to stay late. They also have small snacks like sandwiches and *tramezzini*.

EL SOUK PUB, *Accademia 1056A, Tel. 041/520-0371. Pint of Tennents L5,000.*

A real nightclub/harem atmosphere, with a small dance floor to work off some of the drinks. Located right near the Accademia (take the Accademia's vaporetto stop). To get here, start at the vaporetto stop and go down the road to your right. Take your first right and El Souk will be on your right hand side after a few paces. It's not really a pub. It's more of a disco, so if you want a pint and a conversation, go to one of the two above.

SPORTS & RECREATION

In terms of sporting activities, there really is not much to do in Venice proper except jog along the Grand Canal in the early mornings when the crowds aren't around. For recreation you'll have to go to the island of **Lido**, where you'll find golf, bicycling, horseback riding, tennis and of course, swimming. But I am averse to mentioning Lido, since It really doesn't seem to it into the whole atmosphere of Venice. Why? It was built only recently so the architecture has nothing in common with the beauty of Venice, and most importantly on Lido they allow cars and buses, so that tranquil feeling you get while in Venice leaves instantly when you arrive on Lido. But if you're in need of some sporting fun, go to it.

To get to Lido, take vaporetto no. 6 or no. 11.

Bicycling

Having a leisurely bicycle ride on Sundays is a favorite pastime of the people on Lido. To rent a bike, tandem, or tricycle, *contact Giorgio Barbieri at Via Zara 5, Lido. No phone number.*

Golfing
• **Circolo Golf Venezia**, *Via del Forte, 30011 Alberoni. Tel. 041/731-1333/ 731-015. Fax 041/731-339.* Located 10 km from Venice, this is an 18 hole, par 72, 6,199 meters long course. It's open year round except on Mondays. They have a driving range, pro shop, bar and restaurant.
• **Ca' Amata Golf Club**, *Via Postioma di Salvarosa 44, 31033 Castelfranco Veneto. Tel. 0432/721-833. Fax 0432/721-842.* Located 30 km from both Venice and Padua, this is a nine hole, par 36 course that is 3,311 meters long. Open from February to December and closed Mondays. This place has a driving range, pro shop, putting green, restaurant and swimming pool.
• **Ca' Della Nave Golf Club**, *Piazza della Vittoria 14, 30030 Martellago. Tel. 041/540-1555. Fax 041/540-1926.* Located 12km from Venice on the mainland, this is an 18 hole par 72 course that is a challenging 6,380 meters long. It is open year round except on Tuesdays. They have a putting green, pro shop, tennis courts, restaurant and bar.

Horseback Riding

If you want to go riding, you'll have to pay a kings ransom to rent a horse from the **Venice Riding Club** *at Ca'Bianca on the Lido, Tel. 765-162.*

They have an indoor riding school and paddock with fixed and competitive fences and a variety of competition horses for hire.

Swimming
Your choices are the pools at the **Excelsior Hotel** and the **Hotel des Bains** where you can purchase very expensive daily or seasonal tickets; and the public beaches are at **San Nicolo** and **Alberoni** at both the north and the south ends of **Lido**. The rest of the beaches are private and attached to hotels for the use of their guests.

Tennis
There are tennis courts for rent at the **Lido Tennis Club** *(Via San Gallo 16, Tel. 760-954)*, and from the **Tennis Union** *(Via Fausta, Tel. 968-134)*. Court time is expensive.

SHOPPING
Books & Newspapers in English
Most newsstands in Venice will carry a variety of different international newspapers and magazines. The most current newspaper will most probably be *The International Herald Tribune*, which is a joint venture between The Washington Post and The New York Times and is printed all over Europe. If you can't seem to find a paper, simply go into one of the better hotels and they should have some available for sale. Or if they don't have any, they can surely tell you where to find one.

As for books, listed below are a few bookstores that have English language titles available.

Libreria Pio X, *Studium Veneziano, Calle di Canonica 337, San Marco. Tel 522-2382. Credit cards accepted.*

A religious as well as a general style bookstore near the Ponte della Canonica that also is well stocked with English language books. In conjunction they have many books about Venetian history, architecture, and literature so if you want to bone up on your knowledge of Venice, this bookstore can be of assistance. Everything is laid out in an organized fashion so browsing is easy. I have to mention this because sometimes, here in Italy, some things are not as organized as we expect.

Libreria Internazionale San Giorgio, *Calle Large XXII Marzo 2087, San Marco. Tel. 38-451. Credit cards accepted.*

There is an excellent selection of travel and information books about Venice and other parts of Italy. You'll also find a selection on art, architecture, and history, but only a small section of paperback literature. There also some interesting posters and postcards.

Glass Products

Venice has been making glass products for more than 1,000 years. The glass blowing furnaces were moved in 1292, for fire safety reasons, to the five islands of **Murano** (see *Day Trips & Excursions* below) which are five minutes north of Venice by *vaporetto*. To make sure you're not getting a reproduction or something of inferior quality, always check to see if the letters **VM** are stamped on the bottom of the glasswork. The VM *(Vetro Murano)* is the mark for quality Venetian glass.

All over Venice you'll find these silly glass animals and figurines and you can bet they are not of the highest quality. Yes, they're cute, and I bet your kids go ga-ga over them, but you can find some great glass on Murano. Two of the five major manufacturers on Murano have shops in Venice (**Salviati** and **Venini**) but the rest sell only from the island of Murano. Here's the place to get some fine glass pieces at great prices.

Lace Products

The small island of **Burano** (see *Day Trips & Excursions* below) has been producing intricate hand-made lace work for centuries. Mary Tudor got her wedding gown made on the island. Since that time the style has been widely copied and some say the French make a better lace now, but an excursion to the island to see how the stuff is made is a fun trip.

Masks

Venice is home to one of the world's best **carnivals** (**Carnevale** in Italian), designed for everyone to sow their wild oats before the fasting begins for Lent. The merriment generally begins in February or March and lasts for several weeks before it culminates on **Shrove Tuesday** (**Mardi Gras**), the day before Lent begins on Ash Wednesday. Also, in its history Venetians sometimes wore masks during daily life, allowing men to court and cavort with impunity and women to be able to walk around unchaperoned and meet their secret lovers undetected. Since masks are part of their history, which continues today in the **Carnevale**, Venetians have become quite adept at preparing masks of all kinds.

There are all sorts of traditional masks, many taken from the 16th century *Commedia Dell'Arte*, and any of these masks would make for a great wall ornament or Halloween costume. The craftsmen carve wooden molds from which they make plaster casts – basically negative images of the mask – which are then layered with papiermache to shape the masks. There are plenty of stores where you can watch the mask makers at work.

Paper Products

Venice has been popular for their decorative paper goods for centuries, specifically the marbelling effect they produce for the cover of books, desk blotters, pencils, pens, and many other items. When wandering around the back streets of Venice you will surely stumble upon a small shop making and selling their own versions of marbelized paper products.

Shoes

Now why would shoes be popular in a city that does not allow cars? Because the Venetians have to walk everywhere. Venetians consume the most shoes per capita than anywhere else in the world. Even though Florence, Rome, and Milan all have great shoes, most of the prices in Venice are slightly less expensive.

Markets

The **Erberia** (Vegetable Market) and the **Pescheria** (Fish Market). *Vegetable market is open Monday through Saturday 8:00am to 1:00pm; the fish market is open Tuesday through Saturday 8:00am through 1:00pm.*

The natives and the restaurants of Venice find their daily produce, cheese, fish, meats, and breads in the large Campo and the adjoining streets near the Church of San Giacomo di Rialto and at the base of the Rialto bridge. It is a bustling, crowded, fun adventure just to go there to buy something. By actually going to market with the Venetians you feel almost a part of them since you're sharing one of their truly unique daily experiences.

Look for the *Pescheria* on your map, since that is where most of the fun is located. You'll see a six foot swordfish sliced to perfection for restaurants and home buyers, as well as witnessing a young Venetian peel shrimp faster than you could eat them. Also most stands sell snails. Notice how the persistent buggers attach themselves to the sides of the ladle when the proprietor scoops them out to be weighed. They are only delaying the inevitable transformation into a delectable butter and garlic antipasto. But you have to admire their persistence. A fun place.

Campo San Barnaba, Dorsoduro. *Open Monday and Tuesday, and Thursday through Saturday 9:00am to 1:00pm and 3:30pm to 7:30pm, and Wednesday 9:00am to 1:00pm.*

Located right of the Piazza Santa Margherita, this is a quaint open air floating market where you can mainly buy fresh vegetables.

Campo San Margherita, Dorsoduro. *Open Monday, Tuesday, and Thursday through Saturday from 9:00am to 1:00pm and 3:30pm to 7:30pm.*

A few stalls inter-dispersed around the piazza sell fruits, vegetables, and fish. Not nearly as grand as the Rialto market but one to enjoy nonetheless. This square has to be the best example of true Venetian life there is. Besides the market, come for the mothers playing with their children, the small local shops, and relaxing seating on some of the benches in the square. Don't miss Campo San Margherita.

Calle Regina 2328A. A local pastry factory. Walk by and savor the tantalizing smells that emanate from their open door. You can't go in, but you can watch from the doorway as they prepare the pastries for the shops on the island. But the smell is what brings me back here time after time.

Picnic Supplies
The best place to get picnic supplies is at the **Rialto bridge market** at the base of the bridge on the San Polo section side, which is held every morning except Sundays and Mondays (see *Markets* just above).

PRACTICAL INFORMATION
Bank Hours & Changing Money
Banks in Venice are open Monday through Friday from 8:30am to 1:30pm. Very few re-open in the afternoon, and the few that do only open from 2:45pm to 3:30pm. *Cambi* (money exchanges) follow store hours, which are generally 9:00am to 12:30pm and 4:00pm to 7:30pm Monday through Saturday.

If you're really desperate, the **American Express** office stays open in the summer months from 8:00am to 8:00pm. *They are located at Salizzada San Moise 1471, San Marco, Tel. 520-0844.*

Business Hours
Store hours are generally 9:00am to 12:30pm and 4:00pm to 7:30pm Monday through Saturday. But as is the Italian way, there are many exceptions to the rule. Some stores stay open a half an hour later, some close a half and hour earlier, so don't depend on the stores being open when you want them to be.

Food stores generally close on Wednesday afternoons. Also stores in the main tourist areas generally stay open during the traditional siesta hours and most stores do not close for August as they do almost everyhwere else in Italy. The Venetians are willing to make the necessary sacrifices to get as much of our money as they possibly can.

Consulates
• **United Kingdom**, *Dorsoduro 1051, near the Accademia, Tel. 522-72-07*
• **United States**, *Largo Donegani 1, Milan, Tel. 01/652-841*
• **Canada**, *Via Vito Pisani 19, Milan, Tel. 01/669-74-51. For emergencies 01/66-98-06-00*
• **Australia**, *Via Borgogna 2 , Milan, Tel. 01/76-01-33-30*
Note that for US, Canadian, and Australian citizens, the closest consulate is in Milan. Some of you from other countries may need to contact your embassy in Rome (see our *Rome* chapter, *Practical Information* section).

Mailing Services
The **main post office** is located *at Salizada del Fontegho dei Tedeschi 5554, near the Rialto. Tel. 528-6212 and 520-4143.* Open Monday–Saturady 8:15am–6:45pm. Stamps are sold at *tabacchi* all over town. Venice's **postal code** is *30124.*

Laundry Services
• **Lavaget**, *Cannareggio 1269, Tel. 71-59-76, on the Fondamenta Pescaria.* Located near the station. L15,000 for three kilos of clothes, soap and dry included. Open Monday–Friday 8:30am–12:30pm and 3:00pm–7:00pm. Drop off clothes and pick up later in the day.

Local Festivals & Holidays
• **January 1**, *Primo dell'Anno* (New Years Day)
• **April 25**, *Festa Del Liberazione* (Liberation Day)
• **February**, the two weeks before Lent is **Carnevale**, a time of riotous celebration where costumes are worn both day and night, and grand balls and celebrations occur frequently.
• **March**, First Sunday after Ascension day; anybody piloting an oar powered craft can take part in *La Vogalonga*, the "long row." Participants set off at 9:30am from the Bacino di San Marco and follow a marathon-like course around Venice and its islands. Rowers usually return between 11:00am and 3:00pm
• **May 1**, *Festa del Lavoro* (Labor Day)
• **August 15**, *Ferragosto* (Assumption Day)
• **September**, First Sunday in September is the *Regata Storica*, the historic regatta. The races are preceded by a magnificent procession on the Grand Canal of period boats manned by Venetians in historic costumes. A spectacle to behold. On par with the Palio in Siena.
• **November 1**, *Ognissanti* (All Saints Day)
• **November 21**, *Festa della Madonna della Salute*, which originated as a time of thanks for being spared from the Plague which at one point had decimated over 3/5's of Venice's population. Celebrated on two floating bridges built across the Grand Canal from the Giglio to the Dogana.
• **December 8**, *Festa dell Madonna Immacolata* (Immaulate Conception)
• **December 25**, *Natale* (Christmas)
• **December 26**, *Santo Stefano* (Saint Stephen's Day)

Most stores in Venice take a one or two month vacation in or around Christmas time.

Tourist Information & Maps

• **Ente Provinciale per il Turismo** (three different locations): *Piazza San Marco 71C, Tel. 522-6356; Piazzale Roma, Tel. 522-7402; Sant Lucia Train Station, Tel. 715-016.* They also have an excellent hotel finders service here that comes in real handy if you don't have reservations when you arrive.

• **American Express Travel Service**, *San Marco 1471, Tel. 520-0844.* You don't have to be a card member to get assistance here. A great private travel service.

Tour Operators

• **American Express Travel Service**, *San Marco 1471, Tel. 520-0844.* Same as above. Ask for details on various Venice and area tours, since they change periodically.

• **CIT**, *San Marco 4850, Tel. 528-5480*

• **Wagons-Lit/Cook Travel**, *San Marco 289, Piazzett Leoncini, Tel. 522-3405*

DAY TRIPS & EXCURSIONS

The first three islands mentioned here can all be seen in a three to four hour period. To get to any of them, buy a round-trip ticket for L7,500 *at vaporetto booth #12 at the Fondamente Nuova.* After you have finished your lunch or dinner at one of the fine restaurants on **Torcello** (your last stop) simply stamp your ticket in the yellow machine before boarding the *vaporetto* and you'll be on your way back to Venice.

If you start in the morning around 9:00am and go first to **Murano**, then **Burano**, and then **Torcello**, you will have worked up a powerful hunger. The same goes if you start the trek at 3:00pm or so, after your lunch in Venice. By the time you get to Torcello, you'll be dying to sample their excellent food in a restaurant with wonderful outdoor seating.

To go to just one of the islands, simply purchase a single ticket for L4,000, and stamp it as you leave and again on your return.

MURANO

Located 3/4 of a mile northeast of Venice, **Murano** is a lagoon town that is spread among five little islands. It has a relatively quiet and uncrowded feel to it, especially around dinner time, when all the tourists have returned to the crowds of Venice.

Murano today is what Venice must have been like fifty years ago before international tourism really took off. In Venice every door and building front has been turned into a shop, café, or restaurant for tourists. Here it may only be one out of every four. There are small café's and restaurants dotting the canal-scape, so if you're in the need for a drink, some coffee, a little ice cream or any type of snack, you'll have it. The island group is roughly divided in half by a relatively large canal that is spanned by one bridge, the **Ponte Longo**.

ARRIVALS & DEPARTURES

Take *Vaporetto* 5 or 12 from the Fondamenta Nuove. It takes about five minutes.

SEEING THE SIGHTS

Murano is the perfect place to just stroll around and explore. You feel as if you've entered a time warp as you go down certain streets. Make sure you go off the beaten path. Everything is small enough that it's impossible for you to get lost. This island chain is world-renowned for its **glass blowing** industry, which dates back to 1291 when the furnaces were banned from Venice as a precaution against fire and espionage. At its height in the 16th century, Murano had 37 glass factories and a population of 30,000. Today the population is only a little under 8,000.

What used to be the closely guarded secret of glass blowing is today common knowledge, but Murano glass is still in demand all over the world because of the skilled artisans that prepare the fine works.

And that's what we've come to Murano to see, a glass blowing exhibition. There are number of factories dotting the island group, but the two below are the most interesting:
- **Mazzega SRL**, *Diondamenta Da Mula 147, 31041 Venzia/Murano, Tel. 041/736-888. Fax 041/739-079.* Located directly at the base of the Ponte Longa.
- **Civam**, *Viale Garibaldi 24, Venezia Murano 30141, Tel. 041/739-323. Fax 041/739-323.* Located where the boat lets you off from Venice. Don't go right there, since the other one is actually better; but first simply walk around the island to explore.

Other recommended sights include:
- **Museo dell'Arte Vetraria**, *Fondamenta Giustinian and Fondamenta Manin. Tel 739-586. Open Monday, Tuesday, Thursday and Saturday 10:00am–4:00pm, Sun 9:00am–12:30pm. Closed Wednesdays.* This is the Glass Museum.
- **Santi Maria e Donato**, *Campo San Donato. Open 8:00am - noon, 4:00pm - 7:00pm.*

Also check out the **glass factories** on Fondamenta dei Vetrai, three of which offer glassblowing exhibitions.

BURANO

Located 5 1/2 miles northeast of Venice, **Burano** occupies four tiny islands that are inhabited mainly by fishermen and lace seamstresses. It was first settled in the 5th and 6th centuries by refugees from Altinum fleeing Attila's Huns. Even though it is mainly known for the traditional art of lace making, which the women of the town have been handing down to their daughters for centuries, Burano is also a great place to unwind from the hectic pace of Venice.

The brightly colored houses on the island give it the air of an Italian opera set – a perfect background for some excellent photographs. You'll also find plenty of green space in which to relax. Burano and Torcello (our next destination) have more grass than all of the island chain of Venice proper combined. So for those of you that can get tired of looking at concrete and marble, coming here will be your needed respite.

There are also plenty of little cafés and *gelaterias*, and *trattoria* to quench a hunger or thirst.

ARRIVALS & DEPARTURES

Take *Vaporetto* number 12 from Fondamenta Nuove. It takes about 35 minutes. You'll first stop at Burano.

WHERE TO EAT

1. TRATTORIA AI PESCATORI, *Via Galuppi 371, Tel. 041/730650. Closed Wednesdays and January. All credit cards accepted. Dinner for two L140,000.*

Here you can get great lagoon cooking, which means of course, seafood. Located in the center of the island with a terrace you can enjoy in the summer, this is a nice but expensive local place. Try any of their pasta with fish, like *Spaghetti ai frutti di mare* (with the fruits of the sea) and any of their grilled or fried fish. The name of the place means Fisherman's Trattoria, so fish is the best here.

SEEING THE SIGHTS

Take a look at the lace school and satisfy your curiosity about the inner workings of the lace business. The school is **Consorzio dei Merletti**, *located in the Palazzo dell Podesta in the Piazza B. Galuppi. Tel. 730-034. Open Monday–Saturday 9:00am–6:00pm, and Sunday 9:00am–4:00pm.*

The other interesting sight on Burano is the **Church of San Martino**, *Piazza B. Galuppi,* with its leaning tower. It's no Pisa, but still intriguing nonetheless.

TORCELLO

Located six and a half miles northeast of Venice, **Torcello** is one of the most fascinating spots in the venetian Lagoon. The island was settled between the 5th and 7th centuries by the first wave of refugees from the barbarian hordes. It got its name from the tower (*Torcello* means little tower) from which the bishop of Altinum saw his vision of how to make his people safe.

Now just a solitary village on a lonely island, it was once a flourishing center of commerce and culture whose greatness dimmed as that of Venice grew. Since the 18th century, Torcello has been nearly deserted, with a population today of only about 100 people. All that remains of this long ago splendor is a group of monuments that face out onto the scenic but grassy central piazza.

Most of the land that remains has either been abandoned or has been cultivated, mainly for wine. After you've seen the few sights and walked the few hundred meters of town, the only thing left to do is satisfy your hunger at one of the exquisite outdoor restaurants. Eating, drinking, and making idle conversation is the main activity here. That's why Hemingway liked it so much.

ARRIVALS & DEPARTURES

Take vaporetto number 12 from Fondamenta Nuove. It takes about 45 minutes. You'll stop at Murano, Mazzorbe, and Burano first. After you get off the boat you'll have a little walk beside a canal that has no shops, stores, houses, restaurants or cafés (how amazing).

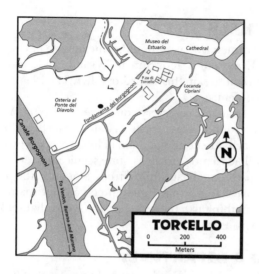

SEEING THE SIGHTS

· **Cathedral**, *Santa Maria Assunta. Tel 730-084. Open 10:00am–12:30pm and 2:00pm–6:30pm. Closes 2 hours earlier in the winter.*
· **Museo dell'Estuario**, *Santa Maria Assunta. Tel. 730-761. Open Tuesday–Sunday 10:30am–12:30pm and 2:00pm–4:00pm. Closed Mondays.*

WHERE TO EAT

If you make it to Torcello, you really should try at least a small meal at one of these places:

LOCANDA CIPRIANI, *Tel. 730-150 or 73.54.33. American Express accepted. Open mid-March–October. Closed Mondays and Tuesdays. Dinner for two L160,000.*

An offshoot of Harry's Bar with the same high prices. This used to be a haunt of Hemingway's too. The place serves traditional dishes like grilled meats and fish. The atmosphere is pleasant, especially the seating in the terrace garden area.

OSTERIA AL PONTE DEL DIAVOLO, VIA CHIESA 10/11. TEL 730-401 OR 730-44*1. American Express and Visa accepted. Open for lunch only. Closed on Thursdays and in January Dinner for two L140,000.*

This restaurant has a relaxing outdoor seating area and serves Venetian specialties like *Tagliatelli con gli scampetti* (tagliatelli pasta with little shrimps). They also make exquisite grilled fish and meats. A high end restaurant that serves great food in a peaceful and calm environment.

SAN MICHELE

If you like cemeteries, you should come here to pay your respects to the graves of Ezra Pound, Igor Stravinsky, and Frederick Rolfe. Otherwise, you may want to skip this stop altogether. The island is located half a mile north of Venice.

This is the strangest cemetery you'll ever see. Why? You can't bury anybody below ground here since its all water, so all they do is stack them one on top of each other and put them in long rows so you can come pay your respects. The island actually is quite scenic and very peaceful, with it's organized paths and beautiful tall trees. Not quite the place to have a picnic, but a place to go that I guarantee you not many tourists visit frequently. Its nothing like the cemetery in Genoa that looks like a little town, but it's still an experience.

ARRIVALS & DEPARTURES

Take *Vaporetto* 5 from Fondamenta Nuove. It takes 5 minutes.

FURTHER AFIELD FROM VENICE
PADUA

A city of 242,000 people just 23 miles west of Venice, **Padua (Padova)** was a rich trading center even before Roman times. The city was an ally of the Romans in the wars against the Gauls but retained its independence. Throughout the Roman period the city was an important cultural and economic center, and was known for its woolen textile industry.

After the Lombard invasions, Padua, like other neighboring towns, became less prosperous because of the financial and social demands placed on the populations. By 1163, Padua was already a part of the **Veneto to Verona League**, a union of smaller towns designed as protection against invading armies. In 1406, the Venetians occupied Padua amicably after the ruler of Padua, Francesco II of Carara, and all his family were killed. The city remained under Venetian rule until 1797, when the city was occupied by the French. From that point on they were ceded to Austria, became part of the Italian Kingdom, were taken over by the Hapsburg Empire, and finally in 1866 became part of modern day Italy.

Today, Padua may be best known as a university city. The **university** was founded in 1222, and is the second oldest in Italy to Bologna's. Padua became the city where the wealthy Venetians studied law and medicine. By the 15th century it also was the creative outlet for artistic expression and intellectual innovation that was not allowed in the more conservative Venice.

Padua is now also an active commercial center in addition to being a highly respected university city. It was severely damaged during bombing

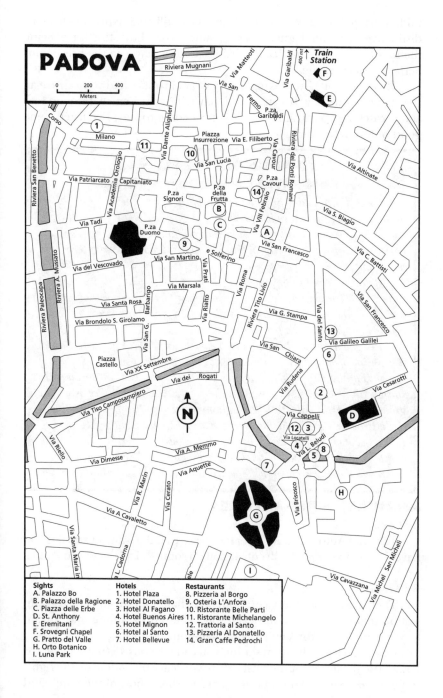

PADOVA

Sights	Hotels	Restaurants
A. Palazzo Bo	1. Hotel Plaza	8. Pizzeria al Borgo
B. Palazzo della Ragione	2. Hotel Donatello	9. Osteria L'Anfora
C. Piazza delle Erbe	3. Hotel Al Fagano	10. Ristorante Belle Parti
D. St. Anthony	4. Hotel Buenos Aires	11. Ristorante Michelangelo
E. Eremitani	5. Hotel Mignon	12. Trattoria al Santo
F. Srovegni Chapel	6. Hotel al Santo	13. Pizzeria Al Donatello
G. Pratto del Valle	7. Hotel Bellevue	14. Gran Caffe Pedrochi
H. Orto Botanico		
I. Luna Park		

raids during World War II but the town still maintains much of its distinctive character. Padua's soccer team also has the distinction of being the first to field an American, Alexi Lalas, as a player in the prestigious Seria A soccer league.

This is a small city, making it easy to get around, and you can see all the sights in one day. If you're on a day trip from Venice, have no fear about catching your train back. If you've come to stay, I've listed some good hotels in the **Centro Storico** area for you to enjoy.

PADUA ON THE FLY –
HIGHLIGHTS FOR A QUICK SIDE TRIP

Gran Caffe Pedrichi is not only a place to get a drink or small bite to eat, but is a fun sight in itself. When it opened in 1831 it was the largest café in Europe, and it still retains that majestic touch. Whatever you get here will cost you an arm and a leg, but the history and ambiance make the money well spent.

*If you're looking for something less expensive and filled with local flavor, the **Trattoria Al Santo** is for you. Don't let its spartan appearance fool you – the food is fantastic. You'll need reservations, since the locals already know this is the place to go.*

*Just down the road from the Trattoria Al Santo is the **Piazza del Santo**, a beautiul open graden in the center of the city that boasts 78 statues of famous Paduans and others that attended the University. Closer to the train station are two interesting sights. The first is the market that is on the ground floor of the Palazzo della Ragione and that spills out into the **Piazza delle Erbe** and **Piazza della Frutta**. Come here for great sights, sounds, and smells of a truly authentic Italian market offering fruit, meat, vegetables, clothing and more. The other sight is the **Scrovegni Chapel**, where you'll find some of the best fresco work that the Master **Giotto** created.*

ARRIVALS & DEPARTURES
By Car

Take the Autostrada A4 just after Mestre all the way to Padua. If you have time, drive along the Brenta Canal on route #11 all the way to Padua.

By Train

There is a frequent service (about every half-hour) from Venice's train station that takes 30 minutes each way. The return is the same: a train leaves from Padua for Venice every half-hour or less.

Once you leave the train station you can take bus #8 (buy a ticket for L1,3000 at the ticket counter just before you leave the station on the right) to the Piazza Santo. Around this square is where most of the hotels and restaurants are located.

By Water

The Burchiello water bus leaves Venice on Tuesdays, Thursdays and Saturdays, May through September, at 9:20am from Ponti Giardinetta near Piazza San Marco. The boat arrives in Padua in early afternoon. This may be the best way to get to Padua if you have a little time on your hands. The boat meanders through the waterways and past Palladian villas that line the Brenta Canal. You return to Venice by bus.

WHERE TO STAY

I really don't recommend that you stay in Padua, unless you're an experienced traveler and want to stay in a city that is a little off the beaten path. The city has great charm and moves at a slower pace than most other Italian cities, so it can be a place to enjoy for a day trip from Venice, or a night or two.

If you choose to stay, here are some of the best places in the **Centro Storico** I found for you.

1. HOTEL PLAZA, *Corso Milano 40, Tel. 049/656-822, Fax 049/661-117. 142 rooms all with bath. All credit cards accepted. Single L130,000-150,000; Double L200,000-220,000. Breakfast included. *****

All the amenities of a good four star hotel in a smaller Italian city. The decor is simple but comfortable as are the rooms. The location is key. Inside the city walls, close to the train station, and near all the sights and sounds that make Padua inviting.

2. HOTEL DONATELLO, *Piazza del Santo, Tel. 049/875-0634. Fax 049/875-0829. 49 rooms, 46 with bath. Single without bath L66,000; Single with bath L70,000-130,000; Double without bath L110,000; Double with bath L110,000-195,000. Breakfast L18,000 extra. Credit cards accepted. *****

How did a four star get away with its rating if all the rooms don't have baths, you ask? It's because it's not in a large town. They have the amenities of a four star but not the look and feel. It's in a great location, and is clean with great service, but this would be a three star at best and more likely a two star in Rome or Florence. And that's what the prices reflect. Still, a good bang for your buck, so if you have the money, go ahead and splurge.

3. HOTEL AL FAGANO, *Via Locatelli 45/47, Tel 049/875-3396. Fax 049/875-0073. 29 rooms all with bath. Single L70,000-80,000; Double L 90,000-100,000. Credit cards accepted. Breakfast L10,000 extra. ***

A quaint little two star that is perfectly inexpensive for a short stay in Padua. The rooms are clean and comfortable and you even have air conditioning, a a must in the summer, as well as television and a lobby bar.

4. HOTEL BUENOS AIRES, *Via B Luca Belludi 37, Tel 049/665-633. fax 049/658-685. 25 rooms all with bath. Single L68,000-73,000; Double L88,000-98,000. ***

Another quaint little two star in a perfect area. They have a nice lobby bar area, and a café right next door that has seating outside. Rooms are a little small with TVs but no air conditioning, which is why the price is lower than the Al Fagano.

5. HOTEL MIGNON, *Via B Luca Belludi 22, Tel. 049/661-722. No fax. 21 rooms all with bath. Single 58,000-78,000; Double 80,000-90,000.* ******

They seem to act as if running a hotel is a hobby, so don't expect much service. Nor will you get TV or air conditioning. A little run down but the rooms are clean if a little cramped. If this is your last resort in Padua, give it a shot.

6. HOTEL AL SANTO, *Via del Santo 147, Tel. 049/875-131. 10 rooms only 4 with bath. Single L37,000-50,000; Double L70,000.* *****

The doubles all come with bath so if you stay here for a night you'll get a great price for a comfortable and clean room. Located on a great street with a variety of shops and restaurants, you couldn't ask for more if you're on a budget.

7. HOTEL BELLEVUE, *Via B Luca Belludi 11, Tel. 049662-493 or 049/ 875-547. 11 rooms 9 with bath. Single L37,000-50,000; Double L70,000.* *****

For all of you that thought a night in Bellevue (the insane asylum) would do you some good, here's your chance. This is not an insane asylum, but rather a wonderfully run little one star that has a hotel attached. The rooms are better than the food, but if you get too tired to go out, they do make some good meat dishes. All the doubles have baths so if you get one, L70,000 is a great price.

WHERE TO EAT

8. PIZZERIA AL BORGO, *56 Via B Luca Belludi, Tel 049/875-8857. Credit cards accepted. Closed Tuesdays and October through March. Pizza for two plus wine L35,000. they have beer on tap but ordering that will escalate the price.*

Based on the months they're open, this place caters solely to the tourist, but if you want a view of the church and the Piazza Santo as well as some appetizing pizza, this is the place to come. With wood beamed ceiling and buttresses as well as tile floors, the ambiance inside is rustic and comfortable. They make all sorts of pizza including the *Musulmana* (mozzarella, tomatoes, and assorted vegetables) as well as a German concoction called *Menestrello* (with Wurstel sausage, onions, and pepperoni) which is excellent.

9. OSTERIA L'ANFORA, *Via del Soncin 13, Tel. 049/656-629. Closed Sundays and Mondays for Dinner. No credit cards accepted. Dinner for two L45,000.*

An informal, lively, local atmosphere. The cuisine is definitely local, simple, rustic and good. Created with care by Alberto Grinzato and his assistants, you'll find great food, excellent wine, and wonderful prices.

10. RISTORANTE BELLE PARTI, *Via Belle Parti 11, Tel. 049/875-1822. Closed Sundays and Mondays for Dinner and three weeks in September. All credit cards accepted. Dinner for two L120,000.*

The prices reflect the experimental cuisine created by owner Angelo Rosi. They take traditional Venetian and Padovan dishes and add a touch of French flair to them. Maybe it has something to do with the French invasion back in the 1700s? Try their *tacchinella in crosta con verdure marinate* (baked turkey in a crust with marinated vegetables) or *la zuppa freda di pomodoro con melone e gambero* (cold tomato, melon, and shrimp soup, kind of like a gazpacho). They also make their own ice creams and sorbet, so don't leave without cleansing your palate with dessert.

11. RISTORANTE MICHELANGELO (ANTICO BROLLO), *Corso Milano 22, Tel. 049/664-555. Closed Mondays and the second and third weeks of September. Credit cards accepted. Dinner for two L110,000.*

Located in a beautiful old building, you may just want to eat here for the atmosphere. They have large windows that look out onto the terrace where you can also eat. This place gets creative with its food too, which is reflected in its prices. Try the *pollicioni al profumo do limone e basilico* (small chicken with a sauce of lemon and basil) or *risotto al melone e fiori di zucca* (rice with melon and pumpkin).

12. TRATTORIA AL SANTO, *Via Locatelli 6/8/ Ri. Businello 6/7. Tel. 049/875-0877. Dinner for two L40,000. No credit cards accepted.*

For my money, this is the most fun place to eat in Padua. A great local place with a plain spartan interior, but the food is fantastic and dirt cheap. Run by an amicable, always silently singing old mama. You'll need reservations if you have a group larger than four, and even then you may have to wait. Your second dish, for example *pollo* or *vitello al forno* (chicken or veal on the grill) only costs L5,000, so have two if you like. Try their succulent and flavorful *patate al forno* (potatoes grilled in oil with a little rosemary) to go with either of those dishes. Your meal here will be something to remember.

13. PUB/PIZZA AL DONATELLO, *Via del Santo 117, Tel. 049/876-0481. No credit cards accepted. Pizza for two with wine L25,000. Open until midnight.*

You'd think the name was al Diavolo, because when you walk in you're confronted with the pizza oven whose lapping flames blaze away in the back. The decor is a garishly hip green with a variety of mirrors and pictures hanging on the walls, as well as a hobby horse from a carousal strategically placed in the entrance. As you enter, before you see the flames, you feel as if the horse is jumping out to trample you. Good food as well as beer on tap, but that will escalate your price L5,000 for each pint. Stick with the pizza and *vino* and you'll be quite pleased.

14. **GRAN CAFFE PEDROCHI**, *Via VIII Febbraio. Credit cards accepted. Drinks L10,000 each.*

When it opened in 1831, this was the largest café in Europe and it still seems that way now. Housed in a neo-classic building near Piazza Garibaldi, this place is *elegantissimo* with its immense ceilings, marble columns and floors, and tuxedoed waiters at your beck and call. You can eat at the overpriced dining rooms or enjoy some pastries and coffee for a little less.

You can either sit inside or have a table outside, in the front or back. Not that it is so good, but the whole place is completely wrapped in history, so if you come to Padua you have to at least stop here and enjoy a drink or coffee.

SEEING THE SIGHTS

If you're looking for a quick day trip, see the sidebar above on *Doing Pauda on the Fly*. But if you want more, here it is:

A. PALAZZO BO, THE UNIVERSITY

Via VIII Febbraio. Anatomical Theater: Tours given Tuesday 9,10, and 11 am. Wednesdays 3, 4, and 5 pm. Thursdays 9, 10, and 11 am and 3, 4, and 5 pm. Friday 3, 4, an 5 pm. Tel. 049/820.97.11; Fax 049/820.97.26.

You need to appear five minutes prior to the scheduled tour, since promptly at the hour the guide leaves and you're out of luck. The entrance is on the side of the building on Canon del Gallo.

The theater was built in 1594 by Girolamo Fabrici d' Acquapendente and was the first permanent anatomical theater to be built in the world. It is made up of six oval wooden galleries of decreasing dimensions leading down to the operating table in the middle. Besides this room, take time to explore the **Hall of Forty**, the **Lecture Hall**, and other well preserved rooms used at the old university.

B. PALAZZO DELLA RAGIONE

Piazza delle Erbe. Tel. 661-377 ext. 423. Open February 1–October 31, 9:00am–7:00pm and November 1–January 31, 9:00am–6:00pm. Closed January 1, May 1, August 15, and December 25, and 26. Admission L7,000.

Don't enter in the Piazza del Erbe – if you're facing the market go down the road to your right, take your first left and enter the gates of the Palazzo Municipiale. Take the stairs in the courtyard up, pay the ridiculously high fee and see the imposing wooden horse. It was commissioned by Annibale Capodilista for a jousting tournament in 1466. Also inside are a series of faded frescoes from the 13th century, but the main draw is the sizable horse sculpture.

WORLD-CLASS SOCCER IN PADUA

*If you're here from October to May, and you want to go see some great soccer, go to the **stadium box office** on Via Carducci #11 and try to get any leftover tickets for the day's game. It's not played at the stadium where you bought the tickets, but outside of the city, so you'll have to arrange for a taxi and spend about L30,000 each way. But if you've never seen a **Serie A** match before, it's a great treat. The box office doesn't have a phone so you'll have to go down there yourself to get tickets.*

C. PIAZZA DELLE ERBA & PIAZZA DELLA FRUTTA

Market Open Every day 7:00am – 1:30pm.

A great market environment, with fruit and vegetable sellers on either side of the **Palazzo della Ragione** building, with cheese and meat sellers in the cool environment inside. At the back, besides fruit you'll also find vendors selling leather goods and clothing. There are some memorable cheese stores with huge wheels of *Parmigiana Regianna* piled up to the ceiling. Come for the sights and smells of a true Italian market. The building in between the two squares is also worth a look.

D. BASILICA OF ST. ANTHONY

Piazza del Santo. Tel 663-944. October–April open 6:30am–7:00pm and May–September open 6:30am–7:45pm.

The basilica is dedicated to St. Anthony of Padua, who was born in Lisbon in 1195. He only lived and worked in Padua for two years but he was so popular that when he died in 1231 the Paduans wanted to keep him as their own. And besides, the city didn't have a patron saint yet, and they were pretty sure the Pope was going to canonize him, so they wouldn't let him go. Pope Gregory IX made him a saint as predicted on the 3rd of May 1232, and this basilica was started immediately afterward.

It was completed between 1256 and 1263 as a single nave church. The other two naves and eight cupolas were added later. The facade has four arches and three bronze doors by Camillo Boito. In the niche above the entrance sits a sculpture of St. Anthony created by Napoleone Martinuzzi in 1940, a copy of the original which is kept in the Anthonian Museum. Above this is a loggia with 17 columns.

Inside (remember not to wear shorts, gentlemen, otherwise you won't be able to enter) you'll find the walls covered with countless old and new frescoes, and any free space is taken up by bas-reliefs and sculptures. The main attraction is the main altar that has seven sculptures accredited to **Donatello**, and St. Anthony's tomb and his chapel which are filled with many sculptures and bas-reliefs depicting the saint's life and miracles.

E♦ EREMITANI

Piazza Eremitani 8. Open summer 9:00am–7:00pm; winter 9:00am–5:30pm. Closed Mondays. Admission is L7,000 which also gains you entrance to the Scrovegni Chapel.

This is the **Civic Museum of Padua**, founded in the nineteenth century. Here you'll find many Pre-Roman, Roman, Greek, Egyptian and Etruscan antiquities. There is not too much to see but what they have is laid out in an appealing, interesting, and educational manner.

F♦ SCROVEGNI CHAPEL

Open summer 9:00am–7:00pm; winter 9:00am–6:00pm. Entrance to the chapel is through the Civic Museum accessed from the Piazza Eremitani 8.

The chapel stands in the Arena gardens and takes its name from Enrico Scrovegni, who built it beside his family home between 1301 and 1303. It is a small simple building that fits a chapel. Inside you'll find a single nave filled with stunning frescoes by **Giotto**, which are the best preserved of the Florentine master.

G♦ PIAZZA DEL SANTO, PRATTO DEL VALLE

In the **Piazza del Santo** sits the **Pratto del Valle**, an open garden in the center of the city that has 78 statues of famous Paduans and people that attended the University. These figures were selected by the members of the families that contributed to the construction cost of the Pratto. It was once the site of an old Roman amphitheater where pagan rituals were held. Begun in 1775, the center island (Memmia Island) used to have small shops surrounding it, but these were later demolished to accommodate the small trees.

There is little shade since the park is wide open, with only a fountain in the center to offer some solace from the sun. Nonetheless it is one of the best sights in Padua. You can get great pictures with statues in the foreground and churches in the rear. If you have kids, you can create a game for them to race around checking up on who's who among the many statues.

H♦ ORTO BOTANICO

Open April–October, 9:00am–1:00pm and 3:00pm–6:00pm everyday.

The oldest **botanical gardens** in Europe. They were founded in 1545 and extend over an area nearly 21,000 square meters. You'll find many exotic and rare plant species, such as the *Palm of Goethe*, which was planted in the sixteenth century. A pleasant walk if it wasn't for the L5,000 charge just to enter.

I. LUNA PARK

Open from May 1 to June 13 every year, and from 4:00pm until midnight every day during that time.

If you or your kids are getting bored in Venice, or you're in Padua and can't think of what to do next, go to **Luna Park**. It's a tiny amusement park with bumper cars, a Ferris wheel, shooting contests, and many other rides as well as your typical food and drink. It's a lot like a county fair in the States. It's hidden away behind a large building past the Pratto della Valle so you have to look to find it.

TOURIST INFORMATION

· **Train Station**, *Tel. 049/875-2077*
· **Museo di Santo**, *Tel. 049/875-3087*
· **Museo Civico Eretani**, *Tel. 049/875-0655*

Each of these locations will supply you with a not-so-good map, but the center city of Padua is not that large and you may not even need it. These places can help you get a hotel room too if you need it.

VERONA

Located 71 miles west of Venice, **Verona** is home to approximately 270,000 people. It is one the most beautiful and romantic of all northern Italian cities. Its presence is dominated by the fast-flowing **Adige River** that curves dramatically through the city. Since Verona was a flourishing Roman city from the first century BC, the city's monuments span over 1,500 years.

Besides its monuments, Verona is also a beautiful city in which to walk because the center is now largely traffic-free, and there are many "Juliet" balconies overlooking the animated streets filled with shops and people. (Did you know that the play *Romeo and Juliet* was actually first written by an Italian from Vicenza, Luigi da Porto, and was only modified by Shakespeare?)

After a brief period of communal government rule in the 12th century, Verona was ruled by the Della Scala family from 1262 to 1387, under whose rule most of Verona's monuments were built. During this time, **Dante Aligheri**, the man who wrote *The Divine Comedy* (*The Inferno*, *Purgatorio*, and *Paradiso*), visited Verona while exiled from Florence. There is a statue commemorating his stay in the Piazza Dei Signori.

Then in 1404, at the same time as nearby Vicenza, Verona became a part of the Venetian Empire until they were conquered by Napoleon's forces some centuries later. Today, Verona is one of the most prosperous cities in Europe because of its central location, which elicited all those pesky unwanted invasions in the past.

There is so much to see and do while in Verona that it may be a good idea to spend at least two days here if you can.

VERONA ON THE FLY - HIGHLIGHTS FOR A QUICK SIDE TRIP

Let's get down to business – food. **Trattoria Imperio** *and* **Ristorante Dante** *are located in the same square,* **Piazza dei Signori.** *The former is down to earth and serves inexpensive but very tasty pizzas in a colorful and playful setting, and the other caters to your every culinary desire while surrounding you with ambiance, charm, and character.*

Just a short distance away from this quaint little piazza with its Baroque buildings is the *sight to see in Verona, the* **Piazza Bra** *and the ancient Roman* **Arena.** *Despite the age of the Arena, opera and other arts are performed in this ancient structure to this day, maintaining its entertainment lineage that dates back to when gladiators were hacked to death inside its walls. Then you must visit the imposing structure of the* **Castelvecchio,** *the old castle, and its magnificent three-arched bridge. Everything else in the city is window dressing – nice, but not essential sights.*

ARRIVALS & DEPARTURES

By Train

From Venice you can catch trains approximately every one and a half hours, and the trip itself takes just that length of time. Once on the ground, the city is within walking distance from the **Porta Nuova Station.** Simply take a right out of the station until you get to the imposing Porta Nuova, then take a left down the Corsa Porta Nuova until you get to the gate with a clock on the imposing arena. From there you have access to everything.

If you want to take the bus from the train station and eliminate the ten minute walk, take either the no. 1, 11, or 12 bus from **Mariapiedi A** (the bus stop) directly in front of the station. You have to buy a ticket first, so spend your L1,300 for a one-way fare at the Tabaccchi in the station. The bus will drop you off at the Arena square.

By Car

Take the Autostrada A4 located just after Marghera. You will have to take one of two exits for Verona which are clearly marked. For a more scenic route take the #11 from Mestre and wind your way through the beautiful scenery in these parts. This will take you directly into the city.

SPECIAL EVENTS

In July and August, operas are performed at the Arena. For informa-tion contact, Entre Lirico, Arena di Verona, Piazza Bra 28, 37100 Verona. Tel 045/800-3204. The ticket office is in the sixth arch of the Arena. In July and August there is a **drama festival**, with an emphasis on Shakespeare's plays, in the **Teatro Romano**.

WHERE TO STAY

1. GABBIA D'ORO, *Corso Porta Bosari 4/a, Tel. 045/590-292. Fax 045/ 590-293. 27 rooms, all with bath or shower. All credit cards accepted. Suite L310,000-540,000; Double L210,000-385,000. Breakfast L35,000 extra.* ***** Located deep in the centro storico just outside of the Piazza Erbe, here you'll really be in the center of things. As befits a five star deluxe hotel, everything here is perfect, except maybe the bathrooms. I can't understand how seven of the rooms only have a shower and not a bath for you to soak in – yet this is still a deluxe. Nonetheless, you'll be treated like royalty while enjoying the beauty and romance of Verona.

2. DUE TORRI HOTEL BAGLIONI, *Piazza S Anastasia 4, 37100 Verona. Tel. 045/595-0444. Fax 045/800-4130. 96 rooms all with bath. Single L180,000-420,000; Double 300,000-490,000. Breakfast included. Credit cards accepted.* **** Located in the city center, this is a truly elegant hotel furnished in period antiques. You have all the modern amenities in your room to make your stay one characteristic of a four star in a smaller market. Probably the best hotel in Verona.

3. HOTEL SAN LUCA, *Via Volto San Luca 8, Tel. 045/591-333. Fax 045/800-2143. 41 rooms all with bath or shower. Credit cards accepted. Single L105,000-125,000; Double L160,000-220,000; Suite L250,000-340,000. Break-fast L25,000 extra.* **** Located near the Arena, this is located on a side street so it is very quiet and tranquil. Here you'll still be in the center of things but this can be your oasis. The rooms are clean but once again I wonder how this place made its rating since 20 of the 41 rooms only have showers. In a big city this would be a three star. But it is well located and the service is superb.

4. GIULETTA E ROMEO, *Vicolo Tre Marchetti 3, 31700 Verona. Tel. 045/800-3554. Fax 045/801-0862. 30 rooms all with bath. Single L80,000-150,000; Double 80,000-220,000. Breakfast included. Credit cards accepted.* *** Situated just off the arena down a small side street, and close to the shopping street Via Mazzini. It is quiet since it's located in the *zona pedonale* (no cars) and comfortable, with its professional staff doing everything they can to make your stay pleasant. After dinner you can return to the hotel and relax in their lounge pub area.

5. HOTEL MASTINO, *Corso Porta Nuova 16. Tel. 045/595-388. Fax 045/597-718. 33 rooms all with bath. All credit cards accepted. Single L98,000-155,000; Double L130,000-197,000. Breakfast included.* ***

Located a few steps from Piazza Bra and the Arena, some of the rooms even have pleasant views of the piazza and the ancient amphitheater. Situated in a historic building, which helps give your stay more cultural significance. The rooms are small but clean, and despite its location the rooms are quiet so you can count on a good nights sleep. A good price for accommodations similar to some four stars in the city.

6. MILANO, *Via Tre Marchetti 11, 31700 Verona. Tel. 045/596-011. Fax 045/801-1299. 50 rooms all with bath. Single L80,000-125,000. Double L100,000-150,000. Breakfast is L15,000 extra. Credit cards accepted.* ***

Almost right next door to the Guiletta e Romeo, this hotel is much more modern in appearance. The only difference is that this place doesn't have a lobby bar. Small rooms which are clean with modern furnishings.

7. HOTEL TOURING, *Via Q Sella 5, 31700 Verona. Tel. 045/590-0944. Fax 045/590-0290. 47 rooms, 45 with bath. Single without bath L75,000-90,000. Single with bath L100,000-143,000; Double without bath L100,000-125,000. Double with bath L125,000-196,000. Breakfast L13,000. Credit cards accepted.* ***

The lobby is charmingly ornate with its marble, wrought iron, Persian carpets, and wood furnishings. The rooms have an intimate appeal since they have all been renovated to achieve modern standards. They are comfortable if a little on the small side. They are also quiet, which is a must for a good night's rest.

8. HOTEL SANMICHELI, *Via Valverde 2, 31700 Verona. Tel. 045/800-3749. Fax 045/800-4508. 15 rooms all with bath. Single L65,000-85,000; Double L76,000-110,000. Breakfast L12,500 extra. Credit cards accepted.* **

A pleasant little two star with tacky leather furniture in the lobby/bar area. They must think it looks international chic. The rooms are quiet and comfortable, if a little on the small side. You're located 150 meters from the Arena, a perfect location for sightseeing and shopping.

9. HOTEL SIENA, *Via Maroni 41, 31700 Verona. Tel. 045/800-3074. fax 045/800-2182. 27 rooms all with bath. Single L 60,000-80,000; Double L75,000-105,000.* **

Located just a little out of the city center, this is pleasantly run hotel that is clean and comfortable. The bathrooms are the kind that get soaked if you use the shower, since the whole room is the shower. The rooms are little small, but you do have TV to keep you company – but no air conditioning. If you face the street and have to keep your window open, you'll get woken up at 7:30am by the shopkeepers raising their iron grates.

10. HOTEL VALVERDE, *Via Valverde 91, 31700 Verona. Tel. 045/ 803-3611. fax 045/803-1267. 19 rooms, 11 with bath. Single (all without bath) L45,000-60,000; Double L65,000-105,000.* **

A pleasant little two star that has a nice little reading room. The decoration here is also leather chic in the lobby area. The rooms are clean, not so quiet, but comfortable. Still, the prices are good.

11. HOTEL CAVOUR, *Via Chiodo 4, 31700 Verona. Tel. 045/590-166. Fax 045/590-508. 12 rooms all doubles with bath. Double L85,000-115,000.* *

A great one star that is shooting for two star status, and they think they deserve it right now, based on the high prices. The service is professional and helpful. The location is great. The rooms are definitely two star status. A good deal.

WHERE TO EAT

There is a row of pizzerias and restaurants on the left side of the Arena and most have seating outside, so you can enjoy the pleasant evenings. You'll also find good restaurants along the **Via Mazzini** or off side streets from this main shopping avenue.

12. RISTORANTE IL DESCO, *Via Dietro S. Sebastiano 7. Tel. 045/595- 358. Closed Sundays, the first week in January and the last half of July. Dinner for two L250,000. All credit cards accepted.*

A few steps from Piazza Erbe, some say this is the best restaurant in the city. You will be received by the owner Elia Rizzo in his beautiful entrance room, and all your food will be prepared and presented with the finest of care. Our suggestion is to try the *menu degustazione* (L100,000 each) which offers you a sampling of antipasto, pasta, entrée, salad, and dessert, all of which are excellent. The wine list has over 500 different options, including some wines from California. Make a night of it.

13. RISTORANTE LE ARCHE, *Via Arche Scaligere. Tel. 045/800- 7415. Closed Sundays and Monday for dinner, as well as the first three weeks of January. Dinner for two L200,000. Formal dress required.*

The owner, Giancarlo Gioco, is like a host of an Italian restaurant out of the movies. He's especially attentive to the women, giving them gifts of dessert, drinks, and sample dishes. He can do all that because his prices are so damned high, an average of $120 for two! Come here if you like fish – fried, boiled, baked, roasted, grilled, whatever. You can order your food in a variety of different portion sizes so you can sample a variety of seafood. It's pleasant enough, but too expensive for my taste. I prefer the Accademia.

14. TRATTORIA SANT'ANASTASIA, *Corso Sant'Anastasia 27. Tel. 045/800-9177. Closed Wednesdays and Sunday nights in the winter, and Sundays and Wednesday nights in the summer. Credit cards accepted. Dinner for two L90,000.*

An excellent local hangout. The menu is limited but the quality is superb. Located in the centro storico, this is a perfect little place where you can sample some local salamis for an appetizer, have home-made pasta next (try the *carbonara*, with egg, cheese, ham and peas), and then finish up with some exquisite roasted meats and potatoes. You won't find many wines that aren't from the area, but they're all good.

15. RISTORANTE RUBIANI, PIAZZETTA SCaletta Rubiani 3, Tel.; 045/800-630. Closed Thursdays. Credit cards accepted. Dinner for two L90,000.

Red jacketed waiters will serve you on the terrace of this almost elegant restaurant. The pink table clothes really match the waiters jackets superbly. The house favorite is the *ravioli alle erbe aromatiche* (made with aromatic herbs). It comes colorfully served with some of the spices and garnish resting on top of the ravioli. A nice presentation. They make other good pastas and are known for the grilled fish and meat.

16. RISTORANTE ADRIATICO, Via Alberto Mario 14, Tel. 045803-1271. Closed Mondays. Credit cards accepted. Dinner for two L80,000.

Located on a small street just off the Via Mazzini, relax on their outside fenced-in terrace. The atmosphere is comfortable and unpretentious, even with the pink table clothes. The pasta is made fresh everyday; tortellini in a variety of sauces is one of their specialties. They also serve great meat dishes, and as the name suggests seafood from the Adriatic.

17. RISTORANTE ACCADEMIA, Via Scala 10, Tel. 045/800-6072. Closed Wednesdays and Sunday nights. Credit cards accepted. Dinner for two L100,000.

A definitely high end, up-scale place. Attached to the four star hotel of the same name this is a place to come on a final night to Verona and have all your whims catered to. They make a great *risotto alla pesce* (rice dish with seafood) that serves two people. After which try their vit*ello al forno* (veal on the grill). Excellent romantic dining environment. Also the place to see and be seen while in Verona.

18.TRATTORIA AL POMPIERE, Viccolo Regina D'Ungheria 5, Tel. 045/803-0537. Closed Wednesdays and Mondays. Credit cards accepted. Dinner for two L65,000.

Great place in a fine location down a small side street off the Via Mazzini. You have to search to find this beauty. No outside seating but it seems as if you are, since they open up all three of their huge bay windows and doors for your pleasure. A typical, local little restaurant that could do without the yellow table clothes. Otherwise everything else is perfect. Try any of their *tortellini* dishes, especially the *in brodo* (in a thick soup). For secondo they grill a wonderful *vitello arrosto* (veal).

19. RISTORANTE NUOVO MARCONI, Via Fogge 4, Tel. 045/591-910. Closed Sundays. Credit cards accepted. Dinner for two L125,000.

If you want to eat at the most respected and elegant restaurant in Verona, this is your chance. You can sit here for hours and savor the romantic setting. Many seats are in a private booth area for your privacy. They specialize in a wide variety of veal concoctions that changes based on the chef's whims. Come here to enjoy the best Verona has to offer.

20. RISTORANTE DANTE, *Piazza dei Singori, Tel. 045/595-249. Closed Sundays. Dinner for two L90,000. Credit cards accepted.*

This place was born over 110 years ago as a café, and it has evolved into a fine restaurant, somber and sophisticated, just like its namesake. You may want to try sitting outside in the piazza, but if the Trattoria Imperio, just next door, is filled with its usual boisterous crowd, you may want to sit inside for some peace and quiet. They make their pasta in house, so give any of them a try. How about the *tagliolini con basilico e scampi* (with basil and shrimp), then a grilled sole (*sogliola alla griglia*) for seconds? If you like wine they have a list of hundreds from all over the world. An excellent choice while in Verona.

21. TRATTORIA IMPERIO, *Piazza dei Signori 8, Tel. 045/803-0160. Fax 045/800-7328. Closed Mondays. Credit cards accepted. Dinner for two L50,000.*

Located in the large Piazza dei Signori, this is a popular local place because of its prices and the food. There is plenty of seating outside as well as in. The tables are covered with different colored tables cloths giving the whole place a festive aura. They have dishes that will make anyone happy: vegetarian, pasta, meat, fish, but they are known for their pizza.

There are 32 different varieties of great pizza; my favorite here is the *Salsiccia* (with tomatoes, cheese, and lots of sausage). The perfect place to come with a large group for an intimate inexpensive dinner (sit inside for that).

22. RISTORANTE CIPETTA, *Vicolo Teatro Filrmonico 2, el. 045/800-843. Closed Friday nights and Saturdays. Credit cards accepted. Dinner for two L80,000.*

Located in a quiet piazza off the Via Roma, this is great place for intimate dining. They specialize in local Verona cooking. Simply try their *tortellini al brodo* (in a thick soup) or any of their superb grilled meat and fish. Ask for their suggestions for what's good when you visit.

SEEING THE SIGHTS

The highlights can be hit rather quicky (see sidebar above, *Doing Verona On The Fly*), or you can take your time and explore thisprettiest of small cities in northern Italy.

A. PIAZZA BRA

The **Forum Boarium** of medieval days of yore is now **Piazza Bra**. The piazza is bounded by the ancient **Roman Arena** to the north, the line of palazzi with their cafés to the west, the 17th century **Gran Guardia** building in the south, and the neo-classic town hall to the east, and has a quaint fountain with a park in the middle. It is the central meeting place for Veronese.

Enjoy a drink or bite to eat at one of the cafés that line the west side of the piazza and soak up the sights and sounds of the city.

B. ARENA

Piazza Bra. Tel. 800-3204. Tuesdays–Sunday 8am–6:30pm in the summer. 8am–1pm in the winter. Admission L6,000.

Originally built during the Roman Republic era, the **Arena** must have been completed about 30AD, judging from mosaics found in an old Roman house in Verona indicating three scenes of gladiators fighting in the arena. These are now in the archeological museum.

After 325 AD, when the emperor Constantine forbade gladiatorial performances, the arena was used less frequently. That's the official line, but historians tell us that gladiators fought all over the Roman empire as magistrates disregarded Rome's orders, until the emperor Honorius violently put an end to this insubordination in the 5th century. During the Middle ages the arena was used for capital punishment and trial by combat (sounds a little like gladiators, doesn't it?). By the 16th and 17th centuries, the arena was used for less violent activities like fairs and tournaments, and a variety of performing arts activities. This tradition lives on today.

The arena went through a variety of expansions and today measures 152 by 122 meters. The ancient structure is formed with four concentric rings, with the outermost only retaining four of its original arches. This outer ring used to encircle the entire arena and had 72 arches. Today the second ring is the outer boundary of the arena.

Despite its age, the arena is still used to today for music and theater festivals. Little has had to been done to it to make it more modern, except that the inner space of the arena was modified between 1569 and 1680 by the Venetian Republic. Even it's old drainage system still works perfectly today.

C. PIAZZA DELLE ERBE

Open 8:00am–1:30pm.

This used to be the Forum of the old Roman city, whose ruins lie a few meters beneath the current piazza. Today the only Roman feature about

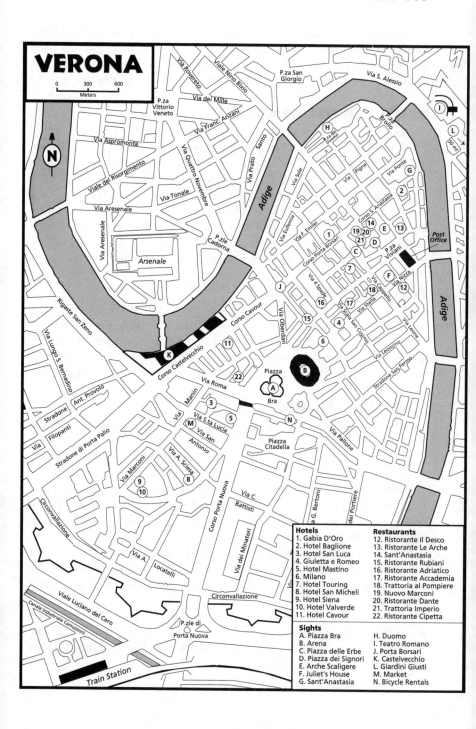

VERONA

0   300   600
Meters

Hotels
1. Gabia D'Oro
2. Hotel Baglione
3. Hotel San Luca
4. Giuletta e Romeo
5. Hotel Mastino
6. Milano
7. Hotel Touring
8. Hotel San Micheli
9. Hotel Siena
10. Hotel Valverde
11. Hotel Cavour

Restaurants
12. Ristorante Il Desco
13. Ristorante Le Arche
14. Sant'Anastasia
15. Ristorante Rubiani
16. Ristorante Adriatico
17. Ristorante Accademia
18. Trattoria al Pompiere
19. Nuovo Marconi
20. Ristorante Dante
21. Trattoria Imperio
22. Ristorante Cipetta

Sights
A. Piazza Bra
B. Arena
C. Piazza delle Erbe
D. Piazza dei Signori
E. Arche Scaligere
F. Juliet's House
G. Sant'Anastasia

H. Duomo
I. Teatro Romano
J. Porta Borsari
K. Castelvecchio
L. Giardini Giusti
M. Market
N. Bicycle Rentals

the square is the *Verona Madonna* statue in the center, placed atop a large marble basin taken from the Roman baths. Today the square is used during the day as an open air market where you can buy fresh fruits, vegetables, and sundries. Don't miss this place while in Verona.

D. PIAZZA DEI SIGNORI

Locally it is known as **Piazza Dante**, because of the statue erected in 1865. It is bounded on the side nearest Piazza Erbe by the **Domus Nova**, a Baroque building of the 17th century. On the opposite side is the **Loggia del Consiglio**, built at the beginning of Veronese Renaissance. This is the second favorite meeting spot in the evenings for Veronese, because of the wide open spaces and the two well-loved restaurants that lay their seating out in the piazza: the **Trattoria Imperio** is a fun- filled local place that is loud and boisterous, whereas **Ristorante Dante** is as somber and sophisticated as its namesake. They compliment each other perfectly.

E. ARCHE SCALIGERE

Just outside of the Piazza Signori, surrounded by the Scalinger palaces, is the Church of Santa Maria Antica and the **cemetery of the Della Scala family** which is known to tourists as the **Arche Scaligere**. Here you will find many elaborate shrines, tombs, and sarcophagi. Take some time to wander through and appreciate the beauty of these death monuments.

F. JULIET'S HOUSE

Via Capello 23, Tel. 803-4303. Open 8am–6:30pm Closed Mondays. Admission L5,000.

The Shakespearean story of *Romeo and Juliet* was actually 'borrowed' from a work by a Vicenza writer named **Luigi da Porto**, who wrote of the vicissitudes of two unhappy lovers named Romeo Montecchi and Juliet Capuleti. We know for sure that these two families did exist. Dante witnessed and wrote about their quarrels when he sojourned here between 1299 and 1304. Besides these facts, we do not know if Romeo and Juliet were actual people and actually fell in love, and so on. But no matter – poetry has triumphed and today we can visit **Juliet's House** in Verona and see the balcony from which she sealed her tryst with Romeo and eventually their demise.

A bronze statue, created by Nereo Costantini, of fair Juliet has been placed in the courtyard in front of the house. Inside the house looks like it would have in the 14th century. If you've ever had romance in your heart, stop in here.

G. SANT'ANASTASIA

Corso San Anastsia. Open 9am–5pm.

Also a Dominican church, **Sant'Anastasia** is quite similar to SS Giovanni e Paolo in Venice. The facade is simple and plain, but what is of interest is inside. The first two columns are flanked by hunchback figures *(gobbi)* holding holy water bowls on their backs. These two figures are something I've never seen in all my travels throughout Italy.

The nave is subdivided by columns of red Veronese marble and connected by arches. The walls of the aisles on either side of the columns contain the large circular windows that let light into the church. Everywhere inside you'll find ornate frescoes, bas-relief altars, and sculptures. The **Miniscalchi Altar**, also known as the Altar of the Holy Spirit, is especially exquisite. This work has been attributed to the Venetian master Agnolo.

H. DUOMO

Piazza del Duomo. Open 7am–Noon and 3pm–7pm.

The **Duomo** is a composite of varying styles, since the original Romanesque building underwent Gothic modifications in the 15th century. The **bell tower**, with its Romanesque base, should have been finished in the 16th century but was only completed in this century. This church is not nearly as interesting and elaborate as Sant'Anastasia but it does have a beautiful work by Titian, *The Assumption of the Virgin*, dating back to 1535-40.

Since this church is near the river and the **Ponte Pietra**, it is a perfect launching place to visit the **archeological zone** and the **Roman Theater** (see below).

I. TEATRO ROMANO

Tel. 800-0360. Open Tuesday–Sunday 8am–6:30pm off-season. Performance days 8am–1:30pm. Admission L5,000.

This ancient theater was excavated between 1834 and 1914. It backs up onto the slope of Colle di San Pietro and has a relatively modern church, SS Siro e Libera, on its steps as a reminder that here in Italy the past, present, and future all fit perfectly together. The orchestra's diameter is almost 30 meters and the two galleries reach a height of 27 meters.

The theater's construction has been carbon-dated to the last quarter of the 1st century BC. If you're interested in archaeology, this is a fun place to roam for a little while.

J. PORTA BORSARI

This is the best preserved of the five **Roman gates** in Verona, and is the easiest to find. It was named **Borsari** in medieval times because of the toll tax *(Bursarii)* that were levied here on goods in transit. It is of interest because the entire facade has remained intact. This gate was probably built (no one knows for sure) during the reign of emperor Claudius (41-54 AD), because of the similarity between it and the Porta Aurea in Ravenna which was made in 43 AD.

The openings on the bottom are 3.5 meters wide and a little more than 4 meters high and are framed by Corinthian columns, which support the rest of the construction. The entire complex rises to a height of 13 meters and is made of white Veronese marble. What is of interest to me is that this ancient arch has been completely incorporated into the life of the modern city, as have most Roman ruins in Italy – even so far as being a part of the modern buildings on either side of it!

K. CASTELVECCHIO

Corso Castelvecchio 2, Tel. 594-734. Open Tuesday–Sunday 8am–6:30pm. Admission L5,000.

This structure was the final residence of the Della Scala family and was built over a period of twenty years from 1354 to 1375. The magnificent three-arched bridge was built for the private use of the residents of the castle. The building itself has served as an army garrison, a military storeroom, and most recently as a museum with an exquisite collection of paintings, sculptures, tapestries, ancient jewelry, frescoes and more. Most of the works are religious in nature, so if you haven't had your fill of the Madonna and Child, there's more here.

A relatively unknown Italian artist, G Francesco Caroto (1480-1555) has many works featured here. He studied under Liberale, Mantegna, and was influenced by Leonardo and Raphael and his works show it. One particular, though simple in nature, seems to come alive. It is his *Young Boy With a Drawing*. You can almost feel the boy's joy at creating the stick figure on the paper he holds in his hand.

L. GIARDINI GIUSTI

Via Giadini Giusti 2, Tel. 803-4029. Open 9am to dusk in summer and 9am–8pm in winter. Admission L5,000.

You'll find the lush garden spaces of the **Palazzo Giusti** on the same side of the river as the Roman Theater, outside the ancient walls. The gardens are well tended and are punctuated by a variety of different statues, fountains, and a fish pond. The gardens also feature a labyrinth, citrus grove, and an aviary to protect birds in danger of extinction.

Sometimes these gardens are the backdrop for summer productions of the **Theater of Verona**. They are a lovely place to come and relax and recharge your batteries if you've had too much of cities.

PRACTICAL INFORMATION

Bike Rental

In **Piazza Bra**, you'll see a fellow who works out of a van the left of the Gran Guardia building as you face it. *They are open 9:00am to 7:00pm. Rates: 1 hour L7,000; 2 hours L10,000; 4 hours L15,000; 1 day L20,000; 1 week L7,000/day; 2 weeks L5,000/day; 1 month L4,000/day.*

Car Rentals
• **Avis**, *Stazione Ponte Nuova 045/800-66-36*
• **Maggiore**, *Stazione Ponte Nuova, 045/800-48-08*

Discos
• **Alter Ego Club**, *9 Via Torricelle, Tel. 045/91-51-30*
• **Excalibur Club**, *24 Stradone Provolo, Tel. 045/59-41-95*

English Language Bookstores
• **The Bookshop**, *3a Interrato Aqua Morta, Tel. 045/800-76-14*

Flower & Fruit Markets

A small local market is in the **Piazza Arditi**, *open 8:00am to 1:30pm every day*. A large market is open in **Piazza delle Erbe** *from 8:00am to 1:30pm daily.*

Pubs
• **Any Capp Pub**, *13v Nievo, Tel. 045/834-80-82*
• **Double A**, *1/a VC Stell, Tel. 045/803-22-23*

Supermarket

If you're going to be in Verona for a day or a week, it's always important to know here you can get fresh supplies of water, fruit, soda, wine, and beer to stick in your room. In Verona, unlike many Italian cities, their is a large supermarket directly in the center of town. You can get everything your heart desires. At the **PAM** supermarket *on Via dei Mutilati #3*, which is just outside the Piazza Bra through the old Roman gate.

Tourist Information

The **tourist office** has branches at:
• *Porta Nuova Station, Tel. 045/800-0861. Open all year long from 8:30am– 7:30pm*

- *Piazza Erbe 42, Tel. 045/803-0086. Open all summer from 9:00am–12:30pm and from 2:30pm–7:00pm*
- *Via Leoncino 61, Tel 045/592-828. fax 045/800-3638. Summer 8:00am– 8:00pm; Winter 8:00am–7:00pm*

You can get any type of information about Verona at these offices, as well as tourist maps that really are not that good but basic enough that you won't get lost.

There's also a **Hotel Booking Office**, *Via Patuzzi 5, Tel. 045/800-9844. Open 9:00am–7:00pm. Closed Sundays.* They can make hotel reservations for you if you have none. They are a private group that represents about three quarters of the better hotels in Verona.

All the representatives at the office speak a variety of languages, and use Macintosh as their computer system, so you'll get what you want quickly.

Travel Agencies
- **American Express**, *Cora Ponte Nuova 11, Tel. 045/800-90-40*

15. BOLOGNA

Bologna the Fat. The Bologna the Learned. Bologna the Turreted. Bologna is considered fat because its food is the best in Italy. Bologna is considered learned because it houses the oldest university in Europe. Bologna is considered turreted because it has many beautiful churches, palazzi, and two leaning towers, and once had the most towers of any city in Italy.

Bologna earns all these nicknames, but even then tourists seem to avoid this beautiful city located just 60 miles north of Florence and about 100 miles southwest of Venice. But then, the loss is theirs. We'll keep the capital of Italy's cuisine, the seat of Europe's oldest university, and the best preserved historic center, after Venice, all to ourselves.

No Italian city has achieved a better balance between progress and preservation as has Bologna. Much of the city center still looks the same way it did centuries ago. In conjunction, Bologna possesses none of the noisy congestion or chaos of Rome or Florence. Instead it offers a glimpse into the lives of real Italians as they go about their business, and it invites you to enjoy life along with them. Just don't expect the romantic ambiance of Lucca, or the Renaissance splendor of Florence, or the charm of Venice – except of course for the miles upon miles of covered (arcaded) sidewalks. This is a real, living, breathing Italian city, virtually free of tourists, where you can enjoy the sights and sounds, and food and drink as they do.

Brief History

Started as an Etruscan settlement of **Felsina**, the town was captured by marauding Gauls, renamed **Bononia**, and kept this name when it became a Roman colony in 139 BC. As you'll notice by the map, the city center today is still dissected in an orderly fashion along the lines of an ancient Roman camp.

After the Roman Empire dissolved, **Ravenna** was the stronger of the two cities in the region, but in the 11th century Bologna broke away from Ravenna. Then it became an independent commune of the **Lombard**

League during the 12th and 13th centuries. In 1278, Bologna became part of the Papal States but was ruled by a succession of local "first citizens."

Bologna's high point, besides being home to the oldest university in Europe (founded in the 5th century AD as the **Imperial School of Bologna**, it later became a university in the 13th century AD), was probably when **Charles V** was crowned emperor in Bologna in 1530 instead of in Rome. That period marked the end of the Renaissance and the beginning of four and a half centuries of foreign rule. In 1796 the town was incorporated into Napoleon's empire. Then in 1815 it reverted back to Papal rule, and eventually became part of the new Italian state in 1860.

Now Bologna is known for its food and its sights, and as the birthplace of **Guglielmo Marconi**, the inventor who gave us the wireless radio.

GETTING AROUND TOWN

By Foot

The center of Bologna is very small, and it is specifically designed for pedestrian traffic since no private cars are allowed. Walking is really the only mode of transport you'll need. Now if you want to explore farther afield and see what the outskirts of town look like, you'll need a cab, but otherwise, Bologna is made for walking.

By Taxi

If you're a long way from your hotel and need a cab, simply flag one down, or call one of these numbers to have one sent to you: *051/53-41-41* or *051/37-27-27*. When you get off the train a taxi stand is on the right outside of the station. Most places suggested in here will be a short taxi ride away, unless you feel like lugging your bags a mile. The fare shouldn't be any more than L10,000 unless you've got loads of luggage.

Renting a Car

If you want to visit the countryside but don't want to take the train, here a few agents that will rent you a car:
• **Hertz**, *Via Amendola 17/22 B, Tel. 051/25-37-43*
• **Avis**, *Via Marco Polo 91A, Tel. 051/634-1623. Fax 051/634-6420*
• **Maggiore**, *Via Cairoli 4, Tel. 051/25-25-25*

ORIENTATION

Bologna, for the purposes of this guide, has been divided into easy to understand quadrants. If you use **Via Ugo Bassi**, **Via Rizzoli**, and **Strada Maggiore** as the line that dissects the city in half horizontally, and **Via M D'Azeglio** and **Via dell'Independenza** as the line that dissects the city vertically, you can easily see the Northwest, Northeast, Southwest, and Southeast quadrants.

At the center of this delineation are the **Piazza Maggiore** and **Nettuno**, the cultural and social centers of downtown Bologna.

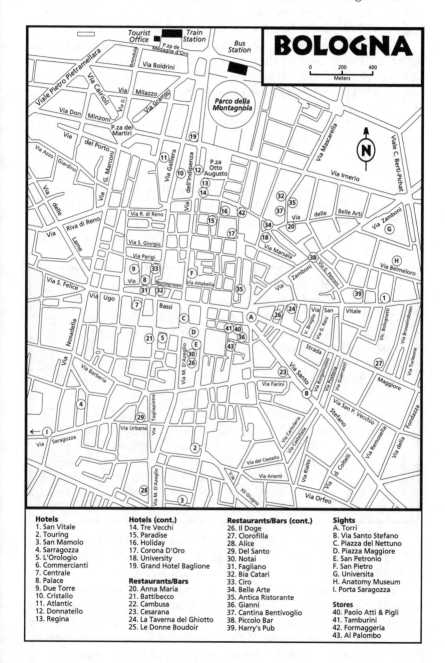

Hotels
1. San Vitale
2. Touring
3. San Mamolo
4. Sarragozza
5. L'Orologio
6. Commercianti
7. Centrale
8. Palace
9. Due Torre
10. Cristallo
11. Atlantic
12. Donnatello
13. Regina

Hotels (cont.)
14. Tre Vecchi
15. Paradise
16. Holiday
17. Corona D'Oro
18. University
19. Grand Hotel Baglione

Restaurants/Bars
20. Anna Maria
21. Battibecco
22. Cambusa
23. Cesarana
24. La Taverna del Ghiotto
25. Le Donne Boudoir

Restaurants/Bars (cont.)
26. Il Doge
27. Clorofilla
28. Alice
29. Del Santo
30. Notai
31. Fagliano
32. Bia Catari
33. Ciro
34. Belle Arte
35. Antica Ristorante
36. Gianni
37. Cantina Bentivoglio
38. Piccolo Bar
39. Harry's Pub

Sights
A. Torri
B. Via Santo Stefano
C. Piazza del Nettuno
D. Piazza Maggiore
E. San Petronio
F. San Pietro
G. Universita
H. Anatomy Museum
I. Porta Saragozza

Stores
40. Paolo Atti & Pigli
41. Tamburini
42. Formaggeria
43. Al Palombo

WHERE TO STAY

1. HOTEL SAN VITALE, *Via San Vitale 94, 40125 Bologna. Tel. 051/ 225-966. Fax 051/239-396. Credit cards accepted. 15 rooms all with bath. Single L60,000-70,000; Double L80,000-95,000.* **

A tranquil little hotel with a small garden in back in which to relax and have a drink from the bar. The rooms are all on the first and second floors with no elevator, but all are clean and very comfortable. And the bespectacled proprietess is very helpful with all your touring interests. A great place to stay, in a quiet area for a wonderful price.

2. HOTEL TOURING,*Via de'Mattuiani 1/2, 20124 Bologna. Tel 051/ 584-305. Fax 051/334-763. 38 rooms all with bath. Single 65,000-115,000; Double 110,000-150,000. Credit cards accepted.* ***

This place is actually two hotels. One old and one renovated. Ask to stay in the renovated section where the accommodations are definitely three star. In the old section they are truly two star. They have a terrace on the road that doesn't offer the greatest views, but at least it's a place to relax other than your room. This is a simple, plain hotel with limited atmosphere.

THE BEST HOTELS IN BOLOGNA

1. HOTEL SAN VITALE, *Via San Vitale 94, 40125 Bologna. Tel. 051/225-966. Fax 051/239-396. Credit cards accepted. 15 rooms all with bath. Single L60,000-70,000; Double L80,000-95,000.* **

6. HOTEL COMMERCIANTI, *Via De' Pignattari 11, 40124 Bologna. Tel. 051/233-052. Fax 051/224-733. 31 rooms all with bath. Single L120,000-160,000; Double L175,000-250,000. Credit cards accepted.* ***

13. HOTEL REGINA, *Via Indipendenza 51, 40121 Bologna. Tel. 051/248-952. ax 051/224-143. 61 rooms all with bath. Single 75,000-120,000; Double L95,000-165,000. Credit cards accepted.* ***

14. HOTEL TRE VECCHI, *Via Indipendenza 47, 40126 Bologna. Tel 051/23-19-91. Fax 051/ 22-14-43. 96 rooms all with bath. Single L 110,000-190,000; Double L140,000-290,000. Credit cards accepted.* ****

---

3. HOTEL SAN MAMOLO, *Via del Falcone 6-8, 40014 Bologna , Tel 051/58-30-56. Fax 051/58-03-86. 19 rooms, 14 with bath. Single L50,000-85,000; Double L80,000-120,000. Credit cards accepted.* **

A small hotel in an out of the way location. There is small local *trattoria* on the corner but that's it. The rooms are tranquil since there's no major street to create traffic noise and they are small but comfortable. The hotel doesn't offer much in the way of extras like breakfast or air conditioning, but they do have TV's in the rooms and a small bar downstairs.

4. HOTEL SARRAGOZZA, *Via Senzanome 10, 40124 Bologna. Tel. 051/330-258. Fax 051/644-6210. 31 rooms, 23 with bath. Single L40,000-75,000; Double L40,000-120,000.* ***

Located on (literally translated) "The street with no name," this is an unspectacular hotel that has a small 'garden' (almost a misnomer) from which the rooms are accessed on the first and second floors, kind of like in the Motel 6 style. It is vaguely clean but dark and dingy. I would only recommend it as a last resort.

5. HOTEL L'OROLOGIO, *Via IV Novembre 10, 40100 Bologna. Tel. 051/231-253. Fax 051/260-552. 29 rooms all with bath. Single 120,000-160,000; Double L175,000-250,000. Credit cards accepted.* ***

A snooty professional hotel that caters mainly to businessmen and did not seem to appreciate a scruffy travel writer staying there, but they do have all the amenities and service you'd expect from a North American hotel. They take their work seriously and professionally, unlike a lot of hotels in Italy, where it's just a way to make money. Part of a group of hotels in the city that also includes the Hotel Corona d'Oro and the Hotel Commercianti.

6. HOTEL COMMERCIANTI, *Via De' Pignattari 11, 40124 Bologna. Tel. 051/233-052. Fax 051/224-733. 31 rooms all with bath. Single L120,000-160,000; Double L175,000-250,000. Credit cards accepted.* ***

Same prices and virtually the same location as its sister hotel, L'Orologio, with the same professional manner and service that caters to traveling business persons. All your needs will be taken care of by the helpful desk staff (more so than at the L'Orologio). Great location for shopping and sight seeing. All the amenities and professional service you'd expect from a North American hotel.

7. HOTEL CENTRALE, *Via della Zucca 2, 40121 Bologna. Tel. 051/ 225-114 . Fax 051/ 223-162. 20 rooms 17 with bath. single L50,000-90,000; Double L70,000-115,000. Credit cards accepted.* **

As the name indicates, this hotel is located in the center of Bologna with shopping and sightseeing all around. On the third floor of a building, you need to catch the lift up to your clean but spartan rooms, some of which have nice views over the rooftops of Bologna. Most rooms face the Via Ugo Bassi and can be noisy in the morning if you have your windows open. In the heat of summer that is necessary because not all the rooms have air conditioning. Make sure you request one that does have air conditioning as well as a private bath and your stay in Bologna will be pleasant and comfortable.

8. PALACE HOTEL, *Via Montegrappa, 40120 Bologna. Tel 051/237-442. Fax 051/231-603. 113 rooms, 110 with bath. Single L 60,000-118,000; Double L95,000-160,000. Credit cards accepted.* ***

One of the oldest hotels in Bologna and it looks it. They've attempted modernization in most of the rooms but you'll still feel as if you've stepped back into the 1950s, which gives the place it's charm. Located on a relatively quiet little street, but don't expect personal service since this place is so big. But you're located in the prime shopping and sightseeing areas of Bologna.

9. HOTEL DUE TORRE, *Via degli Usberti 4, 40210 Bologna. Tel 051/ 269-826. Fax 051/239-944. 15 rooms all with bath. Single L60,000-110,000; Double L75,000-150,000. Credit cards accepted.* ***

Light and airy decor of floral patterns gives life to their relatively large rooms, and their tiny common areas. The bathrooms are all immaculate if small. Your stay here will be very tranquil, not only because of the calming furnishings but also because they're located on a side street with little traffic. You're also situated around all the sights and shops. The place to stay if you can't get into one of the gems.

10. CRISTALLO, *Via San Giuseppe 5, 40100 Bologna.Tel. 051/248-635. American Express, Mastercard and Visa accepted. 42 rooms all with bath. Single L 65,000-85,000; double L90,000-130,000.* ***

Poorly managed hotel just off the Via Indipendenza. The lobby has the look and feel of a place that hasn't been remodeled in a while. The rooms have all been modified to meet the standards of the three star rating so your stay will be pleasant if you choose to stay here.

11. ATLANTIC, *Via Galliera 46, 40121 Bologna Tel 051/ 520-692. fax 051/234-591. 22 rooms, 15 with bath. Single L 40,000-95,000; Double L80,000-140,000. Credit cards accepted.* **

Small, brightly lit, and modern hotel. They have a small bar area on the first floor. The location is a little outside of the old center but you're still within walking distance. Not great atmosphere but clean comfortable rooms.

12. HOTEL DONNATELLO, *Via dell'Indipendenza 65, 40121 Bologna. Tel 051/24-81-74. fax 051/24-81-74. 39 rooms all with bath. Single L70,000-115,000 Double L80,000-150,000. Credit cards accepted.* ***

Another older hotel that looks like it's trying to hang onto its glory. Upstairs the mood is different with slightly modern appointments, making your stay here comfortable. The rooms are quiet since air conditioning means you don't have to open the windows in the heat of the summer. A good choice, but try the Regina first (see below).

13. HOTEL REGINA, *Via Indipendenza 51, 40121 Bologna. Tel. 051/ 248-952. ax 051/224-143. 61 rooms all with bath. Single 75,000-120,000; Double L95,000-165,000. Credit cards accepted.* ***

This hotel is itching to become a four star. The decorations, the service, the amenities all point to this becoming reality soon, so grab the prices while you can. The four star next door charges almost twice the prices. The rooms here are a little smaller and the furnishings not as ornate, but you'll still have plenty of money left over if you stay here instead of at the luxurious Hotel Tre Vecchi. They also have a pleasant bar and dining area.

14. HOTEL TRE VECCHI, *Via Indipendenza 47, 40126 Bologna. Tel 051/23-19-91. Fax 051/ 22-14-43. 96 rooms all with bath. Single L 110,000-190,000; Double L140,000-290,000. Credit cards accepted.* ****

Super luxurious with antiques and faux antiques placed all over. You'll have your every wish tended to here. They even have bicycles for use by the hotel guests. The rooms are all modern but tastefully furnished, and the bathrooms are relatively large and accommodating. If you want to spend one night in heaven while in Bologna try here. But it's very expesnive.

15. HOTEL PARADISE, *Viccolo Cattani 7, 40126 Bologna. Tel. 051/ 231-1792. Fax 051/234-591. 18 rooms all with bath. Single L65,000-135,000; Double 100,000-200,000. Credit cards accepted. Breakfast included.* ***

Clean, modern, professional hotel in the Golden Group Hotel chain that includes the Holiday and University. All done up in a calming purple and green decor, these hotels are the place to stay if you expect professional, courteous service all the time. The rooms are somewhat small but they usually cater to the traveling business person that doesn't need to spread out so much.

16. HOTEL HOLIDAY, *Via Bertiera 13, 40126 Bologna. Tel. and Fax 051/235-326. 36 rooms all with bath. Single L70,000-140,000; Double L105,000-210,000. Break fast included. Credit cards accepted.* ***

Clean, modern, professional hotel in the Golden Group Hotel chain that includes the Paradise and University. Like the Paradise, the decor is purple and green. A good business traveler's choice.

17. HOTEL CORONA D'ORO, *Via Oberdan 12, 40126 Bologna. Tel 051/ 236-456. Fax 051/262-679. 35 rooms all with bath. Single L175,000-270,000; Double L 260,000-390,000. Credit cards accepted. Breakfast included.* ****

The crown prince of the small chain that includes the Orologio and the Commercianti. I think a better value for your money is the Hotel Tre Vecchi, but even so this hotel has everything you could want in a first class place. The elegant design conserves architectural elements from various periods, which makes the ambiance luxurious. Mainly a businessperson's hotel, since Bologna has few tourists. You'll find the rooms spacious and comfortable.

There's an airy lobby with a skylighted atrium, colorful tile floors, frescoes and an abundance of fresh flowers. Most rooms have small balconies, and if you're up high enough you can overlook the rooftops, towers, and domes of Bologna.

18. HOTEL UNIVERSITY, *Via Mentana 7, 40126 Bologna. Tel. and Fax 051/229-713. 21 rooms all with bath. Single L 65,000-135,000; double L100,000-200,000. Credit cards accepted. Breakfast included.* ***

Clean, modern, professional hotel in the Golden Group Hotel chain that includes the Holiday and Paradise. See reviews for these two above.

19. GRAND HOTEL BAGLIONI, *Via Indipendenza 8, 40121 Bologna. Tel. 051/225-4454. Fax 051/234-840. 140 rooms all with bath. Single L185,000-370,000; Double L280,000-560,000.* ****

A former 16th century seminary, this is Bologna's most splendid hotel. The color scheme is of salmon, beige, and light blue, giving the atmosphere a calming effect. A strange feature of the hotel is that it has several yards of early Roman roads on display in the basement, so it's also a museum. The hotel restaurant, I Carracci, is expensive but exquisite.

WHERE TO EAT
Cucina Bolognese

Bologna has many nicknames, but the one that most remember is *Bologna La Grassa* – Bologna the Fat. The reason for this is that Bologna has simply got the best all-round cuisine in Italy and the people enjoy it wholeheartedly. The main local dishes are based on pasta, pork, cream, cheese, and ham; and pasta is so revered here that the city government has a giant golden tagliatelli noodle enshrined in its Chamber of Commerce offices.

The cuisine is so good here because cooks are able to draw on the freshest and best ingredients from the surrounding area. They can get the best *prosciutto* and *formaggio* from Parma (see *Day Trips & Excursions* section), which is world renowned for its excellence. They get the freshest fruits and vegetables from the local farms, and the most succulent pork, salami, and other sausage as well. If you came to Bologna and want to remain on a diet, you came to the wrong place.

Suggested Bolognese Cuisine
ANTIPASTO
• **Prosciutto di Parma con melone** – Local ham with melon.
• **Salsice misto** – plate of grilled local sausages, usually pork.

PRIMO PIATTI
• **Tortellini alla panna** – Cheese filled pasta made with a thick, rich cream sauce, covered with the local parmiggiano cheese. Basically any type of tortellini is a local favorite.
• **Risotto alla parmigiana** – rice cooked with an abundance of the local cheese, Parmigianna Reggianno.

- **Tortellone alla Bolognese** – Large tortellini with ground veal, milk and fresh tomato sauce. Tortellone are also local favorites.
- **Tagliatelli alla Bolognese** – Pasta with a delicate ground veal, milk and fresh tomato sauce.

SECONDO PIATTI
- **Griglia Mista** –Mixed Grill with local pork, beef, vegetables, and sometimes fruit
- **Cotoletta alla Bolognese** – Veal Cutlet smothered in delicate milk and tomato sauce.
- **Maiale arrosto** – Roast pork. Basically any type of porkis good since that's where the excellent local ham comes from too.

Cheese
- **Parmiggiano Reggiano** – local parmesan cheese that is served in chunks. Cut off a piece and just let it melt in you mouth.

Wines
- **Sforza** – A light local carbonated white wine that is served as the house wine at many local restaurants.

BEST RESTAURANTS IN BOLOGNA

20. TRATTORIA ANNA MARIA, *Via Belle Arti 17/a, Tel. 051/ 266-894. Closed Mondays, sic days in January and 15 days in August. All credit cards accepted. Dinner for two L90,000.*

26. RISTORANTE/PIZZERIA IL DOGE, *Via Caldarese 5a. Credit cards accepted. Closed Mondays. Tel. 051/22-79-80. Dinner for two (only pizza) L35,000.*

31. RISTORANTE FAGLIANO, *Calca Vinazzi de Gessi. Credit cards accepted. Closed Thursdays. Dinner for two L65,000.*

33. TRATTORIA CIRO, *5B Via de Gessi. Closed Wednesdays. Credit cards accepted. Dinner for two L60,000.*

37. CANTINA BENTIVOGLIO, *Via Mascarella 4B. Closed Mondays. Open 8:00pm - 2:00am. Snacks and wine for two L45,000.*

---

20. TRATTORIA ANNA MARIA, *Via Belle Arti 17/a, Tel. 051/266-894. Closed Mondays, sic days in January and 15 days in August. All credit cards accepted. Dinner for two L90,000.*

Anna Maria Monari does everything here from prepare the ragu sauce to turning the roast to preparing the check and she does them all well. You'll find plenty of traditional dishes here, including either *tagliatelle, tortellini, tortellone, tagliolini or quadreti in brodo* (different types of pasta in soup); as well as *pasta e fagioli* (pasta and beans) or *trippa coi fagioli* (tripe with beans). They have a great *zuppa di verdure* (vegetable soup), *maiale al forno* (grilled pork) *verdure al forno* (grilled vegetables) or *frittura* (fried). Dining is either inside or outside on their terrace.

21. RISTORANTE BATTIBECCO, *Via Battibecco 4/b, Tel. 051 223-298. Closed Sundays and Holidays as well as August. All credit cards accepted. Dinner for two L140,000.*

This is somewhat of an upper crust place that serves many excellent regional dishes as well as international fare. You'll find that *Prosciutto di Parma, Parmigiana Reggiana*, and local salamis are featured in almost all the appetizers, soups, and pastas. For seconds try some of their seafood concoctions like *antipasti di gamberetti e calamari* (antipasta of small shrimp and squid), or their fresh vegetables either cooked in oven or grilled (*verdure al forno or grigliatta*) or their *scampi reali al whisky* (large shrimp cooked in a whisky sauce. You can also find cold roast beef, which is excellent.

22. TRATTORIA CAMBUSA, *Via Mascarella 8, Tel. 051/266-645. Closed Mondays and August. All credit cards accepted. Dinner for two L76,000.*

If you like fish come here, that's basically all they have. Everything from sardines to crustaceans baked in the oven , cooked over the grill, or lightly fried in a succulent batter. For dessert try their excellent cannoli.

23. RISTORANTE CESARINA, *Via Santo Stefano 19/b, Tel. 051/232-037. Closed Mondays and Tuesdays at Dinner. All credit cards accepted. Dinner for two L140,000.*

Enjoy the beauty of Piazza Santo Stefano from the terrace of this restaurant or savor the smells from the kitchen if you sit inside. This place is a little upscale even though they serve many traditional local dishes. Their *fritto misto* (mixed fried vegetables) is simply great and their *tortellini in brodo* (tortellini in soup) is perfect. They also make an excellent *spaghetti alla vongole verace* (with a spicy clam and oil based sauce), *risotto alla pescatore* (rice with fish), or *scampi alla griglia* (grilled shrimp).

24. LA TAVERNA DEL GHIOTTO, *Via San Vitale 9B, Tel. 051/26-68-51. Closed Sundays. Credit cards accepted. Dinner for two L50,000.*

As you enter you'll see a small bar with a marble counter in front of a beautiful wood frame of large mirrors, and to your right are a few tables in this cute little ristorante. The whitewashed walls really set off both the mirrors and the dark wood beamed ceiling. A friendly local place, try the *tagliatelli al ragu* (with meat sauce) or the *risotto alla parmigiana* (rice with a rich parmesan sauce; you're in the land of *Parmegiano Reggiano* so let's try some it.) for primo. For secondo they have *arrosti misti* (great mixed roasted meats) or *fritto misto* (mixed deep fried meats).

25. LE DONNE BOUDOIR, *Via Mascaarella 5a, Tel 051 23-54-24. No credit cards accepted. Closed Mondays. Open 7:00pm - 4:00am. Dinner for two L90,000.*

An eclectic decorative touch with posters of old, and some dead, American film stars. After getting past the cafe/bar entrance, you enter the cramped surrounding that serves as the dining room. If you're over 5'8" tall, you need to sit at one of the booths against the wall so you can stretch your legs. The food is great especially any of the *tortellini* or *tortelloni* dishes, as well as the *mozzarelle fritte* (fried balls of mozzarella) and *verdure fritte* (fried vegetables). Beware of the waitresses, they are not the most pleasant (to foreigners) but ignore their ignorance and enjoy a fabulous meal.

26. RISTORANTE/PIZZERIA IL DOGE, *Via Caldarese 5a. Credit cards accepted. Closed Mondays. Tel. 051/22-79-80. Dinner for two (only pizza) L35,000.*

A large place on a side street off the Via San Vitale that has a great atmosphere created by wood paneling and stained glass windows and the superb service. As you sit down they bring you a small *bruschetta* (hard garlic bread covered in olive oil and tomatoes). Anything you try here will be good, especially the pizza that they make in the centrally located pizza oven. Each pizza is large, at least 12 inches and they're generous with their toppings. Maybe not like in North America but still a good amount. They also have a good selection of meat and fish dishes.

27. CLOROFILLA, *Strada Maggiore 64c, Tel. 051/235-343. Closed Sundays. Credit cards accepted. Meal for two L 30,000.*

Specializes in vegetarian meals with a large menu from which you're sure to find something you like. They also have wines and beers that were prepared without damaging the environment. You can get fruit salads, regular salads, soybean burgers, couscous, a variety of cheeses, veggie sandwiches, and much more. Even though Italian food itself is fresh and healthy, if you don't even want to see meat on the menu, come here and enjoy your meal in air conditioned comfort.

28. RISTORANTE ALICE, *65a Via D'Azeglio, Tel. 051/583-359. Closed Wednesdays. Credit cards accepted. Dinner for two L L55,000.*

This is a classic, intimate dining establishment a little off the beaten path from the historic center. If you're staying out here please come and enjoy their *risotto al pescecarne* (rice with fish and meat) or the *risotto alla medici* (cheese and ham), otherwise it's not so spectacular that you need to trek all this way. For seconds they make a great *vegetariana con formaggio alla griglia* (vegetarian dish with cheese grilled).

29. TRATTORIA DEL SANTO, *Via Urbana #7F. Credit cards accepted. Dinner for two L60,000*

Real Bolognese cooking at an authentic local place. You can sit outside under the arcaded sidewalk and a canopy on a busy road and breathe exhaust fumes, or sit inside in a plainly furnished place. Try any of their *tortellini* or *tortellone* dishes, especially the *alla panna* (with a thick rich cream sauce that you cover with parmesan). For seconds try the *cotoletta alla bolognese* (veal cutlet covered with milk and tomatoes sauce) or the *scaloppine alla pizzaiolo* (veal covered with melted cheese and tomato sauce).

30. RISTORANTE NOTAI, *Via De' Pignattari, Tel. 051/228-694. Fax 051/265-872. Closed Sunday. Dinner for two L90,000.*

Upper crust dining with a hint of *cucina nuova* thrown in. Some local dishes and some creative ones. Start off with an appetizer of the *prosciutto di Parma* (local ham) or the *salsice in olio d'oliva* (local pork sausages in olive oil). Next try the *tortellini alla bolognese* (cheese stuffed pasta covered in a delicate veal, milk and tomato sauce) or the *spaghetti al pomodoro e salsice fresca* (with tomato sauce and fresh sausages). That should fill you up, but if you're still hungry try their *filetto al tartuffo* (steak covered with truffles).

31. RISTORANTE FAGLIANO, *Calca Vinazzi de Gessi. Credit cards accepted. Closed Thursdays. Dinner for two L65,000.*

On a little side street just off the main road Via Ugo Bassi, they have outside seating under an awning as well as a large inside seating area covered in wood and marble. I despise their lime green tablecloths, but ignore them and enjoy the food. They make great pastas, especially the local favorites *tortellini alla panna* (with cream sauce) and *tagliatelli alla Bolognese* (with veal, milk and tomato sauce.) They also make a dish that is similar to *penne all'arabbiatta* from Rome, called *penne all'diavolo* (devil's pasta, meaning it's hot and spicy with garlic and hot peppers in a tomato and olive oil base). The menu is huge. They also serve pizza, for lunch and dinner, as well as some wonderful dishes cooked over the grill. Try the *Formaggi alla griglia* (grilled cheeses) or the *grigliatta vegetale* (grilled vegetables). Centrally located so it's easy to find.

32. PIZZERIA RISTORANTE BIA CATARI, *Via Montegrappa 7/8, Tel. 22-48-71. Closed Mondays. Credit cards accepted. Dinner for two L75,000.*

If you want some seafood, this place specializes in it. They only have inside seating but it's large, light and comfortable. Try the *antipasto di mare freddo* (cold mixed seafood) or the *cocktail di gamberi* (shrimp cocktail). Skip the pasta altogether and head right to the *fritto misto di mare* (fried mixed seafood) or the *grigliatta mista* (grilled mixed seafood). A great atmposhere with fine service, even for tourists.

33. TRATTORIA CIRO, *5B Via de Gessi. Closed Wednesdays. Credit cards accepted. Dinner for two L60,000.*

Here you can have a peaceful dinner on a private terrace on a small side street away from all the hustle and bustle of Bologna. If you want to watch the pizza chef at work, sit inside around the tile covered oven. Besides pizza they serve great pastas, especially the *spaghetti alla carbonara* (with cheese, ham, and egg) or the *tortellini al piacere* (tortellini made any way you want them). For seconds try any of their pizzas. Knowing that most people in this city like their cheese, they have an option to double the cheese for an extra L2,000. This makes the pizza very much like a North American concoction.

34. TRATTORIA HOSTARIA BELLE ARTE, *Via Belle Arti 6, Tel 051/126-76-48. Closed Sundays. No credit cards accepted. Dinner for two L55,000.*

Set on a side street with outside seating under an awning, and a larger area inside of plain brick with whitewashed walls festooned with pictures, this is a good place to come for a relaxing meal Bologna Style. Try the *Tagliatelle ragu bolognese* or the *tortellini all panna*. They also have some Roman favorites like *amatriciana* and *arrabbiata*. If you're in search of meat try the *braciola di maiale* (arm of pork) or the *grigliatta misto* (mixed grill with pork, lamb and beef).

35. ANTICA RISTORANTE, *San Iobbe 3D. Credit cards accepted. Closed Sundays. Dinner for two L75,000.*

Down a twisting alley that is between the Via del Inferno and the Via Oberdan, here you can enjoy a relatively inexpensive meal in a quiet and comfortable surrounding. (Bring a map to find it). They serve Bolognese specials like *Tagliatelle Bolognese* (with veal, milk and tomato sauce) and *Tortellini al Basilico e pomodoro* (cheese stuffed pasta with a basil and tomato sauce). For secondo they have *castrate* (lamb) and *grigliata mista* (mixed grill with lamb, pork and beef).

36. TRATTORIA GIANNI, *Via Clavature 18. Tel. 051/22-94-34. Credit cards accepted. Closed Mondays. Dinner for two L70,000.*

Down a little alley off of the Via Clavature, you can get a taste of old Bologna here. Both in the decor, which is simple brick walls with pictures of the city interspersed, as well as the menu, which changes daily based on the produce available. The staples you'll find are the *tortellini* or *tortelloni* pasta dishes (small and large cheese stuffed pasta with a variety of sauces) as well as an antipasto of *prosciutto di Parma* and any form of *maiale* (pork) or *vitello* (veal). A great experience for dining because of its hidden location and great food.

Late Night Cafes & Restaurants

Calm by day, Bologna, in large part due to the presence of tens of thousands of students, comes alive at night, especially in the small neighborhood *osterie*. You will find them open late all over town, mainly on the weekends to cater to a late night eating and drinking crowd. Most of them, as you might expect, are around the university.

37. CANTINA BENTIVOGLIO, *Via Mascarella 4B. Closed Mondays. Open 8:00pm–2:00am.*

Enter, walk through an entrance corridor, and descend the stairs to a vast renovated wine cellar. On most nights the place will be packed by

9:30pm, not only to hear the tantalizing live music but also to enjoy the *vino*, plates of pasta and *crostini* (sandwiches, like their *pizzaiolo* with mozzarella, tomatoes and oregano) or the *prosciutto* (with mozzarella and ham). If you want a true Italian late night adventure, try this place out.

38. PICCOLO BAR, *Piazza Giusseppe Verdi 4, Tel 051/227-147. Open 8:30am-3:00am.*

Hip little cafe bar that's open until the wee hours for beer (Bass on tap; pint costs L6,000), wine, drinks, and few snack foods like small pizza or *crostini* (sandwiches) made to order. Deep in the heart of the student section this is where Bologna's version of *P.I.B.s* (people in black) hang out. Try to shed the colorful tourist clothing and put on subtler colors prior to coming here.

If you're generally frightened of people with tattoos and long hair don't come here. Enjoy the ambiance of the evening and the parade of counterculture locals while sitting at the tables on the piazza. If they're all full, and they usually are, settle next to the bar or at one of the small tables inside. Besides drinks they also serve coffee to keep you going until closing. A fun place at night and a relaxing place during the day. Rumor has it that this is the druggie hangout, but I noticed no such activity while I was there. Just good clean alcohol and cigarettes.

39. HARRY'S PUB/OSTERIA, *Via Vinazzetti 5. Closed Sundays. No credit cards accepted. Open 8:00pm-3:00am.*

A dark, rustic wooden decor, definitely not of the same kind we have come to know and love (hate?) in Venice, Florence and Rome. This is a down-to-earth place serving drinks and small snacks like pasta, sandwiches and salads, as well as desserts and ice cream. As always drinks are around L10,000 and the pints are L6,000.

SEEING THE SIGHTS

Bologna is literally made for walking and sightseeing. There are over 20 miles of arcaded sidewalks that make a brief *passegiatta* a veritable stroll into history. Some of these arcades, or *portici*, date back to the 12th century when the *comune* (the government of Bologna) faced a housing shortage as a result of massive enrollment in the University, so they ordered housing to be built onto existing buildings over the sidewalks . As it turned out, the Bolognese grew attached to these *portici*, not only for their beauty, but also for the protection they offer from the elements.

The best part of Bologna as a walkers paradise is that a large part of the historical city center is off-limits to private automobiles, giving you the freedom to move. Like Venice, Bologna is so well preserved that you can walk down medieval streets and witness, side by side, countless historically sacred living exhibitions of northern Italian architecture from the 12th through the 18th centuries.

A. TORRI GARISENDA & ASINELLI, PIAZZA DI PORTA RAVEGNANA

Torre degli Asinelli is open daily from 9am–6pm. In the winter only until 5pm. Admission L3,000.

The **Due Torre** (two towers) were erected in the 12th century as military observation posts. Eventually towers became the fashionable structure to erect as a symbol of your family's wealth (that's why one of Bologna's names is "The Turreted"), as well as a wise military investment for the city. Today only a small handful of them remain, the largest of which is the **Asinelli Tower**, which rises over 320 feet and has a wonderful observation deck from which you can see all of Bologna.

The **Garrisenda Tower** right next to it leans quite a bit more than the other and appears as if it is trying affectionately to touch the Asinelli Tower. From this point, five ancient avenues branch off and lead to a gate on the old city walls. The best of these streets to take is the **Via Santo Stefano**, where great sights await you from the towers.

B. VIA SANTO STEFANO

This is a terrific street to wander along. Stop at the **Piazza del Mercanzi**, which is dominated by the **Merchant's Palace**, an ornate Gothic building that served as the center of Bologna's trade in the 14th century and today houses the chamber of commerce. Go and see the gold plated replica of a pasta noodle inside.

As you proceed down Santo Stefano, it's like walking back in time. With each building you pass, the centuries seem to drop away. You'll pass rows of graceful *palazzi* built by the powerful families of Bologna. Numbers 9 through 11 are interesting because of their sculpted terra cotta facades.

One of the best places along this street is at a small triangular square with a grouping of seven little churches known collectively as **Le Sette Chiese**. You can explore each of their tiny ancient chapels and cloisters of these interconnected buildings and nary see a soul. You will feel as if you are the only one who knows about this humble and hushed place.

C. PIAZZA DEL NETTUNO

You're confronted by a startling nude, hugely muscled statue of *Neptune*, trident in hand, attended by four sirens squirting water from their nipples. Stare at the fountain enough and it seems to come to life.

D. PIAZZA MAGGIORE

This *piazza* is one of the most theatrical public spaces in Italy. This vast, raised square is bordered by Gothic and Romanesque facades and the large basilica of **San Petronio**. It is the place to come and socialize for Bolognese. Just off this piazza is a little neighborhood of streets named after the wares they have sold since the middle ages.

You can find some great stores in this area. For example, try the **Paolo Atti & Pigli** on Via Caprarie that sells a wide array of fresh breads and pastas. A few doors down is the **Pescheria Brunelli** that sells mountains of fresh fish daily. At the corner of the Via Drapperie and Via Caprarie you'll find a great gourmet store, **Tamburini**, which has anything and everything you could imagine. You'll find hams, salamis, sausages, cheses, olive oil, bread, pastas, and the best sight is an immense pig, impaled on a large spit being turned ever so slowly over an open fire. The smell is so tantalizing that you can't help but buy something.

E. SAN PETRONIO

Piazza Maggiore, Tel. 220-637. Open 7:30am-7pm.

Located on the south side of the Piazza Maggiore, this Gothic basilica is the largest church in Bologna and is dedicated to the city's patron saint. It was begun in 1390 but it was never completed according to plan. In fact, construction stopped abruptly in 1650 and never continued. The sculpture on the main doorway of the facade is by Jacopo della Quercia. The interior nave is 117 meters long, 48 meters wide and just over 40 meters high, and the decorations are purely Gothic. A wonderful place to come to get out of the rain, but not that thrilling in and of itself.

F. SAN PIETRO

Via del'Indipendenza. Open 7am-7pm.

If you exit Piazza Maggiore and go up Via dell'Indipendenza towards the train station, you'll run into the Cathedral on the right hand side of the street. It was founded in 910 and has a choir created by Tibaldi in 1575 and a Baroque nave created in 1605 and added to periodically through time. Even though smaller in scale than San Petronio, I found this church to be filled with much more interesting pieces of artwork.

G. UNIVERSITA

Via Zamboni 33, Tel. 259-021.

The **University**, founded in 1088, is the oldest such institution in Europe. By the 13th century it had attracted more than 10,000 students from all over Europe. Its alumni include Dante Aligheri, Petrarch, Thomas a Becket, and more recently Federico Fellini.

The campus, such as it is being in the center of a city, contains both old and new buildings on both sides of the **Via Zamboni** (named after the guy who invented that thing that cleans the ice at hockey games). To see real Italian university life, all you need to do is stroll through the maze of streets with walls covered with graffiti and posters and stop in one of the coffeehouses or *trattoria* catering to the students. The place is alive.

H. ANATOMY MUSEUM OF DOMESTIC ANIMALS

Via Belmeloro 8, Tel. 051/354-243. Open Monday–Saturday 9am–1pm and on Wednesday also open 3–5pm.

You need to call ahead for an appointment to see these samples of dissected pets.

I. PORTA SARAGOZZA & GUARDIA HILL

On my last morning in Bologna during my most recent trip, I went on a long walk that took me out of town through the **Porta Saragozza** and up the **Guardia Hill**, at the top of which stands the sanctuary of the **Madonna di San Luca**. The air was soft with a light rain, just as it had been every morning since I'd arrived. Nonetheless, as I strolled some two miles, I stayed completely dry – thanks to an arcade formed, according to the experts, of no fewer than 666 arches. It is a walk the Bolognese have been taking every May since the 15th century as part of a religious procession in which a revered Byzantine image of the Madonna is carried to the sanctuary.

But it wasn't this sacred object I was hoping to see; it was a view of Bologna. Reaching the top and emerging from under the portico, I turned to look back. The rain had stopped. The day had brightened. For a moment, I glimpsed through the mist that vast carpet of red brick, reposing quietly below.

NIGHTLIFE & ENTERTAINMENT

Nightclubs

If you're into the nightclub scene, the ones in Bologna are a little different. The places are like upscale bars that are frequented by all, but they have an added bonus if you're into this – strippers. If you're not into this, these places will not be right for you.

• **Penny**, *Via delle Moline 18D Tel 051/235-050. Closed Sundays. Open 10:30pm - 5:00am.*
• **La Dolce Vita**, *Via Porta di Castello, 2/II, Tel. 051/22-35-20. Closed Mondays. Open 10:00pm - 5:00am.*

Pubs

There seems to be an affinity for the Irish/English-style pub atmosphere. The drinking is definitely not as heavy, but the ambiance is true to form. Here's a few places you should try if you need a pint of ale.

- **The Irish Times Pub**, *Via Paradiso 1D, Tel. 051/261-648. Happy Hour 7:30pm - 8:30pm from Tuesday - Friday; 6:30pm - 8:30pm Saturday and Sunday. Closed Mondays.* Serves Guiness, Harp and Kilkenny for L6,000 a pint.
- **Il Druido**, *Via Mascarella 26B, Tel 051/22-67-57.* Serves drinks, wine, and pints of Guiness, Harp, and Kilkenny for L6,000 a pint.
- **King's Road Pub**, *Via saragozza 15, Tel 051/644-8426.* Serves food since they are also a restaurant and Labatts for L6,000 a pint.

SPORTS & RECREATION
Golf
- **Golf Club Bologna**, *Via Sabbatini 69, 40050 Monte San Pietro. Tel. 051/969-100. Fax 051/672-0017.* Located 18 km from Bologna, this is a relatively short par 72, 18 hole course. It tops out at 6,171 meters in length. It's open year round except on Mondays. They have a driving range, pro shop, good restaurant, nice bar, and a refreshing pool where your partner can relax while you hit the links.
- **Castenaso Golf & Country Club**, *Via Ca Belfiore 8, 40055 Castenaso. Tel. 051/788-126. Fax 051/789-006.* Located 10 km from Bologna, this is only a nine hole course, 2560 meters in length, and is a par 33. It's open from September to July and is closed Monday mornings. They have a driving range and a putting green.
- **Golf Club Centro**, *Via Dei Tigli 4, 44042 Cento. Tel. 051/683-0504. Fax 051/683-5287.* Located 30 km from Bologna, this is also a nine hole course. It is shorter, only 2,486 meters and is a par 27. The course is open year round except on Mondays. They have a club house, driving range, practice green, and a good practice bunker.
- **Golf Club Molino Del Pero**, *Via Molino del Pero 323, 40036 Monzuno. Tel. 051/677-0506.* Located 25 km from Bologna, this is a par 35, nine hole course that is 2,610 meters long. The course is open year long except on Mondays. The facilities available are a driving range, a nineteenth hole bar, and a pro shop.
- **Argenta Golf Club**, *Via Poderi 2A - SS16, km 100, 44011 Argenta. Tel. 0532/852-545.* Located 45 km from Bologna, 40km from Ravenna, and 32km from Ferrara, this is a par 71, 18 hole course that is 6,400 meters in length. It's open from February 21st to January 5th and is closed Tuesdays. They have a restaurant, bar, driving range and putting green.

Tennis
- **Giardini Margherita**, *Viale R Cristiani 2*
- **Bocciodromo Primavera**, *Via G Bertini*

SHOPPING

Since Bologna has over 20 miles of arcaded sidewalks and most of the historic city center is free from automobile traffic, it is definitely made for walking and window shoppering. All around the **Piazza Maggiore** and **Nettuno**, in the modern **Galleria** just off the **Via Cavour**, and all along the **Via dell' Indipendenza** and **Marconi** are located the small specialized shops that make shopping in Italy so much fun.

Leather goods for many of Italy's most famous designers are manufactured in and around Bologna, which makes all types of shoes, belts, briefcases, wallets, purses, etc., with or without the famous name label, extremely good value. You'll find many of these shops on the major streets listed above. Lately there has been an encroachment of the Benneton's, the McDonalds, and other worldwide chains, but the majority are still homegrown little Italian stores.

Books & Newspapers in English
• **Feltrinelli International**, *Via Zamboni 7, Tel. 051/26-80-70*. Located near the University, this store sells a small amount of books in English.

Department Stores
• **Standa**, *Via Rizzoli 7*
• **Rinascente**, *Via Ugo Bassi 21*
• **COIN**, *Via dei Mille/Piazza Martiri*

Markets
• **Piazza Otto Agosto**, *Friday and Saturday from 8:00am–7:00pm*. Food, clothing, shoes, watches, flea market stuff, antiques. Everything and anything. Come to browse or get a good bargain.
• **Piazza San Francesco**, *Wednesdays from 8:00am–6:00pm*. Flowers and plants.
• **Piazza Aldrovandi**, *every day from 7:00am to 1:00pm and from 4:00pm to 7:30pm*. Great selection of cheese, meat, fruit, and vegetables.
• **Piazza di Porta San Mamolo**, *every day from 7:00am–1:00pm*. Food products, and a variety of clothing, shoes, belts, etc.
• **Via Ugo Bassi**, *Open all day, every day*. This is actually a covered market that sells food products, a variety of goods like clothing shoes, etc.

Picnic Supplies & Miscellaneous Goodies
I've numbered these and placed them on the map in addition to the hotels and restaurants, in part because they're so darn good.
40. Paolo Atti & Pigli, *Via Caprarie*.
Sells a wide array of fresh breads and pastas.

41. Tamburini, *at the corner of the Via Drapperie and Via Caprarie.*
A great gourmet store, which has anything and everything you could imagine. You'll find hams, salamis, sausages, cheses, olive oil, bread, pastas, and the best sight of all – an immense pig, impaled on a large spit being turned ever so slowly over an open fire. The smell is so tantalizing that you can't help but buy something.

42. Formaggeria Al Regno della Forma, *Via G. Oberdan 45a.*
If you want to witness great wheels of cheese stacked one on top of the other to the ceiling, come in here. The aroma is stupendous, as is the sight of all that cheese. If you want to take a picture, be polite and ask the proprietor first. He really doesn't mind, but his customers like to get out of the way of us nosy tourists. Stay for the sights and the smells and even purchase *un etto* (about 1/4 pound) of the wonderful cheese. Remember to let it melt in your mouth.

43. Al Palombo, *Via Clavature.*
This has got to be the best *cartoleria* (stationery store) I've every seen. You can get any type of writing instrument, notebook, paperweight, and other paper product here, all in the Italian fashion mode. So to get something for friends at work or just for yourself, this is the place to shop.

Supermarkets
• **COOP Emilia Veneto**, *Via Montebello 2/3*
• **Conad**, *Via Finelli 8*
• **PAM**, *Via Guglielmo Marcnini 28/A*
• **Conad**, *Via Santo Isaia 67*

PRACTICAL INFORMATION
Bank Hours and Changing Money
Monday to Friday, 8:20 am–1:20 pm and 2:45pm–3:45 pm. All the local banks change money at a variety of different rates and fees. It's best to shop around and ask. The key factor is what fee they charge, since some take a large percentage of the total even when their rate is excellent.
You can also change money in the *cambio* at the train station. Open Monday to Friday, 7:30am–1:15pm and 2:15pm–7:30pm.

Business Hours
Bologna is a shopper's paradise especially along the main drag, the **Via Indipendenza**. Here you'll find the shops open from 9:00am to 1:00pm and then they re-open at 3:30pm and stay open until 8:00pm. The thoroughfare is crowded during the late evening hours as people take their *passegiatta* just prior to their dinner.

Laundries
These are all self-service:
- **Laundry**, *Via Todaro 4. Tel 051/24-07-40. Open Monday to Friday, 8:00am–7:00pm, Saturday 8:30am–1:00pm. Not Open Sunday.*
- **Saragozza**, *Via Saragozza 41, Tel. 051/33-10-62. Open Monday to Friday 8:00am–7:00pm, Saturday 8:30am–1:00pm. Not Open Sunday.*
- **Bolle i Sapone di Masetti Giovanni**, *Via Petroni 22B, Tel. 051/22-17-79. Open Monday to Friday, 8:00am–7:00pm. Saturday 8:30am–1:00pm. Not Open Sunday.*

Postal Services
The only post office I could locate in the entire city was at *Via Guerrazzi #10*, open Monday to Friday, 8:00am–6:00pm.

Tourist Information & Maps
- **IAT Office**, *Piazza Medaglio d'Oro, Stazione Ferroviara, 40121 Bologna. Tel 051/246-541. Open Monday to Saturday, 9:00am–7:00pm.* This is the hotel reservations and information office at the station that can make reservations for you if you have none, and you can get a free, excellent tourist map.
- **Informazione Ferrovie**, *Stazione Ferroviara, Tel. 051/264-490. Open 8:00am–8:00pm.* This is where you get train scheduling information. You need to take a number and wait for it to be called. The service representatives are behind glass doors that only open when they've finished with another customer. Be prepared and quick. They close the doors and change the numbers very fast. Enjoy the spectacle of the chaotic Italians completely baffled by an orderly system, like waiting your turn. Some will simply stand there amazed that they can't cut in line, only later realizing they have to get a ticket. The beauty of Italy is that everything functions even with all this chaos.

Tour Operators
- **Big Tours**, *Via Indipendenza 12, 40121 Bologna, Tel. 051/23-84-11. Fax 051/265-771.*
- **Conray**, *Via Andrea Costa 3a, 40134 Bologna. Tel 051/43-02-06. Fax 051/61-45-252.*
- **Wagon-Lit Travel**, *Piazza Azzarita 1L. Tel 051/52-01-06.*

DAY TRIPS & EXCURSIONS
In this section, explorations include trips to **Parma** and **Ferrara**, both charming, old towns with tons of charm and character.

PARMA

With a population of approximately 180,000, **Parma** is the provincial capital and a well known Italian university town. Back in 183 BC, Parma started off as an isolated Roman outpost and colony. After the fall of the Roman Empire, Parma was controlled by a variety of rulers. First they passed from Milan's control (1346 to 1512) to Papal control (1512 to 1542). Then in 1542, Pope Paul III gave the duchies of Parma and Piacenza to his son (yes, back then not only were the Popes involved in business activities like land grants, but in more carnal activities too), Pier Luigi Farnese.

After the Farnese male line died out in 1731, the duchies were transferred to the Bourbons. Then in 1807, Parma came under the control of the French, and eventually were given to Napoleon's wife, Maria Louise. But then the Italian movement for their own country took hold, and the people of Parma expelled the French in 1859 and Parma was incorporated into the new Italian state.

Now Parma, that warm, medieval city of domes, spires, and bell towers, a city rich in history, is known for its food products: *Prosciutto di Parma*, and especially its famous cheese called *Parmigiano-Reggiano*. Cows in Parma are imported and bred specifically for the richness and quantity of their milk, the milk that will eventually become the King of Cheeses. Cheese making in Parma is considered an art form as well as a respected career, which is passed down from father to son and sometimes from mother to daughter. The whey, which is the byproduct of the cheese making process, becomes the diet of the huge Parma pigs, those that provide the succulent *Prosciutto di Parma*.

As you'll notice when you go to any restaurant in Parma, they all use *Parmiggiano-Reggiano* in immense quantities and with a creative flair, as well as serving large quantities of *Prosciutto di Parma*, usually with melon. Like Bologna the Fat, Parma is a great place to eat.

ARRIVALS & DEPARTURES

By Car
Simply get on the A1 highway from Bologna and follow it all the way to Parma. For a more scenic route, take the smaller road SS 9 which leads directly into the city.

By Train
Trains leave for Parma every hour at the 38th minute, and return to Bologna at the 25th minute of the hour. The trip takes one hour. The **station** is on the north edge of the center, on the Piazzale C. Alberto della Chiesa, and at the end of Via Verdi and Viale Toschi.

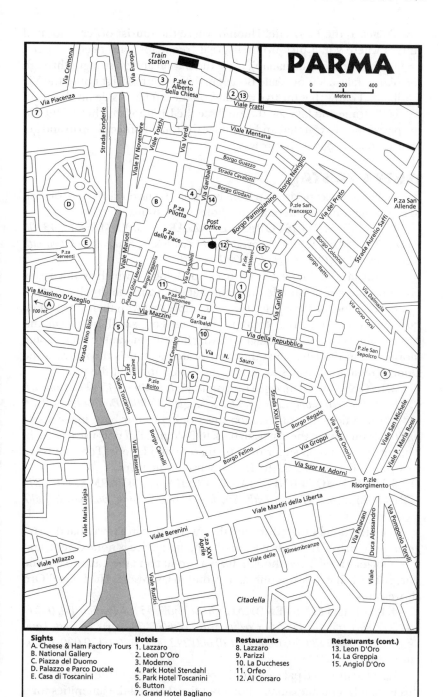

PARMA

0   200   400
Meters

Sights
A. Cheese & Ham Factory Tours
B. National Gallery
C. Piazza del Duomo
D. Palazzo e Parco Ducale
E. Casa di Toscanini

Hotels
1. Lazzaro
2. Leon D'Oro
3. Moderno
4. Park Hotel Stendahl
5. Park Hotel Toscanini
6. Button
7. Grand Hotel Bagliano

Restaurants
8. Lazzaro
9. Parizzi
10. La Duccheses
11. Orfeo
12. Al Corsaro

Restaurants (cont.)
13. Leon D'Oro
14. La Greppia
15. Angiol D'Oro

To get to the Piazza del Duomo where the **tourist office** is located (this is where you'll pick up their great free maps – no need to spend L8,000 for one at a Giornaliao), leave the station and go straight through the piazza, take a left on Viale Boteggo, then your first right onto the Via Garibaldi. Follow that for five minutes on the left hand side until you get to Via Pisacane and take a left. You'll see the Duomo from here. Once in the piazza look to your left and you'll see the tourist office. Stop in and get your map and you're on our way.

WHERE TO STAY

Make Parma a one day trip from Bologna, but if you like it here or wish to stay a night or two, here are my hotel suggestions.

1. HOTEL AND RISTORANTE LAZZARO, *Via XX Marzo 14, 43100 Parma. Tel. 0521/208-944. 8 rooms, 3 doubles with bath, 5 singles, only two with bath. Double L65,000; Single L38,000-42,000.* *

If you missed the last train back to Bologna, which is not really possibly unless you stumbled into the station around midnight, this is a wonderfully inexpensive place to stay. Couple that with their fine restaurant and you have a great combo. The rooms are small, but clean and comfortable. I would even suggest staying here if you want to spend some more time in the city, since they are located a stone's throw from the Duomo on a quiet little side street – and you can't beat the price.

2. LEON D'ORO, *Albergho Ristorante, Viale Fratti 4a, 43100 Parma. tel. 0521/773-182. 16 rooms none with bath. Single L45,000; Double L55,000.* *

Located near the train station this would be your best, inexpensive option if you missed the last train back to Bologna. But only use it as such. Their restaurant is far superior to their accommodations. The rooms are very tiny and are clean in the Italian sense of the word.

3. HOTEL MODERNO, VIA A CECCHI 4, 43100 PARMA. Tel *0521/772-647. 46 rooms, 37 with bath. Single L44,000-57,000; Double L63,000-89,000.* **

A typical hotel situated around the train station in a town that doesn't get many tourists. Basically it is run-down, the service is nonexistent, and the ambiance is nil. Even though this is a two star and the Lazzaro is a one star, go there first. Use this only as a second-to-last resort. The Leon d'Oro above is the last.

4. PARK HOTEL STENDHAL, *Via Boboni 3, 43100 Parma. Tel. 0521/208-057. Fax 0521/285-655. Credit cards accepted. 60 rooms all with bath. Single L115,000-158,000; Double L180,000-242,000. Suite L170,000. Breakfast L18,000 extra.* ****

Located in an old palace near the center of town and the train station, this is mainly a businessman's hotel but they have all the amenities for a fine tourist stay, including a great restaurant featuring *parmiggiano reggianno* and *prosciutto di Parma*. The rooms are immaculate and are large enough to lounge around in.

5. PARK HOTEL TOSCANINI, *Viale A Toscanini 4, 43100 Parma. Tel. 0521/289-141. Fax 0521/283-143. Credit cards accepted. 48 rooms all with bath. Single L105,000-152,000; Double L170,000-220,000. L16,000 extra for breakfast.* ****

Located near the center and the Toscanini museum, this hotel is the perfect place to stay for you music lovers since they have a piano bar. A good four star that caters mainly to the Italian businessman traveling to Parma. Nonetheless you'll find the accommodations clean and comfortable.

6. HOTEL BUTTON, *Borgo Salina 7, 43100 Parma. Tel. 0521/208-039. Fax 0521/238-783. Credit Cards accepted. 41 rooms all with bath. Single L90,000; Double L115,000. Breakfast L12,000.* ***

Centrally located near the university. This place caters to the budgets of visiting professors and families. It's clean and comfortable and quite affordable. The director, Giorgio Cortesi, is pleasant and bends over backwards to make your stay pleasant. A good budget choice while in Parma.

7. GRAND HOTEL BAGLIANO, *Viale Piacenza 12c, 43100 Parma. Tel. 0521/292-929. Fax 292-828. 169 rooms all with bath. Single L120,000-230,000; Double L170,000-320,000. Suite L390,000-700,000. Breakfast included.* ****

If you want to stay in the best that Parma can offer, this is it. But it'll cost you. They have everything from a piano bar to saunas to barbers and hair stylists, as well as a first class restaurant that you can also enjoy from room service. First class, top notch, a number one. The best in Parma.

WHERE TO EAT

8. RISTORANTE LAZZARO, *Via XX Marzo 14, Tel. 0521/208-944. No credit cards accepted. Dinner for two L 55,000.*

If you've ever wanted to try filet of horse (*filleto di cavallo*) look no further. It's really quite good, and no, it doesn't taste like chicken or beef. It's tender and succulent and a true culinary experience, definitely one you can tell your friends about. If that doesn't grab you, try their *costine di agnello* (lamb chop). For primo try some of their truly native pasta dishes like the *tortelli dei erbetta* (pasta stuffed with ricotta and made with butter and covered in *parmigiana*). A great atmosphere with good food just off the Piazza del Duomo.

9. PARIZZI, *Strada Repubblica 71. Tel. 0521/285-952. Credit cards accepted. Dinner for two L90,000. Closed Mondays and in the summer also Sundays.*

A large, friendly place set in an elegant dining environment, after you get past the rather shabby covered walkway you have to use to get to the entrance. Everything here is great, especially the local dishes. For primo try the *tortelli d'erbetta alla parmigiana* (pasta stuffed with ricotta in butter and covered with *parmigiana*). then be adventurous with the *trippa alla parmigiana* (tripe made in local fashion smothered in cheese). For a healthier diet try the *teste di funghi ai ferri* (grilled heads of mushrooms).

10. RISTORANTE/PIZZERIA LA DUCCHESE, *Piazza Garibaldi 1, Tel. 0521/235-962. Credit cards accepted. Closed Mondays. Dinner for two L50,000.*

You have to go with a pasta first course and a pizza second course here. They are both great. Try the local pizza, *Parmigiana* (with tomatoes, mozzarella, ham and cooked egg) or the *prosciutto fungi* (ham and mushrooms) if you're not in the adventurous mood. For pasta they make an excellent *capelleti alla parmigiana* (pasta shaped like little hats with ricotta, spinach, grated cheese and butter) as well as a *carbonara* (with egg, butter and ham).

11. PIZZERIA ORFEO, *Via Carducci 5, Tel 0521/285-483. Credit cards accepted. Dinner for two L50,000.*

The price above reflects if you have two pizzas apiece. A fun local place with over 120 seats in four different rooms. This place gets packed on the weekends and is loud and boisterous. Simple decor except in the *cantina vecchia* in the basement with its arched brick ceilings. The pizzas are great. If you're in the front room you can enjoy the spectacle of the pizzas being prepared. Try any of their offerings and you'll be satisfied, especially with the German beer they offer on tap.

12. PIZZERIA AL CORSARO, *Via Cavour 37, Tel. 0521/235-402 or 221-311. Dinner for two L55,000.*

If you both have a large pizza and an order of their superb pasta, the price above will be expected. You have to look inside if you've seated yourself in their private patio, especially if you have kids, since their bar is half of a twenty foot boat. They are a Neapolitan restaurant, ergo the nautical theme. Try any of their special pastas (*carbonara, arrabiata or amatriciana*) and save yourself for the pizza of the house, the *Napoli* (with tomatoes, mozzarella, oregano and anchovies).

13. RISTORANTE LEON D'ORO, *Viale Fratti 4a, Tel 0521/773-182. Credit cards accepted. Dinner for two L70,000.*

An almost upscale place that has a definitely low-scale hotel attached to it. The decor is plain and simple, but is a favorite of all the locals in the area. Try the *salume misto* (mixed salamis) and/or the *prosciutto Parma* (ham from Parma) as an appetizer, then jump right into some more meat dishes. They have a good *arristi misto* (mixed grill) and a *roost beef* (that's how they spell it).

14. LA GREPPIA, *Strada Garibaldi 39a, Tel. 0521/233-686. Closed Mondays and Tuesdays and all of July. All credit cards accepted. Dinner for two L140,000.*
Housed in a former stable, which lends a country air to the place. There's an excellent *pasta di verdure* (pasta with vegetables) and *tortelli d'erbetta alla parmigiana* (large tortellini with herbs and parmigiana), but overall I found the restaurant to be average.
15. RISTORANTE ANGIOL D'OR, *Vicolo Scutellari 1, Tel. 0521/282-632. Closed Sundays. All credit cards accepted. Dinner for two L130,000.*
An elegant but simple dining experience, you'll still find the packets of bread sticks on the tables, something higher-end establishments frown upon. The kitchen is superb and makes the best of the local ingredients when they are fresh. For this reason, the menu here changes dramatically every three months. I've had some good *tortelli di patate con porcini* (potato tortelli with porcini mushrooms) and *petto di pollo con salsa di vino rosso* (breast of chicken cooked in red wine sauce). You can either choose to sit inside or outside on their quiet terrace.

SEEING THE SIGHTS

In the town where cheese is king, start your touring with a cheese factory – but there are other charms to this wonderful old city too.

A. CHEESE & HAM FACTORY TOURS

If you're interested in going on a tour of cheese factories and stores, please first contact the **Consortio dei Parmigiana** *at Via Gramsci 26a, Tel. 29-70-00 or the Consortio di Prosciutto at Via M. Dell'Arpa 8b, Tel. 24-39-87. Tours available 9am–5pm Mon–Saturday.* You get a guided tour of their facilities and may even get some free samples at the end. Parma is the place to do it, so get going!

B. NATIONAL GALLERY

Palazzo della Pilotta. Open 9am–1:45pm. Admission L5,000.
Located in the **Palazzo della Pilotta**, you'll find *La Scapigliata* here, Leonardo da Vinci's sketch of a young girl, as well as other fine works of art. To enter the gallery you must first pass through the **Farnese Theater**, built in 1615.

C. PIAZZA DEL DUOMO

Baptistry, *Tel. 235-886. Open 9am–12:30pm and 5pm–6pm. Admission L3,000.* **Cathedral**, *Tel. 235-886. Open 9am–Noon and 3pm–7pm.*

Baptistry
This is a pink marble octagonal building, begun in the Romanesque style by Beneddetto Antelami and completed in the Gothic style between 1256 and 1270. The main attractions are the 13th century bas-reliefs and frescoes inside.

Cathedral
This is a Romanesque basilica covered with pillars that dates from the late 12th century. The expansive facade joins together with the *campanile* (bell tower) on the right. The *campanile* is 63 meters high and was built between 1284 and 1294. Inside the church you'll find the amazing fresco of the *Assumption of the Virgin of Correggio* made between 1526 and 1530, as well as the relief work done by Beneddetto Antelami in 1178, *Descent from the Cross*. Look also for the Roman mosaics in the crypt.

D. PALAZZO E PARCO DUCALE
Palazzo is open from Mon–Sat 8am–Noon. Tel. 230-023. Parco is open December/January 7am–5:30pm; November/February 7am–6pm; October/ March/April 6:30am–7pm; May/June/July/August 6am–midnight.

If you need a respite from the city, come here to these extensive Baroque gardens. The building is off-limits since it is currently a military academy, but you can still enjoy the peace and quiet of the gardens.

E. CASA DI TOSCANINI
Tel. 285-499. Open Tuesday–Sunday 10:00am–1:00pm. Tuesday and Thursday also open from 3pm–6pm. Free. Need to make reservations.

Just south of the park on the Borgo Rodolfo Tanzi is the birthplace of **Arturo Toscanini**, the magnificent musical conductor. The house now contains a small museum of memorabilia from the maestro's life.

SHOPPING
The central streets of the town are **Via della Repubblica**, **Via Mazzini**, and **Via Garibaldi**, where the citizens gather to shop and stroll, especially in the early evening hours before their dinner meal. The main square for hanging out and planning which shops to hit is the **Piazza Garibaldi**. With its cafés offering outside seating, this piazza is the meeting area for the citizens of Parma.

Cheese
If you're looking for cheese, look no further than **Formaggeria Del Re**, *Via Garibaldi 46E*, featuring wheels of *parmigiana*, and **Formaggeria**,

Via Borgo Del Gallo 8A. You won't find huge wheels of *parmigiana* but you will find mounds of different types of cheese.

Food Stores & Markets
• **Salumeria**, *Via Garibaldi 42F*
• **Salumeria**, *Via della Repubblica 54a*
• **Market**, *Piazza Ghiaia.* A great source of picnic supplies if you're off to relax in the **Parco Ducale**. They have cheeses, meats, breads, fruits, veggies, as well as clothes and household items. The market atmosphere stretches onto surrounding streets.

Tourist Information
• **IAT Office**, *Piazza del Duomo 5, Tel. 0521/234-735.* They can book your hotel from here as well as offering you map of the city.

FERRARA

Ferrara is a small, walled city with a population of only 155,000. It has many tiny cobblestoned streets that seem right out of the Middle Ages, as well as wide streets and sumptuous palaces that seem directly out of the Renaissance. Ferrara started off as an independent community, but from 1208 to 1598 was controlled by the **Este family** who, history shows, were particularly cruel and despotic, even though they were also tolerant of different religions and great patrons of the arts. After 1598, Ferrara became a papal state, then it was taken over by Napoleon and was ruled by France until it was eventually incorporated into the new Italian state in the nineteenth century.

One of the things I find most appealing about Ferrara is the fact that it is small enough and flat enough, and many of the streets are closed to automobile traffic, that residents will commute to work on bicycles. At rush hour it's fun to sit in a café and watch the swarms pedal on by. You can join them if you like, since Ferrara has plenty of bicycles for rent all over the city by the municipal government.

But one of the best things to do in Ferrara is take a stroll around her walls. Second only in romance to those of Lucca, the walls were the creation of the Renaissance. Here you can see trees and undergrowth covering what once were part of a formidable military defense system.

You can also stroll through the old ghetto where the Jews were housed from 1627 by papal decree. Prior to the church's involvement, Ferrara was an open and tolerant city. When the Jews were expelled from Spain in 1492, Ercole d'Este invited as many as could come to stay in Ferrara. But even after their internment in the ghetto, they were still relatively free to roam the city. Today you can admire the **synagogues** on Via Mazzini as well as the **Jewish Museum** amongst them.

And if you can, try and visit the last Sunday in May since Ferrara celebrates its famous *Palio*. Filled with pageantry and life, this is a spectacle second only to the *Palio* of Siena.

ARRIVALS & DEPARTURES

By Car

Take the A13 highway or a more scenic route (the smaller road 64) straight up to Ferrara. The drive takes between 30 and 40 minutes.

By Train

Trains for Ferrara don't leave as frequently as do those to Parma. Morning trains are: 8:35, 10:26, 10:42, 11:42, 12:26. The return times in the afternoon are spaced about the same, roughly every 45 minutes to an hour, so you can spend a good day of sightseeing then head back to Bologna. Remember to check with the train information to verify times. The trip takes about half an hour.

You can get into the walled town from the train station by walking for fifteen minutes or catching either bus #9 or #1. Once you see the castle with its moat on the right hand side, ring the bell for the bus to stop. It will continue past the castle and stop about fifty feet away. Now you're just past and across the street from the tourist office, where you can rent bicycles and get maps and information about the city.

GETTING AROUND TOWN

By Bicycle

At the **Ufficio Informazioni e Accoglienza Turistica**, *Corso Giovecca 21-23, Tel. 0532/209-370. Fax 0532/212-266,* you can rent bicycles from Monica, a woman who has the most beautiful blue eyes in the world. She speaks wonderful English too. The rates are L4,000 per hour; L10,000 per 3 hours; L18,000 per 6 hours; and L20,000 all day long.

The bikes are all in good shape and are relatively inexpensive to rent. Monica will probably ask you to fill out a questionnaire about where you're from and why you decided to come to Ferrara. You're not obligated to perform the task but take a minute and make her happy.

By Foot

Ferrara is a walker's city. Small and compact. Perfect for short strolls. If you start to get tired, just stop at one of the many cafés and have a pick-me-up and be off again. Along the way you'll be able to soak in the sights and sounds of a magnificent Renaissance capital.

WHERE TO STAY

1. JOLLY HOTEL DE LA VILLE, *Piazzale Stazione 11, 44100 Ferrara. Tel. 0532/53-101. Fax 0532/52-074. American Express, Mastercard and Visa accepted. 85 rooms all with bath. Single L210,000; Double L290,000; Suite 440,000. Breakfast included.* ****

Another Jolly hotel. They are the biggest Italian chain and are in most major cities. Located in the piazza by the station, the location is not grand, but that's Jolly's style. The amenities are modern and comfortable but with limited character; they cater to convenience, not style. For your money I'd stay at either the Ripagrande or the Astra/Best Western.

2. HOTEL ASTRA/BEST WESTERN, *Viale Cavour 55, 44100 Ferrara. Tel. 0532/206-088. Fax 0532/247-002. American Express, Mastercard and Visa accepted. 69 rooms all with bath. Single L210,000; Double L290,000; Suite L360,000-500,000. Breakfast included.* ****

On the main street from the station set in a quiet piazza, they will take care of your every need here. Catering mainly to business travelers, The

Sights	Hotels	Hotels (cont.)	Restaurants
A. Castello Estense	1. Jolly Hotel de La Ville	7. Santo Stefano	11. Buca San Domenico
B. Cathedral	2. Hotel Astra	8. Annunziata	12. Grotta Azzurra
C. Palazzo Schifonoia	3. Ripagrande Hotel	9. Nazionale	13. La Romantica
D. Palazzo dei Diamanti	4. Hotel Carlton	10. Albergho San Paulo	14. Pizzeria Giusseppe
E. Via San Romano	5. Hotel Europa		15. Trattoria delle Volte
F. Mercato Communale	6. Hotel Touring		16. Il Ristorantino
			19. La Trattoria

Astra has air conditioning, a restaurant, room service, bar, mini-bar, TV, air conditioning and more. Located 200 meters from the castle and other sights, it is perfectly situated for both business and pleasure.

3. RIPAGRANDE HOTEL, *Via Ripagrande 21, 44100 Ferrara. Tel. 0532/765-250. Fax. 0532/764-377 American Express, Mastercard and Visa accepted. 40 rooms all with bath. Single L210,000; Double L290,000. Breakfast included. kids stay for only 30% extra in the parents room.* ****

The hotel occupies a former Renaissance *palazzo* in the heart of the historic district. The forty rooms upstairs are all equipped with TVs and air conditioning, and twenty have sitting rooms as well as kitchenettes. There is also a pleasant courtyard in the back with a wonderful restaurant facing out onto it. A truly romantic hotel that offers motorboat tours of the surrounding rivers on the weekends as well as bicycle rentals. They are kid friendly with baby-sitting and a playroom. They do it all.

4. HOTEL CARLTON, *Via Garibaldi 93 (Piazza Sacrati), 44100 Ferrara. Tel. 0532/205-904. Fax 0532/205-766. American Express, Mastercard and Visa accepted. 58 rooms all with bath. Single L90,000-130,000; Double L120,000-190,000. Breakfast L15,000 extra.* ***

Located in a pristine and quiet piazza just off the beaten track but still in walking distance to everything. This is a thoroughly modern hotel that usually caters to the discriminating businessman. The rooms are clean, comfortable, and cozy with their TV and mini-bar. It has little character but everything is taken care of here. They also have a residence just across the piazza with kitchen, dining room, and separate bedroom if you're thinking of a stay of a week or more and really want to make yourself at home.

5. HOTEL EUROPA, *Corso Giovecca 49, 44100 Ferrara. Tel. 0532/205-456. Fax 0532/212-120. American Express, Mastercard and Visa accepted. 42 rooms all with bath. Single L 100,000-115,000; Double 130,000-160,000; Suite L200,000.* ***

Located in a 17th century palazzo with views of the Castello Estense, here you'll have all the amenities of a three star with a splash of antiquity thrown in. Most of the rooms have 16 foot ceilings either frescoed or wood beamed or both so you'll really feel like you're in a palazzo. The sitting room is like something out of a Victorian novel: antique chairs and table, beautiful couches, mirrors and paintings on the wall and more. For a pleasant stay with a touch of class at reasonable prices, stay here.

6. HOTEL TOURING, *Viale Cavour 11, 44100 Ferrara. Tel. 0532/20-62-00. Fax 0532/21-20-00. American Express, Mastercard and Visa accepted. 56 rooms all with bath. Credit cards accepted. Single L70,000-95,000; Double L100,000-150,000.* ***

A modern three-star hotel located in the center of Ferrara a short walk from everything. The trees in the piazza and double-paned windows make your stay quite pleasant, as does the air conditioning in the summer. The rooms are clean and comfortable and some have views of the castle fifty yards away. It's not luxurious but the price is right, and everything is spic and span.

7. SANTA STEFANO, *Via Santo Stefano 21, 44100 Ferrara. Tel. 0532/ 206-924 or 210-261. Fax 0532/210-261. American Express, Mastercard and Visa accepted. 27 rooms, 3 with bath, 8 with shower. Single L40,000 (none have shower or bath); Double L65,000-85,000.* **

Located in the *centro storico* near the cathedral and the castle, this place thinks it's something special but it's not. Stay at the San Paolo instead. They do have a bar and a TV room but chances are you won't be able to find a room with bathroom facilities.

8. ANNUNZIATA, *Piazza Repubblica 5, 44100 Ferrara. Tel. 0532/201-111. Fax 0532/203-233. 26 rooms, all with shower or bath. Credit cards accepted. Single L180,000; Double 280,000; Suite L400,000. Breakfast included.* ****

This used to be a run-down little one star until someone decided that with a little renovation and some private baths it could make a small town listing as a four star. Located in an historic building and set in a tranquil environment you'll find all the necessary amenities for a four star except for a restaurant. But there are plenty around. The rooms are relatively tiny but comfortable.

9. NAZIONALE, *Corso, Porta Reno 32, 44100 Ferrara. Tel. 0532/209-604. No credit cards accepted. 18 rooms 12 with bath. Single L38,000-50,000; Double L78,000-80,000.* **

Located near the cathedral this is a small place that is clean and comfortable for those on a budget. All the doubles have a bath so you can't miss here, especially at the price. There's no air conditioning but there is heat in the winter. And if you're traveling with a dog, Fido's welcome here.

10. ALBERGHO SAN PAULO, *Via Baluardi 9, Tel. 0532/768-333. Fax 0532/762-040. No credit cards accepted. 20 rooms 17 with bath. Single L25,000-60,000; Double L40,000-80,000.* **

Slightly larger rooms and more amenities than the Nazionale. They even have a bar and a TV room. Located in a tranquil setting so you won't be disturbed in the morning. This is also a good place to stay for budget travelers. Fido is also welcome here.

WHERE TO EAT

11. RISTORANTE/PIZZERIA BUCA SAN DOMENICO, *26b Piazza Sacrati. Pizzas cost L3,000. Credit cards accepted.*

In a large rustic decor with wooden booths and tables you can have some really good pizza. Try their alla *Salsiccia or ai funghi* (with sausage or with mushroom). If pizza is not to your liking they have a great *spaghetti con pomodoro e basilico* (with tomatoes and basil). Or try the *zuppa di verdure* (vegetable soup) or their *mozzarella e pomodoro* (mozzarella with tomatoes and olive oil) for something lighter.

12. RISTORANTE GROTTA AZZURRA, *Piazza Sacrista 43, 0532/ 209-152. Fax 0532/210-950. Dinner for two L90,000. Credit cards accepted.*

A high end restaurant and as suggested by its name, which is from the famous grotto on the isle of Capri, this is a seafood place. The decor is maritime and Neapolitan with chandeliers, mirrors, white walls and memorabilia. Try the *antipasto di mare* (seafood antipasto) or the *cocktail di gamberi* (shrimp cocktail) for appetizer. Then try some of their grilled or fried fish such as *grigliatta mista* (mixed grill) or the *fritto di gamberetti* (fried shrimp). If seafood is not to your liking they also have many meat and pasta dishes.

13. TRATTORIA LA ROMANTICA, *Via Ripagrande 36, Tel. 0532/ 765-975. Credit cards accepted. Dinner for two L60,000.*

The dark wooden chairs and beams on the ceiling contrast well with the stark white walls and few plants interspersed around the restaurant. For starters try either their *salumi tipici* (local salamis) or the *patate al forno* (roast potatoes). For seconds either try a great *penne all'arrabiata* (a hot and spicy tomato based pasta dish) or the *costaletto di agnello allo sherry* (lamb cutlet cooked in a sherry sauce).

14. PIZZERIA GIUSEPPE, *71 Via C Mayr, Tel. 0532/761-701. Closed Tuesdays. Credit cards accepted. Dinner for two L30,000.*

There's a wood-burning brick oven in the front, café-looking type room. In the back you can enjoy the privacy of booth tables while munching on perfect pizzas. This is a simple, basic, rustic pizzeria that serves large or small pizzas and serves Fosters on tap.

15. TRATTORIA DELLE VOLTE/ DA MARIO, *Via Delle Volte 37a. Closed Thursdays. No credit cards accepted. Dinner for two L 40,000.*

A small place down a side street with a rustic feel to it that caters to tourists and locals alike. The prices are great, especially the tourist menu for L15,000 that offers a choice of pasta and a choice of meat. Try their *tortellini alla panna* (with cream sauce) and their *braciola di maiale* (arm of pork).

16. IL RISTORANTINO, *Vicolo M Aguchie 15, Tel. 0532/25-922. Closed Sundays. Credit cards accepted. Dinner for two L60,000.*

A great little place, hence the name (the small restaurant), with a friendly simple decor. Try their *spaghetti all'amatriciana, tagliatelle alla bolognese* (with meat sauce), or their *penne all'arrabiata* (with a spicy tomato based sauce) for primo. Then for secondo try the *salamina di Ferrara* (salamis of Ferrara) or the wonderful *scalopina ai funghi porcini* (veal covered with a mushroom sauce).

17. LA TRATTORIA, *Viale Po 13/17, Tel. 0532/55-103. Closed Tuesdays. Credit cards accepted. Dinner for two L 60,000.*

Located near the station and the Porta Po, this is a simple place with a wood beamed ceiling, white washed walls, paintings and ferns hanging haphazardly for color. Their antipasto table seems sparse but it certainly can be filling, especially the sampling of local salamis. They serve excellent grilled meats and make wonderful *tortellini* with cream sauce.

SEEING THE SIGHTS

There's not an awful lot here, but between the castle, the cathedral, and the beautiful palaces, you'll have enough to do in Ferrara.

A. CASTELLO ESTENSE - ESTE CASTLE

Piazza Castello. Tel. 299-279. Open Tuesday–Sunday 9:30am–1:30pm and 2:30pm–5:30pm. Admission L6,000.

Built in 1385 as protection for the Este family, the castle stills has the character of a medieval fortress complete with a moat around its perimeter. The castle was upgraded with marble balconies and tower *loggias* during the 16th century when the building became the local ducal palace. Inside you'll find magnificent frescoes from the Fillippi school of the 16th century.

B. CATHEDRAL

Piazza Cattedrale. Tel. 202-392. Open Monday–Saturday 7:30am–noon and 3pm–6:30pm. Sunday 7:30am–1pm and 4pm–7:30pm.

Built in the 12th century, this large cathedral shows signs of Romanesque, Baroque, and Gothic influences. You should spend some time admiring the marble facade with its many arches, stained glass windows, bas-reliefs, and columns all showing signs of different artistic influences. On the right hand side of the church as you face it you'll find small little stores built into the walls and foundations, a sight you'll not find in too many places. Inside you'll find many tapestries, paintings, sculptures, frescoes and more to admire.

C. PALAZZO SCHIFONOIA

Via Scandiana 23, Tel. 64178. Open 9am–7pm. Admission L6,000.

This palace was built for the rest and relaxation of the ducal family, **Schifonaio**. It contains some of the greatest masterpieces of the Renaissance period, including the **Room of the Months** filled with exquisite frescoes and the **Room of the Stuccoes** with its shining golden roof. All throughout you'll find a vast art collection that spans many centuries.

D. PALAZZO DEI DIAMANTI - PALACE OF DIA-MONDS

Corso Ercole I d'Este, Tel. 205-844. Open Tuesday-Saturday 9am-2pm, and Sun 9am-1pm. Admission L6,000.

When you first see this palace you'll know why it was given its name. The walls appear to be covered with carved stones in the shape of diamonds. When the early morning and the end of the day sun catches and reflects off these many diamonds your photo will be magnificent. On the first floor you'll find the many beautiful paintings of the **Picture Gallery** and on the ground floor you'll find many works of modern art.

SHOPPING

On the **Via San Romano** you'll find narrow curved pedestrian streets graced with elegant old arches and fine small shops. If you took away the neon and modern signs, this small street would make you feel as if you stepped back into the Renaissance. You can taste the market atmosphere. At the end of the street you'll find the Cathedral with shops built into the foundation and wall.

F. Mercato Communale

Located on the corner of Via Santo Stefano and the Via del Mercato, you'll find a quaint little enclosed market bustling with business here every day from 7:00am to 1:00pm. Only on Fridays is it open in the afternoon from 4:30pm to 7:30pm. You can find fruits, vegetables, cheeses, garden supplies, pet supplies, clothes, basically everything an Italian shopper could need or a tourist could want for picnic supplies or a tacky gift for someone at home.

G. Alimentari/Salumeria

At 121 Via San Romano. All the supplies you need for a picnic on the walls of Ferrara.

TOURIST INFORMATION

Ufficio Informazioni e Accoglienza Turistica, *Corso Giovecca 21-23, Tel. 0532/209-370. Fax 0532/212-266. or Via Kennedy 8 Tel. 0532/765-728. Fax 0532/760-225. Open Monday through Saturday 8:00am to 5:00pm.*

To get to the main office at Corso Giovecca, just past the Castello Estense take bus number 1 or 9 from the station. This is where you can rent bicycles and pick up maps an all sorts of tourist information.

16. MILAN

Milan is Italy's chief industrial, financial, and commercial center. Unfortunately 60 percent of the city was destroyed by bombings during World War II, but within a decade the industrious people of Milan had rebuilt their city, making it bigger than ever before.

The city's Gothic **cathedral** is one of the largest and most beautiful churches in the world. It rises like a brilliant white crown in the heart of the city. Another great church is that of **Sant' Ambrogio**, built in the 4th century, where St. Ambrose baptized St. Augustine and many emperors were crowned with the "iron crown" of Lombardy. Nearby stands the former convent of **Santa Maria delle Grazie**, where Leonardo da Vinci's famous *Last Supper* is painted on the refectory wall. If you come to Milan you have to see this.

Brera Palace is the home of the **Academy of Fine Arts and Science**. Its galleries contain works by the great Italian masters and other artists. **La Scala**, Milan's opera house, is world renowned. The city has two famous libraries, three universities, a school of commerce and agriculture, an academy of music, and a celebrated archaeological museum.

As Italy's greatest railway center, Milan commands lines crossing the Alps via the **Simplon Tunnel** and **St. Gotthard passes**. Other lines lead east to Venice and south to Genoa and peninsular Italy. The road network converging upon Milan carries a constant flow of foreign and national tourists. Milan is also the starting point for the famous Italian scenic route called the **Autostrada del Sole** (Highway of the Sun).

Milan is the largest of the industrial cities of northern Italy, where most of the country's manufacturing is done. Electricity from Alpine waterfalls furnishes power for industries. The textile, printing and publishing, chemical, and machinery industries are the most important. Among the products of Milan and its suburbs are airplanes, automobiles, locomotives and railway cars, refrigerators, elevators, bicycles and motorcycles, tires, precision instruments, chemicals and drugs, furniture, and food products. Skilled workers create fine jewelry and art wares. The annual **Milan Fair** attracts international buyers. And Milan has the largest stock market in Italy.

INSIGHT INTO MILAN

Milan is a thoroughly modern city steeped in commerce and high fashion. It's hectic pace, where meals are rushed and greetings, if given at all, are terse is so unlike any other Italian city it is amazing. Big City folk would feel at home here. It is a place where a sneer is usually received instead of a smile. To enjoy Milan, you need a thick skin or a tough composure.

Hotels in Milan mainly cater to businessmen who are attending some convention or another. Tourists are an afterthought here. And the sights, save for the imposing Gothic Cathedral and Da Vinci's Last Supper are few and far between, because Milan was virtually razed during World War II and rebuilt soon after. But if you are an opera fan, La Scala, the most famous opera house in the world, beckons. And if you want to see the most exquisite selection of foods anywhere in the known world, come here to shop and eat at the many Peck's stores. Other than that, Milan can easily be missed.

But if you do come to Milan, you ought to visit Peck's and sample their fine food. Go see the Last Supper. Go up on the observation deck of the Cathedral. Visit the Leonardo Da Vinci Museum of Science and Technology. And go to the Fiera Sinigallia market at Porta Ticinese, which is held every Saturday. Otherwise you haven't been to Milan.

Brief History

Because of its location Milan has a long history of raids and invasions. The city started as Mediolanum, a Gallic town, and was taken over by the Romans in 222 BC. It was burned a number of times – once by the Huns, twice by the Goths, and again by the German Frederick Barbarossa in 1162.

After a period of civil strife, the house of **Visconti** gained control of this powerful city-state. When the last Visconti duke died in 1447, three years later the rule of the **Sforzas** began, and continued until 1535. Most of the ancient beauty of the city was created by the heads of these two great houses. When the Sforza line died out, Spain seized Milan and held it until 1706. Then the city fell to Austria, which governed it until Napoleon created his short-lived Kingdom of Italy and made Milan its capital. After Napoleon's fall, Milan was restored to Austria. Then finally in 1859 it was included in the new united kingdom of Italy.

Milan's industry, trade, and population swelled in the period between the two world wars. Currently the poulation hovers around 1.5 million people. The construction boom after World War II included numerous

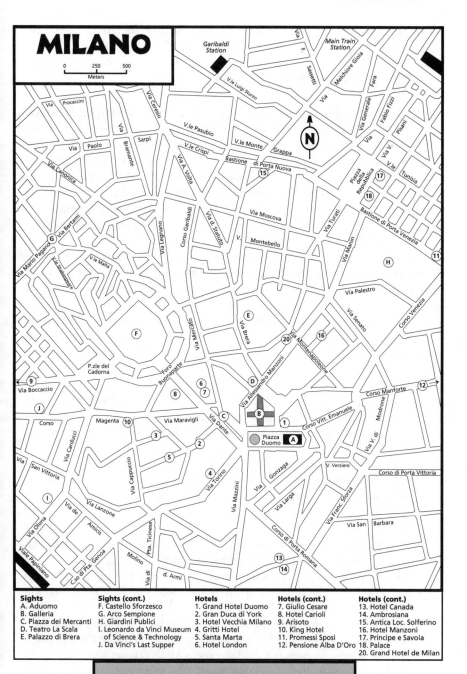

MILANO

0   250   500
Meters

Garibaldi Station

Main Train Station

Sights
A. Aduomo
B. Galleria
C. Piazza dei Mercanti
D. Teatro La Scala
E. Palazzo di Brera

Sights (cont.)
F. Castello Sforzesco
G. Arco Sempione
H. Giardini Publici
I. Leonardo da Vinci Museum
   of Science & Technology
J. Da Vinci's Last Supper

Hotels
1. Grand Hotel Duomo
2. Gran Duca di York
3. Hotel Vecchia Milano
4. Gritti Hotel
5. Santa Marta
6. Hotel London

Hotels (cont.)
7. Giulio Cesare
8. Hotel Carioli
9. Arisoto
10. King Hotel
11. Promessi Sposi
12. Pensione Alba D'Oro

Hotels (cont.)
13. Hotel Canada
14. Ambrosiana
15. Antica Loc. Solferino
16. Hotel Manzoni
17. Principe e Savoia
18. Palace
20. Grand Hotel de Milan

MILAN'S HOTELS & SIGHTS

skyscrapers and factories of modern design, and the streets were widened, eliminating what once was a quaint medieval feel to the city.

ARRIVALS & DEPARTURES

By Air

When coming to Milan you will either arrive at **Malpensa**, which handles all incoming flights from North America, Australia, and the United Kingdom, or **Linate**, which handles most of the domestic air traffic. Not nearly as sophisticated in terms of transport from the airports as is Rome, from Linate there is **bus service** to the Milan Central Train Station leaving every 20 minutes, and **ATM** Municipial Bus Service 73 from Piazza San Babila (corner of Corso Europa) every 15 minutes. Duration for both is 30 minutes. From Malpensa, there is a bus that leaves for the Milan Central Train Station every 30 minutes.

Once at the train station you have access to Milan's extensive Metro system, which takes you virtually everywhere you want to go. If you're in more of a hurry or in need of more comfort, take a taxi from in front of the station.

From the airport into town, the quickest and the most expensive way is to take a taxi. The fare starts at L4,000 and rises rapidly. Be prepared to pay the cost of a night's hotel room for your ride from the airport.

By Bus

Getting in and out of Milan is best done by train – driving is the worst option and bus is almost as bad. Traffic in and around this region is bumper to bumper. The only saving grace for the bus is that you don't actually have to drive. The only time to use a bus around Milan (if you don't have a car) is if the train doesn't go where you're heading.

All intercity buses leave from the **Piazza Castello** (at the Cairioli metro stop). Each company has its own office located here.

By Car

Driving in Milan is worse than any other city in Italy, if you can imagine that. It's not the drivers who are so bad, it's the city that is so immense. As the center of Italian commerce, Milan can be reached by a variety of different avenues from many different locations, making everything completely confusing.

From the east and west the **E64** autostrada bisects the top part of the city. Arriving from the south you would use the **A1** (**E35**) or the **A7** (**E62**). From the north you can get to Milan on the **A9** (**E35**) and **A8** as well as on countless other smaller throroughfares. That old saying about how all roads lead to Rome should actually refer to Milan.

If you want to rent a car while in Milan you can do so at both airports and at the locations given in the **Renting a Car** section of this chapter.
    Sample trip lengths on main roads:
- **Rome**: 6 hours
- **Venice**: 4 1/2 hours
- **Florence**: 4 hours.

By Train

The Stazione Centrale is Milan's primary railway station and it's like a chaotic mini-mall inside. You have all sorts of shops, eateries, a supermarket, two different levels to get lost in, travel agencies, pickpockets, hustlers, and your trusty **tourist office** (*Tel. 02/669-0532*). This station connects Milan with all other major cities in Italy as well as elsewhere in Europe. The other stations (**Stazione Nord**, **Porta Genova**, and **Porta Garibaldi**) connect Milan to smaller municipalities like Como and Asti.
    A word of advice: don't stay around the train station if you can avoid it. Located north of the center of Milan, the area around the station is not the best place around. You will find the best deals here, but you will also have to contend with the underbelly of the city at the same time. As a first time visitor, it's best to hop on the Metro and stay downtown near the Cathedral.
    Sample trip lengths and costs for direct (*diretto*) trains:
- **Rome**: 5 hours, L60,000
- **Venice**: 3 hours, L30,000
- **Florence**: 3 hours, L35,000.

GETTING AROUND TOWN

By Bicycle

They can be rented from **Vittorio Comizzoli**, *Via Washington 60. Tel. 02/498-4694*. I would advise against renting a bike, however, since Milan is such a large city, and is definitely not as picturesque as Rome or Florence, so renting a bike would only put you in harm's way without a reason to do it.

By Foot

Unlike Florence and Venice, and similar to Rome, Milan is a large city that is not the best walking town. That's why they have a Metro system. You can walk the city. It's safe. But to get from point A to point B, why not just take the Metro? It only costs L1,400, which is about 90¢.
    And if the Metro is too much work for you, there's always the ever-present taxis.

By Metro

Find the big red signs with a black "M" indicating that the **Metropolitana Milanese** is just below. Be prepared for a quick, safe, and efficient ride. The metro was built in the 1960s and is surprisingly still clean. There are three lines: **red** (#1), **green** (#2), and **yellow** (#3). Since the lines are all color coded, they can be followed quickly and easily. *The Metro information number is 875-495.*

To catch the train going in the correct direction, find your stop and head in the direction of the end destination. There are maps everywhere inside and outside the trains, so have no fear. This is a simple, easy, intuitive metro system to use. Parts of it are still under construction, since they have to stop periodically and excavate some ancient Roman ruins they uncover.

Tickets cost L1,400 and are sold at local newsstands in the stations, at tobacconist's shops (the ones marked with a blue "T" sign), at each metro stop, or can be bought from machines in the stations. The lines at station ticket counters are invariably long so buy tickets in advance. Also most of the ticket machines only take coins, and the machines that do take bills are usually out of order. Welcome to Italy, and this is their most modern city. All the machines are self explanatory with directions in English, French, Italian, and German – but you know what? I had to show a few Milanese how to use the machines. The Italian culture is so high-touch (i.e., they like to interact with people) that machines scare them, whereas we North Americans have incorporated machines into our daily lives and can figure them out easily.

You can get a map of the Metro system from the FS information counter at the Stazione Centrale, or call Dr. Ibrahim at the Train Station, *0336/330-872.* He'll also try to see if you want to change your room reservation while in Milan, but that's his job (see *Where to Stay*, below).

You can bring bikes on the metro with a special pass.

If you know you're going to be taking the Metro frequently while you're staying in Milan, here are a number of options that can save you money. You can get the following types of tickets at the **Stazione Centrale ATM office** *(tel. 2/669-70-47)* or the **Duomo office** *(tel. 0/89-01-97)*:

• **one day ticket** (24 hours after you stamp it) for L4,8000. If you're going to take five trips or more in a two hour period this will save you money. All you need to do is stamp it once then keep it with you in case an inspector hops on the train. You enter through the gates near the central conductor's booth in every station. If the conductor is around you'll need to show him/her the ticket at this point too.

• **two day ticket** (48 hours after you first stamp it). Same concept and rules as the 1 day (24 hours) ticket.

By Taxi

As in most Italian cities, taxis are everywhere. If you can't locate one on the street, there are plenty of taxi stands all over the city where the taxis line up and wait for fairs. Here a brief list of where some of these taxi stands are located: Piazza del Duomo, Piazza Scala, Piazza Cinque Giornate (D/VE), Largo San Babila (M), Largo Treves (B), Piazzale Baraca (V/M) and Piazza XIV Maggio (PT).

Here some radio taxi numbers that may come in handy if you're caught in the rain somewhere:

• **AAAAAAA**, *S Ambrogio, Tel. 02/53-53. Open 24 hours.*
• **La Martesana**, *Tel. 02/52-51*
• **Cooperitiva Esparia**, *Tel. 02/832-12-13*

Renting a Car

I don't recommend this either unless you want to take a day trip to a place that cannot be reached by train. Driving in Milan is worse than virtually any city in Italy. But if you have the need to be behind the wheel, here are some rental car agencies you can call.

• **Avis**, *Piazza Duomo 6, Tel. 02/86-343-94/89-01-06-45; or Stazione Centrale, Tel. 02/669-02-90/670-16-54*
• **Hertz**, *Viale Marelli 314, Tel. 02/26-22-33-99*
• **Maggiore**, *Stazione Centrale, Tel. 02/669-0934*

WHERE TO STAY

Milan is not the best city for low-budget tourists, unless you want to stay well off the beaten path, that is, nowhere near a Metro line. In the center of the city, the only place to really stay, you only have a few three star hotels and very few two stars. The budget one stars have been relegated to the outskirts, and most are not even near a Metro line. We've listed the best and least expensive three stars we could find, as well as few excellent two stars and all the good four stars.

Another problem with staying in Milan is that it's mainly a convention city, which means that most of the hotels are booked most of the time for some business convention, mainly dealing with fashion or industry. So remember to reserve well in advance.

My recommendation to you if you're traveling on a budget is to contact **Viagi Wasteel**, *Train Station, 0336/330-872* and speak with Dr. Ibrahim Gouda. Contact him also if you've arrived in Milan by train without reservations. He can get you a huge discount on some good three stars, so you'll be staying for the price of a two star. His company, Viagi Wasteel, books many rooms for groups and they can get group rates for individuals, couples, small groups, and so on at the spur of the moment.

I contacted Dr. Ibrahim recently and he got me into a three star hotel with all the amenities for L80,000 plus L10,000 for him per night. I saved L50,000 and stayed in a great room with air conditioning, mini-bar, TV, breakfast in the morning, and more.

The only problem might be the location – you might be staying around the train station. The only real drawback is that you have to take the Metro to and from the sights you're going to see. But to stay in a great room at a great price, I think it's worth it. Give him a call; he speaks perfect English, Italian, French, Japanese, as well as Arabic, since he's Egyptian.

THE BEST HOTELS IN MILAN

*****Five Star*
18. PALACE, Piazza della Repubblica 20, (near the Giardini Publici), Tel. 02/6336. Fax 02/654-485. 193 rooms all with bath. Single L 260,000-440,000; Double L375,000-630,000

****Four Star*
1. GRAND HOTEL DUOMO, Via San Raffaele 1, Tel. 02/8833, Fax 02/8646-2027. 153 rooms all with bath. Single L280,000-360,000; Double L390,000-490,000; Suite L600,000-900,000. Breakfast included. Credit cards accepted.

***Three Star*
3. HOTEL VECCHIA MILANO, Via Borromei 4, 20123 Milano, Tel. 02/875-041. Fax 02/8645-4292. 27 rooms all with bath. Single L80,000-90,000; Double L120,000-140,000. Triples L140,000-170,000; Quad L35,000 over triple.

1. GRAND HOTEL DUOMO, *Via San Raffaele 1, Tel. 02/8833, Fax 02/8646-2027. 153 rooms all with bath. Single L280,000-360,000; Double L390,000-490,000; Suite L600,000-900,000. Breakfast included. Credit cards accepted.* ****

Situated right in the centro storico a stone's throw from the cathedral. If you want location this is the place to stay. The hotel is in an old building, and has great views of the Cathedral from some rooms and the dining room, making a stay here a romantic interlude. This would be my recommendation for anyone who is staying in Milan for the first time, since it is ideally located around all the main shopping and sights.

2. HOTEL GRAN DUCA DI YORK, *Via Moneta 1a, 20123 Milano. Tel. 02/87-48-63. Fax 02/869-03-44. Credit cards accepted. 33 rooms all with bath. Single L140,000; Double L195,000.* ***

Located in the heart of the historic center, only five minutes from the Cathedral and with easy access to a Metro stop. They try to give it a castle-like appearance in the common areas, but the rooms are plainly furnished if comfortable. It seems a little down on its luck since it's located in an historic building, but it has all the necessary amenities and is in a golden location.

3. HOTEL VECCHIA MILANO, *Via Borromei 4, 20123 Milano, Tel. 02/875-041. Fax 02/8645-4292. 27 rooms all with bath. Single L80,000-90,000; Double L120,000-140,000. Triples L140,000-170,000; Quad L35,000 over triple.* ***

You have it all here, location, location, and price. The rooms are clean, comfortable but spartan. The atmosphere is all over this little hotel though, and the staff will do everything to make your stay better. They all seem to speak perfect English too. It's also off the beaten-path enough that your stay will be quiet and tranquil in the evenings.

4. GRITTI HOTEL, *Piazza SM Beltrade 4, 20123 Milano. Tel 02/80-10-56. Fax 02/89-01-09-99. 40 rooms all with bath. Single L140,000; Double L205,000. Breakfast included.* ***

A simply decorated hotel with limited character and somewhat high prices. But that is all outweighed by the location, comfort, and quiet. A good option to choose if the Vecchia Milano is full.

5. HOTEL SANTA MARTA, *Via Santa Marta 4, 20123 Milano. Tel. 02/864-526-61. fax 02/864-526-61. Single L140,000; Double L185,000.* ***

Modern rooms but spartan with all the amenities of a three star. The main problem is the tile floors in the morning, they can be a bit cold. They have a lobby bar in which to relax after a hard day on the town, and they all seem hard in Milano. A perfect location for sightseeing and shopping.

6. HOTEL LONDON, *Via Rovello, 20123 Milano. Tel. 02/7202-0166. fax 02/805-7037. 29 rooms, 22 with bath. Single L80,000-100,000; Double L120,000-150,000. Breakfast L12,000.* **

This place is nice, but it is definitely overpriced. It's only a two-star, granted in a great location, but not all the rooms have bath. Their prices are the same as the Guilio Cesare, a three star across the street and they don't have nearly as many amenities. There is character and charm here, but not enough for these prices.

7. GIULIO CESARE, *Via Rovello 10, Tel. 02/7200-3915. Fax 02/7200-2179. 25 rooms all with bath. Single L92,000-132,000; Double L152,000-180,000. Credit cards accepted.* ***

A small intimate little hotel, ideally located and fairly well priced. The rooms are small and comfortable, but have no character. There is, however, air conditioning and TV. Probably its best feature is that pets are allowed. Try the Vecchia Milano (a two star) before staying here.

8. HOTEL CARIOLI, *Via Porlezza 4. Tel 02/801371. Fax 02/7200-2243. Credit cards accepted. 38 rooms all with bath. Single L100,000-130,000; Double L150,000-190,000. Breakfast included.* ***

Managed by the ever vigilant Andrea Magistradi, this priceless little hotel, is located between the Duomo and the Castello Sforzecca in a tranquil spot. Located on a small side street, they have a sauna and sunroom for relaxing. Also near the Carioli metro stop, they are ideally located away from but accessible to all sights.

9. ARIOSTO, *Via Ariosto 22, Tel. 02/481-78-44. 38 rooms all with bath. Single L150,000; Double L205,000.* ***

A clean, upper-middle class hotel that is plain, plastic, but ultra-hygienic ... and it's located in the middle of nowhere. Why pay these prices out here when you can stay in town where the action is. I can't recommend this place, it's too far out and too sterile.

10. KING HOTEL, *Corso Magenta 18, 20123 Milano. Tel. 02/874-432. Fax 02/8901-0798. 35 rooms all with bath. Single L140,000; Double 195,000.* ***

Ideally located with clean and comfortable rooms. They just seem to be constantly under renovation, year in and year out, so it seems as if you're staying in a construction zone. The place is a little tiny but you have all the necessary amenities for a three star.

11. HOTEL PROMESSI SPOSI, *Piazza Oberdan 12, 20129 Milano. tel. 02/29-51-36-61. fax 02/2940-4182. 40 rooms all with bath. Single L110,000. Double L160,000; Triple L 254,000.* ***

Located in a residential part of Milan just away from the center, but still on a Metro line, this is a quiet, modern hotel that usually caters to business people arriving for Milan's many trade exhibits. The rooms are white, which accentuates the spartan character. For comfort this place can't be beat, but the prices are a little high.

12. PENSIONE ALBA D'ORO, *Viale Piave 5, 20129 Milano. tel. 02/ 760-238-80. 11 rooms none with bath. 3 fully equipped bathrooms in the hallway. Single L50,000; Double L80,000; Triple L110,000; Quad L140,000. Healthy Neapolitan breakfast included.* *

A one star, but so pleasant and peaceful. They have rooms facing out on an interior courtyard that makes your heart soar. The rooms on the main street have their own little balconies from which you can share a snack or a bottle of wine while you look down on the natives. Run by a friendly family of transplanted Neapolitans that have many relatives in the states. Mama Gelsomina will make sure you get your breakfast in the morning, and are tucked in at night. They truly love their work and taking care of the travelers that choose to stay with them. Located about a five minute walk from the cathedral, this quaint place is located in a nice, safe residential neighborhood.

13. HOTEL CANADA, *Via S Sofia 16, 20122 Milano, Tel. 02/5830-4844. fax 02/5830-0282. 45 rooms all with bath. Single L170,000; Double L250,000.* ***

Situated just outside of the tourist section but well connected by Metro, this is a great professional hotel with all the amenities that North

Americans expect – because they're used to catering to discriminating businessmen. The rooms are a little small but the public space, including the bar, make up for that.

14. HOTEL AMBROSIANA, *Via S Sofia 9, 20122 Milano. Tel. 02/58-30-60-44. Fax 02/58-30-50-67. 40 rooms all with bath. Single L145,000; Double L216,000.* ***

A modern professional hotel across the street from the Hotel Canada in a quiet residential neighborhood characteristic of a North American hotel. In conjunction they have a small workout room where you can exercise and unwind after your day. Besides the comfort of the rooms, they offer a beautiful garden where you relax and write your postcards after a tough day of touring. Better priced and with better features than its rival across the street.

15. ANTICA LOCANDA SOLFERINO, *Via Castefidardo 2, Tel. 02/656-905. 11 rooms, 6 with bath. Single L80,000; Double L130,000.* **

In a charming neighborhood with an excellent restaurant literally surrounding the hotel, this place has more character than charm. Meaning, the rooms are somewhat clean, comfortable and well priced, but the proprietess leaves me cold. Also the entrance is located next to the restaurant of the same name which stays open until 1-2:00am, and the rooms are located above it. This does not make for a good night's rest. Try someplace else.

16. HOTEL MANZONI, *Via Santo Spirito 20, Tel. 02/7600-5700. Fax 02/784-212. 35 rooms all with bath. Single L1544,000; Double L200,000; Suite L283,000. Breakfast is L19,000 extra.* ***

Located on a quiet street within walking distance from the Duomo and La Scala. This is a completely modern hotel in a high rent district. The rooms are tranquil, clean and comfortable, and you'll find the service like a four star. If you've come to Milan for shopping, this could be your place of residence.

17. HOTEL PRINCIPE E SAVOIA, *Piazza della Repubblica 17 (near the Giardini Publici), Tel. 02/62-30. Fax 02/659-5838. All credit cards accepted. 285 rooms all with bath. Single L280,000-470,000; Double L380,000-660,000.* ****

The most elegant and prestigious hotel in of all Milan. This place has all the amenities necessary to make even the most discerning traveler relax. As part of the CIGA chain, it prides itself on excellence and that's what you'll receive here.

18. PALACE, *Piazza della Repubblica 20, (near the Giardini Publici), Tel. 02/6336. Fax 02/654-485. 193 rooms all with bath. Single L 260,000-440,000; Double L375,000-630,000.* *****

Another CIGA hotel, this is just a notch below its sister hotel, the Principe e Savoia, but this one has a beautiful roof garden from which you can gaze over the chaos that is Milan. I find the hotel bar to be a welcoming respite from a day's adventures. As can be expected in a five star luxury hotel, the rooms are immaculate and the service exquisite.

19. GRAND HOTEL AT DE MILAN, *Via Manzoni 29 (at the corner of Via Montenapoleone, 20121 Milano. Tel. 02/723-141. Fax 02/8646-0861. 50 rooms all with bath. Superior L330,000-420,000; De Luxe L440,000-530,000; Suites L700,000-900,000. *****

In a great location, especially for avid shoppers, with all the extra amenities to make this a deluxe hotel. There is a convenient reading room with many international newspapers on reading rods like you used to have in school libraries. If that's too sedate for you, the hotel bar attracts a good crowd of locals as wells as tourists, so there's always something happening there.

WHERE TO EAT

Milanese Cuisine

Milanese cuisine is a melting pot not only of Italy but also of neighboring nations, particularly France. Even so, there still remains a distinct Milanese style of cooking that uses butter, cheese, milk and cream in what is usually categorized as **Northern Italian** cooking. One item that is used frequently in Milanese cuisine is rice, which comes from the multitude of rice paddies on the outskirts of town. One of the staples is *risotto al salto*, leftover rice fried like a pancake.

You'll notice that many restaurants in Milan subscribe to the concept of *cucina nuova*, an elegant approach to food preparation. For Milan this type of cuisine is a perfect match, since they push the envelope of traditionalism in so many different industries (fashion, jewelry, furnishings, etc.), but as an old Italophile I prefer the traditional style of food preparation.

Another change you might sense in Milan is that it is no longer considered "bad form" to eat a rushed lunch of a *panino* (sandwich) which you can get from a myriad of *paninoteca* (sandwich bars), or to eat a pizza that takes ten minutes to prepare. This trend is exemplified by the growing numbers of *pizzerie*. And for both of these items you can request any number or type of ingredients. So we tourists can order our sandwiches and pizzas prepared any way we want them, instead of being constrained to the set ingredients for both *panini* and pizza as you are in most other Italian cities.

Suggested Milanese Cuisine

On the next page, I've set out for you the typical offerings of Milanese food.

ANTIPASTO - APPETIZER
- **Antipasto misto** – a variety of different food such as cheese, prosciutto, olives, etc., from a buffet

PRIMO PIATTO - FIRST COURSE
- **Risotto alla Milanese** – a creamy rice dish made with saffron and marrow and is usually bright yellow in color.
- **Risotto** (with a variety of ingredients) – The same creamy sauce as the Milanese risotto but with any number of ingredients such as vegetables, fish, cheese and/or meat.
- **Risotto al salto** – Leftover rice fried like a pancake with the consistency of the fried potatoes you usually get for breakfast in the States.

SECOND PIATTO - ENTRÉE
Pesce – *Fish*
   You can get any type of seafood you want, since many restaurants have fresh fish sent in daily from the coast on ice. As always when you eat fish in a land-locked city, you'll find the prices to be quite astronomical.

Carne – *Meat*
- **Cotoletta alla Milanese** – Breaded thin cutlet of veal sautéed in butter, served crisp on the outside but succulent on the inside.
- **Ossobucco** – Usually served with the *risotto alla milanese*, this is a veal shank cooked with tomatoes and wine then sprinkled with garlic, parsley and a touch of lemon.
- **Rostin Negaa** – Pork or veal slowly cooked in a pot-roast with a variety of herbs, wine and butter. A truly typical Milanese dish.

Formaggio – *Cheese*
- **Gorgonzola** – a sharp, pungent, pale and delicious local cheese usually mistaken for the French Roquefort, but this is made with cow's milk, not ewe's milk. Takes its name from the small town ten miles outside of Milan where it was originally produced.

Milan's Restaurants
   21. OSTERIA DEL MONESTERO, *Corso Magenta 29, Tel. 02/869-3069. Credit cards accepted. Air conditioned dining room. Dinner for two L70,000.*
   A small local place that specializes in seafood. Try the *spaghetti ai calamari alla marinara* (with squid and spicy tomato sauce) then the *misto fritto di gamberini e calamari* (mixed fried shrimp and squid). The atmosphere is intimate and friendly and the food is great.

22. LATTERIA UNIONE, *Via dell Unione 6, Tel. 02/874-401. No credit cards accepted. Open for lunch only. Closed Sundays. Lunch for two L50,000.*

This is actually a *latteria*, or dairy store, which supplies the neighborhood shoppers with cheese, yogurt, butter, milk, eggs, etc., but it also is a fine vegetarian restaurant. It is so popular with the local office workers that it is jam-packed for lunch time, so if you want to try their wares get there a little before noon or just after 2:00pm. They stop serving at 3:00pm, and don't serve on the weekend. It is basically a business lunch crowd place. Their menu includes thick minestrone soup, omelets, stuffed tomatoes and peppers, and *risotti* with a variety of vegetable combinations.

23. ROSTICCERIA PECK, *Via Cantu 3, Tel. 02/869-3017. American Express, Visa and Mastercard accepted. Meal for two L40,000.*

Primarily a takeout place for roasted meats, you can also use their stand-up counter to try what you want. You can get spit roasted chicken as well as pork, beef, and even vegetables all prepared with excellence. They also have perfectly prepared pasta dishes, either hot or cold, that make my mouth water even now. Your meal will be quick, but it will be satisfying.

24. BOTTEGA DEL VINO (PECK), *Via Victor Hugo 4, Tel. 02/861-040. American Express, Visa and Mastercard accepted. Dinner for two L50,000.*

Not just a wine bar and store, this is also a gourmet "fast-food" establishment. At lunch time it is packed with Milanese satisfying their need for excellent cuisine. They have red painted tractor seats set on stools or seating around deli-like counter areas made of beautiful light ash. To wash down all the great food they have in excess of 150 vintages from all over Italy for you to choose from by the glass, or you can sample the beer on tap.

25. IL RISTORANTE (PECK), *Via Victor Hugo 4, Tel. 02/876-774. American Express, Visa and Mastercard accepted. Dinner for two L180,000.*

This is the place to come and sample everything that the Peck food stores have to offer. Located downstairs from the Bottega del Vino, the setting is relaxing even without windows, the service is excellent and, of course, the food is sublime. The amount of potential choices is far beyond human comprehension, so even if you or your travel partner is the pickiest of eaters you are bound to find something to like.

26. BAR RISTORANTE BIFFI, *Galleria Vittorio Emanuele, Tel. 02/805-7961. American Express, Visa and Mastercard accepted. Closed Sundays.*

Located in the Galleria, this is the perfect place to see or be seen. You can get a buffet of cold and hot antipasti, pasta, salad, fish and meat; and you can couple that with a small drink or a cappuccino. They have "outside seating" in the Galleria where you can watch the people walk by, or dine or drink inside in a modern environment. If you come to Milan

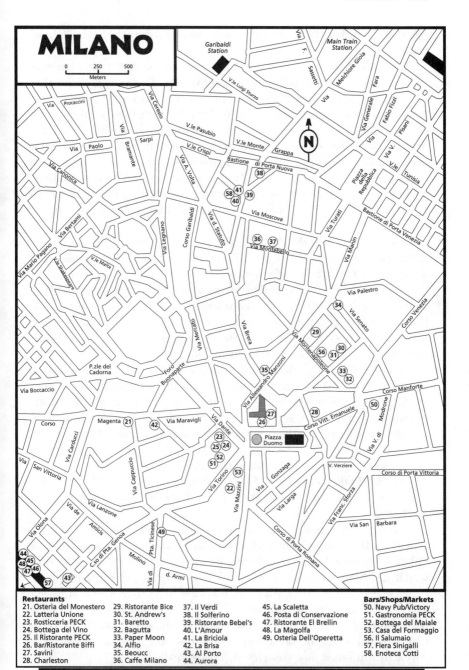

Restaurants

21. Osteria del Monestero
22. Latteria Unione
23. Rosticceria PECK
24. Bottega del Vino
25. Il Ristorante PECK
26. Bar/Ristorante Biffi
27. Savini
28. Charleston
29. Ristorante Bice
30. St. Andrew's
31. Baretto
32. Bagutta
33. Paper Moon
34. Alfio
35. Beoucc
36. Caffe Milano
37. Il Verdi
38. Il Solferino
39. Ristorante Bebel's
40. L'Amour
41. La Briciola
42. La Brisa
43. Al Porto
44. Aurora
45. La Scaletta
46. Posta di Conservazione
47. Ristorante El Brellin
48. La Magolfa
49. Osteria Dell'Operetta

Bars/Shops/Markets

50. Navy Pub/Victory
51. Gastronomia PECK
52. Bottega del Maiale
53. Casa del Formaggio
56. Il Salumaio
57. Fiera Sinigalli
58. Enoteca Cotti

MILAN'S RESTAURANTS, PUBS, & MARKETS

you should try this place for an afternoon *apertivo*, or try the Savini (below) for a ritzy dinner.

27. SAVINI, *Galleria Vittorio Emanuele, Tel. 02/805-8343. American Express, Visa and Mastercard accepted. Closed Sundays. Dinner for two L200,000.*

Also located in the Galleria, this place is a little more expensive than Biffi, but if you want to impress your friends, or at least someone who knows Milan, dine here so you can tell them you did. Everything about the place spells upper crust, from the crystal chandeliers to the impressive wine list to the multilingual waiters. The food, surprisingly enough, is just as good, but very, very expensive. They have an enclosed "outside seating" area in the Galleria where you can enjoy the parade of Milanese as you eat you meal. PS: They won't allow you in shorts or any other inappropriate attire.

28. CHARLESTON, *Piazza Liberty 8, Tel. 02/798-631. Fax 02/7600-1154. American Express, Visa and Mastercard accepted. Closed Mondays and Saturdays for lunch. Dinner for two L60,000.*

An inexpensive pizzeria that serves some of the best pizza in town. You can also have antipasto which is laid out on a vast "L" shaped table just as you walk in. They also have succulent meats, great pasta as well as seafood, but I recommend the pizza. Try the pizza *Charleston*, which is covered with sauce, mozzarella, mushrooms, ham, and egg.

This brightly lit modern restaurant is organized on different levels, with the roaring wood burning pizza oven in the back, all of which gives the impression of much more space. If you're in the mood for outside seating they have it too, and the prices are no different, which is unusual in Italy. Another plus to the place is that is stays open until 1:00am, so you can spend many hours of eating and drinking here with your friends in the tranquillity of a small piazza in the center of town.

29. RISTORANTE BICE, *Via Borgospesso 12, Tel. 02/702-572. American Express, Visa and Mastercard accepted. Closed Mondays. Dinner for two L120,000.*

An expensive restaurant that serves great food from all over Italy, especially their superb cuts of meat, for example the cotolletta alla milanese (breaded veal cutlet lightly pan fried in butter); as well as fish, which in Milan is always a dead giveaway that the restaurant will be expensive. If you're in the fish mood you have to try their *scamponi giganti alla griglia* (giant shrimps on the grill). They now have branches of their restaurant all over the world, including Washington DC, New York, Chicago, Palm Beach, San Diego, Paris, London, Tokyo, and Buenos Aires, so you know how trés chic this place really is.

30. ST. ANDREW'S, *Via Sant'Andrea 23, Tel. 02/7602-3132. Fax 02/798-565. American Express, Visa and Mastercard accepted. Closed Sundays. Dinner for two L90,000.*

Nothing about this place is British, except for some decor and the Beef Wellington, but I guess they think this is what a British place is supposed to look like. Ask the manager, Piero Vezzulli, for his suggestions and you'll have a fine meal. They serve excellent typical Milanese rice and pasta dishes, as well as *Cotoletto alla Milanese*. Needles to say it's expensive since it's around the Via Montenapoleone shopping street.

31. BARETTO, *Via Sant' Andrea 3, Tel. 02/781-255. American Express, Visa and Mastercard accepted. Closed Sundays. Dinner for two L150,000.*

This is a small, expensive restaurant near the Montenapoleone shopping area. The dark wood paneling gives the feel of Germanic influence but the food is all Italian. They have excellent *risotto* dishes here, and if you want to overload on seafood try the superb *salmone can salsa di gamberi* (salmon with shrimp sauce). To get here you enter through an archway and a pleasant courtyard off one of the shopping streets.

32. BAGUTTA, *Via Bagutta 14-16, Tel. 02/7600-2767. American Express, Visa and Mastercard accepted. Closed Sundays. Dinner for two L85,000.*

One of Milan's famous artsy restaurants, which you will instantly notice since the walls are covered with murals, caricatures, and pictures of famous and some not so famous artists. This is a great place to try food from all over Italy, but if you just want the antipasto table, that will surely be enough to satisfy your hunger. They have Roman dishes like *penne all'arrabiata* (spicy tomato based pasta with garlic, oil, parsley, and hot peppers) and the *Saltimbocca alla Romana* (veal shank in a zest tomato based sauce). They also have *tagliatelli alla bolognese* (with light veal, tomato and cream sauce) as well as *trenette al pesto genovese* (with a light pesto sauce). If fish is your desire, try their *fritto misto di mare* (mixed fried seafood) that it perfect.

33. PAPER MOON, *Via Bagutta 1, Tel. 02/792-297. American Express, Visa and Mastercard accepted. Closed Sundays. Dinner for two L80,000.*

This pizzeria serves great light crust pies that come with almost every topping imaginable (if you can't find one you like ask them to put on the toppings you want) as well as pastas, and a strange concoction called *la Bomba* (the bomb). It's a puffed up *calzone* with a *prosciutto* and *formaggio* (ham and cheese) filling.

34. ALFIO, *Via Seneto 31, Tel. 02/7600-0633. American Express, Visa and Mastercard accepted. Closed Saturdays and Sundays at Lunch. Dinner for two L180,000.*

Fish is the flavor here. You can get pasta with seafood such as the *spaghetti alle vongole* (with clams in either a red or white sauce) or *con polpa di granchio* (crabmeat). You can also get fresh fish grilled as well as prime cuts of meat, so this is the place to come to satisfy any palate. The clientele here is definitely as refined as is the decor, even in their inside garden seating area.

35. BOEUCC, *Piazza Belgioioso 2, Tel. 02/7602-0224. American Express accepted. Closed Saturdays and Sundays for lunch as well as the whole month of August. Dinner for two L160,000.*

This is formal but not really stuffy restaurant that is frequented by businessmen and locals alike. The service is perfect and the food is good. Try the v*eal scallopini con porcini* (veal with mushrooms) and *risotto alla milanese* (rice with meat and tomatoes). There is a cover *(coperto)* price, however, and it's a little high.

36. CAFFE MILANO, *Via San Fermo 1, Tel. 02/2900-3300. Credit cards accepted. Closed Mondays. Dinner for two L150,000.*

The place to come for a Sunday brunch in Milan. They even advertise an "American Brunch" but it's not up to speed with all the greasy, fatty, meaty foods we eat. They serve plenty of fresh fruit, luscious breads, juices, coffee, omelets, and only a little pro*sciutto* (ham). Nonetheless, you will love the hearty atmosphere and healthy foods. Also a respected nightlife location because of its artistic flair and after-theater specials. This section, Brera, is known for it's late night dining adventures.

37. IL VERDI, *Piazza Mirabello 5, Tel. 02/651-412. American Express, Visa and Mastercard accepted. Closed Saturdays at lunch and Sundays. Dinner for two L120,000.*

This is the place to come for salads or meat or fish or whatever strikes your fancy. But all the food is prepared in a light healthy fashion and this concept for the meals is reflected in the clean, well-lit, modern decor. You'd better make reservations since if you arrive after 8:30pm without one you'll be waiting for hours. They are known for their many varieties of salads so if you're in a healthy mood stop here to graze.

38. IL SOLFERINO, *Via Castelfidardo 2, Tel. 02/659-9886. Credit cards accepted. Closed Saturdays at lunch and Sundays. Dinner for L120,000.*

Next door to the Locanda Solferino inn, the atmosphere is cozy, romantic, and fashionable but not fancy. Most of the food is made in a simple way without much garnish or presentation but it is excellent. The *Cotoletta alla Milanese* (breaded thin cutlet of veal sautéed in butter, served crisp on the outside but succulent on the inside) is excellent here, as is the *Piccantina di Vitello ai finghi porcini* (veal with mushrooms) The menu includes fresh pastas and homemade patés. La Briciola and L'Amour are right across the street so if you can't find a table in here try those.

39. RISTORANTE BEBEL'S, *Via San Marco 38, Tel. 02/657-1658. Credit cards accepted. Closed Wednesdays. and Saturday mornings. Dinner for Two L85,000.*

You can order great pizza from their prominently situated wood-burning brick oven, or you can try the buffet table that has everything you could want for an entire meal. You can also get fresh fish (they sometimes have live lobsters hanging out on ice) and grilled meats. They make great

Italian staples like *filetto alla griglia* (grilled veal) and *sogliola alla griglia* (grilled sole). Located in the Brera section, you may want to cab back and forth between this restaurant and your hotel.

40. RISTORANTE L'AMOUR, *Via Solferino 25, Tel. 02/659-0176. Open only in the evenings from 7:30pm - 1:00am. Credit cards accepted. Closed Mondays. L85,000.*

The brother restaurant of La Bricciola around the corner, these two may even share a kitchen for all I know, since their food is so similar. A quaint local atmosphere in a restaurant that caters to the late night theater crowd. You can get a wide variety of dishes, including the local favorite *cotolette alla milanese* (veal cutlet lightly breaded and fried in butter).

41. LA BRICIOLA, *Corner of Via Solferino and Via Marsala, Tel. 02/655-1012. Credit cards accepted. Closed Sundays and Mondays. Dinner for two 85,000.*

This place, like its brother L'Amour and the Il Solferino across the street, gathers a rather eclectic crowd in the evenings. Not only does it cater to the theater crowd but the Brera section where the restaurant is located is known as the "artist" section of Milan. Served in a wood floor, glass and pink tableclothed environment, the food here is of local persuasion, with prices to match the upscale clientele but not the peasant fare. You can get the Milanese favorite here, *cotoletto alla milanese* (lightly breaded veal fried in butter) .

42. LA BRISA, *Via Brisa 15, Tel. 02/872-001. American Express, Visa and Mastercard accepted. Closed Sundays at lunch and Saturdays. Dinner for two L85,000.*

Just before you enter you can glimpse some Roman ruins that were dug up during a building construction and left in the open air. The restaurant is a plain and simple local place that serves basic but great food, except for the curried rice called *risotto al' Indiana*. At first I thought, how do people from Indiana make rice that is so good, the I realized they meant from India. A quaint little place especially in their terrace garden. You can get great fish and meats and as well as pastas that are all made in-house. If you're in the area, give it a try.

43. AL PORTO, *Piazzale Generale Contore, Tel. 02/8940-7425. No credit cards accepted. Closed Sundays and Mondays for lunch. Dinner for L120,000.*

What used to be an old canal toll-house is now a great seafood restaurant. You'll feel like you're at the sea with all the maritime decorations of fishing nest, ropes, wheels and more. The menu depends greatly on what fish they are able to purchase from the coast, but they'll always have the freshest and most reasonably priced plates in Milan. You can always find an excellent *risotto* or pasta made with fresh seafood. The best place to enjoy your meal is out on the terrace. I suggest the *scampi alla griglia*, but then I'm partial to any type of shrimp.

44. AURORA, *Via Savona 23, Tel. 02/8940-4978. American Express, Visa and Mastercard accepted. Closed Mondays. Dinner for two L100,000.*

The culinary influence here is definitely Piedmontese with a touch of French. For dinner they have a fixed price menu from which you can choose any dish for appetizer, primo, and secondo. And the cost is only L58,000 without drinks.

Try their *tagliatelli al cavour* (with tomatoes, garlic, basil and olive oil) and their *fritto misto al piemontese* (mixed meat grill). Located in a working class area, you'll need to cab here and back or be prepared for a long metro ride and walk from the station.

45. LA SCALETTA, *Piazzale Stazione Genova 3, Tel. 02/835-0290. American Express, Visa and Mastercard accepted. Closed Sundays and Mondays. Dinner for two L200,000.*

A small, super expensive restaurant. They serve some of the best *cucina nuova* in Milan. The meals here are displayed poetically, but the portions look like some stanzas have been omitted. Reserve days in advance. To get here you have to go way out of your way by cab or car. Go by metro instead. The simplest dish I found was an exquisite ravioli stuffed with veal in a tomato based sauce. A wild dish is truffles, porcini mushrooms, and veal all cooked in a curry sauce. For dessert their chocolate mouse is great.

46. POSTA DI CONSERVAZIONE, *Alzaia Naviglio Grande 6, Tel. 02/ 832-6646. Credit cards accepted. Closed Mondays. Open for dinner only. Dinner for two L85,000.*

Situated along one of the canals in Milan, this down-to-earth restaurant specializes in a variety of grilled meats. You can also try the *vitello alla milanese* here (breaded veal) and come away pleased, but their main fare is creative cooking. So expect to see some strange things on the menu. In a quaint working class section of Milan. You'll need to cab here and back.

47. RISTORANTE EL BRELLIN, *Vicolo dei Lavandai, 20144 Milano. Tel 02/58-10-13-51. fax 02/89-40-27-00. Closed Sundays. Credit cards accepted. Dinner for two L110,000.*

If you want ambiance, character, and great food, it's all here. Located on one of the canals, the building looks like an old farm house, but some of the rooms inside are elegant. Open for the after theater crowd with a piano bar until 1:00am They serve typical Milanese cuisine. For a fun adventure of a meal, this should be the place to begin or end your trip. A little on the expensive side.

48. LA MAGOLFA, *Via Magolfa 15, Tel. 02/832-1696. Credit cards accepted. Closed Sundays. Dinner for Two L75,000*

The food is old style Milanese. None of those *cucina nouva* concoctions here. Try the *risotto alla peperone* (rice with roasted bell peppers) and then their many varieties of veal dishes and you'll go away happy. Located in working class section of Milan, definitely off the tourist path. It's a place to cab to and from.

49. OSTERIA DELL'OPERETTA, *Corso di Porta Ticinese 70, Tel. 02/ 837-5120. American Express, Visa and Mastercard accepted. Closed Sundays. Dinner for two L70,000.*

This is a local night life location with a central bar where patrons can stop for a drink up until 2:00pm, or you can sit down for *trattoria* dining. I love the *tagliatelline* with a cream of mushroom sauce. The menu changes weekly to keep things lively. Weekend evenings you can sometimes find live jazz or blues bands playing.

THE DOMINO'S OF MILAN - PIZZA IN A HURRY!

*If you're in a hotel around the train station, call **Pizza Oggi** at 02/ 6900-1330, and they'll get you a pizza in 30 minutes or less. They serve the train station area since that is also considered the university area. They're open from 6:30-9:30pm every day. They have two different sizes, **Super** (1 person) and **Mega** (2 people). The best order in my opinion is a **Margherita Mega** (L12,000), which is a plain tomato and cheese pizza, then pile on the toppings at L2,500 extra. First get extra cheese (mozzarella), then try either salami, wurstel (sausage), pepperoni, funghi (mushrooms), verdure fresche (mixed fresh vegetables) or salame piccante (spicy salami).*

SEEING THE SIGHTS

Milan may be best known for the world famous **La Scala** opera house and Da Vinci's *Last Supper*, but there are many other worthy sights as well.

A. DUOMO

Piazza del Duomo. Open 7am-7pm. October-May 9am-4:30pm. Access to the top of the cathedral costs L4,000. By elevator L6,000.

If you want Gothic, here you have Gothic at its best. This ornately decorative church was begun in 1386 and is the work of countless architects, artists, and artisans. It is basically unfinished today since it still undergoes many reconstructions, maintenance, and restoration work. This massive structure is crowned by 135 spires with statues and relief work interdispersed everywhere. At night the spires are lit which makes an excellent scene, especially from the dining room at the Hotel Duomo. One of the best ways to get a bird's eye view of the square is to ascend to the outside viewing area above the facade of the cathedral.

The interior, like the exterior, is covered in statues, relief work, and many other decorations. The stained glass windows are of particular interest especially on a bright sunny day. The statue you see in the square is of Vittorio Emanuele, done in 1896 by Ercole Rosa.

B. VITTORIO EMANUELE GALLERIA

Many buildings and houses were demolished to make this huge arcade which was dedicated to Vittorio Emanuele. Started on March 7th, 1865, it was finally finished in 1877 – and so was the architect Mengoni. The day before the opening ceremony the architect plunged to his death from the scaffolding.

Created in the form of a cross, the major wing is 195 meters long and the minor wing is 105 meters long. In the center of the cross you'll find a dome that rises 50 meters above the floor. The inside of the gallery is known as the glass sky since it completely covers all people that enter. It's the perfect place to be in a rainstorm.

Inside you'll find shops and restaurants catering to every need. It is the central meeting place for business people, artists, opera singers, fashion models and tourists alike. It is really the heart and soul of Milan.

C. PIAZZA DEI MERCANTI

The **Merchants Square** (**Piazza dei Mercanti**) is a small, quaint old square that is not really a part of the modern city of Milan. It is bounded by the **Palazzo della Ragione** (**House of Reason**), built in 1233, and the **Loggia of the Osii**, built in 1316, on the north and south; and the **Palatine Schools** and the **Panigalaros house** on the east and west.

In the niches of the Loggia of the Osii, you can find the statues of the Milanese saints. But besides the sculptures and ancient architecture, this is a place to come and get away from the pace of the modern Milan.

D. TEATRO LA SCALA

Piazza della Scala. Tel. 805-3418. Open Monday–Saturday 9am–noon and 2-6pm. Sunday 9:30am-12:30pm and 2:30pm-6pm. Admission L6,000.

If you are an opera fan you've come to Milan to catch a performance at **La Scala**, the most famous and prestigious of all opera houses in the world. Built between 1776 and 1778 on the old site of the church of Santa Maria alla Scala, it is the work of the architect Giusseppe Piermarini. Built in the neoclassical style, the facade has a covered portico and gable with a relief work depicting Apollo's Chariot. The building suffered bomb damage during World War II but was rebuilt perfectly and was re-opened in 1946.

If you can't catch a performance here, just come to visit their museum which offers a variety of operatic costumes, all the way from Ancient Grecian times to the present. There are also many objects that trace the evolution of the theater, as well as 40,000 books that deal with opera and the theater, and records that have over 600 different opera singers recorded.

E. PALAZZO DI BRERA

Via Brera 28, Tel. 862-634. Open Tuesday–Saturday 9am–2pm and Sun 9am–1pm. Admission L8,000.

Built in 1170 by an order of religious men called the **Umiliati** as a monastery and place of worship. Then in the 13th century the **Church of St. Mary of Brera** was added onto the building and it has been so named ever since. In 1772 the building began its new life as an institute of artistic preservation as commissioned by Mary Teresa of Austria. The first part of the collection was donated by the Abbot Giusseppe Bianconi in return for his appointment as secretary to the new museum. Many of its current works were donations from religious orders by decree of Napoleon himself. In the nineteenth century the collection was enriched by many private donations.

All the works were moved for safekeeping during World War II because of the bombings of the city. Because of its industrial nature, Milan was the most badly damaged Italian city. Then on June 9th, 1950, the collection opened for viewing again.

Today you can find works from the 14th century up to present times. Among the most noteworthy are Moccirolo's *Oratorio*, Raphael's well-known *Sposalizio delle Vergine*, Mantegna's *Cristo Morto* and Bramante's *Cristo alla Colonna*.

F. CASTELLO SFORZESCO

Foro Buonaparte. **Metro** *– Carioli. Open Tuesday–Sunday 9:30am–5:30pm.*

What you see today is only part of the original citadel and its many lives. In the beginning it consisted of many forts all enclosed in a great star-shaped ramparted fortress. Despite its reduction in size it is still Italy's largest castle/fortress today.

The current fortress was built in 1450 over the ruins of a viscont's fort, which itself had been built over the ruins of the **Porta Giovia castle**. Under the rule of Lodovico Sforza in 1495, the castle started to take on many artistic accents with works by such masters as Leonardo da Vinci and Bramante. During the Spanish, French, and Austrian control of the area, this beautiful castle was used a military barracks and was treated so poorly that after a while it could only be considered a ruin. Finally in 1890, when the Austrian troops were forced to leave, they decided to restore it and in 1893 the work began. But in 1943 parts of the building and its museums were damaged in the bombings, but these too were reconstructed.

Today you should visit the castle not only to see its immense towers and walls and stroll through the beautiful park inside, but also to see their extensive art collection, underground archaeological museum and Historic Document Archives. In the **Ancient Arts Museum**, you'll find a wide variety of artistic works including fabulous gems by Michelangelo and Leonardo da Vinci, Italy's greatest artists. Look for the *Pieta Rondanini*, Michelangelo's last and unfinished work as well as a hall dedicated to ancient arms such as axes, shields, spiked clubs, spears and more.

In the **Historic Document Archives**, started in 1902, there are preserved documents, some of which date back to 1385. Any bibliophile will love this collection.

G. ARCO SEMPIONE

Piazza Sempione.

This monument is also called the **arch of peace**. Construction began in 1807 to celebrate Napoleon's victories in war. It consists of three barrel vaults supported by Corinthian columns on pedestals and needs to be seen if you can't make it to Paris and see the Arc de Triomphe. The reclining figures near the top represent the four main rivers in Italy.

H. GIARDINI PUBLICI

Located halfway between the main train station and the Duomo. Open 6am-dusk.

These gardens are a fine place to come and get away from the hectic pace of Milan. If you're so inclined there is also a small **zoo** to enjoy. Walk along wooded paths and escape it all.

I. LEONARDO DA VINCI MUSEUM OF SCIENCE & TECHNOLOGY

Via San Vittore 21, Tel. 4801-0040. Metro San Ambrogio. Open Tuesday-Sunday 9am-5pm. Admission L10,000 - Adults; L6,000 kids under 18.

Inaugurated in 1953 for the fifth centenary of Leonardo's birth, this unique museum is a must-see while in Milan. Located on the site of the Olivetano Monastery, this museum now houses a collection of material that gives a complete synthesis of Leonardo da Vinci's work and experiments in many fields.

Here you'll find reproductions of his designs and mechanical models of his inventions, some of which you (and the kid inside you) can actually test out. There are also copies of pages from the *Gates Codex* (used to be the *Codex Hammer*) on display.

If you've had enough of Leonardo's inventions and Codex you can walk through other wonderful exhibits all related to science and technology, like one about the history of aviation, one dealing solely with typewriters, one about land transportation, one dedicated to clocks. Besides all of this there is also an excellent reproduction of Leonardo's

Last Supper painted by Giovanni Mauro Dellarovere at the end of the 16th century. So if you can't get into see the real one come here instead.

J. DA VINCI'S LAST SUPPER

Piazza Santa Maria delle Grazie. Tel. 498–7588. Metro–Carioli. Open Tuesday–Sunday 8:30am–1:30pm. Admission L6,000.

To the left of the **church of Santa Maria delle Grazie** is the refectory of the Dominican convent that houses the most famous of Leonardo's work, *The Last Supper*. Painted between 1495 and 1497, the painting is not standing up to the test of time and man. The humidity in the room doesn't help maintain the fresco and a doorway was built underneath it cutting off one of Christ's legs that was visible under the table. Also restoration work that was done in 1726 and 1770 actually helped to enhance the painting's deterioration. Efforts are underway now, using modern techniques, to save the invaluable work, but if I was you I'd see it sooner rather than later.

NIGHTLIFE & ENTERTAINMENT

The nightlife in Milan centers around the theater, then a light dinner and wine afterwards. Most restaurants stay open after midnight, so this may be your best outlet for subtle entertainment.

There are many theaters in Milan. Contact your travel agent in North America, or your hotel while in Milan about getting tickets. If you want to go to La Scala to see some opera you should plan at least six months in advance (see below).

If theater and a late dinner are not to your liking, here's a small list of pubs that may be more up your alley.

50. NAVY PUB/VICTORY, *Via Borgogna 5, Milano. Tel. 02/76-02-07-18. Half pints L4,000. Pints L7,000.*

Great inside and outside atmosphere. Their terrace is fenced in by beer barrels and pseudo-fish nets and the inside has an English-style wooden bar at which to stand as well as red velvet booths. You can enjoy a Guiness, Harp, or Kilkeny on draft. Enjoy.

HOBBIT PUB, *Via dei Missaglia 59a, tel. 02/89-30-03-66.*

They serve bottle beers from all over the world and stay open until 2:00am for your drinking pleasure. The atmosphere is definitely English-pub style coupled with fun music. If you get hungry they have sandwiches, chips, peanuts etc. to munch on.

BIRROTECA WOODSTOCK, *Via Lodovico Il Moro 3, Tel. 02/89-12-04-79.*

Open until 3:00am, this place also serves beers from around the world. As you can guess by the name, this bar draws a little more eclectic crowd. If you get hungry they have your basic pub fare like sandwiches, chips, and peanuts.

SPORTS & RECREATION

Golf
- **Golf Club Bergam Ol'Albenza**, *Via Congoni 12, 24030 Bergamo. Tel. 035/640-707. Fax 035/640-028.* Located 50 kilometers from Milan and only 13 kilometers from Bergamo this is the home course of the famous Italian golfer Constantino Rocca who came in second to John Daly in the 1995 British Open. The main course is an 18 hole, par 72 that is 6190 meters long. The small course is 9 holes, par 36, and 2462 meters long. Open year round except from December 22nd to January 5th and Mondays. They have a restaurant, bar, driving range, and electric carts.
- **Golf Club Carimate**, *Via Airldi 2, 22060 Carimate. Tel. 031/790-226. Fax 031/790-226.* Located 27km from Milan and 15km from Como this is an 18 hole, par 71 course that is 5,982 meters long. It is open year round except on Mondays. They have a driving range, tennis course, and a fine bar and restaurant.
- **La Pinetta Golf Club**, *Via al Golf 4, 22070 Appiano Gentile. Tel. 031/933-202. Fax 031/890-342.* Located 25km from Milan and 12km from Como this is an 18 hole, par 71 course that is 6,035 meters long. It is open year round except Tuesdays. They have a driving range, pro shop, swimming pool, tennis course, pro shop, and a bar and restaurant. A great place to come for a family outing while you go play golf.
- **Golf Club Milano**, *Viale Mulini S Girogio 7, 20052 Parco di Monza. Tel. 039/303-081/2/3. Fax 039/304-427.* Located 20km from Milan, this is an 18 hole, par 71 course that is 6,083 meters long. Open year round except for Mondays. They have a driving range, pro shop, swimming pool, and restaurant/bar.
- **Molinetto Country Club A.S.**, *SS Padana Superiore 11, 20063 Cenusco sul Naviglio (in Milan). Tel. 02/9210-5128. Fax 02/9210-6635.* Located 10km from the center of Milan, this is an 18 hole par 71 course that is 6,1025 meters long. Open year round except Mondays. They have a driving range, pool, and bar/restaurant. The second closest course to Milan for the addicts.
- **Golf Le Roverdine**,*Via K Marx, 20090 Noverasco di Opera (in Milan). Tel. 02/5760-2730. Fax 02/5760-6405.* Located only 4km from the city center, this is an 18 hole, par 72 course that is 6,322 meters long. It is open year round except on Mondays. The have a driving range, carts, pro shop and a great nineteenth hole bar. This is the closest place to play. Enjoy.
- **Circolo di Campagna Zoate Golf Club**, *Via Verdi 6, 20067 Zoate di Tribiano. Tel. 02/9063-2183. Fax 02/9063-1861.* Located 18km from Milan, this is an 18 hole par 72 course that is 6,122 meters long. It is

open year round except Mondays. They have a pro shop, swimming pool, restaurant and a bar.

• **Barlassina Country Club**, *Via Privata 42, 20030 Birago di Camnago. Tel. 0362/560-621. Fax 0362/560-934.* Located 20km from Milan this is an 18 hole par 72 course that is 6,184 meters in length. It is open year round except Mondays. They have a driving range, pro shop, swimming pool, tennis course, guest house, bar, and a restaurant.

SHOPPING

The best and most expensive shopping streets in Milan are the **Via Montenapoleone** and **Via della Spiga**, and all the little alleys around these two parallel streets. Be prepared to spend through the nose here, but also expect to get the best service and quality of product available. Taking a stroll down these streets you'll witness the opulence and splendor of Milan's stores and the beauty of these elegant streets.

There are so many great stores in Milan that to do them justice would require a separate book – and in fact one excellent resource exists for both Milan and elsewhere in Italy, which I'm pleased to recommend: *Made in Italy* by Anne Brody and Patricia Shultz.

The *salumiere*, where you can get delicious picnic and specialty food supplies, are numbered for you to locate on the map of Milan.

Fashion & Accessories

Milan is the seat of Italian fashion, and plays a close to second to Paris in world fashion. There are plenty of small designer's shops that feature dresses that have either been on the runways during the 'Fashion Week' of spring or fall, or they have deliberately 'copied' these new fashions, or should I say modified them with their own creative direction. Whatever the case, most of these designer outfits will cost you an arm and a leg, but if it's fashion you want, it's fashion Milan has.

If you're looking for leather accessories Milan definitely has the greatest diversity in price and styles than any other city in Italy. Many of their products are made locally and many others come from the many factories that surround Bologna. Wherever the finished leather comes from you'll notice that the selection is gargantuan. The Milanese thrive on taking risks and employing novel new designs. In essence, you'll never have a problem finding something new and different in Milan.

What you may have trouble finding is something in your price range, but if you're here to shop, that doesn't mean you actually have to buy, does it? Go ahead, you're on vacation.

Home & Office Furnishings

In most everything the Milanese are willing to try any new approach as long as it's aesthetically appealing and has practical application. This is probably best expressed in their home furnishings industry. The city thrives on a culture of modernism and its industry allows this creativity to flow through the production into your home or office.

There are a myriad of showrooms and/or retail stores all over Milan in which you can admire and buy the latest and greatest designs in home and office furniture, lighting fixtures. housewares, and accessories for the office and home. Some of them can be much more fun than going to a museum because it seems as if these pieces are alive.

Bookstores (English-Language)

Milan has become the publishing capital of Italy, for magazines, newspapers, and books; and many of Milan's publishers have established their own well stocked, large bookstores. Many of these bookstores contain English-language titles, but even if they didn't I'd suggest that you visit them anyway. Just to wander around the stacks of books in a foreign bookstore helps to give you a feel for what makes the people tick. Listed below are some of the bookstores and newsstands that feature English-language titles:

Rizzoli, *Galleria Vittorio Emanuele 79, Tel. 02/807-348. American Express, Mastercard and Visa accepted.*

The Rizzoli company was founded in 1909 and is currently one of the top publishers in Italy. This is a large two story store, with the a small English language book section along with guidebooks located on the ground floor. But if you're a bibliophile that shouldn't stop you from browsing through the rest of the bookstore.

American Bookstore,*Via Camperio 16, Tel. 02/878-920. Fax 02/7202-0030. American Express, Mastercard and Visa accepted.*

As you guessed, this is exclusively an English-language bookstore. You can find everything from best-sellers to travel books. The best place to replenish your stock of novels for the rest of your trip; and since its open for lunch (as are most bookstores) you can browse here after a light lunch and wait for the museums and stores to open again. There is only a small selection of used books which are priced from L5,000-6,000. The new novels are priced between L15,000-16,000. A great place not only to browse but to hear your native language spoken, and possibly hook up with some ex-pats or tourists for a night out on the town.

Mondadori, *Corso Vittorio Emanuele 34, Tel. 02/705-832. American Express, Mastercard and Visa accepted.*

One of the most respected publishers in Europe and Italy's largest, it is still under the management of the Mondadori family. This store has three floors dedicated to mainly Italian titles, but there is also a fine section of English-language books, including Italian books translated into English.

Marco, *Galleria Passarella 2, Tel. 02/795-866. American Express, Mastercard and Visa accepted. Open on weekdays until 10:30pm.*

Basically a newsstand on hormones, this place has newspapers and magazines from all over Europe, but unfortunately not many English titles. They advertise themselves as a "supermarket of information" and this is obviously the case. They also feature best-selling books in Italian and a few in English. But still the best place for English language titles is over at the American Bookstore.

L'Archivolto, *Via Marsala 2, Tel. 02/659-0842. American Express, Mastercard and Visa accepted.*

Even though this store is not affiliated with one of the giants of Milanese and Italian publishing, it's still a fun place to browse. If you like old and antique architectural drawings this is the place for you. Mainly a bookstore for architecture, city planning, and design enthusiasts, it can still be enjoyable for the average Joe like me.

Salumiere (Picnic Supplies)

When the fashion is put aside, the food comes to the front. The Milanese are well-known for their love of good food, whether in a restaurant or to take home. Milan's *salumierie* (derived from the word salami) are part of the culture of the city, and if you visit Milan try to visit at least one to get a taste (no pun intended) of the local life.

You'll find mountains of cheeses, salamis, prosciutto, pates, home-made pastas, pastries and more. Each of the stores listed below is a perfect place to find a culinary reminder of your voyage to bring back to the States.

There are many other *Alimentaris* in Milan, but you'll not find a better selection, more superior service, or the memories of shopping at Peck's. A must-see.

Peck. There are now five Peck stores that serve carry-out gastronomic excellence and one, **Il Ristorante**, that offers creative cuisine consisting of the many ingredients found in their stores. Peck is the place to go for all forms of prepared foods, salamis, cheeses, fruit, vegetables and wine. They have everything you'll need to create your own picnic or full course meal. Even if you're not in the mood to sample their wares, Peck is a great visual experience. When in Milan you simply have to come and enjoy the visual feast. They make Dean and Deluca, the famous New York-based food specialty store, pale in comparison. Each different store, all located within a stone's throw from one another near the Duomo, carry a variety of different products, obviously designed in this way so you'll have to frequent almost all of them to get the ingredients you need for that special soiree.

Peck was founded by a Czech immigrant who brought his salami making skills with him to Milan in 1883. Now the chain is owned and operated by a quartet of Italian brothers, Stoppani, who have continued the excellence, and expanded it to become the undisputed gourmet delicatessen chain in the world.

Since the choices seem endless, and you may not know what to get, ask for a sample of something before you buy. They will be more than happy to oblige in all of the shops.

51. Gastronomia Peck, *Via Spadari 9, Tel. 02/871-737.*

This is the main deli that offers everything you could ever imagine in Epicurean heaven. The shelves are packed full of platters of prepared foods, fresh pastas, smoked meats, and vegetables and fruits to go. Why the servers wear polka-dotted bow ties I can't tell you, but everything else in here is a self-explanatory food lover's dream.

52. Bottega del Maiale, Via Victor Hugo 3, Tel. 02/ 805-3528.

Just across the street from Gastronomia Peck, this store offers everything possible created from its namesake, **Il Maiale** (The Pig). You'll find snouts, ears, feet (for *Osso Bucco*) as well as salamis, sausages, and cutlets. The hams hanging precariously from the ceiling compete with the salt cured pork for your attention. Try an *etto* (about 1/4 of a pound) of *Salami Milanese* – in my opinion the best salami in Italy.

53. Casa del Formaggio, *Via Speronari 3, Tel. 02/800-858.*

A cheese lover's fantasy with over 300 varieties from all over Italy. You can get the best mozzarella made with buffalo's milk outside of Rome. They also have cheeses made with olives, spices, and nuts. If you missed out on a visit to Parma or Bologna, try a small cut of their *parmiggiano reggiano*. Made from the curds of the cheese making process this dry, brittle cheese simply melts in your mouth.

If you've never seen a skinned rabbit before, look in the window of the *Supermercato* just across the street, they always have a few of them lying there waiting to be bought, heads, tails, eyes and all.

23. Rosticceria, *Via Cantu 3, Tel. 02/ 869-3017.*

This is a meat takeout palace, no vegetarians allowed. You can get spit roasted chicken as well as pork, beef, and even vegetables all prepared with excellence for a quiet picnic in the park. See review above in *Where to Eat, no. 23.*

24. Bottega del Vino (Peck), Via Victor Hugo 4, Tel. 02/861-040.

Not just a wine bar and store, this is also a gourmet "fast-food" establishment. See review above in *Where to Eat, no. 24.*

56. Il Salumaio di Montenapoleone, Via Montenapole*one 12, Tel. 02/701-123. No credit cards accepted. Closed Sundays.*

This place has everything to prepare a five-course gourmet meal, and salami too. Dozens of varieties. You can find home-made pasta, rice, salads, pies, vegetables, barrels of pickles, vats of olives, roasted and cured meats (some of which hang from the ceiling), and cheese. Tons of it. The cheeses here outnumber the salamis.

Then, in the center you can find your dessert. But be prepared to pay for the right to eat these delicacies. Since it's located in this ritzy neighborhood the prices here are quite a bit more than at Peck's. But if you can't get downtown to enjoy the splendor of the many Peck stores, you can find all the gifts and supplies you could imagine here.

Markets

Milan definitely has more flea markets and street markets than any other Italian city. Remember, as we've said earlier in the book, always bargain. Don't just accept the first price given. Since you might be pegged as a tourist the price will usually be close to twice as much as offered to Italians. Also, if you're looking for interesting items and you want to avoid the crowds you have to get to each market early.

57. Fiera Sinigallia, *Porta Ticinese. All day Saturday.*

There are countless peddlers and regular stall holders selling everything from tapes to antiques, as well as books, clothing (new and used) and a variety of curiosities. Definitely the best selection of all the markets. It has grown so big that it merges with the next market on the list, Mercato Papiniano.

Mercato Papiniano, *Viale Papiniamo (Porta Ticinese section). Tuesday Mornings and all day Saturdays.*

Also a good variety of goods including clothes (new and used), housewares, food, and flowers. The main selection here is food and lots of it. Basically this market and the Sinigallia are one and the same. They stretch from the Porta Ticinese past the Porta Genova and encompass the Piazza San Augostino and beyond. These two combined are quite a sight when you're in Milan on a Saturday. You can spend all day here.

Wine

58. Enoteca Cotti, *Via Solferino 42, Tel. 02/2900-1096. Fax 02/2900-1222.*

A large wine shop and liquor store with all kinds of wines from all over Italy and Europe. A great place to find a nice bottle to bring home with you. Located in the Brera section, this might be a little out of the way for some, but it is worth the trip.

PRACTICAL INFORMATION

Bank Hours and Changing Money

Banks in Milan are open Monday through Friday from 8:30am to 1:30pm and from 3:00pm to 4:00pm. All banks are closed on Saturdays and Sundays. Besides banks you also have your trust **American Express** office that will cash your travelers checks. *They are located at Via Brera 3, Tel. 85-571* and are open Monday through Saturday 9:00am to 5:30pm. Also, if you're an American Express Card Holder you can cash personal checks at the office.

You also have the option of using an *Ufficio di cambio*. These exchange offices are located all over the city and generally adhere to regular store hours. Many are located in the area around the Duomo and the Via Vittorio Emanuele.

Business Hours

Stores are generally open 9:00am to 1:00pm and 3:00pm to 7:00pm. Many stores around the Duomo only close for an hour during lunch. Most stores are closed all day Sunday and Monday morning. But ... and there's always a but when it comes to Italian schedules ... food stores open Monday morning but close Monday afternoon.

Consulates

• **US Consulate**, *Via Principe Amadeo 4, Tel. 02/29-00-18-41*
• **Canadian Consulate**, *Via Vittor Pisani 19, Tel. 02/669-74-51. For emergencies 01/66-98-06-00*
• **United Kingdom Consulate**, *Via S. Paolo, Tel. 02/869-34-42*
• **Australian Consulate**, *Via Borgogna 2, Tel. 02/76-01-33-30*

Local Festivals & Holidays

• **First Sunday in June**, *Festa dei Navigli*. Located along the Navigli (canals) in the Ticinese section this is a folkloric celebration with music and a festival. And even thought it is a Sunday most of the stores will be open to accommodate the increased business.
• **December 7**, St. Ambrose day, patron saint of Milan. Features an open-air market surrounding the Basilica of Sant'Ambrogio commonly referred to as "O Bej O Bej."

Postal Services

• **Main Post Office**, *Via Cordusio 4, Tel. 02/869-20-69*. Located near the Duomo, and between it and the castle. Open Monday - Friday 8:45am to 7:30am and Saturdays 8:45am to 5:00pm.

Supermarkets

There are not many near the center of town, so when you're in the need of food in your room and when all the stores are closed during the day and on Sunday, the places listed below will come in handy. They are open from 7:00am until 7:00pm every day.

• **Il Mercato**, *in the train station, lower level.* Open seven days a week featuring all sorts of necessary foods for the traveler and other items that only locals could need. Ideally located for the traveler in need of anything.

• **Standa**, *Via Sarpi 33/Via Paila 2/Via Betrami 2*

• **Unese**, *Viale Bianca Maria 28*

• **SMA**, *Via L Mancin 2/4*

• **Natura Si**, *Via Fara 31.* An environmentalist's dream. Everything in here is natural, biodegradable, recycled, recyclable, organically grown, etc.

Tourist Information & Maps

• **EPT Office**, *in Central Station, Tel. 02/744-065, or at Linate Airport, Tel. 02/80-545.* They have maps of he city that are really no help if what you're looking for is down a side street. In conjunction they have information about hotels and can book them for you if you arrive in Milan without a room.

• **Viagi Wasteel**, *Train Station, 0336/330-872.* Speak with Dr. Ibrahim Gouda if you arrive in Milan without a room reservation since he can get one for you at a hug discount. See *Where to Stay* above for more information.

Tour Operators

• **American Express**, *Via Brera 3, Tel. 02/7200-3694*

• **Wagon-Lit**, *Corso Venezi 53, Tel. 02/7600-4133. Fax 02/7600-4980*

DAY TRIPS & EXCURSIONS

The three nearby towns I'd recommend for day trips or brief excursions are **Bergamo**, **Pavia**, and **Certosa**. Rich in Renaissance history, these towns offer a relaxing escape from the pace of Milan.

BERGAMO

Situated picturesquely at the foot of the **Bergamo Alps**, this is really two different towns. The older **Citta Alta** town consists of narrow winding streets with battlements surrounding them that were built between 1561 and 1592; and then you have the modern **Citta Basso**. The only important information you need to know about the lower city is that it is the home of the famous Italian golfer Costantino Rocca who came in second to American John Daly in the British Open in 1995. But you should concentrate on wandering through and enjoying the tiny medieval streets and buildings of the older Citta Alta.

Bergamo was originally a Gaelic settlement and is first recorded in history in 200 BC as the Roman settlement *Municipium Bergamum*. Quite a mouthful huh? Bergamo remained relatively unimportant until it joined the Lombard League of towns in 1167. The next big political event was when the Kingdom of Milan took control in 1264. As Venice flexed its muscles, it then came under Venetian control from 1428 to 1797. Then France took it over and eventually the unified Italy.

Though Bergamo's past doesn't seem too exciting, it has left us with a scenic old town to wander through on our day trip. Since cars are not allowed in Citta Alta, the town's seven hills can sometimes feel like seventy. But strolling through the streets lined with fourteenth and fifteenth century buildings and *palazzi* that have a definite Venetian influence takes your mind off the climb. Besides the architecture, Bergamo offers you scenic vistas down into the valley, through the town, and up into the Alps. Remember to bring your camera.

Bergamo is the perfect little town to visit when the hectic pace of Milan has begun to grate on you. It's the best place to come to and recharge your batteries, and to give yourself memories that will last a lifetime.

This little town within a town is a perfect place to stay and savor the sights, sounds, and smells of intimate Italian life. If you're staying in Milan and are tired of the brusque manner in which you may be treated, come here for a few days and appreciate the sense of care and community you are given. You'll not want to go back to Milan ... guaranteed.

ONE CHARMING HILL TOWN!

If you are in this area of Italy, come and visit Bergamo Alto. The cobblestone narrow streets, medieval buildings, and squares create an ambiance that is charming, romantic, and out of this world. Stay a day or more and soak up the beauty of Italy in this fantastic hill town.

ARRIVALS & DEPARTURES
By Train

A train leaves from Milan virtually every hour on the quarter hour and takes an hour to get to Bergamo. Once off the train you're in the Citta Basso, the lower city. Where you're going is the Citta Alta (the upper city).

To begin, buy a bus ticket at the *giornalaio* just on the left before you leave the station, and also buy one of their tourist books in English

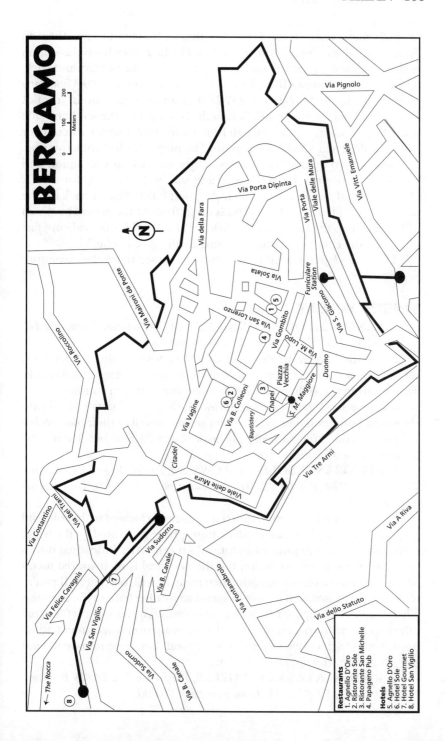

BERGAMO

0 100 200
Meters

Via Pignolo

Via Vitt. Emanuele

Via Porta Dipinta

Via della Fara

Via Maironi da Ponte

Via Roccolino

Via Solata

Viale delle Mura

Via Porta

Via San Lorenzo

Via Gombito

Via S. Giacomo

Funiculare Station

① ⑤

④

Via M. Lupo

Piazza Vecchia

Duomo

Via B. Colleoni

⑥ ②

③

Chapel

Baptistery

S. M. Maggiore

Via Vagine

Citadel

Viale delle Mura

Via Tre Armi

Via A. Riva

Via Sudorno

Via B. Canale

Via Fontanabrolo

Via dello Statuto

⑦

Via Costantino

Via Bel Trami

Via Felice Cavagnis

Via San Vigilio

← The Rocca

⑧

Via Sudorno

Via B. Canale

Restaurants
1. Agnello D'Oro
2. Ristorante Sole
3. Ristorante San Michelle
4. Papageno Pub

Hotels
5. Agnello D'Oro
6. Hotel Sole
7. Hotel Gourmet
8. Hotel San Vigilio

(without map) since in the Citta Alta they only seem to have them in French or Italian. Before you get on bus #1 which goes from the station to the *funiculare*, which will take you up the hill to the old city and back, first stop at the **tourist office**, *located outside of the station on the Viale Papa Giovanni XXIII, #106 (Tel. 035/242-226)*. Just go up the road in front of the station, past the first road. Before the first light on the left hand side in the large building with Banco di Roma is the information office. They have excellent maps and information. The map is perfect for exploring.

Now armed with all necessities, either go back to the station and board bus #1 there or cross the road and wait at the bus stop for the #1. Once on board punch your ticket like a good Italian and sit back for the short five minute ride. The bus pulls up in front of the *funiculare* which will take you up the hill. Your bus ticket is also good for the ride up; just show it to the conductor who is waiting by the gate to check.

The *funiculare* takes all of five minutes. Once there the adventure begins.

WHERE TO EAT

1. AGNELLO D'ORO, *Via Gombito 22, 24129 Bergamo, Citta Alta. Tel. 035/249-883. Fax 035/235-612. Dinner for two L65,000.*

I love the haphazard decor of this place with all the copper pots, ceramic plates and pitchers, as well as plenty of other knickknacks hanging from the ceiling and walls. These intimate surroundings boast some fairly good food, like their *Tortellini alla panna* (pasta stuffed with cheese and smothered in a rich cream sauce) as well as their *filetto di bue alla griglia* (grilled filet of beef). My favorite was the Sole but that may be because of their beautiful patio.

2. RISTORANTE SOLE, *Via B Colleoni 1, 24129 Bergamo, Citta Alta. Tel. 035/218-238. Fax 035/240-011. Tourist menu L30,000; Gastronomes menu L69,000.*

Simply a great restaurant, with the best seating located in the splendid garden area. The place has a festive atmosphere generated by the white walls, red chairs, and pink tablecloths. You can order individual dishes from the menu if you so desire, but the best deal is their tourist menu which offers you a choice of pasta, then meat, as well as a desert. If you're really a hearty eater, and expect to spend some time here in the evenings (always a good idea), their larger menu *gastonomica* comes with the same offerings as the tourist menu, as well as an antipasto, fish or meat, wine, dessert, and Irish coffee to finish up the meal. You have to have at least one meal here while in the Citta Alta.

3. RISTORANTE SAN MICHELLE, *Piazza Vecchia, 24129 Bergamo, Citta Alta. Tel. 035/225-335. Dinner for two L70,000.*

Located on the central square with plenty of seating from which to enjoy the spectacle of this small medieval town, you will also get a good meal. They make excellent pastas like their *Tortellini della casa* (home-made) *con ricotta ed erbetta* (pasta stuffed with ricotta cheese and made with garlic, and other herbs an spices). For seconds try their *misto formaggi alla griglia* (mixed grilled cheese).

There are two other restaurants on the piazza also with outside seating, which will not disappoint if this one is full. They also have a tourist menu for only L40,000 which serves up the best they have to offer, as well as 1/4 liter of wine and 1/2 liter of mineral water. That may be your best bet.

4. PAPAGENO PUB, *Via Gombito, Bergamo, Citta Alta. tel. 035/236-624. Open 1:00am - 2:00am. Closed Tuesdays.*

An ambiance of an English pub here in this small Italian town is hard to believe. they serve Guiness and three German beers on tap for L9,000 a pint. No food is served except in the mornings when they offer coffee and danish to the students that wander by. This is the after hours place to go in Bergamo to enjoy a few pints and try to be a part of the life of the town.

Since the Citta Alta houses a local university, many restaurants stay open at night to cater to the nocturnal yearnings of the younger set. This is the best place to go to be a part of such adventures.

WHERE TO TAY

5. AGNELLO D'ORO, *Via Gombito 22, 24129 Bergamo, Citta Alta. Tel. 035/249-883. Fax 035/235-612. 20 rooms all with bath. Single L55,000; Double L95,000.* **

The small reception area is also the entrance way for their beautifully decorated restaurant. The rooms are all on the small side but they have all the amenities of a three star hotel without the price. Staying here you'll be virtually in the center of things, if such a thing can be said about the calm environs of the Citta Alta. A great place to stay. They have a quaint, small restaurant attached where you can enjoy meals if you don't want to wander out.

6. HOTEL SOLE, *Via B Colleoni 1, 24129 Bergamo, Citta Alta. Tel. 035/218-238. Fax 035/240-011. 10 rooms all with bath. Single L70,000 (double used as a single); Double L100,000.* **

The rooms are all small but they have everything you'd find in a three -star: TV, phone, private bath, etc. The atmosphere is not quite as stuffy as the Agnello and their restaurant is better too. The pace to stay for less in Bergamo. You're in the heart of the Citta Alta. Great for touring and just wandering around.

7. HOTEL GOURMET, *Via San Vigilio 1, 24129 Bergamo, Citta Alta. Tel. and Fax 035/437-3004. 11 rooms. 1 Single (L85,000), 9 Doubles (L120,000); 1 suite (L260,000).* ***

I hope the phone number is correct since they were just installing a new one while I was there and they assured me it would be fine. This being Italy and all, I tend to have my doubts. Anyway, this place is located in the Citta Alta but outside of the walls at the second *funiculare*. Their rooms are a little larger and more comfortable than the ones downtown but you pay a little extra for that comfort. In all a great place to stay. Eating here is another story: their food is good, but the prices are sky high.

8. HOTEL SAN VIGILIO, *Via San Vigilio 15, Bergamo, Citta Alta. Tel. 035/25-31-79. fax 035/40-20-81. 7 rooms, all doubles, L135,000 each.* ***

Located above the Citta Alta. I guess that makes this place the Hotel super-Alta. The views from up here over the Citta Bassa and the Citta Alta are stupendous. You reach here by taking the second *funiculare* all the way to the top. Their restaurant is superb so don't worry about going down to the Citta Alta for dinner and missing the last *funiculare* at 10:00pm (on weekends the last one is 1:00pm). The rooms are Italian-size but comfortable, and I have to say it again, the restaurant is great.

SEEING THE SIGHTS

Let's start off at the Piazza Vecchia, which holds a number of the town's beautiful sights.

PIAZZA VECCHIA

Several outdoor cafes ring this square which is the heart of the old town. In the middle of the square is the **Fontana di Alvise Contarini**, named after the Venetian mayor that gave the fountain to the town in 1780. The buildings that line the square are of 11th and 12th century origin. On the south side is the **Palazzo della Ragione** (palace of Reason). Fires destroyed the ground floor in the second half of the 15th century and the building was restored with arcades instead of walls.

Next to this building is the **Torre Civica** which tolls every evening at 10:00pm 100 times (a tradition dating back to an ancient curfew). On the west side is the **Palazzo del Podesta** and was the home of the Venetian mayors that ran the town many centuries ago. The building is now the seat of the faculty of modern languages and literature for the University. To the north is the **Biblioteca Civica** (the Civic Library) that was started in 1604; the facade was only completed at the beginning of this century. You will find well preserved parchment, scrolls, and other documents inside.

Through an arched passageway under the Palazzo Ragione you can enter the **Piazzetta del Duomo**. In this little piazza you'll find the

Cathedral, the Baptistery, the Colleoni Chapel, and also the Church of Santa Maria Maggiore:

Duomo
Piazza Duomo. Tel. 217–317. Open 8am–Noon and 3pm–6pm.

Started in 1459 and continued in 1699, it was finally completed in the middle of the 19th century. It is a small cathedral but then again Bergamo is a small little hillside town. Inside you'll find the *Madonna and Child* by BG Moroni and a painting by GD Tiepolo, *The Martyrdom of St. John*.

Baptistery
Open by reservations only. Tel. 217–317.

Built in 1340 by Giovanni da Campione, originally it was located at another site and was only moved here in 1898. The upper part has refined columns and eight 14th century statues that represent the virtues. Inside you'll find bas-reliefs of Christ's life and the baptismal font built by Giovanni da Campione.

Colleoni Chapel
Piazza Duomo. March–October open 9am–noon and 2pm–6pm. November–February open 9am–noon and 2:30pm–4:30pm. Closed Monday.

This chapel, created in 1472, is considered one of the earlier works of Renaissance art in the northern Italy, even though the exterior shows definite signs of the flowery Gothic style.

Basilica of Santa Maria Maggiore
Piazza Duomo, Tel. 246–855. November–March open 8am–noon and 3pm–6pm, and open April–October 8am–noon and 5pm–7pm.

Built in 1137, this Romanesque church was once used as a sort of safety deposit box by the rich families of Bergamo. They used to store their jewels and documents here. In the *loggia* of the entrance you'll find a statue of St. Alexander, the patron saint of the town.

CITADEL
Piazza della Citadella, Tel. 242–839. Open 9am–12;30pm and 2:30pm–6pm. Closed Mondays and holidays.

Now the **Natural Science and Archaeological Museum**, this building was built in 1300 and was once part of larger fortresses of that time.

VIALE DELLE MURA
This road leads around the walls and offers scenic views of the lower city and of the Alps. The walls were built by the Venetians in 1561 to

protect this strategically located hill town. From the rampart of San Grata, you can admire the rolling hills at the back of the town. When you come to Bergamo you should spend an afternoon strolling around the walls.

THE ROCCA

Via Rocca, Tel. 262-566. Open October–March, Saturday and Sunday 10am–noon and 2pm–6pm. Open April–September every day from 10am–noon and 3pm–7pm.

Located high above the town you can find the remains of a Viscount's castle from the fourteenth century. All that remains today is the circular dungeon. The fortress itself was built in 1331. Outside you'll find the peaceful **Parco delle Rimembranze**. Inside you'll find the **Risorgimento Museum** and great views of the town from the windows in the dungeon.

TOURIST INFORMATION

• *Viale Papa Giovanni XXIII, #106, Bergamo, Citta Basso. Tel. 035/242-226.* They can give you maps and hotel information but are unable to do the booking for you. The map is very good for both the Citta Alta and the Citta Bassa.

PAVIA & CERTOSA

Pavia is a somewhat interesting city in the area around the University and Duomo, since that is where the old medieval streets are located. But **Certosa** is the prize here.

La Certosa di Pavia (the charterhouse of Pavia) is a gem that you should definitely check out if you're visiting Milan. It has a beautiful marble facade that is the work of Amadeo and Montgegazza, and the portal is covered with reliefs that celebrate the history of the Certosa. In the **Old Sacristy**, you'll find the hippopotamus tooth triptych created by Baldassare degli Embriachi. It is the oldest sculpture in the Certosa, containing 64 ivory molds that feature stories from both the Old and New Testaments. But my favorite part is the **Cloister**, a small building next to the church that contains 24 cells that were used by the Cathusian monks, each with its own garden.

The **Duomo** in Pavia pales in comparison. It is a simple, brick structure that looks like it was part of the dark ages, while the Certosa evokes the beauty of the Renaissance.

ARRIVALS & DEPARTURES

By Train

There are trains every half hour leaving from Milan to **Pavia**. Once in Pavia, leave the station, pass the first street, and turn left at the second

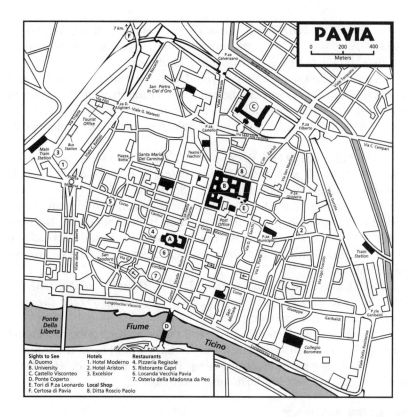

Sights to See	Hotels	Restaurants
A. Duomo	1. Hotel Moderno	4. Pizzeria Regisole
B. University	2. Hotel Ariston	5. Ristorante Capri
C. Castello Visconteo	3. Excelsior	6. Locanda Vecchia Pavia
D. Ponte Coperto		7. Osteria della Madonna da Peo
E. Tori di P.za Leonardo	Local Shop	
F. Certosa di Pavia	8. Ditta Roscio Paolo	

street, Via Trieste. About fifty feet down is the bus station. Here you can get a round trip ticket to **Certosa** for L3,800. The buses leave every half hour and take about 10 minutes to get to the church.

Tourist Information

The Pavia and Certosa **information office** *is located on Via Filzi 12, Tel. 22-156.* They offer first-rate information about the city and the church as well as an excellent map you can use to make your way around.

To get to the information office, leave the station, go past the first street, then take a left on Via Trieste. Go past the bus station to the first corner and take a right. The information office will be on the right hand side in the middle of the street.

WHERE TO STAY

Pavia

If you're interested in staying in Pavia, here is a list of hotels you can contact. Again – it's not that exciting of a place.

1. **HOTEL MODERNO**, *Viale Vittorio Emanuele II 41, Tel. 0382/ 303401. Fax 0382/25-225. Credit cards accepted. 54 rooms all with bath. Single L 130,000; Double L170,000. Breakfast L15,000 extra.* ****
Located near the train station, you'll find all the amenities of four star in small city for a very reasonable price. Even though it's in the center of town you won't notice any noise since it is completely sound-proofed. The rooms are clean, modern, and comfortable. A good and convenient place to stay.

2. **HOTEL ARISTON**, *Via Scopoli 10D, Tel. 0382/34-334. fax 0382/25-667. 60 rooms all with bath. Single L80,000-90,000; Double L120,000-150,000. Breakfast L15,000 extra. All credit cards accepted.* ****
Located deep in the heart of Pavia, here you can explore and enjoy the university and old town much better than at the other places. But then again you're farther away from the train station. You'll have all the amenities of a four star including a decent restaurant. The rooms are small but clean.

3. **EXCELSIOR**, *Piazzale Stazione 25. Tel. 0382/28-596. fax 0382/26-030. 20 rooms all with bath. Single L75,000; Double L105,000. Breakfast L8,000 extra. Credit cards accepted.* ***
Located only 50 meters from the train station, this is good clean hotel managed by Luigi Bricchi. The only drawback would be in the summer since they do not have air conditioning. The price is right for a brief stay but so is the four star Moderno or Ariston above.

WHERE TO EAT

There are not many restaurants in this city, which is a definitive indication that they do not get many tourists. But the ones they do have are pretty good.

4. **PIZZERIA/RISTORANTE REGISOLE**, *Piazza Duomo 1. Closed Mondays. Dinner for two L60,000. Credit cards accepted.*
Known for their varieties of pizza they also have plenty of pasta dishes, including *carbonara* (with cheese, ham, and egg), *vongole* (spicy tomato based clam sauce), and *alla panna* (with a thick cream sauce); and meats and fish. The seating outside facing the Duomo is the best when the weather permits.

5. **RISTORANTE/PIZZERIA CAPRI**, *Via Cavour 32. Credit cards accepted. Dinner for two L55,000. Closed Tuesdays*
A plain little local place on one of the city's busy shopping streets, you'll find plenty here to satisfy your hunger including *pizza al rutta di mare* (pizza with seafood), as well as grilled meats and fish.

6. **LOCANDA VECCHIA PAVIA**, *Via Cardinal Riboldi 2, Tel. 0382/ 304-132. Closed Mondays and Sunday nights as well the first of January and all of August. All credit cards accepted. Dinner for two L180,000.*

Some consider this the best restaurant in Pavia. It certainly is the most chic. Their motto is "We love tradition and we recreate them with a passion" and this fits well with their *cucina nuova*. Located near the cathedral, you can find unique but appetizing dishes such as piccione *alla marinata di verdure e vino rosso* (pigeon in a vegetable and red wine sauce), or *pasta fresca alla scampi e zucchine* (fresh pasta with shrimp and zucchini). The atmosphere is elegant but cramped and the prices are a little high, but for a creative meal in Pavia, come here.

7. OSTERIA DELLA MADONNA DA PEO, *Via Dei Liguri 28, Tel. 0382/302-833. Closed Sundays and August. All credit cards accepted. Dinner for two L120,000.*

In a small room down a tiny side street you can get some great traditional local cooking. Try their salami plate for an appetizer (*salumi tipici*), move onto the *pasta a fagioli* (pasta and beans), and then finish with a succulent *Osso Bucco* (ham hock cooked in sauce and wine)

SEEING THE SIGHTS

Even though I've raved about Certosa, there are some fine examples of Renaissance art and architecture in Pavia. I especially like the University buildings. But the real prize, again, is the charterhouse (see below).

A. THE DUOMO

Piazza del Duomo. Open 7am–7pm.

A notable example of the Lombardy Renaissance period, this structure is the work of Rocchi, Amadeo, and Bramante (1488). It is the shape of a Greek cross surmounted by an immense dome, the third largest in Italy, built in the 19th century by the architect Maciachini. It is an unfinished work since there has been no attempt to put a face or sides of marble over the plain brick exterior.

B. THE UNIVERSITY

Strada Nuova 65. Tel. 24764.

This is one of Italy's finest universities. Built from 1400 to 1500, this is an imposing set of structures developed under the Viscontis and later restructured with a design by Piermarini and Pollach. The northern courtyards retain Pessina's 16th century plan with the Doric columns. Scattered throughout the maze of buildings are monuments to Allessandro Voloto, Antonio Bordoni, Bartolomeo Panizza, and Camillo Golgi.

The best way to explore is to simply wander around and soak up the beauty of the ancient buildings that today are developing Italy's next leaders.

C. CASTELLO VISCONTEO
Tel.33853/308-774. Open Tuesday through Saturday 9:00am to 1:30pm and Sunday 9:00am to 1:00pm. Closed Mondays.

Built between 1360 and 1365, this was an important non-military building during the Lombardy period of the 1300s. The building is surrounded by a deep ditch and protected by drawbridges. It originally was a complete square with four towers, but only two of the towers remain today. You'll find the **Civic Museum** inside as well as a large grassy courtyard.

The Civic Museum has a fine archaeological collection that includes specimens of Roman glass as well as a Romanesque section with an exceptional collection of floors and mosaics.

D. PONTE COPERTO
The covered bridge over the **Ticino** is 1951 reconstruction of a 13th century bridge destroyed during the bombings of the Second World War. Unlike the Ponte Vecchio in Florence, this famous bridge is only used for traffic and not commerce.

E. TORI DI PIAZZA LEONARDO
These are two of what used to be many towers that dotted the city. The towers reach a height of 60 meters. The clock face on one tells the time and the phases of the moon.

F. CERTOSA DI PAVIA
Certosa. Tel. 925-613. Open 9am–11:30pm and 2:30pm–6pm in the summer, and only until 4:30pm in the winter. For March, April, September, and October, only open until 5:30pm. Closed Mondays.

The **Charterhouse of Pavia** is a wonderful example of 15th century Lombard art. It was originally built as a family mausoleum but is now a series of buildings built in different periods.

The church is an ornate marble structure whose portal is covered with bas-reliefs celebrating the history of Certosa. The interior of the church is in three naves with chapels overflowing with rich works of art, such as Perugino's *Eternal Father* and Bergognone's *Saint Ambrose*. The **Old Sacristy**, made in the early 1400s, holds the hippopotamus tooth triptych created by Baldassare degli Embriachi, the oldest sculpture in Certosa. It contains 64 ivory molds featuring stories from the Old and New Testament as well as the *Legend of the Three Wise Men*. On the sides and at the base are 94 statuettes of Saints.

The **Cloister**, a small building annexed to the church, is the most interesting architecturally. Here you'll find 24 cells of the Carthusian monks, each with its own garden, that offer us insight into the domestic religious life of the 15th century. This is a place you cannot miss if you visit Milan or Pavia.

SHOPPING

The main shopping streets are the ones that bisect the city into quarters: the **Strada Nuovo** from north to south and the **Via Cavour** and **Via Mazzini** from east to west. You'll find all sorts of local and international shops here.

One shop not on the main thoroughfares I think you'll like, that I've listed on the map, is:

8. DITTA ROSCIO PAOLO, *Corso Carlo Alberto 32, Tel 0382/22-185.*

Located north of the University just outside its walls, this is small brass shop that features inexpensive old canes, pots, pans, trays, pitchers, and more. If you like brass or antique brass objects, this is great store to visit and get some nice gifts.

17. GENOA

Genoa (**Genova**) is a gritty seaport city that is known for its excellent seafood restaurants and the omnipresent fresh pesto sauce. You can find great food in almost any restaurant from the four star chic to the portside dive. The old town is completely closed off to traffic, making Genoa a great city in which to stroll.

Genoa's white houses are built on the mountain slopes of the **Ligurian Apennines** above a sheltered harbor at the head of the **Gulf of Genoa**. Among the houses stand medieval churches and Renaissance palaces that illustrate the city's historic greatness. Crowded shipping in the harbor and skyscrapers rising in the business district indicate the city's present prosperity as Italy's chief port.

As well as being a shipping center, Genoa's main industry is **shipbuilding**. The port of Genoa leads all other Italian ports in volume of passengers and freight traffic, and is the main source of city income. It handles fuels and raw materials for the factories of Switzerland and southern Germany and is the chief outlet for the products of northern Italy and much of central Europe – mainly cotton and silk textiles, olive oil, and wine. Genoa has been an important port since the Middle Ages. At first its rival, Venice on the Adriatic, was busier and more powerful. Then, as trade shifted westward to the Atlantic, Genoa's location on the west coast became a great advantage.

Because of its location, tucked between the mountains and the sea, Genoa has had to be creative with its resources when expanding. One such situation was when the city began, in the 1950s, filling 250 acres of sea at Sestri Ponente, four miles to the west, for the **Cristoforo Colombo International Airport**, which provides domestic and international flights. Genoa is connected by railroads and highways with the major cities of Western Europe, but only through the creation of extensive tunnels through the mountains surrounding the city.

Genoa is noted for its many examples of medieval, Renaissance, Baroque, and Gothic architecture. The **University of Genoa**, which was founded in 1471, is an important center of higher learning for northern

Italy. The city also has several commercial colleges and a school of navigation.

As you can probably imagine, Genoa is rich in history. Both the Lombards and the Franks once ran the show here, but when Charlemagne's empire broke up, it became an independent city. Genoa also fought a long series of wars with its southern seafaring neighbor Pisa, which was eventually crushed by Genoa in 1284.

INSIGHT INTO GENOA

Genoa is a city of contrasts, a melting pot of people, a provincial port city that is bursting with energy and nationalities. The food here, especially the **pesto sauce**, *placed over a variety of different types of pastas, and the assortment of seafood available, is delicious.*

The main attraction in Genoa is its **Centro Storico**, *a small section of the city with tiny, winding, cobblestone streets that evoke an image of a bustling seafaring medieval town. Tourism is only vaguely apparent on the* **Via XX Settembre**, *a long, arcaded, upscale shopping street complete with international stores like Gucci, Fendi, and more. What makes Genoa run is business. That's why the good hotels lower their rates dramatically on the weekends, because occupancy drops precipitously. So try an get here on a weekend, stay in a four star hotel, and pay great rates.*

If you do come here you can see all that there is to see in a day or two. My favorite sight is the magnificent **cemetery** *a bus ride away, where you can find a virtual city of the dead compete with scaled down chapels, houses, crypts, roads, alleys and more. You'll find exquisite examples of architecture and sculpture throughout this exquisite cemetery.*

If this is your first time in Italy you might prefer the main tourist cities of Rome, Florence, and Venice. Maybe on a subsequent trip you can explore the mysteries of Genoa. But if you have a little time, you'll have fun here!

Genoa's foreign trade and maritime power increased greatly during the Crusades. Young knights and their entourages needed convenient locations from which to begin their voyages of salvation, and Genoa was perfectly located. During this time the city began to develop colonies in Spain and North Africa, conquered from the Saracens; and trading posts and fortresses were established in the eastern Mediterranean and along the Black Sea. During this whole time there were countless commercial wars with Venice, but these ended when Genoa was defeated by Venice at Chioggia in 1380.

Genoa regained her independence but was eventually conquered by Austria in 1746. Then it was ruled by France in the early 19th century. Its neighbor Sardinia-Piedmont acquired the city in 1814. Finally it became part of the kingdom of Italy in 1861. By the early 20th century, Genoa was the major seaport of Italy, and its tunnels, railway system, and industrial development had extended into the **Po Valley**.

Bombing of the city in World War II damaged both the harbor and industrial plants, but the city remains today as if transfixed in time, especially in the **Centro Storico** with its winding, narrow medieval streets.

Excursions from Genoa

Then once you've seen the quaint old world charm of Genoa, which should take a day and a half to explore at the most, it'll be time to really see some sides of Italy not many people experience. Our first stop will be the **Staglieno Cemetery**, which is a veritable city of the dead covering 160 hectares and is so large that it even has its own bus system.

You'll find miniature cathedrals, Romanesque chapels, Egyptian temples, *palazzi*, statues, and more. It's not morbid or macabre. And you are not desecrating their burials grounds by wandering through the monuments erected to celebrate their lives. You are helping to remember these people by appreciating the stone images left behind. I'm confident all members of the family will enjoy visiting here.

Next, we'll take a train ride down to the **Cinque Terre** *(the five lands)* that are in such barren and remote spots no cars can get to them. Each are connected to the other by a small hiking path, which is the main form of transport. These fishing and farming towns, because of their remoteness, are one of Italy's hidden treasures.

You won't find any T-shirt shops or fast food joints in these villages (except in one section of Monterosso al Mare). What you'll find is peace, tranquillity, great food, wonderful, introspective people, beautiful scenery, and memories for a lifetime.

Other highlights in the Genoa area include the postcard-perfect seaside village of **Portofino**, the beautiful small mountain town of **Casella**, and the fun Riviera resort town of **Nervi** very close to Genoa.

ARRIVALS & DEPARTURES

The best and quickest way to get in and out of Genoa is by train. The city's two main train stations are **Stazione Porta Principe** and **Stazione Brignole**.

The main station is Stazione Porta Principe, not too far from the Centro Storico.

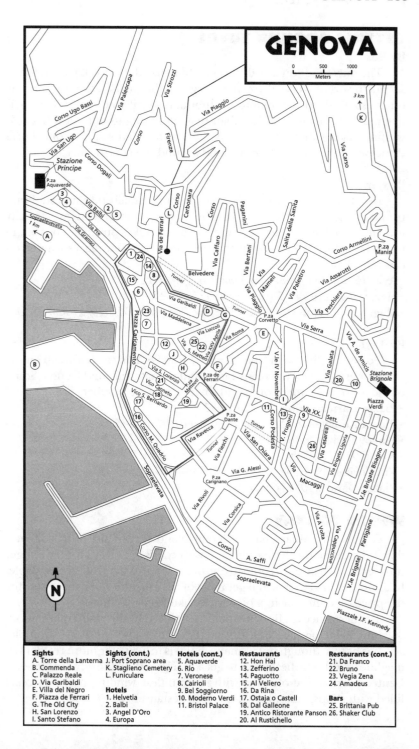

Sights
A. Torre della Lanterna
B. Commenda
C. Palazzo Reale
D. Via Garibaldi
E. Villa del Negro
F. Piazza de Ferrari
G. The Old City
H. San Lorenzo
I. Santo Stefano

Sights (cont.)
J. Port Soprano area
K. Staglieno Cemetery
L. Funiculare

Hotels
1. Helvetia
2. Balbi
3. Angel D'Oro
4. Europa

Hotels (cont.)
5. Aquaverde
6. Rio
7. Veronese
8. Cairioli
9. Bel Soggiorno
10. Moderno Verdi
11. Bristol Palace

Restaurants
12. Hon Hai
13. Zefferino
14. Paguotto
15. Al Veliero
16. Da Rina
17. Ostaja o Castell
18. Dal Galleone
19. Antico Ristorante Panson
20. Al Rustichello

Restaurants (cont.)
21. Da Franco
22. Bruno
23. Vegia Zena
24. Amadeus

Bars
25. Brittania Pub
26. Shaker Club

GETTING AROUND TOWN

By Bus

The only time you'll really ever need to use the bus is if you go to the seaside resort of Nervi, if you have to get to the small station for the ride on the small electric train into the mountain, or if you want to visit their magnificent cemetery. Other than that, all the sights and local flavor is within walking distance between the railway stations, Stazione Porta Principe and Stazione Brignole, and around the centro storico.

By Car

Don't even try to drive in Genoa. The city is small and congested with round-abouts, small streets, and traffic like you've never seen. Also the city is small enough to walk everywhere, or you can take convenient buses and funiculars. But if you do want to drive, here are a few places where you can rent a car:

• **Avis**, *Piazza Aquaverde (Stazione Principe), Tel 01025-55-98*
• **Hertz**, *Via Casaregis 78/a, Tel. 010570-26-25.*
• **Maggiore**, *Piazza Aquaverde (Stazione Principe). Tel. 010/570-26-25*

By Taxi

To get a radio cab in Genoa, *call 010/26-96.* You can hail a cab on the street or grab one of the many **taxi stands** situated around Genoa. Some of the more prominent ones and their telephone numbers are:

• **Piazza Caricamento**, *010/20-46-32*
• **Piazza Aquaverde**, *(Stazione Principe) 010/26-12-46*
• **Piazza Nunziata**, *010/29-82-32*
• **Nervi**, *010/32-15-10.*
• **Via Torino**, *(Stazione Brignole) 010/56-40-07*
• **Piazza Dane**, *010/58-65-24*

WHERE TO STAY

Genoa, like Milan, has either high-end three star, four star, and deluxe hotels, or the flea bag one star variety. It's a great city for the budget traveler if s/he can get a room in one of the few two stars that are available. In a two star in Genoa you'll get most of the amenities of a three star for the price of a one star in a bigger city like Rome. (Whew!)

The best places to find inexpensive hotels is by the main train station, **Stazione Principe**. The area around the other station, Stazione Brignole, also has hotels, though not as many, but it is in a quieter more residential neighborhood. The best place to get a hotel is just on the edge of Genoa's **Centro Storico**, the old city, with its countless winding narrow streets filled with shops, cafes, bars, and a few restaurants.

THE BEST HOTELS IN GENOA

*One star

5. HOTEL AQUAVERDE, *Via Balbi 29/815126 Genoa. Tel. 010/265-427. fax 010/246-4839. 9 rooms, seven with bath. Single without bath L25,000-35,000. Single with bath L35,000-45,000; Double without bath L50,000-60,000; Double with bath L60,000-70,000.*

**Two star

8. HOTEL CAIROLI, *Via Carioli 14/4, 16124 Genoa. Tel. and Fax 010/206-531 and 280-041. 14 rooms, 11 with bath. 1 bathroom in the hall for the other three. 3 singles, the rest doubles. Single L60,000-90,000; Double 90,000-140,000 Triple L125,000. Continental breakfast in the morning costs L5,000-8,000.*

***Three Star

4. HOTEL EUROPA, *Via delle Monachette 8, 15126 Genoa. tel. 010/256-955. Fax 010/261-047. 37 rooms all with bath. Single L78,000-155,000; Double L99,000-198,000.*

****Four star

11. HOTEL BRISTOL PALACE, *Via XX Settembre 35, 16121, Tel. 010/59-25-41. Fax 010/56-17-56. 133 rooms all with bath. Single L 245,000; Double L270,000; Suite L490,000. Single weekends L130,000; Double weekends L170,000. Buffet breakfast included.*

1. HOTEL HELVETIA, *Piazza della Nunziata 1, 16126 Genoa. Tel 010/205-839. Fax 010/247-0627. 32 rooms all with bath. Single L75,000; Double 95,000. ***

A truly run-down three star on a busy street. They have a cheap bar/caffe as their lobby. The prices are good but they don't take the concept of cleanliness and professionalism too seriously. A good place for people on a budget who want a larger room and a TV to watch, but otherwise try and avoid this place.

2. HOTEL BALBI, *Via Balbi 21/3, 16126 Genoa. Tel./010/280-912. 15 rooms only 5 with bath. Single L25,000-45,000; Double L40,000-65,000. ***

Located on the second floor of a rundown building on the street that leads to the train station, this place has absolutely no amenities and their prices reflect it. Perfect for the super-budget traveler.

3. HOTEL ANGELO D'ORO, *Via Monachette 6, 16126 Genoa. Tel. 010246-20-84. fax 010/246-23-27. 29 rooms all with bath. Single L80,000-120,000; Double 90,000-140,000. ****

A pleasant, inexpensive hotel down a side street just off the station. The rooms are clean but a little small. The prices are good for a three star, but that may be because next door is the best three star in the city.

4. HOTEL EUROPA, *Via delle Monachette 8, 15126 Genoa. tel. 010/ 256-955. Fax 010/261-047. 37 rooms all with bath. Single L78,000-155,000; Double L99,000-198,000.* ***

The best three star in the city. Don't get put off by the small little street it's on just off of the Piazza to the Stazione Principe. Inside it's closer to a four star in luxury. The rooms are quiet and comfortable if a little nondescript in their furnishings. They have large common areas and a roof deck that overlooks the entire city. If you can't wait for the weekend to take advantage of the lower rates at the four stars, try and stay here.

5. HOTEL AQUAVERDE, *Via Balbi 29/815126 Genoa. Tel. 010/265-427. fax 010/246-4839. 9 rooms, seven with bath. Single without bath L25,000-35,000. Single with bath L35,000-45,000; Double without bath L50,000-60,000; Double with bath L60,000-70,000.* *

Definitely the best one star in the city, located close to the train station. You get TVs and telephones in your rooms, something usually reserved for a good two star or a three star. The rooms are clean and comfortable and are on the 4th floor of the building. The prices are still reasonable but I know they're trying to get two star status, and when they do their prices are going to rise.

6. HOTEL RIO, *Via Ponte Calvi 5, 16126 Genoa, Tel. 010/29-05-51. Fax 010/29-05-54. 47 rooms, 44 with bath. Single L60,000-80,000; Double 110,000-115,000. Credit cards accepted.* ***

Located deep in the Centro Storico on a relatively wide road, this is a thoroughly modern hotel whose prices are so low because of their location. It's relatively safe, but its not a place that even I would walk alone in at midnight. But what's great is that it's quiet, clean, and comfortable, and you have one of Genoa's best local yet up upscale restaurants just across the street.

7. HOTEL VERONESE,*Vico Cicala (off of the Piazza Caricamento) 16124 Genoa. Tel. and Fax 010/202-551. 20 rooms, 18 with bath. Single L50,000-70,000; Double L60,000-100,000. Breakfast costs L20,000.* **

Located in the heart of the centro storico just off the colorful Piazza Caricamento, where you'll find local shops, eateries, bars, and restaurants (but they all close at night). All the amenities of a three star with the prices of a one star in a big city. They have TV, mini-bar, andphones in the clean and comfortable rooms, but they don't have air conditioning. If you want air conditioning, you have to go to three star. The reason their prices are so low is that they are in the old city, which basically shuts down at night.

8. HOTEL CAIROLI, *Via Carioli 14/4, 16124 Genoa. Tel. and Fax 010/ 206-531 and 280-041.14 rooms, 11 with bath. 1 bathroom in the hall for the other three. 3 singles, the rest doubles. Single L60,000-90,000; Double 90,000-140,000 Triple L125,000. Continental breakfast in the morning costs L5,000-8,000.* **

The maximum prices you see noted here are only if the hotel rooms are booked through a travel agent, since the owner has to give them between L25,000 and L35,000 for that privilege. If you make your own reservation or just show up you'll pay a lot less for your room. Definitely the cleanest, best located, best managed two star I've seen in Italy, and of course at the best prices.

They have everything here, including a European sports channel in English, kind of like ESPN. The only thing they don't have is air conditioning and an entrance on the street, since they're located on the third floor of a building. But they have the best little terrace in Genoa. Your view isn't great but the peace and tranquillity it offers in the mornings, afternoons, and evenings is wonderful. That's where I'm writing this to you now! All I can say is, if you're coming to Genoa, stay here. Also beware of the blind cat.

9. HOTEL BEL SOGGIORNO, *Via XX Settembre 19/2, 16124 Genoa. Tel. 010/542-880. fax 010/581-418. 18 rooms, 17 with bath. Single L55,000-120,000; Double L75,000-140,000.* **

Their prices are outrageous since they are located on the ritzy shopping street Via XX Settembre. They have everything but a street entrance and air conditioning, which will permanently keep them at a two star in Liguria. The rooms are clean and comfortable, except in August, but the prices are ridiculous. I guess they have to pay a high rent for their building.

10. HOTEL MODERNO VERDI, *Piazza G Verdi 5, 16121 Genoa Tel. 010/55-32-104. Fax 010/58-15-62. Internet: hotel.verdi@pn.itnet.it. Credit cards accepted. 100 rooms all with bath. Single L150,000-220,000 (every Friday, Saturday, and Sunday and all of august L120,000); Double L200,000-310,000 (F,S,Sun and August L170,000; Junior Suite L240,000-340,000 (F,S,Sun and August L210,000).* ****

A four star in every sense of the word that offers great deals on the weekends and in August. Why on the weekends? Because Genoa is not a big tourist town, it's mainly a business center, so they lower their rates accordingly to fill up the hotel on the weekends. Here you'll be living in the lap of luxury just a short walk from anything of interest.

11. HOTEL BRISTOL PALACE, *Via XX Settembre 35, 16121, Tel. 010/59-25-41. Fax 010/56-17-56. 133 rooms all with bath. Single L 245,000; Double L270,000; Suite L490,000. Single weekends L130,000; Double weekends L170,000. Buffet breakfast included.* ****

Located on Genoa's premier shopping street, you'll be in the middle of everything here. The rates go down dramatically on the weekends, as with the Moderno Verdi above. So this is the best time to come and stay in the lap of luxury of a four star hotel.

WHERE TO EAT
Genovese Cuisine

Genovese cuisine is dominated by the omnipresent **pesto sauce**, a basil, garlic, and olive oil concoction that they put on everything from lasagna noodles to spaghetti to meat and seafood. Also since they're a port city the "fruits of the sea" (i.e., seafood) are also a big part of any menu you'll find. Essentially the indigenous cuisine reflects the austere tastes and tight budgets of the local fishermen and farmers. Because of this you'll find many creative crépe-type dishes along with the pasta and seafood generally featured. Whatever you'll find, I know you'll enjoy.

Suggested Genovese Cuisine

If you're up for it, try some of these delicious Genovese specialties.

ANTIPASTO - APPETIZER
- **Farinata** – a giant crépe made from chickpea flour sprinkled with olive oil and rosemary and then cooked in a wood–burning stove.
- **Focaccio** – Crunchy flatbread covered in olive oil
- **Focaccio al formaggio** – the local flatbread with cheese, which is not melted on top but baked inside the pouch of the focaccio.
- **Pansotti** – thick chick pea soup

PRIMO PIATTO - FIRST COURSE
Pasta
- **Pansotti** – Small ravioli stuffed with either mushrooms or spinach, or both, covered with a light walnut sauce.
- **Pasta con pesto** – Any type of pasta that is served with the famous light Genovese pesto sauce, which is made from basil, olive oil, and garlic. Usually tossed with thin noodles called trenette.
- **Gnocchi al pesto** – Semolina dumplings with pesto sauce

SECOND PIATTO - ENTRÉE
Carne (Meat)
- **Cima all Genovese** – Breast of veal filled with vegetables and hard boiled eggs.

Pesce – *Fish*
- **Fritto misto di mare** – mixed fried seafood
- **Branzino all griglia** – Grilled slab of sea bass
- **Pesce di Spada con funghi** – Swordfish with mushrooms

Contorno – *Vegetable*
• **Torta Pasqualina** – Vegetables and hard boiled eggs egg rolled in a delicate pastry.
• **Insalata Mista** – mixed salad. You have to prepare your own olive oil and vinegar dressing. American's lust for countless types of salad dressings hasn't hit Italy yet.

THE BEST PLACES TO EAT IN GENOA

12. HON HAI, *Via Conservatori del Mare 35 (near Piazza Banchi), Tel. 010/298-467. Fax 010/297-788. Credit cards accepted. Dinner for two L40,000.*

13. RISTORANTE ZEFFERINO, *Via XX Settembre 20, Tel 010/59-19-90. Fax 010/58-64-64. Credit cards accepted. Closed Wednesdays. Dinner for to L150,000.*

14. POGUOTTO, *Via Lomellini 57. Crêpese, foccace or sandwiches for under L2,000.*

19. ANTICO RISTORANTE PANSON, *Piazza delle Erbe 5r. Tel. 010/294-903. Credit cards accepted. Dinner for two L80,000.*

22. RISTORANTE BRUNO, *Vico della Casana 9, Tel. 010/208.505. Credit cards accepted. Dinner for two L70,000. Closed Saturdays.*

---

12. HON HAI, *Via Conservatori del Mare 35 (near Piazza Banchi), Tel. 010/298-467. Fax 010/297-788. Credit cards accepted. Dinner for two L40,000.*

The best Chinese restaurant I've sampled in Italy. The decor is uniquely Asian (despite the fact that they still use the same dishes as the old Italian place that used to be housed here) and the food is exquisite and inexpensive. With the subtle Chinese music playing in the background and the isolated locale of the restaurant, you'll feel as if you've been transplanted to Canton. And here they make their rice Cantonese style with eggs, ham, and peas that is a meal in and of itself. Also if you're dying for an omelet, they make some of the best.

13. RISTORANTE ZEFFERINO, *Via XX Settembre 20, Tel 010/59-19-90. Fax 010/58-64-64. Credit cards accepted. Closed Wednesdays. Dinner for to L150,000.*

They call themselves the ambassadors for Italian cuisine, and if you're willing to pay their prices the food will not disappoint. The restaurant is filled with brass nautical and kitchen objects, wine bottles, and pictures giving the entire place a rustic ambiance. With their exquisite service and excellent food this is a perfect place for a romantic dinner. Or if you're on a budget it's *the* place to go in Genoa, so why not splurge on your last night in the city? Their *pesto* sauce (garlic, oil and basil) on home-made *fazzoletti* is superb. As are all of their seafood dishes, including the *frittura del golfo* (mixed fried seafood from the gulf of Genoa) and the *Gamberi all Carbone* (succulent shrimp cooked over and open fire).

14. POGUOTTO, *Via Lomellini 57. Crêpese, foccace or sandwiches for under L2,000.*

A local *foccacio* joint that serves up some of the best you'll find in Genoa. As you may know, a *foccacio* is cooked with a variety of fillings in large square trays. The dough is thick but light in texture similar to a croissant. At this place they make them great. Look through the display case which makes an "L" around the small shop to find what you want, then simply order and voila, you have a simple, easy, inexpensive meal. There are no chairs, stools or tables, so this is best visited for a quick afternoon snack. In Genoa, do as the Genoans and eat *foccaccio*.

15. AL VELIERO, *Via Ponte Calvi 10/12. Tel. 010/291-829. Dinner for two L70,000. Credit cards accepted.*

A small, upscale local place that is tucked on a small side street just off the harbor area. The interior is stark white with archways all over the place. It's tiny so get there early or make reservations. They serve great *spaghetti al pesto* (with a garlic, oil, and basil sauce) and *sogliola ai ferri* (sole cooked over an open fire). There other seafood dishes, of which there are plenty around L30,000 each, so if you try any of those besides the *sogliola* your price to eat here will go up. But those in the know in Genoa don't care. This is one place to go if you make it to this beautiful city.

16. TRATTORIA DA RINA, *Mura delle Grazie 3. Nor telephone. No credit cards accepted. Dinner for two L55,000.*

Really in a seedy section off the waterfront, with the highway buzzing by. But once you get inside all you think about is the food, since the smells from the kitchen permeate the entire place. Try some inexpensive *pesto* here. They serve it in a variety of pastas per your request. If you try some seafood dishes the prices will go up. Sit back and enjoy the local flavor.

17. OSTAJA O CASTELL, *Salita Santa Maria di Castello, Tel. 010/298-980. No credit cards accepted. Dinner for two ... it all depends.*

This is a small, local, and irreverent place. They make great food and they have fun making it and serving it. The menu is a dead giveaway to their attitude. It has nothing written on it but snide remarks like "*Antipasto*: we have it/*Primo*: Whatever we have/*Frutta*: costs too much/ *Dolce*: right before the check/*Digestivo*: right after the check/*Vino*: It's good" – and so on and so on. The menu changes daily but if you want a fun, intimate atmosphere in a completely local section of town, and you're a little adventurous, come and give it a try.

18. TRATTORIA DEL GALLEONE, *Via San Bernaro 55r, Tel. 010/ 20-04-22. Credit cards accepted. Dinner for two L55,000.*

A very inexpensive local place that has plenty of seating since it usually fills up for dinner. You can see into the kitchen and watch the cooks slave away over your precious meals if you get a seat in the back room. Simple basic decor and local pasta, meats and fishes that will leave you full and satisfied.

19. ANTICO RISTORANTE PANSON, *Piazza delle Erbe 5r. Tel. 010/ 294-903. Credit cards accepted. Dinner for two L80,000.*

An upscale restaurant in a rustic locale. They've grown huge plants to protect you from the sights in the lively local piazza but the sound still drifts in if you sit on the terrace. Inside seating is better because you can get the true feel of an upscale restaurant in Genoa. Try some of their *risotto di crostacie* (rice with crustaceans) or any of their pasta with *pesto*. They specialize in both seafood and pesto. For seconds the *fritto misto del golfo* (mixed seafood from the gulf) and the *pesce spada* (grilled swordfish) are both excellent.

20. AL RUSTICHELLO, *Via San Vincenzo 59r, Tel. 010/588-556. Credit cards accepted. Dinner for two L70,000.*

A small quaint local place that also caters to tourists. They have a sign out front that indicates they speak English and French. I love the brick walls and arched whitewashed ceilings as well as their pasta, pizza, meat and fish. They say they specialize in Genovese cuisine but they have pasta from all over Italy. So if you're a pasta nut like I am, come here for some. They also have a good *cotolette alla milanese* (lightly breaded veal fried in butter).

21. DA FRANCO, *Archivolto Mongiardino 2. Closed Sundays and Monday. No telephone number. Credit cards accepted. Dinner for two L65,000.*

If you like lobster, this is the place for you. Small and local, down a difficult to find side street, you have to have a good map to locate this excellent lobster and champagne restaurant. Their menu has other dishes, but this is what they do best, serve up succulent lobster so you can wash it down with sparkling wine. Can you think of a better way to spend the evening?

22. RISTORANTE BRUNO, *Vico della Casana 9, Tel. 010/208.505. Credit cards accepted. Dinner for two L70,000. Closed Saturdays.*

Located on the first floor of an old *palazzo*, the dining environment with their tall ceilings is terrific. You feel as if you are outside, this place is so big. Try their *penne ai frutti di mare* (with mixed seafood) or their *ravioli al salmone* (with salmon) for primo. Then move onto either a *filetto ai ferri* (grilled filet of steak) of the *pesce spada ai ferri* (grilled swordfish)

23. TRATTORIA VEGIA ZENA, *Vico del Serragli 15. Tel 010/299-891. Closed Sundays and Monday nights. Credit cards accepted. Dinner for two L70,000.*

Great local seafood place with excellent atmosphere, great service, and a truly wild and crazy owner. They serve a superb *grigliatta mista* (mixed grilled fish for two) as well as almost any other seafood pasta or fish you can imagine. Located in the Centro Storico, this is a place to have dinner from about 7:30pm to 9:30pm, since the area gets dark and deserted after ten in the summer. In the winter only come here for lunch.

24. PIZZERIA/RISTORANTE AMADEUS, *Via PE Bensa 40r (in the Piazza Nunziata), Tel. 010 247-1039. Dinner for two L40,000.*

A popular local pizza place especially for the university students, since they serve huge 16 inch pizzas for great prices. The decor is simple and basic, and the only interesting feature is the red and white tiled wood burning oven in the room on the right. Here you can watch all the pizza being prepared. The food comes super quick since the pizza chef is a maestro, but if you want to linger over a bottle of wine they have no qualms about that. To get the best pizza ask them to put on extra mozzarella.

SEEING THE SIGHTS

Genoa's best sights, in my humble opinion, lie outside of town, but inside this port city are some beautiful palaces, churches, squares, and wonderful old streets that have been alive with people and shops for more than a thousand years.

A. TORRE DELLA LANTERNA

Located near the Stazione Principe, down the Via Andrea Doria.

This is a medieval **lighthouse** last restored in 1543. It stands 117 meters high. Before the advent of electricity, a huge fire would be lit on top of the structure to guide ships into the harbor. If you're into lighthouses, you'll like this one.

B. COMMENDA

Via San Giovanni. Open 7am–7pm.

Located near the Stazione Maritime, this is the home of the **canons of San Sepolcro of Jerusalem**. A rough church with definite Gothic influences, despite construction having begun in the 12th century.

C. PALAZZO REALE

Located at number 10 Via Balbi, Tel. 247–0640. Open Tuesday, Thursday, Saturday and Sunday 9am-1pm.

This is a 12th century *palazzo* which was greatly modified in the 17th century. It has beautiful hanging gardens overlooking the harbor. Here you'll also find a rich collection of Ligurian paintings with works by Tintoretto, Van Dyke, Strozzi, and others.

D. VIA GARIBALDI

This is Genoa's most famous street, laid out in 1558. Many *palazzi* have been converted to banks and offices. **Palazzo Bianci** (No. 11, open Tuesday–Saturday 9 am–1pm and 3pm-6pm, Sunday 9am–Noon, admission fee), **Palazzo Rosso** (no. 18, same hours). In **Palazzo Tursi** is now Genoa's **Municipio** and has a beautiful courtyard, Paganini's violin in the **Sala delle Giunta**, and three letters from Columbus in the **Sala del Sindaco**.

TAKE A BOAT CRUISE

*If you want to try something different and enjoy the beauty of Genoa's harbor at night, try a boat cruise that goes until midnight. Affectionately called a booze cruise by some, they also have karaoke and other entertainment. Call **Calata Zingari**, 010/256-775 or 010/255-975.*

E. VILLA DEL NEGRO

Piazza Corveto. Open Tuesday–Saturday 9am–7pm and Sunday 9am–12:30pm. Admission L5,000.

This is an urban oasis that has streams, cascades, grottoes, and walkways all leading to the **Museo d'Arte Orientale (Museum of Oriental Art)**, featuring samurai swords and helmets and much more. The botanical gardens were created by Ippolito Durazzo.

F. PIAZZA DE FERRARI & PALAZZO DUCALE

Open Tuesday–Saturday 9am–7pm and Sunday 9am–12:30pm. Admission L5,000.

This piazza is the heart of modern Genoa. It is surrounded by many important civic buildings. The piazza was dedicated to the Duke De Ferrari, an outstanding 19th century Genoan who assisted in the creation of a wide range of urban housing in Genoa. Carlo Barbarini is the architect of the square.

The *palazzo* dates back to medieval times and was once the headquarters of the Genovese Doge. One of its sections is the remains of the 13th century **Palazzo del Commune** and the 14th century **Torre del Popolo**. Inside you can admire the lovely frescoes and the **Salone dei Gran Consiglio (Grand Council Chamber)**. The *palazzo* has over 35,00 square yards of displays of precious art, archives, libraries, as well as conference rooms and offices.

G. THE OLD CITY

Just around the corner from the Piazza De Ferrari is the pretty **Piazza San Matteo**. Go south from here and you enter the **old city** of Genoa.

Your best route is down Via Dante to Piazza Dante and the **Porta Soprano**, the twin-towered gateway from 1155, where Columbus's father was supposedly gatekeeper.

This is a place for exploring (but not at night, alone, or in a group with expensive cameras hanging from your necks). Take the Via Ravecca down from Porta Soprana to the 13th century gothic **Church of Sant'Agostino** and its **Museum of Ligurian Sculpture and Architecture** *(Tuesday-Saturday 9am-1pm and 3pm-6pm, Sunday 9am-12:45pm, admission L5,000)*.

From Sant'Agostino take the Strada di Sant'Agostino to the 12th century **San Donato** *(open 9am-dusk)* with its lovely octagonal *campanile* (bell tower). Also near here is the **Santa Maria in Castello** *(open 9am-dusk)* used by the Crusaders as a hostel. It was rebuilt in the 13th century. Today it has a Romanesque facade. The inside has been adorned with chapels representing the noblest Genovese families. The **Convent** with its three cloisters should also be visited. They also have a small museum with paintings by Brea and some beautiful frescoes from the 15th century.

H. CATHEDRAL OF SAN LORENZO

Via San Lorenzo, Open 9am-dusk.

The most elegant and important example of medieval design in and around Genoa. It is beautiful, characterized by its pronounced Roman Gothic style. Over the centuries the cathedral has undergone many reconstructions. In the 13th century the facade was destroyed and replaced by the current black and white striped Gothic styled one we see today. The bell tower was left without a top when constructed in 1427. It eventually got its top two centuries later, and you can see that it just doesn't quite fit with the rest of the church.

The majestic interior is divided into a nave and two aisles. Remember to visit the **chapel of Saint John the Baptist**. It is one of the greatest works of the Renaissance even though it shows persistent influence of Gothic art in its bas-reliefs. And you have to admire the refined mosaic beauty of the stained glass Rose window. A perfect place to be in early morning as the sun shines through.

I. CHURCH OF SANTO STEFANO

Via XX Settembre. Open 8am-7pm.

Set in a small piazza, the church was used as a Benedictine monastery until the 10th century. The facade is plain and simple and looks like a monastery would. Inside, on the right is a painting of the *Martirio di Santo Stefano* (The Martyring of St. Stephen) by Giulio Romano in 1524. Next to it is the statue of *Mary and Jesus* made in the 17th century. You can gain access to the bell tower from the presbytery on the left. The baptismal font was made in 1676. Notice the relief work of San Michele defeating the Devil done in 1453.

J. BETWEEN VIA SAN LORENZO & VIA GARIBALDI

Built up during the Rennaisance, this area's authenticity has survived better than the area around Porta Soprano and the Stazione Principe. Picturesque, old, winding streets containing colorfully local shops, superb traditional restaurants, out of the way pubs, and plenty of interesting people milling about ... at least during daylight hours. Do not even think about coming here at night.

There is a quaint, delightful medieval square, **Campetto**; a couple of centuries-old coffee houses in **Piazza Soziglia** (**Kainguti** at #98r and **Romanegro** at #74r); and the sights and sounds of an ancient seafaring city along the twisting cobblestoned paths. For a scenic route that meanders through the center of this section of the **Centro Storico**, take a series of streets from **Piazza Bianchi** near the water. First in line is the Via Bianchi, which turns into Via degli Orefici to Via Soziglia to Via Luccoli and eventually to the modern **Piazza delle Fontane Marose**. You can take side streets off this main drag of sorts and really grasp the heart of Genoa.

Note: To fully enjoy this section and the entire Centro Storico, I highly reccomend purchasing an orange-covered *F.M.B Pianta di Citta* (map of Genoa). Along with the regular map of the entire city, this map also includes a detailed street map of the Centro Storico on the back. The L8,000 will make your exploring that much more enjoyable.

K. STAGLIENO CEMETERY

Via Piacenza. Open 8am–5pm, October 24th–November 4th from 7:30am–5pm, Christmas Day 8am –Noon.

To get to this fascinating cemetery, take bus 34 from Piazza Acquaverde or Piazza Corvetto. The trip takes fifteen minutes and will set you back L1,300 for a bus ticket that lasts 90 minutes (remember, bus tickets are valid for a given period of time, an hour and a half in this case). So if you get through the place in an hour or a little more, you don't have to buy another ticket at the *giornalaio* near the bus stop.

When you get off the bus at the cemetery, go to your left and around the corner, and the entrance gate is right there. You pass by flower stalls on your way in, so if you want to place a flower on someone's grave, by all means indulge yourself. The best way to start your tour of the cemetery, after you've entered the main gates, is to go past the flower stands and enter the small archway to your right. Walk through the small gravestones, some with tiny pictures on them, until you get to a square of cleared area between the gravestone. On your left is a set of stairs leading up to the interesting stuff. Once up, go to yourright and then begin the process of weaving through this magnificent collection of art and celebration of life.

This is a veritable city of the dead covering 160 hectares (comparable to an acre) and is so large it has its own bus system, centuries-old miniature cathedrals, Romanesque chapels, Egyptian crypts, palaces, statues, all laid out in a haphazard fashion that reminds you of the centro storico. You'll be amazed at the beauty and sadness of the sculptures, some in bronze, others made from marble. Vines and undergrowth twist everywhere, obscuring some of the smaller paths up the hills between the crypts. A perfect place to spend a few hours wondering around.

When you enter there will be numbered marble crypts on the walls and on the floors (Oscar Wilde is buried in the Protestant section). From here go to the center with its small plots. Take a left and go up the stairs to the monuments and chapels. Remember to try and act as serious as possible, especially when you pass other people, which is infrequent. This is a cemetery, even if it does look like a miniature city or a museum.

But even with these restrictions, this is definitely one of the best sights to see in Genoa, and really one of the most interesting in Italy. If you want more information on this place, you can pick up a guidebook at the nearby train station.

L. FUNICULARE ZECCHI RIGHI

Largo Zecca. Open 6am–10pm. Costs the same as a bus ticket.

Take the **Funiculare Zecchi Righi** up to an overlook above the city. Here you can get some great shots of the city itself and other vistas. You can also walk a little way and explore the dilapidated ruins of the **Forts of Begato**, **Puin**, **Sperone**. They are up a small winding road that has cars buzzing around it, so if you're with kids make sure they stick to the sides as you walk. The forts are a little distance away from the funicular, but just follow the signs and you'll make it there. The walk is through dense woods that lends a semblance of tranquillity after the hectic pace of Genoa.

NIGHTLIFE & ENTERTAINMENT

25. BRITANNIA PUB, *Vico della Casana 76A, Tel 010 294-878. Credit cards accepted. Pints L6,000-7,000.*

In a perfect rendition of an English pub, you can enjoy a few pints of Kilkenny (a great Irish beer), Elephant (a superb beer from Denmark), or Dab (an excellent beer from Holland); as well as satisfy your hunger with sandwiches, hamburgers, hot dogs, salads, or simply Italian appetizers like mozzarella and tomatoes. A place to come for lunch, dinner, or late night for drinks and a snack.

26. SHAKER CLUB, *Via Cesarea 45r, Tel. 010-570-5784. Credit cards accepted. Drinks L8,000-10,000.*

You better be dressed well when you come in here, otherwise you'll get the once-over like I did. A piano bar late at night, they serve drinks and light snacks in the early evenings also. Has a bar you can curl up with or small intimate booths in which you can snuggle with your loved one and trade sweet nothings.

SPORTS & RECREATION
Golf
• **Golf Club Arenzano,***Piazza del Golf 3, 16011 Arenzano. Tel. 010/911-1817. Fax 010/911-1270.* Located 20 km from Genoa, this is a 9 hole par 36, 2,770 meters course. Open year round except in October and on Tuesdays. They have a putting green, tennis courts, a quaint bar, and a nice restaurant.
• **Circolo Golf & Tennis Rapallo**, *Via Mameli 377, 16035 Rapallo. Tel. 0185/261-777. Fax 0185/261-779.* Located 25 km from Genoa in the quaint town of Rapallo, this is an 18 hole, par 70, 5,694 meters course that is open year round. Closed on Tuesdays. They have a good restaurant, pro shop, bar, 6 tennis courts, and driving range.

Swimming
Bathing in the sea around here could be a hair-raising or a skin-discoloring situation, so maybe you should try the municipal pools at **Lido d'Albara** on the east side of town. Or better yet, go to **Nervi** just outside of town (see *Day Trips & Excursions* below).

PRACTICAL INFORMATION
Bank Hours & Changing Money
Since this is a maritime and business city there are banks everywhere. But there are not that many *cambios* (small places to change money) since this is not really a tourist city. The banks are open from 8:30 am to 1:30pm and 2:30pm to 3:30pm, Monday through Friday.

There is a *cambio* in the train station that is open from 9:00am to 5:00pm, Monday through Saturday.

Business Hours
The shops are open from 9:00am to 1:30pm and 3:30pm to 8:00pm, except those located in the Centro Storico. These will shut down before it gets dark so they can shutter their stores and get home. The Centro Storico is not a place you want to be caught after dark. Even most restaurants close down.

Consulates
• **United Kingdom**, *Via XII Ottobre 2, Genoa Tel. 010/56-48-33*

Laundry
• *"No Name" Via Pre #34, no telephone.* Drop off your garments in the
   morning and pick them up in the afternoon, all for the small cost of
   L13,000 per machine (washer and dryer). Run by a multilingual
   Senegalese with the greatest disposition and smile you'll find in
   Bologna. He'll write down the number of each of your articles of
   clothing for you as a receipt, so if you don't want your underthings
   flashed around remember to count them beforehand. Ideally situated for almost all travelers.

Local Festivals & Holidays
• **January–April**, Genoa Opera Company performances in the Teatro
   Margherita at Via XX Settembre 16a
• **Summer**, Ballet Festival in Nervi's park

Postal Services
   There is a post office *in the Stazione Principe*, and another one located
just off the piazza that houses the train station. It's down a small side street
on the right hand side across the piazza, *at Salita di San Giovanni #7.*

Tourist Information & Maps
• **EPT**, *Via Roma 11, Tel. 010/581-407*
• **Information Offices** *in both train stations, Stazione Principe and Brignole.*
   They can call hotels for you to see if there are rooms, but they cannot
   book these rooms for you. This service saves you the hassle of walking
   around the city trying to find the hotel of your choice. The office also
   will give you a simple map that is useful everywhere but in the centro
   storico, since there are so many small winding streets. To navigate
   successfully in the centro storico, buy one of the maps you can get at
   a newsstand for L8,000.

DAY TRIPS & EXCURSIONS

   The Genoa area includes some beautiful towns: **Portofino**, now one
of the most photographed and frequented seaside towns anywhere in
Europe; **Cinque Terre**, five isolated towns hidden from most tourists that
are among my favorite destinations in Italy; the relaxing mountain
getaway of **Casella**,and the fun Riviera resort town of **Nervi**.

PORTOFINO

The secluded and protected little fishing village of **Portofino** was discovered many years ago by the super-rich and famous. Accented by the deep blue of the water and the lush green of the nature preserve hillsides, the colorful buildings of Portofino stand out like a fairy tale set. This beauty obviously left the stars themselves awestruck and has now turned the quiet little town into a haven for the not-so-rich-or-famous.

Today, cafes and boutiques line the quaint little hillside streets, and what used to be an exclusive vacation spot is a traffic jam of humanity during the peak summer tourist months. Nonetheless, Portofino will stun you with her beauty despite the summer crowds.

Leaving the piazzetta and its pier lined with fishing nets drying in the sun you can amble up the hill to the **Chiesa** and **Castello di San Giorgio** (*both open 9am–5pm, admission to the Castle is L5,000*). From here you can walk through lush gardens and have superb scenic views over the town and the water on both sides of the peninsula. Portofino is the perfect day trip from Genoa, or a quaint romantic side trip down the coast for a few days.

ARRIVALS & DEPARTURES

Located 36 kilometers from Genoa, trains do not come directly to Portofino, which used to give it some of its exclusivity. You can either come by **car** down the A12 Autostrada, exit at Rapallo, and follow the coast road to Portofino, or you can come by **ferry** from Genoa, which is probably the easiest and least stressful way to get here. Contact one of these numbers for ferry information and reservations: *Tel. 010 265-712 or 0336/688-732*. The ferries leave from the **Aquarium dock** in Genoa.

Another less expensive but far more arduous way to get here is to take the **train** to Santa Margherita Ligure, then catch a bus in Piazza Vittorio Veneto to come to Portofino. The whole trip will take about three hours, however. This will be a little less expensive than a ferry, but is much longer and much more hassle.

WHERE TO STAY

NAZIONALE, VIA ROMA 8, *16024 Portofino, Tel. 0185/269-575. Fax 0185/269-578. 13 rooms all with bath. Single L200,000-320,000; Double L250,000-400,000. Visa accepted.* ****

All you get here is a perfect location a few paces away from the seaside piazza, a romantic old building, great views, clean and comfortable rooms – but not much else. If you come to Portofino, you should stay here to enjoy the ambiance of this tiny little village. Since there are not many hotels in this town, later in the evening after all the ferries and buses have left, the romance begins. If you want to stay here make reservations about a year in advance, and longer for weekend stays.

EDEN, *Vico Dritto 18, 16034 Portofino, Tel. 0185/269-091. Fax 0185/ 269-047. 8 rooms all with bath. Credit cards accepted. Single L120,000- 200,000; Double L160,000-240,000.* **

Only a two star, but boy is it expensive. Location is everything and this is in the center of the little fishing village. Only eight rooms, so reserve well in advance. They have basically the same amenities as the more expensive four star, even a few more, like TVs in the rooms and a sun deck, but their rooms are not quite as clean or as comfortable as the Nazionale.

But if you want the beauty and romance of Portofino at more reasonable prices, stay here.

WHERE TO EAT

IL PITOSFORO, *Via Molo Umberto I 8, Tel. 0185/269-020. Closed Tuesdays and November. All credit cards accepted. Dinner for two L240,000.*

Eating here is not going to be inexpensive, so be prepared. Here you pay for the magnificent view of the harbor and its piazza. Obviously a place designed to fleece the tourists with 130 available seats, but if you're in Portofino come for a bite here. Maybe only a pasta dish and a half carafe of wine. That should cut your bill. Try their *linguine all'aragosta* (pasta with lobster sauce), *risotto di mare* (rice covered with seafood), or any of their other tasty, basic, traditional local dishes.

PUNY, *Piazza Martiri Olivetta 5, Tel. 0185/269-037. Closed Thursdays and January 15 to March 15. No credit cards accepted. Dinner for two L170,000.*

The most famous restaurant in Portofino, located directly in the main port square with a wonderful terrace overlooking the piazza and the port. The green awning shades you from the summer's heat and the baskets of red flowers accent the outside appearance.

Inside this has the look of just another local place but it serves superb seafood, pasta, and fresh vegetables. The prices are high because people will pay them, but you can't go wrong here – except if you forget to bring cash. They don't take credit cards.

TOURIST INFORMATION

• **Information Office**, *Via Roma 35, Tel. 0185/77-10-66*

CINQUE TERRE

If you're searching for something off the beaten path, look no further. These five villages are off limits to cars, and to even find them you have to make five separate detours off the main road far away from the coast since the villages are not linked by any road on which an automobile can travel. Because of this remoteness, these villages have preserved their old world charm and have escaped the onslaught of tourism.

The **Cinque Terre** *(the five lands)* are the five villages of **Monterosso al Mare**, **Vernazza**, **Corniglia**, **Manarola** and **Riomaggiore**. Each is set beautifully in the coastal cliffs and sloping vineyards of Liguria and are connected to each other by a narrow winding country path. Whenever there is a flood, some of the path is washed away but remains traversable on foot – which is the best way to see the Cinque Terra. Settle yourself into a nice hotel in either Monterosso al Mare or Riomaggiore, or a small but nice *pensione* in Vernazza, and walk to the rest. The other two smaller inside villages don't have official hotels or *pensiones* yet. If you get tired and can't walk back, there's always the local train to pick you up and return you to your 'home' village.

The Cinque Terre were initially situated higher up above the coast to protect themselves from marauding pirates. No one knows where these original inhabitants came from since their highland settlements are no longer in existence, but as a result of the high incidence of red hair and light coloring among Cinque Terrans, experts have speculated that they share a Celtic or Nordic background. Nonetheless, when the danger of pirates passed, around 1000 AD, the villages resettled themselves closer to the water's edge to take advantage of the bounty from the sea.

Today most of the permanent residents of each village is either a fisherman or a farmer. But the same rugged terrain that protected them long ago from ocean invaders and that had protected them from a more modern threat, that of T-shirt shops and fast-food joints courtesy of mass tourism, has slowly begun to fail. In the two border towns, tourism is flourishing and in Vernazza, more and more homes are opening themselves up to become *pensiones*. Soon, I fear, the last of Italy's true beauties is going to succumb to the influences of the rest of the world.

The sights, scenery, and tranquillity here are extraordinary. Make the trip and you won't be disappointed, especially in May and September, when you'll have the place virtually to yourself and the approximately 6,500 residents of all five villages. There won't be much to do, except hike from village to village, then casually lunch or dine at a different *trattoria* in a different village each day, and let the cares of the world pass from your mind for a little while.

If you want to swim, **Monterosso al Mare** has the only sandy beach among the Cinque Terre.

ARRIVALS & DEPARTURES
By Boat
You can come by boat, which will take you three hours. The train is an hour quicker. But if you're just going for the day, the boat may well be

what you're looking for: the trip is designed as a boat cruise, then a three hour stay in Vernazza (the best of the villages), then the return trip.

If you're going to stay a day or two, the trip to Vernazza will cost you L33,000 round-trip and L18,000 one way. Contact this number for information and reservations: *Tel. 010 265-712 or 0336/688-732.*

The boat's hours of operation are:

•**July 1–August 26**, *Saturdays, Leave from the Aquarium dock in Genoa at 9:40am*
•**July 2–September 3**, *Sundays, Leave from the Aquarium dock in Genoa at 8:40am*

By Train

Take one of the local trains from Genoa and it will stop in each of the Cinque Terre. A train leaves from Genoa every two hours or so, and the trip takes about two hours as well.

WHERE TO STAY

If you want close to first class hotels, stay in either **Monterosso al Mare** or **Riomaggiore**, then either hike or take the local train to the other villages. If you don't mind small, intimate, rustic accommodations far off the beaten path, then stay at one of the *pensiones* listed in the other three inner villages of the Cinque Terre.

Usually only the most hardy souls will venture to stay in the inner three villages, giving you even more space if solitude is what you're after. If you're looking for a truly Italian holiday adventure, stay is in one of the three smaller villages.

Monterosso al Mare

PORTO ROCA, *Via Corone 1, in Corone, 19016 Monterosso al Mare, Tel. 0187/817-502. Fax 010/817-692. 43 rooms all with bath. Credit cards accepted. Single L140,000-180,000; Double L195,000-250,000.* ****

Built into a cliff above the village, this beautiful romantic setting is perfect for lovers or honeymoons. You have your own private beach, a quaint little restaurant, and great service. There is a shuttle bus that will run you down to the village since it is quite a hike. If you want to stay in luxury in the Cinque Terre but don't want to be a part of the touristy crowd in Moneterosso, stay here.

PALME, *Via IV Novembre 18, 19016 Monterosso al Mare, Tel. 0187/817-541. Fax 0187/818-265. 49 rooms all with bath. Single L93,000-126,000; Double L108,000-170,000. All credit cards accepted.* ****

Located near the beach but still in a tranquil setting, the hotel is small, clean, and comfortable, except when it gets deathly hot in August. I don't understand how it has four stars without air conditioning. A good place to stay if you want access to the beach as well as instant access to town.

JOLIE, *Via Gioberti 1, 19016 Monterosso al Mare, Tel. 0187/817-539. Fax 0187/817-273. 31 rooms all with shower. Credit cards accepted. Single L100,000-150,000; Double L150,000-220,000. Breakfast L20,000 extra.* ***

Located 150 meters from the beach as well as directly in the center of town, here you'll have the best of both worlds. Despite its location, it is well insulated from the sounds of the city. There is an excellent in-house restaurant and a solarium if you don't want to hit the beach for a tan. A clean, quiet, and comfortable hotel.

VILLA ADRIANA, *Via IV Novembre 23, 19016 Monterosso al Mare, Tel. 0187/818-109. Fax is the same. No credit cards accepted. 54 rooms all with bath. Single L60,000; Double L110,000.* **

A two star with its own private beach, a good restaurant, with small, comfortable clean rooms. It's located a little on the outskirts of the town, but they have a shuttle bus you can use to get back and forth. Beware the summer months since they don't have air conditioning.

BAIA,*Via Fegina 88, 19016 Monterosso al Mare, Tel. 0187/817-512. Fax 0187/818-322. 29 rooms all with bath. Credit cards accepted. Single L100,000; Double 100,000-120,000.* *

A one star on the rise. Located a little outside of town, they have their own private beach, accommodating staff, a good restaurant, and clean, comfortable quiet rooms. The only thing missing is air conditioning, but they're looking into that in the future. There is no shuttle bus to get you back and forth like the better hotels.

Vernazza

BARBARA, *Piazza Marconi 10, Vernazza 19018. Tel. 0187/812-201. Nine rooms none with bath. Three bathrooms in the hall way. No credit cards accepted. Single L50,000; Double L70,000. Full board L90,000 per person.* *

A small rustic place with an equally small restaurant and bar (a converted family room). The only real amenity is heat in the winter, but if you're going to stay in Vernazza you didn't come for amenities, you came for the old Italian way of life. Here you can enjoy peaceful evenings secluded from the rest of society and take in the experience of time standing still. The rooms are small but clean and comfortable in a countrified sort of way. To pick up your keys you need to go to the Trattoria del Capitano (see *Where to Eat*, below).

SORRISO, *Via Gavino 4, Vernazza 19018. Tel. 0187/812-224. 11 rooms 1 double with bath. No credit cards accepted. Single L50,000; Double L65,000-75,000. Full board L90,000.* *

Set back from the harbor just outside the little town, this is a perfect place to come for reflection and peace. Once again the only amenity is heat in the winter. They have their own restaurant and small bar. Pets are welcome guests too.

Riomaggiore

CA' D'ANDREAN, *Via Discovolo 25, Riomaggiore 19010, Tel. 0187/ 920-040. 10 rooms all with bath. Single L58,000-61,000; Double L83,000- 87,000. No credit cards accepted.* ***

Located outside of the village of Riomaggiore near Manorola, you'll be completely isolated here. The only real amenities are heat and a phone in the room, as well as a small bar area downstairs. Small rooms which are clean and comfortable.

MARINA PICCOLA, *Via Discovolo 192, Riomaggiore 19010, Tel. 0187/ 920-103. American Express accepted. 6 rooms all with bath. Single L65,000- 70,000; Double L85,000-90,000. Full board L110,000.* ***

Located outside of the little village, thankfully this place has its own restaurant so you don't have to trek out in the night to find food, as you have to do at the Ca' d'Andrean above. On the same street as that hotel too, but a little farther out. This is a pleasant place. The rooms are small but clean and comfortable.

VILLA ARGENTINA, *Via de Gaspari 37, Riomaggiore 19010, Tel. 0187/920-213. 15 rooms all with bath. Single L70,000; Double L80,000. No credit cards accepted.* **

The biggest place around, which isn't saying much since it only has 15 rooms. Also located outside of the village in a tranquil country setting. They have a shuttle bus to bring you back and forth. Besides heat, a phone in the rooms, and being pet-friendly, they also have a small restaurant and bar area.

WHERE TO EAT

Seafood and pesto are the specialties of the Cinque Terre, as they are all over Liguria. There are plenty of restaurants in **Monterosso al Mare**, but only a few in the smaller villages (Vernazza, Corniglia, Manarola, Riomaggiore).

In addition to the restaurants attached to the hotels listed above, most restaurants here are fairly simple affairs.

Vernazza

TRATTORIA DEL CAPITANO, *Tel. 0187/812-224. Dinner for two L100,000. No credit cards accepted.*

This is the best place for a meal in Cinque Terre. You'll have a great view of the sea as it crashes on the rocks below. Pesto and seafood are the specialties. There's a good *zuppa del mare* (seafood soup) for starters.

Follow it with a *pasta con pesto* dish, and finish up with any variety of grilled fish that are pulled from the waters below.

TOURIST INFORMATION

If you want any tourist information about the Cinque Terre, you need to pick it up in Genoa or buy a local guide book. There are no formal tourist operations in any of the villages.

CASELLA

Casella is a small mountain town that is a wonderful place to spend an afternoon away from the port of Genoa. The best part is getting here. The small electric tram you ride through the hills and mountains offer some spectacular views of the surrounding countryside. You'll look over aqueducts, pass through small no-name towns, see ruins on the hills, and truly enjoy the scenery.

Once you arrive there is not much else to do but try one of the local restaurants in the small piazza just off the station, or wander through the side streets and see how the mountain folk of Italy live. There is even a small but fun amusement park near the station that brings life to the villagers in the summer evenings. It's a wonderful place to really see how the other half lives.

ARRIVALS & DEPARTURES
By Train

In Genoa, take the small electric train from the train station at the **Piazza Manin**. To get to the Piazza, take bus number 34. You go through two tunnels, then up a small hill, which at the top is the Piazza Manin. Exit the bus and look to your left. You'll see the large sign "Ferrovia Genoa Casella" just above the Esso station. Follow the arrow which leads you up the stairs, then to the left of the small train station. Your round-trip ticket costs L5,400. Board with the hill natives and the trip takes a little under an hour each way. The first train leaves at 8:10am and the last one that returns is at 7:10pm.

Since this is a small local railway system, your Italorail or Eurorail passes are not valid for this trip.

NERVI

One of the oldest resorts on the **Riviera**, today **Nervi** has been incorporated into the city of Genoa but it still has a life of its own. The town is comprised of green parks and gardens that are nestled among the rocks that lead down to the water. There is a scenic and picturesque cliff walk that is entirely carved out these beautiful rocks.

The beaches are not really sandy, just rocky, kind of like those found halfway up the coast in Maine. Nonetheless it is a peaceful respite from the hectic pace of Genoa. Once you arrive in Nervi, you won't want to leave, so maybe you should simply stay here and commute the 30-40 minute bus or train ride into Genoa to see the sights, sounds, and smells of the big city.

As a seaside resort you'll find all sorts of bars and cafes, ice cream shops, stores, vendors, and restaurants. But the best parts of Nervi are the seemingly inaccessible swimming areas and the pristine park grounds that surround the beach area.

ARRIVALS & DEPARTURES

Located just east of the main city, to get to Nervi simply take bus #17 from Piazza di Ferrari or #15 from Piazza Caricamento. It's about a 30 to 40 minute ride. Try to get to the bus stop a little early, since the bus fills up rapidly. Trains also come here on the half-hour.

WHERE TO STAY

1. ASTOR, *Viale delle Palme 16, Tel. 010/372-8325. Fax 010/372-8486. 41 rooms all with bath. Single L110,000-220,000; Double L123,000-245,000. Credit cards accepted. Breakfast L40,000 extra.* ****

A fashionably elegant hotel located in a lush garden a short walk from the sea and the main street, where all the shops and restaurants are. All the amenities of a good four star hotel, including an excellent restaurant if you choose not to go out for the evening or afternooon. If you have the money, this is *the* place to stay in Nervi.

2. HOTEL ESPERIA, *Via Val Cismon 1, Tel. 010/372-825. fax 010/372-8486. 25 rooms 24 with bath. L60,000-105,000; Double L90,000-140,000. No credit cards accepted. Breakfast L10,000 extra.* ***

Perfectly located on a tranquil side street, your stay will be quiet and pleasant at this good three star hotel. A stone's throw from the beach, the lush public parks, as well as the shopping street. You're in an ideal situation here. The rooms are all modern, clean and comfortable. They also have a restaurant if you do not want to go out in search of food.

3. HOTEL BELSITO, *Via Capolungo 12, Tel. and Fax 010/372-8060. 13 rooms 8 with bath. Single L35,000-48,000; Double L75,000-80,000. Breakfast L5,000 extra. Credit cards accepted.* **

About 300 meters down the road from the Piazza Pittaluga, which is where the buses drop you off from Genoa, and also where the shops come to an end. The only retail outlet nearby is the great restaurant Dai Peatoti (see *Where to Eat*), so you've got the hotel all to yourself. The tranquillity is only accentuated by the hotel's lush garden area, where you can enjoy breakfast in the morning or a drink in the afternoons and evenings.

4. HOTEL LUX, *Via Capolungo 16, Tel. and Fax 010/372-8636. 15 rooms, 8 with bath. Single L40,000-45,000; Double :65,000-75,000. Breakfast L5,000 extra. No credit cards accepted.* **

Located just down the road from the Belsito, this hotel isn't nearly as well run or kept up. The prices charged reflect that difference. The only similarity is that this place also has a tranquil garden area to eat breakfast or relax in after a day at the sea.

5. HOTEL SOGGIORNO AL MARE, *Via Gazzolo 7, Tel. 010/372-8724. 12 rooms none with bath. Single L32,000-38,000; Double L65,000-80,000. No credit cards accepted.* *

A one star with absolutely no amenities. But it's location, on a side street just off Nervi's old fishing village, places you only a stone's throw from the only real authentic life in Nervi. You're also near three good restaurants and a handful of bars and cafes. Perfect for the budget traveler that doesn't demand much.

WHERE TO EAT

There are a few places to eat along the main road parallel to but away from the main beach and walkway of Nervi. Any of these will satisfy your basic hunger, but if you want ambiance, high quality, and slightly out of the way restaurants, here are two I know you'll enjoy.

6. DAI PECATORI, *Via Aldo Casotti 6r, Tel. 010/326-168. Closed Mondays. Credit cards accepted. Dinner for two L80,000.*

In a small out of the way local fish restaurant, run by easy-going and pleasant proprietor who like to enjoy a glass of wine during the evening, this place offers great *gnocchi al pesto* and seafood. The *calamari fritti* (fried squid) as an entrée is superb.

As you enter, you'll pass the local bar/cafe and open kitchen to head to your table. Enjoy the true feeling of a great seafood restaurant.

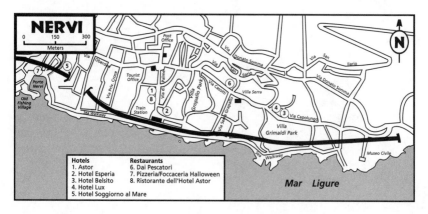

7. PIZZERIA/FOCCACERIA HALLOWEEN, *Via Caboto, Tel. 010/ 372-6154. Closed Wednesdays. Dinner for two L40,000.*

Situated in the center of the old small fishing village of Nervi, here you can sit out on the terrace with a vista of the fishing boats and the harbor. The best place to soak up the past as well as their great pizzas and *foccacci* (pizza-like dish with a light crust and ingredients baked in the middle). The best place to go in Nervi because of the harbor view and the food. Don't let the name fool you.

8. RISTORANTE DELL'HOTEL ASTOR, *Viale delle Palme 16, Tel. 010/372-8325. All credit cards accepted. Dinner for two L110,000. Open all year round.*

In the summer, you can eat your meal in their beautiful tranquil garden setting. Here you can sample the excellent traditional dishes from Liguria, like *tortellone al pesto* (large tortellini with pesto sauce) as well as any manner of fish prepared in a wide variety of ways (grilled, fried, baked, etc.). For dessert try any of their specialties; they're home-made on the premises.

18. TURIN

Located 78 miles southwest of Milan, with a population just topping one million people, **Turin** (**Torino**) is the major city in the **western Alps**. The city lies on the banks of the **Po River** near the foot of the Alps in northwestern Italy. There is enough of interest to justify only a one night stay, but no more.

Because it is the home of automobile makers **Fiat** and **Lancia**, Turin has been called the Detroit of Italy, and that should tell you enough about how interesting it is. Besides automobiles, is also a major industrial center for ball bearings, rubber and tires, clothing, textiles, leather goods, paper, chemicals, and food products.

Turin has also been a center of learning and religion for many years. The **University of Turin** was founded in 1404, and the **Cathedral of St. John the Baptist** was built from 1491 to 1498. This marvelous church houses the chapel of the **Holy Shroud** (sometimes called the **Shroud of Turin**). The chapel contains the urn that holds the cloth formerly believed to have been used to wrap the body of Jesus after his crucifixion. Modern carbon dating and other investigative techniques have recently disproved that theory. But those of you who are still true believers, the shroud should not be missed.

TOURING TORINO

*Walk around and observe the Baroque and Renaissance architecture, and visit the **Royal Armory** (excellent ancient arms and armor), the **Cathedral of St. John the Baptist** (home of the Holy Shroud), the **Palatine Gate** (built by Emperor Augustus), the **Valentino Castle and Park**, **Palazzo Madama** (which houses the **Museum of Ancient Art**), **Carlo Biscaretti di Ruffia auto museum** (with car models dating back to 1893), and maybe the **Egyptian Museum** and the **Galleria Sabauda** (collection of Masters art). If you're interested in Italian industry you could also tour one of the car factories.*

Torino's name comes from the **Taurini Gauls**, who lived here in pre-Roman times. During the reign of Augustus, the Romans rebuilt and walled the city. In 570 AD, it fell to the Lombards, and under Charlemagne it was assigned to the margraves of Susa. Linked to the House of Savoy in 1046 by a noble marriage, it served as the capital of the Piedmont for several centuries. In 1720 it became the capital of the Kingdom of Sardinia, and in the years 1861 to 1865 it was the capital of a newly united Italy. The city was heavily bombed by Allied air raids during World War II because of its industrial nature, but by 1959 its industries and landmarks had been restored.

Three main excursions are detailed in this chapter: the lovely town of **Asti**, with its medieval charms, and the beautiful Alpine resort towns of **Aosta** and **Courmayeur**. Aosta has well-preserved Roman ruins, and both towns are a skier's and hiker's paradise.

ARRIVALS & DEPARTURES

Your best bet is the train; Turin is not far from Milan, and travel time by train from Milan should be about an hour and a half. From Rome, the train trip should take about six hours.

GETTING AROUND TOWN

By Bicycle

You can rent a bicycle at the beautiful and tranquil **Parco Valentino**. The "shop" is located on the Viale Matteoli and is open from 9:30am–12:30pm and 3:00pm–7:00pm, Tuesday through Sunday. You can rent the bikes for L10,000 per day or L3,000 per hour. You need to leave a picture ID and L5,000 cash as a deposit.

By Bus

This is a large industrial city, but the bus system, as in all Italian cities, is excellent so you can get around easily. At a cost of only L1,500 per trip, you can go anywhere in the city quickly and efficiently from 6:00am to 12:30am.

Tickets must be bought at a *Tabacchi* prior to boarding the buses, and convenient maps are available at most main bus terminals and at the APT tourist office on Via Roma.

By Taxi

I wouldn't recommend using your car in this big congested city. You can find taxis all over the streets and at conveniently located taxi stands, but if you want to call one from your hotel try one of these three companies:

- **Central Taxi**, *Tel. 33-99*
- **Pronto Taxi**, *Tel. 57-37*
- **Radio Taxi Torino**, *Tel. 57-30*

Taxis will cost an initial L5,000 plus L1,000 per kilometer. There is a L3,000 surcharge at night and L2,000 on Sundays and holidays.

WHERE TO STAY

Since Turin is an industrial city and the hotels rely mainly on business travelers for income, the city's hotels are virtually empty on the weekends. Therefore most of these hotels are more than willing to offer amazing discounts if you stay over the weekend. All you have to do is ask prior to arriving.

1. CITY HOTEL, *Via F Juvarra 25, 10122 Torino, Tel. 011/540-546. Fax 011/548-188. 60 rooms 38 with bath, 22 with shower. All credit cards accepted. Single L 245,000; Double L380,000. Breakfast included.* *******

A thoroughly modern hotel in a central location, perfect for tourism or business travel. Despite its central location the hotel is peaceful and quiet. The service is professional and the rooms are immaculate and comfortable. Everything you would expect from a five star deluxe hotel. It's relatively small with only 50 rooms, and as the only true five star in Torino, it fills up fast so remember to make reservations.

2. HOLIDAY INN TURIN CITY CENTER, *Via Assietta 3, 10122 Torino, Tel. 011/516-7111. Fax 011/516-699. 57 rooms, 12 with bath, 45 with shower. Single L180,000-235,000; Double L220,000-285,000. Breakfast Included. All credit cards accepted. Full board for L215,000.* ******

Located on one side of the train station in a beautiful park-like site, this beautiful old hotel has been completely modernized by the management of the Holiday Inn. They have an excellent restaurant that you should try even if you do not get the full board option. The rooms are perfectly clean and comfortable, and if you don't want to stay in them the hotel has a quaint little bar area. Another relaxing feature is the availability of a refreshing sauna. And to top it off pets are welcome too. Remember, we're in Italy. This is not your typical Holiday Inn. This place has style and character.

4. GRAND HOTEL SITEA, *Via Carlo Alberto 35, 10122 Torino, Tel. 011/517-1071, Fax 011/548-090. 119 rooms, 92 with bath, 27 with shower. Single L250,000; Double L330,000. Breakfast Included. All credit cards accepted. Full Board L310,000.* ******

Located near the front of the train station, this hotel is perfectly located for all visitors. One of the largest hotels in the city, it doesn't have the charm of the Holiday Inn (did you ever think you'd read that somewhere?), but the service is professional and excellent. The rooms are clean comfortable and large. They have an excellent kitchen that specializes in local Piemontese cuisine as well as dietetic cooking which you can have brought up to your room to enjoy in private. All the amenities of a four star.

5. JOLLY HOTEL AMBASCIATORI, *Corso Vittorio Emanuele II 104, 10122 Torino, Tel. 011/5752, Fax 011/544-978. 199 rooms all with bath. Single L 265,000; Double L 325,000. No credit cards accepted.* ****

Located near the train station in a completely restored old building, this hotel has been in business for quite some years and is now being run by the largest Italian hotel chain, Jolly. There are three other Jolly Hotels in Torino, all within walking distance of one another and all offering the same four star amenities. The service is not up to par with other chains and the decor is a little over modern but their rooms are clean and comfortable. In this hotel you can enjoy evenings in their piano bar.

6. HOTEL ROYAL, *Corso Regina Margherita 249, 10122 Torino, Tel. 011/437-6777. Fax 011/6393. 72 rooms, 15 with bath, 57 with shower. Single L180,000; Double L250,000. Full board L230,000.* ****

If you are an avid tennis player and need a game, this place has courts for you. Located outside of the central area on a main road, you may want to get the full board since not too many restaurants are around you. Their restaurant is small but it serves local cuisine that is quite good, especially their *capunet*, boiled cabbage stuffed with minced meat and a variety of spices. Not the best place to stay for tourists since you can't walk places from here. But if you're a tennis player, this is the only game in town.

7. VALENTINO DU PARC, *Via Giotto 16, 10122 Torino, Tel. 011/673-932. Fax 011/673-932. 12 rooms all with shower. Single L 200,000; Double L250,000. Credit cards accepted.* ****

For those of you tired of the impersonal service at the larger four star hotels, try this little gem near the Parco Valentino. Away from the main city center a little, this quaint hotel is in a tranquil local area but it still has all the amenities you would want from a four star hotel, except maybe a restaurant. But they do have room service for drinks and snacks. They also have a sauna to relax in at the end of the day and are pet friendly.

8. BEST WESTERN PIEMONTESE, *Via Berthollet 21, 10125 Torino, Tel. 011/669-8101. Fax 011/669-0571. 33 rooms, 2 with bath, 31 with shower. Single L90,000-170,000; Double L130,000-210,000. Credit cards accepted.* ***

Located in a quiet street near the station and town center, you will find all the amenities here including air conditioning (just recently installed). They have room service, laundry service, and are pet friendly. The service is North American prompt and courteous, and the rooms try to uphold the same standard but they're not as large as we're used to. They are, however, super clean and comfy. There is a bar downstairs.

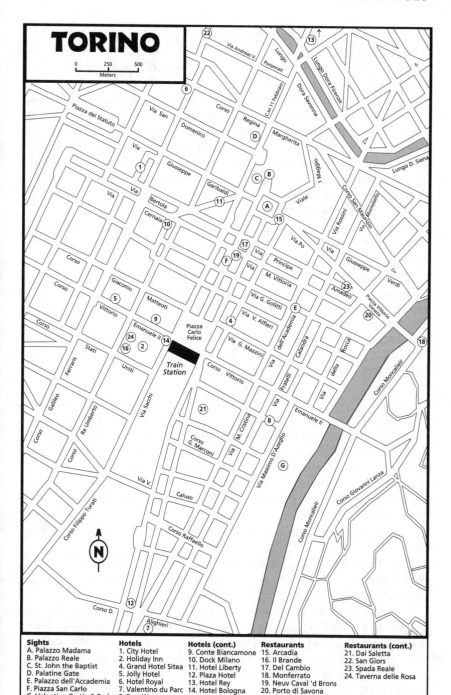

TORINO

0   250   500
Meters

Sights
A. Palazzo Madama
B. Palazzo Reale
C. St. John the Baptist
D. Palatine Gate
E. Palazzo dell'Accademia
F. Piazza San Carlo
G. Valentine Castle & Park

Hotels
1. City Hotel
2. Holiday Inn
4. Grand Hotel Sitea
5. Jolly Hotel
6. Hotel Royal
7. Valentino du Parc
8. Best Western

Hotels (cont.)
9. Conte Biancamone
10. Dock Milano
11. Hotel Liberty
12. Plaza Hotel
13. Hotel Rey
14. Hotel Bologna

Restaurants
15. Arcadia
16. Il Brande
17. Del Cambio
18. Monferrato
19. Neuv Caval 'd Brons
20. Porto di Savona

Restaurants (cont.)
21. Dai Saletta
22. San Giors
23. Spada Reale
24. Taverna delle Rosa

9. CONTE BIANCAMONE, *Corso Vittorio Emanuelle II 73, 10122 Torino, Tel. 011/562-3281. Fax 011/562-3789. 25 rooms, 2 with bath, 23 with shower. Single L 135,000; Double L170,000. Breakfast included. All credit cards accepted.* ***

If you want quaint old restored buildings at a great price, stay here in this beautiful hotel in a peaceful and tranquil area of Torino near the train station. The public areas are a combination of antique and modern. I love the frescoed and relieved high ceilings. The rooms are large, clean and comfortable, if a bit spartan. The only missing ingredient is air conditioning. The staff is always willing to go that extra mile. Stay here when air conditioning is not needed.

10. HOTEL DOCK MILANO, *Via Cernaia 46, 10122 Torino, Tel. 011/562-2622. Fax 011/545-939. 69 rooms, 18 with bath, 51 with shower. Single L110,000; Double L140,000. Breakfast L8,000. Full board L198,000. Extra bed L30,000. Credit cards accepted.* ***

Centrally located, but in a tranquil spot, with clean but spartan rooms. The staff is courteous and professional and the restaurant is actually quite good. They specialize in local Piemontese cuisine. Here you have all the comforts you need including air conditioning.

11. HOTEL LIBERTY, *Via Pietro Micca 15, 10121 Torino, Tel. 011/562-8801. Fax 011/562-8163. 35 rooms, 32 with shower, 3 singles without. Single L80,000-115,000; Double L150,000. Breakfast L10,000 extra. Lunch or Dinner L35,000. Credit cards accepted.* ***

Located on the first floor of a Liberty-style older building in the Parisian and Viennese style of the "fin du siècle," here you have charm, character and taste all rolled into one. In business since the 1800s, this family operated hotel provides meticulous cleaning services, hot and cold buffet breakfast and a local, home-cooking style restaurant. If you like antiques and comfort stay here. Besides the style they also have air conditioning, TV, radios, and direct dial phones in the rooms, as well as prompt room service.

This is the best place to stay in Torino if you're tired of cookie-cutter hotels.

12. PLAZA HOTEL, *Via Ilarione Petiti 18, 10122 Torino, Tel. 011/664-7549. Fax 011/678-351. 65 rooms, 5 with bath, 60 with shower. Single L 110,000; Double L150,000. Credit cards accepted.* ***

Located behind the main train station a little away from the city center, this place has a tranquil location in a restored old building. They have air conditioning, room service, a small bar as well as laundry service. The service is adequate and the rooms are clean, but small.

13. HOTEL REY, *Corso Novara 16, 10122 Torino, Tel. 011/852-335. Fax 011/852-333. 12 rooms all with shower. Single L85,000-125,000; Double L95,000-145,000. Credit cards accepted.* ***

A quaint little hotel with its own restaurant and bar. There are not many amenities but they do have air conditioning, room service, and the intimacy and privacy of a small hotel. Pets are welcome.

14. HOTEL BOLOGNA, *Corso Vittorio Emanuelle II 60, 10122 Torino, Tel. 011/562-0190. Fax 011/562-0193. 47 rooms, 4 with bath, 34 with shower, 10 without. Single L50,000-85,000; Double L70,000-110,000. Credit cards accepted. ***

Located in the center city, this is an inexpensive alternative for all travelers. Clean and comfortable with room service and a bar downstairs. They also have a person at the desk all night long, a rarity in two stars. They have TV in the rooms as well as direct dial phones but no air conditioning.

WHERE TO EAT

Besides being known for its industry, the **Piedmont** region and Torino should also be known for their simple cuisine and their tasty wine. The food is a blend of Northern Italian peasant staples as well as some elegant French flair. You'll find more butter than olive oil in cooking, a blasphemy in the south, and cheese, mushrooms and truffles are used instead of the abundant tomatoes and peppers down south.

During carnival, they have a special dish called *Tofeja* which is prepared with beans that are soaked for 12 hours, then cooked with (I know this doesn't sound appetizing but it's great) minced pork parts like the skin, ears, and snout. These are all spiced with parsley and garlic, then rolled up in a light dough mixture (the *Tofeja*), then cooked over night. When not served at carnival it can be found as an hors-d'oeuvre in many restaurants. They also have another appetizer called *capunet* that is boiled cabbage leaves stuffed with minced meat and a variety of spices, as well as a *fresse*, which is a mixture of minced liver, raisins, salt, pepper and cinnamon roasted in the oven with a sauce of red wine, tomato, and brown sugar. A great pasta dish is *agnolotti*, which is a ravioli-like pasta stuffed with boiled cabbage and roasted lamb.

You can also get some tasty cheeses in this region. There is the *toma* which is aged perfectly for three months and used as snack between dishes but not in cooking. There is also the *tomini*, which is cow and goat milk combined and sold only after 2 or 3 days of production. It's soft and succulent. My favorite is the *savignon*, which is a combination of buttermilk curds, salt, pepper, and spices that is typical of the village of **Settimo Vittone**. There's nothing like spiced cheese curds.

This region of Italy is also know for its desserts, which are usually tarts filled with fresh fruits like peaches, and sweetened with sugar and cocoa, and sometimes almonds.

The **wines** of the region can be bubbly and sweet, like those from **Asti** (most people think that *Asti Spumante* is a champagne, but that type of wine can only come from the Champagne region in France). This is a sparkling wines, like *Carema* or *Erbaluce*. Both of these wines have been produced since the Middle Ages, and were particularly sweet back then since the only preservation method for wine at the time was the application of sugar. Today the wines are light and dry, with a distinct character that can hold its own against the best the world has to offer. These two wines also offer themselves in a Spumante (sparkling) version.

15. RISTORANTE ARCADIA, *Galleria dell'Industria Subalpina 16, Tel. 011/532-029. Closed Sundays and August. All credit cards accepted. Dinner for two L90,000.*

Right in the center of Torino this place is swamped for lunch with the business crowd. They serve a local Piemontese-style menu, including a wonderful mixed vegetable dish made local style (*misto di verdure alla piemontese*) and an assortment of beef dishes like *filetto alla monferrina* (fillet fried in flour). The dessert tray is piled high with local favorites and the waiters are always attentive and alert.

16. TRATTORIA IL BRANDÉ, *Via Massena 5, Tel. 011/537-279. Closed Sundays and Mondays and August. Dinner for two L90,000. No credit cards accepted.*

Reservations are definitely necessary to eat at this wonderful little *trattoria*, since they only have eight tables. Two cousins by the last name of Mottura run the place and offer a set menu, as well as a series of different dishes with mainly a Normandy (French) influence. Try some of their rabbit dishes or their *gnocchi alle erbe* (small dumplings made of flour covered in herbs and spices) and wash it all down with some excellent *Barolo* wine from Piedmont.

17. RISTORANTE DEL CAMBIO, *Piazza Carignamo 2, Tel. 011/546-690. Closed Sundays, the first week in January and all of August. Dinner for two L200,000. All credit cards accepted.*

A super elegant restaurant with over 200 years experience in fine food preparation. Each room is finer than the next and each is a perfect spot for a romantic evening. In this fine environment the service is impeccable and the food exquisite. Their menu changes frequently but this is some of what was available on my last visit: *La tartra di verdurine all'antica con fonduta di Castelmagno* (a plate of vegetables chopped for you to dip in a succulent fondue of Castelmagno cheese) or *tartufo con fiori zucca* (truffles cooked with pumpkin flowers) or the superb *filetto di vitello con funghi e scalogno* (veal filet with mushrooms and scallions).

18. RISTORANTE MONFERRATO, *Via Monferrato 6, Tel. 011/819-0061. Closed Saturdays and Sundays as well as August. Dinner for two L100,000. All credit cards accepted.*

This well-lit, modern restaurant is across the Po River from the center of town. The cuisine is perfect in preparation, presentation, and taste. Try some of their braised, boiled, and exquisitely prepared lamb dishes. I especially like the *agnello con funghi* (lamb with mushrooms). They also have a good set of warm appetizers.

19. RISTORANTE NEUV CAVAL 'D BRONS, *Piazza San Carlo 157, Tel. 011/562-7483. Closed Sundays. Dinner for two L180,000. All credit cards accepted.*

What started out as a beer hall in 1947 became known as the Pub Lancia and Steakhouse, and now has given itself a more refined name. There are three rooms with a few tables and many decorations which lends a refined atmosphere. The menu includes everything from seafood to pasta to meat. Try their *gamberini stufato all'Arneis e zafferano* (shrimp stuffed with cheese and saffron) or the *filetto di trota in pan brioche can salsa di sidro* (trout pan fried in cider).

They also have a vegetarian menu, featuring such dishes as a delicious *ravioli di zucchine e porri* (ravioli made with zucchini and leeks) and the *sformata di spinachi con fonduta* (soufflé/fondue of spinach and cheese). If you're in the mood for cheese, go for the *flan di Castelmagno in salsa* (molded cheese soaked in a great sauce).

20. PORTO DI SAVONA, *Piazza Via Veneto 2, Tel. 011/817-3500. Closed Mondays, Tuesdays for dinner and all of July. Dinner for two L65,000. No credit cards accepted.*

The clientele of this place includes everything from actors to authors to businessmen to students. It is a local favorite. The *cucina piemontese* is superb, all the way from antipasto to dessert. Try anything on the menu, especially their braised or boiled mixed meats or some of their *gnocchi* with different cheese sauces. An inexpensive and delightfully tasty insight into the culture of Torino.

21. TRATTORIA DAI SALETTA, *Via Belfiore 37, Tel. 011/668-7867. Closed Sundays and August. Dinner for two L75,000. Visa accepted.*

Run by the Saletta cousins, this place only has seven small tables from which to enjoy their magnificent pasta dishes, most of which are smothered in creamy cheese sauces. Of course you must sample the local *toma* cheese here, the perfect snack between dishes. All of their braised or roasted meats are excellent but not for the diet conscious. This is another great local place where you can have some perfect Piemontese food and atmosphere. Call for reservations.

22. TRATTORIA SAN GIORS, *Via Borgo Dora 3, Tel. 011/521-1256. Never closes. Dinner for two L 85,000. Visa accepted.*

Not a place for the faint hearted or those in search of a quiet meal. Located in the heart of the Mercato di Porta Palazzo, this place is loud and boisterous, especially at lunch. So if you want a taste of the local flavor come here and sample their *carrello di bolliti misti* (plate of boiled meats which is big enough for two) and soak up the atmosphere.

23. RISTORANTE SPADA REALE, *Principe Amadeo 53, Tel. 011/832-835. Closed Sundays. Dinner for two L95,000. All credit cards accepted.*

One of the most frequented restaurants in the city, thanks mainly to the great food and hospitality of the owner Adriano Stefanini. It is open late and caters to actors from the theater, professional athletes, and a wide variety of locals. The cuisine is creative, to say the least, and changes constantly. Mint and curry seem to be the spice staples in many of the dishes. Come here for something out of the ordinary.

24. TAVERNA DELLE ROSE, *Via Massena 24, Tel. 011/538-345. Closed Saturdays at Dinner, Sundays, and August. Dinner for two L120,000. All credit cards accepted.*

A small, three room, popular local place. The owner and cook Neri Barbieri prepares an excellent antipasto table, some great pasta dishes like *spaghetti all'aragosta* (with lobster) and *papardelle ai funghi* (large strips of pasta in a mushroom sauce), and great grilled and roasted meats. A place for a good down home Piemontese meal.

SEEING THE SIGHTS

There is not all that much to see here, but what there is can be quite enjoyable. Those seeking spiritual experience will no doubt head to the Cathedral of St. John the Baptist to take in the Holy Shroud, but here are a few other ideas as well:

A. PALAZZO MADAMA

Piazza Castello, Tel. 436-1455. Open Tuesday and Thursday 2:30pm–7:30pm, Wednesday, Friday, Saturday 9am–2pm. Admission L6,000.

Located in the central feature of the old town of Torino, the **Piazza Castello**, is this massive *palazzo* which houses the **Museum of Ancient Art**. The core of this building was built in the 13th century on the remains of the Roman east gate to the garrison city.

The building was enlarged in both the 15th and 16th centuries, with the Baroque west front and the magnificent double staircase. The museum is on the ground and second floors and has a valuable collection of sculptures, stained glass, paintings and other works.

B. PALAZZO REALE

Piazza Castello, Tel. 436-1455. Open Tuesday–Saturday 9am–5pm. Admission L6,000. Gardens free.

On the north side of the Piazza Castello is the **Palazzo Reale (Royal Palace)**, which is a plain brick building built between 1646 and 1658. It contains 26 sumptuously decorated apartments (*Reali Apartamenti*). Especially noteworthy is the **Apartamento di Madama Felicita**. In the right wing is the **Royal Armory** with a vast collection of arms and armor dating from the 15th to the 17th centuries.

C. CATHEDRAL OF ST. JOHN THE BAPTIST

Piazza San Giovanni, Tel. 436-6101. Chapel open Tuesday–Saturday 9am–noon and 3–5:30pm. Church open every day 7am–noon and 3–5:30pm.
Home of the **Holy Shroud**, this church was built between 1492 and 1498. The bell tower was added in 1720. The Holy Shroud (Shroud of Turin) was purported to have been the linen cloth in which the body of Christ was wrapped after his descent from the cross. Despite the fact that it has been proven to be a fake, it remains in its chapel and still many believers come and visit it.

D. PALATINE GATE

Located northwest of the Cathedral, the arch was built by Emperor Augustus and was the north gate of the old Roman town. It is a simple structure which has two brick towers, but really is a prime example of how history in Italy all blends together into the present.

E. PALAZZO DELL'ACCADEMIA DELLE SCIENZE

Via Accademia delle Scienze 6, Tel. 61-7776. Open Tuesday–Sunday 9am–2pm. Admission L10,000.
This palace was initially built as a Jesuit college in 1679 and was converted to the **Academy of Sciences** in 1757. Today it houses the **Museum of Antiquities**, with Greco-Roman and Etruscan material mainly from the Piemontese and Ligurian regions; the **Egyptian Museum** (**Museo Egizio**), one of the finest collections of Egyptian antiquities in the world, including a wonderfully evocative statue of Ramses II; and the **Galleria Sabauda**, with its fine collection of Masters paintings and sculptures.

F. PIAZZA SAN CARLO

This symmetrical square was laid out in 1638. Here you'll find the **Church of Santa Cristina** built in 1637 with a facade by Juvara in 1718; and the **Church of San Carlo** built in 1836. In the center of the piazza stands the equestrian statue of Duke Filiberto Emanuele sculpted in 1838. Running through this beautiful Baroque piazza is Turin's main shopping street, **Via Roma**.
A perfect place for a *passegiatta* (stroll) as well as window shopping or people watching.

G. VALENTINO CASTLE & PARK

Via Massimo d'Azeglio, Tel. 669-9372. Open Tuesday–Saturday 9am–6pm and Sunday 10:30am–6pm.

A tranquil respite from the pace of a large city, this park also contains the **Botanical Gardens**, which were established in 1729, and the Renaissance **Castello del Valentino** built in 1640. Towards the south end of the park are the **Borgo Medioevale**, a medieval village and castle created for an exhibition in 1884, which is a great place for kids to visit.

Another great place for kids of all ages is the **Palazzo delle Esposizioni**, which houses the popular **Carlo Biscaretti di Ruffia auto museum** featuring car models dating back to 1893. If you're a car buff, come see the creations of the Henry Fords of Italy.

NIGHTLIFE & ENTERTAINMENT

VINCENZO NEBIOLO, *Via Priocca 10, Tel. 011/436-4558. Closed Sundays and August.*

A quaint little wine bar open from 6:00am to 10:00pm right in the heart of the Mercato di Porta Palazzo. They serve many different wines, most local at L2,000 per liter, as well as superb *Panini* sandwiches with a variety of cheese and salami fillers.

BRITANNIA PUB, *Via Carlo Alberto 34, Tel. 011/54-33-92. Open from 6:00pm until 2:00am. Pints L6,000.*

Your traditional English style pub with Guiness, Harp and Kilkenny on tap. They also serve simple *Panini* and other snacks warm and cold

DUKE OF WELLINGTON, *Via Caboto 26, Tel. 011/59-99-41. Open from 6:00pm until 2:00am. Pints L6,000.*

Another English style pub with a variety of bottled beer and typical English and German offerings on tap. They also serve simple sandwich and *Panini* type food.

LONDON PUB, *Via Tripoli 38, Tel. 011/39-99-86. Open from 6:00pm to 2:00am. Pints L5,000.*

Yet another English style pub. These establishments are definitely catching on in style with the Italians. Ten years ago you would have found just one in most cities. Guiness, Harp and Kilkenny on tap.

SPORTS & RECREATION

Golf

• **A.S. Golf Club Le Fronde**, *Via S Agostino 68, 10051 Avigiliano, Tel. 011/938-053. Fax 011/930-928.* Located 25 kilometers from Torino, this is an 18 hole, par 72, 6000 meter course that is open from February to December except on Mondays. They have a driving range, carts, pull-carts, a pro shop, bar & restaurant, and a pool (for your companion to lounge around while you hit the links).

• **Golf Club La Mergherita**, *Strada Pralormo 29, 10002 Carmagnola, Tel 011/979-5113. Fax 011/979-5204.* Located 25 kilometers from Torino, this is an 18 hole, par 72, 6278 meter course that is open from March to December except on Tuesdays. They have a driving range, pool, pro shop, and restaurant/bar.

• **Golf Club Margara**, *Via Tenuta Margara 5, 15043 Fubine, Tel. 0131/778-555. Fax 0131/778-772.* Located 65 kilometers from Torino, this is an 18 hole, par 72, 6043 meter course that is open from February to December except for Mondays. They have two tennis courts, an Olympic size swimming pool, guest house, pro shop, restaurant and bar. Conceivably you and your family could spend a few enjoyable days playing tennis, golf, swimming, and dining here.

• **Golf Club Associazione Sportiva I Roveri**, *Rotta Cerbiatta 24, 10070 Fiano, Tel. 011/923-5667. Fax 011/923-5669.* Located 20 kilometers from Torino, you can either play the 18 hole, par 72, 6218 meter course or the 9 hole, par 36, 3306 meter course. They are open from March to November except on Mondays. There's a driving range, gymnasium, putting green, pro shop and restaurant/bar.

• **Circolo Golf Stupinigi**, *Corso Unione Sovietica 506 A, 10135 Torino, Tel. 011/347-2640. Fax 011/397-8038.* Located only 4 kilometers from Torino, this is a 9 hole, par 33, smallish 2170 meter course. They are open year round except August and Mondays. They have a driving range and a restaurant/bar. Good for day trips and short rounds of golf.

• **Vinovo Golf**, *Via Stupinigi 182, 10048 Vinovo, Tel. 011/965-3880. Fax 011/962-3748.* Located 3 kilometers from Torino, this is a 9 hole, par 32, short 2082 meter course that is open from January 10th to December 20th except for Mondays. They have a driving range, restaurant, and pro shop. Perfect for day trips and short rounds of golf.

• **AS Golf Club Cherasco**, *Loc. Fraschetta Cascina Roma, 12062 Cherasco, Tel. 0172/489-772. Fax 0172/488-304.* Located 50 kilometers from Torino and 40 kilometers from Asti, this is an 18 hole, par 72, 5987 meter course that is open from March through November except on Tuesdays. They have a driving range, tennis courts, pro shop, and restaurant.

SHOPPING

Since there's not many sights to see in Turin, you might as well go shopping, and the best place for that is the elegant **Via Roma** where you can find all sorts of stuff, including shoe stores, tailors, *alimentari*, cafés, restaurants, jewelers, department stores (like UPIM and STANDA), furriers, and much more. Even if you don't spend any money it still is a fun place to window shop and people watch.

Books & Newspapers in English
• **Libreria International Luxembourg**, *Via Accademia dell Scienze 3, Tel. 011/561-38-96. Monday 3:00am to 7:30pm. Tuesday through Friday 8:00am to 7:30pm. Closed Sundays.* There's a good selection of travel books, fiction, and non-fiction works as well as books relating to science and industry.

PRACTICAL INFORMATION
Bank Hours & Changing Money
Banks in Turin are open Monday through Friday from 8:30am to 1:30pm. Very few re-open in the afternoon, and the few that do only open from 2:45pm to 3:30pm. *Cambi* follow store hours which are generally 9:00am to 12:30pm and 4:00pm to 7:30pm, Monday through Saturday.
Below is a list of some centrally located bank branches:
• **Banca Commerciale Italiana**, *Via Roma 343*
• **Banca CRT**, *Piazza CLN 230*
• **Banca Popolare di Novara**, *Piazza San Carlo 196*
• **Istituto Bancario San Paolo di Torino**, *Piazza San Carlo 156*

Business Hours
Store hours are generally 9:00am to 12:30pm and 4:00pm to 7:30pm, Monday through Saturday. But as is the Italian way, there are many exceptions to the rule. Some stores stay open a half-hour later, some close a half-hour earlier, so don't depend on the stores being open when you want them to be.
Food stores generally close on Wednesday afternoons. Stores in the main business and commercial center generally stay open during the traditional siesta hours.

Laundry Services
• **Lavanderia Vizzini**, *Via San Secondo 30, Tel 011/54-58-82. Open Monday–Friday 8:00am to 12:30pm, and 3:30pm to 6:30pm.* Bring in your wash in the morning and pick it up at night. Cost for 4 kilos is L15,000; 6 kilos is L20,000.

Postal Services
• **Central Post Office**, *Via Alfieri 10 and Via Arsenale 13, Tel. 011/54-70-97. Open Monday through Friday 8:30am - 5:00pm, Saturday 9:00am to 12 noon.*

Tourist Information & Maps
- **APT Office**, *Via Roma 226, Tel. 011/53-59-01*
- **Information Office**, *Porta Nuova Train Station, Tel. 011/53-13-27*
     Both of these offices will supply you with a workable map of the city and help you find a room if you've arrived without one. In conjunction you can pick up the latest information on what's happening during your stay *(Un Ospite a Torino)* in town and throughout the province.

Tour Operators
- **AviaTour**, *Via Pomba 29, Tel. 011/557-6066*
- **Comitours**, *Via Carlo Alberto 29, Tel. 011/55-471*
- **Wagons-Lit Turismo**, *Piazza San Carlo 132, Tel. 011/548-456 and Largo Orbassano 62, Tel. 011/318-1933*

DAY TRIPS & EXCURSIONS

     The excursions below will be more fun for most people than a sojourn in Turin. You've got medieval **Asti** and the skiing/hiking resorts of **Aosta** and **Courmayeur**. These towns are perfect escapes, whether you're in the mood for simple relaxation or whether you're going to hit the slopes or trails.

ASTI

     Asti hit the big time back in 89 BC, when it became a Roman garrison town, and over time it emerged as one of the most powerful of the city republics in Italy during the Middle Ages. Bologna was known as the city of towers in its day, but Asti should be known as the city of towers today. Despite the many wars that were fought for its control during the Middle Ages and after, more than one hundred 13th century towers still remain intact for tourists to admire.

     Today the city and its region are best known not for these incredible towers, but rather for their renowned bubbly, *Asti Spumante*.

ARRIVALS & DEPARTURES

     There are trains from Turin every half hour that cost L5,000. The trip takes a little under 40 minutes. You will disembark at the station in **Piazza Marconi**, which is only a short walk from the center of town to the triangle-shaped **Piazza Vittorio Alfieri** via a series of twists and turns down some medieval streets. You'll need to take the five minute walk to get to the **tourist office** to pick up a map of the city and get help with hotel reservations if needed.

WHERE TO STAY

1. LIS HOTEL, *Via Fratelli Rosselli 10, 14100 Asti, Tel. 0141/595-051. Fax 0141/353-845. 29 rooms, 1 with bath, 28 with shower. Credit cards accepted. Single L100,000-110,000; Double L150,000-160,000; Suite L180,000. Breakfast L12,000 extra. Extra bed L36,000.* ****

Located in the center of the old city down some side streets in an old renovated building, here you can experience the feel of Asti at a tranquil four star hotel. They have all the services you'd expect from a good hotel, except maybe a restaurant, but there are quite a few in the immediate area. The rooms are clean, comfortable, and quiet.

2. PALIO HOTEL, *Via Cavour 106, 14100 Asti, Tel. 0141/34-371 or 599-282. Fax 0141/34-373. 34 rooms, 1 with bath, 33 with shower. 4 suites all with bath. Credit cards accepted. Single L130,000; Double L200,000; Suite L230,000. Breakfast included. Extra bed L30,000.* ****

Also housed in a renovated old building and located in the center of the city down some small medieval streets, this hotel is perfectly situated for exploring. They have all the amenities of the Lis and more, including hydro-massage tubs in all the rooms. No restaurant here either, but they too are in the middle of everything. The rooms are a little larger than Lis, spotlessly clean, and immensely comfortable.

3. HOTEL CAVOUR, *Piazza Marconi 18, 14100 Asti, Tel. 0141/530-222. 19 rooms only 16 with shower. Single L45,000-58,000; Double L65,000-83,000. Breakfast L10,000 extra. Extra bed L30,000.* **

Located in the piazza of the train station, this is the best inexpensive alternative available. Situated in an historic old building that has been beautifully renovated, they have good amenities for a two star like TVs, direct dial phones, a night porter, room service, a bar, parking and more. But they don't have air conditioning, so if it's hot stay elsewhere. A step up for the budget traveler.

WHERE TO EAT

4. L'ANGOLO DEL BEATO, *Via Gattuati 12, Tel. 0141/531-668. Closed Sundays, the first ten days of February, and the first twenty days of August. Dinner for two L100,000. All credit cards accepted.*

The food here is superb with a nice ambiance to boot, despite the fact that the restaurant is located near the train station. The *gallina bollita* (broiled chicken) is perfectly cooked and spiced and comes with an excellent array of freshly cooked vegetables. Since you're in the mountains now, they also serve an excellent variety of *conniglio* (rabbit), so maybe this is the time to try some.

5. BAROLO & CO., *Via Cesare Battisti 14, Tel. 0141/592-059. Closed Sunday nights and Mondays as well as the last three weeks of August. Dinner for two L90,000. Credit cards accepted.*

Located near the Torre Troyana, the tallest tower in Asti, this place is a restaurant on top and a wine bar on the bottom floor. You can get some great *lardo* (smoked pork fat which is surprisingly tasty) local salami, *crostini caldi con formaggio* (baked dough with cheese inside), *insalatina di funghi freschi* (salad of fresh mushrooms) and a scrumptious *stracotto al vino rosso* (beef stew with red wine sauce). A wonderful local place in taste and atmosphere.

6. IL CONVIVIO VINI E CUCINA, *Via GB Giuliani 4/6, Tel. 0141/ 594-188. Closed Sundays and ten days in August. Dinner for two L100,000. Credit cards accepted.*

Located in the Centro Storico of Asti, this place is a cantina in the early afternoons that offers some great Italian wines, and at night it is a restaurant that features local, traditional, simple, peasant fare like chicken, rabbit, gnocchi and more. There's also an afternoon wine sampling.

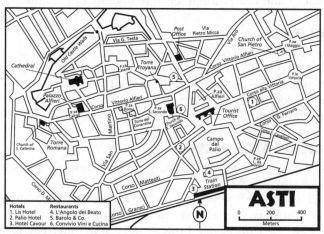

SEEING THE SIGHTS

The main attraction are the towers dotting the city, but there are other pleasures here too. If you like wine tasting, there are some great nearby vineyards.

THE TOWERS OF ASTI

Torre de Troyana is located in the Piazza Medici; Torre Rossa is in Corso Vittorio Alfieri; and Torre dei Conentina in Corso Vittorio Alfieri.

In Asti not only can you can find over one hundred medieval towers, but you can also locate the highest tower in the Piedmont region, the **Torre de Troyana**. Built in the 13th century, it is accompanied by other of its brethren, including the **Torre Rossa**, a sixteen-sided structure which is Asti's oldest, and where it is purported that the patron saint of the town,

San Secondo, was imprisoned and beheaded. Another interesting tower to look for is the **Torre dei Conentina**.

PALIO OF ASTI

Held on the third Sunday in September every year, this festival recreates the city's liberation in 1200. In period garb, townspeople and horses parade the streets to the triangular **Piazza Alfieri** where they re-enact the oldest known horse race in Italy. A great sight to see if you're in Asti at the time. About as good as the Palio of Siena.

CAMPO DI PALIO

Every Monday and Wednesday from 8:30am to 1:30pm vendors sell every imaginable type of fruit and vegetable. A wonderful typical local setting that shouldn't be missed if you're in town at that time.

CATHEDRAL

Piazza Cattedrale. Open 7:30am–noon and 3–7pm.

Built between 1309 and 1348 on the site of an earlier church, this simple church with its brick facade is decorated with statues and has many Baroque frescoes covering the walls inside. You'll also notice mosaics decorating the floor of the main altar.

CHURCH OF SAN PIETRO

Corso Vittorio Alfieri. Open Tuesday–Saturday 9am–noon and 3–6pm. Sunday 10am–Noon.

This 15th century church is better known for its 12th century octagonal baptistery. The church itself contains many fine terra cotta works as well as a cloister that brings you back in time. The baptistery usually contains exhibits of local artists.

VINEYARD & CASTLE TOURS

*You can get information about the wine tours from the **tourist office** at Piazza Alfieri, Tel. 53-03-57, open Monday through Friday 9:30am-12:30pm and 3:30pm-6:00pm, and Saturday 9:30am-12:30pm.*

Surrounding the city are many vineyards, some of which still have ancient castles on their grounds. The tours last for 2 to 3 hours and are offered year round. At the tourist office you can also find information about visiting Asti's extensive **wine cellar**.

AOSTA

If you're interested in Roman ruins with a backdrop of snow-capped mountains, and medieval churches, buildings, and towers as a foreground, this unique scene can be yours in **Aosta**. Sitting in the flat lands of the nearby mountains of **Monte Emilius** (3,600 meters) and **Becca di Nona** (3,200 meters) this town was built as a Roman fort and the gateway through the **Great** and **Little St. Bernard** passes.

The Roman fort was erected in 25 BC and was then called Augustus Praetoria Salassorum, and today an arch dedicated to Augustus remains in the city. The plan of the town still retains the simple structured layout of its Roman origins and the old town is still surrounded by the walls erected at that time. These walls form a rectangle 725 meters by 572 meters, and contains twenty lookout towers. The city is the capital of the autonomous region known as **Val D'Aosta** and is a prime location for skiing, kayaking, rafting, hiking and more. Aosta is a good jumping off point for each of these activities.

SKI ITALY!

*The **Aosta valley** is the place to ski while in Italy. The two best locations are the larger, more historic town of **Aosta** and the smaller **Courmayeur**. Aosta offers excellent skiing on the slopes of **Mount Emilius**, while Courmayeur is located at the base of **Mont Blanc**, the highest peak in the Alps, just over the border from France. Both areas deliver some of the most challenging skiing in the world. So if you enjoy the rush of adrenaline you get from speeding down sheer mountain sides on waxed extensions of your feet, give these two places a try.*

ARRIVALS & DEPARTURES

Aosta is 98 kilometers from Turin, from which three trains leave daily: one in the early am, one at 1:00pm, and one in the late pm. The trip takes about an hour each way. If you don't want to rush, stay the night.

WHERE TO STAY

1. HOLIDAY INN AOSTA, *Corso Battaglione 30, 1100 Aosta, Tel. 0165/23-63-56. Fax 0165/23-68-37. 50 rooms all with bath. Single L190,000; Double L230,000. Breakfast L15,000 extra. Credit cards accepted.* ****

Located in the heart of the city in a building that was renovated in 1994. The rooms are what you would expect in a high class hotel: clean, comfortable, and quiet. There are fitness and sauna facilities available as well as an excellent restaurant, La Taverne Provencale, and a nice bar that makes a cozy retreat.

2. HOTEL EUROPA, *Piazza Narbone 8, 11100 Aosta, Tel. 0165/236-363. Fax 0165/40-566. 71 rooms, all with bath. Single L 190,000; Double L230,000. Suite L440,000. Credit cards accepted.* ****

Located in the heart of the city, this is an exceptional hotel complete with elegant furnishing, a fitness center, piano bar, two-tiered restaurant that serves local and international food. The rooms are perfect with everything you could want, even a video cassette player for rent.

3. HOTEL BUS, *Via Malherbes 18, 11100 Aosta, Tel. 016543-645. Fax 0165/236-962. 39 rooms, 20 with bath, 19 with shower. Single L73,000-85,000; Double L104,000-123,000. Breakfast L15,000 extra. Credit cards accepted.* ***

A slight step down in decor from the local four stars, but you have most of the amenities including an in-house restaurant that serves local cuisine, room service, a downstairs bar, satellite TV, and more, all in a tranquil location. The rooms are clean, if not as large as their four star brethren. All in all a good, inexpensive place to stay.

4. HOTEL ROMA, *Via Torino 7, 11100 Aosta, Tel. 0165/40821. Fax 0165/32404. 33 rooms, 3 with bath, 30 with shower. Single L60,000-70,000; Double L90,000-110,000. Credit cards accepted.* ***

Located near the Arch of Augustus, this is a hospitable, clean and comfortable three star housed in a renovated older building. Once of the oldest hotels in town the renovations have improved the look and feel of the place. Their restaurant creates some wonderfully appetizing local dishes and their downstairs bar is a place to relax after a tough day. The only thing they do not have is TVs in the rooms.

5. HOTEL TORINO, *Via Torino 14, 11100 Aosta, Tel. 016544593. Fax 0165/361-377. 50 room only 45 with bath. Single L52,000-74,000; Double 90,000-110,000. Breakfast L10,000 extra. Credit cards accepted.* ***

Same type of amenities as the Hotel Roma, which is just down and across the street from this location, except they have TVs in the room. The hotel restaurant is not as good, but is adequate. The rooms are clean, quiet, and comfortable. Be sure to ask for a room with private bathing facilities.

WHERE TO STAY

6. LA TAVERNA PROVENCALE, *Via Guido Saba 1, Tel. 0165/236-356. Credit cards accepted. Dinner for two L90,000.*

A two-tiered brightly lit hotel restaurant attached to the Holiday Inn. They serve local flavors here and the food is very good. Try the *Bouilla-baisse* for primo, after a fine plate of *Grigliatta di Verdure* (grilled vegetables) for starters. Then you can either move onto a fine fish dish like *Pesce Persico alle verdure di stagione* (filets of perch cooked with seasonal vegetables) or a great meat dish like *Tagliata di manzo ai Petali di Carciofi* (beef steak with artichoke leaves). Or if you want to save a little money and still get two courses plus dessert, try one of their four fixed price menus from L45,000–L25,000.

7. GROTTA AZZURRA, *Via Croix de Ville 97, Tel. 0165/262-474. Closed Wednesdays. Dinner for two L80,000. No credit cards accepted.*

A great little pizzeria, and, as the name suggests (the *grotta azzurra* is the famous grotto under the Isle of Capri in the Bay of Naples), also serves fine fish dishes. Try their *insalata di mare* (seafood salad) and their *spaghetti alla vongole verace* (with a spicy clam sauce), or a fine *zuppa di mare* (seafood soup). And if you can't choose between the fish options, you can always select a pizza made with mounds of cheese.

8. VECCHIA AOSTA, *Piazza Porte Pretoriane 2, Tel. 0165/361-186. Closed Tuesday Nights and Wednesdays, two weeks in July and two weeks in October. Dinner for two L90,000. Credit cards accepted.*

A nice internal ambiance with an ancient Roman feel and look about it. You can be served outside on their terrace also. Here they make some fine local specialties like *ravioli al sugo di arrosto* (roasted ravioli) as well as some great fondues. You can also get a tourist menu for L28,000 per person, as well as a gastronomic menu for L35,000. A great place to come and relax and eat simple hearty food.

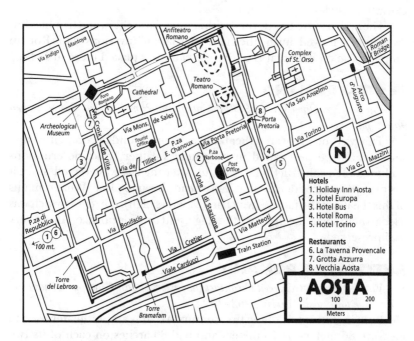

Hotels
1. Holiday Inn Aosta
2. Hotel Europa
3. Hotel Bus
4. Hotel Roma
5. Hotel Torino

Restaurants
6. La Taverna Provencale
7. Grotta Azzurra
8. Vecchia Aosta

AOSTA

SEEING THE SIGHTS

Take in the Roman ruins as well as the extant Roman structures, or wander around the medieval and Gothic churches gracing this pleasing town.

PONTE ROMANO

Located over the **Butheir River** at the eastern part of the city, this is an ancient Roman bridge still in use (after centuries of renovations, of course), even though during the Middle Ages the course of the Butheir changed and didn't flow underneath. The humpbacked bridge is 6 meters wide and 17 meters long and was built in the time of Augustus, at the end of the first century BC.

ARCO D'AUGUSTA

Piazza Arco d'Augusto.

Not grand or imposing by comparison to those found in Rome, but this **arch** is astounding in that it was built in 25 BC in homage to Augustus and to commemorate the victory by the Romans over a local tribe called Salassi. This monument, which is perfectly aligned with the Praetorian gate, is 11.5 meters high and represents a combination of Dorian and Corinthian styles.

The arch used to be adorned with statues, bas-reliefs, and trophies but these were removed during the many "Barbarian" invasions of the Roman Empire. The crucifix that is under the vault was placed there in 1542.

TEATRO ROMANO

Via Bailage. Open Winter 9:30am–noon and 2pm–4:30pm. Summer open 9am–7pm.

This was once a covered **theater** like the one found in Pompeii, so that shows could be performed in inclement weather (volcanic eruptions excluded). It's construction was begun after the city was erected, since it sits over private residences that had already been in place. What remains of this theater is the facade (which is 22 meters high), the *cavea* (which was used to help cover the theater), the stage, and the side portico. All are very well preserved.

ANFITEATRO ROMANO

Via dell'Anfiteatro. Need to contact the Sisters of San Giuseppe in advance to arrange for a visit at 0165/262-149.

Built in the middle of the first century AD, this **amphitheater** used to measure 86 meters by 76 meters and had 60 arches on each of its two floors. It could hold over 2,000 spectators (double the number of inhabitants in the city). It is a little worse for wear, and all that remains today are eight arches that have been incorporated into the **Convent of the Sisters of San Giuseppe**. This could be a more interesting ruin if the city would bother to take the time and money to excavate it properly.

PORTA PRAETORIA

Located between via Sant'Anselmo and Via Porte Pretoriane.

This once was the eastern entrance to the town and dates back to 25 BC, when the city was founded. It is made of parallel double stone walls and is open at the bottom by three arches. The external wall is 4.5 meters thick and the internal wall is about 3.5 meters. The space between the walls was used as a weapons storeroom. Today over three meters of the gate and wall lie under the ground, due to the periodic flooding of the Dora over the years.

The tower next to the gate was built in the 12th century as a residence for the lords of Quart. Today the ground floor is used as a local photographic exhibit.

CATTEDRALE

Piazza Cattedrale. Open 7am–7pm.

Built on the sight of the Roman forum that dates from the fourth century AD, this Romanesque **cathedral** was constructed from 994 to 1026. It was altered many times over the centuries, with addition of the cloister, a neo-classic facade, and cross vaults inside. On a bright sunny day you will really appreciate looking out the 23 stained glass windows.

COMPLEX OF SAINT ORSO

Via and Piazzatta dell'Orso. Tel. 0165-262-026. Winter 9:30am–noon and 2pm–5:30pm. Summer 9am–7pm.

This Romanesque and Gothic complex includes the church of Saints Peter and Orso, the bell tower clock, the crypt, the Museum of Treasure, the cloister of Saint Orso, the buildings of the Priorate, and the ancient cemetery. Everything about this complex gives us an insight into the religious day to day life from the fifth century to the fifteenth century.

SPORTS & RECREATION

Hiking

The best time to hike in this area is July, August, and the first two weeks of September. Otherwise it can be a little chilly. Contact the tourist office in Aosta listed above, and request a free list of campgrounds, trails, and alpine refuges *(rifugi alpini)* for rent along the many twisting trails of the surrounding peaks. For more detailed information, contact the **Club**

Alpino Italiano, *located above the tourist office in Aosta at Tel. 0165/40-194. Fax 0165/36-32-44.*

Skiing

High season is November through March, and as such can be very crowded. It is best to make reservations well in advance. Contact the local tourist office in Aosta *(Piazza Chanoux, 11110 Aosta, Tel 0165/23-66-27, Fax 0165/34-667)* for a pamphlet they distribute for free called *Winter Season, Aosta Valley.* The pamphlet contains up-to-date information about skiing, hotels, events, and more. Courmayeur is the most well known ski resort in the area and is Italy's oldest (see below).

Aosta has a *funiculare* to carry skiers up **Mount Emilius**. It is located just behind the train station away from the historic part of town. In the winter, Aosta fills up with skiers from all over the world – not only to sample her slopes but to also bathe in her beauty and charm.

COURMAYEUR

Courmayeur and its sister city five kilometers down the road, **Entreve**, are located at the base of **Mont Blanc**, the highest peak in the Alps. Entreve is also the at the entrance to the Mont Blanc Tunnel and offers easy access to France. Both towns serve up some of the best skiing in Italy. The economy of Courmayeur and Entreve are completely geared towards winter sporting activities, and to a lesser but not insignificant degree summer relaxation and hiking, since many hotels stay open year round.

Courmayeur is Italy's oldest Alpine resort and as such is able to offer skiers of all levels everything they need to have the time of their lives. Just a few hundred meters from the main square, **Piazzale Monte Bianco**, is the **Funivia Courmayeur**, which transports skiers and sightseers up the first leg of the mountain to reach the choicest slopes this area has to offer. In Entreve there are two more such *funivie* running up Mont Blanc for your skiing pleasure.

In the summer these same *funivie* carry hikers and nature lovers up into the mountains to explore the natural beauty of the area. Courmayeur and Entreve are year round paradises, whatever your pleasure.

ARRIVALS & DEPARTURES

If you're driving from Aosta, take the **E 25** straight into Courmayeur. Be aware that during most times of the year there will be a lot of traffic, since this road leads to the Mont Blanc Tunnel that cuts through the mountain into France and the ski center of Chamonix.

The only other way to get here other than car is by bus.

WHERE TO STAY

Wherever you stay, you're going to pay through the nose. This is another of those places that was created by the rich and famous many years ago for their pleasure, then left for the not-so-rich-and-famous to enjoy later. But the prices stayed the same.

I strongly recommend making reservations at least 6 months in advance, summer or winter (in June virtually everything shuts down so shop keepers, restaurateurs, and hoteliers can take their vacations), especially if you want to stay on a weekend.

GALLIA GRAN BAITA, *Strada Larzy, 11013 Courmayeur. Tel. 0165/ 844-040, Fax 0165/844-805 (USA & Canada Tel. 402/398-3200, Fax 402/ 398-5484; Australia Toll Free 1-800-810-862; England Tel. 071/413-8886, Fax 071/413-8883). 50 rooms and 3 junior suites all with bath. Single L235,000; Double L390,000; Suite L590,000. Breakfast L25,000 extra. Credit cards accepted.* ****

Located on the edge of town on the way to Entreve, you don't have to worry about the location since the hotel has a free shuttle bus to pick you up and drop you off wherever and whenever you choose. Wood and stone is the motif inside giving this place a truly rustic Alpine appeal. There's a relaxing bar to return to after a day of skiing with an adjacent fireplace. Or you can take a dip in their heated indoor pool, relax in the sauna or sun room, or tone a few more muscles in the gym.

If any of this doesn't grab you they have their own spa that offers everything from being wrapped in seaweed to getting a wax treatment. They also have baby-sitting services. A truly great place to stay.

HOTEL PALACE BRON, *Via Plan Gorret 41, 11013 Courmayeur. Tel. 0165/846-742. Fax 0165/844-015. 27 rooms, 1 junior suite all with bath. Single L130,000-170,000; Double L220,000-290,000; Suite L480,000-660,000. Breakfast L25,000 extra. Credit cards accepted.* ****

Located above the town of Courmayeur, here you can feel a part of the hustle and bustle of the area while also being able to get away from it. The view from the restaurant, lounge, and piano bar is breathtaking. Windows are everywhere to make sure you don't miss the snow-capped beauty. Whitewashed walls, wood paneling and fireplaces dominate the decor downstairs and the rooms come with floral patterned bed spreads, curtains and chairs. Not quite as down to earth as the Gran Baita but that may be because they are up in the clouds. They have a spectacular garden in the summer and a shuttle bus to take guests to and from various locations all year round.

HOTEL PAVILION, *Strada Regionale 62, 11013 Courmayeur. Tel. 0165/846-120. Fax 0165/8460-122. 50 rooms, 10 of which are junior suites, all with bath. Single L 160,000-210,000; Double L250,000-340,000; Suites L430,000-640,000. Credit cards accepted.* ****

Near the *funivia* that takes skiers up the mountain, this is one of the largest places in town, and it only has 50 rooms. The exterior with its stone, dark wood, yellow awnings and cascading red flowers is quite impressive. The lobby and the rooms are finished with light wood and earth tones, creating a calming effect. Their restaurant, Le Bistroquet, has magnificent views of the mountains and serves superb food. Other than that they have an indoor swimming pool, sauna, sun deck, weight rooms, and shuttle bus to cart guests back and forth to their destinations. Right in the middle of things. Basically in stumbling distance from many watering holes.

HOTEL DEL VIALE, *Viale Monte Bianco 74, 11013 Courmayeur. Tel. 0165/846-712. fax 0165/844-513. 23 rooms, 12 with bath, 11 with shower. Single L80,000-180,000; Double L100,000-240,000. Credit cards accepted.* ***

Located on the way to Entreve and near the Gran Baita, this is a rustic looking little hotel with great interior decor. The restaurant is the best, with its open kitchen separated by only a thick wooden table for the dining area, and with the roaring flame in the fireplace oven. All the ambiance seems to have been used up in the common areas, for the rooms are whitewashed and the furniture is basic Italian modern; they are comfortable and clean. The best hotel in this category in Courmayeur.

CHALET PLAN GORRET, *Via Plan Gorret 45, 11013 Courmayeur. Tel. 0165/844-832. Fax 0165/844-842. 6 rooms all with shower. Double L95,000-126,000. No credit cards accepted.* ***

Do you want to stay in a real chalet? Talk about quaint and rustic, and filled with character and ambiance, and you've got this place. It is so intimate and romantic you'll fall in love all over again just by staying here. No real amenities except for privacy (you're up a hill from the main town near the Palace Bron), great views, a small bar area, and good food served with the meal plan, and of course romance. If you like staying in country inns or Bed and Breakfasts, this is the place for you.

WHERE TO EAT

Many of the hotels will require you to purchase a half meal plan depending on the season, which means you get to eat breakfast and one other meal of the day at the hotel. With your other meal here are two restaurants I know you'll love. If these don't please your palate, there are plenty more around.

PIERRE ALEXIS 1877, *Via Marconi 54, Tel. 0165/843-517. Closed Mondays. Visa Accepted. Dinner for two L90,000.*

A seemingly authentic rustic local place that serves salami as an appetizer. The soups and most other plates have a strong base of cheese in them and then you get to the fish and meat dishes and the cook goes wild. Maybe its some sort of French influence, but they have a great *trota in salsa delicata al pepe rosa* (trout in a delicate red pepper sauce) and other interesting dishes. There are also plenty of hearty meat dishes for you Alpine food lovers.

LE RELAIS DU MONT BLANC, *S.S. 26 #18, Tel. 0165/846-777. Closed Tuesdays and Wednesdays for lunch as well as all of June as well as October 15 through November 30. All credit cards accepted. Dinner for two L100,000.*

A large place, over 100 people can be seated at one time. The restaurant features exquisite fondues. Anything to do with cheese this place does great: *minestra di formaggi* (mixed cheese soup), *maccheroni ai formaggi alpini* (macaroni and alpine cheese). Besides the cheeses, the chef seems to roast the meats to perfection too. You can't go wrong here.

SPORTS & RECREATION

Funivia Ticket Prices

- **1 day pass**, *L49,000*
- **2 day pass**, *L93,000*
- **3 day pass**, *L131,000*
- **4 day pass**, *L167,000*
- **5 day pass**, *L208,000*
- **6 day pass**, *L242,000*
- **7 day pass**, *L277,000*
- **8 day pass**, *L307,000*

Ski Guides

You can hire **Alpine ski guides** to take you on guided skiing through the mountains. You need a group of at least two and no more than eight including the guide. Cost per person (excluding the guide, of course) is L76,000.

You get to ski or hike from Italy to France or vise versa, then take a bus in the other direction. Loads of fun but exhausting.

Ski School Rates Per Hour

- **1-2 People**, *L52,000*
- **3 People**, *L58,000*
- **4 People**, *L63,000*

Rates for a daily ski instructor for 1-2 people are L355,000, and for each other person add another L33,000.

TOURIST INFORMATION

- **Tourist Office**, *Piazza Monte Bianco, Tel. 0165/842-060.* Located in the same building as the bus terminal. Here you can get up to date information about skiing, hiking, alpine huts, hotel availability, etc. They also supply superb maps.

19. SOUTHERN ITALY

Southern Italy is still a land of immigrants waiting to move, but today instead of moving to America like their great grandfathers or grandfathers would have, they move to northern industrial cities like Milan or Turin. Without jobs in the south, Southern Italians are forced to move even if they know they will be cursed because of their accents and their place of birth. The discrimination against Southern Italians from too many of their cousins in the north is unfortunately still alive and well.

The main work for people in the south is still in small-scale agriculture, local fishing activities, and small-scale crafts manufacturing, with a smattering of limited industrial activities. Despite its poverty, Southern Italy can be a wonderful place to visit for an experienced Italy traveler. The sights to see, many of which have a definite Middle Eastern or Moorish influence, are few and far between.

But if you've never been to Italy, or still haven't seen all there is to see in Rome, Florence, Venice and other cities, Southern Italy, with the exception of Naples, would not be a vacation for you.

Naples has as much to offer as many of the northern cities, despite its unsavory reputation in northern Italy. Naples is not the cleanest of cities, nor the safest, but you can find museums stocked with ancient Roman antiquities as well as *palazzi* filled with paintings by such masters as Titian. But the rest of Southern Italy is only for the hardiest travelers. In 1993, two American tourists, roaming the quaint country roads of Southern Italy, suddenly stumbled into a situation they weren't supposed to see in a small village (it was reported to be Mafia related). They didn't come back alive. Don't wander aimlessly through Southern Italy.

NAPLES

Naples is a welcoming city. In many neighborhoods, life is still lived in the streets, where old and young interact and the day or evening entertainment is right in front of you, whether it's a family quarrel or two lovers at the corner cuddling away from onlookers. As Dickens wrote,

Neapolitans don't just live their lives, they enact them. To people here, life is a performance and as such it must be lived with gusto. You'll see this quality all over Naples, especially in its **Centro Storico** (old town), and that's what makes Naples so irresistibly Italian.

Naples is a city that has been conquered, destroyed by wars, and leveled by earthquakes, but it still keeps on ticking. As a port city, Naples is filled with all sorts of characters from all over the world, as well as some great seafood. Though Naples is not really known for its cuisine, you can find some good restaurants and pizzerias. Naples claims that it is the birthplace of the pizza so you'll have to try at least one while here.

There is much to see in Naples if you can get used to the clutter of cars, buses, motorcycles and people all interweaving themselves through the tapestry of life. You can see everything from Roman ruins to medieval castles, and all can be seen by using quick and convenient underground metro or above ground funicular.

BE ALERT

In your travels in Naples, be prepared. For all its charm and vibrancy, Naples at night is not very safe if you do not know where you are going. As a port city, like Genoa, it attracts undesirables from all over the world. So be aware, and make sure you perform all necessary safety precautions.

Brief History

Naples was originally a Greek settlement. In the 8th century BC (800s), it was called Parthenope and settled by people from Rhodes. Near this site, Ionian settlers founded the 'old town' in 7th century BC, which they called Palaipolis. In the 5th century BC, the 'new town' of **Neapolis** was founded by newcomers from Chalcis, and the name, only with slight changes, remains today.

These three settlements interacted freely but never merged. In 326 BC, they became allies of Rome and united. Though faithful to the alliance, Naples still retained its strong Greek traditions and characteristics until late into the Roman Imperial period. The town itself became a favorite of many wealthy Roman merchants and magistrates because of its beautiful scenery.

But the peace that Rome brought was not to last. In 543 AD, the town fell into the hands of the Goths. Ten years later it was returned to the rule of the Byzantine Empire. After that it began to assert its independence and was free until 1139, when conquered by the Normans and incorporated into the Kingdom of Sicily by Roger II. Frederick the I, Roger II's grandson, founded the **University in Naples** that still exists today. Only forty years later, the capital of the Kingdom of Sicily was moved to Naples.

But still peace was not to last. Spain gained control of the kingdom from 1503 to 1707, and in 1713 the territory passed to the Hapsburgs. Then in 1748 the Bourbons gained control, and kept control until 1860, when the territory was incorporated into the united Italy we see today.

GETTING AROUND TOWN

By Bus

Buses can take forever to get you where you want to go, especially at rush hour, but there are times you'll need to take them. For example, when you want to get up to Campodimonte and the National Gallery. The buses congregate at the Piazza Garibaldi outside the train station and each route is posted on the signs at all bus stops for ease of use. You can also get a convenient map from the tourist office that details the main map routes, or you can buy an even better one from a newsstand that lists all the bus routes.

To use the map simply find where you are and where you want to go. Then match up the black numbers (which are the numbers of the bus routes) where you are with those located at where you want to go. For example, if you're at Piazza Garibaldi which is marked number 8 on the map, and you want to go to Piazza Municipio which is also marked number 8 on the map, that means the bus number 8 goes from Piazza Garibaldi to Piazza Municipio.

Riding the bus during rush hour is very tight, so try to avoid the hours of 8:00am to 9:00am, 12:30pm to 1:30pm, 3:30 to 4:30pm, and 7:30pm to 8:30pm. They have an added rush hour in the middle of the day because of their siesta time in the afternoon.

By Foot

You'll obviously need to combine the use of one of the above modes of transport with bi-ped movement. You'll love the strolls through the Centro Storico and university area, but always be alert. Don't walk at night, especially alone. Remember, this is a port city. During the day, don't go down alleys that are empty of people. Just play it smart.

By Funicular

These hill-side trams connect the lower city of Naples to the hills of Vomero, where you can see the Castel San Elmo and the Certosa di San Martino. There are three funiculars that can assist in your ascent, the **Centrale** that leaves from Via Toledo, the **Montesanto** that leaves from Piazza Montesanto, and the **Chiai** that leaves from Piazza Amadeo. A one way ticket costs L1,500.

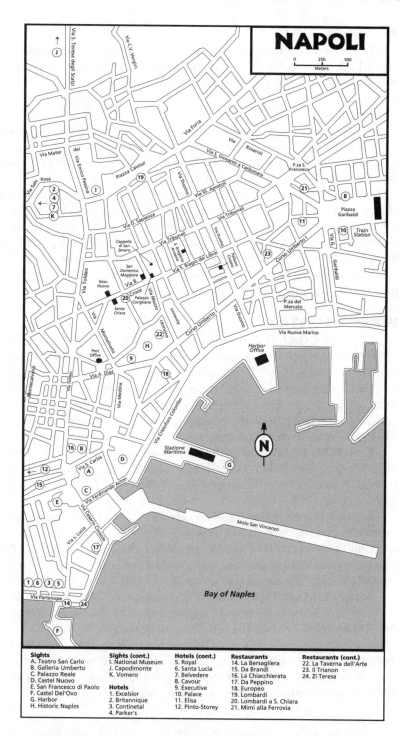

NAPOLI

0   250   500
Meters

Bay of Naples

Sights
A. Teatro San Carlo
B. Galleria Umberto
C. Palazzo Reale
D. Castel Nuovo
E. San Francesco di Paolo
F. Castel Del'Ovo
G. Harbor
H. Historic Naples

Sights (cont.)
I. National Museum
J. Capodimonte
K. Vomero

Hotels
1. Excelsior
2. Britannique
3. Continental
4. Parker's

Hotels (cont.)
5. Royal
6. Santa Lucia
7. Belvedere
8. Cavour
9. Executive
10. Palace
11. Elisa
12. Pinto-Storey

Restaurants
14. La Bersagliera
15. Da Brandi
16. La Chiacchierata
17. Da Peppino
18. Europeo
19. Lombardi
20. Lombardi a S. Chiara
21. Mimi alla Ferrovia

Restaurants (cont.)
22. La Taverna dell'Arte
23. Il Trianon
24. Zi Teresa

By Metro

You can take the metro almost anywhere you want to go in Naples for only L1,500 a trip each way. It's fast, inexpensive, and safe, but always keep a lookout for pickpockets. They flourish here in Naples.

By Taxi

Naples is a very congested city, and as such it will cost you an arm and a leg whenever you choose to transport yourself by taxi, especialy during rush hour. But if you want to spend the equivalent of a meal at a good restaurant just to get from point A to point B, by all means.

The going rate as of publication was L4,500 for the first 2/3 of a kilometer or the first minute (which usually comes first during the rush hours), then its L500 every 1/3 of a kilometer or minute. At night you'll also pay a surcharge of L3,000, and Sundays you'll pay L1,000 extra. If you bring bags aboard you'll be charged L500 extra for each bag.

Besides having to rely on flagging down a cab, there are strategically placed cab stands all over the city.

WHERE TO STAY

1. EXCELSIOR HOTEL, *Via Partenope 48, 80121 Napoli Tel. 081/764-9743. Fax 081/411-742. 136 rooms all with bath. Single L257,000-286,000; Double L386,000-428,000. Credit cards accepted.* *****

This it *the* place to stay in Naples. Located to the southeast of the Centro Storico right on the water's edge, within walking distance of all the sights as well as being located in a relaxing place. All the amenities of a five star deluxe hotel including a swimming pool.

2. HOTEL BRITANNIQUE, *Corso Vittorio Emanuelle 133, 80121 Napoli Tel. 081/7611-4145. Fax 081/669-760. 86 rooms all with bath. Single L180,000; Double L240,000; Suite L260,000. Breakfast L11,000 extra. Credit cards accepted.* ****

Situated above the city in the Vomero section, with great panoramic views of the harbor as well as of Vesuvius, here you'll be in a quaint little romantic building and area complete with everything you'll need to make your stay pleasant. Besides clean, comfortable, and large rooms, you have access to a great restaurant that serves local food.

3. HOTEL CONTINENTAL, *Via Partenope 44, 80121 Napoli Tel. 081/764-4636. Fax 081/764-4661. 166 rooms all with bath. Single L200,000-245,000; Double L290,000-370,000. Credit cards accepted.* ****

Located right next to the Excelsior within walking distance to all the sights, but located outside of the Centro Storico and business districts right on the Bay of Naples. A tranquil sight with its own swimming pool. Besides a good restaurant, they also have a separate American style bar and a piano bar for your evening's entertainment. This street is a beautiful one to stay on, with a panoramic view of the bay. Basically all hotels on it are superb.

4. PARKER'S HOTEL, *Corso Vittorio Emanuelle, 80121 Napoli Tel. 081/761-2474. Fax 081/663-527. 83 rooms, 47 with bath, 36 with shower. Single L 180,000-220,000; Double L290,000-330,000; Suite L750,000-1,500,000. Breakfast included. L70,000 extra bed. Kids stay for 10% of cost in you room. Credit cards accepted.* ****

In a renovate historic building, this is a romantic spot with great panoramic views of the harbor and Vesuvius. You can get local or international cuisine in the restaurant, and you have entertainment in the piano bar. The rooms come with whirlpool tubs. A tranquil, relaxing place to stay.

5. ROYAL HOTEL, *Via Partenope 38, 80121 Naples, Tel. 081/764-4800. Fax 081/764-5707. 300 rooms all with bath. Single L 200,000-245,000; Double L290,000-370,000. Credit cards accepted.* ****

The second largest hotel in Naples, located on the panoramic street Via Partenope next to the Excelsior. This is elite hotel row. The hotel also has its own swimming pool as well as a fine restaurant. The rooms are clean and comfortable befitting a good four star in a major Italian city. For entertainment, they offer a piano bar at night. Within walking distance of all Naples major sights.

6. SANTA LUCIA, *Via Partenope 46, 80121 Naples, Tel. 081/764-0666. Fax 081/764-8580. 102 rooms, 90 with bath, 12 with shower. Single L250,000; Double L350,000; Suite L600,000. Breakfast L20,000 extra. Credit cards accepted.* ****

Located within walking distance of the Centro Storico as well as the other major sites, this tranquil romantic hotel is located with a perfect panoramic view of the bay and Mount Vesuvius. Like its brethren on the Via Partenope, this is an excellent choice with all the necessary amenities. The only thing it doesn't have is a swimming pool.

7. HOTEL BELVEDERE, *Via T Angelini 51, 80121 Naples, Tel. 081/578-8169. Fax 081/578-5417. 27 rooms, 2 singles with bath. Single without bath L90,000-150,000; Single with bath L150,000; Double L200,000. Credit cards accepted.* ***

Located by the Castel Sant'Elmo, here you're just a funicular ride away from the Centro Storico. But you are free from all the hassles of staying in the city. This is a small, intimate, romantic hotel located in a renovated historic building. It's tranquil and secluded. Their excellent local restaurant has, as do a number of the rooms, the perfect panoramic view of the Bay of Naples and Mount Vesuvius. At night for entertainment they have a piano bar. Stay here if you're tired of the number-in-a-crowd way you feel at one of the larger hotels.

8. HOTEL CAVOUR, *Piazza Garibaldi 32, 80142 Naples, Tel. 081/283-122. Fax 081/287-488. 98 rooms, 40 with bath, 58 with shower. Single L95,000-150,000; Double L150,000-190,000. Suite L200,000-230,000. Breakfast included.* ***

In a renovated historic building in the busy Piazza Garibaldi. The double paned glass keeps out most of the sound but some of it leaks through. The staff is professional and courteous and do everything to make up for the location. You have air conditioning, satellite TV, and a restaurant that serves local dishes and international cuisine.

9. HOTEL EXECUTIVE, *Via del Cerriglio 10, 80134 Naples, Tel. 081/552-0611. Fax the same. 19 rooms all with bath. Single L120,000-160,000. Double L140,000-220,000. Credit cards accepted.* ***

In the Centro Storico in a renovated old building, this place has a gym, sauna, and sun room. It's a good alternative to the larger hotels in Naples. Here you are made to feel special. The rooms are clean and comfortable and have air conditioning, TV, mini bar and more. A romantic place to stay, but my favorite in this price range is still the Hotel Belvedere.

10. PALACE HOTEL,*Piazza Garibaldi 9, 80142 Napoli, Tel. 081/267-044. Fax 081/264-306. 1002 rooms, 52 with bath, 50 with shower. Single L95,000-150,000; Double L150,000-190,000. Breakfast included. Extra bed L60,000. Credit Cards accepted.* ***

In the busy Piazza Garibaldi, this place has many amenities but they can't make up for the intruding chaos of Naples. The rooms are clean, small, but comfortable. The restaurant serves international and local cuisine and you have air conditioning and TV in your rooms.

11. HOTEL ELISA, *Piazza Mancini 11, 80139 Napoli, Tel. 081/269-494. 16 rooms all with bath. Single L 35,000-60,000; Double L65,000-98,000. Credit cards accepted.* **

A small two star near the station with air conditioning and TV in the rooms, a downstairs bar, and a night porter. A good option for the budget traveler who wants to stay in a little more upscale place. The rooms are kept immaculate but they are a little small.

12. HOTEL PINTO-STOREY, *Via G Martucci 72, 80121 Napoli, Tel. 081/681-260. Fax 081/667-536. 25 rooms, only 19 with bath. Single without bath 80,000; Single with bath L130,000. Double without bath L110,000; Double with bath 180,000. Credit cards accepted.* **

This is two star that thinks it should be a three star, except for the six rooms without bath. Located in a quiet area of Naples just below the Villa Floridiana, it's a short walk to the bay. They have air conditioning and TV in the rooms and a small bar downstairs. For your money, I'd recommend instead the Hotel Belvedere.

WHERE TO EAT

14. LA BERSAGLIERA, *Borgo Marinaro Sant Lucia, Tel. 081/764-6016. Closed Tuesdays and August. Credit cards accepted. Dinner for two L140,000.*

The best thing about this place is its location with a view of the Castel dell'Ovo, especially on their terrace overlooking the water. The food is good, but not for these exorbitant prices. If you want romantic atmosphere, come here. Try their *spaghetti con vongole* (with clams) or their *linguine agli scampi* (with shrimp). For seconds try their fried or grilled fish.

15. PIZZERIA DA BRANDI, *Salta San Anna di Palazzo 1, Tel. 081/416-928. Closed Mondays and one week in August. Dinner for two L60,000. Credit cards accepted.*

As you know Neapolitans claim to have made the first pizza, and this place claims to have made the first *Pizza Margherita* (simple pizza with fresh tomato sauce, oil, and mozzarella cheese). This place is famous throughout Naples not only for their *Margherita* but also for their *Pizza Biancha* (dough and oil only) which is superb. Located in the Spanish Quarter, it's a little walk from the Centro Storico. If in Naples, you have to try this place.

16. LA CHIACCHIERATA, *Piazzetta M Serao 37, Tel. 081/411-465. Closed Sundays and August. American Express Cards accepted. Dinner for two L60,000.*

A small *trattoria* with only a few tables at the end of the Via Toledo near the Palazzo Reale. They use a lot of vegetables here, especially on their pizza on which they pile mozzarella and provolone. You can also get some *pasta e fagioli* (pasta and beans), some good *pesce arrosto* (grilled fish), and a some superb *capretto al forno* (kid goat on the grilled). The food here is great.

17. PIZZERIA DA PEPPINO, *Via Palepoli 6a/b, Tel. 081/764-9582. Closed Sundays. American Express card accepted. Dinner for two L80,000.*

In the Santa Lucia area near the Castel dell'Ovo this place is open late for you revelers. Here you not only can get great pizza, but a tasty seafood appetizer, superb *bruschetta* (garlic bread with oil and tomatoes), some *linguine alla putanesca* (whores pasta made with tomatoes, oil, garlic and tuna), and great grilled or fried fish. A fun place to come any time day or night.

18. EUROPEO, *Via Marchese Campodisola 4/8, Tel. 081/552-1323. Closed Sundays and two weeks in August. Only open for lunch on Friday and Saturday. American Express and Visa accepted. Dinner for two L80,000.*

This is a small local *trattoria* that is frequented by academics, since it's near the University, as well as manual laborers. Eating here gives you an insight into the people of Naples. They serve a tasty *ostriche e frutti di mare* (oysters and other sea food) appetizer. Then try their *Pizza Margherita* (simple pizza with fresh tomato sauce, oil and mozzarella cheese) or have them put some great sausage on the pizza as well. Or try their superb *spaghetti alla vongole verace* (with spicy clam sauce). For seconds they make a great *frittura di pesce* (fried fish dish).

19. PIZZERIA LOMBARDI, *Via Foria 12, Tel. 081/456-220. Closed Mondays. All credit cards accepted. Dinner for two L55,000.*

Located near the Museo Archeologico Nazionale, this place definitely has the best *Pizza Napoletana* anywhere. Covered in ricotta, mozzarella, vegetables, and almost everything imaginable, this is the tastiest pizza around. If this is a little complicated for you, look over their extensive list of other excellent pizza. You can order anything from the basic *Margherita* to a pizza with wurstel sausage, with local sausage and more. Also, the no smoking signs on the walls .... nobody adheres to them, so take note.

20. PIZZERIA LOMBARDI A SANTA CHIARA, *Via B Croce 59, Tel. 081/522-0780. Closed Sundays and three weeks in August. Credit cards accepted. Dinner for two L65,000.*

Located in the heart of the Centro Storico right next to the Santa Chiara church and their beautiful cloisters, this place makes great pizza of all kinds. For an appetizer try their *mozzarella di bufala* (buffalo mozzarella) *peperoni, melanzane* (eggplant), and *zucchine* plate. A perfectly situated place to stop for a bite to eat in the middle of a day of touring. The food is excellent and inexpensive.

21. MIMI ALLA FERROVIA, *Via A d'Aragona 21, Tel. 081/553-8525. Closed Sundays and a week in August. Credit cards accepted. Dinner for two L120,000.*

Choose either the terrace or inside in which to dine. At both you will be more than happy. Start with their appetizer of *mozzarella of bufala, peperoni* or *assagi di paste povere* (a tasty sampling of their pasta dishes). For pasta try their *linguine alla Mimi* (which comes with a great shrimp sauce), then move onto their *frutti di mare e pomodorini* (mixed seafood and small tomatoes). The *calamaretti fritti* (fried calamari) is also good.

22. LA TAVERNA DELL'ARTE, *Rampa S. Giovanni Maggiore 1a, Tel. 081/552-7558. Closed Sundays and August. No credit cards accepted. Dinner for two L80,000.*

A small local place situated in the center of the Centro Storico near the University. The service is excellent, either on the terrace or inside. Try the traditional appetizer of *pizze rustice* (literally country pizza, with a variety of toppings), *salumi artigianali* (literally craftsmen salami – great local salami), *mozzarrelle fresche* (fresh mozzarella) and *sformato di cipolle* (baked onions). This will definitely fill you up so move directly to a great main course of *maiale in agrodolce* (a sweet and sour pork dish).

23. IL TRIANON, *Via P Colletta 46, Tel. 081/553-9426. Closed Sundays and for lunch, New Years Eve and Christmas. No credit cards accepted. Dinner for two L50,000.*

Located in the Centro Storico, this is the best pizza in Naples, and that's saying a lot. Besides the many varieties of pizza that come out of their wood burning brick oven, you'll love the high ceilings, slate-yellow walls, tacky print motifs that they call decoration, and the long communal tables. Mainly frequented by University students this place has a fun filled crowd. Try their filling pizza/lasagna that is loaded with sauce, cheese and meat if a pizza sounds too boring to you, but do not miss this place when in Naples. Great food, local atmosphere.

24. RISTORANTE ZI TERESA, *Via Partenope 1, Tel. 081/764-2565. Closed Sunday nights and Saturdays as well as two weeks in August. Credit cards accepted. Dinner for two L130,000.*

Located across from the Castel dell'Ovo on the water, this is a famous and popular eating spot, and because of that it's rather expensive. It's also surrounded by some of the best hotels in the city, like the Excelsior and the Continental which doesn't help keep prices down. Their terrace is a perfectly romantic spot to have lunch or dinner, but remember to reserve well in advance. Start off with their *antipasto di mare* (seafood antipasto), then move on to their *spaghetti alla vongole* (with clam sauce), then if you're still hungry settle on any of their grilled fish.

SEEING THE SIGHTS

Naples has plenty to offer, from high culture like opera, museums, and centuries-old castles and palaces, to the simple pleasures of just strolling along the harbor. Use common sense, don't wander down lonely alleys, and Naples can be a fun town.

A. TEATRO SAN CARLO

Via San Carlo, Tel. 797–2331. Ticket office open Tuesday – Sunday 10am–1pm and 4:30pm–6pm.

This is the most distinguished opera in house in Italy after La Scala in Milan. Its neoclassic facade dates from its rebuilding in 1816. The season runs from October to June. Most tickets are always sold out, but you can check at the ticket office between 10:00am and 1:00pm and 4:30pm to 6:00pm Sunday through Tuesday during the season.

B. GALLERIA UMBERTO

Between Via San Carlo and Via Toledo. Open 24 hours.

Modeled after the Galleria Emanuelle in Milan, this glass ceilinged and arcaded shopping area is also laid out in a cross pattern. The blending of iron and glass gives it an almost futuristic appeal. A place to visit even if you're going to Milan, just to compare the two structures. And if you like to shop, this should be one of your stops.

C. PALAZZO REALE

Via Ferdinando Acton. Open 9am–noon and 3pm–5:30pm.

The former **Royal Palace** was begun in 1600 by Domenico Fontana and was restored between 1837 and 1841. You'll see statues of eight former kings who ruled Naples on the facade. This extensive palace contains a magnificent marble staircase built in 1651, 17 heavily decorated apartments, and the **Biblioteca Nazionale** that contains over 1,500,000 volumes as well as many ancient manuscripts and relics. You should come to the Royal Palace just to see the National Library, because it is like nothing you can find in North America.

D. CASTEL NUOVO

Via Ferdinando Acton. Open 9am–Noon and 3pm–5:30pm.

Behind the palace is the magnificent, five towered **Castel Nuovo**, also referred to as **Maschio Angionino**. This was once the residence of kings and viceroys who ruled the Kingdom of Naples. Built between 1279 and 1283, it pre-dated the Palazzo Reale and was constantly being upgraded. Surrounded by parkland, it seems as if it is an oasis in the sea of Neapolitan chaos. An imposing structure that adults and children alike love to explore. Other gardens you can explore are those located next to the Palazzo Reale near the water. A great place to get away for a few hours.

E. CHURCH OF SAN FRANCESCO DI PAOLO

Piazza del Plebiscito. Open 7am–noon and 4pm–5:30pm.

The **Church of San Francesco di Paolo** was built between 1818 and 1831, and is a fine imitation of the Pantheon in Rome.

F. CASTEL DEL'OVO

Borgo Marinaro, Open 9am–noon and 3pm–5:30pm.

If your kids like exploring castles, there is another one nearby the Castel Nuovo and the Palazzo Reale. The **Castel del'Ovo** is located off a causeway from the Via Partenope and sits on a small rocky islet. It was begun in the 12th century and completed in the 16th century. It was used as lighthouse and as the line of first defense of the harbor.

G. THE HARBOR

Always a bustle of activity, since Naples is one of Italy's biggest ports. You can get more information about the history of the location at the

Marine Station on Molo Angioino just past the heliport. From this heliport you can take regular helicopter service to Capri and Ischia as well as the Airport. This is the same location from which you would catch a ferry or hydrofoil over to these two islands.

H. HISTORIC NAPLES - CENTRO STORICO

Located just north of the harbor, this part of Naples is the most fun to walk, since it has winding streets that seem to lead nowhere but to another small local church. A fun place to explore in the day (be careful at night), especially along the old main street through the center.

The old main street is a combination of all the streets, from the Via Toledo, the Via Maddaloni, moving to the Via D. Capatelli, and ending at the **Piazza Nolana** with the Via Nolana. This old main street, as well as the small streets and alleys that are offshoots, is lined with shops of traditional artisans like the **Calace of Strumenti Musical** at Vico San Domenico Maggiore #9 in front of the church of the same name. Up the stairs to the first floor you'll find guitars and other instruments being crafted by hand.

Another unique shop is the **L'Ospedale delle Bambole** (**The Doll Hospital**), located on Via S Biagio dei Librai in the Centro Storico. This is the world famous shop where you'll find ancient dolls and puppets hanging everywhere or just lying around. Walk in and have a look around, the proprietor is very friendly.

Another can't-miss street in the Centro Storico is the **Via San Gregorio Aremeno**, which is commonly known as the Nativity scene streetsince they sell figurines for crèches year round.

Via Toledo

Formerly **Via Roma**, this street runs through the heart of the Centro Storico. Sometimes referred to in other guidebooks or on other maps as Via Roma, the natives refer to the street by both names. Officially it is Via Toledo, since it was built by and named after Don Pedro de Toledo.

Montecalvario

On the left of this street is the **Montecalvario** section that rises steeply to the **Via Vittorio Emanuelle**. Many of these 'streets' are actually steps. An interesting place to walk.

Church of Santa Anna del Lombardi

Piazza Mondayteoliveto, Open daily 7:15am–1pm.

This church, in the **Piazza Monteoliveto** just off the Piazza della Carita, is a great collection of Renaissance sculpture. The church was built in 1411 and later continued in the Renaissance style. Here you'll find the

Pieta, created in 1492 by Guido Mazzoni. You'll also find some wonderful terra cotta statues as well as a beautiful 16th century choir stall.

Church of Santa Chiara & Gesu Nuovo

Piazza del Gesu Nuovo. Santa Chiara open daily 8am–12:30pm and 4:30pm–7:30pm. Gesu Nuovo open daily 7:15am–1pm asnd 4pm–7:15pm.

Try to see these two churches. The Jesuit **Gesu Nuovo** was erected between 1585 and 1600 and still maintains its triangular grid-like facade. There are also some beautiful cloisters here. The place is full of roses and cats. It's a great place to relax among the Mediterranean-style tiles covered with bucolic scenes of Naples. There are benches on which to sit where you can enjoy the aroma of the roses and escape from the hectic pace of Naples, at least for a few minutes.

The **Santa Chiara** is one of the main monuments to medieval Naples. It was built in 1310 and was recreated in the Gothic style after being bombed during World War II. Inside you'll find many medieval tombs and sarcophagi that belong to the house of Anjou. And don't miss the Nun's choir that sits behind the High Altar, where secluded nuns could watch mass without being seen. This church has a wonderful courtyard that seems to always be empty. There are beautiful frescoes and a lazy palm leaning in the center. The church also has some great art work on its ceiling. They have thoughtfully placed slanted mirrors for you to see the ceiling without having to crane your neck.

Church of San Domenico Maggiore

Piazza San Domenico Maggiore. Open daily 8am–12:30pm and 4:30pm–7pm.

From the two churches above, go east down the Benedetto Croce to the next piazza on the left to the church of **San Domenico Maggiore**. Built around 1300, with a Gothic facade added in the 19th century, this is one of the most interesting churches in Naples. It has early Renaissance art as well as over 40 sarcophagi of the Anjou family. Here you'll find a combination of Gothic and Baroque architecture.

Capella di San Severo

Via F de Sanctis. Open Monday and Wednesday–Saturday 10am–5pm, Tuesday and Sunday 10am–1:30pm. Admission L6,000.

The **Chapel of San Severo** is a short distance east of the church of San Domenico Maggiore, hidden down the small side street of Via F de Sanctis. Built in 1590 as a burial chamber for the Sangro family, it was embellished with the Baroque style in the 18th century. Now a private museum, the chapel is filled with many fine statues including an eerie *Christ in a Winding Sheet* by Sammartino. You can also find two grisly corpses located downstairs. They are leftovers from the experiments of the Prince Raimondo.

Palazzo Corigliano
Piazza San Domenico Maggiore. Open daily 9am–7pm.

In the 4th floor library of the **Palazzo Corigliano** (currently a university building dating from the 18th century), located in the Piazza San Domenico Maggiore, you'll find a place to leisurely read a periodical or book and escape the pace of Naples. You can also see the remains of Greek walls in the basement.

Cloisters of San Gregorio Armeno
Between Via Tribunali and Via S. Baglio S. Librai. Hardly ever open. You need to go there and request entrance.

Often closed, you have to ask the nuns if you can enter. But if you gain access you'll adore the beauty of the flowering plants, the splashing fountain, and the comfortable benches. There's a place where you can enter the choir chamber which is all made of wood and peer through the wrought iron grating down onto the church itself. This was where the cloistered nuns celebrated mass, but themselves could not be seen.

Most often they'll only allow women in and usually only on special Sundays, but it doesn't hurt to try. Here you'll be able to see what the life of a cloistered nun is like.

Palazzo Cuomo
Via Duomo. Open 9am–2pm.

The beautiful Renaissance **Palazzo Cuomo**, built from 1464 to 1490, is located on the corner of the Via Duomo and the Via San Biago ai Librai. The building now houses the **Museo Filangieri** that contains arms and armor, as well as porcelain and pictures.

Duomo
Via Duomo. Open daily 8am–12:30pm amd 5–7pm.

Up the Via Duomo from the Palazzo Cuomo is the **Cathedral**. It is dedicated to San Gennaro, the patron saint of Naples. Built over the 4th century ruins of a paleo-Christian basilica, this church was erected between 1295 and 1324 in the French Gothic style. After an earthquake destroyed part of it in 1456 it was rebuilt, restored, and altered. It was further updated in the 19th century when part of the facade was replaced, but the church retains its original doors.

On the main altar you'll find a silver bust of **San Gennaro** that contains his skull. In the tabernacle are two vials of hardened blood from the saint. Believers say that this blood liquefies three times, as well as a few minutes, every morning. To find the saint's tomb, look under the high altar.

Gite Sotteranea – The Underground City

This is one cool sight. You can go on underground tours of two different **catacombs**, as well as **aqueducts, cisterns**, and **Roman** and **Greek cities** that lie below Naples. You'll be given candles to help guide you through the slim passages and damp darkness.

One trip starts from the Caffe Gambrinus (there are only a few accessible entrances to the underground city; another entrance is from the Piazza San Gaetano in the Centro Storico). You'll find aqueducts, caves, quarries, Greek markets, medieval houses, Greek tombs, catacombs. There are also special tours that start from the Chiesa di S. Lorenzo. You need to ask a priest to guide you through the courtyard and underground to the location where they are still excavating the jumbled layers of Greek, Roman, and medieval streets, houses, and markets. You have to do a little talking in Italian to get where you want to go but it's worth the trip.

Go to the tourist office in the Piazza del Gesu Nuovo for more complete times, locations, and information about touring the underground city.

I♦ NATIONAL MUSEUM

Piazza Cavour. Tel. 440-166. Open daily 9am–7pm. Open September–May, Monday–Saturday 9am–2pm, Sunday 9am–1pm. Admission L10,000.

On the northwestern outskirts of the Centro Storico just off of **Piazza Cavour** is the **National Museum**, which boasts one of the world's finest collections of antiquities. The building was originally erected as a barracks in 1586, then was the home of the University from 1616 to 1790. During this time the University began to house the art treasures of the kings of Naples, the Farnese collections from Rome, and material from Pompeii, Herculaneum, and Cumae. A great museum.

J♦ CAPODIMONTE

Park open daily 7:30am–8pm. In off-seasojn open 7:30am–5pm. Museum open Tuesday–Saturday 9am–2pm, Sunday 9am–1pm. Admission L10,000. Take bus 110 or 127 from the train station or 22 or 23 from Piazza del Plebiscito. If walking, take the Corso Amadeo di Savoia about two kilometers north up the hill from the National Museum to arrive at the park of Capodimonte and the Catacombs of San Gennaro.

The **Catacombs** are only open Saturday and Sunday mornings and like their Roman counterparts, these contain a maze of passageways and tomb chambers. But these are slightly better preserved and have much more artistic representation.

Just across the piazza Tondo di Capodimonte is the entrance to the park. This 297 acre park commands some wonderful panoramic views of Naples. It is a peaceful respite from the hectic pace of Naples. If you don't get to Vomero you must try and get here. Also located at the park is the **Capodimonte Museum** of arms, armor, porcelain, and pictures. In particular, there are some great works by **Titian**.

K. VOMERO & THE SURROUNDING HILLS

Certosa di San Martino, Museum Tel. 578-1769. Open Tuesday–Sunday 9am–2pm. Admission L8,000; Castel Sant'Elmo, Open Tuesday–Saturday 9am–2pm, and Sunday 9am–1pm.

If you want to get away from the smog and congestion of Naples just hop on one of the *funiculares* and enter a calm antidote in a residential district high above the city. The district was built from 1885 onwards. You can also get here by climbing the streets in the Montecalvario section.

The Villa Floridiana public park in the southern part of Vomero has a terrace with a wonderful view overlooking the **Bay of Naples**. You'll also find a small museum, **Duca di Martina Museum**, with paintings, porcelain, ivory, china, and pottery here.

Of great interest is the **Certosa di San Martino**, an old monastery erected in the 14th century and remodeled during the Renaissance and Baroque periods. You should take the time to the see the cloisters because they give you a glimpse into the monastic life of the times. Their museum contains some interesting nativity scenes (crèches).

Just north of the monastery is the **Castel Sant'Elmo** that was built in 1329 and added to between the 15th and 17th centuries. Come here for the view from the ramparts, as well a chance to explore the many passageways that were used for the defense of the harbor.

NAPOLI PORTA APERTE - OPEN DOOR NAPLES
Be aware that at infrequent times and in true Italian fashion, unannounced, the city opens of all the churches, monuments, and gardens for free. Ask at the tourist office or your concierge whether this rare event will occur during your stay.

NIGHTLIFE & ENTERTAINMENT

RIOT, *Located in an old building at Via S Biagio dei Librai 26 in the Centro Storico. Open from 9:00pm until 3:00am. No phone.*

To enter come through a wooden door, cross an open courtyard, climb a staircase, and on the right is the secret garden that is the club. It consists of a few rooms in an old building from the 18th century with tall French windows opening out onto a lush terrace of palm trees, pebble paths, and tables at which to sit and enjoy a drink or a smoke.

During the summer they have art exhibits and late night bands, mostly American blues and jazz. The waitresses here are all hip and have a definite attitude. Even so they will serve you drinks and sandwiches outside. Its a bit expensive but the crowd is fun and the atmosphere is like nothing you'll find in the States. I mean how many nightclubs do you know are in 18th century *palazzi*? It's like something out of an Anne Rice vampire novel. They are so hip they don't have a phone.

SPORTS & RECREATION
Golf
• **Circolo Golf Napoli**, *Via Campiglione 11, 80072 Arco Felice. Tel. 081/526-4296.* Located only 5 km from Naples, this is a 9 hole, par 35, course that is 2,601 meters long. It is open year round except Mondays and Tuesdays. They also have a driving range, pull carts, and a bar/restaurant. A good place to come if you're going through golf withdrawal.

SHOPPING
The main shopping streets with fancy shops are the **Corso Umberto**, **Via Toledo**, and **Via Chiaia**. Along these streets you'll find your international style, upscale, expensive stores.

For additional shopping suggestions, see Seeing the Sights: H. Historic Naples above.

English Language Bookstores
• **Feltrinelli,** *Via San T. d'Aquino 70. Open Monday through Friday 9:00am to 8:00pm, Saturday 9:00am to 1:00pm.* They have an extensive selection of English language travel guides as well as some paperback novels.
• **Universal Books,** *Rione Sirignano.* This store has books in many different languages and only a small selection of paperbacks in English.

PRACTICAL INFORMATION
Bank Hours & Changing Money
Banks are open Monday through Friday from 8:30am to 1:30pm and some do reopen from 2:30pm or so to 4:30pm or so. Most exchange money but strangely enough some do not in Naples. The **Stazione Centrale** has a *cambio* inside that is open from 8:00am to 1:30pm and 2:30pm to 8:00pm.

If you're looking for an **American Express** office you'll have to go all the way to **Sorrento** *(Tel. 081/807-3088)*.

Business Hours

From October to June, most shops are open from 9:00am to 1:00pm and from 3:30pm to 7:30pm, and are closed all day Sundays and on Monday morning. Then from June to September, when it really starts to get hot in Naples, the morning hours remain the same, but the mid-day siesta time is slightly extended to 4:00pm and sometimes 4:30pm, which then pushes closing time back to 7:30pm or 8:00pm. And also, in conjunction with being closed on Sunday and Monday mornings, shops are also closed half-days on Saturday.

Food stores, like *alimentari*, generally are open from 8:30am to 1:30pm (so stock up on your picnic supplies before you need them) and from 5:00pm to 7:30pm, and during the winter months they are closed on Thursdays.

Consulates

• **United States**, *Piazza della Repubblica, Naples, Tel. 081/583-8111*

Postal Services

You can buy stamps at local tobacconists (they are marked with a "T" outside) as well as post offices. Mail boxes are colored red. Post offices are open from 8:00am to 2:00pm on weekdays. The two exceptions to this rule are the **main post office** (**Palazzo delle Poste**) at Piazza Matteoti and the office at the Stazione Centrale, both of which are open Monday through Friday from 8:00am to 7:30pm, and Saturday from 8:00am to noon.

Tourist Information & Maps

The **EPT** has an extensive office at the Stazione Centrale, where you can get some pretty good maps, as well information on ferries, reservations for hotels, and pick up a copy of the necessary *Qui Napoli* publication that tells you what's going on around the city *(Tel. 081/268-779)*.

EXCURSIONS FROM NAPLES

Two must-see area excursions are **Pompeii** and **Herculaneum**, the Roman Empire-era cities that were engulfed in lava after Mt. Vesuvius erupted in 79 AD. They're only 15 minutes away from Naples (take the *Circumvesuviana* high speed train to get to Ercolano (Herculaneum) or Pompeii Scavi at the central station, one floor underground. Cost L5,000).

For detailed information about these world-renowned sites, see Chapter 12, *Rome,* the section on *Day Trips & Excursions.*

A beautiful side trip to the magical **Isle of Capri** is also an easy trip from Naples: Go to **Mole Beverello** in the harbor to catch the ferry or hydrofoil to the island (tourist cars are not allowed on the island so you'll have to leave it in Naples. Not a good idea.) Or go to the same spot and catch a helicopter ride. There are many different companies that offer services to Capri. There are plenty of signs indicating the departure times and costs for each company at the dock.

Again, for complete information including hotels, restaurants, and sights, see Chapter 12, *Rome,* the section on *Day Trips & Excursions.*

BARI

Bari is known in Italy as the 'gateway to the East' because as a port city it is heavily involved in trade with the Eastern Mediterranean. Bari also is the chief embarkation point for passenger ships to Greece and beyond, as it was an embarkation point centuries before for many of the Crusades.

Because of its location and port, Bari became the cornerstone of several ancient Empires and was a major stronghold of Byzantine power. The old city still has some remnants of the look and feel of many centuries ago and should be explored – during the day, not at night. Like Naples, this is a port city.

As the capital of **Apulia**, Bari also is the seat of an archbishop, a major university, and a naval college. Besides shipping, the city's other industries include shipbuilding, petrochemical refinement, and tourism. Bari also is the site of Italy's first atomic power station.

BARI'S SANTA CLAUS

Have you ever wanted to see Santa? In Italy he is the patron saint of seafarers, prisoners, and children. **Saint Nicholas of Bari** *is buried in the* **Church of San Nicola.** *Better known to us as Saint Nick or Santa Claus, here's your chance to finally see that portly, paramount, patriarchal provider of presents.*

Not far away from Bari are two other attractions: the **Castellana Grottoes**, limestone caves that are 48 km (30 miles) south, and the Apulian **Trulli** dwellings – rock houses built in a spiral design, thought to have been influenced by ancient Middle Eastern structures (in **Alberobello**, just a few miles farther south of Castellana). On your way to Bari, look out the car or train window for a sight of some of these Trulli dwellings. They look like something from another planet. Other regional sights you'll see on your way to Bari are fields upon fields of olive trees.

In all, Bari is a good place to place to stay and explore the region and its local flavor. It's also a perfect place to stop over on your way to points east.

Again, a word of warning: This is a port city like Genoa and Naples and as such you need to be aware of your surroundings. The crime that comes with a port city is doubled since this is the country's poorest region. Don't wear flashy jewelry, carry your handbag on the arm that is not towards the street, and always walk down streets that are populated.

The most important rule you can follow is do not go into the Old City after dark, ever. They don't call Bari *scippoladdri* (the land of petty thieves) for nothing.

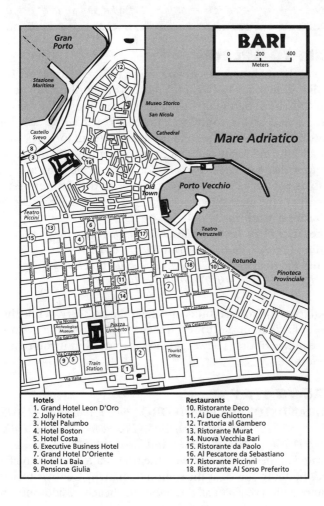

Hotels
1. Grand Hotel Leon D'Oro
2. Jolly Hotel
3. Hotel Palumbo
4. Hotel Boston
5. Hotel Costa
6. Executive Business Hotel
7. Grand Hotel D'Oriente
8. Hotel La Baia
9. Pensione Giulia

Restaurants
10. Ristorante Deco
11. Ai Due Ghiottoni
12. Trattoria al Gambero
13. Ristorante Murat
14. Nuova Vecchia Bari
15. Ristorante da Paolo
16. Al Pescatore da Sebastiano
17. Ristorante Piccinni
18. Ristorante Al Sorso Preferito

STOP OVER IN BARI

The city has a program by just that name (Stop Over In Bari), which is in place from June to September and assists all travelers under 30 who are not residents of the region in finding inexpensive lodging or camp sites. You can also get information about food stores, restaurants, laundromats, and more when you arrive in Bari. You can get all this information at the **Information Office** *in the train station at the* **Stazione Maritima** *or at their main office on Via Dante Aligheri 111 (Tel. 080/521-45-38). This program is designed to encourage travelers to stay a few extra nights in Bari and it seems to be working. During the summer, Bari has become a backpackers heaven and is a great place to find a party and a companion.*

FERRIES TO GREECE

One of the main reasons people come to Bari is use their **ferry** and **hydrofoil** system to get to Greece. Your Eurorail or Interrail pass do not give you a discount on the fares, but most ferry lines offer discounts for students as well as for round-trip tickets. You have to ask for these discounts since they don't automatically offer them to you.

For all information about prices and schedules, go to the Stazione **Maritima** *on Molo San Vito in the port* (not the Stazione Maritima for trains on the Corso Vittorio Veneto) and check with the different ferry lines. Below is a list of the main offices ferry lines. They also have a ticket window at the **Stazione Maritima.**
• **Marlines**, *Car Ferry Terminal Box 3-4, Tel. 080/521-76-99*
• **Poseidon**, *Corso de Tullio 40, Tel. 080/521-0022*
• **Ventours Ferries**, *Corso de Tullio 16, Tel. 080/521-05-56*
• **Yasco**, *Corso de Tullio 40, Tel. 080/521-0022*

Taking the hydrofoil is much quicker than the ferry. While the ferries take most of a 24 hour day to reach their destinations, the hydrofoils get you there in five hours. They cost twice as much, but if you're in a hurry they're perfect.

WHERE TO STAY

1. GRAND HOTEL LEON D'ORO, *Piazza Aldo Moro 4, 70122 Bari. Tel. 080/523-5040. Fax 080/521-1555. 110 rooms all with bath. Single L120,000; Double L200,000. Credit cards accepted.* ****

Located in the same piazza with the train station, this is the first time I'll say it's better to stay near the station than in the Centro Storico. From here you're within reach of all the sights, the beach, restaurants and bars, and it's safe to walk around at night. The rooms are clean and comfortable with TV and air conditioning. The hotel has an acceptable restaurant and a relaxing bar.

2. JOLLY HOTEL, *Via G. Petroni 15, 70122 Bari. Tel. 080/536-4366. Fax 080/536-5219. 164 rooms all with shower. Single L 110,000-210,000; Double L150,000-275,000. Credit cards accepted.* ****

Jolly hotels seem to be everywhere in Italy. The Jollys are not up to the standards of a Western hotel chain but they are clean, comfortable and the help sincerely tries. The rooms come with air conditioning, satellite TV and room service but are tiny in the Jolly mode. The chain caters mainly to Italians who are shorter in stature and don't see to need as much room as we do. The hotel restaurant is good enough to eat one meal there. The Manager Gabriele Delli Passeri really makes an effort to ensure your stay is pleasant.

3. HOTEL PALUMBO, *Via Vittorio Veneto 31-33, 70057 Bari. Tel. 080/ 552-0222. Fax the same. 15 rooms all with bath. Single L90,000; Double L120,000-170,000. Credit cards accepted.* ****

I just love smaller four star hotels. They make your stay so much more intimate. Located outside of town in a truly romantic old building, this hotel has its own private beach. They also have shuttle service to pick you up and drop you off if necessary, in part because they do not have an in-house restaurant. The rooms are beautifully furnished and very clean and comfortable.

4. HOTEL BOSTON, *Via Piccinni 155, 70122 Bari. Tel. 080/521-6633. Fax 080/524-6802. 70 rooms, 20 with bath, 50 with shower. Single L100,000-140,000; Double L150,000-210,000. Breakfast included. Credit cards accepted.* ***

Located just on the edge of the Old City, this is as close as you want to get to the Old City at night. Since the hotel is located near the Municipio (Town Hall), you're safe here. This is a three star hotel with four star prices and about three and a half star amenities. The rooms are relatively tiny but are spotless, as are the bathrooms. There is air conditioning, satellite TV, room service, laundry service, and a welcoming bar downstairs.

5. HOTEL COSTA, *Via Crisanzio 12, 70122 Bari. Tel. 080/521-9015. Fax 080/521-0006. 23 room, only 18 with bath. Single without bath L50,000-60,000; Single with bath L60,000-70,000; Double without bath L70,000-85,000; Double with bath L97,000-110,000. Credit cards accepted.* ***

Located two streets up and two streets over from the station, this is an inexpensive hotel option in Bari. All the amenities of a three star in a small city like direct dial phones, TV, room service, laundry service, but no air conditioning. The rooms are somewhat small but kept clean. A good place to stay for the budget traveler.

6. EXECUTIVE BUSINESS HOTEL, *Corso Vittorio Emanuelle 201, 70122 Bari. Tel. 080/521-6810. Fax 080/524-5178. 21 rooms all with shower. Single L80,000; Double L120,000. Breakfast L5,000 extra. Credit cards accepted.* ***

Located in a renovated older building near the Municipio (Town Hall), this is, as the name suggests, a businessman's hotel. The rooms are immaculate but small as are the bathrooms, and the amenities are simple but good. There are direct dial phones, air conditioning, TV, room service, and a downstairs bar. For the price it is a good place to stay.

7. GRAND HOTEL D'ORIENTE, *Via Cavour 32, 70121 Bari. Tel. 080524-4011. Fax 080/524-3914. 120 rooms, 60 with bath, 60 with shower. Single L130,000-150,000; Double L200,000-250,000; Suite L180,000-285,000. Credit cards accepted.* ***

On the upscale Via Cavour near the beach, here you can have all the amenities of a four star hotel, in a three star hotel – with four star prices. Does that makes sense to you? The only reason they're a three star is that their rooms have showers, a minus mark in the ratings game. Located in a renovated historical building, the rooms here are impeccably clean and perfectly comfortable, and staff bends over backwards to make you feel comfortable.

8. HOTEL LA BAIA, *Via Vittorio Veneto 29a, 70057 Bari. Tel. 080/552-0288. Fax the same. 56 rooms all with bath. Single L 79,000; Double L105,000-132,000. Full board L20,000. Credit cards accepted.* ***

Located outside of town in a tranquil setting, this quaint little hotel even has its own private beach. They also have a shuttle bus to ferry you back and forth into town. All the amenities you could want including TV, air conditioning, rooms service, and laundry service as well as a beautifully panoramic view. If you don't want to stay in town, try either this place or the Hotel Palumbo almost next door.

9. PENSIONE GIULIA, *Via Crisanzio 12, 70122 Bari. Tel. 080/521-6630. Fax 080/521-8271. 14 rooms only 10 with shower. Single without bath L45,000; Single with bath L65,000; Double without bath L70,000; Double with bath L80,000. Breakfast included. Credit cards accepted.* **

This is definitely the best budget traveler's alternative in Bari, with its location a few blocks up and over from the train station. It's in a safe and quiet neighborhood and the prices are good. You don't have air conditioning and need to make reservations for the rooms with bath, but this is good place to stay. The rooms are clean if a little worn, and they're comfortable. There is a little sitting room and bar area.

WHERE TO EAT

10. RISTORANTE DECO, *Largo Adua 5, Tel. 080/524-6070. Closed Mondays and August. Credit cards accepted. Dinner for two L120,000.*

A good restaurant inside an interesting structure that makes some great *cucina nuova* dishes made mainly with the ingredients that are found locally, such as leafy greens, other vegetables, fresh pasta, local cheeses and meats in large quantities. Creatively rustic servings that change all the time.

11. AI DUE GHIOTTONI, *Via Putignani 11, Tel. 080/523-2240. Closed Sundays and two weeks in August. All credit cards accepted. Dinner for two L120,000.*

What a perfect name, *The Two Gluttons*, for the restaurant that is the symbol of the city for the Barese (i.e., the people of Bari). Here you had better come ready to eat since their portions are large. Heck, you wouldn't even be able to finish your antipasto if it was your main meal. They make excellent pasta dishes, as well as a variety of fish plates. When in Bari, eat at least one meal here.

12. TRATTORIA AL GAMBERO, *Corso a de Tullio 8, Tel. 080/521-6018. Closed Sundays, Christmas and August. No Credit cards accepted. Meal for two L90,000.*

Located deep in the heart of the old city, I recommend you eat lunch here, not dinner, but eat here you must. Their terrace has a wonderful view of the port area and they make superb *spaghetti alla cozze* (with mussels), *alla vongole verace* (with a spicy clam sauce) and *al frutti di mare* (with a variety of sea food). They always have a fire burning outside where they cook the specialty of the region, grilled fish. In the winter they still cook outside, but mainly meats like *vitello* (veal).

13. RISTORANTE MURAT, *Via Lombardy 13, Tel. 080/521-6551. Closed Sundays and August. All credit cards accepted. Dinner for two L120,000.*

One of the finer restaurants in Bari. This place is refined and elegant both on the terrace and inside. They have a great gourmet menu with wine included for L60,000 per person that includes native dishes and some simple *cucina nuova* creations. Try some of their *minestra di verdure* (vegetable soup), *stracceti di pasta alla cozze* (pasta with mussels), *filetto di spigola gratinato con mozzarella* (sea bass au gratin with mozzarella).

14. NUOVA VECCHIA BARI, *Via Dante Alighieri 47, Tel. 080/521-6496. Closed Tuesdays and three weeks in August. Credit cards accepted. Dinner for two L90,000.*

A rustic location in the new city, this place is famous for its ancient local cuisine creations. All the specials are made in the tradition of regional Apulian cooking. Try some great game dishes and their fresh home-made pasta with a spicy tomato-based sauces, as well as an excellent vegetable soup.

15. RISTORANTE DA PAOLO, *Via Q Selia 13a, Tel. 080/521-1662. Closed Mondays and the last two weeks of August. Credit cards accepted. Dinner for two L80,000.*

Located in the center of new Bari, this restaurant, owned by Paolo Anaclero, makes excellent food despite the thoroughly modern decorations. And at great prices. Try some of his famous *spigola al sale* (sea bass with salt) and the scrumptious *misto di pesce arrosto* (mixed roasted fish).

16. AL PESCATORE DA SEBASTIANO, *Via Frederico II di Svevia 6, Tel. 080/523-7039. Closed Mondays. All credit cards accepted. Meal for two L120,000.*

Located in the old town right by the castle, this is a place to come for lunch, not dinner. A good restaurant that cooks mainly fish and seafood over an open fire, but they also specialize in some great home-made pasta dishes. The best place to sit in the summer is outside on their terrace where you can gaze at the majestic Castle across the piazza.

17. RISTORANTE PICCINNI, *Via Piccinni 28, Tel. 080/521-1227. Closed Sundays and August. All credit cards accepted. Dinner for two L140,000.*

The ambiance here is refined, elegant, and discreet, especially in their inside garden seating area. One of the higher-end restaurants in Bari. Here you'll find many of the magistrates from the town hall just down the road. The menu consists of a variety of local, national, creative and international dishes. Sample dishes include *filetto di Angus al pepe verde* (filet of Scottish Angus beef with pepper), *spaghetti con fiori di zucchine* (with zucchini flowers), and *pappardelle con radicchio e gamberi* (wide strips of pasta with radish and shrimp). There's something for everyone here, but you'll pay the price.

18. RISTORANTE AL SORSO PREFERITO, *Via de Nicolo 46, Tel. 080/523-5747. Closed Sundays and 15 days in August. Credit cards accepted. Dinner for two L100,000.*

Located near the Porto Vecchio, this is a well respected and frequented local place that serves both local and national dishes. They feature a wide variety of pasta dishes as well as a great bi*stecca alla fiorentina alla brace* (steak cooked over an open flame), and my favorite *agnello al forno* (lamb cooked over a fire pit). The prices are a little high but the food is superb.

SEEING THE SIGHTS

Bari is an easy town to walk around and enjoy the town's castles, churches, and harborfront area. In Bari there is a new town and an old town. Most of the interesting sights are located in the **old town** and around the **Porto Vecchio (Old Port)**.

NEW TOWN

The main feature of the new town is the palm-shaded **Piazza Umberto I**, located two blocks in front of the train station. Another sight to see in the new town is the **Teatro Piccinni**, which is located in the **Town Hall** (**Municipio**) in the **Piazza della Liberta** and on the Via Vittorio Emanuelle I (*Corso Vittorio Emanuele. Tel. 521-3717. Concert season is in the spring; the rest of the year the theater is closed*). This is the city's busiest streets and it conveniently divides the new town from the old town. Another theater to see is the **Teatro Petruzzelli**, which was almost completed destroyed by insurance-related arson, located on the Corso Cavour (*Concert season is in the spring; the rest of the year the theater is closed*).

Behind the theater is the **Lungomare Nazario**, a beautiful seafront promenade that runs past the old harbor. If you go in the other direction you'll find the **Pinoteca Provinciale** in its gray and white towered building, about a kilometer down the promenade. This is the home of the provincial picture gallery with works by Tintoretto, Bellini, Vivarini, and Veronese (*Lungomare Nazario Saura. Tel. 392-421. Open Tuesday–Saturday, 9am–1pm and 4pm–7pm. Sunday 9am–1pm.*)

LEVANT FAIR

Fair takes place in the fairground by the municipial stadium, off of Lungomare Starita.

This is the annual fair that runs for 10 days in mid-September, located about 2.5 kilometers from the center of town. This is the largest fair in southern Italy and goods from all over the world are exhibited and sold here. A festive atmosphere. Don't miss it if you're in Bari while it's being held.

OLD TOWN

Around the old city is a peaceful seaside promenade. Strolling here is the perfect way to get a feel for Bari as it used to be. To the left of the old city is the **Gran Porto** (**Grand Harbor**), where the big liners and ferries dock. To the right of the old city is the **Porto Vecchio** (**Old Port**) that evokes a feel of sailors past.

CATHEDRAL

Piazza Duomo. Open daily 8am–noon and 4pm–7pm.

This 12th century church with a Romanesque facade and Baroque influences resides in the center of the old city. You can find in the crypt an ornate painting of the Virgin from Constinantinople, and the church's archives contain many large scripture rolls from the 11th century. Also notice the Romanesque architecture characteristic of the choir and chapel protruding ever so perfectly from the Nave.

CHURCH OF SAN NICOLA

Via Palazzo Citta. Open daily 8am–noon and 4pm–7pm.

This is a large church built over an ancient Byzantine castle that once occupied the site. The funding came from Crusaders and pilgrims money in 1087, but it sat incomplete until the late 13th century. Besides being one of the finest achievements of Romanesque architecture in the region, the church contains the remains of **Saint Nicholas of Bari**. This patron saint of seamen, prisoners, and children,better known to us as **Saint Nick** or **Santa Claus** (ignore those northern European claims to Sinter Klaas, Father Christmas, and all their other Santa Claus allegations – this is the real deal, or so my Bari sources tell me!)

So if you or the kids really want to see Santa, bring them to San Nicola here in Bari.

CASTELLO SVEVO

Piazza Federico II di Svevia. Museum open daily 9am–1:30pm and 3:30pm–7pm. Admission L5,000.

The **Castle** is located on the outskirts of the old town, almost directly in front of the Cathedral. Begun by Frederick II in 1233 and converted into a palace by Bona Sforza, the wife of Sigismund II of Poland and the last duchess of Bari in the 16th century (her remains are located in San Nicola). It was later used as a prison and a light house/signal station. Recently a **Roman city** was discovered on the site. There is also a small **museum** containing copies of Apulo-Norman sculpture.

PRACTICAL INFORMATION

Bank Hours & Changing Money

Banks are open Monday through Friday from 8:30am to 1:30pm and some do reopen from 2:30pm or so to 4:30pm or so. The **Stazione Centrale** has a *cambio* inside that is open from 8:00am to 1:30pm and 2:30pm to 8:00pm Monday through Saturday.

The **American Express** office *is on Corso de Tullio in the offices of Morfimare at #40, Tel. 080/521-0022 near the Stazione Maritima.*

Business Hours

From October to June, most shops are open from 9:00am to 1:00pm and from 3:30pm to 7:30pm, and are closed all day Sundays and on Monday morning. Then from June to September, when it really starts to get hot in Southern Italy, the morning hours remain the same, but the mid-day siesta time is slightly extended to 4:00pm and sometimes 4:30pm, which then pushes closing time back to 7:30pm or 8:00pm.

In conjunction with being closed on Sunday and Monday mornings, shops are also close half-days on Saturday. Food stores, like *alimentari* generally are open from 8:30am to 1:30pm (so stock up on food if you're taking a picnic) and from 5:00pm to 7:30pm, and during the winter months they are closed on Thursdays.

English Language Bookstores
- **Feltrinelli**, *Via Dante Aligheri 91. Open Monday through Friday 9:00am to 8:00pm, Saturday 9:00am to 1:00pm.* They have an extensive selection of English language travel guides as well as some paperback novels. Located a half block away from Stop Over in Bari's main office.

Postal Services
You can buy stamps at local tobacconists (they are marked with a "T" outside) as well as post offices. Mail boxes are colored red. Post offices are open from 8:00am to 2:00pm on weekdays. The one exception to this rule is the **main post office (Palazzo delle Poste)** located behind the university at **Piazza Batista** *(Tel. 080/521-0381)* which is open Monday through Friday from 8:00am to 7:30pm, and Saturday from 8:00am to noon.

Tourist Information & Maps
- **Stop Over in Bari,** *Via Dante Aligheri 111, Tel. 080521-4538. Open Monday through Saturday 9:00am - 8:00pm and Sunday 10:00am to 5:00pm.* They also have offices in the Stazione Centrale as well as the Stazione Maritima. They can supply you with all the information you need to know.
- **EPT**, *Piazza Aldo Moro 33A, Tel. 080/524-2244.* Located just to the right as you leave the station. In perfect Italian disorganization, the government is sponsoring two different agencies to give out virtually the same information. If you don't get everything you need from **Stop Over in Bari**, try here.

BARLETTA
Barletta is small compact town and is one of the principal ports in the region. It has a few sights of interest and can be easily walked. If you're up for swimming in the Adriatic Sea, here's your opportunity.

ARRIVALS & DEPARTURES
Barletta is 40 minutes from Bari by train (L5,000) or 50 minutes by car, taking the **coastal highway 16**.

WHERE TO STAY

1. HOTEL ARTU, *Piazza Castello 67, 70051 Barletta. Tel. 0883/332-121. Fax 0883/332-214. 32 rooms, 8 with bath, 24 with shower. Single L120,000; Double L190,000. Breakfast included. Credit cards accepted.* ****
Located right in the center of all the sights that Barletta has to offer, you are also close to the beach at this hotel. This is a renovated old building that is perfect for a romantic weekend. All the amenities are here, including a restaurant that features local and international cuisine as well as great pizzas, and a piano bar for nightly entertainment. The rooms are super clean and very comfortable.

2. HOTEL LA TERRAZZA, *Litoranea di Levante, 70051 Barletta. Tel. 0883/535-662. Fax 0883/535-662. 12 rooms, all with shower. Single L65,000; Double L90,000. Credit cards accepted.* ***
Located outside of town along the sea, this is an inexpensive alternative to the other hotels in the area, and there are not that many. This place has somewhat tiny rooms, but they and the bathrooms are spotless. Amazing for a seaside hotel and restaurant. And what a restaurant it is. Great local food and perfectly made pizzas. They also have a discotheque and piano bar attached to the hotel. Not really a place to come and relax at night. One main drawback is they have no air conditioning.

WHERE TO EAT

3. ANTICA CUCINA, *Via Milano 73, Tel. 0883/521-718. Closed Sunday nights and Mondays as well as the last week in January and the month of July. Dinner for two L140,000. Credit cards accepted.*
This place has sort of a rustic sophisticated charm with its antiques hanging on the wall and tables laid out for an elegant dinner. Open for a little over ten years, this is one of Apulia's best restaurants. Their cooking is an expression of the region with the traditional dishes they make and the local ingredients they use. If you like anchovies try their *alici marinate in olio e aceto* (anchovies marinated in oil and vinegar) or the *melanzane arrosto con polpa di granchio e merluzzo* (roasted eggplant covered with crab meat and pulped cod meat). Their *spaghetti con fiori di zucchine al profumo di aglio* (with zucchine flowers and garlic) is also good, as is the *Frittura alla Barlettana* (local fried seafood: calamari, octopus, mullet, and whatever else is caught that day).

4. RISTORANTE BACCO, *Via Sipontina 10, Tel. 0883/571-000. Closed Sunday nights and Mondays, as well as August. Dinner for two L160,000. Credit cards accepted.*
Another great restaurant in the city, as well as the region. The owner, Franco Ricatti, recently opened a second Bacco in Rome, so business must be good. The atmosphere is always friendly and the menu includes two

different gastronomic options, so you can sample a wide variety of food at a lower cost. They make traditional dishes ass well as creative ones. Their *zuppetta di fagioli e cozze* (soup of beans and muscles) is particularly good as is the *fusilli al ragu di scorfano* (twisted pasta with a ragu sauce of scorpion fish).

   5. IL BRIGANTINO, *Litoranea di Levante, Tel. 0883/533-345. Dinner for two L100,000. Credit cards accepted.*

   Located outside of town on the sea this place never closes, ever. It's open every day and year round. This is an institution in Barletta, which is why the place is always crowded. The view of the Adriatic from the terrace is a perfectly romantic spot. The food is all of the local, traditional flavor. A good place to come for an evening's repast. During lunch they offer a "work menu" (*colazione di lavoro*) for L35,000 that includes soup, pasta, and fish.

SEEING THE SIGHTS

   From the train station, walk straight ahead down the Viale Giannone to the second street on the right, Corso Garibaldi. Take a right and walk a couple hundred meters to the **Church of San Sepolcro** on the left hand side (*Corso Vittorio Emanuele. Open summer Monday–Saturday 10am–Noon and 6:30pm–8:30pm. Open winter 10am–noon and 5:30pm–8pm*). This is a 12th century Gothic church whose facade is a little worse for wear. You'll know it is the right church by the five meter tall **Colosso** next to the church towers. This is a 4th century bronze statue which represents a Byzantine emperor holding the cross and globe, the symbols of his two realms of power. Inside the church the only ornate item left is the large baptismal font.

Go back to the Corso Garibaldi and follow it to the **Duomo** *(Piazza Duomo. Open 7am–noon and 4pm–7pm daily)*. As you walk, the street name changes to the Via Duomo and curves to the right. Also known as the church of **Santa Maria Maggiore**, this is part Romanesque and part Gothic. The west end and *campanile*, built between 1147 and 1193, are Romanesque; the nave and choir inside, built in the 14th century, are Gothic. Some items to admire are the fine pulpit and tabernacle built in the 13th century.

From the Piazza del Duomo you can see the enormous **castle** *(Via del Duomo. Tel. 31114. Open October–April, Tuesday–Sunday 9:30am–1pm and 4–6:30pm)*. This was first a Saracen and Moor outpost, then it was enlarged by the Hohenstaufens (Normans) in the 13th century, and finally the four bastions were added in 1537 by Carl V. The castle is now home to a **museum** and **picture gallery**.

After you've explored the twisting streets of this beautiful medieval town take a walk east of the harbor and go to their **public bathing beach** for a dip in the Adriatic.

If you have a car, take the time to drive 30 km south down **route #170** to **Castel del Monte** *(Route 170. Open Tuesday–Sunday 10am–12:30pm and 4pm–7pm)*. This is the most amazing Norman castle in Italy. It was built circa 1241 to be a hunting lodge for Frederick II. This early Gothic structure is a perfect octagon, ringed by eight towers with eight rooms of the same size on each floor. The rooms on the upper floor, with their particularly fine windows, are believed to have been Frederick II's apartments. The structure was also the final prison for Frederick II's grandsons.

TRANI

Known for its scenic old city and peaceful gardens at the **Villa Communale**, this is a seaport city seemingly trapped in time. You'll just adore the quaint little harbor with the old city surrounding it. But as in all port cities, no matter how small, especially if they are in the South of Italy, always be aware of your surroundings.

ARRIVALS & DEPARTURES

Trani is between Barletta and Bari. You can take a train from Bari and get here in 30 minutes, or a train from Barletta and get here in 10 minutes. Also if you drive on **highway 16** along the coast between Barletta and Bari, you'll pass through Trani.

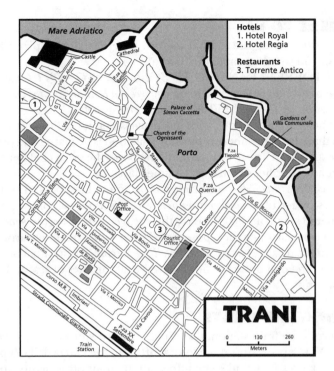

Hotels
1. Hotel Royal
2. Hotel Regia

Restaurants
3. Torrente Antico

TRANI

WHERE TO STAY

1. HOTEL ROYAL, *Via de Robertis 29, 70059 Trani. Tel. 0883/588-777. Fax 0883/582-224. 46 rooms all with shower. Single L 109,000; Double L179,000. Breakfast included. Credit cards accepted.* ****

Situated a short distance outside of the town center, the Royal offers the luxuries of four star living including a wonderful little restaurant that serves regional, Italian, and international dishes. If you're looking for peace, quiet and comfort stay here.

2. HOTEL REGIA, *Piazza Archivia 2, 70059 Trani. Tel. 0883/584-527. Fax 0883/586-568. 9 rooms all with shower. Breakfast L5,000 extra. Credit cards accepted.* ***

Located near the beach and the center of town this is a perfectly located hotel in the middle of everything. The rooms are immaculate and comfortable, even if the bathrooms are a little small. The building has beautiful high ceilings and looks as if it has been around forever. They have an excellent pizzeria/restaurant and piano bar if you don't want to venture out at night.

WHERE TO EAT

Besides trying the food at the two hotel restaurant/pizzerias listed above, you should sample the food at:

3. TORRENTE ANTICO, *Via E Fusco, Tel. 0883/47911. Closed Sunday Nights and Mondays, as well as the second week in January and the last two weeks of July. Dinner for two L160,000. Credit cards accepted.*

The only thing wrong with this place is that it is a little pricey. Other than that, the atmosphere is pleasant, the food is prepared and presented perfectly, and it's taste is superb. All thanks to the great chef here, Savino Pasquadibisceglie (say that three times fast).

Try their *filetto di spigola con zucchine* (filet of sea bass with zucchini) or the wonderful *salmone gratinato con erba cipollina* (salmon au gratin with herbs and small onions). Also try their *spaghetti alla vongole verace* (with a spicy clam sauce) or their *pennette alla marinara* (small macaroni with a tomato meat sauce) or their *tagliatelli ai porcini* (pasta with a mushroom sauce sautéed in butter). They also serve all varieties of seafood and fish for seconds.

SEEING THE SIGHTS

From the train station, take Via Cavour (if you want to, as you walk down Via Cavour, stop at the **tourist office** in the Piazza della Repubblica and pick up a map and some information about other sights) for about half a mile to the **Piazza Plebiscito** and the **Villa Communale gardens**. Here you can enjoy a relaxing picnic, a scenic view out over the Adriatic, or a panoramic sight of the old city and its cathedral across the harbor.

To get to the cathedral, walk around the harbor. You'll pass the **church of the Ognissanti** (*Via Ognissanti. Open 8am–noon and 4pm–7pm*) with its deep porch and beautiful Romanesque carvings above the door. Keep going around the harbor and take a left into the **Piazza Trieste**. In this piazza is the **Palace of Simone Caccetta** built in the 15th century (*Open 9am–1pm and 4pm–7pm.*)

Go through this piazza and into an open area facing the sea. The **cathedral** sits in this area almost on the water's edge (*Piazza Duomo. Open 9am–1pm and 4pm–7pm*). Built between 1150 and 1250, this church and bell tower dominate this small town. You'll find beautiful bronze doors made in 1160 and a stone doorway carved in the 13th century. The interior is magnificent with its double columns, the only example of such a construction in Apulia. You'll find the **Crypt of St. Nicholas the Pilgrim** (died 1094) under the transept and the **Crypt of St. Leucius** (died 670) under the nave.

One last sight to see is the **castle** to the west of the cathedral. Built between 1233 and 1249 by Frederick II, it is no longer open to the public since it is now a prison.

LECCE

Situated halfway along the **Salentine peninsula** (the heel of the Italian boot), **Lecce** is the capital of its province and is one of the most interesting towns in Southern Italy. Virtually untouristed, Lecce boasts an array of 17th century Baroque architecture.

The palaces, buildings, churches, and arches are covered with intricate swirls and designs that characterize *barocco leccese*. Even though many different conquerors swept through this area – Greeks, Cretans, Romans, Saracens, Moors, Swabians, and more – as you'll see from the architecture the main influence was the **Spanish Hapsburgs** during the 16th and 17th centuries. It's almost as if everything else was discarded outright and the Spanish remade this town and others in their own image. Some people call the city the *Athens of Apulia* because of its beauty.

Besides viewing Lecce's architecture, the city is the perfect jumping off point to explore the Salentine peninsula, where the countryside is dotted with medieval fortresses and castles. You'll also see countless olive tree groves and hill towns. Exploring the base of Italy's heel is like going back in time, but it is an adventure not to be undertaken except by the most experienced travelers. I would recommend Lecce and this area only to those who know Italy, Italians, and have at least a decent command of the language.

ARRIVALS & DEPARTURES

Located about 100 kilometers from Bari, there are three trains a day that go between the two cities. The trip takes about an hour and a half to two hours depending on the number of stops the train makes.

To get into town from the train station, you can either walk for 10-15 minutes sraight out of the station down the Viale Oronzo Quarta into the Centro Storico, or you can take bus #1, 2, 3, or 15 from the station. You need to buy a ticket at the newsstand in the station first. The cost is L700 one way.

WHERE TO STAY

1. GRAND HOTEL TIZIANO E DEI CONGRESSI, *Superstrada Brindisi-Lecce, 73100 Lecce. Tel. 0832/4718. Fax the same. 184 rooms 60 with bath, 134 with shower. Single L124,000-127,000; Double L190,000-225,000. Credit cards accepted.* ****

Located a little way outside of town near the Autostrada here you have all the amenities you could want when traveling through the south. There's an indoor pool, a gymnasium, sauna, a good restaurant, a piano bar and more. The hotel and rooms are modern but appear in need of slight upkeep – but that's just Southern Italy taking its toll. The bathrooms are clean and there is air conditioning, which is needed in the deadly summers down here.

2. GRAND HOTEL, *Viale O. Quarta 28, 73100 Lecce. Tel. 0832/309-405. Fax 0832/309-891. 71 rooms, 7 with bath, only 50 with shower. Single without L46,000; Single with L63,000; Double without 72,000; Double with L110,000. Credit cards accepted.* ***

Not many amenities in this place except for air conditioning, clean rooms, and an acceptable restaurant. At least it's convenient to both the train station and sights in town. Make sure you ask for a room with a bath or shower, otherwise you could get stuck using one in the hall.

3. HOTEL CAPPELLO, *Via Montegrappa 4, 73100 Lecce, Tel. 0832/308-881. Fax 0832/301-535. 32 rooms all with shower. Single L 45,000-50,000; Double L75,000-80,000. Credit cards accepted.* **

Clean rooms, immaculate bathrooms, air conditioning, and a shower in every room. This place is bucking for three star status but they won't get it. The rooms aren't big enough, nor are the bathrooms. But if you want comfort (in small spaces) near the train station and access to the sights at a good price, stay here.

WHERE TO EAT

4. BARBABLU, *Via Umberto I #7, Tel. 0832/241183. Closed Mondays, the last week in June, and the first week in September. Credit cards accepted. Dinner for two L100,000.*

Located in an old building in the Centro Storico, this place has great atmosphere both inside and outside on the terrace and serves wonderful food. The antipasto table is overflowing with goodies like eggplant, peperoni, local sausage, zucchini, cheeses, and more. For your first course, try the *spaghetti alla vongole verace* (with a spicy clam sauce), it's excellent in these parts. For seconds, they make great fish or meat dishes, so try either. I like the *Saltimbocca alla leccese* (ham shank cooked in tomatoes and spices). It's better than the Roman version. The ingredients are fresher.

5. TAVERNA DI CARLO V, *Via G Palmieri 46, Tel. 0832/248-818. Closed Sunday nights and Mondays. In the summer also closed Saturdays. In Winter Saturday for lunch. Closed all of August. Visa accepted. Dinner for two L70,000.*

A classic atmosphere of an old tavern, this place is located on the bottom floor of a building that dates to 500 AD and is located in the Centro Storico of Lecce. You can also sit outside on the terrace and watch Lecce go by as you eat. They make many traditional Lecce dishes here, including *zuppa di farro con ceci o fagioli* (soup made with flour and chickpeas or beans), *zuppa di lenticchie* (lentil soup) and a thick and tasty *stufato di verdure fresche* (fresh vegetable stew). For seconds try some local favorites like the *pezzetti di cavallo alla griglia* (small pieces of grilled horse meat) or *involtini di trippa con patate* (rolled tripe with potatoes). They also have a plentiful supply of fish dishes.

6. RISTORANTE VIA MONTI, *Via Monti 13, Tel. 0832/390-174. Closed Wednesdays and the last three weeks of August. Credit cards accepted. Dinner for two L120,000.*

On the outskirts of town, take a cab to and from this restaurant. It is an elegant dining experience, so come appropriately dressed. My favorites are the *linguine ai frutti di mare* (linguine with mounds of seafood) and the *involtini di vitello alla crema di parmigiano* (rolled veal covered with a creamy parmigian sauce). They have plenty of other meat and fish dishes.

SEEING THE SIGHTS

The old town of Lecce is a maze of small winding streets which are a joy to wander. Start in the center of town at the **Piazza San Oronzo** where the information office is. In the center of the piazza is a the **Colonna di San Oronzo**, with a statue of the saint on top, which once stood, saintless, in Brindisi to mark the end of the Appian Way. Also in the piazza is a partially excavated **Anfiteatro Romano** that dates from the 2nd century.

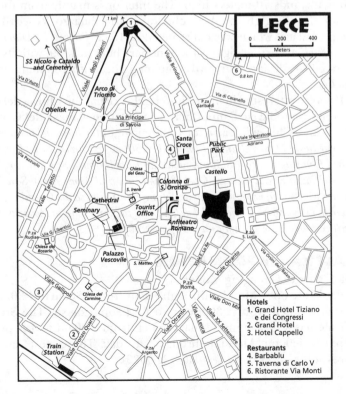

LECCE

0   200   400
Meters

SS Nicolo e Cataldo and Cemetery

Via D'Aurio

Arco di Triomfo

Obelisk

Viale degli Studenti

Viale Brindisi

P.za Garibaldi

Via di Casanello

Viale Imperatore
Adriano

Via Principe di Savoia

Santa Croce

Public Park

Viale Taranto

Via Pazzuolo

Chiesa del Gesu

S. Irene

Colonna di S. Oronzo

Castello

Cathedral

Seminary

Via G. Libertini

Tourist Office

Anfiteatro Romano

Viale Luce

P.za S. Lucia

P.za Rudiae

Chiesa del Rosario

Palazzo Vescovile

S. Matteo

Via Orsini del Balzo

Viale Otranto

Viale Gallipoli

Chiesa del Carmine

P.za Roma

Viale Don Min

Viale Orozo Quarta

Via di Leuca

Viale XX Settembre

Train Station

P.za Argento

Hotels
1. Grand Hotel Tiziano e dei Congressi
2. Grand Hotel
3. Hotel Cappello

Restaurants
4. Barbablu
5. Taverna di Carlo V
6. Ristorante Via Monti

North of the piazza in the **Piazza della Profettura** is the best church to see in Lecce, **Church of Santa Croce**, built between 1549 and 1697 (*Open 9am–1pm and 5:30pm–7:30pm*). It has an ornately decorated facade and a beautiful exterior. The interior is only two simple rows of columns supporting bare white walls. Behind the church are the peaceful **Giardini Publici** where you can relax with a picnic lunch.

East of the Piazza San Oronzo is the imposing trapezoid **Castello**, built from 1539 to 1548 during the reign of Charles V (*not open to public*). To the west of this sight is the **Arco di Trionfo**, erected in 1548 in honor of Charles V. If you're interested in cemeteries, go up the Viale San Nicolo to the church of **SS Nicolo e Cataldo**, founded in 1180, and the cemetery it tends to. The **cemetery** is filled with small mausoleums of every imaginable style and shape all clustered together on tiny paths (*Viale San Nicolo. Open 8am–1pm and 4–7pm; cemetery is open 9am–6pm. Sundaydays 9am–1pm*).

Back in the center of the city is the **Piazza del Duomo** (*Piazza del Duomo. Open 8am–11am and 4:30pm–7:30pm*). This is an entire complex of buildings that stand out because of their white facades. First you have the looming **Cathedral of Sant Oronzo** and *campanile* built from 1658 to 1570 that stands 70 meters high. The interior is mainly from the 18th century. To the right of the cathedral is the **Palazzo Vescovile**, the Bishop's Palace, which was constructed in 1652 (*Piazza del Duomo. Not open to public*). Further right is the **seminary** built in 1709, with its richly decorated facade and courtyard containing a beautiful fountain (*not open to public*).

If you're interested in more churches Lecce has the **Chiesa del Gesu**, **San Irene**, **San Marco**, **Santa Chiara**, **San Matteo**, **Chiesa del Carmine**, and the large **Chiesa Rosario** for your enjoyment. *Chiesa del Gesu (Piazza Gastromediano, Open 8am–11am and 3:30pm–5:30pm), San Irene (Via Vittorio Emanuele, Open 8:30am–noon and 3pm–6pm), San Marco , Santa Chiara (Piazza Santa Chiara, Open 8am–11am and 4pm–7pm), San Matteo (Via San Matteo, Open 8am–noon and 4pm–6pm), Chiesa del Carmine (Piazza Tancredi, Open 8am–11am and 4–7pm), and the large Chiesa Rosario (Via G. Libertini, Open 8am–11am and 3:30pm–5:30pm).*

PRACTICAL INFORMATION
Bank Hours & Changing Money
Banks are open Monday through Friday from 8:30am to 1:30pm and some do reopen from 2:30pm or so to 4:30pm or so. The **Stazione Centrale** has a *cambio* inside that is open from 8:00am to 1:30pm and 2:30pm to 8:00pm Monday through Saturday. The closest **American Express** office *is in Bari (Tel. 080/521-0022).*

Business Hours

From October to June, most shops are open from 9:00am to 1:00pm and from 3:30pm to 7:30pm, and are closed all day Sundays and on Monday morning. Then from June to September, when it really starts to get hot in Lecce, the morning hours remain the same, but the mid-day siesta time is slightly extended to 4:00pm and sometimes 4:30pm, which then pushes closing time back to 7:30pm or 8:00pm. In conjunction with being closed on Sunday and Monday mornings, shops are also closed half-days on Saturday.

Food stores, like *alimentari*, generally are open from 8:30am to 1:30pm (so stock up on your picnic supplies before you need them) and from 5:00pm to 7:30pm, and during the winter months they are closed on Thursdays.

Postal Services

You can buy stamps at local tobacconists (they are marked with a "T" outside) as well as post offices. Mail boxes are colored red. Post offices are open from 8:00am to 2:00pm on weekdays. The one exception to this rule is the **main post office** (**Palazzo delle Poste**) *located in Piazza Libertini (Tel. 0832/303-000)* which is open Monday through Friday from 8:00am to 7:30pm, and Saturday from 8:00am to noon. You can't miss it, it's basically in the shadow of the castle.

Tourist Information & Maps

• **EPT tourist office**, *in the center of town in the Piazza San Oronzo between the Duomo and castle. Tel. 0832/316-461.* Here they can supply you with maps of Lecce as well as Gallipoli (Not the Gallipoli that was immortalized by that Australian World War I movie – that one was in Turkey.)

If you want to charter a bus to take you to the sights, contact the travel office of **CTS** *at Via Palmieri 91, Tel. 0832/301-862.*

ACAIA

This is the closest castle to Lecce, making it the most convenient. You can reach it by taking one of the three daily buses that leave from the bus station on Via Adua. Contact the EPT office for more specific schedule information.

Located only 10 kilometers from Lecce, and thus only a ten or fifteen minute drive, this castle has long been abandoned and is overgrown with weeds and shrubbery. But you can easily see its former majesty from the mosaic remnants, narrow medieval staircases, huge rooms, and eerily quiet courtyards. This is a good place to start your adventure exploring Southern Italian castles.

WHERE TO EAT

LOCANDO DEL GALLO, *Piazza Castello 1, Tel 0832/861-102. Closed Mondays, 15 days in September and 15 days in January. Credit cards accepted. Dinner for two L90,000.*

The best place to be in this restaurant is sitting in the shadow of the castle on the terrace. There is a fixed price menu (L40,000 per person) that offers some wonderful local flavor, like the *tubetini con la cernia* (pasta with sea bass or grouper), *meurzi fritte* (pieces of bread and peperoni fried), and any of their fine game caught in the hills around the castle.

GALLIPOLI

Located on the edge of the Gulf of Taranto and the Ionian Sea, this little port town is situated on a rocky island connected to the more modern city by an ancient bridge, the **Ponte Citta Vecchia**.

The beautiful **old town**, with its narrow winding streets evokes images of centuries past. This is a fun place for a day or two.

ARRIVALS & DEPARTURES

There is a train from Lecce every two hours. The trip takes 45 minutes and costs L5,000. If you go by car, simply take **highway 101** straight to Gallipoli. You'll pass through the country town of **Galapone**. Stop there for a brief visit and enjoy the town's beautiful cathedral and their Baroque **Church of the Crucifixion**.

WHERE TO STAY

1. GRAND HOTEL COSTA BRADA, *Litoranea Santa Maria di Leuca, 73014 Gallipoli. Tel. 0833/22-551. Fax is the same. 80 rooms, 10 with bath, only 68 with shower. Single without L100,000; Single with L140,000; Double L230,000. Credit cards accepted.* ****

Located outside of the city, this place has everything you could want to keep you entertained: private beach, tennis courts, outdoor pool, snorkeling equipment, horseback riding, sauna, discotheque, piano bar, superb restaurant that makes local dishes, a hairdresser and more. This is a prime vacation spot for Italians so you may need to make reservations in the high season.

2. HOTEL SPINOLA, *Corso Roma 129, 73014 Gallipoli. Tel. 0833/ 261-916. Fax 0833/261-917. 13 rooms all with shower. Single L 120,000; Double L190,000. Breakfast L8,000 extra. Credit cards accepted.* ****

Located in the center of the city near the train station, you are within walking distance of all the sights. A quaint little hotel that makes you feel special. The bathrooms are a little tiny, the rooms are clean, and all have air conditioning and TV. A well located place to stay.

3. HOTEL JOLI PARK, *Piazza Salento 2, 73014 Gallipoli. Tel. 0833/ 263-321. Fax is the same. 87 rooms all with shower. Single L 71,000; Double L115,000. Credit cards accepted.* ***

Located near the beach and the center of town, which isn't hard in Gallipoli, since it's surrounded by water. Housed in a renovated old building that also has a good restaurant that makes traditional dishes. A good, clean, comfortable place to stay. The furniture is a bit eclectic but it fits. You have air conditioning and TV in the all the rooms as well as a bus to ferry you back and forth to the old town or the station.

4. HOTEL LE SIRENUSE, *Litoranea Santa Maria di Leuca, 73014 Gallipoli. Tel. 0833/22536. Fax 0833/22539. 120 rooms all with bath. Single L82,000; Double L136,000. Credit cards accepted.* ***

If you want the luxury and activities of the Grand Hotel Costa Brada but at almost half the price, this is your place. They're located a little farther out from Gallipoli but they also have a private beach, snorkeling equipment, horseback riding, tennis, and outdoor pool, a disco, a piano bar – wait, there's more – mini-golf, a bocce course, and a superb restaurant that offers a beautifully romantic view. They also have hair-dressers and a nursery for kids as well as a bus to take you back and forth to the city.

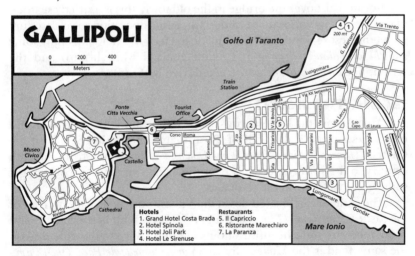

WHERE TO EAT

5. IL CAPRICCIO, *Viale G. Bovio 14, Tel. 0833/261-545. Closed Mondays in the summer and all of October. Credit cards accepted. Dinner for two L120,000.*

The menu here is a combination of traditional dishes and regular Italian fare. A direct result of the many Italian tourists that flock to the beaches in the area during the summer (mainly in August). So if you know your Italian food you can always find something you like. For example: *tagliatelle alla bolognese* (with a tasty meat sauce) *spaghetti all vongole verace* (with a spicy clam sauce), *spaghetti ai frutti di mare* (with mounds of seafood). For seconds, you can't go wrong with the *grigliatta mista* (mixed grill of meat and fish) or the *zuppa di pesce* (a thick fish soup). Pleasant atmosphere both inside and out – on their terrace under an awning.

6. RISTORANTE MARECHIARO, *Lungomare G Marconi, 0833/266-143. Closed Tuesdays. Credit cards accepted. Dinner for L120,000.*

Located just before the Ponte Citta Vecchia, this place used to be a dump frequented by local fishermen, but it has slowly upgraded its decor. The food is as filling and robust as before. Enjoy their many fish dishes either inside with the rustic decor or outside where you can gaze at the sea. It's a large place, over 200 seats, but reservations would be advised in the high season. For firsts, try the *zuppa di pesce alla gallipolina* (fish soup made Gallipoli style with mounds of seafood) which is so filling it can take the place of a pasta. For seconds try any of the many fish they make roasted over an open flame and you'll come away satisfied.

7. LA PARANZA, *Largo Dogana, Tel. 0833/266-639. Closed Wednesdays in Winter. Visa accepted. Dinner for two L100,000.*

Located just over the bridge in the old town, this is a strictly seafood place. The owners also run a seafood wholesale operation so you are sure to get the best seafood here. Sit outside to enjoy the view and enjoy some *gnocchi di patate con gamberi* (potato gnocchi with shrimp) and the scrumptious *fritto misti di mare* (mixed fried seafood).

SEEING THE SIGHTS

An old road, the **Riviera**, runs all the way around this small town and offers views of both the **Gulf of Taranto** and the **Ionian Sea**. Visit the **Castello** (*Piazza Imbiani. Open 9am–1pm and 4–7pm*), built from the 13th century to the 17th century just over the bridge on the left. You can get some great views from the ramparts.

The **cathedral** is located down the Via Antoinette de Pace in front of the castle (*Open 8am–11am and 3:30pm–5:30pm*). Built between 1629 and 1696, there are some beautiful choir stalls here. Beyond the cathedral on the same road is the **Museo Civico**, (*Via Antoinette de Pace, Open 9am–1:30pm and 4pm–7pm Tuesday–Sunday*) which contains many artifacts, sculptures, and paintings of the region's past. If you arrive in the morning, don't miss the fruit and vegetable **market** in front of the castle in the **Piazza Imbriani**.

After you've visited this scenic, beautiful, and unique little town head up the coast on the Gulf of Taranto side to some wonderful beaches and resorts. During the *Ferragosto* holidays in August, this seaside town of 20,000 people swells to many more than that with Italian vacationers.

For more information about the town and the surrounding area, stop at the **information office** *just across the bridge from the old town at Corso Roma 225, Tel. 0863/476-202.*

OTRANTO

A little fishing village situated panoramically on a beautiful bay. Founded in the 6th century BC by the Greeks (Hydrus), the small port then came under Roman rule (Hydruntum), and later became the capital of Byzantine Apulia. It was razed to the ground in 1480 by the Ottoman Turks and all its citizens were slaughtered.

There are some ancient churches here, and a castle with a terrific view where you can gaza across at the Republic of Albania.

ARRIVALS & DEPARTURES

There are two trains a day from Lecce to Otranto. The trip takes 45 minutes and costs L5,000. By car from Lecce, go through the seaside resort of San Cataldo with its lighthouse, and take the scenic coast road. The trip will take about 45 minutes.

Once you arrive, from the train station go around the right side of the circle and bear left down the hill on **Via Pantaleone**. There will be signs indicating that you should go right. Follow them and you'll have a much longer walk. Instead, go through the stoplight and go to the **Lungomare d'Otranto**, which runs along the beach. Go three blocks to the right and you'll hit the **Piazza de Donno**. Bear to the left down **Via Vittorio Emanuele II** and you'll enter the old town in a few blocks.

Turn right on **Via Basilica** to get to the local tourist office and the cathedral. Pick up a map here and begin your exploration into the byways of this charming seaside escape.

WHERE TO STAY

HOTEL DEGLI HAETHEY, *Via Sforza 33, 73028 Otranto. Tel. 0836/ 801548. Fax 0836/801576. 21 rooms all with shower. Single L 99,000; Double L139,000. Credit cards accepted* ****

Located just away from the center of town, this country four star has impressive amenities. There's a pool, piano bar, great views from the terrace and most importantly a shuttle bus to bring you back and forth to the sights. Clean and comfortable rooms with relatively small bathrooms.

GRAND HOTEL DANIELA, *Litoranea San Cataldo, 73028 Otranto. Tel. 0836/806-648. Fax 0836/806-667. 146 rooms all with shower. Single L90,000-180,000; Double L180,000-360,000. Credit cards accepted.* ****

Ooo-la-la – what luxury! Great views, a private beach, snorkeling equipment, sauna, gymnasium, bocce courts, tennis courts, horseback riding, swimming pool, nursery for the kids, hairdressers, piano bar and much more. This is the place to stay to have all the luxuries of the world at your fingertips when you're in the middle of nowhere. Located outside of town, they also have a shuttle bus to take you to the sights and back.

HOTEL VALLE DELL'IDRO, *Via D. Grasso 4, 73028 Otranto. Tel. 0836/801-224. Fax 0836/802-374. 27 rooms all with shower. Single L75,000-90,000; Double L90,000-130,000. Credit cards accepted.* ****

Another inexpensive four-star. This place doesn't have nearly as many amenities as the Grand Hotel Daniela but they make you feel taken care of. Located outside of town near the beach, this is really only a place to rest your head for a few days and not for a full vacation. They have a passable restaurant and a welcoming bar for an evenings *aperitif*.

HOTEL BELLAVISTA, *Via Vittorio Emanuelle 19, 73028 Otranto. Tel. 0836/801-058. 22 rooms, 2 with bath, 20 with shower. Single L40,000-50,000; Double L60,000-70,000. No credit cards accepted.* **

The best budget choice in the area in terms of cost, and you get air conditioning, which is imperative in the summertime down here. They have their own restaurant attached to the hotel and they serve great local food. There's a full board option for only L82,000 per couple.

WHERE TO EAT

TRATTORIA DA SERGIO, *Corso Garibaldi 9. Tel. 0836/801-408. Closed Wednesday in Winter, February and November. American Express accepted. Dinner for two L120,000.*

Exclusively a local style seafood restaurant. Some great dishes here are *frutti di mare con linguini or risotto* (linguini or rice with mounds of fresh seafood), *gamberoni alla griglia* (large grilled shrimp) or some great *pesce spada alla griglia* (grilled swordfish). You can enjoy both inside and outside seating.

TRATTORIA VECCHIA OTRANTO, *Corso Garibaldi 96, Tel. 0836/801-575. Closed Mondays in Winter and November. Credit cards accepted. Dinner for two L100,000.*

Opened in 1981, this rustic restaurant on Otranto's main street is a well respected local place that serves traditional dishes like *tonnarelli alla polpa di ricci e peperoni* (wide strips of pasta with sea urchins and pepperoni) or *zuppa di pesce all'otrantina* (special local seafood soup). They have inside and outside seating. I'd recommend the local flavor inside.

SEEING THE SIGHTS

The **cathedral of Santissima Annunziata**, begun in 1080, is the last home for the remains of those slaughtered by the Ottomans. The church contains ancient columns that have had 12th century capitals placed on them. You'll also find some unique well-preserved 12th century mosaic tile floors that depict the passing of the months and of battles won in the area (*Piazza Duomo. Open 8am–noon and 3–5pm*).

A smaller church, **San Pietro**, of 19th century origin sits on a side street in the upper part of town with its Byzantine dome and frescoes. Next visit the **Castello di Aragonese** (*Via Castello. Currently under reconstruction. Open 9am–1pm and 4–7pm. Admission L5,000*). The castle affords wonderful views, on clear days, across the **Straits of Otranto**. The straits are 75 kilometers wide, and you can see across to the mountains of Albania – a country once ruled by Italy.

For more information about Otranto, and to get a map of the city and surrounding area, contact the local **tourist office** *at Via Basilica 8, Tel. 0836/801-436, which rest at the foot of the cathedral.*

20. SICILY

Sicily (**Sicilia**) is a mountainous, arid island that is a geological extension of the Apennine Mountains, only separated from the mainland by the **Straits of Messina**. Many powers have occupied this strategically important area over the centuries: Greeks, Romans, Arabs, Phoenicians and today, unofficially of course, the Mafia. The extensive historical sites related to these former powers are part of the island's attraction.

And not just the powers from the past: for probably the strangest tours anywhere, you can actually contact local travel agencies and go on a **Mafia tour** that visits various Family activities and the graves of infamous godfathers and victims.

Among the ancient Greek and Roman ruins on the island are the Greek **Taormina theater** and **San Domenico Monastery** near **Messina**, the Greek theater in **Syracuse**, and the 5th-century BC **Temple of Concord** in **Agrigento**. It's also a fun adventure to visit the **Isole Eolie**, off the north shore by Messina.

Early Settlements

Before invaders came to Sicily, we know, based on excavations at **Realmonte** near Agrigento, that man's history in Sicily dates back to the early Paleolithic period. There are also early settlements at **Stentinello** and **Lipari** that have been carbon dated to the Neolithic period. During the Copper and Bronze ages, the island's inhabitants traded with many of the other developing Mediterranean settlements. During this time the **Isole Eolie** and its capital Lipari rose in power and began to go off on its own tangent separate from Sicily. They were more influenced by Malta and the western Peloponnesian culture, while Sicily came mainly under the influence of **Greece** and the **Phoenicians**.

Near the end of the Bronze Age, a contingent of people called **Siculi** (thus the island's name) came from the mainland and began to dominate the small settlements of the island, which broke up and headed inland to the mountains for protection. These new people prospered, but were mainly just vassals to the Phoenician and Greek traders. Even though Phoenicia had a great influence in Sicily, especially the port cities, they left the main colonization to the Greeks. They started their settlements on the east coast and gradually pushed the Siculi people westward.

By the fifth century BC, **Syracuse** on the east coast had become the strongest settlement and had Helenized almost all of Sicily. The Siculi looked to the western Phoenician towns of Marsala and Trapani for assistance; they were holding fast against the Greek colonization. As a result a war was fought between the two Sicilian factions, which had to be settled by Roman intervention with the two **Punic Wars** of 264–212 BC.

With the Roman domination, the interior of the island began to prosper. Splendid villas and fertile fields sprung up throughout Sicily, providing much of Rome's produce.

Foreign Invasions

After the fall of Rome, the island was invaded by the Vandals in the 5th century AD, then by the Goths. Eventually the Byzantine Empire took control and almost three centuries of peace lasted until 826. Then the Moors and Saracens took control of Sicily. Their biggest change to the island was to move the capital from Syracuse to **Palermo**, where it remains today.

In 1061, the Norman conquest began (five years before their successful invasion of another island, England) and the island enjoyed its most successful period in history. In 1302, the era of peace and prosperity ended with the Spanish domination. This period saw the rich get richer and the poor get poorer, creating a division between the people and their governors that still exists today. It may be an exaggeration to say that history passed by the Sicilians for the next five hundred years, but not an awful lot of consequence occurred during this long period.

Then on May 11, 1860, **Garibaldi** landed at Marsala and began to dismantle the Kingdom of Sicily and merge it with the Kingdom of Italy. During this time the people were greatly oppressed, which gave rise to the beginnings of what we know today as the **Mafia**. At the beginning of the twentieth century, a massive emigration began, mainly to America and Australia, spreading the tentacles of the Mafia all over the world.

Sicily Today

Sicily has since to recover economically and remains a poverty stricken island off the coast of Italy, still basically controlled by the Mafia. Everything from the government to industry bends to their will, making it even more difficult for the island to recover. But the Sicilians are fiercely independent people, and most are working hard to combat organized crime and overcome their poor economic situation.

Besides its rich ancient history, there are many other reasons to visit Sicily: water sports, beaches of rock and sand (including black sand), natural beauty, great food and friendly people (for the most part). For touring, the island can be roughly divided into the north shore and south shore areas. The **north shore** has reefs, olive groves, secluded coves and countless seaside resorts, including **Cefalu**, a gorgeous Arab-Norman city with good beaches.

In the center of the north coast is **Palermo**, the ancient and current capital and the island's largest city with a population of approximately 801,000. Be sure to visit the central market and 12th-century **Monreale Cathedral**, which has impressive biblical mosaics. About 80 km west of Palermo lies the ancient village of **Erice**, atop a mountain, where you can still find the remains of a temple dedicated to Venus.

The **southern coast** has an even milder climate than the North, which means you can enjoy swimming most of the year, although between November and March it can get quite chilly. Among the areas not to be missed are **Agrigento** (to see the **Valley of the Temples**) and **Mt. Etna**, an active volcano just topping 3,200 meters on the east coast. The last time the volcano erupted was in January 1992. The time previous to that was in March 1987, when two people were killed. Although scientists say it can erupt at any time, if you play it safe you shouldn't be in any danger. There is also good winter skiing around Mt. Etna that offers great ocean views.

ARRIVALS & DEPARTURES
By Air
As of press time, there were no direct flights from North America or Australia to either Catania in the east or Palermo in the west. You will have to fly through Milan or Rome first, then transfer to **Alitalia** to get to Sicily. Fares today are changing very rapidly, but expect to pay about $266 US for a round-trip between Rome and Palermo, and about $302 US for a round-trip between Rome and Catania. It may be slightly cheaper if you purchase your tickets in Italy, but it might also be more expensive ... go figure.

You can get direct flights from London to both Palermo and Catania, so this could be an option for you when traveling from North America or Australia. There are also direct flights from Dublin to both Palermo and Catania. In conjunction, you can catch a flight from all major Italian cities directly to Palermo or Catania, so if you're already in Italy and have the urge to see Sicily it is easy, but not inexpensive, to get to the island.

By Car
The drive down to Sicily through Southern Italy is beautifully scenic, especially down the coast, but it takes quite a while. From Rome it will take

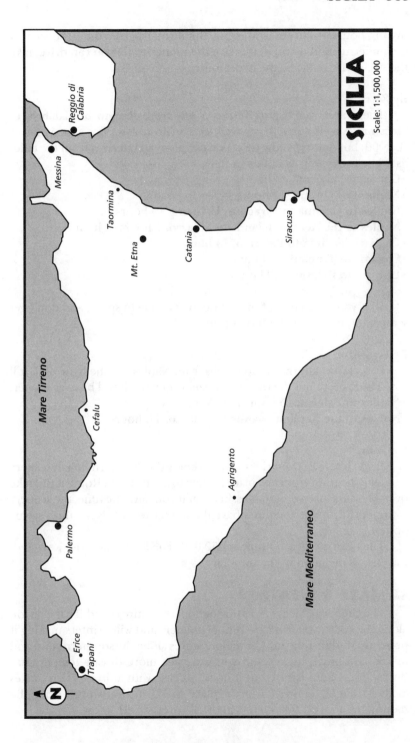

over 14 hours just to get to Messina. But if you have the time, the scenery is wonderful, and if you don't have the money to fly you can drive, take the train, the ferry, or the hydrofoil.

By Ferry

There are over twenty ferries a day from **Reggio di Calabria** to **Messina** (cost is L5,000), as well as a hydrofoil service that is faster (L6,000) but doesn't allow cars. You can also catch ferries from the cities listed below as well as others in Italy:

- **Genoa to Palermo**, 23 hours
- **Naples to Palermo**, 11 hours
- **Naples to Catania to Syracuse**, 15 hours/19 hours
- **Naples to the Aeolian Islands to Milazzo**, 7 hours/8 hours
- **Cagliari Sardinia to Palermo**, 14 hours
- **Cagliari to Trapani**, 11 hours
- **Livorno to Palermo**, 19 hours

So if you are in one of these cities, have time to spare, and don't get seasick too easily, try the ferry option.

By Hydrofoil

For a faster alternative to ferries from Naples, try the hydrofoil. It'll cost a little more but the ride will be smoother and it will be over sooner.

- **Naples to Palermo**, 5 hours and 30 minutes
- **Naples to the Aeolian Islands to Milazzo**, 4-6 hours

By Train

If you like long train rides you can enjoy the Southern Italian scenery and take the train from any place in Italy to Sicily. From Rome it will take over 14 hours just to get to Messina. But if you have the time, the scenery is wonderful, and if you don't have the money to fly this is a nice, scenic option.

The train fare from Rome is L50,000. The ferry ride from Reggio di Calabria is included in the train fare.

CLIMATE & WEATHER

The climate of Sicily varies throughout the entire island. To the north, along the coast, you can expect hot summers and wild winters making it perfectly Mediterranean. The temperatures along the southern coast and inland, are much higher and you can have more drastic temperature fluctuations. Rain is rare but it does increase with altitude. This makes Sicily, strangely enough, a great place to ski in the winter, since the mountains above 1,600 meters get well covered with snow.

In the summer expect to experience the hot and humid *Scirocco* that blows in from the Sahara, bringing with it discomfort and clouds of reddish dust.

When to Go

Anytime is good time to travel to Sicily. The climate doesn't vary greatly, making Sicily a pleasant trip any time of year – although the summers can get unbearably hot at times. The northern coast's climate is more stable than that of the southern coast and inland. If you want to try the beach from November to March, it's not a good idea, since it will be like autumn back in the US.

So the best time to Sicily to enjoy good warm weather is September through the first week in November. To enjoy good skiing, go between December and March.

PUBLIC HOLIDAYS & FESTIVALS

Offices and shops in Sicily are closed on the following dates, so prepare for the eventuality of having virtually everything closed. This is your cue to stock up on picnic snacks, soda, whatever, because in most cities and towns there is no such thing as a 24 hour a day 7-11.

- **January 1**, New Year's Day
- **January 6**, Epiphany
- **April 25**, Liberation Day (1945)
- **Easter Monday**
- **May 1**, Labor Day
- **August 15**, *Ferragosto* and Assumption of the Blessed Virgin (climax of Italian family holiday season. Hardly anything stays open in the big cities through the month of August)
- **November 1**, All Saints Day
- **December 8**, Immaculate Conception
- **December 25/26**, Christmas

Local Events & Festivals

- **Agrigento**, *Sagra del Mandorlo in Fiore*, 1st to 2nd Sunday in February
- **Catania**, *Festa di San Agata*, February 3-5
- **Acireale**, *Carnevale acese*, Sunday and Shrove Tuesday
- **Sciacca**, *Carnevale*, Sunday and Shrove Tuesday
- **Trapani**, *Processione del misteri*, Good Friday and Easter Sunday
- **Marsala**, *Sacra rappresentazione*, Holy Thursday
- **Acata**, *Festa di San Vincenzo*, 3rd Sunday after Easter
- **Pergusa**, *Sagra del Lago*, 1st Sunday in May
- **Naro**, *Festa di San Calogero*, June 18

- **Palermo**, *Festa di U Fistinu*, July 11-15
- **Marsala**, *Sagra del Vino Marsala*, 3rd Sunday in July
- **Messina**, *Passeggiata dei giganti*, August 14
- **Siracusa**, *Festa di San Lucia*, December 13

GETTING AROUND SICILY

Sicily is interconnected by an extensive highway system, a superb train system, and naturally, since Sicily is an island, a complete shipping service involving ferries, hydrofoils, and liners. Your mode of transport will depend on how long you're staying in Sicily and what you want to see.

If you're only visiting coastal towns, it might be fun to take a ferry between them. If you are going to rural, off the beaten path locations, you'll need a car, because even if the train did go to where you're going, the *Locale* would take forever since it stops at every town on its tracks.

By Train

You can get most anywhere in Sicily by train, much the same as on the mainland. There are more extensive rail systems on the east of the island to accommodate the flow of trains from the mainland. Here you should expect delays since the trains may have had trouble getting across on the ferry.

There are some small towns that the trains do not go to, but you should avoid these anyway. You never know when you're going to stumble onto something better left unseen in one of the mountain villages.

By Car

The expressways, called **autostradas**, are superhighways and toll roads. They connect all major Sicilian cities and have contributed to the tremendous increase in tourist travel. Car is the best way to see Sicily since you don't have to wait for the trains, which are inevitably delayed, something that rarely happens on the mainland.

Driving is the perfect way to see the entire variety of Sicily's towns, villages, seascapes, landscapes, and monuments. The Sicilian drivers may be a little *pazzo* (crazy), but if you drive confidently you'll be fine. A word of caution, again: Sicily is best explored along its coastline and a little inland. Once you start roaming through the mountain towns, unless you know what you're doing, anything could happen.

CAR RENTAL IN SICILY

You have all the major international and national players in the car rental business here in Sicily. Below please find a list of their addresses and phones numbers separated by city.

In Catania
• *Avis*, Via Federico de Roberto 10, Tel. 095/374-905; Via Giuseppe La Rena 87, Tel. 095/347-975; Aeroporto Fontanarossa, Tel. 095/340-500
• *Hertz*, Via Toselli 45, Tel. 095322-560
• *Maggiore*, Piazza Gioeni 6, Tel. 095/338-305; Piazza Verga 48, Tel. 095/310-002; Aeroporto Fontanarossa, Tel. 095/340-594

In Messina
• *Avis*, Via Vittorio Emanuele 35, Tel. 090/58404
• *Hertz*, Via Vittorio Emanuele 113, Tel. 090/363-740
• *Maggiore*, Via T. Cannizzaro 46, Tel. 090/775-476

In Palermo
• *Avis*, Via Principe di Scordia 12, Tel. 091/586-940; Aeroporto di Punta Raisi, Tel. 091/591-684
• *Hertz*, Viale Michelangelo 200, Tel. 091/204-277; Aeroporto di Punta Raisi, Tel. 091/591-682
• *Maggiore*, Via Agrigento 27, Tel. 091/625-9286; Aeroporto di Punta Raisi, Tel. 091/591-681

In Syracuse
• *Avis*, Piazza dell Repubblica 11, Tel. 0931/69635
• *Maggiore*, Via Tevere 14, Tel. 0931/66548

In Trapani
• *Maggiore*, Via Torre, Tel. 0923/21567

BASIC INFORMATION
Banking Hours
Banks in Sicily are open Monday through Friday 8:35am to 1:35pm and from 3:00pm to 4:00pm, and are closed all day Saturday and Sunday and on national holidays. In some cities the afternoon open hour may not even exist. These are true bankers' hours!

Even if the bank is closed most travelers checks can be exchanged for Italian lire at most hotels and shops and at the many foreign exchange offices in railway stations and at airports.

Business Hours

Store hours are usually Monday through Friday 9:00am to 1:00pm, 3:30/4:00pm to 7:30/8:00pm, and Saturday 9:00am to 1:00pm. Most stores are closed on Sunday and on national holidays. Don't expect to find any 24-hour convenience stores just around the corner. If you want to have some soda in your room after a long day of touring you need to plan ahead.

Also, you must plan on most stores not being open from 1:00pm to 4:00pm. This is Sicily's siesta time. Don't expect to get a lot done except find a nice restaurant and enjoy the pleasant afternoons.

Consulates
• **United States**, *Via GB Vaccarini 1, Palermo. Tel. 091/302-590*

Safety & Precautions

Sicilian cities are definitely much safer than any equivalent American city. You can walk most anywhere without fear of harm, but that doesn't mean you shouldn't play it safe. Listed below are some simple rules to follow to ensure that nothing bad occurs:
• At night, make sure the streets you are walking on have plenty of other people. Like I said, most cities are safe, but at night the rules change.
• Always have your knapsack or purse flung over the shoulder that is not directly next to the road. Why? There have been cases of Italians on motorbike snatching purses off old ladies and in some cases dragging them a few blocks.
• Better yet, have your companion walk on the street side, while you walk on the inside of the sidewalk with the knapsack or purse.
• Better still is to buy one of those tummy wallets that goes under your shirt so no one can even be tempted to purse snatch you. That's really all you should need, but always follow basic common sense; if you feel threatened, scared, alone, retrace your steps back to a place where there are other people.
• Be especially on guard against street thieves and pickpockets in Palermo and other large towns.

SPORTS & RECREATION

Sicily is an island, thus the water sports at their beach resorts are prevalent. But they are also a mountainous island, so their skiing is actually quite good too, despite the fact that they are close to Africa. Sicily is a prime vacation spot for both winter and summer sports, so if you're in the mood for either while on the island you can find what you want.

FOOD & WINE
Food
Most Sicilian food is cooked with fresh ingredients raised or caught a short distance from the restaurant, making their dishes healthy, fresh, and satisfying. There are many restaurants in Sicily of international renown, but you shouldn't limit yourself only to the upper echelon. In most cases you can find as good a meal at a fraction the cost at any *trattoria*. Also, many of the upper echelon restaurants you read about are only in business because they cater to the tourist trade. Their food is good, but the atmosphere is a little hokey.

The traditional Sicilian meal has been influenced by the Middle East, Greece, France, and Spain as a result of the island's past conquests. Other influences include the sea (what better place to find a meal) and the fact that the island's climate is perfect for raising all sorts of herbs and spices, and vegetables and fruits.

Suggested Sicilian Cuisine
As I've said in other chapters, you don't have to eat all the traditional courses listed below. Our constitution just isn't prepared for such mass consumption.

ANTIPASTO - APPETIZER
- **Arancine di Riso** – Rice balls filled with meat sauce and peas. Very Middle Eastern.
- **Antipasto Di Mare** – Mixed seafood appetizer plate. Differs from restaurant to restaurant
- **Tomate, Mozzarella ed olio** – Tomato and mozzarella slices covered in olive oil with a hint of basil
- **Minestre di pesce** – Fish soup. Varies by region and restaurant.

PRIMO PIATTO - FIRST COURSE
Pasta
- **Pasta con le sarde** – Made with sardines, raisins, pine nuts, onions, tomatoes, fennel and saffron.
- **Spaghetti alla Norma** – Made with tomato, fried eggplant and ricotta cheese. Typical of Eastern Sicily.
- **Penne alla Paola** – Short ribbed pasta tubes made with broccoli, pine nuts and raisins.
- **CousCous** – Made with fish, chicken, beans or broccoli. Middle Eastern.

Zuppa – *Soup*
- **Minestre di pesce** – Fish soup. Varies by region and restaurant.

SECOND PIATTO - ENTRÉE
Carne – *Meat*
- **Involtini** – Meat stuffed with cheese and onions
- **Salso Magro** – Meat stuffed with salami, hard–boiled eggs and cheese
- **Conniglio alla cacciatore** – Rabbit cooked with red wine, tomatoes and spices.

Pesce – *Fish*
- **Tonno alla cipollata** – Tuna made with onions.
- **Pesce spada alla ghiotta** – Swordfish made with tomatoes, olives and capers.
- **Pesce Spada alla griglia** – Grilled swordfish

Contorno – *Vegetable*
- **Caponata** – Eggplant, tomatoes, spices, capers, olives, tuna eggs and shrimps cooked together.
- **Fritella** – tomatoes, onions, artichokes, beans and peas all stewed together.

Formaggio – *Cheese*
- **Pecorino** – Sheep's cheese
- **Piacentino** – Pecorino flavored with peppercorns and saffron.

DOLCE - DESSERT
- **Cassata** – Sponge cakes made with ricotta, almond paste, chocolate and candied fruits
- **Cannoli** – fried pastry with a mixture like the Cassata

Wine

Sicily's best wines are *Etna* (red and white, wide variety) from the Catania area and *Marsala* (white, dry or sweet) from the Trapani province. You should also try some *Casteldaccio,* a dry white from around Palermo, and if you like sweet wine, an *Eloro* from around Syracuse should suffice. If you're on the Eolie Islands, try their unique red and white *Malvasia*.

MESSINA

Ninety percent of **Messina** was destroyed in the earthquake of 1908, after which the city was rebuilt with wide avenues intersecting at right angles, making her an entirely modern looking city. Some of the most famous buildings were painstakingly reconstructed, but they too met their demise during the Allied bombings during World War II. But prior to all this destruction the city was so quaint and charming that William Shakespeare used it as the setting for his play *Much Ado About Nothing* (see sidebar on *Shakespeare's Italy,* page 86).

Messina is your main point of entry into Sicily from the mainland, so you will most probably have to pass through this unimpressive city. This is a place to stay only if you're so exhausted from your journey down to Sicily that you cannot make it any further. Otherwise continue on with your journey.

Women should not walk alone in Messina at night, and no one should walk around the area near the train station or the harbor after dark. Your best bet is to stay close to the streets around the Duomo, where you'll find people out and about. Never go down a street that is deserted and always be on the lookout for pickpockets and purse-snatchers, especially the ones on motor scooters roaring by.

GETTING AROUND TOWN

By Bus

If you want to catch the bus to save your weary feet, you need to purchase tickets from any *tabacchi* or newsstand for L700, or get an all day pass for L2,500. To get to the Museo Regionale, you need to catch the northbound yellow buses traveling on the Via Garibaldi numbered 8, 27, or 28.

By Foot

The city is walkable from the train station, the hydrofoil station, or the Stazione Maritima to any of the sights and each other. The only sight not accessible from the main disembarkation points in the Museo Regionale, which is about 45 minutes on foot from the train station.

WHERE TO STAY

1. JOLLY HOTEL DELLO STRETTO, *Via Garibaldi 126, 98100 Messina. Tel. 090/363-860. Fax 090/590-2526. 96 rooms, 48 with bath, 48 with shower. Single L 90,000-180,000; Double L120,000-210,000. No credit cards accepted.* ****

Located in harbor off the main street Via Garibaldi, this is the only really good hotel in the city. They have their own private beach air conditioning, Satellite TV, room service, laundry service, a passable restaurant and an inviting bar. The rooms are kept clean and comfortable (the air conditioning helps in the summer) and bathrooms are immaculate.

2. EXCELSIOR HOTEL, *Via Maddalena 32, 98100 Messina. Tel. 090/ 293-8721. 44 rooms, 7 with bath, only 22 with shower. Single without L19,000-38,000; Single with L32,000-63,000; Double without L35,000-70,000; Double with L52,000-103,000. Visa accepted. ****

Located near the train station, this hotel is not in the best area but the prices are cheap. But then again so are the amenities in this place: no air conditioning, no TV, no room service, not all the rooms have bath or shower. How did it get a three star rating? If you're a budget traveler this is the least expensive place to stay with any star rating.

3. HOTEL MONZA, *Viale San Martino 63, 98100 Messina. Tel. 090/ 673-755. Fax is the same. 58 rooms only 36 with shower. Single without L30,000-40,000; Single with L46,000-66,000; Double without L46,000-66,000; Double with L66,000-110,000. No credit cards accepted. ****

Also located near the train station, this place has absolutely no amenities except for phones in the room, that have to go through a switchboard and passable heat in the winter. Only stay here as a last resort, or if you can't afford anything else.

WHERE TO EAT

4. TRATTORIA DUDU, *Via C Battisti 122, Tel. 090/674-393. Closed Mondays and the last week in September. American Express accepted. Dinner for two L70,000.*

Located between the train station and the Duomo, this is a small place with seating for only 30 patrons. Dudu serves wonderful local dishes and has a down home rustic atmosphere. The specialty of the house is the *stoccafisso "alla ghiotta,"* a pungent and tasty ensemble of stock fish made with tomatoes, capers, olives and onions. For dessert try their *torta di limone* (lemon pie). Seating outside available.

5. GIARDINO D'INVERNO NINO LIBRO, *Viale Boccetta 381, Tel. 090/362-413. Closed Mondays and 15 days in August. Credit cards accepted. Dinner for two L100,000.*

Located a small distance from the harbor and the center of the city. You'll need to take a cab here and back. They make local, traditional favorites as well as creating new and different dishes. They have the local *pesce stocco "alla ghiotta"* (stock fish made with tomatoes, capers, olives and onions) as well as *crespelle ai profumi di Sicilia* (pasta pancakes stuffed with tomatoes, basil, eggplant, and beef or horse meat).

6. RISTORANTE PIPPO NUNNARI, *Via Ugo Bassi 157, Tel. 090/ 293-8584. Closed Mondays and August. Credit cards accepted. Dinner for two L100,000.*

A classic and elegant environment. Remember to dress appropriately for a meal here. The food is simple but satisfying. Open with an antipasto of marinated fish or the basic *insalata di mare* (seafood salad). For the next course you have to try the *fettucine alla "Nunnari"* which is pasta with eggplant, ham, tomatoes and mozzarella. For the final dish try any of their fish *alla brace* (cooked over open flames) especially the *pesce spada* (swordfish), which was probably caught that morning.

SEEING THE SIGHTS

Not too much going on here, but the Regional Museum really is worth a trip.

MUSEO REGIONALE

Via della Liberta 465. Open Monday–Saturday 9am–1:30pm and 3pm–5:30pm, Sunday 9am–12;30pm. Admission L3,000. Take bus 8, 27, or 28.

Really the only place to visit when in Messina, if you're interested in the artistic history of Sicily. Here you'll find many paintings and sculptures, including works by **Caravaggio**, including the *Adoration of the Shepherds* and the *Resurrection of Lazarus*. You can also find Sicilian hand-crafted works including embroidery, silver, and fabric work.

DUOMO

Piazza Duomo. Open 8am–noon and 4–7pm.

Originally built by Roger II, this **cathedral** has undergone many reconstructions and the only original parts that remain are her basilica-style floor plan with three aisles. Destroyed by two earthquakes and engulfed in flames, all the precious mosaics and frescoes perished years ago. Today it's a rather bland example of what it used to be. The best sight to see here is the **Fontana di Orione** in the middle of the square. Designed in 1547 by Florentine artist Montorosoli, a pupil of Michelangelo's, this statue depicts several reclining nudes.

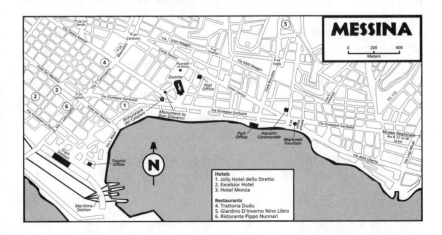

CHIESA ANNUNZIATA DEI CATALANI

Via Giuseepe Garibaldi. Open 8:30am–noon and 3:30pm–6:30pm.

Across the piazza from the Duomo is the smaller **Chiesa Annunziata dei Catalani** built in the same period. Another bland church, but one that is a little more interesting architecturally than the Duomo. In the Piazzetta dei Catalini near the church is the 16th century **Monument to Don Giovanni d'Austria**.

AQUARIO COMMUNALE

Via Mazzini, Tel. 48897. Open 9am–2pm. Admission L3,000.

A relaxing place to come when everything else is closed. Here you can enjoy the colorful fish as they float in their tranquil world.

PRACTICAL INFORMATION

Banking Hours & Changing Money

Banks are open Monday through Friday from 8:30am to 1:30pm and some do reopen from 2:30pm or so to 3:30pm or so. Besides banks there are plenty of exchange bureaus around (*casa di cambio*). One that is open until 9:00pm on weekdays, and until 2:00pm on Saturdays, is in the **Train Station**.

Another option, if all else is closed, is to simply change your money at your hotel. You won't get the best rate but at least you'll have money.

Business Hours

From October to June, most shops are open from 9:00am to 1:00pm and from 3:30pm to 7:30pm, and are closed all day Sundays and on Monday mornings. Then from June to August, when it really starts to get hot in Sicily, the morning hours remain the same, but the mid-day siesta time is slightly extended to 4:00pm and sometimes 4:30pm, which then pushes closing time back to 7:30pm or 8:00pm. And also, in conjunction with the Sunday and Monday morning closings, shops also close half-days on Saturday.

Food stores like *alimentari* generally are open from 8:30am to 1:30pm (so stock up on your picnic supplies before you need them) and from 5:00pm to 7:30pm, and during the winter months they are closed on Thursdays.

Local Festivals & Holidays

The *Ferragosto Messinese* on August 14th and 15th every year features a parade of over 100,000 people dressed as Giants. A sight to behold.

Postal Services

The **central post office** in Messina *is in the Piazza Antonello (Tel. 090/ 77-41-90) near the Duomo.* Open Monday through Friday 8:30am–5:00pm, Saturday 9:00am–12 noon. But if you're in a hurry, stamps can be bought at any tobacconist (stores indicated by a **T** sign outside), and mailed at any mailbox, which are red and marked with the words *Poste* or *Lettere.*

Tourist Information & Maps

There is a **tourist office** outside of the train station to the right *in Piazza della Repubblica (Tel. 090/674-236) and another in Piazza Carioli (Tel. 090/293-5292), both of which are only open from 8:30am to 1:00pm, Monday through Saturday.*

Both places will give you tourist information about the surrounding areas and useful city and area maps.

CEFALU

Cefalu is a small port of exquisite beauty located on the north shore of Sicily. Once a quiet little fishing village, today it is one of Sicily's main tourist attractions, because Cefalu has lost little of its charm and character. It's a great place to spend a couple of days exploring the winding streets surrounded by Norman, Arab and medieval architecture.

You can walk along the Vittorio Emanuelle and escape back in time as you see fishermen mending ageless nets in the high vaulted boathouses that line the water. On the same street is a relic from the Saracen occupation, the **lavatoio**, an ancient bath house and laundromat (*Via Vittorio Emanuele. Open 8am–1pm and 3:30pm–7pm*). You can also enjoy the pristine beaches that surround the city. From the train station to the south and into the Centro Storico of Cefalu, everything is within easy walking distance.

Palermo is only an hour away by train, so conceivably you could venture here as a day trip from the capital. If you haven't done so yet, you can also get to the **Lipari Islands** from here by taking a hydrofoil.

WHERE TO STAY

Most of the hotels in the area are outside of the old city and near the spectacular beaches, none of which is a four star. I have listed here the best three hotels near the Centro Storico and the best beach side resort near the city at the Beach Mezzaforno.

1. BAIA DEL CAPITANO, *Spiaggia Mazzaforno, 90015 Cefalu. Tel. 0921/20005. Fax 0921/21063. 39 rooms, 9 with bath, 30 with shower. Single L 50,000-110,000; Double L65,000-170,000. Full board L180,000 per couple. Visa accepted.* ***

Located a short distance out of town on one of the two best beaches around, this is the best hotel in the area. They have their own private beach, snorkeling equipment for rent, water skiing, beautiful views, a swimming pool, tennis courts, sauna, day care for little kids and a wonderful restaurant. The hotel is small which helps make the service extra attentive. They also have a shuttle bus to pick you up at the train station and to transport you back and forth into town.

2. HOTEL TOURIST, *Via Lungomare, 90015 Cefalu. Tel. 0921/ 21750. Fax is the same. 6 rooms, 36 with bath, 10 with shower. Single L 100,000; Double L160,000. American Express accepted. ***

Located near the Centro Storico and train station, this place is perfectly situated for sightseeing. They also have a private beach and their own swimming pool, as well as a shuttle bus to take you to and from town even though it isn't needed. The rooms are clean and comfortable if a little run down. The bathrooms are larger than normal. They also have a decent restaurant attached if you don't want to go out at night.

3. HOTEL ASTRO, *Via Roma 105, 90015 Cefalu. Tel. 0921/21639. Fax 0921/23103. 29 rooms, 2 with bath, 27 with shower. Single L35,000-90,000; Double L45,000-110,000. Full board per person costs L150,000. Visa accepted. ***

Near the train station, which is a slight walk from the Centro Storico, this little hotel has few amenities save for air conditioning in the rooms and a good restaurant. As you can see from their prices, they think that's all that's necessary to charge three star prices. Even so, the place is clean, comfortable, and has a shuttle bus to take you to and from the town and train station.

4. RIVA DEL SOLE, *Via Lungomare 25, 90015 Cefalu. Tel. 0921/ 21230. Fax 0921/21984. 28 rooms, 4 with bath, 24 with shower. Double L95,000. Full board costs L120,000 per person. American Express and Visa accepted. ***

Perfectly located and wonderfully priced. You won't actually be in the lap of luxury but you will have your own private beach and you'll be within walking distance of the Centro Storico. There's a great restaurant and bar, and your rooms will be clean, a little small, but comfortable.

WHERE TO EAT

There are many little restaurants and *trattorias* that have sprouted up because of the tourist trade. These are three of the best:

5. TRATTORIA L'ANTICA CORTE, *Cortille Pepe 7, Tel. 0921/ 23228. Closed Thursdays and all of November and December. Credit cards accepted. Dinner for two L60,000.*

Located in a small courtyard that exudes ambiance, here you can feel as if you walked back in time while also enjoying fantastic food. Their

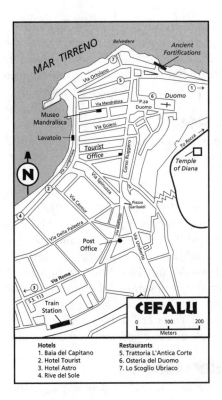

terrace in the small courtyard is the best place to enjoy your meal. Here you'll have plenty of options since their menu is super extensive. Try any of their pastas, especially a local favorite *taglierine all'anchova e mollica* (pasta with anchovies bread crumbs and oil) or *spaghetti al ragu* (with a super tasty meat and tomato sauce). Most of the ingredients come from the area so everything is fresh. They even make their own pasta.

6. OSTERIA DEL DUOMO, *Via Seminario 5, Tel. 0921/21838. Closed Mondays and December. Credit cards accepted. Dinner for two L80,000.*

The ambiance here, with the cathedral so close you can almost touch it, is historically exciting, especially out on their terrace. The owner Enzo Barranco will greet you at the door and is as hospitable as can be, even if his English is not that good. Try the amazing and incredible *penne in barca* (tubular pasta in a tasty clam and oil sauce). Try any of their grilled fish, whose smell permeates the inside of the place.

7. LO SCOGLIO UBRIACO, *Via CO di Bordonaro 24, Tel. 0921/ 23370. Closed Tuesdays, but not in summer, and November. Credit cards accepted. Dinner for two L70,000.*

Sit at their beautiful terrace by the sea that offers magnificent panoramic views. Reserve well in advance to get a good table outside. The atmosphere is peaceful, the service professional, and the food perfect. Try some of their *spaghetti al cartoccio* (with a spicy tomato-based sauce and a variety of seafood) or *spaghetti alla barcola* (with a subtle tomato based sauce and swordfish). For seconds, sample the exquisite *fritti misti* (fried calamari and shrimp) and you'll leave truly satisfied.

SEEING THE SIGHTS

The views from the mountain are especially rewarding, so try and get up it. It's a great walk.

DUOMO

Piazza Duomo. Open 9am–noon and 3:30–7pm.

An austere 12th century Norman cathedral built during the reign of Roger II. The scene of the fortress-like **Duomo** located at the base of the **Rocca**, the large head-shaped hillock that dominates the town is quite impressive. Inside you'll find 16 columns supporting beautiful Saracen style horseshoe arches, and some of the most impressive mosaics left in Sicily. These mosaics stand out even more since the rest of the interior is quite bland. To enter you need to be wearing proper dress. No shorts, short skirts, thin-strapped dresses, tank tops, etc., allowed.

MUSEO MANDRALISCA

Via Mandralisca 13. Tel. 21547. Open 9am–12;30pm and 4pm–7pm. Admission L5,000.

Situated on Via Mandralisca which connects with the Piazza Duomo, this little **museum** houses a fine collection of Greek ceramics, paintings, pottery and more. My favorite is the *Portrait of an Unknown Man* by the 15th century artist Antonello de Messina.

THE ROCCA

To get a great view of the city and its harbor, take the half-hour walk up the mountain. Follow the steps of the Salita Saraceni, and the signs that start near the Piazza Garibaldi just off the Via Ruggero. On the mountain you'll be following walkways lined with medieval walls that lead to the **Temple of Diana**. Built in the 5th century BC, it was first used as a place of worship and sacrifice, then later was employed in defense of the city.

BEACHES

You can catch a bus to the best beaches around in front of the train station or from the Piazza Garibaldi, halfway to the center of town. The cost to go to either **Spiaggia Mazzaforno** or **Spiaggia Settefrati**, two of the better beaches, is L2,500 each way.

PRACTICAL INFORMATION
Banking Hours & Changing Money
Banks are open Monday through Friday from 8:30am to 1:30pm and some do reopen from 2:30pm or so to 3:30pm or so. Besides banks there a plenty of exchange bureaus (*casa di cambio*) around, or you can always use your hotel's exchange.

Business Hours
From October to June, most shops are open from 9:00am to 1:00pm and from 3:30pm to 7:30pm, and are closed all day Sundays and on Monday mornings. Then from June to August, when it really starts to get hot in Sicily, the morning hours remain the same, but the mid-day siesta time is slightly extended to 4:00pm and sometimes 4:30pm, which then pushes closing time back to 7:30pm or 8:00pm. And also, in conjunction with the Sunday and Monday morning closings, shops also close half-days on Saturday.

Food stores like *alimentari* generally are open from 8:30am to 1:30pm (so stock up on your picnic supplies before you need them) and from 5:00pm to 7:30pm, and during the winter months they are closed on Thursdays.

Local Festivals & Holidays
During the summer months there are many music, dance, and performing arts exhibitions on the beaches of Cefalu and in the Cathedral. The best celebration is the **Festa di San Salvatore**, the town's patron saint, which includes fireworks and marching bands and singers.

Postal Services
The **central post office** in Cefalu *is on the Via Vazzana off of Via Roma (Tel. 0921/215-28) near the station.* Open Monday through Friday 8:30am–5:00pm, Saturday 9:00am–Noon. But if you're in a hurry, stamps can be bought at any tobacconist (stores indicated by a **T** sign outside), and mailed at any mailbox, which are red and marked with the words *Poste* or *Lettere*.

Tourist Information & Maps
• **Tourist Office**, *Via Corso Ruggero 77 (Tel. 0921/21-050) in the old city.* Open Monday–Friday, 8:30am–2:00pm, 4:30pm–7:30pm, and Saturday 9:00am–2:00pm. They can supply you with useful maps of the city and area, information about bus schedules to get to the beaches around Cefalu, and more. They also help with finding accommodations if you arrive without reservations.

PALERMO

Palermo started off as a Phoenician city, which the Greeks referred to as Panormos. The city then came under Roman rule during the two **Punic Wars** in 254 BC. After that they endured Byzantine rule (353–830 AD), then Saracen domination (830-1072). Finally Norman (1072-1194) influence placed its stamp on the city. These conquerors were succeeded by the Hohenstaufens in 1194, then the House of Anjou ruled from 1266 until a popular uprising in 1282.

After that, Palermo came under Argonese and Spanish rule and eventually passed to the Bourbons in the 18th century. It finally became part of Italy on May 27, 1860, when it was liberated by Garibaldi. Today Palermo is Italian but ruled by the Mafia.

Palermo is large, busy, noisy, congested and polluted, the perfect capital for the Mafia. Today there is the beginning of a popular backlash against *La Cosa Nostra's* influence in the city, evidenced by anti-Mafia posters on the walls. But as a tourist you have little to worry about from the Mafia. In Palermo you need to protect yourself against pickpockets and purse snatchers, especially if you roam away from the Centro Storico.

Centuries ago the city was divided into four quarters, which all merged at the square known as the **Quattro Canti** (four corners) in the center of town. This square is at the intersection of **Corso Vittorio Emanuelle** and **Via Maqueda**. The **Albergheria** is northwest of the *quattro canti*, **Capo** is southwest, **Vucciria** is northeast and **La Kalsa** is southeast. Each of these quarters had distinct dialects, cultures, trading practices and markets for their products. There was limited intermingling and intermarriage would result in being ostracized.

Today, the area around the Quattro Canti is where most of the sights are located. Today the area is an eclectic mix of medieval streets and Norman, Oriental, and Baroque architecture, broad modern avenues and large buildings, and bombed-out vacant lots from World War II.

As such it is not nearly as charming as Florence or Venice, and it also has less historical architecture and museums than Rome. But Palermo is still an interesting city to explore. There's a heavy Middle Eastern influence, almost a *souk*-like atmosphere at some markets that differentiates Palermo from other Italian cities. Stay to see Palermo's sights, marvel in its sounds and smells (sometimes only traffic and pollution), and then hop on a train and go explore some other less hectic part of Sicily.

ARRIVALS & DEPARTURES

By Air

You can fly into Palermo from Rome or Milan. The fare is changing all the time, but at last check it was $266 from Rome. It may be even higher

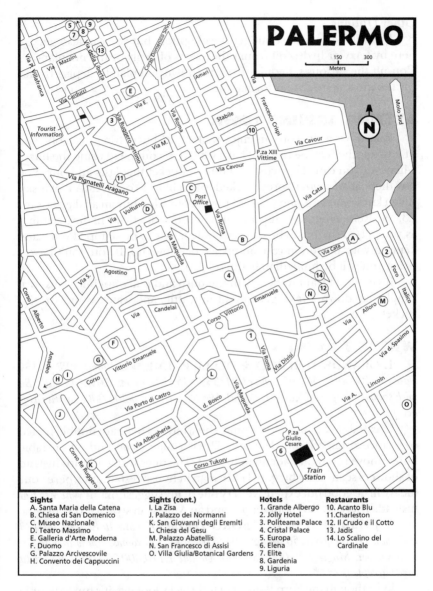

PALERMO

150   300
Meters

Sights
A. Santa Maria della Catena
B. Chiesa di San Domenico
C. Museo Nazionale
D. Teatro Massimo
E. Galleria d'Arte Moderna
F. Duomo
G. Palazzo Arcivescovile
H. Convento dei Cappuccini

Sights (cont.)
I. La Zisa
J. Palazzo dei Normanni
K. San Giovanni degli Eremiti
L. Chiesa del Gesu
M. Palazzo Abatellis
N. San Francesco di Assisi
O. Villa Giulia/Botanical Gardens

Hotels
1. Grande Albergo
2. Jolly Hotel
3. Politeama Palace
4. Cristal Palace
5. Europa
6. Elena
7. Elite
8. Gardenia
9. Liguria

Restaurants
10. Acanto Blu
11. Charleston
12. Il Crudo e il Cotto
13. Jadis
14. Lo Scalino del
    Cardinale

by the time you read this, but look for various excursion fares or even package deals with **Alitalia** or **Lufthansa**, the major airlines flying in and out of Sicily. You can also get direct flights from London or Dublin to Palermo, so this could be an option for you if you're crossing the Atlantic.

By Train

Palermo is about one hour away from Cefalu by train.

Other Options

Bus will be your best budget travel option, but you can also get here by ferry or hydrofoil from other parts of Sicily or the mainland. Consult the various schedules from the town you plan to depart from for the most up-to-date information.

GETTING AROUND TOWN

Palermo is a city you can enjoy walking in, but getting from one end of it to another can be tiring. That's why we recommend using the **buses** whenever you can. They cost L1,000 for a ticket that lasts an hour. You buy them at *tabacchis* (stores marked with a blue **T**) or at AMAT's kiosks. If you know you're going to be taking the bus a lot, buy an all day pass for L3,000. Remember to stamp a single ticket or a day ticket in the machines as you get on the bus. The day pass only needs to be stamped once and kept on your person in case an inspector shows up. If you don't have a ticket you will be immediately fined L50,000.

If you don't want to deal with the push and pull of public transport, simply flag down a **taxi**, get caught in traffic, and watch your fare sky-rocket.

WHERE TO STAY

1. GRANDE ALBERGO & DELLE PALME, *Via Roma 398, 90139 Palermo. Tel. 091/583-933. Fax 091/331-545. 187 rooms, 103 with bath, 84 with shower. Single L75,000-150,000; Double L100,000-200,000. Credit cards accepted.* ***

Located on the busy Via Roma, the windows here are double-paned so you are insulated from the noise. This is a huge, clean, and comfortable hotel whose rooms are adequately sized. The ones with bathtubs instead of showers seem to be bigger. There is an in-house restaurant where your meal will be good but expensive. Try one of my suggestions in *Where to Eat* instead. There is also room service and an American style bar downstairs.

2. JOLLY HOTEL DEL FORO ITALICO, *Foro Italico 22, 90133 Palermo. Tel. 091/616-5090. Fax 091/616-1441. 277 rooms, 207 with bath, 70 with shower. Single L90,000-180,000; Double L110,000-220,000. No credit cards accepted.* ****

Even though the Foro Italico is a little tacky looking, it's fun to people watch in the evenings. It's also well located so you can walk to most of the sights. The hotel has a pool, nice restaurant, room service, laundry service, air conditioning and Satellite TV in the rooms. The place, like all Jolly hotels, is as modern as they come, but it is mainly a businessman's hotel – meaning the rooms are little tiny.

3. POLITEAMA PALACE HOTEL, *Piazza Ruggero Settimo 15, 90124 Palermo. Tel. 091/322-777. Fax 091/611-1589. 102 rooms, 37 with bath, 65 with shower. Single L150,000; Double L200,000. American Express and Visa accepted.* ****

Another businessman's hotel, this one is located in the new Palermo by the Modern Art Gallery and the tourist office. It's a long ways away from most of the sights, and beside cleanliness and comfort it doesn't have many other amenities, except air conditioning, TV, and an in-house restaurant that is acceptable.

4. CRISTAL PALACE HOTEL, *Via Roma 477, 90139 Palermo. Tel. 091/611-2580. Fax 091/611-2589. 90 rooms, 39 with bath, 51 with shower. Single L115,000; Double L170,000. American Express and Visa accepted.* ***

Located on the busy and noisy Via Roma, this place has kept out most of the street sounds with double-paned glass. Besides super clean rooms with air conditioning and satellite TV, the hotel offers a restaurant, a piano bar, a disco, an American Style bar and a gymnasium. This is the kind of place you don't leave after returning to it at night. Comfortable but still a little pricey.

5. HOTEL EUROPA, *Via Agrigento 3, 90141 Palermo. Tel. 091/625-6323. Fax is the same. 73 rooms, 58 with bath, 15 with shower. Single L95,000; Double L140,000. Credit cards accepted.* ***

A thoroughly modern place with air conditioning, TV, and spotless bathrooms and rooms. Located in the modern section of Palermo six blocks north of the Modern Art Museum, they also have a fine restaurant that is well priced. Coupled with an American style bar and quick room service, you can have a pleasant stay here.

6. HOTEL ELENA, *Piazza Giulio Cesare 14, 90127 Palermo. Tel. 091/616-2021. Fax 091/616-2984. 56 rooms only 22 with bath. Single without L38,000; Single with L50,000; Double without L55,000; Double with L70,000. No credit cards accepted.* **

Located at the train station, this hotel should be used as quick stopover if you're only going to be in Palermo a day or two and are leaving by train. You don't want to go walking at night around the station, so make sure you get a comfortable room with a bath. The rooms are as clean as can be expected from a two star by a train station. One big minus is that there is no air conditioning, a must in the summer in Palermo. Definitely a budget travelers stop.

7. HOTEL ELITE, *Via M Stabile 136, 90139 Palermo. Tel. 091/329-318. Fax 091/588-614. 18 rooms, 5 with bath, 13 with shower. 2 sets of two rooms share a connecting bathroom. Single L 55,000-60,000; Double L70,000-85,000. Credit cards accepted.* **

You can get full board at their adequate restaurant for only L85,000. Located between the Modern Art Gallery and the Archaeological Museum, this place is kind of in between total modern and decaying. They do have room and laundry service, as well as TVs in the rooms but no air conditioning, a necessity in summer. Even so the price is right and they offer a clean environment for budget travelers.

8. HOTEL GARDENIA, *Via M Stabile 136, 90139 Palermo. Tel. 091/ 322-761. Fax 091/333-732. 9 rooms, 7 with shower. Single without L55,000; Single with L70,000; Double without L70,000; Double with L85,000. No credit cards accepted.* **

Located in the same building as the Hotel Elite, this place is a little smaller and has a lot fewer amenities, except they do have air conditioning in the rooms. The rooms are tiny, as clean as can be expected, all decorated differently just like a country inn, and are comfortable enough to lounge around in. Definitely a budget travelers haunt.

9. HOTEL LIGURIA, *Via M Stabile, 90139 Palermo. Tel. 091/581-588. 16 rooms, 2 with bath, 6 with shower. Single without L33,000; Double without L49,000; Double with L64,000. American Express accepted.* **

If you want to save money stay at this two star on the same street as the Elite and Gardenia. Only L64,000 for a double with shower, which is pretty good. But they don't have TV or air conditioning or matching bed spreads and curtains. Only rugs on the floors, no carpeting. and without the double-paned glass it can get a little noisy. But if you want to save money, stay here.

WHERE TO EAT

10. TRATTORIA ACANTO BLU, *Via F Guardinone 19, Tel. 091/326-258. Closed Sundays and September. No credit cards accepted. Dinner for two L50,000.*

A small little place that serves basic rustic cuisine. You can either enjoy the air conditioning inside or the terrace outside. Try some of the extensive antipasto table, especially the fried vegetables with a spicy hot sauce. Next try what they call *riso dei poeti* (rice of the poets), which contains apple, radish and fish. Its quite delectable. Then save the best for last, *funghi infornati cotti nella mollica condita con olio e peperoncini* (fresh mushrooms baked in a mold of bread served up with fresh olive oil and peperoncini).

11. RISTORANTE CHARLESTON, *Piazzale Ungheria 30, tel. 091/ 321-366. Closed Sundays. All credit cards accepted. Dinner for two L130,000.*

One of "the" places to go in Palermo, but that doesn't mean they're any good. This restaurant is known for their fish dishes, but they can't seem to get them right. Their sauces are too thick or too pungent, the fish is overcooked and the presentation is horrible. Maybe it's one of "the" places to go because it's Mafia owned? I didn't want to ask. What saved the meal was a great wine list and a *sambuca con mosche* (a sweet liquor with coffee beans) afterwards.

12. IL CRUDO E IL COTTO, *Piazza Marina 45a, Tel. 091/616-9261. Closed Tuesdays and variable holidays. No credit cards accepted. Dinner for two L70,000.*

In the beautiful Piazza Marina you can get a great meal at this tiny family run *trattoria*. You have Laura in the kitchen and Franchino and Giovanni greeting people and working as waiters. Get a seat outside so you can enjoy the view. Try their *riso ai frutti di mare* (rice with mixed seafood) then a succulent *bistecca* (steak) or *pesce spada alla griglia* (grilled swordfish for seconds). To wash it all down get some of their house wine, which comes from the local mountains.

13. JADIS, *Via Liberta 121, Tel. 091/349-323. Closed Sundays and Mondays and August. Open only at night. No credit cards accepted. Dinner for two L70,000.*

Located a few blocks north of the Museum of Modern Art, this is a very popular place with the arts crowd as well as with people that appreciate good food. You have a choice of outside seating, which is wonderful on cool evenings. Try their *carpaccio di vitello* or their *carpaccio di pesce spada* (steak of veal or sword fish)

14. LO SCALINO DEL CARDINALE, *Via Bottai 18, Tel. 091/ 3310124. Closed Mondays, for Lunch, and the last half of September. Credit cards accepted. Dinner for two L70,000.*

A great local place that is always packed during the week. With its terrace in use in the summer there seems to be plenty of space, but in the winter it's difficult to find a spot to eat. Try some of their *crocchette al latte* (croquets with milk) or *al primo sale fritto* (fried with a local cheese). For seconds, try their *pesce spada al profumo di Cardinale* (swordfish with a creamy sauce with sliced bell peppers).

SEEING THE SIGHTS

North of Corso Vittorio Emanuelle

As you move from the east of Corso Vittorio Emanuelle to the west, you may want to catch rides on the frequent bus #27 to quicken your pace.

A. SANTA MARIA DELLA CATENA

Via Vittorio Emanuele. Open 8am–11:30am and 3:30pm–7pm.

Built in the early 16th century, this church is named after the chain that used to be dragged across the old harbor, **La Cala**, at night to protect the vessels inside. This used to be the main port of Palermo until it started silting up in the late sixteenth century. The main industrial shipping moved north and this little inlet was left to the fishermen. It's a great place to take a short stroll and take in the sights, smells, and sounds of the Sicilian seafarers.

Not far away, located almost at the eastern part of the city, is the **Porta Felice**, which was built in 1582 to compliment the slightly older **Porta Nuova**, which is all the way to the west. Since these two gates were once the ancient boundaries of old Palermo, this is a good place to start your tour, because from here you can get a good feel for the true extent of ancient Palermo.

Past Porta Felice is the popular but relatively tacky promenade, **Foro Italico**, with its own little **amusement park**. On summer nights residents come out here to sit, talk, walk, stare, and share the beautiful evenings with each other.

B. CHIESA DI SAN DOMENICO

Piazza San Domenico. Open 7:30am–noon.

Walk down Via Vittorio Emanuelle towards the Porta Nuova and take a right on Via Roma to get to the Piazza San Domenico and the **Church of San Domenico**. This beautiful 17th century church with an 18th century facade is the burial site of many famous Sicilians. At night the facade and the statue-topped marble column are lit up, creating quite a spectacle. The perfect spot to sip an *aperitivo* at one of the outdoor cafes surrounding the piazza.

Just behind the church, on Via dei Bambinai #16, is the **Oratorio del Rosario di San Domenico**, which contains some interesting stucco work created by Giacomo Serpotta as well as a magnificent altar piece by Van Dyke (*open 7:30am–Noon*).

C. MUSEO NAZIONALE

Piazza Olivella. Tel. 662-0220. Open Monday–Saturday 9am–1:30pm, Tuesday and Fridayday also open 3pm–5:30pm. Sunday and holidays only open 9am–12:30pm. Admission L3,000.

Go back to the Via Roma and walk north to the **National Museum**. Also known as the Museo Archeologico Regionale, if you've been out discovering Sicily's archaeological sites or intend to do so, you'll love this museum. Located in a former monastery, their collection of pre-historic relics, Etruscan, Greek, Egyptian and Roman pieces is quite extensive and well presented.

The museum has frescoes from Pompeii, bronze works from Greece, Roman sculptures, and much more. Especially imposing are the 56 lion head water spouts taken from Himera in the 5th century BC. This is one of the finest museums in all of Italy.

D. TEATRO MASSIMO

Piazza G Verdi. Undergoing re-construction. Not open to public. Usual hours 9am–1pm and 4pm–7pm. Admission L3,000.

The **Teatro Massimo** is down Via Maqueda from the Archaeological Museum. Also known as **Teatro Vittorio Emanuelle**, this theater was built from 1875 to 1897 and can seat 3,200 attendees. As such it is the second largest theater in Europe, second only to the Opera house in Paris. Currently under renovation, you probably will not be able to get a tour inside, but it doesn't hurt to ask.

E. GALLERIA D'ARTE MODERNA

Gallery open Tuesday–Sunday 9am–1pm and 3–6pm. Admission L6,000.

I know you didn't come to Sicily to look at modern art, but a trip to the **Modern Art Museum** is a breath of fresh air after looking at relics all day long. Italy's art treasures don't all belong to the past, so visit here and see some beautiful and interesting modern works.

Nearby is the main **tourist office**, past the English gardens in front and past the equestrian statue of Garibaldi in the square. Stop here to get ideas about current happenings and what else to see in Palermo and elsewhere in Sicily.

Walk back down Via Roma to the **Quattro Canti** (The Four Corners) – Via Roma, Via Vittorio Emanuelle and Via Maqueda converge here at what is the imagined center of the old city.

F. DUOMO

Piazza del Cattedrale. Open 7am–noon and 4pm–7pm.

The **Duomo** is three hundred meters past the Quattro Canti on the Via Vittorio Emanuelle. The church was begun by the Normans in 1185, and thereafter underwent many architectural transformations from the 13th century to the 18th, though the Norman towers and triple-apsed eastern side remain today. With it's many styles, the intricate exterior is a joy to study. The same can't be said for the interior, which was recreated in a bland neoclassic style.

To the left as you enter you'll find six imposing tombs contains the bodies of past kings of Palermo, including Frederick II and Roger II. In the chapel to the right of the choir is the silver sarcophagus that contains the remains of the city's patron saint, Rosalia. The **treasury**, located to the right of the apse, is infinitely more interesting since it contains some exquisite, jewel encrusted ancient clothing (L1,500 to enter). You also find pieces of some saints preserved here.

G. PALAZZO ARCIVESCOVILE

Via Papireto Bonnello. Open Tuesday–Sunday 9am–1pm and 3pm–6pm.
Immediately southwest of the cathedral is the one-time **Archbishop's Palace** that contains the **Dioclesan Museum**. The museum features many works of art that were salvaged from other churches during the Allied bombings of World War II. If this is closed check out the **Mercato delle Pulci**, just up Via Bonello (next to the Palace) in **Piazza Peranni**. This is a great junk/antique market held everyday from 8:00am to 2:00pm.

A little further down the Via Vittorio Emanuelle is the **Porta Nuova**, which was erected in 1535 to commemorate the Tunisian exploits of Charles V.

H. CONVENTO DEI CAPPUCCINI

Open Monday–Saturday 9:00am–Noon and 3:00pm–5:00pm. The visit is free but a donation of about L2,000 per person is expected.
No, this isn't a shrine to that wonderful frothing espresso product. This is a bizarre yet fascinating place, in a morbid kind of way. To get here, walk 1.5 km west past the Porta Nuova or catch bus #27 going west from the Via Vittorio Emanuelle to the Via Pindemonte. After you get off, it's a short walk to the convent. Just follow the signs.

This is like something out of a horror movie. Bodies stacked everywhere. Almost 800 of them. For many centuries this convent was the burial place not only for church members but also for rich laymen. You'll find bodies preserved with a variety of methods with differing results. Some bodies still have their hair and skin. Others have decomposed completely. The saddest sight here, though, are the remains of the tiny infants and young children that never made it into adulthood. A gruesome place to visit, yes. But an experience you will never forget.

I. LA ZISA

Open Monday –Saturday 9:00am–2:00pm. Sunday 9:00am–1:00pm. The visit is free.
Since you're already out here, you might as well walk a short way north to **La Zisa**, a huge palace begun by William I in 1160 and finished by his son William II. Take the Via Corradino di Svevia, take a right on Via Eugenio L'Emiro (the first road), then take an immediate left onto Via Edersi, then take the second right onto Viale Luigi Castiglia and you'll turn left after about fifty meters into the piazza that houses La Zisa.

This is a wonderful replica of an Arabian palace (Zisa means *magnificent* in Arabic) and was used as a retreat for the king where he had lush exotic gardens tended and wild animals housed.

South of Corso Vittorio Emanuelle
J. PALAZZO DEI NORMANNI

Open Monday–Friday 9:00am–Noon and 3:00pm–5:00pm and Saturday and Sunday 9:00am–11:00am. The chapel is closed Sunday.

The **Norman** or **Royal Palace**, just past the Porta Nuova going east on Corso Vittorio Emanuelle, is a terrific place. Originally built by the Saracens and remodeled and reinforced by the Normans, this is an imposing fortress-like building that sits on the high ground overlooking the city below. Since the palazzo is the current seat of the Sicilian Parliament, you must be escorted by a guide through the rooms. Don't playfully attempt to sneak off; security is pretty tight because of the Mafia problems.

One room you can't miss is the **Cappella Palatina**, the Palatine Chapel, which contains some of the best **mosaics** outside of Istanbul and Ravenna. The tile art describes scenes from the Old Testament. Another room adorned with mosaics, twith a flora and fauna motif, is the **Sala di Ruggero**, King Rogers Hall.

K. SAN GIOVANNI DEGLI EREMITI

Corso Re Ruggero. Open 9am–1pm. On Tuesday, Wednesday, and Fridayday also open 3–5pm.

Founded by Roger II, and built in 1132, the architecture of **St. John of the Hermits** has Arabic influence. Just down the road from the Norman Palace, this church was built over a mosque and is dominated by five Arab-looking domes. To get to the church you must walk up a path lined with citrus trees, behind which are some 13th century cloisters. A beautiful sight to see.

L. CHIESA DEL OF GESU

Via Porto di Castro. Open 7am–noon and 5–6:30pm.

Follow Via Porto di Castro from the Norman Palace to this small church with its green mosaic dome. It has a multicolored marble interior and an almost surreal interpretation of the *Last Judgment*. In the church's small courtyard, you can still see the effect of Allied bombings during World War II. You can see this same bombing effect near the **Palazzo Abatellis** that is home to the **Galleria Nazionale Siciliana** (see below).

M. PALAZZO ABATELLIS

Via Alloro. Open 9am–1:30pm and also open on Tuesday, Thursdays and Fridayday 4–7pm. Sunday and holidays 9am–12;30pm. Admission L4,000.

This palace houses the **Galleria Nazionale Siciliana**, one of Sicily's wonderful regional art museums. The gallery gives a comprehensive insight into Sicilian painting and sculpture. Some of the work is quite crude, some is magnificent, but if you've never been exposed to Sicilian art, this is your chance to learn.

N. CHURCH OF SAN FRANCESCO DI ASSISI

Via Paternostro. Open only from 7:00am–11:00am every day.

You have to be an early bird to catch this sight: the church is known for its intricate rose window that looks magnificent from the inside when the early morning sun streams through it. The zig-zag design on its exterior is common to many of the churches in the area. Built in the 13th century, there were two side chapels added in the 14th and 15th centuries.

O. VILLA GIULIA PARK & BOTANICAL GARDENS

Via Lincoln. Park open until dark. Botanical Gardens open Monday–Fridayday 9am–Noon and Saturday 9am–11am. Admission L2,000.

This is Palermo's best centrally-located park, which gives you a respite from the hectic pace of Palermo. Besides wildlife roaming around like deer and ducks, there are gardens, a small kiddy train and a pretty **Botanical Gardens**. The gardens feature tropical plants from all over the world. It's an uplifting spot after a few days touring through Palermo.

NIGHTLIFE & ENTERTAINMENT

There is plenty to do at night in Palermo, but I recommend that you enjoy a nice meal, then retire to your room. Crime is a problem, including violent crime – I don't want you walking down the wrong street. If just having dinner is too boring for you, locate a restaurant near your hotel and stop there for after-dinner drinks before making the short walk back to your hotel.

SHOPPING

Food shopping can be done at the markets that are located off Via Roma on the **Via Divisi**, as well as between the **Palazzo dei Normani** and the train station at **Piazza Ballaro**.

For inexpensive clothing, try the **Via Bandiera** near Chiesa San Domenico. For more expensive clothing, try along the main thorough-fares of **Via Roma** and **Via Maqueda**.

PRACTICAL INFORMATION

Banking Hours & Changing Money

Banks are open Monday through Friday from 8:30am to 1:30pm and some do reopen from 2:30pm or so to 3:30pm or so. Besides banks there a plenty of exchange bureaus (*casa di cambio*). One that is open until

9:00pm on weekdays, and until 2:00pm on Saturdays is in the Train Station. Another option, if all else is closed is to simply change your money at your hotel. You won't get the best rate but at least you'll have money. If you need **American Express** service, contact Giovanni Ruggeri e Figli *at Via E Amari 40, Tel 091/587-144. Open regular business hours.*

Business Hours

From October to June, most shops are open from 9:00am to 1:00pm and from 3:30pm to 7:30pm, and are closed all day Sundays and on Monday mornings. Then from June to August, when it really starts to get hot in Sicily, the morning hours remain the same, but the mid-day siesta time is slightly extended to 4:00pm and sometimes 4:30pm, which then pushes closing time back to 7:30pm or 8:00pm. And also, in conjunction with the Sunday and Monday morning closings, shops also close half-days on Saturday.

Food stores like *alimentari* generally are open from 8:30am to 1:30pm (so stock up on your picnic supplies before you need them) and from 5:00pm to 7:30pm, and during the winter months they are closed on Thursdays.

Local Festivals & Holidays
• **July 11-15**, Festival of Santa Rosalia with fireworks and insanity
• **September 4**, pilgrimage-like walk to Monte Pelligrino in honor of Santa Rosalia
• **Last week in September**, International Tennis Tournament

Postal Services

The **central post office** in Palermo *is at Via Roma 322.* Open Monday through Friday 8:30am–5:00pm, Saturday 9:00am–Noon. But if you're in a hurry, stamps can be bought at any tobacconist (stores indicated by a **T** sign outside), and mailed at any mailbox, which are red and marked with the words *Poste* or *Lettere.*

Tourist Information & Maps
• **Main Information Office**, *Piazza Castelnuovo 34 (Tel. 091/583-847) across from the Modern Art Museum*
• **Information Office**, *in the train station, open Monday–Friday, 8:00am–8:00pm*
If the office at the station is out of information and maps, take bus #101 to the piazza and the main office. They both supply detailed maps and information about Palermo and other places of interest. There is also a tourist office in the Stazione Maritima and at the airport.

TRAPANI

Located on a sickle shaped peninsula on the northwest coast of Sicily, **Trapani** is the island's largest fishing port. The city, called *Drapanon* (which means sickle) by locals, used to be the main port for the ancient Greek city of **Eryx** (Erice – see next section). Trapani flourished as a trading center, mainly with customers in Africa and the Middle East. The town has an ancient elegant **Centro Storico** out on the end of the sickle of a peninsula.

Today the city's lifeblood still depends on the trading of salt, wine, and fish. It's a modern city, developed after most everything else was destroyed during Allied bombing in World War II. Trapani is also a friendly city and should be one of your destinations while in Sicily.

GETTING AROUND TOWN

The **Centro Storico** occupies about a square kilometer on the peninsula, so everything in it is within walking distance. The **train station** lets you off just on the edge of the old town, and the docks along **Via Ammiraglio Staiti** (which runs half the southern length of the old town) are where you can catch ferries to the **Egadi Islands**.

To get to the city's museum in the new section of town, you'll need to catch bus #1 or #10 from the train station.

WHERE TO STAY

Most of the hotels in Trapani are located in the new city. The two below are the best and closest to the town's old city.

1. HOTEL VITTORIA, *Via F. Crispi 4, 91100 Trapani. Tel. 0923/873-0444. Fax 0923/29870. 65 rooms all with bath. Single L70,000; Double L125,000. American Express and Diners Club accepted.* ***

Located about two blocks from the train station. Exit and walk to the right down Via F. Crispi and you'll run right into it. Really the only good hotel in the Centro Storico area, and is perfectly situated for exploring the old town as well as getting to the station quickly to explore points outside of Trapani. The rooms have air conditioning, room and laundry service, great views over the sea and the park, and are clean and comfortable. Also, the bathrooms are immaculate and large for an Italian hotel.

2. CAVALLINO BIANCO, *Lungomare D. Aligheri, 91100 Trapani. Tel. 0923/21549. Fax 0923/873-002. 43 rooms all with shower. Single L 50,000; Double L88,000. Full board L95,000 per person.* **

Located along the shore road in the new town, this is not the most scenic place to stay, but it is clean, comfortable, and kid friendly. Their restaurant is also quite good and they do have a shuttle bus to pick you up from the train station and to ferry you into town for sightseeing.

WHERE TO EAT

3. RISTORANTE P&G, *Via Spalti 1, Tel. 0923/547-701. Closed Sundays and August. Credit cards accepted. Dinner for two L90,000.*

The decorations are not something to write home about, but the food here is excellent. Once you start digging into your antipasto, your mouth will come alive with the flavors of the Mediterranean, not just Italian. Try some of their *cuscus con la cernia* (couscous with stone bass) for primo, then move onto some *tonno al forno* (oven cooked tuna steak) or *alla brace* (grilled tuna steak). You should have at least one meal here while in Trapani, especially if you work for Proctor and Gamble (P&G, get it?). There's only 50 seats so make reservations or come early.

4. RISTORANTE DA PEPE, *Via Spalti 50, Tel. 0923/28246. Closed Mondays. Credit cards accepted. Dinner for two L90,000.*

Just down the road from P&G, they're known for their house pasta dish made with the local pasta, *busiati*, which is actually just *fusilli*, a spiral shaped pasta. The sauce is made with cooked garlic, tomatoes, and basil and is fantastic. And of course for seconds try any of their varieties of *pesce spada* (swordfish) or *tonno* (tuna) steaks.

SEEING THE SIGHTS

The look and feel of this medieval port city, with its European and Arab influences, makes you feel as if you've stepped back in time. The medieval and Renaissance fabric of the streets blends well with the tapestry of the Baroque buildings. It should take one full day to see everything that Trapani has to offer if you want to do it right.

And when you're done here, use the city as a jumping off point to visit **Erice** and other sights in the area.

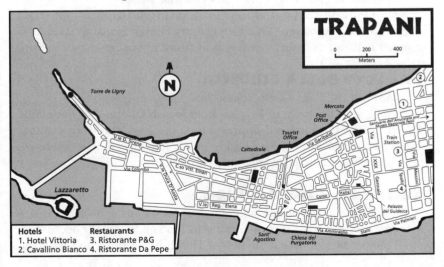

CATTEDRALE

Corso Vittorio Emanuele. Open 8am–noon and 3–6pm.

With its Baroque portico and immense exterior, and with it's colorful dome and stucco walls, the **Cathedral** can be an imposing sight compared to the other tiny churches in the old city. Most of the others have been closed for years for restoration, but you may be in luck and find one of them open. A number of them have an interesting mix of Muslim and Christian influences.

TORRE DE LIGNY

Located at the most eastern point of the city, this is a great spot to watch the sunset, and since the town seems to close down around 9:00pm, you can watch the sunset then retire for a romantic evening at your hotel. The tower also houses the surprisingly interesting **Museo di Preistoria** *(Open Monday–Saturday 9:00am-1:00pm and 4:00pm to 8:00pm; admission L2,500)*, which contains Neanderthal bones, skulls and tools, as well as the remains of prehistoric animals.

MERCATO DI PESCE

Walk up the Via Mura di Tramontana Ovest on the north side of the peninsula from the tower and you'll come to the bustling fish market. Here you can see fishermen selling their catch, and fruit and vegetable vendors clamoring for your attention. But remember to get here in the morning, because it shuts down by 1:30pm.

SANT' AGOSTINO

Piazzetta Saturdayurno. Open 8am–noon and 3–6pm.

Near the cathedral and adjacent to the main tourist office is the small church of **Sant'Agostino**. This 14th century church is mainly used as a **concert hall** and its main attraction is its stunning rose colored window.

PALAZZO DELLA GUIDECCA

Via della Guidecaa 43. Open 9am-1pm and 4pm-7pm

Located in the heart of Trapani's old **Jewish Ghetto** that was established during the medieval oppression of the Jews, this 16th century building has a plaque-studded facade with some Spanish-style windows. An elaborate and intricate architectural piece.

CHIESA DEL PURGATORIO

Via Cassaretto. Open mon–Saturday 10am–noon and 4:30–6:30pm.

The most fascinating church to see in Trapani, not really because of itself but because of what it has inside. The church is home to a large set of life-sized wooden statues called the **Misteri** that have been paraded through town during Good Friday celebrations every year for the past 600 years. Each statue represents a member of one of the trades, such as fishermen, cobblers, etc. It's quite a sight to see.

SANTUARIO DELL'ANUNZIATA
Via Conte Pepoli. Open 8:30am–noon and 4–6pm. No Charge.

Really the only reason to venture into the new city is to come see these last two sights. If you don't want to hike 3 km down a large boulevard, catch either bus #1 or #10 from the station out here. Remember to buy a ticket at a Newsstand or *Tabacchi* first (L800).

This 14th century convent and church contains the town's main treasure, the smiling *Madonna and Child*. This statue has supposedly been responsible for a number of miracles, so it is kept secured here and is usually surrounded by many kneeling worshipers.

MUSEO NAZIONALE PEPOLI
Via Conte Pepoli. Open Monday–Saturday 9am–1:30pm. Sunday until 12:30pm. On Tuesday, Thursdays and Saturday also open 4–6:30pm. Admission L3,000.

Fans of numismatics (that's the study of coins to you and me), hang on to your hats! Next to the convent and church is a **museum** with a wide variety of artifacts, including an extensive Roman, Greek, and Arab coin collection. Don't miss the 18th century guillotine, the local coral carvings, or the quaint folk-art figurines. It's a great museum for kids of all ages, but remember to come during the day since the lighting doesn't seem to be adequate in the evening.

NIGHTLIFE & ENTERTAINMENT

Trapani closes down around 9:00pm, but before that people are out, just after dinner, along the **Via Vittorio Emanuelle** for a stroll or a sip of Sambuca at a sidewalk cafe. If you're interested in sampling a local delicacy try a *biscotto coi fichi*, a very tasty fig newton-like cookie.

PRACTICAL INFORMATION
Banking Hours & Changing Money

Banks are open Monday through Friday, 8:30am–1:30pm and some reopen from 2:30pm or so to 3:30pm or so. Besides banks there a plenty of exchange bureaus (*casa di cambio*). One that is open until 9:00pm on weekdays, and until 2:00pm on Saturdays is in the Train Station. Another option, if all else is closed is to simply change your money at your hotel. You won't get the best rate but at least you'll have money.

Business Hours

From October to June, most shops are open from 9:00am to 1:00pm and from 3:30pm to 7:30pm, and are closed all day Sundays and on Monday mornings. Then from June to August, when it really starts to get hot in Sicily, the morning hours remain the same, but the mid-day siesta time is slightly extended to 4:00pm and sometimes 4:30pm, which then pushes closing time back to 7:30pm or 8:00pm. And also, in conjunction with the Sunday and Monday morning closings, shops also close half-days on Saturday.

Food stores like *alimentari* generally are open from 8:30am to 1:30pm (so stock up on your picnic supplies before you need them) and from 5:00pm to 7:30pm, and during the winter months they are closed on Thursdays.

Local Festivals & Holidays
• **Good Friday**, Procession of Wooden Statues from 3:00pm to 7:00pm
• **Last Three weeks of July**, Luglio Musicale Trapanese. Musical festival in the Villa Margherita at 9:00pm each night.

Postal Services

The **central post office** in Trapani *is in the Piazza Vittorio Veneto (Tel. 0923/873-038) at the ends of Via Garibaldi.* Open Monday through Friday 8:00am–5:00pm, Saturday 9:00am–Noon. But if you're in a hurry, stamps can be bought at any tobacconist (stores indicated by a T sign outside), and mailed at any mailbox, which are red and marked with the words *Poste* or *Lettere.*

Tourist Information & Maps
• **Main tourist office**, *Piazza Saturno (Tel. 0923/29000).* They have maps, brochures, and all sorts of information about the town and surrounding area.

ERICE

Only a forty-five minute bus ride from Trapani, don't miss **Erice** when in Sicily. It is a walled mountain town that used to the biggest in the area (Trapani was just its port), but is still completely medieval with its winding streets, alleys, and ancient buildings. You may actually want to stay here rather than in Trapani and do the reverse commute into the larger city, then escape back to this town's silent charms at the end of the day. It's what I should have done on my last trip here.

The views from Erice's terraces are fantastic. You can see all of Trapani as well as the **Egadi Islands** (Isole Egadi) and on a good day the coast of Africa. Besides the views and the charming streets there is little of importance to see in Erice, but these are types of ancient towns you came to Sicily to see. Don't be upset if there's no Michelangelo's *David* to admire – the town is a masterpiece in itself.

ARRIVALS & DEPARTURES

After a 45 minute bus ride from Trapani, the bus will drop you off at the **Porta Trapani** at the southwest edge of town. From here cross the piazza to the **tourist office** *(open regular business hours, closed Sundays; Tel. 0923/869-388)* and pick up any information you think you might need.

WHERE TO STAY

If you want to stay in Erice during the summer months, make reservations well in advance. Listed below are the three hotels in the town.

1. ELIMO HOTEL, *Via Vittorio Emanuelle, 91016 Erice. Tel. 0923/869-377. 21 rooms all with bath. Single L 80,000-100,000; Double L120,000-160,000. No credit cards accepted.* ***

A quaint little hotel that is the best in the city. It has a fine restaurant and a relaxing bar for an evening's refreshments, and quaint old surroundings. The rooms have heat since it can get chilly here at night, as well as a TV if you get bored with ambiance and views. They are also smallish but clean and very comfortable.

ERICE

0   200   400
Meters

Hotels
1. Elimo Hotel
2. Hotel Moderno
3. Pensione Edelweiss

Restaurants
4. Cortile di Venere
5. Monte San Giuliano

2. HOTEL MODERNO, *Via Vittorio Emanuelle 63, 91016 Erice, Tel. 0923/869-300. Fax 0923/869-139. 40 rooms, 6 with bath, 34 with shower. Single L100,000-120,000; Double L140,000-180,000. American Express and Visa accepted.* **

The second best hotel in the city with clean rooms and relatively modern furnishings. They have laundry and room service as well as good in-house restaurant that is large, elegant, and serves superb food, especially their *cous cous di pesce* (a Middle Eastern rice dish with fish) or their *vitello al forno* (veal cooked perfectly in the oven). Request a room with a view; the views from some of the rooms are spectacular.

3. PENSIONE EDELWEISS, *Cortile Piazza Vincenzo 5, 91016 Erice. Tel. 0923/869-420. Fax 0923/869-252. 13 rooms, 13 with bath. Single L80,000; Double L120,000. American Express and Visa accepted.* **

Since there are only three good hotels in Erice, this makes the Edelweiss the third best hotel in town. In a quiet alley off the Piazzetta San Domenico, this is a simple family-run place that is comfortable and clean, even if the furnishings don't seem to match. If you're a budget traveler this is your only option, even though the accommodations are better than budget.

WHERE TO EAT

You're not going to find an inexpensive meal in Erice unless you grab a sandwich at a sidewalk cafe, but if you try one of these places, at least you'll be eating well.

4. CORTILE DI VENERE, *Via Sales 31, Tel. 0923/869-362. Closed Wednesdays. All credit cards accepted. Dinner for two L100,000.*

In the summer you can eat in a splendid courtyard surrounded by buildings from the 17th century. The *gamberi marinati* (marinated grilled shrimp), *spaghetti al pesto ericino* (with a pesto sauce Erice-style) and the ta*gliolini al uova di tonno* (thin pasta with a sauce of tuna eggs) are all great. For seconds try some of their *involtini di pesce spada* (rolled swordfish steaks stuffed with spices), *calamari ripieni* (stuffed calamari), or a *costata di Angus alla brace* (an Angus steak grilled over an open flame). Definitely the best food and atmosphere in town.

5. MONTE SAN GIULIANO, *Via San Rocco 7, Tel. 0923/869-595. Closed Mondays. All credit cards accepted. Dinner for two L100,000.*

If you want to get one of the tables that looks out over the water and the Isole Egadi, you need to get here early or reserve in advance. Their *busiati con pesto ericino* (twisted pasta made with almond paste, garlic, tomatoes, and basil) is exquisite. For seconds, I love their grig*liata di calamari, gamberi e pesce spada* (grilled calamari, shrimp, and swordfish).

SEEING THE SIGHTS

As you enter the town you'll be confronted by the **Chiesa Matrice**, whose tower served as a lookout post, then a prison before getting religion (*Via Vito Carvini, open 8am-noon and 3-6pm*). There are five other churches, much smaller in scale, in Erice. When you find them, stick your head inside and take a peek. They are definitely not St. Peter's or the Duomo in Florence, but they help you step back in time to medieval Erice.

There's a small, really insignificant **museum** (*Corso Vittorio Emanuelle, open Monday-Saturday 8:30am-1:30pm, Sunday 9am-noon*). So if you want a dose of art stop in here; it's free. After wandering through the streets, avoiding the hordes of tourists in the summertime, walk up past the public gardens and the ancient **Torretta Pepoli**, a restored 15th century tower, and go to the **Castello San Venere** (*open Saturday-Thursdays 10am-1pm and 3-5pm*). Built on the site of an ancient temple to the Greek god Aphrodite and later the Roman god Venus, from here you can get the great views we spoke of earlier. Don't forget your camera.

AGRIGENTO

Nobody comes to **Agrigento** to visit its quaint medieval streets and buildings, where butchers and bakers share storefronts with Fendi. Even though the city is quaint beyond compare and is exciting to explore, tourists come for another reason. It's also not the more than four kilometers of pristine beaches, the reason people come here is for the most captivating and well-preserved set of Greek remains and Doric temples outside of Greece – the Valley of Temples.

These temples were erected during the 5th century BC, below the Greek town of Akragas, the forerunner to Agrigento, as testament to the wealth and prosperity of the town. Today Agrigento survives from the tourist trade, and ,it is rumored, through Mafia money.

GETTING AROUND TOWN

You can easily walk every in the town itself, and explore the tiny medieval streets. To get the Valley of Temples, you'll need to catch either bus #8, 9 or 10 from the train station. Ask to be let off at the **Museo** (the museum) when you get there.

WHERE TO STAY

1. **HOTEL DELLE VALLE**, *Via dei Templi 94, 92100 Agrigento, Tel. 0922/26966. Fax 0922/26412. 93 rooms, 89 with bath, 4 with shower. Single L110,000; Double L170,000. Full board L200,000. American Express and Visa accepted.* ****

Located on the road to the temples, you need to take tbus #8, 9, or 10 from the station to get here. They have a swimming pool, tranquil gardens, a fine restaurant, air conditioning, TV and clean and comfortable rooms.

2. HOTEL VILLA ATHENA, *Via dei Templi 33, 92100 Agrigento. Tel. 0922/596-288. Fax 0922/598-770. 40 rooms, 8 with bath, 32 with shower. Single L170,000; Double L250,000. Full board L200,000. American Express and Visa accepted.* ****

Located in the Valley of the Temples itself, this place has all the amenities you could want, including an indoor and outdoor pool, tranquil gardens, a good restaurant, laundry and room service, air conditioning and more. Located in a quaint old romantic building, your rooms are clean as are the bathrooms. The rooms are comfortable and the view from many of the rooms, onto the temples, is exquisite, especially at night.

3. HOTEL BELVEDERE, *Via San Vito 20, 92100 Agrigento. Tel. 0922/ 20051. 35 rooms, 5 with bath, 13 with shower. Single without L35,000; Single with L55,000; Double without L40,000; Double with L70,000. American Express and Visa accepted.* **

Located near the train station, I would advise getting a bathroom of your own because there are not many in the halls and they don't look too inviting. Little or no amenities, except a good view from some of the rooms. Try to reserve room #30, which has a large balcony where you can relax in the evenings.

WHERE TO EAT

There are plenty of little bars and cafes at which you can grab a snack, as well as some local restaurants. Below is the one I feel is the best.

4. KALOS, *Piazza San Calogero, Tel. 0922/26389. Closed Sunday Nights. Credit cards accepted. Dinner for two L80,000.*

Located in the small piazza near the station and the church of San Calogero, this is a clean, modern looking place, with professional service. Try their *Macceroncelli al pistacchio* (macaroni with pistachio sauce, gorgonzola and parmesan cheese). For seconds, get any of their succulent fish or meat cooked on the grill.

SEEING THE SIGHTS

There are only a few sights to see in town. The main show is out at The Valley of the Temples.

A. THE VALLEY OF THE TEMPLES

Open Sunday–Friday 8am–Dusk.

After being dropped off by the bus #8, 9, or 10 from town, walk down the hill to the **Museo Nazionale Archeologico di San Nicola** *(open Tuesday–Friday 9am–1:30pm and 3–5pm, Weekends 9am–12:30pm)* to admire the artifacts removed from the ruins for safekeeping. This museum will help give you a feel for the people that used to worship at these temples. You can find vases, candlestick holders, lion's head water spouts, excellent model reconstructions of the site below, coins, sarcophagi and more.

The **church** that the museum is named after is next door and contains many Roman sarcophagi with intricate relief work. The church isn't open too often. Walking down the road in front will lead you to the Valley of the Temples.

Most of these temples were destroyed by earthquakes and human destruction. Despite the state of the temples, it's still awe inspiring to walk among structures that once stood erect in the 5th century BC.

The **Tempio di Giove (Temple of Zeus)** would have been the largest Doric temple ever built had it been completed. It was to be dedicated to the Olympian god Zeus, as you can guess from its name (Jove in English, or *Giove* in Latin, is Zeus). You can still see the remains of one of the standing *telemones*, human figures that were to be the support columns.

The **Tempio della Concordia (Temple of Concord)** is probably the best preserved most probably because it was converted to a Christian church in the 6th century AD. It has been fenced off to keep scavenging tourists from tearing it apart. But even from a distance it is a joy to behold.

The **Tempio di Giunone (Temple of Juno/Hera)** is not as well preserved but it is still an engaging structure. You may notice some red and black marks in the stone. These could be remnants of fires that were set when the temple was sacked many centuries ago.

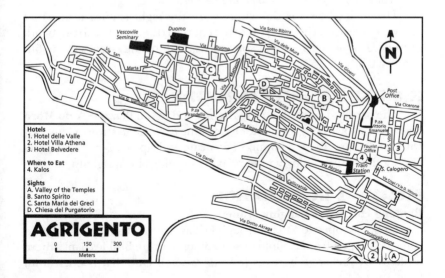

IT'S A BEAUTIFUL NIGHT
IN THE VALLEY OF THE TEMPLES

*At night the monuments are illuminated, so be sure to take a night stroll down the **Viale della Vittoria**, the street that leads to the temples from just in front of the train station. Bring your camera and some high speed film. This is one of my favorite scenes in all of Italy, and I think you'll like it too.*

The Town

B. SANTO SPIRITO

Piazza Santo Spirito. Accessible 9am–noon and 3–6pm.

Built by Cisterian nuns in 1290, this complex contains a church, convent, and charterhouse. The church contains some fine stucco work. You'll need to ring the bell on the church to gain admittance. Be patient. It's considered rude to keep ringing the bell.

C. CHURCH OF SANTA MARIA DEI GRECI

Via Santa Maria dei Greci. Open 8am–noon and 3–5pm.

Built on a 5th century BC Greek temple, you can still see evidence of the columns in the walls, as well as the base of the columns in the foundation below the church. Make time to search out the entrance in the courtyard. Also inside are some interesting Byzantine frescoes.

D. CHIESA DEL PURGATORIO

Via Fodera. Open 8am–noon and 4–7pm.

The main draw for this church are the eight statues inside that represent the eight virtues. Next to the church is the entrance to a network of underground avenues and courtyards, built by the Greeks in the 5th century BC.

NIGHTLIFE & ENTERTAINMENT

The bars and cafes along **Via Atenea** and in the **Piazzale Aldo Moro** is where the town congregates for its evening *passegiatta* (stroll). Come out with the Italians about 8:00pm, sit at a cafe and sip an *aperitivo*, or stroll among the natives enjoying the relaxing evenings in Agrigento.

PRACTICAL INFORMATION

Banking Hours & Changing Money

Banks are open Monday through Friday from 8:30am to 1:30pm and some do reopen from 2:30pm or so to 3:30pm or so. Besides banks there a plenty of exchange bureaus (*casa di cambio*). One that is open until

9:00pm on weekdays, and until 2:00pm on Saturdays is in the Train Station. Another option, if all else is closed is to simply change your money at your hotel.

Business Hours

From October to June, most shops are open from 9:00am to 1:00pm and from 3:30pm to 7:30pm, and are closed all day Sundays and on Monday mornings. Then from June to August, when it really starts to get hot in Sicily, the morning hours remain the same, but the mid-day siesta time is slightly extended to 4:00pm and sometimes 4:30pm, which then pushes closing time back to 7:30pm or 8:00pm. And also, in conjunction with the Sunday and Monday morning closings, shops also close half-days on Saturday.

Food stores like *alimentari* generally are open from 8:30am to 1:30pm (so stock up on your picnic supplies before you need them) and from 5:00pm to 7:30pm, and during the winter months they are closed on Thursdays.

Local Festivals & Holidays
• **First Sunday of February**, Almond Blossom Festival in the Valley of The Temples
• **Late July/Early August**, *Settimana Pirandelliana*. A week long festival of plays, opera and ballets all performed in the Piazza Kaos.

Postal Services

The **central post office** in Agrigento *is in the circular building in Piazza Vittorio Emanuelle.* Open Monday through Friday, 8:30am–5:00pm, Saturday 9:00am–Noon. But if you're in a hurry, stamps can be bought at any tobacconist (stores indicated by a T sign outside), and mailed at any mailbox, which are red and marked with the words *Poste* or *Lettere*. There is a currency exchange window inside that is open in the mornings.

Tourist Information & Maps
• **Tourist Office**, *Piazza Aldo Moro #123 (Tel. 0922/20391), just to the left as you exit the train station.* Here you can get free maps and information about the town and the Valley of the Temples.

SIRACUSA

Most of the city of **Siracusa** (**Syracuse**) is situated on an island separated by a narrow channel from the east coast of Sicily. Because of the quaint older town, the scenic **Bay of Porto Grande**, its beautiful natural surroundings, and the monuments and relics of a glorious past, Siracusa is one of the most frequented spots in Sicily for tourists.

Founded in 743 BC on the island by a few colonists from Corinth, **Ortygia** (later to be named Siracusa) grew into a feared and powerful city in the Greek world. In 415 BC, the city was drawn into the conflict between Athens and Sparta, but when an expedition from Athens in 413 BC ended in the complete annihilation of the Athenian fleet and army, the Greeks began to leave the locals alone as they concentrated on their internal strife. Siracusa detained over 7,000 Athenians in squalid conditions for over 7 years. From that point until 212 BC, Siracusa was arguably the greatest and most powerful city in the world.

Just after that time, the city expanded from its easily defensible island to the mainland. The ruler at the time, Gelon, built the market area and necropolis which is now the famous **Archaeological Park** with its preserved buildings, temples, and theaters that people from all over the world come to see.

After the first Punic War, in which Siracusa was allied with the Romans, the city changed its alliance in the second Punic War to the Carthaginians. Big mistake. The Romans attacked and conquered the city in 212 BC, and thus began the city's decline. During this two year assault, the city defended itself with an ingenious variety of devices created by the great scientist and inventor Archimedes. This last great thinker of the Hellenic world was hacked to death in retribution after the Romans finally sacked the city.

The city never really recovered its past glory, but it did remain the main port in Sicily. It also briefly became the capital of the Byzantine Empire in 663 AD, when the Emperor Constans moved his court here. After that the city, like much of Sicily, was overrun by waves of Arab, Norman, and other conquerors. In conjunction the area was repeatedly devastated by earthquakes and other natural disasters. But today it is a great city to visit.

GETTING AROUND TOWN

If you're staying in a hotel in or around the center city, Siracusa is a perfect city for walking. From the train station, located almost on the edge of the island, you are within walking distance of the **Centro Storico** and **Stazione Maritima** on the island, as well as the **Archaeological Park** to the north on the mainland.

The Archaeological Park and Museum are about a fifteen minute walk away, so if you're tired you may want to catch either bus # 4, 5 12, or 15 from the Piazza della Poste or from Largo XXV Luglio, which will pass by both of these stops.

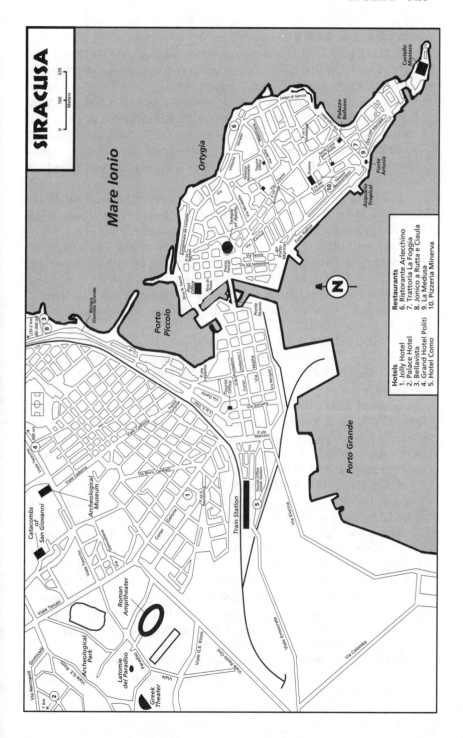

SIRACUSA

0   160   320
Meters

Mare Ionio

Ortygia

Largo di Gancia

Palazzo Bellomn

Castello Maniace

Via Leo Maniace

Fonte Artusia

Duomo

Palazzo Municipio

Acquário Tropical

Temple of Apollo

Riva N. Sauro

Post Office

Riva di Posta

Porto Piccolo

Piazza Pancali

Via Savoia

Via XX Settembre

Foro Italico

Lgo Porto Marina

Ponte Nuovo

Riviera Dionisio Grande

Corso Umberto

Via Bengasi

Via Malta

Via Savoia

Via Dante

Piazza Euripide

Via Somalia

P.zle Marconi

Porto Grande

Archeological Museum

Catacombs of San Giovanni

Viale Teocrito

Viale Cadorna

Viale Paolo Orsi

Roman Ampitheater

Latomie del Paradiso

Greek Theater

Archeological Park

Via Necropoli Grotticelli

Viale E. Rizzo

Viale Tercati

Train Station

Via Elorina

Via Colomba

Viale Ermocrate

Hotels
1. Jolly Hotel
2. Palace Hotel
3. Bellavista
4. Grand Hotel Politi
5. Hotel Como

Restaurants
6. Ristorante Arlecchino
7. Trattoria La Foggia
8. Jonico a Rutta e Ciaula
9. La Medusa
10. Pizzeria Minerva

WHERE TO STAY

1. JOLLY HOTEL, *Corso Gelone, 96110 Siracusa. Tel. 0931/461-111. Fax 0931/461-126. 100 rooms, 56 with bath, 44 with shower. Single L190,000; Double L210,000. No credit cards accepted.* ****

These Jolly hotels are everywhere, but why don't most of them accept Mastercard, Visa, or American Express I'll never know. A clean and comfortable hotel that has a good restaurant (L270,000 for full board if you're interested), a little American-style bar, room service and laundry service, but little else. Located near the train station you'll find air conditioning and satellite TVs in the rooms.

2. PALACE HOTEL, *Viale Scala Greca 201, 96100 Siracusa. Tel. 0931/ 491-566. Fax 0931/756-612. 136 rooms, 39 with bath, 97 with shower. Single L150,000; Double L200,000. No credit cards accepted.* ****

Located outside of town and north of the Greek Theater in the Archaeological Park, this place is a little way from everything, so getting their L200,000 full board option at their in-house restaurant would be a good idea. The rooms are old and somewhat small and they don't have air conditioning, which is a necessity in the summer. An option if nowhere else has rooms available.

3. BELLAVISTA, *Via Diodoro Siculo 4, 96100 Siracusa. Tel. 0931/411-355. Fax 0931/37927. 49 rooms, 6 with bath, 31 with shower. Single without L44,000; Single with L75,000; Double without L68,000; Double with L120,000. Credit cards accepted.* ***

Located quite a distance from the Centro Storico and the Archaeological Park, this is a place for people that want to try and get away from it all. They have a good restaurant that offers full board for only L115,000. Besides that and the fact that they take credit cards, the only other amenity is a tranquil garden in which to relax.

4. GRAND HOTEL VILLA POLITI, *Via M Politi Laudien 2, 96100 Siracusa. Tel. 0931/412-121. Fax 0931/36061. 94 rooms, 85 with bath, 9 with shower. 2 Suites. Single L95,000; Double L159,000. Credit cards accepted.* ***

This is *the* place to stay in Siracusa. The rooms are a little run down, but are clean and comfortable, the restaurant offers great local cuisine (L170,000 full board), and the hotel is located in a quaint historic building. You have air conditioning in the rooms, a disco for dancing at night, a swimming pool, tennis courts, bocce courts, and great views over the sea. It's located a short distance outside of town, but is about equidistant from the town and the Archaeological Park. For a three star, this place offers many options and is priced well.

5. HOTEL COMO, *Piazza Stazione 10, 96100 Siracusa. Tel. 0931/464-055. Fax 0931/61210. 14 rooms all with shower. Single L72,000; Double L102,000. Credit cards accepted.* **

A tranquil setting with good views, air conditioning in the rooms, Satellite TV, room service and laundry service, which may seem a bit much for a two star, but they're at the high end. Near everything, this small hotel has clean rooms and bathrooms and small but comfortable rooms.

WHERE TO EAT

6. RISTORANTE ARLECCHINO, *Via del Tolomei 5, Tel. 0931/ 66386. Closed Mondays. All credit cards accepted. Dinner for two L100,000.*

Located in Ortygia, from the entrance you have a great view of the sea. This modern, well-lit place is huge; over 260 people can be seated at the same time. It caters to tourists, but mainly of the Italian variety so the food is good. Try their antipasto buffet table for starters that is overflowing with seafood. Then for more seafood with the spaghetti *ai ricci di mare* (with the riches of the sea) or the *tortelloni con scampi allo zafferano* (large cheese stuffed pasta with a shrimp and sauce). For seconds try any of their oven roasted fish as well as their many meat dishes.

7. TRATTORIA LA FOGLIA, *Via Capodieci 29, Tel. 0931/66233. Closed Tuesdays. All credit cards accepted. Dinner for two L80,000.*

Located in Ortygia, this is a small local place that changes its menu daily based on whatever ingredients chef Nicoletta was able to get at the market. Usually the antipasto will be vegetables, like *fritelle di finocchietto* (fried small fennel). Try one of their soups for your primo to save yourself for their exquisite fish dishes. Only 25 seats, so make a reservation.

8. JONICO A RUTTA E CIAULU, *Riviera Rionisio il Grande 194, Tel. 0931/65540. Closed Tuesdays, the end of the year and Easter. All credit cards accepted. Dinner for two L110,000.*

Located up the coast near the Grand Hotel Villa Politi, the best place to eat is on the terrace where you have a fine view of the Ionian Sea. Here you can get some good local dishes at somewhat high prices. Try some of their *spaghetti alla siracusano* (with anchovies and scraped toasted bread sauce), which doesn't sound too appetizing but I like it, or some *spaghetti con tonno fresca* (with fresh tuna sauce). For seconds they serve some great tuna and swordfish steaks.

9. LA MEDUSA, *Via San Teresa 21, Tel. 0931/61403. Closed Mondays and August 15 to September 15. American Express accepted. Dinner for two L40,000.*

Another restaurant in the Ortygia district, this place is run by a Tunisian who has been in Siracusa for over 15 years. You can get some great couscous with either *pesce* or *carne* (a rice based dish with either fish or meat) for primo. The antipasto is good too with the *pesce spada marinata* (marinated swordfish), *gamberetti* (small shrimp) and more. For seconds try their *arrosto misto di pesce* (mixed roast fish). Great atmosphere and good food.

10. PIZZERIA MINERVA, *Piazza Duomo 20, Tel. 0931/69404. Closed Mondays and November. No credit cards accepted. Dinner for two L40,000.*

In the summer this is the perfect pace to end a long walk through Ortygia. The place seats over 130 people, but not all outside in the piazza facing the Duomo. Try and get one of these outside seats. You can get any pizza imaginable here, but if you want it American style you have to order doppio moz*zarella* (double cheese).

SEEING THE SIGHTS

The archaeological park and museum is the big draw here, but there are some lovely squares and churches in town that are great for poking around.

ORTYGIA

On the island of **Ortygia**, the ancient nucleus of Siracusa, you can find remains from over 2,500 years of history. A small area, almost half a kilometer across and only one in length, this little parcel of land contains much of the charm and adventure from all of those centuries.

TEMPLE OF APOLLO

Just over the **Ponte Nuovo** from the mainland is the oldest Doric temple in Sicily. Built in the 7th century BC, little remains of this once glorious temple except for two pillars and parts of some walls. To really get an idea of what it used to look like, go to the Archaeological Museum for a scale model.

PIAZZA ARCHIMEDE

This is Ortygia's **central piazza**. The square has some bars and cafes with outside seating where you can sit and enjoy the sight of the 12th century fountain with a woodland nymph cavorting under a cover of modern moss. Down a small road from the square is the **Via del Montalto** on which you can find the **Palazzo Montalto** (*not open to public*), with its fabulous double and triple arched windows. The building's construction was begun in 1397 and is constantly undergoing renovations.

PIAZZA DEL DUOMO

A piazza surrounded by some beautiful 17th and 18th century palazzos and dominated by the impressive Baroque **Duomo**. The square was built over and encompasses an earlier Greek temple, the 5th century BC Ionic temple of Athena. You can still see evidence of the previous structure in the walls, where 26 of the original 34 columns remain. Because much of its earlier wealth was stolen and a majority of it was destroyed in the earthquake of 1693, this cathedral contains a wide variety of differing architectural styles, from Greek to Byzantine to Baroque.

The **Palazzo Benevantano** *(at #24 on the piazza, not open to the public)* is worth a look because of its attractive 18th century facade and serpentine balcony. At the far end of the piazza is the small church of **Santa Lucia alla Badia** built from 1695 to 1703 *(open 8am–noon and 3:30pm–6pm)*. The church is significant because it contains the remains of the city's patron saint, Santa Lucia.

GALLERIA DI PALAZZO BELLOMO

Via Capodieci 14. Open Tuesday–Sunday 9am–1pm. Admission L3,000.

Almost behind **Santa Lucia alla Badia** is the **Palazzo Bellomo**, a 15th century palazzo that contains a wonderful gallery of all kinds of artwork, including ancient bibles, medieval carriages, sculptures, tombs, paintings and more. The most famous painting is the *Annunciation* by Antonello da Messina.

Walk down to the Via Capodieci to arrive at the **Foro Italico**, the main promenade for the citizens of Ortygia. On this tree-lined promenade you'll find rows of bars and cafes on the land side, and rows of yachts lining the water. It's where the local citizens come to enjoy the evenings before they retire home. At the beginning of this promenade is the fresh water fountain **Fonte Aretusa**. If you take notice, this fountain is located virtually out to sea so it is considered some kind of miracle that it serves fresh water. Just past the fountain is the **Acquario Tropical** *(open Saturday–Thursdays 9am–1pm, admission L3,000)* that offers 35 different species of tropical fish for your aquarium-viewing pleasure.

CATACOMBS

Via San Giovanni. Open 9am–1pm and 2pm–7pm. Closed Wednesday. Guide tours of catacombs cost L3,000.

The **catacombs of San Giovanni** are located under the basilica of the same name, and contain a quantity of faded frescoes. This is an ominous tour through a labyrinth of passageways, but you won't encounter any bodies. Most of these were destroyed by looters and their riches stolen, so to see a sarcophagus you need to go to the Archaeological Museum.

ARCHAEOLOGICAL MUSEUM

Viale Teocrito. Open Tuesday–Saturday 9am–1pm and Sunday 9am–12:30pm.

To get to the museum, you can take the 15 minute walk or catch bus #4, 5 12, or 15 from the Piazza della Poste or from Largo XXV Luglio. Since this museum is the most extensive antiquities museum in Sicily, you should spend some time browsing through the collection. The museum contains fossils, skeletons, figurines, sarcophagi and more, but the collection's tour de force is the *Venus Anadiomene*, the coy statue of Venus rising from the sea. If you're into antiquities, this is a great place to spend a few hours.

ARCHAEOLOGICAL PARK

Open Tuesday–Sunday 9am to an hour before sunset. Admission L3,000.

To get to the park, you can take the 15 minute walk or catch bus #4, 5 12, or 15 from the Piazza della Poste or from Largo XXV Luglio. The structures preserved here were constructed between 475 BC and the 3rd century AD and many remain somewhat intact. An example of this preservation is the **Greek Theater**, originally made from the side of the hill around 475 BC. The structure was enlarged in 335 BC and could seat up to 15,000 people. If you want to see a performance here, come in May and June on the alternate year when Classical Greek plays are staged. They are quite stirring.

Next door to the Greek Theater is the **Latomie del Paradiso**, the **Paradise Quarry**, so named because many of the 7,000 Athenians captured in 413 BC went to the afterlife from here. In the quarry are two interesting caves: **Grotta dei Cordari**, where rope makers used to work at their craft because the damp cave kept the strands of rope from breaking, and the **Orecchio di Dionisio** (Ear of Dionysis), so called because the entrance resembles and ear and the cave has amazing acoustic qualities.

Up from the grotto is the **Roman Amphitheater** which was built in the 3rd century AD, by, you guessed it, the Romans. Here they held their vicious gladiatorial games pitting man against man as well as beast. Just one hundred and forty meters long, it's not quite as impressive as the Coliseum in Rome, but knowing that countless people and animals lost their lives here, it has an effect on you.

NIGHTLIFE & ENTERTAINMENT

The only nightlife to speak of is along the **Foro Italico** promenade, where you can sip a drink or have a light meal and watch the citizens of Siracusa walk by.

PRACTICAL INFORMATION

Banking Hours & Changing Money

Banks are open Monday through Friday from 8:30am to 1:30pm and some do reopen from 2:30pm or so to 3:30pm or so. Besides banks there a plenty of exchange bureaus (*casa di cambio*). One that is open until 9:00pm on weekdays, and until 2:00pm on Saturdays is in the Train

Station. Another option, if all else is closed is to simply change your money at your hotel.

Business Hours

From October to June, most shops are open from 9:00am to 1:00pm and from 3:30pm to 7:30pm, and are closed all day Sundays and on Monday mornings. Then from June to August, when it really starts to get hot in Sicily, the morning hours remain the same, but the mid-day siesta time is slightly extended to 4:00pm and sometimes 4:30pm, which then pushes closing time back to 7:30pm or 8:00pm. And also, in conjunction with the Sunday and Monday morning closings, shops also close half-days on Saturday.

Food stores like *alimentari* generally are open from 8:30am to 1:30pm (so stock up on your picnic supplies before you need them) and from 5:00pm to 7:30pm, and during the winter months they are closed on Thursdays.

Local Festivals & Holidays

• **May to June**, every even numbered year Classical Greek drama is performed at the Greek theater. Reservations required.

Postal Services

The **central post office** in Siracusa *is in the Piazza delle Poste (Tel. 0931/ 684-16) located in the Centro Storico island just over the bridge from the mainland.* Open Monday through Friday 8:30am–6:30pm, Saturday 9:00am–Noon. But if you're in a hurry, stamps can be bought at any tobacconist (stores indicated by a T sign outside), and mailed at any mailbox, which are red and marked with the words *Poste* or *Lettere*.

Tourist Information & Maps

• **Tourist office**, *just outside the train station*
• **Tourist office**, *on the island at Via Maestranza 33, Tel. 0931/652-01*
• **Tourist office**, *on the mainland near the catacombs at Via San Sebastiano 45, Tel. 093/677-10*

All three can offer you maps of the area and the Archaeological Park, as well as brochures and information about hotels.

CATANIA

Catania is the second largest city in Sicily and a main point of arrival for many international travelers, who land at the airport just outside the city. The city was destroyed by an earthquake in 1693, but even so there is a mix of architectural influences and sights to be seen. Catania is best enjoyed as a stopover for a few days from which you can visit**Mt. Etna**, or rest for a day and then pop over to the beautiful **Taormina**.

Don't get me wrong – Catania is a pleasant city with many 17th century sights to see, and can offer an enjoyable few days, but it is not the safest city and can appear dirty and crowded after a few days.

The city was founded about 729 BC and was named **Katana** by Greek settlers. Throughout its history it has been destroyed by **Mount Etna** then rebuilt. As a Greek city it was of small importance compared to Siracusa, but under Roman rule the city was built into one of the largest towns in Sicily. After their rule ended, the city went into a decline that can be seen today.

Be cautious here as you would in most other cities in Sicily: women should not walk alone in Catania at night, and no one should walk around the area near the train station or the harbor after dark. Your best bet is to stay close to the streets around the Duomo where you'll find people out and about. As usual, beware deserted streets and use common sense whenever you're out at night.

ARRIVALS & DEPARTURES

By Air

You can fly to **Fontarossa Airport** in Catania from Milan, Rome, and quite a few other Italian cities. The best fares usually are on either Alitalia or **Lufthansa**, but it's usually cheaper to fly into Palermo. You can get direct flights from London to Catania, so this could be an option for you when traveling from North America or Australia. There are also direct flights from Dublin to Catania.

Getting In From the Airport

Located only five kilometers south of the city, Fontarossa is easily accessible. Bus #24 leaves from right outside the international terminal and drops you off at the Piazza Duomo in twenty minutes. You can get tickets for the bus (L1,500) at the *Tabacchi* in the Departure Hall. If you want to take a taxi it will cost about L40,000, depending on how much traffic there is.

Other Options

Bus and train are your best travel options, but you can get here by ferry or hydrofoil from other parts of Sicily or the mainland as well. Consult the various schedules from the town you plan to depart from for the most up-to-date information.

GETTING AROUND TOWN

Most of the sights you will want to see are located around the **Piazza Duomo**, so you can easily walk around the city (during the day, never at night) with a map, since the city is laid out haphazardly. The Piazza Duomo is about a twenty minute walk from the train station; to get there from the station, make a left down **Via VI Aprile** to the plant-covered semi-circular **Piazza del Martiri**, then right along the **Via Vittorio Emanuelle**.

If you don't want to walk or lug your bag that far, catch one of the following buses: #27, 29, 33, 36, and 39 that will take you from the station to the Piazza. Tickets cost L1,500 and can be bought at any newsstand or *Tabacchi*.

WHERE TO STAY

As Sicily's second largest city, don't be shocked to discover that hotel accommodations are quite expensive.

HOTEL CENTRAL PALACE, *Via Etnea 218, 95131 Catania. Tel. 095/325-344. Fax 095/715/8939. 99 rooms all with bath. Single L85,000-150,000; Double L150,000-237,000. Credit cards accepted. Breakfast included.* ****

Located in the center of the city near the train station and Duomo, other than the Excelsior this is the place to stay while in Catania. The rooms have air conditioning and TV and are clean, modern, and comfortable. Service is impeccable. Meals are good at their in-house restaurant and you're located in the middle of everything.

EXCELSIOR, *Piazza G Verga 39, 95129 Catania. Tel. 095/537-071. Fax 095/537-015. 150 rooms all with bath. Single L145,000; Double L200,000-245.000. Credit cards accepted. Breakfast L35,000 extra.* ****

This is the the best luxury hotel Catania has to offer. The rooms are large, well tended, clean and comfortable with a sprinkling of antiques to give it them an alluring air. Of course there's air conditioning, TV, and mini-bar, as well as fast room service and competent laundry service. They have a bus to shuttle to the airport, train station, or wherever. Centrally located to all the sights. Their in-house restaurant is quite good, but expensive.

HOTEL MODERNO, *Via Alessi 9, 95124 Catania. Tel. 095/326-250. Fax 095/326-674. 47 rooms, 28 with bath. Single without L30,000-55,000; Single with L45,000-85,000; Double with 70,000-135,000. Visa Accepted. Breakfast L20,000 extra.* ***

All the doubles have bathroom facilities, but they are small. Still, the rooms are quite nice except for the lack of air conditioning. No real amenities in the hotel except for a small bar downstairs. A place to stay if you're on a budget, since you're located near all the sights.

VILLA DINA, *Via Caronda 129, 95128 Catania. Tel. 095/447-103. Fax the same. 22 rooms all with bath. Single L90,000-100; Double L140,000-180,000. Credit cards accepted. Breakfast L15,000 extra.* ***

Located near everything, this place is situated in a quaint old building with a beautiful garden. It has virtually everything you could want except for air conditioning and an in-house restaurant. I think that's why it's still a three star, since the rooms are kept immaculate and they are quite comfortable.

HOTEL SAVONA, *Via Vittorio Emanuelle 210, 95124 Catania. Tel. 326-982. Fax 095/715-8169. 25 rooms, 20 with bath. Single without L37,000; Single with L60,000; Double without L56,000; Double with L94,000. No credit cards accepted. Breakfast included.* **

Smack dab in the middle of town, ideally located for touring. A small clean hotel that is trying to move up in the rankings. Little to no amenities except TV and phone in the rooms, a small bar downstairs, and laundry service. But the price is right for the high end of budget travel.

WHERE TO EAT

There are plenty of little *trattoria* and restaurants located in the **Centro Storico** and all over Catania. I've chosen four of the best for you.

FINOCCHIARO, *Via E. Reina 13, Tel. 095/234-765. Closed Sundays. No credit cards accepted. Dinner for two L80,000.*

Located just off the Piazza dell'Universita, this place is set back in a courtyard making your meal quite relaxing. This is a place frequented by professors and students with some money. Try their extensive appetizer table complete with seafood and vegetables. You can get the Catania special, *spaghetti alla Norma* here. The sauce is made with tomatoes, garlic, ricotta cheese, basil and eggplant and is fantastic. They also have plenty of meat and fish cooked on the grill.

LA CANTINACCIA, *Via Messina 245a, Tel. 095/382-009. Closed Mondays and August. All credit cards accepted. Dinner for two L90,000.*

If you like meat, especially sausage, you'll love this place. You can get an *antipasto di salsicce cinghiale e prosciutto di selvaggina* (sausage and ham made from wild boar). For primo try their *pasticcio d'orzo alla Henry* (barley pastries made with pumpkin, ricotta cheese and asparagus) or the *tagliolini alla Rossella* (with wild mushrooms, olives, pistacchio, egg and truffle). If you want fish for seconds they only serve it on Fridays, otherwise try some of their excellent roast meats. Located outside of the Centro Storico, and the taxi ride will run you L6,000 each way.

I VICERE, *Via Grotte Bianche 97, Tel. 095/320-188. Closed Sundays and June 15 to September 15. Open only at night. All credit cards accepted. Dinner for two L90,000.*

Located near the north end of the Villa Bellini, it is always a joy to return to this restaurant. The ambiance is refined, the attention of the waiters attentive, and the food created by the chef Saverio is sublime. For appetizers, try any and all available at the huge antipasto table. For primi, try some *finocchietto e gamberi* (fennel with shrimp), or a *minestra di fave* (bean soup), or *ravioli fusi al ragu* (molded ravioli with a tasty ragu sauce). For seconds try any of their creative meat dishes like the *filletini di maiale al mandarino* (small filets of pork with an orange sauce) or one of the normal grilled or roasted varieties.

LA SICILIANA, *Viale Marco Polo 52a, Tel. 095/376-6400. Closed Sunday nights and Mondays and the first two weeks of August. All credit cards accepted. Dinner for two L130,000.*

You'll need to take a taxi back and forth to this place (about L8,000 each way) but if you have the money, this is the most famous restaurant in and around Catania. Operated by three brothers (Vito, Salvo, and Ettore La Rosa) this is wonderful place to come for a relaxing evening on their garden terrace under an awning. Their seafood antipasti are magnificent. Ask Ettore, who works the floor, which one is best that day.

For primo, try their *Ripiddu Nivicatu* (rice with cuttlefish and ricotta cheese and a touch of tomato sauce). For seconds try *il tonno con le cipole* (tuna steak made with onions) or the fantastic *lo spiedino di pesce spada e gamberoni gratinati alla brace* (swordfish and large shrimp au gratin cooked on a spit over and open fire).

SEEING THE SIGHTS

Between the sights on the main piazza and the lovely Bellini Gardens, you'll have an enjoyable time wandering the streets during the day.

PIAZZA DEL DUOMO

This is Catania's main square. From here everything is within walking distance. The central feature of the square is the **Fontana dell'Elefante** in the center. This is an 18th century fountain made from lava that supports an Egyptian obelisk on its back. On the east side of the piazza is the **Duomo** itself (*open 8am–noon and 5–7pm*), of which only the medieval apses survived the earthquake of 1693. The facade has incorporated some of the granite columns 'borrowed' from the Roman Amphitheater.

The ornate Baroque interior contains a beautiful **Cappella dell Madonna** in which resides a Roman sarcophagus and a statue of the Virgin. As you leave, take note of **Bellini's tomb** located to the left of the entrance.

CASTELLO URSINO

The **Castello Ursino** is a slight walk south from the Piazza del Duomo, which used to be the castle of Frederick II. The whole area is quite dilapidated since it has been almost completely neglected after the last earthquake. Just recently they've tried to restore as much as they can and remove the truck loads of junk thrown into the moat. They are developing a museum inside and when it opens, I hear it will be fantabulous.

GRECO ROMAN THEATER & ODEON

Via Teatro Greco. Open 9am–1pm.

If you head back north up the twisting streets just past the Via Vittorio Emanuelle, you'll end up at the **Teatro Romano** and the **Odeon**. Both were built from marble in the second century AD, most of which was pilfered to make other buildings, and today both sites have been covered with lava from the last eruption.

BELLINI GARDENS

Via S Tomaselli. Open Monday–Saturday 9am–1pm.

North up the Via Etnea are the magnificent **Bellini Gardens**. Here you can take a relaxing walk through their serpentine promenades. A great place to come for a picnic and escape the hectic pace of Catania. Just before you arrive at the gardens there is a **Roman Amphitheater** located just below street level. Built in the 3rd century AD, it is the grandest of Catania's Roman remains. This amphitheater could hold close to 16,000, even though its hard to tell since most of the structure is covered up by surrounding buildings. You can enter the vaults under the buildings to see a little more of the structure.

NIGHTLIFE & ENTERTAINMENT

As a university city, Catania has an entertaining nightlife, but I would not recommend wandering the streets at night unless you've been here before and know where you are going. I've traveled here before and still choose to take a late dinner as my entertainment, then return home early to bed.

PRACTICAL INFORMATION

Banking Hours & Changing Money

Banks are open Monday through Friday from 8:30am to 1:30pm and some reopen from 2:30pm or so to 3:30pm or so. Besides banks, there are plenty of exchange bureaus around (*casa di cambio*). Try the one at the train station, open Monday–Saturday, 9:00am–Noon and 1:00pm–8:00pm.

Business Hours

From October to June, most shops are open from 9:00am to 1:00pm and from 3:30pm to 7:30pm, and are closed all day Sundays and on Monday mornings. Then from June to August, when it really starts to get hot in Sicily, the morning hours remain the same, but the mid-day siesta time is slightly extended to 4:00pm and sometimes 4:30pm, which then pushes closing time back to 7:30pm or 8:00pm. And also, in conjunction with the Sunday and Monday morning closings, shops also close half-days on Saturday.

Food stores like *alimentari* generally are open from 8:30am to 1:30pm (so stock up on your picnic supplies before you need them) and from 5:00pm to 7:30pm, and during the winter months they are closed on Thursdays.

Local Festivals & Holidays
• **February 3-5**, *Festa di Sant'Agata*. Fireworks, procession with statue of saint and long candles, stalls selling sweets
• **November to April**, Catania Jazz Festival

Postal Services

The **central post office** in Catania *is at Via Etnea 215 (Tel. 095/311-506) near the Duomo.* Open Monday–Friday, 8:30am–5:00pm, Saturday 9:00am–Noon. But if you're in a hurry, stamps can be bought at any tobacconist (stores indicated by a T sign outside), and mailed at any mailbox, which are red and marked with the words *Poste* or *Lettere*.

Tourist Information & Maps
• **Tourist Office**, *at the Train Station, Tel. 095/531-802*
• **Tourist Office**, *at the Airport, Tel. 095/341-900*

Both are open Monday–Saturday, 9:00am–Noon and 1:00pm–8:00pm. They can offer you free hotel listings, city maps, and information about Catania and the surrounding area.

MOUNT ETNA

One of the world's largest active volcanoes, **Mount Etna's** presence dominates the skyline of this coastal area. The last two eruptions have, in 1985 and 1992, destroyed local roads and threatened local villagers, who, for some reason, continue to live at the base of this accident waiting to happen. Despite the possibility that the volcano could erupt at any time, Mount Etna is still a great tourist draw.

There are two ways to see the volcano, from the safety of a train that tours the base, or from the volcano itself.

By Train Around the Volcano

The first option can be achieved by riding the private railway **Ferrovia Circumetnea**, which goes from Catania around Mount Etna to **Riposto**, up north on the coast. This three hour ride is quite scenic, even if you're not going up the side of the volcano. The train passes through small towns and settlements along the way (**Adrano**, **Randazzo**, and **Giarre**) complete with castles and medieval walls. If you wish, you can disembark, walk around for a while then catch the next train for the coast. But remember there are only three trains a day. Ask the conductor if another is coming along behind.

You can catch this private train, that does not accept Eurorail or Italorail passes, in Catania at **Stazione Borgo** *(Via Coraonda 350 just north of the Bellini Gardens; cost is L12,000 one way)*. Once you reach **Riposto**, you'll need to catch a one way regular local train back to Catania which should cost L5,000 and tack another half an hour onto your trip.

By Bus To the Volcano

Skirting the base of the volcano will give you perspective on this natural landmark and afford you some nice views, but actually ascending to the top first-hand will give you a better feel for the awesome strength of this volcano. To get to the mountain, catch a bus from Catania's central train station at 8:00am and return at 4:00pm. The round-trip ticket costs L5,000. Buy it inside the train station at the AST window. The bus reaches its destination at the **Rifugio Sapienza**, 1,440 meters below the summit.

Ascending Mt. Etna

You have three options to get near the top: walk, cable car, or mini-van. The highest you're allowed to go is to the **Torre del Filosofo**, a lava tower built by the Romans to commemorate Hadrian's climb to the top. From this spot you're not far from the top and should be treated to gaseous explosions and molten rocks being spit up from the crater. The whole landscape is otherworldly in appearance.

The **cable car** option, if working, costs L45,000 per person, takes two hours, and gives you about 45 minutes of walking around. The **minivan option** costs L40,000 and gives you about the same amount of time. **Walking** can be tiring and treacherous, since the footing is not too secure with lava pebbles hindering your traction. You'll also be climbing a little over 1,000 meters in oxygen-thin air, so you must be prepared.

TAORMINA

Despite being Sicily's main tourist attraction, **Taormina** still retains much of its medieval hilltown charm to make it worth a visit. Since it is rather expensive to stay here, and considering how quick and easy it is to get here from Catania, you may want to come early in the morning and leave late in the evening for a full day's enjoyment.

This town is situated in a place of unsurpassed beauty. Located on a cliff top with two coves below, I am hard pressed to imagine a more beautiful sight. Lately some high rise hotels have sprung up along some of the outlying beaches below, but if you stay in the old town or just visit the old town you'll see none of that. But you will see tourists, in numbers that make Taormina uncomfortable in the summer. So the best time to come here is between October and March, when you'll have the whole place, almost, to yourself.

The town is tiny and filled with 15th to 19th century buildings along its main street and in its twisting alleys. Besides wandering through the town's medieval beauty, you can also visit the quiet hill town of **Castelmola**, or frequent the beaches below. There is a cable car that runs between Taormina and its closest beach, **Mazzaro**.

ARRIVALS & DEPARTURES

If you took the train around the base of Mount Etna to Riposto and are not returning to Catania, Taormina is only a short train ride away. If you're leaving from Catania, there are 30 trains a day that take 45 minutes each way and cost L5,000.

The train station is located far below the town of Taormina and you must catch one of the frequent buses up the mountain. They run until 10:30pm.

WHERE TO STAY

Since this is a tourist town there are plenty of places to stay, but if you arrive in the peak months from April through September without a reservation, you may not be able to find a room or you'll have to settle for less than stellar accommodations.

Below are the best options in each category.

1. SAN DOMENICO PALACE, *Piazza San Domenico 5, 98039 Taormina. Tel. 0942/23701. Fax 0942/625-506. 101 rooms, 100 with bath, 1 with shower. Single L250,000-380,000; Double L400,000-620,000. Credit cards accepted.* *****

This is the best place to stay in Taormina. An excellent five star deluxe hotel with super professional service and every amenity under the sun. Here you can rub elbows with some of Europe's glitterati while enjoy superb dining, a swimming pool, tennis courts, a great view, and a private beach. The hotel is located in an old building that is filled with character, ambiance and romance. If you have the money, a perfect place to stay.

2. BRISTOL PARK, *Via Bagnoli Croci 92, 98039 Taormina. Tel. 0942/ 23006. Fax 0942/24519. 52 rooms, 42 with bath, 12 with shower. Single L100,000-135,000; Double L180,000-210,000. No credit cards accepted.* **** Not as many amenities as the San Domenico but still a luxurious four star accommodation. Their restaurant is also good and their swimming pool is relaxing, as is their garden terrace, after a tough day walking the alleys of Taormina. The rooms are a little small, but they have everything you need: air conditioning, TV, and mini-bar.

3. JOLLY HOTEL DIODORO, *Via Bagnoli Croce 75, 98039 Taormina. Tel. 0942/23312. Fax 0942/23391. 103 rooms, 58 with bath, 45 with shower. Single L95,000-180,000; Double L125,000-240,000.* **** Located on the same street as the Bristol Park, this place wins out in the contest of the four stars. The restaurant and many of their rooms have superb views, making this a rather romantic place to stay. In the evening there is a piano bar, a swimming pool, and a garden terrace. The rooms are quite comfortable and immaculately maintained.

4. HOTEL ISABELLA, *Corso Umberto 58, 98039 Taormina. Tel. 0942/ 23153. Fax 0942/23155. 29 rooms, 10 with bath, 19 with shower. Double L107,000-165,000. American Express and Visa accepted.* *** Though located in the medieval town itself, this little hotel has its own private beach below. You can rent snorkeling gear from the hotel. Besides the great views from some of the rooms, you also have a relaxing garden area in which to take your evening after-dinner drink. They have a baby-sitting service and a sun room to catch some rays in the winter time.

5. HOTEL SIRIUS, *Via Guardiola Vecchia 34, 98039 Taormina. Tel. 0942/23477. Fax 0942/23208. 41 rooms, 12 with bath, 29 with shower. Single L60,000-100; Double L80,000-140,000. Diners Club accepted.* *** Not quite as nice as the Belvedere or the Isabella, this is still a pleasant place to stay. They have a tiny swimming pool, enjoy a meal at their fine restaurant, or hand over the kids to the hotel nursery for a peaceful and romantic day or evening on your own. Not many other amenities– the most apparent is the lack of air conditioning or TV in the rooms.

6. VILLA BELVEDERE, *Via Bagnoli Croce 79, 98039 Taormina. Tel. 0942/23791. Fax 0942/625-830. 47 rooms 14 with bath, 33 with shower. Single L55,000-88,000; Double L85,000-140,000. Visa accepted.* *** The rooms here are clean and comfortably relaxing and they have air conditioning. But if you don't want to stay in your room you can swim in the pool, play a little tennis at their court, or relax with a drink in their garden. A small, friendly, well located place to stay in Taormina.

7. PRESIDENT HOTEL SPLENDID, *Via Dietro Cappuccini 10, 98039 Taormina. Tel. 0942/23500. Fax 0942/625-289. 50 rooms all with bath. Single L35,00-50,000; Double L65,000-80,000. American Express, Visa accepted.* **

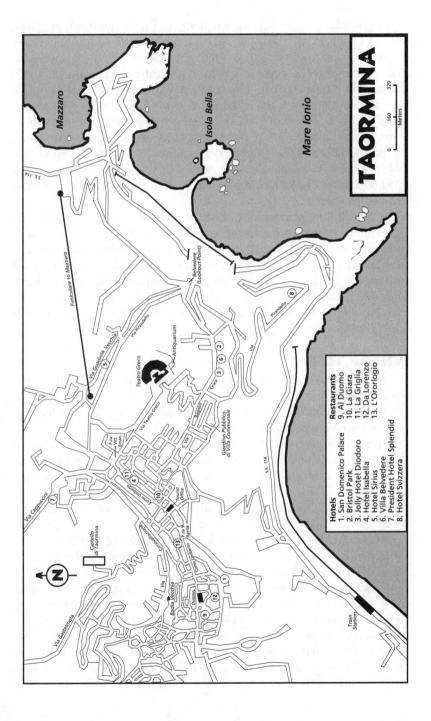

TAORMINA

0   160   320
Meters

Mazzaro

Isola Bella

Mare Ionio

S.S. 114

Funiculare to Mazzaro

Belvedere
(Lookout Point)

Via Pirandello

Via Giardola Vecchia

Antiquarium

Teatro Greco

Via Teatro Greco

Giardino Pubblico
di Villa Communale

P.za Vitt. Eman.

Corso Umberto

Tourist Office

Via Bagnoli Croce

Via Pirandello

S.S. 114

Via Cappuccini

Castello
di Taormina

Via Circonvallazione

Corso Umberto

P.za S.ta Agata

Via Gastelnola

Badia Vecchia

Via Duomo

Train
Station

N

Hotels
1. San Domenico Palace
2. Bristol Park
3. Jolly Hotel Diodoro
4. Hotel Isabella
5. Hotel Sirius
6. Villa Belvedere
7. President Hotel Splendid
8. Hotel Svizzera

Restaurants
9. Al Duomo
10. La Giara
11. La Griglia
12. Da Lorenzo
13. L'Ororlogio

A fantastic place to stay for any budget. A little run down in places, but the rooms at the front have great panoramic views and most have balconies from which you can sit, enjoy room service, and enjoy the view. The restaurant serves superb local food (the full board for only L80,000 is a steal) and the view from most of the tables is magnificent. They also have an outside pool and a relaxing bar downstairs. Located about 150 meters from the center of town, this place is trying to upgrade its facilities to get three stars. Their next step is to get air conditioning in the rooms.

8. HOTEL SVIZZERA, *Via L Pirandelo 26, 98039 Taormina. Tel. 0942/23970. Fax 0942/625-906. 16 rooms, 4 with bath, 12 with shower. Single L25,000-35,000; Double L41,000-56,000. No credit cards accepted. Full board L85,000 per person.***

A quaint little place on the outskirts of town near the water. This is a great inexpensive option for budget travelers. Only 16 rooms though, so remember to reserve well in advance. Their restaurant is good and might be an option since they're a little away from everything. There is a relaxing garden setting from which you can enjoy an after-dinner drink. They also have a shuttle service to pick you up at the train station. No air conditioning or TV in the rooms, but they are clean and comfortable enough to sleep in.

WHERE TO EAT

As a tourist town, there a plenty of little places to eat. Listed below are the restaurants I think are best.

9. AL DUOMO, *Vico Erbrei 11, Tel. 0942/625-656. Closed Wednesdays. All credit cards accepted. Dinner for two L80,000.*

In the summer the best place to eat is on their little terrace facing the Piazza Duomo. They have a small antipasto plate of cheese and salad that I can't recommend. But their pasta dishes are superb, especially the *pennette vecchia Taormina* (little macaronis with a spicy tomato and vegetable sauce). For seconds, try their *polpette arrostite nelle foglie di limone* (roasted meatballs with a touch of lemon sauce).

10. LA GIARA, *Vico La Floresta 1, Tel. 0942/23360. Closed Mondays but not from July to October. Only open on weekends in November, February and March. All credit cards accepted. Dinner for two L120,000.*

Elegant and sophisticated, this large place is located in the heart of the old town, and has a great terrace that is used year round with wonderful views all the way to the beach at Giardini Naxos two kilometers away. The cooks serve the regular local dishes here, as well as creative adaptations of them. Try the *foie gras* for an antipasto or the *insalatina di crostacei* (little salad with crustaceans). For primo try the *raviolini di Crostacei in salsa di scampi* (ravioli stuffed with crustaceans in a shrimp sauce). For seconds try any of their regularly prepared meats or fish, or *mignon di carne al tartufo nero* (filet mignon covered with black truffles). You can prolong the evening after dinner by getting a drink at their piano bar.

11. LA GRIGLIA, *Corso Umberto 54, Tel. 0942/23980. Closed Tuesdays and November 20-December 20. All credit cards accepted. Dinner for two L110,000.*

On the main street in Taormina, this place is known for their aquarium stuffed with lobsters and fish that you can choose for your meal. This is a rustic but refined place, with professional service preparing you for fine Sicilian food. Try the *vermiccelli incasciati* (fried vermicelli pasta made with a tomato sauce) or the classic *penne con sarde e finicchietto* (tubular pasta with sardines and fennel). For seconds try anything they have on the grill – after all, the name of the place means "The Grill."

12. DA LORENZO, *Via M Amari 4, Tel. 0942/23480. Closed Wednesdays and November 15 to December 15. All credit cards accepted. Dinner for two L90,000.*

Situated a stone's throw away from the Piazza Duomo, during the summer the best place to eat is out on their patio. In this small intimate restaurant that only seats around 45 people, the best antipasto samplings are the *ricci di mare* (a large plate of mixed seafood), *occhie di bue* (oxen eyeballs - go ahead, be adventurous, they're much better than mountain oysters), or *calamaretti fritti* (fried small squid). For primo try their *fussilli al carciofo* (pasta with a tasty artichoke sauce) and for seconds try any of their roasted or grilled meat or fish.

13. L'OROLOGIO, *Via Don Bosco 37a, Tel. 0942/625-572. Closed Mondays and November. All credit cards accepted. Dinner for two L100,000.*

You can sit outside on their enclosed terrace year round. For antipasto try their *gamberetti con rucola* (small shrimp with cheese), or il *prosciutto di porcellino* (ham from a young pig) that comes with *bruschette* (garlic and oil smothered bread covered with tomatoes). Next try their *ravioli di carne di cinghiale al finocchietto* (ravioli stuffed with wild boar meat in a fennel sauce). Then for seconds try their excellent *Fantasia dell'Orologio* (mixed fried seafood, meats and cheeses).

SEEING THE SIGHTS

Taormina's main attractions are really the steep stepped medieval streets, quaint old buildings, and scenic views over the water, but here are a few other sights of interest.

TEATRO GRECO

Via Teatro Greco. Open 9am–1 hour before sunset. Admission L3,000.

Founded by the Greeks in the 3rd century BC, this theater was almost completely redone by the Romans in the 1st century AD to accommodate their gladiatorial displays. It's so well-preserved that tourists are still allowed to clamber around on the stone seats still in existence today.

GIARDINO PUBBLICO

Via Bagnoli Croce. Open during daylight hours.

Directly in front of the Greek (Roman) theater are the gardens of the **Villa Communale**, where you can enjoy a peaceful stroll or relax on a bench sunk into a flower bush. From the walls there are some wonderful views over the water and the beach areas.

TEATRO ROMANO

Via Corso Umberto. Open all the time.

Back in town there is a smaller Roman theater that is partially covered under the **Church of Santa Caterina**. You can peer down from the railings in the street or enter the church to see more of the theater through the floor. Located right next to the tourist office.

CASTELLO

Castle is open to the public 9am–1pm and 4–7pm.

If you're in the mood to climb small steep steps up a mountainside for about 30 minutes, then you can enjoy the best views of the area. Located above town, this tumble-down medieval castle isn't much in itself, but the panoramic views are superb.

NIGHTLIFE & ENTERTAINMENT

There are plenty of discos to choose from, all of which will cost you between L10,000 and L20,000 just to get in. If you want a more relaxing evening there is nothing better than sipping a good Sicilian wine at one of the outdoor cafes and watching the world go by. That will be a little expensive too, about L6,000 per glass, but your eardrums will still be intact.

PRACTICAL INFORMATION

Banking Hours & Changing Money

Since this is a big tourist town, during the high season banks are open Monday through Saturday, 8:30am–1:30pm and from 4:00pm–7:30pm. Besides banks there a plenty of exchange bureaus (casa di ca*mbio*) around and **American Express** is represented in the offices of **La Duca Viaggi** *at Via Don Bosco 39, Tel. 0942/625-255.*

Also there is a *cambio* in the train station at the information office that is open Monday–Sunday, 9:00am–9:00pm.

Business Hours
Most shops are open from 9:00am–1:00pm and from 3:30pm–7:30pm Monday–Saturday, and Sunday 9:00am–1:00pm.

English Language Bookstore
• **Libreria Interpress**, *Corso Umberto 37, Tel. 0942/24989*. Open regular business hours. Not exclusively an English-language bookstore, but they do carry a few popular titles in English.

Local Festivals
• **May**, *Sfilato del Carretto*. A display of Sicilian carts
• **July to September**, *Taormina Arte*. Theatrical, film and musical productions all over the city.
• **Christmas**, Festive parade

Moped Rental
• **Sicily on Wheels**, *Via Bagnoli Croce 90, Tel. 0942/625-657*. Must be over 16 to rent. Open daily from 9:00am–1:00pm and 4:00pm–7:00pm. You can also rent cars here. A great way to see the countryside or just go for a spin down to the beach is by moped.

Postal Services
The central post office in Taormina is *at Piazza San Antonio (Tel. 0942/23010)*. Open Monday through Saturday 8:30am–5:00pm, and since this is a tourist town Sunday 9:00am–Noon. Stamps can be bought at any tobacconist (stores indicated by a T sign outside), and mailed at any mailbox, which are red and marked with the words *Poste* or *Lettere*.

Tourist Information & Maps
• **Tourist Office**, *Piazza Santa Caterina, Tel. 0942/232-43*. Can help you find a place to stay and give out maps and other information. Open Monday–Saturday, 8:30am–2:00pm and 4:00pm–7:00pm.

ISOLE EOLIE
The **Isole Eolie**, named after the Greek God of the Wind, are also known as the **Lipari Islands** in reference to the largest island in the chain. There are seven inhabited islands in total that lie between 30 and 80 km off the north coast of Sicily. The population of the islands today is about 14,000, which is a decrease, since the islands were once used as ancient penal colonies.

Today the islands attract people interested in scuba diving and snorkeling, as well as those wishing to enjoy one of the most unspoiled seashores in Italy. The main island, **Lipari**, is more prepared for dealing with tourists. It also has a beautiful Castle, archaeological ruins, and a variety of churches. **Vulcano** is aptly named since it is basically a bubbling volcano itself. **Stromboli** is also an active volcano and is the most scenic of all the islands. These three islands are horribly crowded in the summertime with tourists, but you can visit the other four **Panarea**, **Salina**, **Filicudi** and **Alicudi** and enjoy a bit of solitude. These islands really should be enjoyed as a relaxing vacation in and of themselves.

ARRIVALS & DEPARTURES

Access to the islands is easiest from **Milazzo** on the north shore of Sicily. There are year round ferries and hydrofoils that leave several times a day. These ferries stop first at Vulcano, then at the main island Lipari. Here you can disembark and catch a smaller local ferry to any of the other islands.

But you can also catch ferries and hydrofoils to the islands from cities in Sicily (**Palermo**, **Cefalu**, and **Messina**) as well as **Naples** and **Reggio di Calabria** on the mainland, and **Calabria** in Sardinia.

Ferries & Hydrofoil Companies in Milazzo
•**SNAV**, *Via L. Rizzo 14, Tel. 090/928-4509.* Hydrofoils (L32,000) only.
•**Siremar**, *Via dei Mille 32, Tel. 090/928-3242.* Ferries (L16,000) and hydrofoils (L32,500).
•**Navigazione Generale Italiano**, *Via dei Mille 26 Tel. 090/928-4091.* Ferries (L16,000) only.

LIPARI

The island of **Lipari** is the most visited since it is the largest and most beautiful. The main town of the same name has quaint little pastel colored houses, and is surrounded by the medieval **Castello** that crowns the small town. Inside the castle walls there are four churches, the town's **Duomo**, and an **archaeological park**, which reveals that there were people in Lipari as far back as 1600 BC.

GETTING AROUND TOWN

There are buses every 45 minutes or so that leave Lipari and traverse the island. Any of the other villages are no more than half an hour away by bus. If you're feeling adventurous, rent a moped and ride around the island. They can be rented at one of the many rental shops along the **Via Marina Lunga**.

North of the town of Lipari is the village of **Cannetto**. Visitors come to enjoy the **Spiaggia Bianca**, a small walk north of the village, where topless and bottomless bathing (sometimes). If you're in for a climb, walk

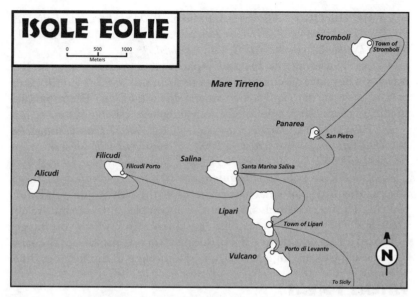

the four kilometers uphill to **Quattroochi**. You get a magnificent view of the town of Lipari, and the island of **Vulcano** in the background. Remember to bring your camera.

WHERE TO STAY

1. HOTEL MELIGUNIS, *Via Marte 7, 98055 Lipari. Isole Eolie. Tel. 090/981-2426. Fax 090/988-0149. 32 rooms all with shower. Double L150,000-300,000. Credit cards accepted.* ****

Not far outside of the town of Lipari, this is one of the two four star hotels on any of the islands. The other is on Vulcano. They have a private beach, their own restaurant, a tranquil little park, and first class service. The rooms are luxurious and comfortable with mini-bar, TV, and air conditioning. They also have shuttle bus that runs guests back and forth all over the island.

2. HOTEL CARASCO, *Porto delle Genti, 98055 Lipari. Isole Eolie. Tel. 090/981-1605. Fax 090/981-1828. 89 rooms, 20 with bath, 69 with shower. Single L90,000-120,000; Double L160,000-220,000. Visa accepted.* ***

Located out of reach of Lipari and even the smaller villages on the island, this is truly a resort type environment. Set in a romantic old building, this place has a swimming pool, disco, piano bar, a private beach, great views of the water and other islands, a great restaurant and an accommodating bar. The rooms are relatively large, very clean, quite charming, and extremely comfortable. This is the place that Italians come to relax in the Isole Eolie. They have a shuttle bus that can take you all over the island.

3. HOTEL ORIENTE, *Via G Marconi 35, 98055 Lipari. Isole Eolie. Tel. 090/981-1493. Fax 090/988-0198. 24 rooms all with shower. Single L30,000-60,000; Double L50,000-100,000. Visa Accepted.* **

A small place in the town of Lipari that is geared to the budget traveler. They have air conditioning, a rarity in two stars, a beautiful little private park/garden, and a comfortable downstairs bar. The rooms are small and clean but are definitely not someplace to hang out in.

4. HOTEL MACOMBO, *Via C Battisti 192, 98055 Lipari. Isole Eolie. Tel. 090/981-1442. Fax 090/981-1062. 14 rooms all with shower. Single L68,000-135,000; Double L85,000-170,000. No credit cards accepted.* **

Located in the village of Canneto north of the town of Lipari, this is an expensive little place that has easy access to the area's topless and nude beaches. The hotel's rooms are quaint, comfortable, and clean but are not luxurious. They have their own little restaurant from which you can get full board for L100,000, the price of one meal for two elsewhere. They also have a small bar and importantly, air conditioning in the summer time.

WHERE TO EAT

There are plenty of family-run restaurants all over the island. Most are open only in the high season to fleece the tourists. Below you'll find the best choice on any of the seven islands.

5. RISTORANTE FILIPPINO, *Piazza del Municipio, Tel. 090/911-002. Closed Mondays (but not in high season) and all November 15 to December 15. Credit cards accepted. Dinner for two L100,000.*

Great local food, especially the *maccaruna alla Filippino*, a tasty home-made pasta dish with a sauce of tomatoes, eggplant, mozzarella and ham, as well as other culinary delights. You can expect to taste some of the best prepared fish anywhere. I don't know what they do or how they do it but any fish you try, whether it's baked, fried, or grilled will melt in your mouth. They also make their own bread in-house and it is stupendous.

PRACTICAL INFORMATION

Banking Hours & Changing Money

Banks are open Monday through Friday, 8:30am–5:30pm. Most of them are located on the **Via Vittorio Emanuelle**. Besides banks there are a few exchange bureaus (casa di *cambio*) around. Another option, if all else is closed is to simply change your money at your hotel.

Business Hours

During high season most shops are open from 9:00am–1:00pm and from 3:30pm–7:30pm, and are closed all day Sundays and on Monday mornings. In the off-season, the shops that cater specifically to the tourists close down entirely.

Food stores, like *alimentari*, generally are open from 8:30am–1:30pm (so stock up on your picnic supplies before you need them) and from 5:00pm–7:30pm, and during the winter months they are closed on Thursdays.

Postal Services
The **central post office** in Lipari *is on the Corso Vittorio Emanuelle 207 (Tel. 090/981-1379).* Open Monday through Friday 8:30am–5:00pm, Saturday 9:00am– Noon. Stamps can also be bought at any tobacconist (stores indicated by a T sign outside), and mailed at any mailbox, which are red and marked with the words *Poste* or *Lettere*.

Tourist Information & Maps
• **Tourist Office**, *Via Vittorio Emanuelle 202 (Tel. 090/988-0095)* and is open regular business hours. You can get free information on buses, sights, and a not very useful map.

VULCANO

Some geologists think this small volcano of an island (hence the name, **Vulcano**) will explode sometime in the next decade, so beware when you go. Despite the pungent sulfurous smell, you can enjoy a relaxing bath in the heated bubbling water around the island, or coat yourself in the famous **fanghi**, or mud baths. These are located just up the Via Provinciale from the Porto di Levante, where the ferries dock on the east side of the island on the way to the beach. The mud is slightly radioactive, so don't sit in it too long, and pregnant women and small children shouldn't even think of going in.

If caking yourself with mud is not for you, walk down to the beach and immerse yourself in the bubbling **aquacalda** (hot water). You can also go up and peer into the **Gran Crater** (Great Crater) that simmers and boils. You need to be in reasonable shape to get up to the top. Once there you'll have some fabulous photo opportunities of the surrounding islands. You'll need to go in the early morning or late afternoon, since the face of the volcano gets quite hot from the sun and the lava inside at midday.

Almost everything on the island is closed before June and after September, so if you want to stay on the island or grab a bite to eat when it's low season, you may be out of luck.

WHERE TO STAY

LES SABLES NOIRS, *Porto Ponente, 98050 Vulcano. Isole Eolie. Tel. 090/985-2461. Fax 090/985-2454. 33 rooms. 8 with bath. 25 with shower. Single L130,000-200,000; Double L185,000-270,000. No credit cards.* ****

Quite an exclusive establishment located in a truly romantic setting. They have their own private beach where you rent snorkeling equipment, a swimming pool, a sun deck, a beautiful view, a piano bar and really good hotel restaurant that serves local cuisine as well as dietetic food. They also have bus service that can take you around the island. The rooms are quaint and comfortable. This place deserves its four star rating.

HOTEL CONTI, *Porto Ponente, 98050 Vulcano. Isole Eolie. Tel. 090/ 985-2012. Fax 090/988-0150. 62 rooms, only 61 with shower. Single with or without shower L50,000-100,000; Double L70,000-140,000. Visa accepted.* **

One of the bigger establishments on the island, they have their own private beach, a fine restaurant, a relaxing garden, a shuttle bus service – but no air conditioning. Stay here if you can stand the heat. The rooms are relatively large, with inconsistent furnishings, but they are clean and quite comfortable.

STROMBOLI

Another volcano in this chain of islands, **Stromboli** is the furthest from Sicily. This place is super-crowded in high season and is almost completely shut down in the low season. If you want to stay here you need to make reservations well in advance. The year round population of the island is only about 400, but when the tourists come you can have as many as 300 more staying here and many more coming to visit or to camp.

There are two towns on the island, tiny Ginostra on the southern end, and a combination of Piscita, Fiocogrande, San Vincenzo, and Scari which make up what is popularly called **Villaggio Stromboli** (**Stromboli Town**). You'll find most places to eat and stay in Stromboli Town, with only one small no-star pensione in Ginostra. But Stromboli is an island to visit for the day and is not really a destination in itself.

The only real attraction here is the climb up the **volcano**. To legally do this you need to go with an official guide, who can be hired from the **Club Alpino Italiano** at their offices *in Piazza Vincenzo (Tel. 090/986-263)*. The cost will be between L20,000 and 25,000, depending on how well you bargain. You start off in Piscita and the trip should take around three hours up and two hours down, so you have to be in really good shape. You'll also need to wear well-soled boots and bring along at least 1.5 liters of water. Don't drink it all at once. You'll want it later.

About halfway up you'll come across the **Sciara del Fuoco**, the volcanic trail that vents the lava directly into the sea. At the top, be careful not to lean over too far. Once you drop in you'll be hard-boiled forever.

On your descent from the top you may decide to go down the other side to **Ginostra** (follow the red, yellow and orange marked rocks) where you can enjoy a less touristy environment. There are ferries from here back to Stromboli Town, as well as Lipari.

Another fun side trip here is a visit to the **lighthouse** on the small rock island of **Strombolicchio**. From Via Marina and the ferry dock, you can hire a boat to take you out there for between L15,000 and L25,000, depending on how well you bargain.

WHERE TO STAY

LA SCIARA RESIDENCE, *Via Soldato Cincotta, 98050 Stromboli. Isole Eolie. Tel. 090/986-121. Fax 090/986-284. 62 rooms, only 59 with shower. Single without L 37,000; Double without L65,000; Single with L80,000-90,000; Double with L150,000-180,000. No credit cards accepted. ****

A truly romantic and relaxing place to stay. They have their own private beach, a swimming pool, tennis courts, magnificent views and a good hotel restaurant. The one thing they do not have is air conditioning, but try to get a seaview room, open your window, and the sea breeze will cool down the place quickly. A quaint, clean, and comfortable place.

SALINA

Salina is an uncrowded alternative to the three main islands, but that may soon change, so come here soon to enjoy the peaceful tranquillity of a place where time stands still. You arrive at **Porto Santa Maria**, the island's main port, where you can rent mopeds or bicycles to traverse the island, or take one of the many buses to any of your destinations.

Just three kilometers south of the port is the little village of **Lingua**, that is really only a small clean beach and a tiny cluster of *pensiones* and *trattorias* with great views of Lipari. A nice place to grab a bite to eat. If you head north from the port you'll pass through **Malfa**, a quaint little village that has a backdrop of decaying fishermen's huts. There is also a good beach here. Further along you come to **Pollara**, the site of the last eruption on the island back some 12,500 years ago. The village sits on a crescent-shaped crater from that eruption.

If you arrive on the island on August 15, you will be surrounded by pilgrims celebrating the Assumption of the Virgin festival, enroute to the **Sanctuary of the Madonna del Terziot** in **Valdichiesa**.

WHERE TO STAY

If you really want to get away from it all, here's one of the better little hotels on the island:

LA MARINARA, *Via Alfieri, Lingua. Salina. Isole Eolie. Tel. 090/984-3022. 14 rooms all with bath. Single L40,000; Double L75,000. No credit cards accepted. **

A small place with a great restaurant. You can get full board for L95,000 a couple. But since there are a few other restaurants in Lingua you may want to sample some of these. The rooms are simple and rustic but if you decided to stay on this island you should be expecting this. They also have a relaxing little garden where you can relax in the evenings.

PANAREA

Located between Lipari and Stromboli, **Panarea** is the smallest of the seven islands as well as the prettiest. That's why it is slowly becoming the hangout for more and more members of the jet set. From this island you can venture to some smaller islets that surround the east side for some great swimming. You should be able to hire a boat at the ferry dock at **San Pietro** for about L25,000 per person.

At **Punta Milazzese**, you can explore an archaeological dig of a Bronze Age settlement. There is little else to do on the island except eat, drink, and relax.

WHERE TO STAY

HOTEL CINCOTTA, V*ia San Pietro, 98050 San Pietro. Panarea. Isole Eolie. Tel. 090/993-014. Fax 090/983211. 29 rooms all with showers. Double L180,000-250,000. No credit cards accepted.*

A rustic little place that has small, clean, and comfortable rooms. You can get full board at their fine local style restaurant for L210,000 per couple, which is rather expensive. But you won't do any better at any other place on the island. Since everything has to be imported, food prices are sky-high. They also have a swimming pool surrounded by lush and relaxing gardens.

FILUCIDI

From the **Porto Filucida** where the ferry docks, take a walk north up to the almost abandoned village of **Valdichiesa**. If you keep walking all the way to the west side of the island, you'll be able to see the huge phallic rock formation **La Canna** thrusting out of the sea. You'll see lots of couples here. If you don't want to walk all the way there, you can hire a boat at the ferry pier to take you for about L25,000 per person.

You can also go across the island over the thin peninsula to the other coast to the tiny village of **Pecorino**. If you walk along the peninsula east, you'll come to the archaeological site of **Capo Graziano**, where there is a site of Bronze Age structures that predates those on Panarea.

One last place to see here is the **Grotta del Bue Marino** (**The Seal Grotto**), which can only be reached by boat.

WHERE TO STAY

HOTEL PHENICUSA, *Via Porto, 98050 Filicudi. Isole Eolie. Tel. 090/ 984-4185. fax 090/988-9966. 36 rooms, 2 with bath, 34 with shower. Single L 46,000; Double L70,000. No credit cards accepted.* ***

Located at the ferry port, this place has its own private beach and a really good restaurant. Take the option of the full board for L121,000 per couple since you only have one or two other options on the entire desolate island. The rooms with bathtubs are the best, but there's only two of them, so reserve early. The other bathrooms are tiny but clean. The rooms are all decorated in whatever furniture and bedding the hotel could find, but they are comfortable and clean.

ALICUDI

This is the place to go if you really want to get away from it all. There are only 125 inhabitants, one hotel, electricity only recently installed, and no paved roads. This tiny island used to be a rocky penitentiary maintained by the Italian government, but now the island is all but abandoned. From the island's only town and the ferry dock, **Alicudi Porto**, you can follow a path north to the ruins of a **castle** that used to house the prisoners. Other than that, and swimming along the rocky shore, there's nothing to do here except relax and enjoy the escape from the commercial world.

On your way here you will pass by the large rock phallus, **La Cana**, off the west coast of Filucidi.

WHERE TO STAY

HOTEL ERICUSA, *Via Regina Elena, 98050. Alicudi. Isole Eolie. Tel. 090/988-9902. 12 rooms all with shower. Double L90,000. No credit cards accepted.* *

I suggest you take the full board of breakfast, lunch, and dinner for L95,000 extra, since your options will be limited on Alicudi. Besides small but comfortable rooms, and tiny but clean bathrooms, the hotel has little else to offer. Very rustic, but oh so peaceful and relaxing.

21. SARDINIA

Roughly oblong in shape, **Sardinia** is the second largest island, after Sicily, in the Mediterranean Sea. It is located just south of the French island of Corsica. Sardinia is rugged, wild, and rather remote from Italy. Because of its isolation, even more so than Sicily, many of the old Sardinian customs and traditions live on today. The Sardinian language, which developed independently from Italian, still retains many old characteristics, despite the *Italophiling*, i.e. modernizing, of the island in more recent years.

What is today an autonomous region in the Republic of Italy started off as home to Bronze Age refugees cast onto Sardinia's shores about 2,000 BC. Evidence of their existence is seen in the over 700 remaining **nuraghi**, massive towers built with large stones without mortar that still dot the island. The **Phoenicians** were the first to invade this pristine isle in the 9th century BC. **Rome** was attracted to the island's mineral riches needed to maintain her Legions, so a Roman fleet invaded in 238 BC.

Around 455 AD, Sardinia fell into the hands of the **Vandals**, then later was fused into the **Byzantine empire**. But repeated **Saracen** attacks weakened the empire's hold so that four independent districts emerged called **Guidacati** that were governed by popular decree. These fours independent states remained even after the seafaring cities of Pisa and Genoa, with the Pope's backing, drove off the repeated incursions of Saracens and claimed the island as their own. For the next several centuries Sardinia became a protectorate of many different nations including Aragon, Spain, and Austria. **Vittorio Emanuelle**, who became king of Italy in 1863, started his campaign to unite the country from Sardinia with the help of a native son, **Giuseppe Garibaldi**.

Sardinia today lags economically behind much of the rest of Europe. Their main industry is agriculture and pastoral farming, as well as fishing, but recently the island has begun to succumb to the siren call of tourism. Sardinia is also a mining center. It produces four-fifths of Italy's lead. The islands large mineral deposits are largely found in the southwest and include zinc, lignite, fluorite, bauxite, copper, silver, antimony, manganese, and iron.

The island is divided into four provinces: **Cagliari**, **Nuoro**, **Oristano**, and **Sassari**. Each province is named for its capital city. Most tourists visit the northern Sassari Province, including the **Costa Smeralda**, or **Emerald Coast**. But there are many rustic sights to sea in Sardinia besides the beach, most of which are off the beaten path in the mountains. If you decide to search these out, however, be careful. This is a poor island and if you roam into the mountains, you or your belongings might not return.

Women traveling alone in particular could be targets, so please be careful. Try to hook up with someone if you plan on heading into the mountains, especially at night, since there are still bandits around. When in any major city never go down a street that is deserted and always be on the lookout for pickpockets and purse-snatchers, especially the ones on motor scooters roaring by.

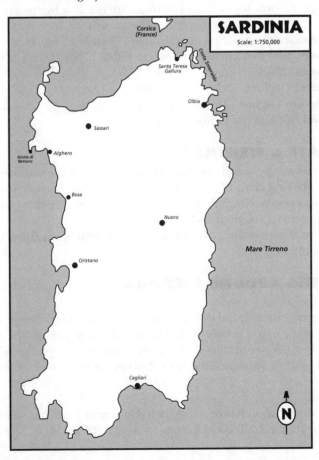

ARRIVALS & DEPARTURES
By Air
Cagliari has an international airport that does not accept flights from North America. But you can get a flight from most European capitals and a number of Italian cities directly to Cagliari.

From the airport you can take a bus directly to the city center near the train station. The bus leaves every twenty minutes from outside the international terminal and drops you off at the Piazza Matteoti. The ride is free. Check with your travel agent for details.

By Ferry
The most popular way to get to Sardinia is by ferry from one of the ports in Italy, especially **Civitavecchia**, whose ferries land in **Olbia**. If you're travelling in the high season – May to September – you need to book passage on your ferry weeks in advance, since there are so many people going over to Sardinia and there are not that many ferries.

The company **Tirrenia** operates the majority of ferries to and from the destinations below. You can purchase tickets from most travel agents:
- **Civitavecchia (just north of Rome) to Olbia**, 7 hours, fare is L34,000
- **Genoa to Olbia**, 13 hours, L58,000
- **Naples to Cagliari**, 16 hours, L54,000
- **Palermo to Cagliari**, 13 hours L50,000
- **Trapani to Cagliari**, 11 hours L45,000

CLIMATE & WEATHER
Anytime is a good time to travel to Sardinia. The climate doesn't vary greatly, making Sardinia a pleasant trip any time of year – with the following caveats: November to March is not prime beach weather, and the summers can sometimes be overbearingly hot.

For the best weather, visit between early September and the first week in November.

GETTING AROUND SARDINIA
By Car
The most prized, and thus the most remote and most dangerous sites to visit on the island simply cannot be visited unless you go by car. If this is your first time to Sardinia, stick with the train until you get a feel for Sardinia and its customs. Rental car listings are in each city's section.

By Train
Service by train has been upgraded in recent years but still remains light years behind the rest of Europe (this is a third world country in many

respects). Unlike Italy's mainland, there are frequent delays. But the views you'll see from the train are stupendous. And you won't have to worry about driving on the treacherous mountain roads.

BASIC INFORMATION

Banking Hours

Banks in Sardinia are open Monday through Friday, 8:35am-1:35pm and only the larger branches are open in the afternoon from 3:00pm-4:00pm. All are closed Saturday and Sunday and on national holidays. In some cities, the afternoon hour may not even exist. Even if the banks are closed, most travelers checks can be exchanged for Italian lire at most hotels and shops and at the foreign exchange offices in railway stations and at airports.

If you arrive in Sardinia without Italian currency, the **airport** at Cagliari has a few banks and monetary exchange offices *(Ufficio di Cambio).*

Business Hours

Store hours are usually Monday through Friday, 9:00am-1:00pm, 3:30/4:00pm -7:30/8:00pm, and Saturday 9:00am-1:00pm. Most stores are closed on Sunday and on national holidays. Don't expect to find any 24-hour convenience stores just around the corner. If you want to have some soda in your room after a long day of touring, you need to plan ahead. Don't expect to get a lot done from 1:00pm to 4:00pm, except find a nice restaurant and enjoy a pleasant afternoon.

Consulates

As you have probably surmised, there are no embassies or consulates on Sardinia, so if you need their assistance you'll have to make do with the embassies in Rome (see Chapter 7, Basic Information, for a full list of embassies and consulates).

Public Holidays in Sardinia

Offices and shops in Sardinia are closed on certain dates, so prepare for the eventuality of having virtually everything closed by stocking up on snacks, soda, whatever. For more details, see Chapter 20, Sicily, page 585, the same holidays are observed here in Sardinia.

FOOD & WINE

Food

As in Sicily, most Sardinian food is cooked with fresh ingredients raised or caught a short distance from the restaurant, so the food is healthy and satisfying. The traditional Sardinian meal has been influenced by the Middle East, France, and Spain as a result of the past conquests of the island. Other influences include the sea and the climate, perfect for raising many herbs and spices, as well as vegetables and fruits.

Suggested Sardinian Cuisine
These are traditional Sardinian dishes. Enjoy!

ANTIPASTO - APPETIZER
- **Antipasto Di Mare** – Mixed seafood appetizer plate. Differs from restaurant to restaurant
- **Pane frattau** – The local thin unleavened bread *carta di musica* covered with eggs and tomato sauce
- **Minestre di pesce** – Fish soup. Varies by region and restaurant.

PRIMO PIATTO - FIRST COURSE
Pasta
- **Sa fregula** – Pasta in broth with saffron
- **Culurgione** – Ravioli stuffed with beet roots, local cheese, and covered with tomato sauce and sausage made from lamb

SECOND PIATTO - ENTRÉE
Carne – *Meat*
- **Maiale arrosto** – Pig roasted on a spit
- **Capra arrosto** – Goat roasted on a spit
- **Cordula** – Lamb entrails baked with saffron and other spices

Pesce – *Fish*
- **Aragosto** – Lobster
- **Sogliola alla griglia** – Grilled sole

DOLCE - DESSERT
- **Sebada** – Dough stuffed with cheese, sugar and honey

CAGLIARI

Cagliari is the capital of Sardinia, the islands main port, and the main commercial and trade center on the island. The city was founded by the Phoenicians, who called it Caralis, and was later taken over by the Romans and renamed Carales, and eventually passed through the rule of Spaniards and Pisans and was overrun by Saracens. The town's nickname is Castello, which in Sardinian is pronounced *Casteddu*, which is the official name for the city.

The old city sits picturesquely on the slopes of a large hill, at the base of which away from the water are the newer suburbs and developments. In the **Centro Storico**, though, you can find a charming blend of Roman ruins, Spanish churches and medieval streets, castle walls and old town gates.

ARRIVALS & DEPARTURES

See *Arrivals & Departures* above (for all of Sardinia) and choose your preferred mode of transportation.

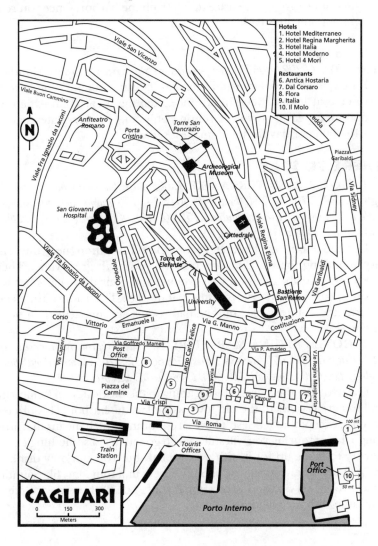

Hotels
1. Hotel Mediterraneo
2. Hotel Regina Margherita
3. Hotel Italia
4. Hotel Moderno
5. Hotel 4 Mori

Restaurants
6. Antica Hostaria
7. Dal Corsaro
8. Flora
9. Italia
10. Il Molo

CAGLIARI

GETTING AROUND TOWN

By Bus

The buses all depart from the central location of Piazza Matteoti and cost L1,500 one way. You can purchase tickets at any newsstand or tabacchio. There is a newsstand in the train station and the bus station. Bus #8 goes up the hill to the old town. Bus P goes out to the beach.

By Foot

Besides getting to the beach, Cagliari is a walkable city even though the sights you're going to see are uphill from the harbor. Once you're at the top the going gets easier.

By Rental Car

• **Hertz**, *Tel. 07/024-0037, office located at the airport.* Open Monday-Friday, 9:00am–6:00pm and Saturday 9:00am–1:00pm. You need to reserve at least a week in advance. Renting a car is an expensive option, especially if you're renting only for one day. Rates start at L150,000 per day for their smallest sedan.

WHERE TO STAY

1. HOTEL MEDITERRANEO, *Lungomare C. Colombo 46, 09125 Cagliari. Tel. 070/301271. Fax 070/301-274. 136 rooms, all with shower. Single L 134,000-161,000; Double L157,000-188,000. Credit cards accepted. Breakfast L19,000 extra.* ****

Located about one kilometer from the train station, near the cemetery and along the sea. This is a tranquil spot with great views. Their restaurant is worth trying for one evening and their downstairs bar is a relaxing place to settle down after a long day. The rooms are clean, modern, and comfortable, and the bathrooms are immaculate. A good place to stay.

2. HOTEL REGINA MARGHERITA, *Viale Regina Margherita 44, 09124 Cagliari. Tel. 070/670-342. Fax 070/668-325. 100 rooms, all with bath. Single L 190,000; Double L230,000. Credit cards accepted.* ****

Located near the marble steps leading to the Bastione San Remo, this hotel has great views of the old town as well as the harbor. This place is very nice, except that it doesn't have a restaurant, which means that after a tough day of touring you will still have to go out to get something to eat. They try to make up for it with a piano bar, but you can only drink so much. Every other service you should expect in a four star, like laundry service, room service and professional staff. The bathrooms are pleasantly large with nice big tubs.

3. HOTEL ITALIA, *Via Sardegna 31, 09124 Cagliari. Tel. 070/660-410. Fax 070/650-240. 113 rooms, 5 with bath and 108 with shower. Single L 70,000-90,000; Double L90,000-125,000. Credit cards accepted. Breakfast L10,000 extra.* ***

Located near the train station, you're in the center of everything but the noise is eliminated with the hotel's double paned windows. The rooms are slightly small but comfortable, and they are kept quite clean – but there are some ridiculous furnishings. I think Pee Wee Herman must be their decorator. Besides air conditioning, TV, bar downstairs, they also have laundry service and room service. One of the city's better restaurants is located next door (see *Where To Eat*)

4. HOTEL MODERNO, *Via Roma 159, 09124 Cagliari. Tel. 070/660-306. Fax 070/660-260. 93 rooms, 47 with bath, 46 with showers. Single L 105,000; Double L130,000. Credit cards accepted. Breakfast L14,000 extra.* ***

What a quaint hotel! Situated in an old building near the train station, try to get one of the rooms with a tub since these are the oldest and best. The showers were added later to the other rooms making the bathrooms a little cramped. No restaurant but an antique filled sitting and bar area. There is air conditioning and TV in the rooms. Laundry and room service too.

5. HOTEL 4 MORI, *Via G.M. Angioj 27, 09124 Cagliari, Tel. 070/668-535. Fax 070/666-087. 21 rooms only 8 with bath. Single without L60,000; Single with L88,000; Double without L82,000; Double with L110,000.* **

This place has everything a small three star would have such as room service, cocktail lounge, sitting room, air conditioning, TV and mini-bar in the rooms, and other amenities. The one drawback is that the majority of the rooms do not have bathrooms. Their prices don't reflect this absence, so I recommend using this only as a last resort or if you want to save a little money.

WHERE TO EAT

6. ANTICA HOSTARIA, *Via Cavour 60, Tel. 070/665-870. Closed Sundays, August and National Holidays. All credit cards accepted. Dinner for two L130,000.*

It's always a pleasure to eat at this terrific seafood place. You can get shrimp cocktail, *antipasto di mare* (mixed seafood antipasto) and great grilled steaks of *pesce spada* (swordfish) They also serve a tasty local stew made with lamb called *ghisau*. Their house wine is a superb local wine, but if your palate is more refined their list contains many mainland Italian labels also.

7. DAL CORSARO, *Viale Regina Margherita 28, Tel. 070/664-318. Closed Sundays and December. All credit cards accepted. Dinner for two L160,000.*

At this place you get fantastic food, but you have to pay for it. In my opinion this is the best restaurant in Cagliari. It has a wonderful selection of menu options, a perfect selection of local, national and international wines, and the service is impeccable. All this is thanks to Giancarlo and Gianliugi Deidda, who make it their mission in life to give you the best meal possible. If you want something that's not on the menu they will try their best to have the cooks make an equivalent for you. You should try some of their home-made pastas especially the delicious *tagliolini freschi con zucchine e vongole* (pasta with zucchini and clams) or the *lasagna ai filletti di scorfano e pomodoro fresco* (lasagna with scorpion fish and fresh tomato sauce).

8. FLORA, *Via Sassari 45, Tel. 070/664-735. Closed Sundays. All credit cards accepted. Dinner for two L140,000.*

Simple traditional dishes are served in an elegant environment, either outside on their terrace or inside. Start with an *insalata di gamberi* (shrimp cocktail), then move onto the *zuppa di verdure* (vegetable soup) and finish with a succulent *stinco di maiale al forno* (pork shank roasted in the oven). A good place to get local dishes at somewhat high prices.

9. ITALIA, *Via Sardegna 30, Tel. 070/657-9870. Closed Sundays. All credit cards accepted. Dinner for two L100,000.*

Located by the hotel of the same name, this place has a committed clientele. The Italia serves many local specialties and the menu is equally divided between surf and turf. Start off with the *insalata di polpo* (octopus salad), and move to the *zuppetta di cozze* (muscle soup) so you can save room for the tasty and large *spiedino di carne miste* (mixed meat grilled on a spit). If you want to stick with fish they make excellent grilled and fried of all varieties.

10. IL MOLO, *Calata dei Trinitari, Tel. 070/308959. Closed Sunday and Monday nights, and November. All credit cards accepted. Dinner for two L100,000.*

Located almost right on the water, this place was a nautical club for many years, but today it is one of the best places to go to savor the seafood of the region. The *menu digestivo* is inviting, offering you a different seafood dish for every course. If you don't want to eat that much, try the flavorful and filling *grigliate miste di pesce* (mixed grilled fish).

SEEING THE SIGHTS

To get to the old town from the harbor, walk past the tree-lined Via Roma up the hill to the **Piazza Costituzione**. Walk up the flight of marble steps to the **Bastione San Remo**, which offers you magnificent views over the city, the harbor, and beyond. These medieval bastions are partially restored and are the best place to begin your exploration of Cagliari's old town.

Pass through the **Porta dei Due Leoni** to the Via Universita and go past the **University** (*Via Universita, open 8am-7pm*). If you're so inclined, stop in and see for yourself what a Sardinian university is like. They have peaceful gardens in the back of the main building. As you pass the University, take note of the massive tower, **Torre di Elefante**, on the right hand side of the street. Take a right past the tower and enter the steep lanes, dark alleys, and imposing archways that make up the streets of the old city.

Weave your up to the **Piazza del Palazzo** where you can find the 14th century **Cattedrale** on the right. Built by the Pisans in 1312, the cathedral (*Piazza Palazzo, open 8am-noon and 3-7pm*) is a prime example of their expressive architectural style. On either side of the entrance are two pieces of a pulpit that was created by the Pisan master Gugliemo Pisano, whose family worked on the cathedral and leaning tower in Pisa. The pulpit is covered with magnificent New Testament scenes. Make sure you visit the crypt where the remains of many Sardinian saints are stored. Exit the cathedral and walk to your right to get to the **Museo Nazionale Archeologico** (*Piazza Indipendenza. Open 9am-7pm. Admission L5,000*)

The museum contains some well preserved, and some not so well preserved, relics and artifacts from Greece and Rome, as well as the largest collection of Sardinian antiquities anywhere. On the upper floors is the National **Painting Museum** that contains pictures from the 14th through the 18th centuries.

In the same piazza as the museum is the **Torre San Pancrazio**. Together with the aforementioned Torre di Elefante, they were part of the defense structure of Cagliari's castle. From the tower, pass through the **Porta Cristina** to get the Viale Buon Cammino. This will lead you to the **Anfiteatro Romano** (*Viale Fra Ignazio Da Laconi, open 9am-7pm*), which was constructed in the 2nd century AD in a natural depression in the rock. It is definitely one of the most imposing and well preserved Roman ruins in Sardinia. Today the structure is used for open air concerts and theater presentations. Just south of the theater are the lush **Botanical Gardens** where you can go and relax among a variety of flowers and plants (*Viale Fra Ignazio Da Laconi. Open 8:30am-8pm. Admission L2,000*).

PRACTICAL INFORMATION
Banking Hours & Changing Money
Banks are open Monday through Friday, 8:30am-1:30pm and some re-open from 2:30pm or so to 3:30pm or so.

Besides banks there is a *casa di cambio* in the train station open from 9:00am until 7:00pm, Monday to Saturday. Another option, if all else is closed is to simply change your money at your hotel, where you won't get as good a rate.

Business Hours

Most shops are open from 9:00am–1:00pm and from 3:30pm–7:30pm, and are closed all day Sundays and on Monday mornings. In conjunction with the Sunday and Monday morning closings, shops also closed half-days on Saturday.

Food stores, like *alimentari*, generally are open from 8:30am–1:30pm (so stock up on your picnic supplies before you need them) and from 5:00pm–7:30pm, and during the winter months they are closed on Thursdays.

Laundry Services
• **Lavanderia Erica**, *Via Ospedale 109*. Located across from the hospital on the way up the hill to the Roman Amphitheater. Bus #8 goes right up there from the Piazza Matteoti. Open Monday through Saturday 8:00am to 8:00pm. L12,000 for drop-off service that will wash, dry, and fold your clothes.

Postal Services

The **central post office** in Cagliari *is in the Piazza del Carmine (Tel. 070/668-356) near the train station*. Open Monday through Saturday 8:30am–5:00pm. But if you're in a hurry, stamps can be bought at any tobacconist (stores indicated by a T sign outside), and mailed at any mailbox, which are red and marked with the words *Poste* or *Lettere*.

Travel Agencies
• **Cosmorama**, *Piazza Repubblica 8, Tel. 070/49-78-72. Fax 070/49-78-73*. If you don't want to rent a car, but you still want to see the sights outside of the city, contact this excellent travel agency to arrange for a private tour. Some of the staff speak decent English.

Tourist Information & Maps
• **Tourist Office**, *outside of the train station in the Piazza Matteoti (Tel. 070/669-255)* which is open from 8:30am–8:00pm Monday through Friday, and Saturday 9:00am –1:00pm. Pick up tourist information about the surrounding areas and useful city and area maps.

EXCURSIONS FROM CAGLIARI

Spiaggia di Poetto

This is Cagliari's most popular bathing beach. **Spiaggia di Poetto** is a white sand paradise extends 10 km along the **Golfo di Quarta**. On summer weekends, the place is packed with people so try and get here during the week. Take bus **P** from a bus stop on the south side (harbor side) of Via Roma. It will take about 25 minutes to get here.

Remember to buy a bus ticket for L1,500 first from a *tabacchi* or newsstand, or risk getting nabbed by the inspectors and fined about L50,000.

Nuraghi di San Nuraxi

These are the best preserved complex of **nuraghi** (tall stone structures held together without mortar) in all of Sardinia. Located on the top of a hill, these structures are obviously placed together for defensive purposes, giving us some insight into the culture of the ancient prehistoric civilization that built them. The only easy way to get here is to rent a car and ride the 60 km through rolling countryside outside of Cagliari.

If you want to take public transportation you can get out to the sight, but you won't be able to return the same day.

Nora

Settled by the Phoenicians around 850BC, and later taken over by the Romans, the strategic town of Nora sits at the end of peninsula. After a series of disastrous Saracen raids, the stronghold was abandoned to the elements. Today there are some well preserved Roman ruins, including a forum, amphitheater, temples, and villas with mosaic tiles on the floors. This sight is only easily accessible by car. Public transportation in Sardinia is not up to par with the rest of Italy.

ALGHERO

Bypass the large and industrial city of Sassari altogether and make your way to **Alghero**, one of the most romantic medieval villages by the sea you'll ever find. There really is not too much to do or visit in Alghero, but it is so beautiful that visiting here should be your main reason for coming to Sardinia. You'll find tiny alleyways, fantastic vistas, medieval towers, Gothic churches, wonderful restaurants and an ambiance and environment that can't be beat.

ARRIVALS & DEPARTURES

By **train** it is three hours from Cagliari and an hour from Olbia. Trains leave three times a day from Cagliari and four times a day from Olbia.

If you don't want to wait that long, you can catch a flight into the small domestic **Fortilia Airport** just outside of town. Small commuter flights from mainland Italy, Cagliari, and Sicily fly into this airport.

Renting A Car
• **Budget**, *Fortilia Airport, Tel. 079/986-050*. L100,000 per day, must be at least 21 years old.
• **Avis**, *Fortilia Airport, Tel. 079/935-064*. L110,000 per day, must be at least 21 years old.

WHERE TO STAY

1. VILLA LAS TRONAS, *Lungomare Valencia 1, 07041 Alghero. Tel. 079/981-818. Fax 079/981-044. 30 rooms all with bath. Single L170,000-180,000; Double L280,000. Breakfast included. Credit cards accepted.* ****

A quaint old hotel housed in a romantic old building and run ever so smoothly by Dirretore Antonio La Spina. Here you have access to the old town of Alghero as well as having the privacy of your own beach, a swimming pool, great views over the water, bocce courts, and a fine restaurant that serves local cuisine. The service and care given you here makes it feel like a home away from home.

2. HOTEL EL BALEAR, *Lungomare Dante 32, 07041 Alghero. Tel. 079/975-229. Fax 079/974-847. 57 rooms all with bath. Single L 70,000; Double L100,000. Credit cards accepted. Breakfast L10,000 extra.* ***

A respectable place just on the edge of the old town with wonderful views over the water from their garden terrace. The rooms are nice size but they don't have air conditioning. The bathrooms are clean and modernized. Their restaurant serves authentic local food prepared very well and there is a downstairs piano bar for your evening's entertainment.

3. HOTEL SAN FRANCESO, *Via Ambrogio Machin 2, 07041 Alghero. Tel. 079/980-330. Fax is the same. 21 rooms all with shower. Single L 40,000-50,000; Double L65,000-85,000. Breakfast included. Visa accepted.* **

A tiny place located in a renovated historic building. The rooms are large with high ceiling but they don't have air conditioning or TV but they are comfortable. The furnishings are kind of a hodge-podge of whatever seemed to be around, but that only adds to the quaint charm of this place. A good option for budget travelers, and everyone else too.

4. MANNU HOTEL, *Viale Alghero, Bosa 08013. Tel. 0785/375306. Fax 0785/375-308. 22 rooms all with shower. Single L50,000-60,000; Double L90,000-120,000. Breakfast included. Credit cards accepted.* ***

If you decide you want to stay in Bosa, a very quiet but incredibly charming small town about 45 km away from Alghero, this is the place for you. It's located in a building of recent construction in a quiet tranquil area with great romantic panoramic views and wonderful service. The rooms are large with high ceilings and the bathrooms are kept immaculate. They have air conditioning, TV, rooms and laundry service and more. The restaurant serves excellent food and is featured below.

WHERE TO EAT

5. CAVAL MARI, *Lungomare Dante, Tel. 079/981-570. Closed Tuesdays (not in summer) and 15 days in November. Credit cards accepted. Dinner for two L120,000.*

Located near the Hotel El Belear, this hotel has a large verandah on the rocks near the water where you can admire the Bay of Alghero. The large dining room is subdivided into sections, giving the place a more intimate feel. The food is a mix of regional traditional, meaning it has some Ligurian and Catalan influences, as well as being a bit creative.

Try their *polpo tiepido all'olio e aglio* (warm roasted octopus served in an oil and garlic sauce) or the *spigola marinata* (seafood grilled on a skewer). But first you must try their many versions of spaghetti, especially *alle cozze* (with mussels) and *ai ricci di mare* (with the riches of the sea, i.e., mixed seafood). The grilled meats are also good.

Mar di Sardegna

Train Station

Port Office

Via Catalogna

Torre De Maddelena

Torre di Porta Terra

Via Vittorio Emanuele

Cathedral

Casa Doria

Via Mazzini

Via XX Settembre

San Francesco

Torre San Giacomo

Torre L'Espero Reyal

Via Sassari

Via Giovanni XXIII

Via Tarditi

Post Office

45 km

ALGHERO

0   150   300
Meters

Kennedy

Hotels
1. Villa Las Tronas
2. Hotel El Balear
3. Hotle San Francesco
4. Mannu Hotel

Restaurants
4. Ristorante Mannu
5. Caval Mari
6. La Lepanto
7. Ai Tuguri

6. LA LEPANTO, *Via Carlo Alberto 135, Tel. 079/979-116. Closed Mondays in the winter. All credit cards accepted. Dinner for two L140,000.*

A fine place with a quaint terrace located in the heart of old city, but the preparation of dishes is haphazard. Sometimes it's great, other times so-so. Maybe its because they try to do too much. The menu is extensive and seems to have everything that surf and turf could offer. I've always been pleased with the *i polpi tiepido con le patate* (roasted octopus in an oil and garlic sauce with roasted potatoes) and the *spaghetti con gamberi e melanzane* (with shrimp and eggplant). For antipasto try the exquisite *antipasto misto di pesce spada affumicato* (smoked swordfish) or the *insalata mista* (mixed salad) with fresh vegetables from the region.

7. AL TUGURI, *Via Maiorca 113, Tel. 079/976-722. Closed Sundays and December 20 to January 20. Visa accepted. Dinner for two L100,000.*

This is a small place spread out over three floors with just enough room to seat about 35 people, and because of this it has an authentic local Algherese feel to it. The owner, Enrico Carbonella, walks among the tables making all feel welcome. The menu isn't extensive, but what they do serve is prepared perfectly.

For antipasto try the code *di gamberi e nuvole di funghi* (shrimps tails and mushroom heads) or the *marinate di pesce fresca* (marinated fresh fish). For pasta you simply must try the *linguine bianche* (made with an oil, garlic and pepper sauce). For seconds their huge *aragosta alla catalana con cipole e pomodorini freschi* (lobster Catalan style with onions and tomatoes) is terrific.

4. RISTORANTE MANNU, *Viale Alghero, **Bosa** 08013. Tel. 0785/ 375306. Visa accepted. Dinner for two L100,00.*

Note: this restaurant is part of the Mannu Hotel, so it is also no. 4 on our map.

Located inside the Mannu Hotel, the decor is classic modern. There aren't many options on the menu and most of the selections are seafood. Try their *gattuccio e la razza in agliata* (dogfish grilled with an oily garlic sauce) for seconds. For primo, try either the *risotto alla pescatora* (rice with seafood), *penne alle cozze* (tubular pasta with a mussel sauce), or *spaghetti al'aragosta* (with a lobster sauce).

SEEING THE SIGHTS

In town you'll find the **Chiesa di San Franceso** *(Via Carlo Alberto, open 8am–Noon and 3–5pm)*, begun in the 14th century and completed in the 16th. The different color stones give a clear indication where work recommenced. At Via Principe Umberto #7, you'll find the **Casa Doria** *(not open to the public)* a beautiful 16th century building built by the Doria family of Genoa who played a large part in the fortification and development of the city.

Down the street is the **Cathedral** (*Via Principe Umberto. Open 8am-noon and 3:30pm-6pm*), which is a jumble of architectural styles that can be seen from its Gothic/Catalan/Renaissance facade. There are three medieval towers located around the town: the **Torre di Porta Terra** to the east that was once one of only two access points into Alghero; the **Torre de L'Espero Reyal** to the south that is circular in design and once served as prison; and the **Torre de San Giacomo** facing the sea that once served as an 18th century dog pound.

In the vicinity of Alghero you can find quaint mountain towns, a necropolis, *nuraghi*, and more. The best sight outside of town are the **Grotte di Nettuno**, eerie but beautiful caverns complete with stalactites and stalagmites that can either be reached by car or by sea. Boats leave from the port near the train station hourly in the summer time. Round-trip takes about 2 1/2 hours and costs L16,000 per person. If you go by car, the admission is L10,000 and you'll have to descend over 600 steps to get down to the sea.

Also, only 10 km west of Alghero near the **Capo Caccia** (where there are great beaches, incidentally) are the **Nuraghi di Palmavera** that date back to 1500 BC. In another direction, just 10 km north of Alghero are the famous **Necropolis di Aghelu Ruju**, a group of 38 tombs built around 3000 BC.

Then if you go 45 km south of Alghero, you'll stumble upon the most quaint medieval hill town you'll ever find, **Bosa**. If you want to stay the night, or just for a meal to soak up more of the pristine beauty, see the *Where to Stay* and *Where to Eat* sections above. If you want the taste and feel of Sardinia's past merged with its present, Alghero and its environs is the place to visit. But you better hurry before everybody else finds out.

PRACTICAL INFORMATION
Banking Hours & Changing Money
Banks are open Monday through Friday, 8:30am-1:30pm and the **Banco Nazionale de Lavoro** *on Via Sassari* reopens from 2:30pm to 3:30pm. Besides banks there is a *casa di cambio* in the train station open from 9:00am until 7:00pm, Monday to Saturday. Another option, if all else is closed is to simply change your money at your hotel, where you won't get as good a rate.

Business Hours
Most shops are open from 9:00am-1:00pm and from 3:30pm-7:30pm, and are closed all day Sundays and on Monday mornings. In conjunction with the Sunday and Monday morning closings, shops also closed half-days on Saturday.

Food stores, like *alimentari*, generally are open from 8:30am–1:30pm and from 5:00pm–7:30pm, and during the winter months they are closed on Thursdays.

Postal Services
The **central post office** in Alghero *is on the corner of Via Carducci and Via Giovanni XIII.* Open Monday through Friday, 8:30am–5:00pm, Saturday 9:00am–Noon. Stamps can also be bought at any tobacconist (stores indicated by a T sign outside), and mailed at any mailbox, which are red and marked with the words *Poste* or *Lettere*.

Tourist Information & Maps
• **Tourist Office**, *Piazza Porta Terra, Tel. 097/979-054.* You can get maps, a list of possible accommodations, and bus and train schedules.

OLBIA

Olbia is like Messina in Sicily, in that you have to come here because this is where the ferry docks, but you definitely don't have to stay. I'm mentioning it since it is a trans-shipment point and you may have to pass through if you take one of the ferries from **Civitavecchia**. And if worse comes to worse and you have to spend the night here, I've listed some decent lodgings and good restaurants.

There are two real sights, **Chiesa San Simplicio** (*Via San Simplicio, open 9am–noon and 3pm–6pm*) a 12th century Pisan Romanesque church, and the **Chiesa Primaziale** (*Piazza Primaziale, accessible 9am–Noon and 4pm–6pm*) a 14th century convent complex that you can gain entrance to just by asking. From Olbia you can head south by bus to the beaches around **San Teodoro**, hop the train to **San Teresa Gallura** for a ferry over to the French island of **Corsica**, or start your journey by train across Sardinia to **Alghero** or south to **Cagliari**.

Put simply, since all traces of Olbia's Greek, Roman, and medieval past have been obliterated for the sake of modernization, this is a place that has little of interest. Pass through as quickly as you can.

GETTING AROUND TOWN

When you disembark from your ferry, the **train station** is only a couple hundred meters northeast of you. Follow the main road Corso Umberto I until you see the station on your right. The **bus station** is at the end of Corso Umberto I conveniently near the port.

You can walk anywhere, but if you need a taxi late at night there should be some around the port. Or call the 24-hour taxi line (*0789/ 31039*).

Renting a Car

• **Avis**, *at the airport in Loiri, 10 kilometers outside of town. Tel. 0789/22420.*
Call beforehand to have them send a van to pick you up at the ferry.

WHERE TO STAY

If you don't stay in a three or four star hotel, the accommodations you get will be rather poor here. The three below are my picks for their service and convenience.

1. HOTEL MARTINI, *Via G D'Annunzio, 07026 Olbia. Tel. 0789/ 26066. Fax 0789/26418. 66 rooms all with shower. Single L 118,000-147,000; Double L184,000-230,000. Credit cards accepted. Breakfast included.* ****

Romantic little hotel set near the beach with a great view of the water. No restaurant inside but Bacchus is just down the road. The rooms are smallish but comfortable and clean, as a four star should be. They have air conditioning, TV, laundry service, room service, minibar and more. A restful place a short ride from the train station, so you can get out of this town.

2. HOTEL PRESIDENT, *Via Umberto 9, 07026 Olbia. Tel. 0789/ 27501. Fax 0789/21551. 44 rooms all with bath. Single L118,000; Double L198,000. Credit cards accepted. Breakfast included.* ****

They have a bus service that will pick you up at the ferry if you call and tell them when you're arriving. If you don't call you'll just have to wait until they can rustle somebody up to get down there, and since this is Sardinia you never know how long that is going to take. They have a fine restaurant of their own, so you don't have to leave the place if you don't want to. The rooms have air conditioning, TV, and mini-bar, and are decently sized and immaculately maintained.

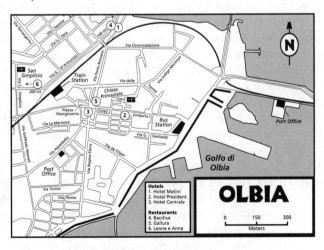

3. HOTEL CENTRALE, *Corso Umberto I 85, 07026, Tel. 0789/23017. Fax 0789/26464. 23 rooms all with shower. Single L 100,000; Double L140,000. Breakfast L10,000 extra. Diner Club accepted.* ***

Simply a place to lay your head for a night's rest. The rooms are small but they do have air conditioning, TV, and a phone. There's a small area they call a bar downstairs, as well meeting rooms. Other than that, this place is an empty shell. Clean, nondescript, but aptly named since it is in the center of things in Olbia.

WHERE TO EAT

4. BACCHUS, *Via G. D'Annunzio 2p, Centro Martini, Tel. 0789/21612. Closed Sundays, but in the summer only Sunday lunch, and 20 days in January. Credit cards accepted. Dinner for two L110,000.*

Located on the bay of the old Porta Romana, there are nice views from their terrace dining area over the water and the Isola Biancha. The atmosphere inside is grandiose with a touch of elegance, and the food, mainly seafood, is perfectly fresh and appetizing. If you want an antipasto try the *calamaro ripieno al profumo di basilico* (large squid stuffed with the taste of basil) it is truly delicious. For primo try any of their fantastic pasta options especially the *spaghetti ai gamberoni* (with small shrimp sauce). For seconds don't leave without sampling the *filetto di triglia con dadolata di pomodoro* (filet of mullet covered with diced tomatoes).

5. GALLURA, *Corso Umberto 145, Tel. 0789/24648. Closed Mondays, 10 days in November and 20 days between December and January. All credit cards accepted. Dinner for two L160,000.*

Ouch. The prices here really hurt. The atmosphere is nice, a little stuffy and formal but comfortable. If you don't want to spend too much but also get a great meal try the following: *zuppa di verdure* (vegetable soup) as an appetizer, then jump straight to an entree. This way your meal will be about L90,000. For entrée, avoid the pricey fish and try either the *l'agnello in tegame* (pan-fried lamb) or the *cinghiale in agrodolce* (sweat and sour wild boar). To finish things off sample some of their succulent *pecorino*. They have a selection of this cheese at different aged stages, each tasting wonderful and amazingly different from one another.

6. LEONE E ANNA, *Via Barcellona 90, Tel. 0789/26333. Closed Wednesdays (not in the summer) and January. Credit cards accepted. Dinner for two L160,000.*

Ouch again. But here too, if you avoid the fish dishes you can get a great meal at a more reasonable price. After a period, when this place was on the skids, it has finally regained the vitality, energy, and warmth it used to have years ago. Skip the antipasto, most of the seafood, and get some *pappardelle ai funghi porcini*, a scrumptious pasta dish made with butter and *porcini* mushrooms. Then for seconds dig into either the succulent *porcetto al forno* (baby pork on the grill) or the *capretto al forno* (baby goat on the grill).

PRACTICAL INFORMATION

Banking Hours & Changing Money

The banks on Corso Umberto I are open Monday through Friday, 8:30am–1:30pm and some reopen from 2:30pm or so to 3:30pm or so. There is an exchange at the ferry office that gives very bad rates, but that may be your only option if you don't have lire.

There is an American Express representative in the offices of **Avitur**, *Corso Umberto I 139, Tel. 0789 24327.*

Business Hours

From October to June, most shops are open from 9:00am–1:00pm and from 3:30pm–7:30pm, and are closed all day Sundays and on Monday mornings. Food stores, like *alimentari*, generally are open from 8:30am–1:30pm and from 5:00pm–7:30pm, and during the winter months they are closed on Thursdays.

There is a **STANDA** food store *on Corso Umberto I on the way to the train station*, open Monday to Saturday, 9:00am–8:00pm.

Postal Services

The **central post office** in Olbia *is on the Via Aquadotte (Tel. 0987/ 22251) near the open air market that takes place each the morning.* Open Monday through Saturday 8:30am–5:00pm. But if you're in a hurry, stamps can be bought at any tobacconist (stores indicated by a **T** sign outside), and mailed at any mailbox, which are red and marked with the words *Poste* or *Lettere.*

Tourist Information & Maps

• **Tourist Office**, *just off the Corso Umberto I on the Via Piro (Tel. 0789/ 21453).* Open from 8:30am–1:00pm and 4:00pm–7:00pm Monday through Friday, and 9:00am–1:00pm Saturday. If the town is not much to see, the tourist office makes up for it with all the information you can get here: maps of the city and surrounding areas; itineraries for exploring Sardinia's lush beaches and ancient archaeological sites, and most importantly a list of hotels in Sardinia including almost all the little towns and villages.

COSTA SMERALDA

The **Emerald Coast** (**Costa Smeralda**) is located just north of Olbia. This coastline at one time used to be nothing but a series of small subsistence level fishing villages. Then in 1962, it began to be developed as the playground for the rich and famous. Now all you can see for miles are high-rise luxury and some not-so-luxury hotels. Avoid the congestion and rank consumerism that this area is known for. There is little to see except lots of people crammed like sardines next to each other on the beach, and anything to do costs a small fortune.

The same goes for the once-beautiful islands of **La Maddalena** and **Caprerra**, now nothing but one big tourist trap. Some of the smaller outlying islands, like **Santa Maria** and **Budelli**, have not yet succumbed completely but they are on their way. If you are so inclined they can all be reached from the port at **Palau**.

One reason you may be interested, but only for short period of time, in visiting La Maddelena is that in the small town of **Caprera** lie the remains of the Italian and Sardinian hero **Giussepe Garibaldi**. You can catch a bus from the port to take you there.

22. THE LAKES OF NORTHERN ITALY

The northern lake region of Italy has offered vacationers respite from their daily troubles for centuries. The most famous visitor is probably **Julius Caesar**, whose legions left a lasting impression on the landscape with the remains of the forts and cities they built many years ago.

The quaint medieval charm of the lake towns, many of which were founded by the Romans, with their terraced gardens and terracotta roof-tiled villas, pale in comparison to the natural splendor of the breathtaking scenery. What used to be a relatively untouristed region that you could enjoy in calm serenity is now inundated with tons of tourists during certain times of the year. If you visit in July, August, or early September, the traditional time for Europeans to take their vacations, you will feel as if you've visited the Jersey shore instead of the vast expanse of **Lago Maggiore**, or **Como**.

But even during those hectic months, when most of Italy is swamped with tourists, you can still find some small lakeside town to escape from it all. Or you can hike up into the mountains for some stirringly fresh air, or hitch a ride on a ferry boat and float on the tranquil waters of the lakes on your way to a remote villa or garden.

Without the use of an automobile, you may want to restrict yourself to exploring just one lake by ferry or local bus service that moves along the *lungolago*, the lakeshore drive. With a car you'll have the freedom to explore all the lakes and you can also take excursions to wonderful hill towns like Bergamo's Citta Alta, or experience the romantic beauty of Verona or Venice.

When to Go

Most hotels, restaurants, and shops close during the winter, and ferry service is cut back dramatically. The time to avoid is July through September, when it seems as if all of Europe has descended on the lakes.

The best time to come is during the Spring months (March to early June) or the Fall months (late September through October). During these periods the ferries operate on a curtailed schedule and some hotels and restaurants are closed, but you will usually have the lakes virtually all to yourself. During these months you may encounter a mist or haze settling over the lakes and obscuring the mountains, but that sometimes can add to the medieval, mystical charm of this wonderful location.

TOURING THE LAKES

The best way to tour the lakes is by **ferry**, whether it is a **car ferry** *(traghetto auto)* or a **passenger-only ferry** *(traghetto)*. The ferries take longer than driving a car around the *lungolago* road, but on the water you will be blessed with far superior views of obscure villas and gardens, and best of all you will avoid the maddening traffic that descends during the peak months and even on the weekends in the off-season. The ferries go to all the main towns on each respective lake, so you can enjoy a complete lake experience only by utilizing them.

But don't expect to be able to see everything quickly. The ferries take time, and you can't do everything in a day.

To save time, consider packing a sandwich and eating on the ferry as it skims the calm waters of the lake. You can also take **hydrofoils** both ways or in one direction. But hydrofoils do not go to all the destinations on the lakes and they cost about twice as much as the ferries.

What to Do

Besides bathing in the spectacular scenery, and sometimes bathing in the waters of **Lake Orta** and **Garda** – but not in Lake Como or Maggiore; pollution has invaded even these pristine locations – you can try your hand at water skiing, windsurfing, jet skiing, and sailing. These water sports, hiking in the mountains surrounding the lakes, and exploring the charming little medieval towns is my idea of a great travel experience – but not from July through September if you can help it! Remember, the lakes are supremely busy then.

HOTEL MEAL PLANS ON THE LAKES

Most hotels on the Northern Lakes require you to purchase a full board meal plan, which could effectively double the cost of your stay. In some places this is a blessing, since there is not much around, but in places like Riva del Garda or Desnzano it really isn't necessary. Unfortunately, you may have to live with it. Inquire about the meal plan prior to arrival. It's better not to get it if you have the option, because if you decide you would like full board after you've settled in, you can simply purchase it on-site.

LAKE MAGGIORE

The second largest of the Alpine lakes after Garda, **Lake Maggiore** (**Lago Maggiore** in Italian, and it's also known as **Verbano**) was formed during the Ice Age from the movement of glaciers. This is evidenced by the U-shaped shoreline, it's extended length, and the wide inlets advancing into the valley. The majority of the lake is in Italy, but a small section extends into Switzerland in its northern reaches. The lake has been inhabited since around the ninth century BC. There have been recent archaeological discoveries that indicate an Iron Age people lived here, now referred to as **Golasecca**, after the site of one of the most important burial mounds found here.

The climate here is splendidly mild, which not only assisted human settlement but also a stable agricultural life. These ancient visitors were in all likelihood attracted to the stunning northern scenery and the beautiful, pristine waters. Since these early settlers, there have been plenty of visitors to this lake, many of them quite famous – Byron, Goethe, and Wagner among them.

It would take volumes to list all of the magnificent towns to visit, with their medieval streets, impressive churches, imposing castles, and more, so I've compiled a list of the best of the best. Once here, use your hotel as a jumping-off point for area sights.

Lakeside Attractions

Visit the Villa Taranto, a house built in 1875 and located on the Castagnola between the towns of Intra and Pallanza. (These two towns are so close together it is almost as if they are one.) At the villa you'll find over 20,000 species of plants flourishing on over 20 hectares of land. Besides the lovely botanical gardens, the grounds are lovely. Take a relaxing stroll through terraces, lawns, and fountains. If you're here at the end of April through the beginning of May, you will have stumbled upon the magnificent **Tulip Week**.

If architecture is your pleasure, see the fabulous **Santa Caterina del Sasso**, located between Reno and Cerro on the water. The best way to approach is by boat, where you can get the perfect view of the buildings hewn out of the rock walls of the **Sasso Ballaro**. This monastery was built in the 13th century and added onto over the centuries, giving it a vibrant charm.

Another building of architectural interest is the fortified palace on the **Rocca** in **Angera**. Built by the Visconti family in 1350 on the ruins of an earlier fortress, this place is worth a visit because of the vaulted ceilings and its medieval charm. I also love the tiny village set at the palace's feet that looks as if it hasn't changed in centuries.

Another architectural and historical sight are the remains of the **Vitaliano castle**, built by Count Ludovico Borromeo between 1519 and 1526 that now rests on one of the three islands that are between Canero and Cannobio. The ferry doesn't stop here (it's really just a speck of an island with a fortified castle on it) but does get close enough for pictures to be taken. Truly magnificent.

Looking for something to being back home, either for yourself or a friend? Don't miss the **Wednesday market** at **Luino**, where you can get crafts, food, local clothing, and more. At the same time you can enjoy the sights and sounds of a boisterous local market.

STRESA

For those of you that insist on the best hotels with all the amenities, like swimming pools (you'll need them on Maggiore if you want to swim, since the lake is not yet pollution-free), saunas, tennis courts, and more, then you'll want to come to **Stresa**.

Called the *Pearl of Verbano*, Stresa sits below the green slopes of **Mottarone** and offers a cool climate in the summer and mild emperatures in the winter, as well as picturesque beaches, beautiful landscaped gardens, fine restaurants, and much more. Stresa is the perfect place from which you can explore the rest of Lago Maggiore.

ARRIVALS & DEPARTURES

Located 80 miles northwest of Milan, there are a number of daily trains from Milan. If driving, take the **E 62** to the **SS 33**, which brings you into Stresa.

WHERE TO STAY

GRAND HOTEL DES ILES BORROMEES, *Corso Umberto I 67, Stresa 28049. Tel. 0323/30431. Fax 0323/32405. 182 rooms all with bath. Single L310,000; Double L490,000. All credit cards accepted.* *****

This is Stresa's best five star deluxe hotel. Located in a picturesque, romantic old building, this fine hotel is superbly situated on the town's main street as well as the lake's edge. They have their own indoor and outdoor swimming pool, tennis courts, health club, sauna, massage parlor, sun room, private beach, and snorkeling equipment for rent. On top of all that there is a piano bar, a restaurant with a scenic view over the lake, and everything else you can imagine that comes with a deluxe hotel. The rooms have high ceilings, antique furniture, and magnificent views, either of lake or the mountains.

REGINA PALACE HOTEL, *Corso Umberto I, Stresa 28049. Tel. 0323/933-777. Fax 0323/933-776. 162 rooms all with bath. Single L 200,000-210,000; Double L300,000-340,000; Suite L450,000-550,000. Breakfast included. All credit cards accepted.* ****

Another hotel situated in an historic and romantic building. Overlooking the lake, this place has its own private beach, outdoor swimming pool, tennis and squash courts, gymnasium, sun room, sauna, snorkeling equipment, day care, discounts on golf at local courses, and more. The restaurant has perfect views of the lake and the Borromean Islands, and the piano bar offers relaxation in the evening.

Since they are only a four star they seem to try harder than the five star deluxe, and offer a better price. The only real difference is that the Grand Hotel has an indoor pool, a plus in the winter time. The rooms here have high ceilings, quaint antique furnishings, and spectacular views of the lake and/or the mountains.

LA PALMA, *Corso Umberto I 33, Stresa 28049. Tel. 0323/32401. Fax 0323/933-930. 126 rooms all with bath. Single L175,000; Double L240,000. Breakfast L18,000. All credit cards accepted.* ****

Located on the main street and on the water's edge, this hotel also has its own private beach and a swimming pool. Situated in a more modern building than the Regina Palace and Grand Hotel, it is not nearly as charming and romantic but its location is perfect and the views over the water and the islands just as good, especially from the restaurant and the swimming pool. They have a health club, sauna, sun room, and snorkeling equipment, plus a quiet lounge for a drink in the evening.

HOTEL DU PARC, *Via Gignous 1, Stresa 28049. Tel. 0323/30335. Fax 0323/33596. 22 rooms, all with bath. Single L50,000-100,000; Double L70,000-140,000. Breakfast L15,000. All credit cards accepted.* ***

Located right by the local tourist information office, this hotel is set a short distance back from the main street and the shoreline. Situated in a romantic little building, this is the perfect choice for those travelers wanting a nice place to stay for not a lot of money. The only real amenities are a small restaurant that serves good food, room service, cable TV and air conditioning. The rooms seem a little small compared with the four and five stars but they are clean and comfortable.

SEMPIONE, *Corso Italia 46, Stresa 28049. 0323/30463. No fax. 17 rooms, 6 with bath, 11 with shower. Single L51,000; Double L75,000. No credit cards accepted.* **

Not much of a place, but the rooms are clean and comfortable, if a little small. The rooms with shower have tiny bathrooms, but the facilities are more modern. They have their own restaurant service, but I suggest eating out, especially at L'Emiliano almost next door (see Where to Eat). This is a budget travelers option.

WHERE TO EAT

L'EMILIANO, *Corso Italia 50, Tel. 0323/31396. Closed Tuesdays, Wednesdays for lunch, and January and February. All credit cards accepted. Dinner for two L160,000.*

The atmosphere is functional and the food is fabulous. If you want to save some money, order their *menu degustazione* for L55,000 per person that gives you a first and second course. Their menu is a twist between traditional and nouvelle and mainly consists of fish from the lake. Try their *ravioli di pesce con bisque di crostacei* (ravioli stuffed with fish and served with a crustacean sauce) or *their spaghetti freddi con cozze ed erba cipollina* (cold spaghetti with a sauce of mussels and baby onions). If mountain meat is what you need, try their *costoletto d'agnello profumate al rosmarino* (lamb cutlets cooked with a touch of rosemary), a succulently exquisite alternative to seafood.

PIEMONTESE, *Via Mazzini 25, Tel. 0323/30235. Closed Mondays and holidays. Credit cards accepted. Dinner for two L120,000.*

Located in the center of Stresa away from the water, the restaurant of the brothers Bellossi specializes in seafood and fish from the lake. In this elegant environment, try some of the *taglierini con vongole verace* (thin spaghetti like pasta with a spicy oil based clam sauce) or the tasty *involtini di sogliola e salmone* (rolled filets of sole and salmon). They also offer meat dishes like *costolette d'agnello al timo con patate arrosto* (lamb cutlet cooked with thyme and served with roast potatoes).

TOURIST INFORMATION

•**Piazzale Europe 3**, *Tel. 0323/31050-30416*

BORROMEAN ISLANDS

Just off shore from Stresa, the three enchanting little **Borromean Islands** will make you feel like you've stepped back in time. The **Isola dei Pescatori** has an ancient and picturesque little fishing village and that's about it, but it is a great place to escape for a while. The **Isola Bella** has its imposing **Palazzo Borromeo**, complete with a spectacular terraced garden. A tour through the palace brings you in contact with the wealth of the Borromeo family, furnished with Venetian chandeliers and mirrors, puppets, and more. If you come to this island, take the guided tour (*Tel. 30556. Open April–November 9am–Noon and 1:30pm–5:30pm. Admission L10,000*).

The **Isola Madre** is world-famous for its **villa** and landscaped **gardens** featuring a wide variety of exotic birds (*open April–November 9am–noon and 1:30pm–5:30pm; admission L10,000*). Inside the villa you'll find a cute little collection of dolls and puppets dating from the 16th to the 19th centuries. All the islands are just a short ferry ride or small personal boat taxi ride away from Stresa, and are so close that you can see them all in less than a day. If you wish to stay or to eat on the islands, here's where you should go:

WHERE TO STAY

VERBANO, *Via Ugo Ara 2, Isola dei Pescatori. Tel. 0323/30408. Fax 0323/33129. 12 rooms, 8 with bath, 4 with shower. Double L120,000. Breakfast Included. Full boar L150,000. All credit cards accepted.* ***

Isolated but still a ferry ride away from Stresa, here you'll have peace and quiet in the evenings and get the opposite view from the tourists on the mainland. Gaze at the lights of the small town of Stresa, which are very pretty. Located in a romantic old building, the hotel has its own private beach – but that's about it. Take them up on the full board meal option, since there are virtually no other places to eat on the island. A place to feel like you're getting away from it all. The rooms are small but clean and comfortable.

BELVEDERE, *Via di Mezzo 20, Isola dei Pescatori. Tel. 0323/30047. No Fax. 11 rooms, only 5 with bath. Double L65,000. American Express and Visa accepted.* *

No amenities except isolation, clean rooms, and a good meal. A great place for the budget traveler to stay.

ELVEZIA, *Lungolago Vittorio Emanuele 18, Isola Bella. Tel. 0323/ 30043. 9 rooms, none with bath. Three bathrooms in the hallway. Single L40,000; Double L55,000. Full board L75,000. Credit cards accepted.* *

Only for the budget traveler extraordinaire. Some of the rooms are mere closets and no room has a private bath, but you're able to stay on a quaint little island that looks like it rose out of a fairy tale. Don't take the full board, since you can find better food elsewhere on the island (see below, Where to Eat).

WHERE TO EAT

ELVEZIA, *Isola Bella, Tel. 0323/30043. Open only in the evenings by reservation only. Closed Mondays and November and March. All credit cards accepted. Dinner for two L90,000.*

This place has been in the Rossi family for generations. Even though this is a large place, about 140 seats available, that caters mainly to tourists, they still offer personal, attentive service and great food. It's best to find a seat on the verandah porch area overlooking the water. Try their *antipasto di pesce all'isolana* (fish appetizer made island style), or *le lasagnette alle verdure* (small vegetable lasagna). For seconds any of their fish dishes are superb.

PALLANZA

Pallanza is a tiny resort town, more commonly known as **Verbania** to Italians, that has the luck of not having the main *lungolago*, SS 33, run right through the center of town. The main draw here, as mentioned earlier, is the **Villa Taranto**, a house built in 1875 and located two kilometers north of town. Here you'll find over 20,000 species of plants flourishing on over 20 hectares of land.

Besides the lovely botanical gardens, there are quaint grounds in which you can take relaxing strolls through terraces, lawns, and fountains (*Villa Taranto, Open Apr–Oct 8:30am–7:30pm. Admission L10,000.*)

ARRIVALS & DEPARTURES

Located on the north shore of Lago Maggiore across from Stresa. You can reach here by ferry from Stresa, or by car take the **SS 33** to the **SS 34** around the lake to Pallanza.

WHERE TO STAY

You'll find that many of the hotels require you to also purchase a full-board meal plan. Inquire about this when making your reservation.

GRAND HOTEL MAJESTIC, *Via Vittorio Veneto 32, 28048 Verbania Pallanza. Tel. 0323/504-305. Fax 0323/556-379. 119 rooms 56 with bath, 63 with shower. Single L150,000-180,000; Double L200,000-250,000; Suite L400,000. Breakfast included.* ****

Located directly on the lake shore, the hotel is situated in a romantic old building complete with private beach, indoor swimming pool, private gardens, tennis courts, health club, piano bar, sun bathing terrace, and two restaurants with scenic views over the water. Definitely the place to stay in Pallanza.

IL CHIOSTRO, *Via del Ceretti 11, 28048 **Verbania Intra**. Tel. 0323/53151. Fax 0323/401-231. 49 rooms, only 40 with shower. Single L75,000; Double L120,000. Breakfast included. Credit cards accepted.* ***

Located in Pallanza's sister town of Intra, this beautiful, quaint, charismatic, romantic hotel is located in a 17th century monastery. The second best place to stay while in Verbania, even though it's only a three star. You'll be up the slope of the mountain here, with a stunningly beautiful inner garden courtyard surrounded by arcaded walkways where you can sit and relax. Similar in style to colonial Spanish architecture, you'll find peace and tranquillity as well as a good restaurant, room service, lobby bar, tennis courts and more.

The rooms have been completely refitted to contain every modern comfort. If only the monks had it so good when they lived here.

CASTAGNOLA, *Via al Collegio 18, Verbania Pallanza. Tel. 0323/503-414. Fax 0323/556-341. 107 rooms, 5 with bath, 104 with shower. Single L50,000-70,000; Double L80,000-100,000. Visa and Diners Club accepted.* ** What a two star! Located on the mountain overlooking the water and the sister cities of Pallanza and Intra, here you'll find yourself in a tranquil, romantic environment complete with tennis courts, ample park lands for bocce or soccer, a gymnasium, an excellent restaurant and more.

The hotel has huge ceilings, creating the feeling of immense space in your rooms. The bathrooms have been modernized with showers, but are quite small. A great place to stay for the budget traveler and anyone else.

WHERE TO EAT

MILANO, *Corso Zanitello 2, Tel. 0323/556-816. Closed Tuesdays, January 10-February 10 and the first 10 days of August. All credit cards accepted. Dinner for two L100,000.*

Located on the shoreline and next to the information office, this is the best place to eat in Pallanza, especially on their lakeside terrace with the view of the water and the little island of San Giovanni. Situated in an old villa with beautiful gardens and elegant dining rooms, you can't go wrong with the setting or the food.

The chef/owner Egidio Sala makes sure of that. Some of his dishes are a little exotic, like the appetizer *trota alla menta e aceta rossa* (trout with a mint and red vinegar sauce) and the pasta dish *tagliolini agli scampi e zafferano* (thin spaghetti-like pasta with shrimp and saffron) but they all taste fantastic. For seconds their meats are superbly and simply prepared, as are their fish dishes.

LA CAVE, *Viale delle Magnolie 16, Tel. 0323/503-346. Closed Wednesdays and the first two weeks of November. All credit cards accepted. Dinner for two L90,000.*

Located along the lake shore, the atmosphere here is comfortable and relaxing. Couple that with fantastic service and superb food, and you have a great place to eat. They present their dishes at your table in a covered cart so you can get an idea of what you're going to get. Try any of their fish and seafood antipasti. For primo, sample the exquisite *tagliolini all'astice* (pasta with lobster). For seconds you have a wide variety of options from seafood to meat, many of them roasted over an open flame. The second best place to try after the Milano.

TOURIST INFORMATION

• **Corso Zanitello 8**, *Tel. 0323/503-249*

LAKE ORTA

Lake Orta is less populated, less touristed, more attractive, and exceedingly more romantic than Lago Maggiore. Only half a mile across and eight miles long, it has an almost spiritual air about it that perhaps emanates from the chapels and monasteries and churches surrounding its shores, or maybe these structures were placed here because the lake has a gentle, tranquil, and almost indescribable beauty.

Besides the village of Orta San Giulio and its accompanying island, the only other real attractions around the lake is the **Sacro Monte complex** above the town with twenty chapels dedicated to St. Francis, and the **Sanctuary of Madonna del Sasso** that sits perched on a rocky outcrop near Boletta and the lake.

ORTA SAN GIULIO

This small medieval town with its twisting cobblestoned streets and Baroque buildings is the perfect place to stay and use as an embarkation point to explore the lake. The main square, closed to traffic, with its cafes and quaint **Palazetto della Communita**, is the meeting place of the town and has a calm demeanor about it. While here, visit the **island of San Giulio** only a short boat ride away.

Life on the island moves at a relaxed and slow pace. From the cloistered **convent** of the Closed Benedictine nuns to the **San Giulio Basilica**, you will feel transported back to medieval Europe. There's not much to do here but take it easy, eat, and poke around.

ARRIVALS & DEPARTURES

Orta San Giulio is located 75 km northwest of Milan. You can either take the train, or drive; by car, take the **E 62** past Lago Maggiore to **SS 229**. Take this north to Orta San Giulio.

WHERE TO STAY

HOTEL SAN ROCCO, *Via Gippini 11, 28016 Orta San Giulio. Tel. 0322/911-977. Fax 0322/911-964. 74 rooms, 61 with bath, 13 with shower. Single L160,000-220,000; Double L240,000-320,000; Suite L340,000. Breakfast L20,000. Credit cards accepted.* ****

Seventy percent of the rooms here have views of the lake, so make sure you request one of these. This is a beautiful, old, romantic building with a swimming pool, sauna, private beach, health club, sun room and great views. Just outside the main town, you'll find tranquillity galore, as well as a fine restaurant and relaxing piano bar. The rooms are large, with high ceilings and all imaginable modern amenities. Without a doubt, the place to stay on Lake Orta.

LEON D'ORO, *Piazza Motta 43, 28016 Orta San Giulio. Tel. 0322/911-991. Fax 0322/90303. 37 rooms, 5 with bath, 32 with shower. Single L80,000; Double L100,000. Credit cards accepted.****

Located in the center of town, the only amenities this place can offer is location, a private beach, a lobby bar, and a restaurant with a panoramic view. The rooms are clean and comfortable, but if you want a TV you won't find it here. A good place to stay for budget travelers.

ORTA, *Piazza Motta 1, 28016 Orta San Giulio. Tel. 0322/90253. Fax 0322/905-646. 35 rooms 13 with bath, 23 with shower. Single L85,000; Double L130,000. Credit cards accepted.* ***

A better place to stay than the Leon d'Oro. Not because of its location, since they are in the same square, but because of the beautiful romantic building this place is in, with its larger rooms and more modern amenities, such as TV, room service, laundry service, etc. They also have a good restaurant with wonderful panoramic views.

WHERE TO EAT

VILLA CRESPI, *Via G. Fava 18, Tel. 0322/911-902. Closed Mondays in the summer. Dinner for two L120,000. Credit cards accepted.*

Near the gates of the town this is a magical restaurant. If you want an alternative to a la carte ordering, try one of their *menu degustazione* where you can sample a variety of their dishes. The fare is mostly local dishes influenced by fish from the lake and game from the mountains.

TOURIST INFORMATION
· **Tourist Office**, *Via Olina 9/11, Tel. 0322/90355*

LAKE COMO

This lake is a European tourist paradise – or hell depending on how you look at it. Over the centuries **Lake Como** has become famous with royalty, and most recently with the glitterati for its intense landscapes and scenery, and has evolved into a playground for the rich and not-so-famous. You can find every imaginable activity around Lake Como including swimming (in pools, not the lake), sailing, canoeing, water skiing, sailing, fishing, golf, hunting, tennis, hiking, rock climbing and much more.

If you're not into active vacations and prefer the more sedate pursuits like sight seeing, Como will not disappoint. There are vast parks, exotic gardens, lush villas, picturesque villages, and ancient castles, basilicas, art galleries and museums scattered along the lake.

In this way, it is a tourist paradise since there is so much to do, but as with the rest of the lakes in Northern Italy, if you visit between July and September it will be a tourist hell, since the shoreline and tiny villages will packed with many, many vacationers.

COMO

Como produces almost one-fifth of the world's silk supply. Ancient merchants stole the secret of the silk worm from the Chinese many centuries ago, and began production of the seductive cloth along the banks of Lake Como and on the outskirts of the city. As such, you can find many bargains on silk in Como. If shopping is of little interest, you should visit the neo-classic **Villa Olmo** also on the outskirts of town. It is currently the seat of the local government, but the magnificent gardens are open to the public year round *(9am–noon and 1:30pm–6pm)*.

Como is the perfect jumping off point from which to explore the Lake and its many little towns either by ferry or car. You can also hop on the *funiculare*, located on the north edge of the city, and go up to the **Brunate** section of Como that is dotted with exquisite mansions and gardens. A short way outside of town (5 km) is the village of **Cernobbio**, where you can find the princely **Villa D'Este** (not to be confused with the Villa D'Este outside of Rome) with its lush gardens and enormous grounds. The villa is now the area's best five star deluxe hotel. You can still wander through the grounds even if you're not staying there.

ARRIVALS & DEPARTURES

Located 70 kilometers north of Milan, you can either take the train from there (four times a day) or drive up the autostrada **A9** straight to the city.

WHERE TO STAY

GRAND HOTEL VILLA D'ESTE, *Via Regina 40, Cernobbio 22012. Tel. 031/511-471. Fax 031/512-027. 113 rooms, 45 suites all with bath. Singles L340,000-510,000. Doubles/Suites L595,000-670,000. All credit cards accepted.* *****

What grandeur. If you stay here just for the building, the gardens, and the romantic atmosphere, it is well worth it. Besides the beauty you have an indoor swimming pool, tennis courts, sauna, private beach, glorious views over the water and the most attentive staff this side of Buckingham Palace.

COMO, *Via Mentana 28, 22100 Como. Tel. 031/266-173. Fax 031/266-020. 66 rooms, 6 suites all with bath. Single L110,000-150,000; Double/Suites L135,000-200,000. Credit cards accepted.* ****

Located in the center of Como you'll also have a private beach, swimming pool, sauna, a scenic restaurant overlooking the water, a relaxing garden, and thermal baths all in and around a renovated old building. The rooms are small by American standards but comfortable and clean.

PALACE HOTEL, *Via Lungo Lago Trieste 16, Como 22100. Tel. 031/303-303. Fax 031/303-170. 99 rooms all with bath. Single L150,000-170,000; Double L200,000-250,000. Credit cards accepted.* ****

Located a little north of town near the funicular to the Brunate region of Como, here you'll find a luxurious hotel in a quaint romantic old building. They have all the facilities for water sport activities as well as a relaxing piano bar and good restaurant. A quiet, peaceful place to stay with great views.

HOTEL CONTINENTAL, *Via Innocenzo XI 15, 22100 Como. Tel. 031/260-485. Fax 031/273-343. 65 rooms all but one single with shower. Single without shower L50,000-55,000; Single with shower L75,000-90,000; Double L100,000-130,000. Credit cards accepted.* ***

Located in a renovated old building closer to the train station than the lake, this is still a nice place to stay, especially for the price. It's quiet and peaceful and has a nice restaurant so you don't need to go out at night. They have all the facilities for you to engage in water sports, for a price. Perfect for people that are traveling by train and on somewhat of a budget. The rooms are clean and comfortable if a little crowded, with TV, mini-bar, radio, and phone which are necessities for a three star hotel.

ENGADINA, *Viale Fratelli Rossi, 22100 Como. Tel. 031/570-008. Fax 031/570-204. 21 rooms 6 with bath, 15 with shower. Single L53,000-68,000; Double L68,000-86,000. Visa accepted.* **

Located near the lush public gardens on the lake shore this is the best choice for the budget minded. Located on a main street near the water, the ferries, and the train station. The rooms are small but tidy and clean. The furniture is a little eclectic but the accommodations are comfortable. The only real amenity is a place to park your car, a bar in the lobby, and a night porter.

WHERE TO EAT

DA ANGELA, *Via Foscolo 16, Tel. 031/304-656. Closed Sundays and August. All credit cards accepted. Dinner for two L150,000.*

Local food at luxury prices. Located near the Stazione F.N. Lago (not the main train station), this is a popular place in Como. An elegant but rustic atmosphere, try their *conniglio alle olive* (rabbit with olives) or their fantastic *gnocchetti al sugo di salsicce e pomodoro* (little gnocchi in a sauce of tomatoes and sausage).

DEL GESUMIN, *Via Cinque Giornate 46, Tel. 031/266-030. Closed Sundays and 10 days in August. Dinner for two L180,000.*

This place, simply put, has average food at ridiculous prices, and the service stinks. The only saving grace is the ambiance created by the decor and beautiful garden terrace. So if you like elegant dining (you have to dress the part here), enjoy the romantic atmosphere, sample the food, and be prepared for the prices.

IMBARCADERO, *Via Cavour 20, Tel. 031/277-341. Closed the first ten days in January. Credit cards accepted. Dinner for L120,000.*

Located a few meters from the water's edge, this relaxed place offers great traditional dishes, simple in preparation but bursting with flavor. In the summer they open up their terrace so you can enjoy a great meal and the sounds, sights, and smells of the lake. An inexpensive and quite satisfying alternative to ordering a la carte is their *menu del giorno,* which offers a different primo and secondo each day for only L35,000 per person. Fish, soup, pasta, and meat all find their place onto this menu.

TOURIST INFORMATION
• **Tourist Office**, *Piazza Cavour 17, Tel. 031/274-064*

BELLAGIO

The location of this village is utterly divine. Surrounded by the lake on three sides, you have fantastic views over the water as well as the east and west shores of the lake. You can enjoy strolls through the winding medieval streets or engage ina any number of water sports.

Down on the eastern shore of the peninsula is the quiet port of **Pescallo** with its many boats. The most famous sights here are the Villa Melzi and the Villa Serbelloni. The **Villa Melzi** *(Lungolario Marconi, open 9am–noon and 2pm–dark)* is known for its gardens ornately strewn with monuments and a small little pond of its own covered with lily pads and flowers. The **Villa Serbelloni** is now five star hotel whose gardens are only open to non-guests for two hours a day *(9am–11am)*. Also known for its intricate gardens, the only way to truly appreciate them is by staying there – but the price is rather high.

ARRIVALS & DEPARTURES

Located 80 kilometers north of Milan, you can drive here by taking the autostrada **A9** to Como, go through town to the north end near the funicular. Here the *lungolago* road turns into the **SS 583**, which will lead you along the Lake to Bellagio.

You can also take the train to Como, and simply take a ferry from there to Bellagio.

WHERE TO STAY

GRAND HOTEL VILLA SERBELLONI, *Via Roma 1, 22021 Bellagio. Tel. 031/950-216. Fax 031/951-529. 66 rooms, 28 suites all with bath. Single L280,000; Double L407,000; Suites L600,000. Credit cards accepted.* *****
This is an incredible place – supreme grandeur overlooking the town of Bellagio and Lake Como. Here you'll find everything you could imagine in a hotel, including pool, tennis courts, bus service, private beach down at the lake, water sports equipment, day care, a piano bar, an excellent restaurant, room service, laundry service and more, all presented in a gorgeous old romantic mansion that will make your heart soar.

EXCELSIOR SPLENDIDE, *Via Lungo Lago Manzoni 26, 22021 Bellagio. Tel. 031/950-225. Fax 031/951-224. 47 rooms, 13 with bath, 34 with shower. Single L68,000; Double L100,000. American Express and Visa accepted.* ***
Located outside of town along the lakeside road near the funicular, this hotel is situated in a romantic old building and has its own heated indoor swimming pool. Other amenities include a good restaurant with a scenic view over the water and a piano bar for entertainment at night. They actually feature a small orchestra with three and sometimes four pieces. A great place to stay for the price.

HOTEL FIRENZE, *Piazza Mazzini, 22021 Bellagio. Tel. 031/950-342. Fax 031/951-722. 34 rooms, all but one single with bath. Single without bath L68,000; Single with bath L100,110,000; Double L140,000-155,000. No credit cards accepted.* ***
In the center of town, this hotel occupies a romantic old building. There's a private beach, swimming pool, tennis court, as well as a restaurant and lobby bar. Not the fanciest of places, but its clean, comfortable, and affordable.

WHERE TO EAT

SILVIO, *Via Loppia 10, Tel. 031/950-322. Closed only in January. Credit cards accepted. Dinner for two L70,000.*
A family-run place near the Villa Melzi. Mom's in the kitchen, and her son is serving and greeting in the dining room with Dad. All you'll find here is whatever they caught on the lake in the morning or during the day. They fry, grill, or bake the fish to perfection and also mix it with *risotto* (rice) or ladle it over pasta. They have a relaxing terrace area that should be enjoyed in the summer. The best place to eat while in Bellagio.

TOURIST INFORMATION

• **Tourist Office**, *Lungolago A. Manzoni, Tel. 031/950-204*

LAKE GARDA

At 32 miles long, and 10 miles at its widest point, **Lake Garda** is the biggest Northern Italian lake. It is also the mildest in climate, causing the waters to teem with all sorts of fish and water craft. The shoreline abounds with all sorts of produce, vegetation, and tourists. As Italy's most visited lake, over the years the hotel and restaurant service has become first class. You can get from town to town by ferry, hydrofoil, or the **Gardesana highways** which pass along the shore and through any mountains that get in the way.

Besides scenic natural beauty and your fellow tourists, you'll be able to enjoy some of the most impressive and well preserved medieval architecture in the region, especially the **Torre San Marco** at **Gardone Riviera**, as well as the remains of an ancient Roman villa near **Sirmione**. There are smaller villages along the shore of the lake that warrant exploring as well.

One of the best ways to do this is during market day. So on Monday visit **Manerba**, Tuesday visit **Desenzano** and **Limone**, Wednesday visit **Gargnano**, Thursday visit **Lonato** and **Toscolano**, Friday is the market day of rest, Saturday visit **Salo** and **Sirmione**, and on Sunday visit **Padenghe**. You'll be able to find all sorts of arts, crafts, local produce, cheese, meats, bread, and more at each of these colorful markets. If you're in the area on the first weekend of the month, head to Desenzano for their small antiques market.

DESENZANO

From this city you can gain easy access to any of the other lakeside towns by ferry or the Gardesana road, which follows the water's edge and cuts through a variety of mountainous outcroppings along the way. The second largest city on the lake to Riva del Garda, Desenzano lies in a wide gulf and has some fine beaches, but is not nearly as picturesque as **Sirmione** or **Gardone Riviera**.

This is a good starting point for a tour, but not the best base of operations to explore the lake. Their 16th century **cathedral** is virtually non-descript, save for the *Last Supper* painted by Tiepolo (*Via Mazzini, open 9am–noon and 3:30pm–5pm*). There is also a luxurious **Roman villa** built in the 2nd century AD that contains some well-preserved mosaics (*Via Villa Romana, open 9:30am–1:30pm and 3:30pm–6pm*).

ARRIVALS & DEPARTURES

Located only about 30 km away from Verona and 90 km from Milan on the Autostrada **A4**. You can also get here by train from both Verona and Milan.

WHERE TO STAY

This is not the best place to stay on Lake Garda, since it is one of the biggest towns. For a more romantic and scenic adventure, try and stay at **Sirmione** or **Gardone Riviera**.

HOTEL DESENZANO, *Viale Cavour 40-42, Desenzano 25015. Tel. 030/914-590. Fax 030/914–0294. 40 rooms all with bath. Single L90,000-95,000; Double L110,000-130,000. Breakfast L10,000 extra. Credit cards accepted.* ****

Located on the road from the train station, this is a relatively old building that has been renovated and lends a romantic air to your stay. They have a swimming pool, sun deck, and a restaurant that serves national, local, and international food. All the amenities of a good four star: satellite TV, direct dial phone, air conditioning, room service, and clean and comfortable rooms at a great price.

LIDO INTERNATIONAL, *Via Tommaso dal Molin 43, 25015 Desenzano. Tel. 030/914-1027. Fax 030/914-3736. 25 rooms, 2 with bath, 23 with shower. Single L90,000-120,000; Double L160,000-180,000. Credit cards accepted.* ****

Located near the port, here you'll find yourself in another quaint old restored building that has a great pizza restaurant with a scenic view over the water. They have a private beach, swimming pool and sun deck, day care, and all the other amenities of a lake side four star hotel. They cost a little more than the Desenzano because the hotel offers a few more amenities.

AURORA, *Lungolago C. Battisti 53, 25105 Desenzano. Tel. 030/914-1018. Fax 030/991-1662. 18 rooms all with shower. Single L68,00; Double L90,000. Visa accepted.* ***

Located on the lake shore drive, this is a good inexpensive choice. They have great views from most of the rooms, a sun deck, TVs in the rooms, direct dial phones, a lobby bar and a garden to enjoy. Limited amenities but a good location at a good price.

WHERE TO EAT

CAVALLINO, *Via Murachette 9, Tel. 030/912-0217. Closed Sunday nights and Tuesday at lunch. All credit cards accepted. Dinner for two L160,000.*

A wonderful little restaurant that serves everything from game to fish to pasta. Their terrace in the summer is an ideal place to savor their *anatra e conniglio in salsa al pepe* (duck and rabbit in a pepper sauce) or *trenette all'astice* (long flat noodle in a lobster sauce), definitely their most tasty dish. A great place to sample the food from the region.

ESPLANADE, *Via Lario 10, Tel. 030/914-3361. Closed Wednesdays. Credit cards accepted. Dinner for two L150,000.*

About 500 meters outside of town along the shore road to the south, this is an elegant place with a nice terrace in the summer from which you can have a romantic view of the area. Mainly a menu of fish from the sea and the lake, they also serve local specialties like rabbit and duck.

TOURIST INFORMATION
· **Tourist Office**, *Piazza Mateoti, Tel. 030/914-1510*

SIRMIONE

Located on the south side of the lake extending out into the water on a slender peninsula, **Sirmione** is a truly romantic and historic town to spend a few beautiful days. An impressive sight here is the **Rocca Scaligera fortress** in the center of town, built in the 12th century to guard the lake. This massive construction with towers and battlements extending out into the water to create a safe harbor is still imposing today (*Piazza Carducci. Open 9am–12:30pm and 2–6pm in summer. and 9am–1pm in winter. Closed Monday. Admission L5,000*).

Out on the tip of the peninsula is the **Grotte di Catullo**, a grandiose Roman villa complex with rooms, corridors, and underground areas still very well preserved (*Via Catullo. Open 9am–6pm in summer and only until 4pm in winter. Closed Monday.*) Other features of the town are the well-known **thermal baths** and the enchanting, winding medieval streets.

ARRIVALS & DEPARTURES

From Verona, only about 30 km away, take either train or bus. By car, take the autostrada **A4** and then the **SS 11** at Pescheria del Garda to Sirmione.

From Milan, about 90 km away, take either train or bus. By car, take the autostrada **A4** to Desenzano, then take the SS 572 just over six km to the lone road the branches left to Sirmione and its peninsula.

WHERE TO STAY

VILLA CORTINE PALACE HOTEL, *Via Grotte di Catullo 6, 25019 Sirmione. Tel. 030/990-5890. Fax 030/916-390. 55 rooms all with bath. Single L240,000-280,000; Double L340,000-480,000. Credit cards accepted.* *****

What a beautiful old building, located out near the ruins of the ancient Roman villa. Here you'll have peace and quiet at your private beach, swimming pool, and tennis courts. They also have a nice restaurant, relaxing bar, room service, TV and superb service. The rooms have large ceilings and are clean and comfortable.

HOTEL CONTINENTAL, *Via Punta Staffalo 1/9, 25019 Sirmione. Tel. 030/990-5711. Fax 030/916-278. 53 rooms all with bath. Single L107,000-120,000; Double L180,000-220,000. Breakfast L13,000 extra.* ****

A modern hotel with a balcony in every room. Located on the lakeside, they have a private beach, swimming pool, water sports equipment and great views from the rooms and the restaurant. A step down from the ambiance of the Villa Cortine but still a perfect place to relax. The rooms are modern, clean, and comfortable with satellite TV, air conditioning, and mini bar.

IDEAL, *Via Grotte di Catullo 31, 25109 Sirmione. Tel. 030/990-4245. Fax same. 26 rooms all with bath. Single L85,000; Double L110,000-130,000. Visa Accepted.* ****

Just five years ago, this used to be a one star hotel. But after upgrading their facilities and maintaining a private beach, they are now able to proudly display themselves as a four star, but as the reasonable prices demonstrate the new rating hasn't gone to their heads. Little to no amenities save for the beach and a garden terrace restaurant, but the price is right. Rooms are nice and quiet. Located outside of town near the ancient ruins of the Roman villa.

WHERE TO EAT

VECCHIA LUGANA, *Piazzale Vecchia Lugana 1, Tel. 030/919-012. Closed Sunday nights and Tuesdays. All credit cards accepted. Dinner for two L160,000.*

An expensive place that has started to serve superb food in the past year or so. The dishes are prepared with the best ingredients, presented well, and taste superb. One of their best pastas was *ravioli di pesce al profumo d'erba cipollina* (seafood ravioli with a baby onion sauce). You can also get a buffet of vegetables or fish as a meal or appetizer. They also make great meats and fish on the grill. You can savor the succulent taste of the food either in the elegance of the inside dining or outside on their terrace facing the water.

LA RUCOLA, *Via Strentelle 7, Tel. 030/916-326. Closed Thursdays and January. All credit cards accepted. Dinner for two L150,000.*

An elegant local restaurant, some of their dishes seem a little odd to me. It's as if they're just mixing things together to be creative and get a reputation. The smells were good, the tastes the same but the ingredients ... I don't know. One of the strangest dishes is their *astice freddo con patate calde* (cold lobster with hot roasted potatoes). For a different meal, however, come here.

TOURIST INFORMATION

· **Tourist Office**, *Viale Marconi 2. Tel. 030/916-114*

GARDONE RIVIERA

A place of beauty and tranquillity, when not being swarmed by zillions of invading tourists like you and me. The majestic **Torre San Marco** rises from the water to greet you; it is a beautiful medieval and Renaissance lighthouse and private harbor area (*open 9am–1pm and 3pm–6pm. and only until 4pm in the winter*).

Other features of the town are its splendid mansions, particularly the **Villa Turati** that contains one of Europe's most entertaining and extensive botanical gardens, with plants from the Mediterranean, Africa, and the Alpine regions (*Via Roma, open 10am–noon and 2pm–6pm and only until 4pm in the winter*). **Villa Cargnacco**, also known as **Il Vittoriale**, is also worth visiting, with its amphitheater where the plays of Gabriele d'Annunzio are performed in July and August (*open 8:30am–12:30pm and 2–6pm. Only unitl 5pm in winter. Closed Mondays. Admission L5,000*).

Besides the villas and the tower at Gardone Riviera, you can take quiet, relaxing walks through the lush mountain trails, and appreciate the majestic beauty all around you.

ARRIVALS & DEPARTURES

By car, make your way to Desenzano (see above). Once at Desenzano take the **SS 572** along the lake shore to the town. Alternatively, take the ferry from Desenzano, Sirmione, or Riva del Garda.

WHERE TO STAY

GRAND HOTEL, *Corso Zanardelli 72, 25083 Gardone Riviera. Tel. 0365/20261. Fax 0365/22695. 180 rooms all with bath. Single L145,000-185,000; Double L220,000-315,000. Credit cards accepted.* ****

Not to be confused with the Fasano Grand Hotel just down the road, this wonderful hotel has been in existence for more than 100 years. Located in a quaint and romantic old *palazzo*, this has been the playground for the jet set for decades. Enjoy the private beach, swimming pool, disco, a good restaurant, and a relaxing bar. The rooms are large and comfortable and all come with satellite TV for you CNN junkies.

MONTEFIORI, *Via del Lauri 12, 25083 Gardone Riviera. Tel. 0365/290-235. Fax 0365/25083. 31 rooms all with bath. Single L80,000-90,000; Double L130,000-140,000. Credit cards accepted.* ***

Set off in a park above the lake, this nice hotel radiates peace and tranquillity. Located in a small old *palazzo* with tennis courts, swimming pool, and great views over the area. A great inexpensive place to stay.

WHERE TO EAT

VILLA FIORDALISO, *Corso Zanardelli 132, Tel. 0365/20158. Closed Mondays and the 10th of January through the 25th of February. Dinner for two L180,000.*

Super elegant dining, whether on the terrace in the garden during summer or in the rooms decorated in the intricate Liberty style. The food is excellent and the presentation is refined, but the portions are minuscule. Many of their dishes are made from the day's catch from the lake or the Adriatic.

Try their *tagliolini con calamaretti e asparagi* (with small calamari and asparagus) and then some *filetto di pesce persico e menta* (perch with a light mint sauce). They also have a *menu degustazione* for L60,000 per person which is good, just as non-filling, and a lot less expensive.

TOURIST INFORMATION

· **Tourist Office**, *Corso Repubblica 35, Tel. 0365/20347*

RIVA DEL GARDA

At the northernmost end of Lake Garda, **Riva del Garda** has plenty of winding medieval streets to keep you entranced and occupied exploring. On the west side of town are short cliffs, and on the east side is a small pebble-strewn beach. Surrounding the city beach (there is another beach just further west) are gardens that make for a pleasant picnic, stroll, or just a lazy afternoon doing nothing at all.

In the middle of these both is the imposing 12th century moated **Rocca fortress**. Now a local **museum**, Roman artifacts and other goodies from the past are on display (*Piazza Battisti. Open 9am–1pm and 3–5pm. Only until 4pm in the winter. Closed Mondays.*)

ARRIVALS & DEPARTURES

All the way at the north end of this expansive lake, Riva del Garda is one of the two largest towns (the other is Desenzano) and can be reached by ferry from any other town on the lake with service.

Or you can get yourself stuck in traffic following the lake road around Lago Garda. I recommend the ferry.

TOURIST INFORMATION

· **Tourist Office**, *Giardino di Porta Orientale, Tel. 0464/554-444*

WHERE TO STAY

Most hotels are located to the east of the medieval city and offer little in the way of ambiance and romance. The only exception is the first hotel on my list.

HOTEL DU LAC ET DU PARC, *Viale Roverto 44, 38066 Riva del Garda, Tel. 0464/551-500. Fax 0464/555-200. 170 rooms, 145 with bath, 45 with shower. Also available are 32 private bungalows. Single L125,000-160,000; Double L220,000-360,000; Bungalow L370,000-480,000. Breakfast L15,000 extra. Credit cards accepted.* ****

This very nice hotel is not too far outside of town, and is situated in the middle of lush green gardens and lawns right on the lake shore. An old building filled with character, stay here for a holiday paradise, complete with indoor and outdoor pool, tennis courts, gymnasium, health spa, sauna, sun room, piano bar, several restaurants, water sports equipment and more.

LIDO PALACE HOTEL, *Viale Carducci 108, 38066 Riva del Garda. Tel. 0464/552-664. No fax. 63 rooms all with bath. Double L180,000-240,000. Credit cards accepted.* ****

One of the few good hotels located in the center of town near the Rocca. They have few amenities save for a swimming pool and a good restaurant, but you'll be staying amidst the town's medieval splendor, in clean and comfortable rooms. The prices are reasonable for a four star.

ASTORIA, *Viale Trento 9, 38066 Riva del Garda. Tel. 0464/552-658. No fax. 96 rooms, all with bath. Single L60,000-80,000; Double L90,000-130,000. Credit cards accepted.* ***

Also located in the center of town, this three star's only real amenity is a swimming pool. Their restaurant is suspect, but in this location you'll have access to outside dining establishments. The price is right and the rooms, though a little small, are clean, modernized, and comfortable. No TV or air conditioning.

WHERE TO EAT

VECCHIA RIVA, *Via Bastione 3, Tel. 0464/555-061. Closed Tuesdays (not in high season) and January. All credit cards accepted. Dinner for two L120,000.*

A super classy restaurant that takes classic dishes and explores the possibilities with them. They have a terrace that is perfect for summer dining. They make great *crepes al caviale* (with caviar) served with a yogurt sauce. Most of the second courses are based on the fresh catch of the day from the lake, many of which, unlike the San Marco, are covered in a creative sauce in an attempt to enhance the fish's flavor. If you like culinary adventure, come here. For basic food try the San Marco.

SAN MARCO, *Via Roma 20, Tel. 0464/554-477. Closed Mondays. All credit cards accepted. Dinner for two L100,000.*
An elegant environment in which many international recipes as well as national Italian dishes are prepared. Many options contain your basic fresh local ingredients and fish from the lake. If you don't want to order from the menu, they offer an inexpensive tourist menu every day that covers two courses, and is tasty and filling.

23. GLOSSARY

The following is a glossary of art, architectural, and historical terms used in the book, both Italian and English. The glossary of food terms is in Chapter 11, *Food & Wine.*

Agriturismo, a program that allows tourists to stay in farmhouses throughout Italy Depending on the region, the cost of the stay may be offset by laboring on the farm

Aisle, sides of a church flanking the nave, separated from it by a series of columns

Amphora, large antique vase, usually used to hold oil or wine

Apse, a semicircular, domed projection at the east (altar) end of a church

Atrium, entrance court, usually to an ancient Roman house or a Byzantine church

Basilica, in ancient Rome, a building used for public administration Christians adopted the architectural style, a rectangular building with aisle and apse but no transepts, for their churches

Battistero, a baptistery, (almost always) a separate building near the town's *Duomo* where all city baptisms were performed

Borgo, a suburb or street leading into a suburb from the center of town (these suburbs are now often just another section of town)

Campanile, a bell tower, usually free-standing

Camposanto, a cemetery literally means holy ground

Cantoria, choir gallery of a church Literally means the place to sing

Caryatid, a column in the shape of a female figure

Camillo Cavour, Vittorio Emanuelle's minister during the *risorgimento*

Cell, cells of a monastery

Cloister, a quadrangle with covered walkways along its edges, usually with a garden in the center

Comune, the government of a free city of the Middle Ages

Corso, principal street

Cupola, dome, usually in a church

Duomo, cathedral, the official seat of a diocesan bishop, and usually the central church of an Italian town

Facade, the front of a building, or any other wall given special architectural treatment

Fiume, a river

Forum, in an ancient Roman town, the central square containing most of the municipal buildings

Frescoe, a water-color painting made on wet plaster When it dries, the painting becomes part of the wall

Funiculare, funicular, a cable railway ascending a mountain

Garibaldi, the popular hero of the risorgimento First name Giuseppe

Giardino, garden

Grotesque, painted, carved, or stucco decorations (often heads) on a Roman or Etruscan homes, named for the work found in Nero's buried (grotto) Golden House in Rome

Latin Cross, a cross whose vertical arm is longer than its horizontal arm

Loggia, the covered gallery or balcony of a building

Lungo, Lung, literally "along," so that a *lungomare* is a boardwalk or promenade alongside the ocean. For example, the *Lungarno* in Florence is a street running alongside the river Arno, and in Rome the *Lungatevere* is the road running alongside the river Tevere

Lunette, a circular frame in the ceiling or vault of a building that holds a painting or sculpture

Nave, the central body of a church

Palazzo, an important building Even though the word literally mens palace many of the buildings don;t appear as if they are But in their day theu were

Palio, a banner Now is also used as the name for a reenactment of a medieval horse race in which the neighborhoods of a city compete for a banner

Pensione, *Pensione* originally meant a boarding house, and started to be used interchangeably with *albergo* (hotel), but is now being phased out of use

Piazza, a city square In Venice, the term *campo* (literally field) is usually used instead

Pieta, a scene of the Virgin, sometimes accompanied, mourning the dead Christ

Piscina, a swimming pool

Rifugio, (plural *rifugi*) refuges (alpine huts) scattered all over the Alps and Dolomites which offer beds and meals for hikers

Scuola, the Venetian name for a confraternity, and now means school

Stigmata, miraculous body pains or bleeding the resemble the wounds of the crucified Christ

Strada, street

Tabacchi, tobacconist where you can buy stamps as well as tickets for local
city buses

Telamones, supporting columns sculpted as male figures (the counterparts to caryatids)

Transept, either one of the arms of a cruciform church

Via, street

Villa, a country house, usually a large estate with a formal garden

Vittorio Emanuelle II, the main street of just about every town in Italy is
named after the first King of Italy

INDEX

FROM THE PUBLISHER

Our goal is to provide you with a guide book that is second to none. Please remember, however, that things do change: phone numbers, prices, addresses, quality of food served, value, etc. Should you come across any new information, we'd appreciate hearing from you. No item is too small, so if you have any recommendations or suggested changes, please write to us.

Have a great trip!

Open Road Publishing
P.O. Box 20226
Columbus Circle Station
New York, NY 10023

And now you can e-mail us at:
Jopenroad@aol.com

OPEN ROAD PUBLISHING
Your Passport to Great Travel!

Going abroad? Our books have been praised by **Travel & Leisure, Booklist, US News & World Report, Endless Vacation, American Bookseller,** and many other magazines and newspapers!

Don't leave home without an Open Road travel guide to one of these great destinations:

France Guide, $16.95
Italy Guide, $17.95
Paris Guide, $12.95
Portugal Guide, $16.95
Spain Guide, $17.95
London Guide, $13.95
Holland Guide, $14.95
Austria Guide, $14.95
Israel Guide, $16.95

Central America Guide, $17.95
Costa Rica Guide, $16.95
Belize Guide, $14.95
Honduras & Bay Islands Guide, $14.95
Guatemala Guide, $16.95
Southern Mexico & Yucatan Guide, $14.95
Bermuda Guide, $14.95
Hong Kong & Macau Guide, $13.95
China Guide, $18.95 (10th Edition!)

Forthcoming foreign guides in 1996 and 1997: Greece, Turkey, Ireland, Czech & Slovak Republics, India, Vietnam, Japan, Mexico, Kenya.

Closer to home, check out Open Road's US travel guide series:
Las Vegas Guide, $12.95
Disney World & Orlando Theme Parks, $13.95
America's Most Charming Towns & Villages, $15.95
Florida Golf Guide, $16.95

Forthcoming US guides in 1996 and 1997: Colorado, San Francisco, California Wine Country, Alaska, and more!

Look for Open Road travel guides in your favorite bookstore. To order any guide directly from us, send a check or money order to: **Open Road Publishing, P.O. Box 20226, Columbus Circle Station, New York, NY 10023.** Orders must include the price of each book **plus** $3.00 for shipping/handling for the first book and $1.00 for each book thereafter.

We also offer special bulk order discounts.
And thanks for hitting the open road with Open Road Publishing!